Therapeutic Recreation
Processes and Techniques

Evidence-Based Recreational Therapy

7th
edition

David R. Austin

SAGAMORE
PUBLISHING

Publishers: Joseph J. Bannon and Peter L. Bannon
Director of Sales and Marketing: William A. Anderson
Marketing Coordinator: Emily Wakefield
Director of Development and Production: Susan M. Davis
Technology Manager: Christopher Thompson
Production Coordinator: Amy S. Dagit

ISBN print edition: 978-1-57167-751-8
ISBN ebook: 978-1-57167- 752-5
LCCN: 2013943128

SAGAMORE
P U B L I S H I N G
1807 N. Federal Dr.
Urbana, IL 61801
www.sagamorepub.com

This book is dedicated to my wife, Joan,
whose love and support allowed me to write this book.

Contents

About the Author

David R. Austin

Dr. Austin's research has focused upon the social psychology of recreational therapy and professional preparation. Topics of over 140 publications have included attitudes toward serving persons with disabilities, burnout, and recreational therapy curricula. He is the author or coauthor of five widely used textbooks: *Therapeutic Recreation Processes and Techniques* (7th edition); *Inclusive and Special Recreation: Opportunities for Diverse Populations to Flourish* (6th edition); *Therapeutic Recreation: An Introduction* (3rd edition); *Conceptual Foundations for Therapeutic Recreation;* and *Lessons Learned: An Open Letter to Recreational Therapy Students and Practitioners.* Dr. Austin produced 23 instructional videos through the federally funded Recreation Therapy Video (RTV) Project, and he is author of the Health Protection/Health Promotion Model of Practice. Dr. Austin has served on editorial boards for the *Journal of Leisure Research, Schole, Annual in Therapeutic Recreation,* and *Leisure Today.* He is a past president of ATRA, the Society of Park and Recreation Educators, and the Academy of Leisure Sciences, as well as a past member of the NRPA Board of Trustees. Dr. Austin is a fellow in the Academy of Leisure Sciences and a founding fellow of the National Academy of Recreational Therapists. He is the only individual to have received the NTRS Distinguished Service Award, the ATRA Distinguished Fellow Award, and the SPRE Distinguished Fellow Award. He has been awarded Indiana University's highest teaching award, the Frederic Bachman Lieber Memorial Award for Distinguished Teaching. He has been named to the Union College Hall of Fame and was presented the Brightbill Award by the University of Illinois. In 1998, Dr. Austin received the NRPA Literary Award.

Preface

This seventh edition of *Therapeutic Recreation Processes and Techniques* is a revision of the last edition published in 2009. Being the seventh edition makes the book unique among recreational therapy books as it is the first RT book to be published in seven editions. The material has been extensively updated, and new information has been included to expand the breadth and depth of the topics covered in order to make this edition of the book more comprehensive than ever.

My goal in writing from the first edition of this book in 1982 to the current edition has been to produce a text that would add to the practice knowledge of the profession, as well as enhance the technical abilities of recreational therapy students and clinicians. Ultimately, the purpose of this book has always been to improve the quality of recreational therapy services available to clients.

Today's recreational therapists must possess a broad knowledge base that offers them a foundation for practice. Recreational therapists need to know strategies for applying the latest techniques and possess the best evidence available to help their clients to achieve the most optimal outcomes. Consistent with those aims, the purpose of this book is to inform practice. While dealing with the practice of recreational therapy, it provides the theoretical and empirical evidence needed to support practice.

I wrote the original edition because there was a need for a book that explained how to practice recreational therapy. Instead of providing information about recreational therapy services and client characteristics, I wrote a book that emphasized substantive concerns involved in actual practice. Throughout the book, I have discussed not only theory, but the implications of theory for the practice of recreational therapy.

This text was written to go beyond the common-sense approach that utilizes knowledge gained primarily through personal experience. The content of this book includes literature from psychiatry, education, nursing, social work, rehabilitation, and counseling, as well as academic disciplines representing the behavioral sciences. This broad-based foundation provides a scholarly basis for understanding and applying recreational therapy processes and techniques. In sum, it can be a valuable resource for those who engage in evidence-based practice. In fact, the subtitle of *Evidence-Based Recreational Therapy* has been added to the title of this seventh edition to emphasize the focus within the book on evidence-based practice.

Finally, I wished to provide a book that is readable and easy to follow. Each chapter adheres to a set format that includes objectives to guide the reader's learning and a set of reading comprehension questions. This structure is explained in detail in Chapter 1.

There have been a number of changes in this edition. Chapter 2, "Theories and Therapies," includes expanded and updated coverage of an emerging theoretical perspective for recreational therapy, positive psychology. A new table titled "Positive Psychology in a Nutshell" has been added to succinctly interpret positive psychology. Chapter 3, "Facilitation

Techniques," now includes scores of up-to-date research studies to guide evidence-based practice. Ample empirical evidence is cited to support the use of many facilitation techniques such as adventure therapy, animal-assisted therapy, aquatic therapy, progressive relaxation training, imagery, yoga, exercise and physical activity, humor, creative arts (e.g., music listening, expressive writing), remotivation therapy, and life review. New segments have been added on Cognitive Stimulation Therapy, robotic therapy, and retail therapy. Chapter 4, "The Recreational Therapy Process," has increased emphasis on theory-based practice and the assessment of strengths. In Chapter 5, "Helping Others," the section on cultural diversity has undergone updating and expansion. Chapter 6, "Communication Skills," contains expanded information on communicating with clients from a number of specific groups. Chapter 7, "Being a Leader," has been extensively revised to provide a wealth of information to help recreational therapists perform well in their roles as group leaders. Detailed information on group processing is provided within the chapter. Chapter 9, "Clinical Supervision," has been updated and enlarged to include developmental stages in clinical supervision and multiculturalism in clinical supervision. Throughout the book, sections have been augmented and additional tables have been added. Unique elements found in earlier editions of the book have been updated. These include information on drug therapy, therapeutic communication skills, developing self-awareness, conceptual models, the Transtheoretical Model and motivational interviewing, the International Classification of Functioning, Disability and Health (ICF), and formulating goals and objectives. Over 325 new references appear in this seventh edition. In short, I am excited to be able to present what I believe are, by far, the most extensive and best revisions ever made to this book.

I wish to acknowledge and express appreciation to Sagamore Publishing for allowing an expansion in the number of pages in the chapters on the recreational therapy process and facilitation techniques. The facilitation techniques chapter, in particular, has been greatly enlarged to accommodate an increased emphasis on research evidence related to the various facilitation techniques.

A word about the choice of terms in this book is in order. The term *client* has been used because it is widely accepted in the world of recreational therapy today and is a more universal term than patient, student, or resident. Also, the terms *recreational therapist* or *therapist* have been consistently applied when referring to practitioners.

As in prior editions, in this seventh edition many practical guidelines, exercises, and examples are provided throughout the book. Instructors may obtain an Instructor's Guide for the book at www.sagamorepub.com.

I am indebted to many individuals and institutions for assistance in preparation of this book. I am particularly grateful for the work done by my wife, Joan; in addition to coauthoring Chapter 10, she made many suggestions and edited drafts of the manuscript.

David R. Austin, PhD

Chapter 1

Basic Concepts

■ Chapter Purpose

Recreational therapy accomplishes its goals through the actions of specialists who, as helping professionals, serve clients. To become a competent helping professional, recreational therapists must gain both the theoretical and the technical knowledge necessary for successful practice. An introduction to helping others and to the content and format of the book is presented within this chapter.

■ Key Terms

- Helping relationships
- Objectives
- Theory

■ Objectives

- Comprehend the nature of the content contained within this book.
- Grasp what makes the recreational therapist different from the layperson.
- Know the major topics to be covered in this book.
- Understand the format followed in each chapter.
- Recognize that the approach taken within this book is to make the reader the focus of instruction.

Since there are other books on recreational therapy, one might ask, "Why add another to the collection?" One reason might be that an improved version of prior works is needed. However, there are already several well-prepared works among the current recreational therapy textbooks. There is, however, a great deal of information regarding recreational therapy that has not been covered in previously published textbooks.

Introductory recreational therapy textbooks necessarily provide information about recreational therapy services and client characteristics but do not deal extensively with the actual delivery of direct client service. This book marks a departure from the survey type of textbooks that have served the profession well as literature for introductory courses in recreational therapy. This book will examine the methods of recreational therapy. It is directed at the *how* of recreational therapy. Although it is based largely on theory, the book covers basic helping skills required in the practice of recreational therapy. In short, *Therapeutic Recreation Processes and Techniques* deals with a client-centered, evidence-based approach to practice.

On Helping Others

Those in recreational therapy require literature that will expand knowledge of the processes and techniques central to the delivery of evidence-based direct client services. In successful **helping relationships,** we assist the client to meet a problem or need. If we are to be able to do this better than the client can alone or with family or friends, we must possess more than good intentions. The difference between a layperson's approach to the client and that of the trained practitioner is that the practitioner bases his or her service on processes and techniques drawn from the theoretical, scientific, and experiential knowledge of his or her profession. People rely on recreational therapists to have the theory and skills that will enable them to do things they could not otherwise accomplish alone.

It is therefore critical that basic processes and techniques of recreational therapy be thoroughly understood and skillfully applied by those practicing in the profession. This book provides professional information to assist those developing themselves for careers in recreational therapy to gain competencies necessary for the provision of quality services.

Major Topics Covered

Chapter 1: Basic Concepts
Chapter 1 offers a brief overview and discussion of this book's major concepts, purposes, and its organization.

Chapter 2: Theories and Therapies
One distinction between the layperson and the professional is that the professional draws on **theory** as a basis for action. Chapter 2 differentiates among psychoanalytic, behavioristic, cognitive-behavioral, growth psychology, positive psychology, and other theories—and therapeutic approaches related to these orientations—and provides a fundamental level of knowledge about theoretical perspectives for recreational therapists.

Chapter 3: Facilitation Techniques
Chapter 3 discusses facilitation techniques such as values clarification, horticulture therapy, therapeutic touch, social skills training, progressive relaxation training, yoga, animal-assisted therapy, and reminiscence therapy that are less comprehensive in their development than the major theories and therapies presented in Chapter 2. Nevertheless, many facilitation techniques can be used as interventions by recreational therapists. Research support provided for each of the facilitation techniques offers recreational therapists empirical evidence on which evidence-based practice may rest.

Chapter 4: The Recreational Therapy Process
The recreational therapy process (sometimes referred to as the therapeutic recreation process) is a systematic method of problem solving applied in recreational therapy. Chapter 4 shows how, through a progression of steps involving assessment, planning, implementation, and evaluation, the process is utilized to bring about changes in the client and the client's

environment. Closely related to the recreational therapy process is theory that is expressed in conceptual models for recreational therapy practice. The chapter contains an explanation of how conceptual models inform recreational therapy practice. Also included is information on evidence-based practice.

Chapter 5: Helping Others

Recreational therapy takes place through interpersonal relations. Helping people is a complex act requiring an understanding of both human behavior and what constitutes an effective helper and a helping relationship. Chapter 5 explains how this understanding is an essential ingredient for the recreational therapist in order to bring about the therapeutic use of self. The development of self-awareness is vital to recreational therapists, because knowing one's self is a basic competency necessary for helping others.

Chapter 6: Communication Skills

All interpersonal relationships depend on communication, the topic of Chapter 6. Without communication, no relationship can exist, because relationships depend on a two-way sharing of ideas and experiences (Sundeen, Stuart, Rankin, & Cohen, 1998). This is unquestionably true in recreational therapy; good interpersonal communication is necessary for effectively relating to clients in clinical practice.

Chapter 7: Being a Leader

One of the most critical elements in recreational therapy is leadership. Chapter 7 looks at the interactions that occur between the leader and the client, and among clients, that are central to the success of recreational therapy programs. Skills in leadership help the recreational therapist use therapeutic interventions or facilitate client growth. Leadership in recreational therapy calls for competencies in dealing with both individuals and groups.

Chapter 8: Specific Leadership Tasks and Concerns

Leadership in recreational therapy, covered in Chapter 8, requires knowledge of a number of specific tasks and concerns. Among these tasks and concerns are (1) individual client documentation, (2) incident reports, (3) teaching/learning principles, (4) motivating clients, (5) teamwork, (6) advocacy, (7) the International Classification of Functioning, Disability and Health (ICF), and (8) understanding transactions with clients. Areas covered within the section on understanding transactions are self-concept, learned helplessness, the self-fulfilling prophecy, labeling, loneliness, self-efficacy, and attributional processes.

Chapter 9: Clinical Supervision

Chapter 9 discusses clinical supervision, a cooperative process between a supervisor and an individual who has direct responsibility for carrying out the agency's clinical program through work with clients. The supervisor helps the supervisee to improve his or her clinical abilities and to achieve the goals sought for the clinical program. The clinical supervision process has come to be recognized as a key to successful clinical practice of recreational therapy.

Chapter 10: Health and Safety Considerations

Theory forms the underpinnings for professional practice; however, recreational therapists also must possess certain technical knowledge and skills as discussed in Chapter 10. Among the areas of technical knowledge that may be required in recreational therapy are the use of first-aid and safety procedures with members of specific client groups, the proper use of mechanical aids, procedures for transfers and assistive techniques, and information on the effects of commonly used psychotropic and anticonvulsant drugs.

This Book's Format

Each chapter begins with a brief statement of purpose and key terms, followed by a listing of the major objectives for the chapter. At the conclusion of each chapter, reading comprehension questions are provided to guide your reading. They also serve the instructor and students as questions for class discussion. Within each chapter you will find questions or statements heading each section. These questions or statements are often designed to further break down the objectives for the chapter into smaller, more digestible parts.

The Focus of Instruction

You, the reader, are the central point of focus for this book. The focus is on you and the **objectives** you must achieve to possess competencies necessary to meet the personal and professional demands that you will face as a recreational therapist. Your mastery of the skills, attitudes, and knowledge required for professional service in recreational therapy is critical to your personal success and that of your profession.

The Objectives

The objectives at the beginning of each chapter form a road map for learning. Making the purpose clear by the listing of major objectives enhances learning and removes the mystique that sometimes accompanies and plagues instruction.

Reading Comprehension Questions

1. How does this book claim to differ from the traditional "survey" textbooks often used in recreational therapy courses?
2. Why does a recreational therapist need more than "good intentions" in order to practice successfully?
3. What makes the recreational therapist, or any professional helper, different from the layperson?
4. Outline the parts or items found in each chapter.
5. Where is the focus of the book directed?

Chapter 2

Theories and Therapies

■ Chapter Purpose

There is no one preferred therapeutic approach found in recreational therapy. Instead, a great variety of methods are applied in the clinical, rehabilitative, continued care, educational, and other environments in which recreational therapy takes place. Understandably, emerging recreational therapists may be confused by the diversity of approaches in practice today. This chapter will help the reader to grasp a fundamental understanding of the five major theories of helping that apply to interventions in the wide range of settings in which recreational therapy services are delivered. These are the psychoanalytic, behavioristic, humanistic, cognitive-behavioral, and positive psychology theories. Also discussed are developed theories (i.e., family therapy, psychodrama, and multimodal therapy) and related theoretical perspectives (i.e., constructivism, feminist therapies, and multicultural perspectives).

■ Key Terms

- Eclecticism
- Behavior therapy
- Classical conditioning
- Psychoanalytic approach
- Positive reinforcement
- Extinction
- Chaining
- Premack principle
- Gestalt therapy
- Cognitive-behavioral therapy
- Humanistic psychology
- Positive psychology
- Positive emotions
- Family therapy
- Constructivism
- Feminist therapies

- Ego defense mechanisms
- Behavior modification
- Operant conditioning
- Principle of reinforcement
- Negative reinforcement
- Shaping
- Modeling
- Person-centered therapy
- Rational-emotive therapy
- Reality therapy
- Transactional analysis
- Positive strengths
- Positive institutions
- Psychodrama
- Multimodal therapy
- Multicultural perspectives

◼ Objectives

- Appreciate the role of theory in influencing the practice of recreational therapy.
- Know what is meant by eclectic approach.
- Differentiate among psychoanalytic, behavioristic, humanistic, cognitive behavioral, and positive psychology theories.
- Assess selected therapeutic approaches to understand implications for practice in recreational therapy.
- Define basic terminology and concepts of therapeutic approaches related to recreational therapy.
- Examine inclusive viewpoints that transcend established theories of helping.
- Accept responsibility to begin to formulate personal theoretical notions in harmony with abilities, beliefs, and interests.

Theory is a unifying focus for the assumptions that underlie therapeutic approaches. A case can be made for the necessity of theory to direct methods of practice. Following this reasoning, theory furnishes a basis for action, because it provides beliefs, concepts, and assumptions that directly bear on the selection of specific therapeutic techniques. Even without formally studying the theories related to helping, each of us forms personal beliefs and assumptions that operate to guide our everyday actions (Austin, 2011a; Okun, 2002). No doubt you have already begun to develop your own theory for practice, although you may not have systematically analyzed your theory to determine if it consistently and comprehensively integrates the beliefs, concepts, and assumptions of which it is composed.

The Eclectic Approach

Recreational therapy is characterized by **eclecticism**, or the utilization of approaches and techniques drawn from several sources. The rationale for this eclectic approach is that even though each of the widely accepted therapeutic approaches has strong points, no single one has all the answers.

Therefore, instead of imposing a specific approach on all clients, methods are dictated by the nature of client needs. By gaining familiarity with major theories and approaches, the recreational therapist can select and combine the most appropriate techniques from a variety of sources. Of course, techniques chosen for actual practice should be in harmony with the personal abilities, beliefs, and interests of the recreational therapist, as well as with the policies and practices of the agency in which he or she is employed.

A bewildering number of therapeutic approaches exist; therefore, the material within this chapter is organized into several sections in an attempt to present the approaches in digestible portions. First discussed are the five major theoretical approaches to human behavior and the techniques that relate to them. Then a separate section titled *Developed Therapies* deals with the most fully developed therapeutic approaches and discusses therapies such as multimodal therapy and family therapy. Finally, constructivism, feminist therapies, and multicultural perspectives are covered as viewpoints that may transcend the previously presented approaches.

Facilitation techniques and less fully developed therapeutic approaches are covered in Chapter 3. There coverage is given to approaches such as leisure education/counseling, values clarification, relaxation techniques, adventure therapy, animal-assisted therapy, and reminiscence therapy.

The five major theories of human behavior related to helping are the psychoanalytic, behavioristic, humanistic psychology, cognitive-behavioral, and positive psychology theories. All of these perspectives have been embraced by recreational therapy at various times (Austin, 2005-06). In this section each of these major theoretical orientations will be briefly described. (See Table 2.1 for a brief introduction to the orientations.)

Psychoanalytic Approach

Sigmund Freud's (1856-1939) work represents a great contribution to the world of psychiatry, clinical psychology, and psychological theory.

Table 2.1

Five Major Theories of Helping

Theory	Theorists	Concepts	Approaches
Psychoanalytic	Freud Adler Horney Erickson Sullivan	Instincts motivate behaviors. A great deal of significance is given to unconscious factors.	Therapist's interpretations Catharsis Psychoanalysis Psychotherapy
Behavioristic	Watson Pavlov Thorndike Skinner Premack	Behavior is learned. Abnormal behavior is a type of learned behavior and so it can be changed.	Reinforcement Modeling Token economies Premack Principle Social Skills Training

Humanistic Psychology	Rogers
	Perls
	Bern
	Maslow
	Allport
		People identify thoughts and beliefs they hold about themselves and the world in order to change the way they think about themselves and the world.	Person-Centered
			  Therapy
			Gestalt Therapy
			Transactional
			  Analysis

Cognitive Behavioral	Ellis Glasser Beck	Sees people as being self-aware, able to deal with environmental influences, and generally in control of their own destinies.	Rational-Emotive Therapy Reality Therapy Cognitive-Behavioral Therapy

Positive Psychology	Seligman
	Csikszentmihalyi
		People reach optimal functioning through positive emotions, positive traits, and positive institutions.	Broaden-and-Build
			  Theory
			Activities foster
			  positive emotions
			Development of
			  strengths and
			  abilities

As a physician who proposed a psychological view of mental disorders in contrast to the then-traditional organic view, Freud was not accepted by his medical colleagues. For the greater part of his career, he was viewed by the medical community as an extremist obsessed by sex (Maddi, 1996). Yet no other individual had the profound influence on psychological theory and treatment that Freud ultimately produced through the development of his **psychoanalytic approach,** the processes for which he termed the psychodynamic processes (Craighead, Craighead, Kazdin, & Mahoney, 1994).

Freud proposed that there are basic instincts common to all people. These instincts have biological origin, but they are at the core of personality because of the powerful influence they have on thought and behavior. When an instinct is felt, it is an indication that the person is in a state of deprivation. This state of deprivation produces tension that the individual must somehow handle. Therefore, the goal of instincts is to relieve tension produced by biologically induced deprivation. These instinctual drives energize humans into action (Maddi, 1996).

Central to Freud's view is the assumption that there exists within each person a basic tendency to allow the maximum gratification of the primitive instincts while giving minimum attention to the demands of society. This clash between maximizing instinctual desires and minimizing punishment and guilt resulting from society's social controls is the source of all goal-directed behavior. Adjustments in life center on the ability to meet this conflict by working out a compromise among self-centered, selfish, instinctual demand, and the requirements of society (Maddi, 1996; Alderman, 1974).

Freud proposed a balance model in order to conceptualize the dynamics underlying this basic conflict. Under his model he identified three divisions of personality: the id, superego, and ego. All goal-directed behavior results from the interaction of these three systems.

The *id* is the primitive part of us. It is propelled by three major instinctual, biological drives. The first, the *self-preservation instinct*, preserves biological life. It deals with our basic needs for food, water, and oxygen. The other two major forces are the *sexual instinct* and the *aggression instinct* (which Freud later developed into the death instinct).

Freud gave much attention to the sexual instinct, which played an integral part in his theory. He termed the energy for sexual urges the *libido.* The libido induces action when sexual expression has been deprived. According to Freud's early writings, complete gratification of the sexual instinct was produced only by having intercourse with a person of the opposite sex. Other sexual activity was seen to lead to only partial fulfillment (Maddi, 1996). Later, however, Freud broadened his view of the sexual instinct to include pleasurable sensation from the erogenous zones and unidentified "inner" responses that produce pleasurable sensations (Ford & Urban, 1963). Therefore, it may be noted that Freud eventually broadly defined the term "sex" to refer to almost anything pleasurable. The sexual instinct was perceived by Freud to develop to an adult level of maturity through five psychosexual stages (see Table 2.2). However, if a child were overindulged or too greatly restricted during any stage, a partial fixation with that stage could develop. Such a fixation would later be revealed in adult life (Borden & Stone, 1976).

Table 2.2

Freud's Stages of Psychosexual Development

Oral Stage. From birth until about 18 months. Characterized by preoccupation with feeding. The mouth is the primary erogenous zone, thus giving the stage its name. The early source of pleasure is sucking and, when teeth are developed, in biting.

Table 2.2 (cont.)

Anal Stage. From around 18 months to 3 years of age. It is marked by a shift of erotic activity from the mouth to the anus. As the child becomes capable of voluntary control over defecation, he or she begins to express feelings of autonomy through pleasing or annoying parenting adults by retaining or expelling feces. A major developmental task is learning independence and control. The critical experience of this stage is, of course, toilet training.

Phallic Stage. From the end of the third year through the fifth year, during which time the libido is centered in the genital region. During this stage, the questioning of adults about sex, masturbation, and interest in the genitals of the opposite sex are common. The *Oedipus Complex* occurs when the child falls in love with the parent of the opposite sex and develops feelings of rivalry and aggression toward the same-sex parent. The resolution of this conflict occurs with identification with the parent of the same sex. The developmental task of sexual identity takes place as the child begins the socialization process by adopting characteristics of adults of the same sex.

Latency Stage. The stage from about age 6 to puberty in which the child's sexual urges remain dormant. The primary developmental task is identification with groups of peers at school and in recreational activities. During this stage, there is increased intellectual activity and a weakening of home ties.

Genital Stage. This stage begins with puberty when the adolescent becomes sexually mature with the capacity for orgasm. The libido is once again centered on the genital area. The early phase of the stage is characterized by selfish interests. After this, there is for many teens a temporary homosexual phase when adolescents desire to meet with those of the same sex. Finally, attraction to the opposite sex asserts itself and most individuals enter into heterosexual relationships. Persons also strive for independence as they begin to assume adult roles.

Sources: Murray, R. B., & Huelskotter, M. M. W. (1991). *Psychiatric/mental health nursing* (3rd ed.). Norwalk, CT: Appleton & Lange; Okun, B. F. (2002). *Effective helping: Interviewing and counseling techniques* (6th ed.). Pacific Grove, CA: Brooks/Cole; Rawlins, R. P., Williams, S. R., & Beck, C. K. (1993). *Mental health-psychiatric nursing: A holistic life-cycle approach* (3rd ed.). St. Louis: Mosby Year Book; Rowe, C. J., & Mink, W. D. (1993). *An outline of psychiatry* (10th ed.). Madison, WI: Brown and Benchmark; Townsend, M. C. (2000). *Psychiatric mental health nursing: Concepts of care* (3rd ed.). Philadelphia: F. A. Davis Company.

The aggressive instinct leads to free-floating aggressive energy that builds up to the point that aggression must be expressed, according to psychoanalytic theory. Even though it may be displaced or sublimated, the aggressive urge will rebuild and, once again, must be released. The release of aggression is therefore a continual process (Austin, 1971).

The sexual and aggressive urges and emotions of the id are extremely selfish and self-centered. The id is propelled by raw forces of biological necessity, without accompanying social refinement. The process of seeking immediate gratification without concern for reality or moral constraint was termed by Freud as *pleasure principle functioning*. The message of the id is: "This is what I want, what I really really want" (Milne, 1999, p. 125).

The second system of personality is the *superego*. The superego is the person's social conscience. Its crucial role is to incorporate societal values that balance the impulsiveness of the id. Through the superego we take in, or internalize, socializing forces. Not surprisingly, much of the content for internalization comes from our parents or parent figures. Other prime teachers of societal values and beliefs are family members, peer group members, and other significant people in our lives. Once the roles of society are internalized, individuals are no longer controlled primarily by threat of punishment but by the guilt they experience if they transgress against their personal moral codes. Young people commonly have not formed their own value systems. Having not yet learned the rules of society, they are more likely to function at the level of the pleasure principle, and, therefore, must be controlled by threat from parents, police, and other authority figures who have the power to levy punishment. At the other extreme, "mental illness" may occur when the superego has become too strict or unrealistic, and the person cannot cope with the resulting conflict.

The final system of personality is the *ego*. The ego is the moderator between the id and superego. It balances the primitive forces of the id with the structures that the superego attempts to impose. Two functions are thus performed by the ego. The first is to aid in the satisfaction of instincts within the reality demands of the external world. The second function is to allow the expression of instinctual urges consistent with the demands of the superego. In carrying out these functions, the ego is guided by *reality principle functioning*, which leads to the realistic integration of the id's urges by arriving at a compromise that will meet the requirements of society. Thus, the ego is the socialized unit of personality that allows people to make intelligent choices, taking into consideration the demands of the id, the superego, and the environment. It is the part of the mind that controls higher cognitive powers and engages in realistic thinking based on accumulated experiences and perceptions of the environment.

Ego Defense Mechanisms

In order to meet the instinctual demands of the id while defending against the moral structures of the superego, the ego may turn to the use of **defense mechanisms**. Defense mechanisms function unconsciously to protect us when we feel a threat to the integrity of our ego, or sense of self-concept. They put up a protective shield against psychic pain (i.e., guilt, anxiety, shame) by displacing the energy of instinctive urges of the id toward objects or actions other than those from which they originated (Alderman, 1974; Okun, 2002; Tamparo & Lindh, 2000). Among commonly employed defenses are denial, repression, compensation, displacement, regression, projection, sublimation, substitution, rationalization, minimization, and intellectualization (Ramont & Niedringhaus, 2008).

Psychoanalysis, Transference, and Countertransference

Although the terms *psychoanalysis* and *psychodynamic* are often used to mean the same thing, there is a distinction between *psychoanalysis* and treatment based on psychodynamic principles. *Psychoanalysis* is a long-term therapy based primarily on exploring the unconscious to make it conscious. Treatment often involves the patient attending three to five sessions weekly in which he or she lies on a couch with the psychoanalyst sitting behind him or her. In orthodox psychoanalysis, the patient is encouraged to transfer unknowingly to the psychoanalyst (analyst) attitudes and feelings the patient has held toward significant others. Through this expression of attitudes and feelings, the analyst can examine the patient's reactions. This process of identifying the analyst with a person from the patient's past is called **transference**. Supposedly the awareness gained by the patient through transference allows him or her to become free from past confusion and conflict. Aasheim (2011) has explained, "Transference refers to the unconscious experience in which a client displaces thoughts, feelings, and behaviors onto the counselor (i.e., analyst or therapist), although these thoughts, feelings, and behaviors originally stemmed from a relation with another significant figure in his or her life" (p. 169). The term *countertransference* is used to describe the process when the therapist responds to the client as though he or she were someone from the therapist's past. Countertransference is not sought and must be guarded against by the therapist so that the client is responded to genuinely and not like another person from the therapist's past. *Psychodynamic psychotherapy*, on the other hand, is briefer and less intensive than psychoanalysis. It does not deal with extensive probing of the unconscious but employs psychoanalytic principles in dealing with specific problems in living (Blackham, 1977; Carson & Trubowitz, 2006; Hill & O'Brien, 1999; Kovel, 1976; Levy, 2009).

Play Therapy

Children's play was seen by Freud as a partial means to master painful or tension-producing experiences by acting them out over and over again. Through play, children grasp the situation and feel mastery, or control, over reality (Ellis, 1973). Play therapy, as developed by psychoanalytic theorists, is based on this basic idea that symbolic play offers a means for the child to bring real-life problems to the surface in order to be able to deal with them and establish control over them. In play therapy children are allowed to play out traumatic experiences under the direction of a therapist schooled in psychoanalytic theory. Play therapy has now broadened from its original psychoanalytic basis that primarily emphasized the unconscious "to include the child's conscious cognition, observable behaviors, recent experiences, family interactions, and peer and social interactions" (Critchley, 1995, p. 335). Nondirective and behavioral approaches have joined the psychoanalytic approach as theoretical bases for play therapy.

Recreation and Psychoanalytic Theory

Psychoanalytic theorists have presented the positive effects of recreation in helping people to lead happier lives. Among these theorists have been the eminent psychiatrists Karl and William Menninger, who have suggested recreation activities as a means to discharging sexual and aggressive impulses in a socially acceptable manner (Menninger, 1960; Gussen, 1967). The influence of psychoanalytic theory also found its way into recreational therapy literature of the 1960s and 1970s. In a paper titled "The Rationale of Recreation as Therapy," Meyer (1962) discussed the strengthening of defense mechanisms through recreation activities. Included was information on the substitution of acceptable activities for aggressive impulses, the sublimation of sexual urges through dance and other art forms, and the development of skills to compensate for real or imagined inadequacies. O'Morrow (1971), in an article entitled "The Whys of Recreation Activities for Psychiatric Patients," suggested that recreation activities provide approved outlets for aggression and other emotions by facilitating sublimation and permitting unconscious conflicts to be expressed.

The Cathartic Notion

The idea that recreation can provide outlets for pent-up aggressive urges was once widely accepted. It was thought that ventilating aggression provided a safe opportunity to rid the individual of aggressive energy. Both viewing and taking part in aggressive sports were seen as proper outlets through which to release aggression. Supposedly this produced what has been termed a cathartic effect. Freud is credited with developing the **cathartic notion**, although, from the days of Aristotle, people have felt that venting an emotion can free a person from that emotion. Two ideas underlie the cathartic notion. One is that the expression of aggression can provide relief from the tension or make a person feel better. The second is that the person who expresses aggression will have a tendency to be less aggressive (Austin, 1971).

Reviews by social psychologists have found fault with the cathartic notion (e.g., Berkowitz, 1978; Martens, 1975; Parke & Sawin, 1975; Quanty, 1976). Following their review of the research evidence, Baron and Byrne (1994) wrote that "Contrary to popular belief, then, catharsis does not appear to be as effective a means for reducing aggression as is widely assumed" (p. 471). Feldman (1995) stated, "The idea of catharsis is appealing, because it suggests that permitting people to 'let off steam' can reduce their subsequent penchant for violence. Despite its appeal, though, results of experiments investigating catharsis do little to buttress the claims of theorists (who favor the cathartic notion)" (p. 293). Widmeyer, Bray, Dorsch and McGuire (2002) similarly concluded, "Thus, it appears that behaving aggressively tends to exercise (i.e., develop aggression) rather than exorcise hostility" (p. 354). It now seems clear that allowing aggressive behavior simply brings about further aggression. If children and adults are encouraged to behave aggressively during recreation participation, it would be expected that they will become more aggressive, not less aggressive, as once hypothesized.

Quanty (1976) has suggested that the social learning model (i.e., behavior can be socially reinforced) contains the implication that prosocial responses to anger and frustration can be just as effectively reinforced as aggressive responses. One prosocial behavior that can help clients to deal with anger aggression is to take part in vigorous physical activities. As in other forms of stress, anger reactions produce high levels of adrenaline in the bloodstream. This is part of the "flight or fight" reaction in which our bodies prepare for action. Being "hyped up" brings about a higher level of arousal that will likely lead to even more negative thoughts and feelings. At this point the cycle needs to be broken. This can occur by the tension reduction produced by physical activity when a parasympathetic reaction is produced. Exercise uses up adrenaline and has a calming effect on the body. Taking part in a physical activity that the person particularly likes can add to the effect by producing enjoyment and positive reactions. Doing something pleasurable also provides the participant with a positive "mental set" while, in addition, serving as a distraction from the situation that produced the original anger (Hayes, 2001). It is best to avoid competitive activities because such activities can lead to frustration for those who lose. Therefore, for clients dealing with anger aggression, noncompetitive physical activities (e.g., swimming, jogging) that clients enjoy would be the best.

In sum, the cathartic notion that aggression may be reduced through viewing or participating in aggressive recreation activities has been refuted. Yet, the general influence of psychoanalytic theory has been felt in the practice of recreational therapy since at least the 1960s. Even today, some unenlightened recreational therapists still subscribe to the cathartic notion.

The Neoanalytic Theorists

Well-known neoanalytic theorists, such as Alfred Adler, Carl Jung, Karen Horney, Harry Stack Sullivan, and Erik Erickson, have brought about many modifications in psychoanalytic theory over the years. Adler developed the concept of the inferiority complex. Jung brought a more optimistic view of human beings that emphasized that maladaptive behaviors arise largely from social and environmental factors. Sullivan's interpersonal theory of personality focused on understandings gained from knowledge of clients' interpersonal histories (Murray & Huelskotter, 1991; Okun, 2002; Rowe & Mink, 1993). Erickson formulated a model of psychosocial development containing eight stages, the first five of which roughly parallel Freud's psychosexual stages (Rawlins, Williams, & Beck, 1993).

Summary

Within this section, Freud's psychoanalytic theory has been presented as a conflict model involving three systems of personality (id, ego, and superego) and two primary instinctual drives (sex and aggression). His theory attached a great deal of significance to unconscious factors operating in the id and superego and to the mediating role of the ego. Freud's classic psychoanalytic theory also placed great emphasis on the biological determinism reflected in the instinctual urges that supposedly propel behavior (although neo-Freudians have placed greater emphasis on social and cultural aspects as determinants of behavior). Even though it is no longer the sole form of psychotherapy, as it once was, the psychoanalytic approach is usually what comes to mind when the average person thinks of therapy (Kovel, 1976), and it continues to represent an influence on recreational therapy.

Implications for Recreational Therapy

Recreational therapists will not conduct psychoanalytically oriented psychotherapy, but the theoretical ideas represented by the psychoanalytic viewpoint will likely pervade the practice of recreational therapists. Recreational therapists must recognize that unconscious motivational factors may affect behavior, the use of defense mechanisms in protecting against threats to self-concept, and the effects the developmental years have on adult behavior (Okun, 2002).

The once accepted psychoanalytic concept of the cathartic notion has been refuted by numerous researchers and theorists. The literature is clear that allowing aggression just brings about more aggression. Aggression begets aggression. Ideas concerning the cathartic notion of releasing aggressive urges have common sense appeal, but the evidence strongly suggests that these concepts lack the validity once afforded them by recreational therapists. Instead of acting aggressively, clients should be encouraged to take part in physical activities that are not aggressive in nature and are not competitive. Participation in such physical activities has the potential to produce a calming effect that leads to a reduction in anger aggression.

Behavioristic Approach

In the 1960s, there emerged a form of intervention that became known as behavior therapy or behavior modification. Many use the terms interchangeably; however, the term **behavior therapy** seems to be employed mostly in psychiatric practice, while **behavior modification** is associated with other client groups, such as persons with intellectual disabilities. No matter what terminology is used to describe the behavioristic approach, it is concerned with bringing about changes in behavior. The theory and techniques used to bring about behavioral changes are based on the psychological theory of behaviorism.

Behaviorism arose as a protest to the psychoanalytic model. In contrast to the psychoanalytic approach, where emphasis is on hidden, unconscious forces that underlie behavior, the basis for behaviorism comes from academic learning theory. John B. Watson (1878-1958) is noted as the founder of behaviorism. In 1913 he wrote the paper "Psychology as the Behaviorist Sees It," in which he set down basic positions of behaviorism. Watson attacked subjectivity, saying that psychology should not be concerned with subjective experiences but with overtly observable behavior.

Followers of this new school of psychology also rejected the concept of mental illness. Instead, they assumed that abnormal behavior was not a disease, but rather that it was learned. The behavioral assumption is that all maladaptive behaviors are learned and that they can be modified through learning. Some behaviorists, therefore, contend that the term *therapy* is not appropriate for their approach because change occurs by means of an educational experience that involves a teaching/learning process (Corey, 1985; Waughfield, 2002).

Pavlov, Thorndike, and Skinner

The basic concepts of behaviorism spring from the early work of Pavlov and Thorndike. Pavlov (1849-1936), a Russian physiologist, emphasized the simple association of events that become linked when they repeatedly occur together. This theory, which became known as **classical conditioning**, or respondent conditioning, involves substituting one stimulus-evoking response for another. In Pavlov's famous dog study there was the pairing of one stimulus to which there was already a set response (salivation to food) with a neutral stimulus (the sound of a bell). After a number of pairings, the neutral stimulus (in this case, the bell) begins to take on the characteristics of the first stimulus (food bringing on salivation). The *unconditioned stimulus* (food) and *the conditioned stimulus* (bell) become connected to bring about the *response* (saliva).

Thorndike (1874-1949) emphasized that behavior is controlled by its consequences. That is, it rewards function to reinforce certain behaviors, whereas negative outcomes tend to eliminate the occurrence of behavior. A reinforcer is basically anything that reinforces behavior. Commonly employed reinforcers include food, money, attention, affection, and approval or praise. The potency of a reinforcer depends on the need state of the person. For example, food would be a poor reinforcer after dinner. Candy would not be a good reinforcer for someone on a diet.

Noted former Indiana University and Harvard University psychologist B. F. Skinner (1904-1990) has also been associated with this line of thought, which has been termed **operant conditioning**, or *instrumental conditioning*. The terms come from the idea that it involves voluntary actions that operate on the environment instead of just responding to the environment, as in respondent conditioning. Craighead and her colleagues (1994) explained operant conditioning as follows: "Much of human behavior is not involuntary or elicited by stimuli in the sense of reflexive reactions. Rather, behavior is emitted and is controlled primarily by the consequences that follow. Behaviors amenable to control by a change in the consequences that follow them are referred to as operants, because they are responses that operate on or have some influence on the environment and generate consequences" (p. 30). Most everyday behaviors (e.g., talking, smiling, working) fit this category because they are not reflexive but are freely emitted.

Pavlov's classical or respondent conditioning theory involves the **principle of association**, while Thorndike's theory (operant or instrumental conditioning) involves the **principle of reinforcement**. These two basic principles help to form the foundation for techniques of the behavioral approach (Milne, 1999; Seaward, 2002). "Reinforcement in some form is probably the procedure most readily associated with behavior therapy," according to Franks (2006, p. 39).

What specific intervention techniques have resulted from the behavioral approach? Terms such as positive reinforcement, negative reinforcement, extinction, modeling, shaping, chaining, prompting, fading, time-out, token economies, behavioral contracts, and the Premack principle may be familiar as techniques that have a basis in the behavioral approach. The following section will briefly review each of these techniques.

Positive and Negative Reinforcement

Dattilo and Wolfe (2002) stated, "Positive reinforcement represents a powerful tool for promoting appropriate behavior and is the most commonly applied behavior modification procedure" (p. 37). The idea of **positive reinforcement** is that people tend to repeat behaviors that provide rewards. Any behavior that is followed by a positive reinforcer (reward) is likely to be repeated. Teaching new behaviors or increasing the occurrence of existing behaviors therefore depends on the participants finding the behaviors rewarding. Following this train of thought logically, even frequently repeated behaviors that seem to be inappropriate or unproductive must somehow be rewarding for those who perform them.

Negative reinforcement involves *the removal of an aversive stimulus* in order to increase the future occurrence of a desired behavior. The rationale behind negative reinforcement is that if an individual is subjected to unpleasant or painful stimulation, any behavior that results in the withdrawal of the stimulus is reinforced. Negative reinforcement is sometimes confused with punishment, a procedure used to decrease the future occurrence of an undesired behavior. The two are different, as Milne (1999) has noted. He states: **Positive reinforcement** describes the strengthening of a response by the incentive of a stimulus as reward. **Negative reinforcement** describes the strengthening of a response by removing an unpleasant stimulus (e.g., by removing a loud noise)" (p. 168). Dattilo and Wolfe (2002) explained, "*Negative reinforcement* increases the strength of a behavior by removing or postponing an aversive antecedent, contingent on the occurrence of the behavior." Further, they stated, "When the individual engages in a behavior that avoids or allows the person to escape from the aversive condition, negative reinforcement has occurred. Therefore, the consequence of the behavior is avoidance of or escape from an ongoing aversive condition" (p. 39). Because negative reinforcement is rarely employed in recreational therapy, the focus of this section will be on positive reinforcement.

Kinds of Reinforcement

While we may first think of M&M's™ candies as a reinforcer, people find many things to be rewarding. As previously mentioned, rewards include food and money as well as social reinforcers such as attention, affection, and approval. More subtle are rewards gained from discovery or learning that people may gain as outcomes of educational or recreational experiences (Vernon, 1972). According to Vernon, children are least affected by subtle reinforcers. Therefore food is often initially used as a reinforcer in programs serving children. After a short while, praise is given along with the food and, occasionally, praise is given alone. Gradually, praise is used more and more by itself as a reinforcer.

Attention can be a potent reinforcer, whether provided in the form of praise or approval or just paying attention to the person. As a matter of fact, the leader must be on guard not to give too much attention to those who act out or behave inappropriately. People who feel neglected may cause problems just to draw attention to themselves. Positive outlets must be found for these persons so that they can receive rewards for appropriate behaviors.

If undesirable behavior exists, it has been reinforced. It follows that the simplest way to get rid of a behavior is to stop reinforcing it and it will go away. Each time a behavior is emitted without being reinforced, the strength or frequency of that behavior is diminished. This process of withholding reinforcement is termed **extinction.**

Reinforcement Techniques

The timing of the delivery of reinforcers is critical to their success. To have the greatest effect, they should come immediately after the behavior occurs. For this reason, athletes in Special Olympics competitions are rewarded immediately following completion of their events. The frequency of reinforcers is likewise important. During the time when behaviors are first being established, a continuous schedule of reinforcement seems to be best. The reward should occur every time the person performs the behavior, if at all practical. Once the behavior has been established, it is possible to change to a partial schedule of rewarding the person only once in a while. This should be done slowly by gradually reducing the frequency of giving reinforcement. Diebert and Harmon (1977) suggest first decreasing reinforcement patterns to reinforce 80% of the time, then 50%, then 30% and, finally, only once in a while.

Shaping is another technique in reinforcement or operant conditioning. It is the process by which reinforcement is differentially applied to the responses that are made toward approximating a desired behavior. Reinforcement is delivered only when a particular standard is reached. Once reached, the standard is continually raised until the person being rewarded makes a closer and closer approximation of the behavior that is being conditioned. Eventually, the final form of desired behavior is reached. **Chaining** is an associated concept that involves linking one learned response with another to build to a more complex response.

Modeling is a form of social learning that may employ reinforcement. Through modeling, new responses can be acquired more quickly if the learner can see a model demonstrate the desired behavior, especially if this is combined with positive reinforcement. Responses can be learned through modeling combined with either seeing the model rewarded or the learner directly receiving a reward. Models who are physically attractive or who are seen as prestigious or influential are most likely to be imitated (Townsend, 2000). Rawson (1978) has reported success in the use of modeling and reinforcement to alter the behavior of children with behavioral disorders in a camping program. Reynolds and Arthur (1982) used modeling as a technique to alter the social play of children with emotional problems.

Wehman (1977) has also reported using various other behavior modification techniques to help children with intellectual disabilities develop play patterns. Among the techniques employed were prompting and fading. In **prompting**, the leader physically guides the child through the desired play skill. For instance, the child is manually guided to pull a wagon or roll a ball. Successes are followed by praise and affection. **Fading** involves gradually removing the physical guidance of the prompts when the play skill has become learned.

A procedure often employed in behavior modification programs for children is time-out. **Time-out** is a type of negative reinforcement because it involves the removing of a reinforcer or time away from positive reinforcement (Johnson, 1995). Time-out is used as an alternative to punishment when the behavior of an individual is disruptive or may be harmful to himself or herself or to the group. It involves simply removing the person for a short time from the setting in which others are able to gain positive reinforcement. This is done matter-of-factly, without berating the person. Typically, the time-out room is a small, plain room devoid of stimuli so that there is nothing for the child to do. Therefore, time-out involves stimulus removal in contrast to punishment's stimulus delivery.

When irrational fears (i.e., phobias) require therapy, two techniques may be used. **Systematic desensitization** is a gradual approach in which the client is taught to relax while in the situation, or with the object, that brings on the fear. **Implosion therapy** exposes the client to a level of the feared stimulus so that eventually the fear is reduced (Hayes, 2001).

Token economy systems may be applied to change behavior. Tokens (also called "exchangeables") are given by staff members to clients as rewards for performing selected behaviors that have been determined to be desirable. The tokens are made of plastic or some other inexpensive material and have no value in themselves, but they can be redeemed for items or privileges that have value to the residents (e.g., candy, television viewing time). Research published in the *Therapeutic Recreation Journal* (Wolfe, Dattilo, & Gast, 2003) reported a token economy system produced an immediate increase in the numbers of pro-social behaviors of adolescents with emotional and behavioral disorders.

Behavioral **contracts** are written agreements, typically between client and therapist, in which the consequences of specified client behaviors are set in advance. The contract usually specifies reinforcers to be received by the client upon completing certain behaviors within a given time period. Therapists should encourage clients to become involved in the writing of the contract so they may help decide on the behaviors to be specified, the accepted length of time, and appropriate reinforcers. It is generally agreed that clients who cooperate in formulating contracts will be motivated to fulfill them.

Premack Principle

The final behavior modification procedure to be discussed is the widely accepted **Premack principle**. Premack introduced the idea that naturally, highly preferred behavior can be used to reinforce a less-preferred behavior. For example, quiet activity of children (the less-preferred behavior) might be reinforced by allowing the children to have outside play on the playground (a naturally, highly preferred activity). Another example would be allowing a teen to talk with friends on the telephone if she completes her homework (Townsend, 2000). This procedure has two obvious advantages. One is that highly preferred behaviors are easily observed, so appropriate reinforcers can be predicted relatively simply for a given individual. Second, because activities are used as reinforcers, a behavior can be increased without depending on outside rewards such as candy or other food.

Schmokel (1980), in an unpublished student research project, called into question the validity of the Premack principle alone to predict behavioral outcomes adequately. According to Schmokel, a better explanation is the *response deprivation hypothesis* proposed by Timberlake and Allison (1974). Under this hypothesis, either a highly preferred behavior or a less-preferred (low-rate) behavior can serve as a reinforcer. The key is that the individual is deprived of his or her normal level of activity until he or she increases the sought behavior above its accustomed level. Even a relatively low-rate behavior can be used as a reinforcer if the person is deprived from participating in it at the accustomed level. On the other hand, a high-preference activity will not serve as a reinforcer unless the individual feels deprived of participation at the normal level of activity.

Implications for Recreational Therapy

The focus of the behavioristic approach is clearly on the objective observation of overt behavior and the learning of new behaviors. This approach emphasizes the need to make precise behavioral observations and to consider conditions that may alter behavior. Recreational therapists must be accountable by providing outcome measures resulting from designated plans and continually examining reward systems that surround and influence client behavior (Dattilo & Wolfe, 2002; Okun, 2002). Recreational therapists can also apply behavioral techniques covered in this section of the chapter, such as positive reinforcement, negative reinforcement, shaping, chaining, modeling, fading, time-outs, token economies, behavioral contracts, and the response deprivation hypothesis.

Three therapeutic approaches, which have come to be viewed as entities unto themselves, are related to the behavioral approach. Assertiveness training and progressive relaxation training rest upon behaviorism. Social skills training has been influenced by several theoretical perspectives, including behaviorism. These approaches and their implications for recreational therapy are covered later in the following chapter on "Facilitation Techniques."

The Growth Psychology Approach: Humanistic Psychology

The term growth psychology is taken from Schultz's (1977) book *Growth Psychology: Models of the Healthy Personality*, in which he presents the humanistic psychology views of figures such as Maslow, Berne, Rogers, and Perls. Humanistic psychology is a way of looking at human nature that rejects what many consider to be the negative and deterministic views presented by the psychoanalytic and behavioristic approaches. Humanistic psychology does not see people as being primarily driven by instinctual urges (as psychoanalytic theory) or conditioned by the environment in a robotic manner (as behavioristic theory). Smither (2009) has emphasized that "humanistic psychotherapists categorically reject the idea that human behavior is controlled by either unconscious motivation or conditions in the client's environment" (p. 309).

The humanistic approach recognizes biological drives and the influence of past learning, but it goes beyond previous theories to see people as being self-aware, capable of accepting or rejecting environmental influences, and generally in conscious control of their own destiny. Furthermore, under this growth-orientated model, the emphasis is not so much on past failures and conflicts, but on tapping previously unused creative talents and energies. In short, humanistic psychology takes a positive view of human nature in contrast to the relatively pessimistic picture offered by psychoanalytic theory and behaviorism.

Critical Review

Humanistic, or third-force, psychologists have been critical of the psychoanalytic and behavioristic approaches. A number of these criticisms are apparent in the following quotation taken from Shapiro and Astin (1998). They have written:

> Textbooks summarize the first force, the psychodynamic position, as saying we are controlled by unconscious biological, instinctual forces. Behaviorism, the second force, ascribes control to environmental factors. Both theories argue that humans are influenced by powerful internal and external forces largely outside their conscious awareness and control. The third force, humanistic/existential, is seen in many ways a rejoinder emphasizing the importance of personal choice, individual freedom, and the right and responsibility of individuals to be in control of their own lives. (p. 12)

Thus, both the biological determinism of Freudians and the environmental determinism of the behaviorists have been rejected by humanistic theorists. Instead of behavior being determined by biology or the environment, these third-force followers perceive people as having freedom of choice. Because people direct their own behavior, they must assume responsibility for their actions. This notion is central to humanistic psychology, which views people as striving toward self-fulfillment in a self-aware, self-directed manner (Smither, 2009).

Schultz (1977) has referred to humanistic psychology as *health psychology*, since it is concerned with wellness. Humanistic psychologists view mental health as more than the mere absence of neurosis or psychosis. Healthy persons are self-aware. They realize their strengths and weaknesses, and they do not pretend to be something they are not. They live in the present instead of dwelling on the past or fantasizing about the future. They are not satisfied to maintain the status quo, but seek challenges and experiences in life.

Those following the humanistic approach believe that the relationship between the therapist and client are at the heart of the therapeutic enterprise. Smither (2009) wrote:

> ...humanistic psychotherapy puts special emphasis on the actual interpersonal relationship between the therapist and client. In fact, this relationship is key to the success of humanistic therapy. Humanistic psychologists believe that an individual's

inability to solve his or her problems—which is the reason for seeking professional help—originates in flawed interpersonal relationships from the past. Because of this, the humanistic psychotherapist takes special precautions not to convey any kind of evaluation or judgment other than his or her warm acceptance of the client as a person (pp. 318-319).

Person-Centered Therapy, Gestalt Therapy, and Transactional Analysis are therapeutic approaches that come from growth-oriented traditions of humanistic psychology. These approaches are covered in the sections that follow.

Person-Centered Therapy

One of the most widely accepted growth-oriented therapeutic approaches is the **person-centered therapy** of Carl Rogers (1902-1987). Rogers believed people have the capacity to be rational thinkers who can assume responsibility for themselves and whose behavior will be constructive when given the freedom to set directions in life. People are seen as motivated by a basic tendency to seek growth (to actualize potentials) and self-enhancement (to feel positive regard).

As each person grows up, a sense of self begins to form. A positive concept of self is developed when a person receives love (positive regard) from others. If parents and significant others freely give love (unconditional positive regard), there is no need for defensive behavior or to feel guilty or unworthy. The person will feel good about himself or herself and will experience congruence between positive self-concept and life experiences with others.

On the other hand, when parents withdraw love and affection when children misbehave, children may learn to feel that they are only worthy of love when they behave in ideal ways. Hayes (2001) has explained:

> As a result, Rogers argued, they tend to develop unrealistically high ideals. They feel that it isn't they themselves who are loved, but some ideal person. So their view of themselves—their self-concept—is that, if they are just being themselves, they are unlovable. (p. 70)

When incongruence between the concepts of self and life experiences occurs, it is disturbing and poses a threat to established self-perception. Anxiety results and defense mechanisms become aroused. Through defense mechanisms, experiences are distorted or denied in order to bring them in line with self-perceptions. Therefore, psychological problems arise when incongruencies exist between life experience and self-concepts. Intervention through person-centered therapy allows the person to reestablish congruence and once again begin to pursue self-actualization.

The role of the helping professional in person-centered therapy is to display unconditional positive regard (complete acceptance) for the client. The basic hypothesis on which person-centered therapy rests is that the support of an empathetic, genuine, accepting helper will enable the client to change. Techniques are secondary to attitude, since the helper is not an expert with insight who can condition the client but someone to strengthen and support the client in efforts to become responsible for his or her own life. The helper never tells the client what to do. Cain (2002) has explained that the Rogerian therapist ever keeps in mind the "belief that the direction and local of control in therapy [are]...clearly centered in the person seeking help" (p. 17).

Hayes (2001), a British author, has explained the importance of the therapist creating an atmosphere of unconditional positive regard and of being nondirective. He has written that this means

> it is important that the counselor, or therapist, is able to create an atmosphere of unconditional positive regard. That means a relationship in which the person feels safe and approved of, no matter what they reveal about their inner selves. At the same time, Rogers believed, the therapist also needs to be as nondirective as possible. That means encouraging the client to say what they want or need, rather than suggesting anything. (p. 71)

Therefore, the helper is nonjudgmental and nondirective, providing an accepting atmosphere that will allow the client to assume the same positive self-regard the helper has shown the client. Since the client is obviously valued and cared for by the helper, the client begins to feel he or she is a person worth being cared for. In such a nurturing climate, feelings are brought into awareness, and the client learns to revise his or her concepts of self to bring them into congruence with life experiences. Once this process is complete, the client no longer feels threatened and is open to new experiences (Hill & O'Brien, 1999; Raskin & Rogers, 2000; Okun, 2002; Schultz, 1977; Smither, 2009). Thus the therapeutic relationship is a key. As Milne (1999) has explained, "The quality of the interpersonal relationship—supportive, warm, empathic, accepting—provides a safe, validating environment for the client to explore, examine and accept the whole of their being" (p. 159).

The element of an empathic response provides the focus for Bennett's (2001) book, *The Empathic Healer: An Endangered Species?* In this book empathy is described as "a mode of relating in which one person comes to know the mental content of another, both affectively and cognitively, at a particular moment in time and as product of the relationship that exists between them" (p. 7).

Empathy represents the core of Rogers' person-centered therapy, according to Bennett. Bennett explained the role of the therapist under person-centered therapy:

> The role was not to treat in the ordinary sense, but to promote recovery of health through creating an ambience that might reawaken the innate capacity for such growth. Under such circumstances, healing would come from within. This ambience is characterized by an attitude that includes three features: *congruence* (genuineness on the part of the therapist), *unconditional positive regard for the patient* (acceptance of the patient's communicated experience without judgment or criticism), and empathy. (p. 39)

Rogers believed that six vital conditions need to exist in order for change to occur. These are outlined in Table 2.3.

Gestalt Therapy

A second well-known growth-oriented approach is *Gestalt therapy.* Frederick (Fritz) Perls conceived Gestalt therapy after he became disenchanted with Freud and psychoanalysis. The term *Gestalt* is a German word that implies an organized whole or sense of wholeness.

Perls felt that many people repress impulses and wishes so that they become aware of only parts of themselves instead of knowing the whole self. Preconceived perfectionistic ideas cause these people to inhibit their feelings and impulses and to become afraid to express them. They live as they believe others expect them to behave. Instead of following

Table 2.3

Six Conditions for Change

1. The client and helper must be in psychological contact. A therapeutic relationship or emotional connection between the helper and client is essential.
2. The client must be in a state of incongruence....If a client feels no anxiety, she or he is unlikely to be motivated enough to engage in the helping process.
3. The helper must be congruent (genuine) or integrated in the relationship....The helper cannot be phony in the helping relationship.
4. The helper must feel unconditional positive regard for the client....Essentially, a helper is trying to understand a client's feelings and experience but is not trying to judge whether the person "should" or "should not" have the feelings or whether the feelings are "right" or "wrong."
5. The helper must experience empathy for the client....We can distinguish empathy from sympathy, in which the helper feels pity for the client and often acts from a one-up power position rather than as an equal.
6. The client must experience the helper's congruence, unconditional positive regard, and empathy. If the client does not experience the facilitative conditions, for all practical purposes they do not exist for the client and the sessions are not likely to be helpful.

Source: Hill, C. E., & O'Brien, K. M. (1999). *Helping skills: Facilitating, exploration, insight, and action.* Washington, D.C.: American Psychological Association, pp. 68, 69.

natural and spontaneous responses guided by a true awareness of self and the world, they allow external controls to move them in stereotyped, predetermined ways. In short, they are directed by their environment rather than being self-directed.

Because they are unable to accept their own impulses and feelings, they project these onto others. By distorting the situation, they do not have to own up to their feelings. They may also deny that parts of themselves exist. Nevertheless, their hidden impulses and feelings will seek release in some indirect form such as a nervous tic or an ulcer.

The goal of Gestalt therapy is to restore the personality to wholeness. This is done by helping the client to gain a full awareness of what is really happening to him or her so that the person may recognize that he or she can be free of external regulations (including those that have become internalized). Without such awareness, the person will be unable to be himself or herself and will continue to assume roles that he or she feels others expect.

Panman and Panman (2006) emphasized, "The focus of Gestalt Therapy is always on what is, on awareness of the present moment, and not what might have been (regrets about the past) or what should be (worry about the future)" (p. 53). Techniques of Gestalt therapy are aimed at opening up direct, immediate experiences so that the client can become aware of what he or she is feeling, thinking, and doing. The emphasis is always on present behavior (the "here and now") and on the direct expression of impulses, thoughts, and feelings instead of on following stereotyped social roles that keep people from becoming aware of their needs and feelings. The critical aspect of Gestalt therapy is, therefore, opening the person's awareness of real needs and feelings (which avoidance mechanisms have excluded from awareness) and having the person assume the responsibility to act directly to express his or her impulses and feelings.

In addition to awareness of the self, Perls presented two other levels of awareness: awareness of the world, and awareness of intervening fantasy between the self and the world. Gestalt therapy helps persons to become aware of the aspects of the personality that contain fantasy and irrational prejudices and to discontinue them so that they are no longer barriers between the self and the real world. In becoming aware of intervening fantasy, people see things as they really exist. They can then experience the world in the present instead of consuming energy dealing with prejudices and fantasies.

The methods of Gestalt therapy revolve around training people to observe themselves by bringing experiences into awareness so they can be examined. Techniques such as role-playing and group awareness exercises are used to help clients get in touch with what they are experiencing so that they may become more deeply aware of themselves. The therapist remains active during therapy in order to redirect the client when he or she tries to avoid problems. Thus the therapist must remain alert to signals in tone of voice, posture, or other nonverbal cues that indicate true feelings are being denied so that the client's attention may be drawn to them.

The facilitation of client awareness is seen as the therapist's main responsibility. Once healthy awareness of the self and the world are established, unhealthy processes that substitute for growth and block self-actualization are removed. The healthy person can then actualize his or her potentials by responding spontaneously and naturally to needs and feelings (Okun, 2002; Matson, 1977; Schultz, 1977).

Transactional Analysis

Transactional analysis (TA) is a theory of personality and social interaction conceived by Eric Berne (1910-1970). It is most commonly used as a basis for group therapy. Along with rational-emotive therapy and reality therapy, transaction analysis emerged in the 1950s. It was not, however, until Berne's book, *Games People Play* (1964), became a best seller in the mid-1960s that transactional analysis gained popularity.

According to Berne's theory, there are four primary methods used to understand human behavior: structural analysis (to understand ego states within a given individual); transactional analysis (to understand interactions between two people's ego states); racket and game analysis (to understand repetitive transactions that are useless and of a devious nature); and script analysis (to understand life plans formed in childhood on which adults base choices on how their lives should be lived) (Harris, 1976; Woollams, Brown, & Huige, 1976). Following Berne's death in 1970, another element of transaction analysis emerged, the egogram (to symbolize the amount of time and energy the individual exudes in each ego state) (Dusay & Dusay, 1984).

Structural analysis. People have the capacity to store recordings, or "tapes," of past experiences in the brain. From these, they can recall both information and feelings related to specific events, the most significant of which occur during the preschool years. Different tapes play back, depending on which of three ego states a person is operating in—the Parent, Child, or Adult (Harris, 1976). Through structural analysis, the ego state that is operating in a given individual at a particular time is identified.

The source of the *Parent ego state* is a massive tape of external experiences absorbed during the most formative years (birth to age 6). An enormous store of attitudes, beliefs, values, and rules for living learned primarily from parents (or parent substitutes) directs patterns of behavior of the Parent. A person's Parent can be nurturing or controlling and critical. In either case, these attitudes can be expressed directly in the individual's words, demeanor, voice tone, and expressions or gestures—or indirectly as an effect on the Adult or Child.

Associated with the Critical Parent would be words such as bad, should, ought, and always; a stern and judgmental demeanor; a critical or condescending tone of voice, and gestures such as pointing the index finger. The Nurturing Parent would use words such as good, nice, cute, and I love you, a caring demeanor; a warm tone of voice; and expressions and gestures such as smiling and open arms.

The *Child ego state* is based on another tape that has been made simultaneously with the Parent tape. This tape has recorded the internal reactions or feelings of the child to external events (Harris, 1976). Thus the Child ego state is made up of all the emotions that spring from early experiences in addition to natural or innate feelings. As with the Parent, the Child can be divided into two major parts: the Adapted child and the Natural child (or Free child). The Adapted child responds in ways that gain acceptance from "big people." The Natural child is spontaneous and free from worry about pleasing others (Woollams et al., 1976).

The *Adult ego state* is the rational part of the person that weighs facts before making decisions. It begins to develop late in the first year of life. Through exploration and testing, the infant begins to take in and respond to information (as the Parent and Child) and to gain control over the environment. The Adult ego state is the computer-like data processor that makes decisions based on information from the Parent, the Child, and from data the Adult has collected and continues to gather (Harris, 1976). By the time the person has reached 12 years of age, the Adult has matured to the point of becoming fully functional (Woollams et al., 1976).

The emotionally healthy individual can function appropriately from the ego state of his or her choosing, whether it is serving as a Nurturing Parent to a youngster, the Adult making a decision, or the Natural Child enjoying recreation (Woollams et al., 1976). Problems develop when a person is unable to work from the appropriate ego state in a particular situation. For example, the person who lets the Critical Parent pattern his or her behavior during leisure deprives himself or herself of a true recreational experience and may be a disruptive force in the recreational enjoyment of others.

Transactional analysis. Transactions are interactions between two people's ego states. For example, two mature persons might interact on an Adult-to-Adult level. Through transactional analysis, such interactions are examined. In the example given, a parallel transaction exists. In such parallel transactions, the response comes from the ego state at which it was directed, and the returned response is aimed at the original ego state that initiated the transaction. In parallel transactions, the flow of communication continues.

In contrast, nonparallel (crossed) transactions always cause a breakdown in communication. For example, one person may ask from the Adult, "Where are the cards?" Another person responds, "Why can't you take care of things?" The second person responded from his or her Parent to the Child of the first. It is easy to see how this transaction could lead to a communication breakdown.

Rackets and games analysis. The phrase "collecting stamps" is used to describe the process by which people collect feelings, much as shoppers used to collect trading stamps. These stamps (feelings) are later cashed in to justify some behavior. People cash in their stamps toward any number of things, from getting drunk to attempting suicide. Their logic is that they deserve whatever "prize" they desire (Woollams et al., 1976).

Healthy persons do not collect stamps. Instead, they deal with feelings as they occur. The actual act of pursuing and saving stamps is the person's *racket*. Different rackets exist, including anger rackets and depression rackets, in which people collect anger stamps or depression stamps, depending on their particular racket.

Games substitute for intimate relations. Essentially, they are a series of dishonest transactions people repeat over and over in order to accomplish ulterior motives.

Script analysis. Early in life most people determine a life plan by which they live their lives. This plan, or script, preordains the roles they will assume in later life (Steiner, 1974). If the script results mostly in positive strokes (recognition), it is a winner's script. If the strokes are generally negative, it is a loser's script. Routine, boring scripts that look good superficially but in which people actually do not take chances and avoid emotionally charged situations are termed nonwinning or banal scripts (Woollams et al., 1976).

Scripts are closely related to *life positions,* because scripts are formed out of the vantage point of one of four life positions: (a) I'm OK–You're OK; (b) I'm OK–You're not OK; (c) I'm not OK–You're OK; and (d) I'm not OK–You're not OK.

When an infant enters the world, he or she naturally assumes the healthy I'm OK–You're OK position. This position is maintained as long as the person receives positive strokes (recognition). These can be nonverbal (a pat on the back) or verbal ("You're beautiful"). When a person's stroke bank is full, a stroke reserve is built to draw on and the person feels OK. When the reserve is depleted, the person feels not OK (Campos & McCormick, 1980).

Three needs (hungers) underlie the development of ego states in the child and all transactions. Recognition hunger is a need for sensations provided by other people. It can be met by gaining strokes. Sensation hunger is the need for stimulus. Structure hunger is the need to create order and be a part of social structures (Burton & Dimbleby, 1990). There are six ways of structuring time.

Withdrawal is removing oneself from others. By withdrawal, people avoid strokes. *Rituals* are predictable exchanges of strokes. *Pastimes* are goal-directed communications. Both are superficial and result in minimum stroking. *Games* are useless time fillers that substitute for intimate relations. They result only in negative strokes. *Activities* have to do with accomplishing things people want to do or have to do. *Intimacy* is represented in genuine caring relationships that are totally free from games or exploitation. Activities and intimacy provide positive strokes that reinforce OK feelings (James & Jongward, 1996).

Implications of the Humanistic Approach for Recreational Therapy

Recreational therapy (RT) has been heavily influenced by the humanistic approach (Austin, 2011a; Kunstler & Stavola Daly, 2010) and, specifically, the **person-centered therapy** of Carl Rogers. First, like the Rogerian approach, RT applies to all people, not just those who are "ill and disabled." It is the process followed to assist people to grow that is the primary element, not the population being served. Second, similar to the Rogerian approach, RT follows a developmental model, rather than a medical model. The aim of RT is to do more than simply remove barriers to health. It is growth-oriented. Like Rogerian Therapy, the focus of RT remains on the development of the individual, not on pathology. The goal is more than problem removal, it is the highest degree of self-actualization possible. Finally, RT, similar to the Rogerian approach, deals primarily with the here and now, rather than the past or future. Additionally, many of the skills used in person-centered therapy are regularly applied in the daily practice of RT. Healthy interpersonal relationships, empathetic listening without levying judgment, and a warm, accepting climate are elements basic to the practice of recreational therapy.

Like **Gestalt therapists**, recreational therapists are interested in clients talking but also gaining personal awareness through experiences—including trying out new expressions of impulses and feelings in the "here and now." While certain skills of Gestalt therapy may be helpful in the practice of recreational therapy (such as Gestalt awareness exercises in leisure counseling), the emerging recreational therapist should be warned that Gestalt techniques tend to take on a gimmicky quality in the hands of persons who have not had training in their use.

Transactional analysis also has many elements that may have application within RT. For example, every person needs positive stroking. Positive stroking encourages young persons to grow into the winner roles they were born to assume. Ignoring individuals or giving negative strokes pushes young persons toward losers' scripts and reinforces losers' scripts for older people (James & Jongward, 1996). By structuring opportunities for activities and intimacy, recreational therapists will lead people to give and obtain positive strokes. Leaders following TA traditions create a safe, protective climate where clients feel free to be themselves and to experiment in developing new cognitions and behaviors (Corey, 1995; Okun 2002). Recreational therapists can also help people release the script-free Natural Child in order to be able to experience the freedom and joy found in play and recreation. Transaction analysis additionally can be used to help clients improve interpersonal communications. Since transaction analysis is not the private domain of any single professional group, it can be employed by recreational therapists who have studied its theories and processes. Transaction analysis offers the leisure counselor a common sense, understandable approach through which clients can gain insights and make choices to change leisure behaviors. James and Jongward (1996), in their best-selling book on transactional analysis, *Born to Win*, have presented exercises related both to people's childhoods and current play that are appropriate for use in leisure counseling.

Cognitive-Behavioral Approaches

Albert Ellis, William Glasser, and Aaron Beck have provided leadership for cognitive-behavioral approaches that focus on helping clients to examine thinking processes and the effects of those processes on behaviors and emotions. Cognitive-behavioral approaches assist clients to identify thoughts and beliefs they hold about themselves and the world, to examine the validity and usefulness of these cognitions, and if deemed necessary, to change the way they think about themselves and their environments. Clients then are assisted in acting on their cognitions in their daily lives, including their leisure. In sum, cognitive-behavioral theorists hold that there is an interdependence of thoughts, behaviors, and emotions (Craighead et al., 1994; Okun, 2002; Stuart, 2001).

An important element common to all cognitive-behavioral approaches is to help clients to question and revise their views of the world. Shealy (1999) has explained, "Self-defeating and self-denigrating thoughts are replaced by positive ones, and specific problems are addressed in the context of the whole" (p. 198).

Ellis developed rational-emotive therapy (RET), Glasser brought about reality therapy (RT), and Beck produced cognitive-behavioral therapy. These three major approaches are covered in the material that follows.

Rational-emotive Therapy
Rational-emotive therapy (RET) is a system of philosophy, a theory of personality, and a psychological treatment approach (Ellis, 1976). Albert Ellis' (1913-2007) rational-emotive therapy relies heavily on the cognitive processes, or people's thinking processes. Its philosophical origins go back to a notion first put forth by Epictelus, an early philosopher, who wrote, "Men are disturbed not by things, but by the view which they make of them." Later this same thought was expressed by Shakespeare in Hamlet, when he wrote, "There's nothing either good or bad but thinking makes it so" (Ellis, 2000).

Ellis (1976, 2000) uses an A-B-C theory. The A is the activating experience (or what the person irrationally believes causes C). C stands for the consequences (e.g., feel upset, worthless, depressed). B represents beliefs about A. B is the critical intervening variable that influences the way we look at what happens to us. Ellis holds that we value, perceive, or conceptualize first; then we feel. Therefore it is what we bring to each experience in the way of our beliefs, concepts, and attitudes (or our way of thinking) that influences our feelings.

According to RET, we have a predisposition to expand ourselves, to be creative, and to experience enjoyment in the here and now. Ellis (1976) has written:

> RET clearly defines appropriate feelings and rational beliefs as those aiding human survival and happiness—particularly those enabling you to accept objective reality, live amicably in a social group, relate intimately to a few members of this group, engage in productive work, and enjoy selectively chosen recreational pursuits. (p. 21)

However, we can also engage in irrational thinking involving absolutes ("I must") or perfection ("I should") or other irrational beliefs leading to inappropriate feelings. In short, we can be rigid and intolerant of ourselves to the point of destroying our health and happiness (Ellis, 2000). By entering into self-defeating thinking, we may become the creators of our own psychological disturbances. It is the task of RET to assist in changing basic self-defeating beliefs and attitudes in order to correct irrational thinking. Once this is done, we are rid of the emotional blockages that have prevented us from reaching our true potentials. Thus the basic goal of RET is not helping the client to solve a particular problem but to develop a new philosophy of life.

During therapy, RET therapists help the client identify irrational beliefs: they attack these beliefs, show the client they cannot be validated, and ultimately teach the client to change his or her irrational belief system (Ellis, 1976, 2000). In addition to therapy sessions, homework assignments utilizing behavioral techniques are also employed with RET clients.

Implications for Recreational Therapy

The most obvious implications of RET for the recreational therapist are the strong relationship between cognitive processes (beliefs and attitudes) and feelings and the need for people to discard irrational thinking that prevents enjoyment in the here and now. It is particularly important that those doing leisure counseling be aware that beliefs and attitudes may block leisure enjoyment for many persons. For example, some people cannot escape work, and feel guilty about having free time. Such persons might profit by examining the thinking that prevents them from enjoying leisure.

Reality Therapy

The focus of the **reality therapy** of William Glasser (1925-) is on present behavior, facing reality, and taking responsibility for one's own needs. Responsibility and reality are central to Glasser's approach. Responsibility deals with achieving personal needs without depriving others of fulfilling their needs. Reality has to do with facing instead of denying the world around us (Glasser, 1965).

According to Glasser, the basic human needs are to find love and worth—or relatedness and respect. Those who fail to meet these psychological needs (those who feel lonely and worthless) escape hurt and pain by denying the world of reality. Psychotic persons who cannot make it in the real world cope with loneliness and worthlessness by withdrawing and creating their own worlds of reality. Some deny the laws of society and engage in crime or antisocial acts. Others may become physically ill and seek help for backaches, headaches, or other illnesses. Still others drink to escape feelings of inadequacy. Any one of these and other denying responses are seen by Glasser to be irresponsible coping behaviors that have been learned throughout life (Glasser, 1965).

Reality therapy does not dwell on feelings, but instead helps clients to examine their present behavior, confront irresponsible actions, and establish commitment to change. Once a client makes a plan, the therapist does not accept any excuses from the client. No matter what has occurred in the past, no excuse is accepted for irresponsible behavior in the present. Therefore, unlike conventional therapy, reality therapy emphasizes the present, not the past. Even though personal insights may be interesting, the therapist's interest lies in the actual behavior of the client, not the unconscious motivations that may be offered as an excuse for irresponsible behavior (Glasser & Wubbolding, 1995).

Because clients have the need to love and be loved and to feel worthwhile to themselves and others, it is necessary that the therapist build a firm relationship with the client. Involvement on the part of the therapist begins immediately to reduce the client's loneliness and worthlessness. Therefore, a warm, caring attitude is mandated on the part of the therapist. Nevertheless, cautions Glasser (1976), the helping professional must be careful never to promise more involvement than he or she plans to provide.

Implications for Recreational Therapy

Perhaps the major implication of reality therapy for recreational therapists is that all helping relationships demand an accepting and understanding attitude and that positive involvement by the helper may immediately reduce client feelings of loneliness and worthlessness. Through his or her personal relationship with the client, the recreational therapist can provide a feeling of involvement and being cared for. The client can then become actively involved with others through participation in recreational therapy groups, ultimately leading to expanded involvements within ongoing recreation groups. Without such involvements, people cannot help themselves to fulfill their needs to feel cared for and to care for others.

A second implication is that clients can take responsibility to alter irresponsible behavior. Recreational therapists must provide opportunities for clients to learn and try out social behaviors that will lead to new relationships and more satisfying involvements. The climate created in recreational therapy should provide an accepting atmosphere that encourages positive social interaction.

The final implication from reality therapy is to help clients to live in the present. Recreational therapy, like reality therapy, is geared primarily toward helping people function in the here and now. Robert Wubbolding, author of the book *Using Reality Therapy* (1988b), has encouraged those in recreational therapy to employ reality therapy principles in his article (1988a) "Reality Therapy: A Method made for the Recreation Therapist."

Cognitive-Behavioral Therapy

The central feature of Aaron Beck's (1921-   ) **cognitive-behavioral therapy** is the concept that people's cognitions influence the way they react to life situations. Cognitive-behavioral therapy was first used by Beck (1976) to treat clients with major depressions. His approach has more recently been extended to successfully treat individuals with anxiety disorders, personality disorders, eating disorders, and substance abuse (Hales & Hales, 1995; Ivey, Ivey, & Simek-Morgan, 1997).

Cognitive-behavioral therapy arose from a dissatisfaction with a strictly behavioral approach to clinical problems (Oakley & Freeman, 2009). The basis for cognitive-behavioral therapy is that maladaptive assumptions underlie individuals' thoughts and beliefs. Kielhofner (2009) has explained: "Cognitive-behavioral therapy is guided by the cognitive model. This model proposes that dysfunctional thinking and unrealistic cognitive appraisals of life events can negatively influence feelings and behavior" (p. 242).

Distorted thought patterns (irrational ideas or faulty reasoning) then cause problems for individuals as they deal with life situations, particularly in times of stress. The purpose of therapy is to help these troubled individuals to acknowledge and change their distorted thinking. In order to learn to think differently, clients first have to identify inappropriate or distorted ways of thinking. The therapist elicits the client's thoughts and self-talk and how these are interpreted by the client. Discussion then turns to the validity of the client's interpretations and, finally, to testing the client's interpretations (perhaps through homework assignments), which, in turn, provides for further discussion (Okun, 2002).

Examples of irrational ideas or faulty reasoning that produce distorted thought patterns have been delineated by Hales and Hales (1995). They include *overgeneralizing* (making global conclusions from a single negative event), *arbitrary inference* (drawing a mistaken conclusion from an event or experience), *selective abstractions* (focusing on a single negative detail taken out of context), *dichotomous thinking* (all-or-nothing thinking or seeing only in terms of extremes), *magnifying or minimizing* (overstating the worst aspects of an event or underestimating the importance of an event), *personalization* (taking events that have nothing to do with the individual and personalizing them) and *automatic thoughts* (spontaneously thinking negative ideas such as "You're stupid" or "You can't do anything right").

In cognitive-behavioral therapy, the therapist helps the client to identify irrational thoughts, such as those listed in the previous paragraph, and to take steps to establish new thought patterns. One specific strategy to develop new thought patterns is the use of cognitive rehearsal. During cognitive rehearsal, the client envisions a situation that in the past has been disconcerting and imagines just how he or she would overcome it by breaking it down into manageable steps that he or she rehearses mentally (Hales & Hales, 1995). Other strategies include the use of a number of techniques drawn from various sources. Role-playing, exposure therapy, homework assignments, relaxation training, and social skills training are all psychoeducational techniques employed by therapists in cognitive-behavioral therapy (Ivey, et al., 1997). No matter what strategy is selected, the focus of cognitive-behavioral therapy remains on problem solving in the here and now (Hales & Hales, 1995).

Frisch and Frisch (2002) have listed three distinct characteristics of cognitive-behavioral therapy: (1) It is goal-focused and result-oriented; (2) It is short term; and (3) It is self-help oriented, with the therapist coaching the client, who is learning new tools for living and coping with life's challenges (p. 674).

Implications for Recreational Therapy

Cognitive-behavioral therapists recognize the complex interdependence of thoughts and behaviors. Recreational therapists must be aware of the interrelation of thoughts, feelings, and behaviors as they plan and conduct interventions with their clients. Cognitive-behavioral therapists also stress the notion that clients have the capacity to examine themselves and to develop insights into themselves. The focus of cognitive-behavioral therapy on helping clients to identify their assumptions, beliefs, and expectations, and the effects of these on behaviors and emotions, can be easily transferred to leisure education/counseling. In leisure counseling, counselors are helping clients to appraise leisure beliefs, values, and attitudes and to understand how these affect leisure feelings and behaviors.

Additionally, cognitive-behavioral therapists readily draw on strategies and techniques from other theories. Recreational therapists doing leisure counseling or using other interventions need to understand there are a wide variety of strategies and techniques upon which to draw from the various theories of helping. Finally, like cognitive-behavioral therapists, recreational therapists largely assist clients to deal with the here and now. Malkin, writing with Cook (Malkin & Cook, 1997) and with Kastrinos (Malkin & Kastrinos, 1997), has outlined specific cognitive-behavioral techniques for application in recreational therapy.

Positive Psychology

Just as the 21st Century was beginning, a new approach termed positive psychology jumped upon the scene. Positive psychology has been championed by Martin E. P. Seligman. Seligman's 2002 book titled *Authentic Happiness: Using the New Positive Psychology to Realize Your Potential for Lasting Fulfillment* was one of the earliest works to present positive psychology. Other books on positive psychology quickly followed. These included Aspinwall and Staudinger's (2003) *A Psychology of Human Strengths*, Keyes and Haidt's (2003) *Flourishing: Positive Psychology and the Life Well-Lived*, Linley and Joseph's (2004) *Positive Psychology in Practice*, Fredrickson's (2009) *Positivity*, Donaldson, Csikszentmihalyi, and Nakamura's (2011) *Applied Positive Psychology*, and Seligman's (2011) *Flourish: A Visionary New Understanding of Happiness and Well-being*.

The growth of positive psychology is reflected in Azar's (2011) article on the advancement of positive psychology. She wrote that within a few years "…almost 1,000 articles related to the field (were) published in peer-reviewed journals between 2000 and 2010 on topics that include well-being, pride, forgiveness, happiness, mindfulness and psychological strength—and how these attributes are related to both mental and physical health" (p. 34).

Linley and Joseph (2004b) have explained that "Positive psychology came about in response to the predominant late twentieth-century orientation of mainstream psychology to disease and the medical model" (p. 719). Instead of focusing on the negative side of human beings, positive psychology focuses on the positive side. Rather than concentrating on the study of pathology, positive psychology displays concern for human strengths and optimal functioning. Or as Biswas-Diener and Dean (2007) have put it, "(Positive psychology is a) branch of psychology that focuses on what is going right, rather than what is going wrong with people" (p. x). It moves psychological thought away from pessimistic views of human nature. In short, positive psychology accentuates the positive.

Thus the emphasis of positive psychology is very much on the development of human strengths and potentials. The language of positive psychology that talks about human strengths and optimal functioning, in fact, seems to echo terms used by humanistic psychology and brings to mind Roger's self-actualizing tendency and Maslow's notion of self-actualization (Austin, 2011b). Jorgensen and Nafstad (2004) have gone so far as to make a case that positive psychology may be perceived as simply an outgrowth of humanistic psychology.

Seligman, Steen, Park, and Peterson (2005), in fact, have acknowledged that positive psychology builds on humanistic traditions but believe positive psychology's emphasis on empirical data derived through experiments and science sets it apart. The scientific bent of positive psychology is reflected in the writings of two pioneers in positive psychology, Seligman and Csikszentmihalyi (2001), who stated, "We are, unblushingly, scientists first. The work we seek to support and encourage must be nothing less than replicable, cumulative, and objective" (pp. 89–90).

Defining Positive Psychology

From the introduction to positive psychology, it may be surmised that a brief definition of positive psychology would be that it is "the psychology of human strengths and optimal functioning." It would seem that authors' definitions are similar to this statement but expand upon it. Biswas-Diener and Dean (2007) provided this definition of positive psychology: "In short, it is a new branch of psychology that focuses on what is going right, rather than what is going wrong with people" (p. x). Duckworth, Steen, and Seligman (2004) wrote, "Positive psychology is the scientific study of positive experiences and positive individual traits, and the institutions that facilitate their development" (p. 630). Gable and Hatch (2005) stated, "Positive psychology is the study of conditions and processes that contribute to the flourishing or optimal functioning of people, groups, and institutions" (p. 104). The definition of positive psychology advanced by the founders of positive psychology, Seligman and Csikszentmihalyi (2000), follows:

> The field of positive psychology at the subjective level is about valued subjective experiences: well-being, contentment, and satisfaction (in the past); hope and optimism (for the future); and flow and happiness (in the present). At the individual level, it is about positive individual traits; the capacity for love and vocation, courage, interpersonal skill, aesthetic sensibility, perseverance, forgiveness, originality, future mindedness, spirituality, high talent, and wisdom. At the group level, it is about the civic virtues and the institutions that move individuals toward better citizenship: responsibility, nurturance, altruism, civility, moderation, tolerance, and work ethic. (p. 5)

Helpful to recreational therapists may be an applied approach to defining positive psychology provided by Linley and Joseph (2004). These authors stated, "Applied positive psychology is the application of positive psychology research to the facilitation of optimal functioning." They went on to say, "Applied positive psychologists work to promote optimal functioning across the full range of human functioning, from disorder and distress to health and fulfillment" (p. 4). This view is similar to that of Linley and Stephen (2004a), who proclaimed, "Applied positive psychologists may work both to alleviate distress and to promote optimal functioning" (p. 6).

Linley and Joseph's definition is also in keeping with Skerrett's (2010) view of positive psychology. She wrote that "positive psychology is devoted to understanding what goes well in a life and examines how and why, and under what conditions, human beings flourish." She went on to say that while positive psychology is "not a replacement to the more problem-focused or deficit-based paradigms, it is conceptualized as a complementary and important dimension to understand the full range of human experience" (p. 488).

It would seem that these definitions of applied positive psychology, along with the more general definition provided by Seligman and Csikszentmihalyi (2000), naturally lead to the notion that positive psychology deals with positive subjective feelings, positive traits, and the institutions that support individuals in both their efforts to overcome disorders and distress and in their endeavors to achieve health and personal fulfillment.

Three Pillars of Positive Psychology

Seligman (2002) has identified positive emotions, positive traits, and positive institutions as *the three pillars of positive psychology*. He wrote, "First is the study of positive emotion. Second is the study of positive traits, foremost among them the strengths and virtues, but also the 'abilities' such as intelligence and athleticism. Third is the study of the positive

Table 2.4

Positive Psychology in a Nutshell

1. Positive psychology looks at what is right with people, focuses on when people are at their best, and attends to individual and group flourishing.
2. Positive psychology is not the focus of the positive at the expense of the negative. Positive psychologists recognize negative emotions, failure, problems, and other unpleasantries as natural and important aspects of life.
3. Positive psychology is, first and foremost, a science. As such, it is principally concerned with evidence, measurement, and testing. That said, positive psychology is also an applied science, and there is a common understanding that research results will lead to the creation of real-world interventions that will improve aspects of individual and social life through evidence-based practice.
4. Interventions produced by positive psychologists are, by and large, positive interventions.

Adapted from Biswas-Diener, R. (2010). *Practicing positive psychology coaching.* Hoboken, NJ: John Wiley & Sons, Inc., p. 5.

institutions, such as democracy, strong families, and free inquiry, that support the virtues, which in turn support positive emotions" (p. ix). It is to these three areas that we now turn our attention.

Positive Emotions

Positive psychology is about such positive emotional experiences as: contentment and satisfaction encountered in the past; current feelings such as happiness, flow, and sensual pleasure; and optimistic and hopeful emotions in anticipation of the future (Seligman, 2002). One of the best-known perspectives on positive emotion is Fredrickson's (2001, 2009) *Broaden-and-Build Theory of Positive Emotion.* This theory has arguably made her the leading advocate for the idea of positive emotion helping people to better function in both the short run and long term.

According to Fredrickson (2001), *emotion* "begins with an individual's assessment of the personal meaning of some antecedent event. This appraisal process may be either conscious or unconscious, and it triggers a cascade of response tendencies manifest across loosely coupled components systems, such as subjective experience, facial expression, cognitive processing, and physiological changes" (p. 218).

Emotions then are seen to be relatively short-term feelings that have an object that brings them about. Further, negative emotions can be adaptive because a specific negative emotion will likely propel us to act (e.g., feeling fear leads to escaping the situation). Positive emotions, however, have not been found to trigger such specific reactions. As an example, Fredrickson (2001) has explained that joy brings about general tendencies such as "aimless activation, interest with attending, and contentment with inactivity" (p. 219), rather than one specific response.

In order to better explain positive emotions (e.g., joy, pride), Fredrickson has developed the *Broaden-and-Build Theory of Positive Emotion.* This theory sees positive emotions as having the effect of broadening the range of thoughts and actions that people will consider with the result that this broadening of the range of choices allows persons to build their strengths. The broadening aspect opens people up to thoughts and actions (the Broaden part of the theory) and following these possibilities allows for the building of strengths (the Building portion of the theory).

Or, put another way, when people experience positive emotions, they feel free or unencumbered. They open up. They are receptive to new thoughts and actions. When this occurs they are prone to take more risks, to challenge themselves. Stretching themselves can lead them to try things they might not otherwise attempt and to build strengths.

In addition to broadening and building, a third component of the Broaden-and-Build Theory is that positive emotions are seen as serving as antidotes for lingering effects of negative emotions. Fredrickson refers to good feelings negating lingering negative emotions as *the undoing hypothesis.*

Additionally, continuing to experience positive emotions tends to create a spiraling effect over time. These positive emotions not only ward off lingering negative emotions but as more and more positive emotions are experienced, thinking further broadens, increasing the probability of perceiving positive meaning in events that follow, resulting in improved emotional well-being. This, in turn, builds psychological resiliency or individuals' coping abilities. Fredrickson has cited empirical research she published with Joiner (2002) to support the upward spiraling effect with gains in resiliency and increased positive emotions. She has stated:

> Our data revealed clear evidence for an upward spiral. Individuals who experienced more positive emotions than others became more resilient to adversity over time, as indexed by increases in broad-minded coping. In turn, these enhanced coping skills predicted increased positive emotions over time. (Fredrickson, 2001, p. 223)

In summary, under the Broaden-and-Build Theory, *undoing* is the process of positive emotions serving as antidotes for the lingering effects of negative emotions. *Broadening* is the concept that positive emotions expand the range of thoughts and actions that people will consider. *Building* is the notion that positive emotions build personal resources or strengths.

Further, empirical research (see Fredrickson, 2001, 2009) suggests that positive emotions not only make people feel good at the time they experience the emotions but may produce an upward spiraling effect as they begin to build skills that lead to improved coping and that result in additional positive emotions, enhanced emotional well-being, and more optimistic views of the future.

Skerrett (2010) has succinctly summarized the Broaden-and-Build Theory. She has written it "suggests that positive emotions (a) broaden people's attention and thinking, (b) undo lingering negative emotional arousal, (c) fuel psychological resilience, (d) build consequential personal resources, and (e) trigger upward spirals toward greater well-being in the future" (p. 494).

Positive Traits

Positive Traits are said to be the second pillar or component of positive psychology (Seligman, 2002). Positive traits include *abilities* that we inherit, such as intellectual and athletic abilities, as well as *strengths* or *virtues* that we develop. While what is meant by intellectual and athletic abilities is relatively apparent, it may be less clear as to what constitute strengths or virtues. Seligman (2000) has explained that strengths and virtues are simply moral traits that have to do with one's character.

Potential personal strengths and virtues include those under the following six categories: (a) wisdom and knowledge, (b) courage, (c) love, (d) justice, (e) temperance;

and (f) transcendence. *Wisdom strengths* are curiosity, interest, love of learning, judgment, critical thinking, open-mindedness, practical intelligence, creativity, originality, ingenuity, and perspective. *Courage strengths* include valor, industry, perseverance, integrity, honesty, authenticity, zest, and enthusiasm. Under *love* fall intimacy, reciprocal attachment, kindness, generosity, nurturance, social intelligence, personal intelligence, and emotional intelligence. Strengths listed under the category of *justice* include citizenship, duty, loyalty, teamwork, equity, fairness, and leadership. Under *temperance* are forgiveness, mercy, modesty, humility, prudence, caution, self-control, and self-regulation. Finally, under *transcendence* are the strengths of awe, wonder, appreciation of beauty and excellence, gratitude, hope, optimism, future-mindedness, playfulness, humor, spirituality, sense of purpose, faith, and religiousness. It is probably best to think of the strengths delineated as examples of strengths that can be built, rather than as an exhaustive list (Seligman & Peterson, 2003).

In a similar fashion to Roger's actualizing tendency and Maslow's self-actualization tendency, positive psychology emphasizes inherent human potentials for developing character traits. Whereas traditional psychology saw human beings as self-serving and asocial, positive psychology views people as being social and moral individuals, not as just taking care of their own needs in egotistical ways.

This is in the Greek tradition of Aristotle who believed people wish to maintain positive relationships with others and that these relationships are mutually beneficial, according to Jorgensen and Nafstad (2004). These authors stated, "The Aristotelian model focuses on the virtuous individual and those inner traits, dispositions, and motives that qualify the individual to be virtuous" (p. 20).

Seligman and Csikszentmihalyi (2000) reflected an Aristotelian view when they explained, "Enjoyment…refers to the good feelings people experience when they break through the limits of homeostasis—when they do something that stretches them beyond what they were—in an athletic event, an artistic performance, a good deed, a stimulating conversation. Enjoyment, rather than pleasure, is what leads to personal growth and long term happiness…" (p. 12).

Of course, both inherited and cultivated traits must be developed. It is up to those applying positive psychology to understand these traits, to learn how to access them, and then how to help people to develop them. Once positive strengths are established, Seligman (2000) has proclaimed, "Engaging in a strength usually produces authentic positive emotion in the doer: pride, satisfaction, joy, fulfillment, or harmony" (p. 138). Thus, the development of human potentials provides a source of happiness and well-being.

Positive Institutions

Positive institutions represent the third pillar of positive psychology. Positive institutions are those influences that cultivate abilities and strengths, which in turn produce positive emotions (Seligman & Peterson, 2003). It is only through transactions within the environment that persons grow toward self-realization (Nakamura & Csikszentmihalyi, 2004).

The concept of positive institutions can vary widely. It can include broadly framed institutions such as democratic communities, or even democratic nations. Or it can be narrowly conceived as in the institution of a strong family (Seligman, 2000). Seligman and Peterson (2003) have given little league sports and high school student councils as examples of positive institutions that allow children and adolescents to develop their abilities and strengths in protected environments under the guidance of adult leadership.

Unfortunately, the pillar of positive institutions is less well developed than the pillars of positive emotions and positive traits. Lacking seems to be a well-defined concept of positive institutions. Nor is there the presentation of depth understandings of the concept of positive institutions. Stokols (2003) has indicated that positive psychology has not fully considered perspectives from environmental and ecological psychology in terms of the environment and its effect on behavior. For the purpose of our discussion, I have approached positive institutions as being those aspects of the environment that allow for the development of abilities and strengths that ultimately result in positive emotions.

Of course, both positive and negative aspects of the environment can influence people's well-being. It is the enhancement of the positive elements of the environment, however, that are of particular concern to positive psychology. These include both physical and social features. An example of a physical element would be a tranquil wilderness environment where people can get away from their normal routines and enjoy the restorative qualities of the natural setting. An example of a social element is a community group that provides friendships and social support (Stokols, 2003).

In order for people to enjoy psychological well-being, it is important that contextual factors surrounding them are taken into consideration. For example, Stokols (2003) has cited research showing "that when individuals encounter environments that are too predictable and too controllable, they experience those settings as boring and unchallenging....Ideally, people prefer environments that offer opportunities for exploration and for acquiring new information and skills" (p. 337). Thus, those applying positive psychology interventions need to examine environments so that they are not negative but positive ones that will foster the growth of strengths, with resulting positive emotions.

Implications for Recreational Therapy

Seasoned recreational therapists who examine positive psychology may well react by thinking, "They are speaking our language!" Recreational therapy does seem to have an excellent fit with positive psychology.

As a part of their philosophical underpinnings, both recreational therapy and positive psychology have the goals and concerns of Rogers and other humanistic psychologists as a part of their lineage. This includes the notion of a self-actualizing tendency in humans is a central part of humanistic psychology. Next, both take the approach that one of the best ways to help those who are suffering is by focusing on positive things. Finally, both are strength-based. They focus on human strengths, rather than weaknesses. They share the assumption that people possess the capacity for change through strength-building successes that, in turn, produce positive emotions.

Let us look more closely at elements of recreational therapy and positive psychology to more specifically examine their relationships and ensuing implications for practice. First, recreational therapists, like those in positive psychology, have concentrated on positive experiences and positive traits that allow clients to exercise their actualizing tendencies. As Joseph and Linley (2004) have indicated, "The actualizing tendency provides a holistic framework that simultaneously spans psychopathology and well-being. In facilitating the actualizing tendency, the therapist is both alleviating psychopathology and promoting well-being" (p. 364).

Like positive psychologists, recreational therapists should then go beyond exclusive concerns with distress, disease and dysfunction to promote optimal functioning. As positive psychology, recreational therapy can be perceived as being "health-building oriented rather than reactive, and repair or containment-oriented" (Cowen & Kilmer, 2002, p. 450). Linley and Joseph (2004b) echoed this theme in writing that interventions "do not begin and end with the target of the client being symptom-free" (p. 724).

Thus, both positive psychology and recreational therapy may have concern simultaneously with both relieving suffering (health protection) and promoting well-being (health promotion). An example might be therapists using engaging, enjoyable activities to focus interventions on the "intact areas" of clients having severe problems in mental health, with the intent of using client strengths to both overcome problems and promote resilience.

Approaches that flow out of Fredrickson's (2001, 2009) *Broaden-and-Build Theory of Positive Emotion* have much in common with what has gone on in recreational therapy practice for many years. Yet, this theory offers a basis for practice that may not have been previously made explicit to recreational therapists.

In short, the Broaden-and-Build Theory provides recreational therapists with a solid foundation for practice. First, the *undoing hypothesis* states that positive emotions can help negate negative feelings. Certainly, participation in recreational activities offers people a high potential for experiencing positive emotions that ward off lingering negative emotions. Next, the experiencing of positive emotions, such as joy and satisfaction during recreation activities, opens people up to new thoughts and behaviors. They are ready to broaden their cognitive and behavioral repertoires and, thus, open themselves to build strengths that, in turn, result in experiencing positive emotions. In the build portion of the theory, the safe and secure atmosphere provided in recreation offers means to engage the world and to build personal and social strengths or resources (e.g., skills, abilities, social support) to use in the future. Further, positive emotions experienced during this process have the potential to produce an upward spiraling effect as people begin to build skills that lead to improved coping and that result in additional positive emotions, enhanced emotional well-being, and more optimistic views of the future.

Biswas-Diener and Dean (2007) have explained, "Foul moods can sap energy from clients and interfere with good relationships while positivity offers the best possible change for success. It is important that you consider happiness and other pleasant emotions as more than a desirable finish line. Positivity, research shows, is a vital resource that helps clients to reach their goals" (p. 27). These words serve as good reminders to recreational therapists that positive emotions experienced in activities offer clients much more than an occasion to "feel good;" they open doors for growth.

Therefore, it is critical that clients are provided opportunities within recreational therapy to pursue activities they find interesting and engaging so that they gain positive emotions and build strengths from their participation. Of course, in order to produce successes with ensuring positive emotions, the activities selected have to be carefully chosen so they have the right "person-activity fit," according to Sheldon and Lyubomirsky (2004). These authors have written, "People have enduring strengths, interests, values, and inclinations, which predispose them to benefit more from some activities than others" (p. 138). Further, Berman and Davis-Berman (2005) have provided a note of caution for recreational therapists who have typically relied upon disequilibrium in outdoor activities as a means to change behavior. They suggest that "Consistent with the ideas form positive psychology, outdoor education programs, who goals are to encourage both personal growth and change, should take steps to try to reduce the perception of risk in programs. Underlying this assumption is the belief that, for many, just participating in a program increases one's sense of threat and instability, and that further threat potentially could be damaging" (p. 22).

The second pillar of *positive traits* features the strengths and abilities of clients. Recreational therapists have typically assessed clients to determine the strengths and abilities they possess. This focus on client strengths helps to reinforce the notion that clients have strengths and abilities that they have used in the past to resolve problems. It also sets a positive tone as the emphasis on the positive presents a hopeful and optimistic approach for treatment. This positive, strength-based method is one that is shared by social workers who use a strengths perspective as interpreted in Glicken's (2004) insightful work titled *Using the Strengths Perspective in Social Work Practice.*

Recreational therapists have also long striven to develop the abilities and strengths of their clients, something positive psychology emphases in its second pillar of positive traits. Clients develop their abilities and strengths when they break through old limits and stretch themselves to accomplish things they have not been able to achieve. From such accomplishment comes enjoyment. In order to assist clients toward reaching their abilities and developing their strengths, recreational therapists need to understand potential abilities and strengths, how to bring these out, and, finally, how to use interventions that will help their clients to develop them.

Positive psychology's approach to building abilities and strengths should not be lost when serving persons with disabilities. Positive psychology sees health as far more than the absence of deviations from the norm. Those with disabilities can access their abilities and strengths in order to develop themselves to the maximum possible for them within the environments in which they reside. Research has shown that participation in challenging, recreational activities by persons with disabilities produced optimal experiences, which yielded developmental gains for those individuals. The researchers, Fave and Massimini (2004), reported, "Although most participants reported disablement among the negative life influences, they also stressed their effort to effectively overcome the related social, behavioral, and biological constraints, focusing on the positive and constructive components of their life history and daily experiences" (pp. 593 – 594). This reinforces the need for recreational therapists to help clients achieve growth and move toward their optimal levels of health despite their disabilities.

The third pillar of positive psychology stresses *positive institutions* that can affect the development of human abilities and strengths. Yet, Austin (2002c) has indicated that recreational therapy "has given insufficient attention to the environment." He has gone on to state: "In assessing clients, consideration should be given not only to clients' needs, strengths, and limitations but also to the environment as well" (p. 18). Recreational therapists need to access what environmental conditions have affected the client negatively and which offer potential future benefit.

Certainly within recreational therapy there can be fostered an optimal environment for change. By their nature, recreational therapy groups tend to offer a safe, warm, caring, and nurturing atmosphere in which clients may gain and practice their skills. The optimistic approach commonly reflected by recreational therapists working with their groups also can instill hope in clients who have faced hopelessness and demoralization (Austin, 2002a).

Additionally, recreational therapy groups may offer clients a sense of social support as a part of their environment (McCormick, 2002). Because feelings of being loved and cared for by others are important to clients, recreational therapists must be aware of the effects of their therapy groups on clients. It is also advisable for recreational therapists to be cognizant of potential support to be found in the communities in which their clients reside and to prepare their clients to take advantage of these. Frisch (2006) has warned: "Many clients fail to use important social outlets such as area health clubs, singles clubs, churches, and hobby groups because of social anxiety and social skill deficits" (p. 306).

It should be emphasized that psychological elements, such as social support (along with optimism, perceived control or mastery, and self-esteem), can have beneficial effects for physical health as well as mental health (Donaldson, Csikszentmihalyi, & Nakamura, 2011). Empirical research has regularly found relationships between psychological variables and physical health. Pettit et al. (2001) acknowledged this when they stated that "a notable amount of research has identified relationships between psychological events and physical health" (p. 521). Likewise, Taylor et al. (2000) indicated that "the research suggests that psychological benefits such as meaning, control, and optimism act as resources, which may not only preserve mental health in the context of traumatic or life-threatening events but be protective of physical health as well" (p. 99). Thus, positive psychology clearly has implications for recreational therapists practicing in physical rehabilitation.

In closing this section, it would seem that the major implication from positive psychology may be that activities clients enjoy and derive pleasure from can serve as linchpins to their well-being. Recreational therapists need to introduce their clients to this connection so they may understand the benefits to be obtained through participation in activities that produce positive emotion, along with the development of positive strengths and abilities.

Austin (2005/2006) has predicted that positive psychology will have a significant impact on recreational therapy practice. He wrote:

> It is likely that, as positive psychology becomes better known, recreation therapists will embrace it because positive psychology tends to extend the ideas already accepted by recreation therapists through the influence of humanistic psychology. With the welcoming of positive psychology, recreation therapists will likely more strongly embrace health promotion. Health promotion will then join health protection (i.e., treatment and rehabilitation) to provide two primary thrusts for recreation therapy practice in the years ahead. Already, models of practice such as the Health Protection/Health Promotion Model (Austin, 2002a, 2002b) and the Therapeutic Recreation Service Delivery Model (Carter, Van Andel, & Robb, 1995), have included the notion of the importance of health promotion in recreation therapy practice. (p. 9)

Developed Theories

Developed theories have more fully evolved than others. These perspectives have generally existed longer than less complete approaches and, therefore, have undergone testing and revision overtime. Yet, they do not have the standing of the five major theories.

Developed approaches include family therapy, psychodrama, and multimodal therapy.

Family Therapy

The foundation for family therapy is that the family has a tremendous impact on its members. The nature of families may be understood traditionally or be more broadly construed, as Skerrett (2010) has done in defining the family "as two or more individuals who depend on each other for support, membership being self-defined" (p. 489). No matter how families are perceived, within family therapy each client needs to be considered within the context of his or her family group. Sturges (2006) has underscored the crucial role the family plays in the life of each individual. She has written:

> No family can be understood by analyzing its members individually. That would be like trying to understand the workings of a complicated piece of machinery by disassembling it and studying each part separately, rather than learning how all the parts fit and work together as a whole. (p. 359)

Family therapy arose in the United States due to observed inadequacies of prevailing individual-based treatment approaches. It has evolved out of group therapy over the last quarter-century, gaining increasing popularity within mental health circles within the past decade. In fact, it may be categorized as a type of group therapy done with the family, a natural, preformed group. There is no one accepted theoretical basis for family therapy, but, instead, eclectic approaches are commonly employed by practitioners (Carr, 2000).

Kovel (1976) has termed family therapy "the most pragmatic of all therapies" (p. 196), largely because it "enables a person to focus more directly on the real behaviors that affect life with those closest to him" (p. 196). He goes on to say: "Certain aspects of the emotional world that appear right away in family treatment may remain inaccessible to any form of individual therapy, or even other group therapy" (p. 196).

Shealy's (1999) description of family therapy provides helpful understandings. He writes:

> Family therapy is based on the premise that the family forms an organic unit, in which anything that affects one part of the unit will affect the rest as well. If one member of a family is in emotional distress, the whole family suffers in one way or another, and the family's response to this distress is crucial in determining whether the problem gets better or worse. (p. 206)

Hayes (2001) has offered this description of family therapy:

> Modern family therapists tend to look at the family in terms of working systems, with everyone being interlinked and affecting everyone else. Therapy aims to teach the members of the family to become aware of their impact on others, learning to respond sensitively to one another instead of just reacting to the other family members as a source of irritation or discomfort. (p. 67)

General goals for family therapy are the development of cohesion and adaptability in the family unit, within the context of developmental issues that affect the family. Effective families allow members to become enmeshed into the family but still permit them to be alone at times. Cohesion exists when there is neither total enmeshment nor disengagement. Effective families also allow for flexibility in the face of stressful circumstances. Leadership within the adaptable family is neither authoritarian nor chaotic.

Specific goals for family therapy have been listed by Gladding (2002) and Mueser and Glynn (1999). These include to (a) reduce stress in family relationships; (b) improve communication skills to enhance communications within the family; (c) increase family's understanding and acceptance of their family member's disorder; (d) foster the ability of the family to develop problem-solving strategies; (e) increase emotional closeness of family members; (f) break down defenses, enhance self-esteem, and renew potentials for emotional experiencing; (g) combat rigidity and promote flexibility, spontaneity, and playfulness; and (h) bring about greater awareness of family dynamics.

Understanding family developmental issues is important to helping families. Developmental transitions are marked by events such as the birth of a child, the child leaving home, or events such as illness or relocations (Brammer et al., 1993; Ivey et al., 1997).

Family resilience has been "defined as those properties of individuals that help them bounce back from crisis or disruption" (Skerrett, 2010, p. 489). Included among key elements to build family resilience has been shared recreation (Black & Lobo, 2008). Even so, family therapy has not been prominently featured within recreational therapy.

Even though family programming in recreational therapy has been limited to date, the general goals of pioneering programs have been congruent with the overall philosophy and purposes of family therapy. Monroe (1987), in describing the program at the Portsmouth Psychiatric Center, has stipulated the purpose of the program is "to enhance family relationships through participation in structured family leisure activities" (p. 47). Objectives of the program are to (a) develop communication or cooperative skills; (b) improve leisure attitudes, skills, and abilities; (c) learn to make family decisions; (d) develop parenting skills; and (e) develop family self-esteem (p. 47).

DeSalvatore, with Rosenman (1986), and writing alone (DeSalvatore, 1989) has described the family therapy program on the children's psychiatric unit at the New England Memorial Hospital. The goals of the program are to assess and treat families in terms of family process and family structure. Areas covered include parenting, communication, discipline and limit setting, positive reinforcement, playing with children, feelings, and self-esteem (Ayers, Colman, & DeSalvatore, n.d.).

Malkin, Phillips, and Chumbler (1991) have described an interdisciplinary family leisure education program (termed the "Family Lab") designed for families of adolescents in substance abuse treatment. The Family Lab provides the family with greater leisure awareness and an increased range of leisure interests. The program also allows parents opportunities to practice parenting and communication skills they have previously learned in a parent's class and to have experiences that later can be discussed in family therapy sessions.

Dupuis and Pedlar (1995) presented evidence of the success of a structured family leisure program in improving the quality of family visits and enhancing social support. These outcomes lead to increasing the coping capacity of family members serving as caregivers for institutionalized older adults with Alzheimer's disease.

Research by Freeman and Zabriskie (2003) and Townsend and Zabriskie (2010) has established empirical evidence of a strong relationship between families' participation in leisure and positive family functioning. Thus, family therapy interventions within recreational therapy would seem to hold promise for positive outcomes.

Implications for Recreational Therapy

Perhaps because recreational therapy for many years transpired largely in hospitals, institutions, and long-term care facilities, instead of in clients' homes and communities, family therapy has been limited within the recreational therapy profession. With more and more recreational therapy occurring in the community, it would appear a natural consequence may be an enlarging role for family-centered programs. Obviously, recreational therapists may wish to consider establishing family therapy programs similar to those described by Monroe (1987), DeSalvatore (1989), Malkin, et al. (1991), and Dupuis and Pedlar (1995).

Recreational therapists need to have adequate preparation in order to engage in conducting family therapy programs. Needed are a knowledge of family assessment, family therapy models, and intervention skills to employ with families. Unfortunately, there has been a paucity of knowledge provided on family-centered approaches within most recreational therapy curricula. There is a real need for those preparing students for careers in recreational therapy to give more attention to the emerging area of family therapy.

All recreational therapists should be aware of the danger in treating the individual in isolation, without giving consideration to other family members or including them in the treatment program. Secondly, recreational therapists, through family therapy, are reminded of the advantages of programming in the nonthreatening atmosphere of activities where people can be themselves. Finally, family therapy approaches also remind recreational therapists that recreational therapy programs often allow for the direct observation and learning of behaviors that may be used daily in interactions with family members and others.

Psychodrama

Psychodrama is a form of psychiatric treatment developed by Austrian psychiatrist Jacob Moreno (Panman & Panman, 2006). Psychiatrist Adam Blatner (2000) has explained, "Psychodrama is a method for exploring psychological and social problems by having participants enact the relevant events in their lives instead of simply talking about them" (p. 1).

The goal of psychodrama is to help the client gain increased awareness of feelings and behaviors through personal insights and the perceptions of others resulting from dramatizing situations centering on past, current, or anticipated difficulties. The client discovers more about his or her difficulties and learns to cope with them by means of the cathartic expression of acting out problems. Corey (1995) has explained, "The techniques of psychodrama lend themselves very well to producing lively group interaction, exploring interpersonal problems, experimenting with novel ways of approaching significant others in one's life, and reducing one's feelings of isolation" (p. 206-207).

Elements involved in psychodrama include the stage director (therapist or leader), subject or protagonist (client), alter ego, auxiliary ego, and audience. The psychodrama takes place on a stage and is directed by the *director*, who facilitates by interjecting comments when necessary and who interprets the drama. It is also the director's job to convey a warm, caring, and supportive attitude conducive to encouraging spontaneity. The subject has the opportunity of playing the *protagonist* (i.e., leading role or main character), which may be himself or herself or someone else. It is the protagonist who is attempting "to work out a problem, gain insight, or develop an alternative response pattern" (Blatner, 2000, p.3). This person, or any character in the drama, may have an *alter ego* (or double) who stands immediately behind the person and states aloud whatever that character is probably thinking (in contrast to what the person is actually saying). Thus the alter ego is an extension of the person's ego. *Auxiliary egos* (supporting players) are persons who portray significant others in the life of the subject. The *audience* is made up of those in the group not assuming roles as director, protagonist, alter ego, or an auxiliary ego (Blatner, 1999; 2000; Cohen & Lipkin, 1979; Corey, 1995).

The director uses various techniques to facilitate the client's ability to experience feelings. An example of a technique would be "Empty Chair," in which the person is asked to imagine the dress, appearance, and posture of a particular person sitting before him or her in an empty chair. Another example of a facilitation technique is "One Day to Relive," in which the client chooses one day to relive if he or she could do so. These techniques yield scenes that can then be acted out in a psychodrama. The *sharing integrative process* element involves the entire group sharing how they felt about what took place. In this phase, the director attempts to build empathy and an atmosphere of trust. The final element is the *closure of the group*. At this time support is provided for the client (protagonist) and he or she is thanked for his or her efforts. This is also the time for the group to offer applause, verbal support, and perhaps a group hug (Nathan & Mirviss, 1998).

Implications for Recreational Therapy

Recreational therapists should not be tempted to conduct psychodrama without extensive preparation. The psychodrama leader must obtain a high level of training under expert direction. Nevertheless, aspects of psychodrama such as role-playing and rehearsal for future situations may be used by recreational therapists. Role-playing and rehearsal are facilitation techniques that you can use to help clients gain insights into themselves and others. For example, role-playing may be used to practice social situations that are difficult for clients, and then changes in behaviors can be rehearsed in further role plays. Nathan and Mirviss (1998) have suggested role-playing may be used

- whenever you want group members to see themselves as others do;
- when a group needs a change of pace from what is normally done in the group.;
- for couples, siblings, co-workers, and other relationships where problems may have developed; and
- as a way to laugh at ourselves. (p. 172)

It is important to understand that role playing and rehearsal for future situations are techniques that should be employed only by qualified recreational therapists who are experienced in their use. Even then, complications can arise when material surfaces that is highly threatening. Like leaders of psychodrama, recreational therapists should attempt to create a warm, accepting atmosphere so clients feel free to express themselves and feel supported while doing so. Also, like leaders of psychodrama, recreational therapists should promote client enjoyment through participation.

It is interesting to note that psychiatrist Adam Blatner and Allee Blatner have used psychodrama techniques to teach adults to play. Their 1988 book on reawaking playfulness in adults is titled, *The Art of Play: An Adult's Guide to Reclaiming Imagination and Spontaneity*.

Multimodal Therapy

The **multimodal therapy** of Arnold A. Lazarus (1932-   ) is a systematic and comprehensive psychotherapeutic approach with the goal of reducing psychological suffering and promoting personal growth. Lazarus' principle of *technical eclecticism* encourages the employment of a diverse range of assessment and treatment methods drawn from different sources without adhering to the theories that spawned them. While operating within the framework of social learning theory, multimodal therapy transcends behavioral traditions to use an array of techniques ranging from behavioral (e.g., modeling, contracting, biofeedback, assertiveness training), to cognitive (e.g., Ellis' paradigm, thought-blocking, bibliotherapy), to Gestalt (e.g., empty chair), to sex therapy (e.g., tactile stimulation), to meditation. Flexibility is inherent in multimodal therapy, since the therapist is constantly searching for new techniques or refining or eliminating old ones to determine what works best for each individual under particular circumstances (Lazarus, 1989; 1992).

While subscribing to the *principle of parity* (we are equal to one another), Lazarus views each of us as different and unique because he believes our personalities are produced out of an interplay among our genetic endowment, our physical environment, and our social learning history. From this belief, Lazarus developed the acronym BASIC I.D. (**B**ehavior, **A**ffect, **S**ensation, **I**magery, **C**ognition, **I**nterpersonal Relationships, and **D**rugs/biological factors) to represent the "human personality." In multimodal therapy, assessment and treatment are specifically and systematically divided into these seven discrete but interactive modalities (Lazarus, 1989; 2000). Meaningful improvement is expected only when concern is given to all of the modalities (Lazarus, 1992).

Because of this perspective, multimodal therapy is, by necessity, personalistic and individualistic. A fundamental premise of multimodal therapy is that clients are seen as usually being troubled by a number of specific problems that need to be treated using a multitude of techniques. Therefore, in multimodal therapy there is no typical treatment format. Instead, clients are assessed using the BASIC I.D. Chart or Modality Profile that is structured around the seven modalities. This assessment serves as a blueprint in that stipulating salient features of the client's BASIC I.D. enables the client and therapist to establish objectives, specify therapeutic techniques, and formulate a comprehensive evaluation plan (Lazarus, 1989).

Implications for Recreational Therapy

Multimodal therapists are drawn from a wide range of health service professionals including (but not limited to) psychologists, social workers, psychiatric nurses, and pastoral counselors. A multimodal therapy approach has been suggested for leisure counseling with elderly clients (Munson & Munson, 1986). Therefore, recreational therapists with strong counseling backgrounds, who are well versed in multimodal methods, may utilize it in leisure counseling. More likely, however, would be the use by recreational therapists of concepts shared bet been multimodal therapy and therapeutic recreation. The following represent such concepts:

- Multiple areas are covered in completing a comprehensive assessment.
- Following assessment information, treatment procedures are individually tailored to meet the unique needs of each client.
- A vast array of therapeutic approaches may be used with clients to meet a wide spectrum of concerns.
- An egalitarian approach is followed in the therapist-client relationship.
- Objectives are clearly stated and an evaluation plan is developed to measure results.

Related Theoretical Perspectives

New ways of thinking have come with the 21st Century. Theorists have raised questions related to previously existing theories. Okun (2002) has indicated, "Some of these questions were about the universality of the theoretical principles and values as well as about the lack of acknowledgment of the significant impact of sociocultural, economic, and political variables on human development." She has gone on to say, "They are inclusive viewpoints that transcend the basic theoretical models and are likely to be integrated with one's theory-of-use in current practice" (p.148). The constructivism, feminist, and multicultural perspectives surveyed in this section provide elements that may be missing or incomplete in theories previously proposed.

Constructivism

Constructivism follows a cognitive-behavioral perspective that presents thinking, feeling, and doing as interdependent elements that impact on people. It is a phenomenological approach that sees people as creating their own realities. Based on past experiences, people construct their views of the world. Their reaction to the environment is then affected by this perspective. Under constructivism, therapy therefore revolves around helping the client to understand his or her fundamental assumptions and how they came about. The goal of therapy is to alter these assumptions, which may involve deep structural change or new constructions of the self, others, and the world in general. As Okun (2002) has stated, "The collaborative deconstruction of defeating core assumptions and co-construction of empowering constructs in a warm, collaborative helping relationship is a major vehicle for change" (p. 149).

Implications of constructivism for practice are (a) both thoughts and feelings are important in affecting people's future cognitions, emotions, and actions; (b) objective and subjective and conscious and unconscious thinking enters into people's perspectives; (c) as people examine their perspectives they become more aware of their thought processes and discover alternative ways to think or act; and d) creating a warm, comfortable atmosphere in therapy allows clients to examine themselves and to reconstruct ways of thinking and feeling (Okun, 2002).

Feminist Therapies

Because established theories were primarily developed by men, they necessarily have a male bias. They do not represent a feminist perspective. According to Okun (2002), "**Feminist therapies** focus on understanding gender as both a cause and a consequence of women's experiences in a male-dominated culture. They expose the limitations and constraints of the traditional normative value bases of existing psychological theories and the helping process" (p. 150).

Critical to success within feminist therapies are: (a) an egalitarian relationship between the client and therapist; and (b) understandings gained of the affect of sociocultural factors in the lives of women whose problems are often linked to their oppression by society (Okun, 2002).

Results from feminist therapies have include (a) opening the door for multicultural approaches to therapy to develop, (b) emphasis on the importance of an egalitarian relationship between therapist and client, (c) acknowledgment of the impact of gender role socialization on both women and men in society, (d) recognition of the potential for sexism to have an influence on people, (e) the need to increase clients' feelings of self-efficacy, and (f) the need to acknowledge women's unique attributes (Okun, 2002).

Multicultural Perspective

Cultural issues are at the center of the multicultural perspective. This perspective stresses the importance of therapists being aware of themselves and their clients having been affected by multicultural factors. In one of the earlier helping theory books written from a multicultural perspective, Ivey, Ivey, and Simek-Morgan (1993) indicated, "It is critical that as a counselor/therapist you develop awareness in yourself and others of how issues such as race/ethnicity, culture, and gender affect the way you and your clients construct meaning in the world (p. 1).

Implications from the multicultural perspective include the need for helpers to (a) develop sensitivity to and appreciation of cultural differences; (b) realize that sociocultural factors may underlie clients' problems; (c) know that cultural influences affect clients' sense of the world, including their views of relationships; (d) understand that people from different cultures may have different ways of coping; and (e) know that cultural influences may affect the ways clients express themselves verbally, nonverbally, and emotionally (Okun, 2002). Further discussion on cultural diversity is found in Chapter 5 on Helping Others.

Chapter Summary

Some approaches covered in this chapter, such as psychoanalytic psychotherapy and psychodrama, are beyond the normal bounds of recreational therapy and are utilized by other helping disciplines. Nevertheless, theoretical notions or actual techniques drawn from these approaches may have application in recreational therapy. Other approaches, such as behavior modification and transactional analysis are more likely to be used in recreational therapy interventions and leisure counseling. The information from this chapter will hopefully act as a catalyst for the interested reader to develop expertise in several of these therapeutic approaches.

Reading Comprehension Questions

1. Provide an example from your own experience that shows how theory affects practice.
2. What is meant by the eclectic approach? Do you agree that therapeutic recreation is characterized by eclecticism?
3. Differentiate between the psychoanalytic and behavioristic approaches. Contrast these with the humanistic psychology approach.
4. What are the id, ego, and superego?
5. Think of possible conflicts you have personally experienced between your id and superego.
6. What is the narcissistic phase?
7. What is psychoanalysis? Transference? Countertransference?
8. Do you accept the cathartic notion? Why or why not?
9. Describe play therapy.
10. How do behaviorists view "mental illness"?
11. Compare classical conditioning with operant conditioning.
12. Discuss what is meant by shaping, prompting, and fading.
13. What is modeling? Suggest ways to use it in recreational therapy.
14. What is time-out? Do you think it should be used by recreation therapists as a behavior modification technique?
15. What are token economies?
16. Should recreation be used as a privilege to be earned with tokens?
17. Explain the Premack principle. Do you think the response deprivation hypothesis is a better explanation of reinforcement patterns?
18. What is humanistic or growth psychology? Who is associated with humanistic psychology?
19. What do you consider to be the major implications of Rogers' client-centered therapy for practice in recreational therapy?
20. Briefly describe Gestalt therapy. Do you see any way its techniques could be used in leisure counseling? Do you believe positive psychology has a good fit with recreational therapy? Explain.
22. Which of the five major orientations do you personally favor (psychoanalytic, behavioristic, humanistic cognitive-behavioral, or positive psychology)? Why?
23. Do you agree that rational-emotive therapy can have useful application in leisure counseling?
24. Do you agree with Glasser's basic propositions regarding responsibility and reality? Would you place the same level of importance on involvements as Glasser does in his theory?
25. What are the four primary methods by which those using transaction analysis attempt to understand behavior?
26. What are the transaction analysis ego states?
27. Do you allow your Natural Child to come out in play and recreation?
28. What are positive strokes?
29. Should recreational therapists be involved with family therapy?
30. Does psychodrama have implications for recreational therapy practice?
31. Do you concur with Lazarus' principle of technical eclecticism?
32. Do you concur with the constructivism, feminist, and multicultural perspectives?

Chapter 3

Facilitation Techniques

■ Chapter Purpose

In addition to the more developed and comprehensive helping theories and therapeutic approaches discussed in Chapter 2, there are a number of facilitation techniques that may be employed as interventions. This chapter will help the reader to gain an understanding of a variety of techniques that may be used by recreational therapists and the research evidence related to each technique.

■ Key Terms

- Leisure education/ counseling
- Cinematherapy
- Horticulture therapy
- Therapeutic touch
- Breathing techniques
- Autogenic training
- Benson's technique
- Self-massage
- Aromatherapy
- Tai chi
- Debriefing
- Social skills training
- Cognitive rehabilitation
- Retail therapy
- Validation therapy
- Resocialization
- Reminiscence therapy

- Values clarification
- Bibliotherapy
- Therapeutic community
- Humor
- Progressive relaxation training
- Transcendental meditation
- Biofeedback
- Adventure therapy
- Oigorg
- Aquatic therapy
- Assertiveness training
- Animal-assisted therapy
- Technology as an intervention
- Creative arts
- Cognitive stimulation therapy
- Remotivation therapy
- Sensory training

■ Objectives

- Assess selected facilitation techniques to understand implications for practice in recreational therapy.
- Define basic terminology and concepts related to facilitation techniques.
- Evaluate facilitation techniques for possible use in recreational therapy.

The approaches discussed in this chapter are diverse. Some have been used primarily (but not exclusively) in psychiatric settings. Bibliotherapy, relaxation techniques, adventure therapy, and therapeutic community fall into this category. Others, such as cognitive stimulation therapy, remotivation therapy, resocialization, sensory training, and reminiscence therapy, have been employed mostly with persons who are elderly. Still others, such as horticulture therapy, humor, and values clarification have been used in an array of settings with a variety of client groups. Because the approaches presented in this section do not fit together into neat packages, no attempt has been made to group or arrange them systematically (with the exception of those primarily employed with persons who are elderly, which are placed together). Therefore, the order in which a particular approach is presented has nothing to do with its importance or possible value to recreational therapy.

Leisure Education/Counseling

In a survey of Certified Therapeutic Recreation Specialists (CTRSs) from the northeastern United States, Kinney, Warren, Kinney, and Witman (1999) discovered that leisure education/counseling was the facilitation technique most used in RT practice. A similar national study (Kinney, Kinney, & Witman, 2004) also identified leisure education/counseling as one of the most used facilitation techniques. In this same national study, CTRSs also identified leisure education/counseling as a facilitation technique that should be taught in all university professional preparation programs.

Dattilo and Williams (2011) have written that while there once were distinctive differences in the use of the terms *leisure education* and *leisure counseling,* these distinctions have largely been lost. The term leisure education is today commonly used to encompass all educational enterprises, including leisure counseling, that involve learning about leisure-related information, values, attitudes, and skills.

Dattilo (2008), citing earlier work of Askins (1997), has written that leisure education "is more than learning the skill needed to play a sport, tend a garden, or paint a picture; it involves developing leisure values, an understanding of the benefits of leisure, problem-solving skills, assertiveness, and learning about leisure resources in the community" (p. 10). According to Dattilo and Williams (2011), components of leisure education include (a) leisure appreciation, (b) self-awareness, (c) decision making, (d) self-determination, (e) leisure activity skills, (f) community skills, (g) social skills, and (h) leisure resources (p.168). Such elements are strikingly similar to the four major areas described by McDowell (1980) in his early writings on leisure counseling.

McDowell listed four major areas: (a) leisure-related behavioral concerns, (b) leisure lifestyle awareness concerns, (c) leisure resource guidance concerns, and (d) leisure-related skills-development concerns (See McDowell's levels of counseling in Table 3.1.) This similarity between Dattilo and Williams' leisure education components and McDowell's areas of leisure counseling certainly strengthens the notion of using the term leisure education to include concerns once addressed under the term, leisure counseling. Nevertheless, authors (e.g., Leitner & Leitner, 2012) do differentiate between leisure education and leisure counseling. Therefore, while there is obvious overlap between the terms leisure education and leisure counseling, because leisure education and leisure counseling are both employed in the literature and the term leisure education/counseling is found in the literature (e.g., Kinney, et al., 1999), the expression "leisure education/counseling" is employed within this book.

Table 3.1

McDowell's Levels of Counseling

Leisure-Related Behavioral Problems

To help clients resolve behavioral concerns. Clients develop effective coping skills and problem-solving abilities to deal with chronic or excessively expressed leisure-related behavioral concerns (e.g., boredom, TV watching).

Leisure Lifestyle Awareness Orientation

To help clients improve self-knowledge and understanding pertaining to leisure values, beliefs, and attitudes. Clients develop understanding regarding leisure and issues such as personal lifestyle, family relations, and transitions (e.g., aging, retirement, relocation, divorce).

Leisure Resource Guidance Orientation

To help clients match leisure interests with community resources. Clients need to identify leisure interests, or what to do in their free time, and information regarding opportunities needs to be provided to them.

Leisure-Related Skills-Development Orientation

To help clients develop the leisure-related skills and abilities that they lack. Clients develop skills in areas such as assertiveness, social skills, grooming, motor abilities, effective use of transportation, and recreation activities.

Source: McDowell, C. F. (1984). Leisure: Consciousness, well-being, and counseling. In E. T. Dowd (Ed.), *Leisure counseling: Concepts and applications.* Springfield, IL: Charles C. Thomas.

Developments in Leisure Education/Counseling

The need to educate for leisure has long been a part of the professional literature of recreation and leisure studies. Brightbill's (1966) *Educating for Leisure-Centered Living* is a case in point. It was, however, Mundy and Odum's (1979) book, *Leisure Education: Theory and Practice*, that seems to have brought leisure education to the forefront of recreational therapy. While leisure education had long been a part of recreational therapy, Mundy and Odum's textbook was influential in bringing the term *leisure education* into wide usage. At the same time, the book helped to infuse formal knowledge regarding leisure education into recreational therapy practice. Dattilo (2008) continued the traditions of leisure education found in Mundy and Odum's book in his authorship of his book, *Leisure Education Program Planning: A Systematic Approach,* as have Bullock, Mahon, and Killingsworth (2010), who provided an extensive chapter on leisure education in their book on recreation for persons with disabilities.

Leisure counseling (then referred to as recreation counseling) has been a much discussed topic since the 1960s and 1970s. Several extensive reviews of the leisure counseling literature appeared at that time (e.g., Compton, Witt, & Sanchez, 1980; Fikes, 1976; Shank & Kennedy, 1976) as scholars attempted to define the area and analyze empirical studies completed on the topic. In the 1980s, authorities (Tinsley & Tinsley, 1981; Munson & Munson, 1986) agreed that what had gone on in leisure counseling in the early years was largely information giving. Staff assisted clients to identify leisure interests and then gave them the information needed to locate opportunities to pursue those interests. Many then conducting leisure counseling had not been adequately prepared in the dynamics of counseling and, therefore, lacked the conceptualization of the counseling process and knowledge of counseling skills (Tinsley & Tinsley, 1981).

As time went on, a growing sophistication in leisure counseling was reflected by the publication of research in the area. For instance, Wolfe and Riddick (1984) reported on a program for adult psychiatric outpatients directed toward bringing about changes in leisure attitudes and self-esteem. Caldwell, Adolph, and Gilbert (1989) reported on research findings regarding the long-term effects of leisure counseling on leisure participation and satisfaction. The need for establishing theoretical underpinnings for leisure counseling practice also seemed to be better understood. Iso-Ahola (1984) formulated social psychological foundations for leisure with implications for counseling. Munson and Munson (1986) and Hultsman, Black, Seehafer, and Howell (1987) offered specific theory-based models for leisure counseling.

The development of models (e.g., McDowell, 1980; 1984; Hultsman et al., 1987) and the appearance of thoughtful writings (e.g., Iso-Ahola, 1984; Tinsley & Tinsley, 1981) have allowed us to realize that leisure counseling can extend far beyond the narrow bounds of information giving into such areas as lifestyle awareness and decision making, which more closely resemble traditional counseling. Other lessons learned have been the necessity to adopt models and theory to support practice and the need for those conducting leisure counseling to possess well-developed counseling skills.

Unfortunately, during the 1990s leisure counseling did not seem to advance as it had in the previous decade. Nevertheless, now that we have entered the 21st Century, leisure counseling seems to be poised for a leap forward in its development. Interestingly, most 21st Century articles on leisure counseling seem to have appeared in British journals (Juniper, 2003, 2005; Leitner & Leitner, 2005). Authors of these articles have emphasized that leisure counseling can offer the potential for helping clients to attain therapeutic objectives. American authors Leitner and Leitner (2012), have provided a chapter on leisure counseling geared toward counseling with older clients in their book titled *Leisure in Later Life*. Within the chapter, Leitner and Leitner present an 11-step developmental educational approach to leisure counseling.

Components of Leisure Education/Counseling

Eight areas of leisure education/counseling have been identified by Dattilo and Williams (2011). These eight areas represent goals that clients may achieve through leisure education/counseling. They are discussed in the section that follows.

Leisure appreciation. The goal of leisure appreciation is to assist clients to become aware of leisure as a phenomenon and of ensuring benefits (e.g., enjoyment, satisfaction) to be gained in leisure. Assessing attitudes toward leisure can be an important component within leisure appreciation.

Self-awareness. Here clients examine their leisure lifestyles so that they may become aware of values, patterns, and behaviors reflected in their lifestyles, as well as barriers to achieving the leisure lifestyle they seek. Having such an understanding allows clients to plan to make alterations in their leisure lifestyles.

Decision making. Unfortunately, many persons with disabilities have not had opportunities to engage in decision making. Yet decision-making skills can be learned by clients through leisure education/counseling.

Self-determination. Building on the work of Wehmeyer (1996), Dattilo and Williams (2011) have defined self-determination as "being in control of the course a life takes" (p. 192). Because self-determination is a central defining property of leisure (Austin, 2001b), it is critical that clients experience self-determination in order to experience leisure. Therapists can help clients to identify leisure preferences and then assert themselves in order to achieve those leisure preferences.

Leisure activity skills. People need a repertoire of activities in order to enjoy recreation and leisure participation. Through leisure education programs, clients learn the skills they need in order to take part in activities that may range from archery to yoga.

Community skills. Community skills are those that allow clients to participate in community life. Perhaps the community skill most needed by persons with disabilities is that of knowing how to use transportation so that they can get around the community. Another community skill is learning how to handle money.

Social skills. The expression *increasing socialization* is commonly used by recreational therapists to indicate the development and use of social skills by clients. Because clients with disabilities often experience social skills deficits, a variety of approaches is employed to teach social skills to clients. These include modeling appropriate behaviors for clients; using role playing as a technique; providing opportunities for social recreation in order for clients to try out their social skills; and reinforcing clients for using appropriate social skills. Formal social skills training programs may also be conducted.

Leisure resources. Early leisure counseling efforts often involved matching clients with community resources. Following the assessment of client leisure interests, therapists provided clients with information about possible resources (i.e., places, programs, and people) to meet their interests. The role of assisting clients to use leisure resources retains its importance among today's recreational therapists. In addition to leisure counseling, recreational therapists may hold leisure education classes or may coach clients to use resources in the community.

Implications for Recreational Therapy

It is evident that leisure education/counseling is a widely used facilitation technique in recreational therapy. A large number of outcomes may be achieved through leisure education/counseling. These range from gaining an appreciation for leisure to obtaining concrete information about possible community leisure resources. A variety of structures for leisure education/counseling exist in recreational therapy practice, including leisure education classes, social skills training groups, community reintegration programs, group leisure counseling, and individual leisure counseling.

A useful resource is Witman and Ligon's (2011b) *Reflection, Recognition, Reaffirmation: An Engaging Frame of Reference for Leisure Education.* The book contains a number of goal-directed exercises to use in leisure education.

Bullock, Mahon, and Killingsworth (2010) have presented a number of research studies to support the value of leisure education programs to clients with physical disabilities, intellectual disabilities, and mental illnesses, as well as older adults. Studies have also been published on successful leisure education programs provided for caregivers (e.g., Bedini & Phoenix, 1999; Hutchinson et al., 2011).

Even though it is evident that leisure counseling may be subsumed under the term leisure education, in this discussion the term leisure education/counseling has been used to emphasize counseling as a major means to leisure education. It is anticipated that in the future that authors within recreational therapy will further advance leisure counseling as an approach to leisure education. Recreational therapists should have a solid foundation for doing leisure counseling, if they possess the basic helping characteristics for recreational therapists (outlined in Chapter 5) that include the ability to communicate therapeutically.

Values Clarification

Values clarification is a facilitation technique that can be used to help clients in making autonomous decisions consistent with their values. Health care professionals can assist clients to explore their values and to make decisions regarding their values, which are important beliefs and principles by which people live their lives.

Purtilo and Haddad (2002) have defined values. They have written:

Values are deeply held attitudes and beliefs we have about the truth, beauty, or worth of a person, object, action, or idea. One criterion of a "true" value is that it has become a part of a pattern of a person's life. In other words, values must not only be identified, but embraced and expressed. (p. 5)

Prominent among authorities associated with values clarification is Sidney B. Simon, who has presented an approach to valuing made up of seven steps. These seven steps fall under three major categories—choosing, cherishing, and acting—each of which represents a plateau. The first category or plateau deals with choosing one's beliefs and behaviors. It has three subprocesses: option exploration or determining alternatives, appraising the consequences of a particular choice, and freely choosing a value after rational consideration. The second plateau deals with cherishing beliefs and behaviors. It contains the fourth step, which asks if you feel good or are happy with your choice and if you are ready to let others know of your choice. The third plateau contains the final two steps. Step six is determining action or what you are willing to do about your value. Step seven is making the value a regular part of your life (Simon & Olds, 1977).

Simon has also presented a number of values clarification strategies. Included within these are many that directly concern leisure choices. Among exercises from the book by Simon, Howe, and Kirschenbaum (1995) that I have used with groups are "The Pie of Life" (strategy 33) and "Twenty Things You Love to Do" (strategy 1).

Pie of Life

The purpose of this strategy is to take an inventory in terms of how time is spent during typical work or leisure days. Value/time inconsistencies may be discovered as participants find out if they are getting what they want out of life. The strategy also can produce thought-provoking issues about how individuals spend their lives.

The procedure involves the leader drawing a large circle on the board while indicating that the circle represents a typical 24-hour day. Participants are then asked to draw their own circles and divide them into quarters, representing six-hour blocks, using broken lines. One circle can be used to represent a work day (or school day) and the other, a leisure day. Participants then use the following categories (additional categories may be included) to draw in slices of the pie to depict how they spend their time: sleep, school, work, with friends, alone, with family, on chores around the house, exercise or sports, eating, or other miscellaneous pastimes.

After completing the pies, participants are asked to think about the following questions:

- Are you satisfied with the relative sizes of your slices?
- Ideally, how big would you want each slice to be? Draw your ideal pie.
- Realistically, is there anything you can do to begin to change the size of some of your slices?
- Is there a Self-Contract (see strategy number 59) you'd be willing to make and sign your name to?

Twenty Things You Love to Do

The question asked by this strategy is "Am I really getting what I want out of life?" Rewarding living includes taking part in highly prized activities. Until participants engage in this strategy, they may not know whether they are getting what they really want from life. In Appendix A at the end of this chapter (p. 140), you will find the directions for this activity. The activity encourages participants to evaluate how they really feel about things they do by insisting that they note various conditions about these activities.

Other exercises I have used from the 1995 Simon book are strategies 3, 4, 23, 27, 28, 57, and 71. With some of these the leader must choose parts or adapt them in a way that emphasizes leisure aspects. A very helpful strategy to use in conjunction with a number of exercises is strategy 15, "I Learned Statements." This exercise stimulates group discussion about the previous strategy by allowing participants to complete phrases such as "I learned that I ...," "I realized that I ...," and "I was surprised that I ..."

It is important for those leading values clarification strategies to keep in mind that the goal of values clarification is not to impose a value or course of action on participants but to encourage them to look at alternatives and their consequences. Such clarification on leisure lifestyle can be meaningful to individuals who have not adequately worked through value issues related to leisure.

Spending an Unexpected Free Day

Still another values clarification exercise for clients has been suggested by Taylor, Lillis and LeMone (2001; p. 83). The therapist asks the client to rank behaviors as to how he or she would *most likely* spend an unexpected free day. Options include:

_____ Enjoy some quiet time alone (e.g., thinking, readings, listening to music)
_____ Spend time with family, friends
_____ Do something active (e.g., hiking, playing ball, swimming)

____ Watch television
____ Volunteer time and energy to help someone else
____ Use time for my job
____ Other

Following making their decisions, their choices are discussed to determine what they say about the client's values. The client is then asked how he or she wished he or she could spend the free day, versus how he or she would *most likely* spend it. This choice is then discussed.

Implications for Recreational Therapy

Values clarification has direct implications for recreational therapists who may employ values clarification strategies in leisure education/counseling programs. Through these exercises, individuals can discover leisure values and initiate plans to act on their values. Usually exercises are completed in a group, with the leader providing the instructions for each exercise. No particular equipment is necessary, although it is helpful to have a blackboard available. Participants may need paper and pencils to complete some exercises. In Dattilo and McKenney's (2011) book on *Facilitation Techniques in Therapeutic Recreation*, within the chapter on values clarification are specific approaches to conducting values clarification programs.

Bibliotherapy

The term *bibliotherapy* was first coined in 1916 by Samuel Crothers (Yusuf & Taharem, 2006). Bibliotherapy has enjoyed a "long and rich history" (Jack & Ronan, 2008, p. 178) that has included receiving support from esteemed figures in the history of medicine such as Drs. Benjamin Rush and William C. Menninger (Jack & Ronan, 2008).

Bibliotherapy employs reading materials such as novels, plays, short stories, booklets, and pamphlets to help clients become aware that others share problems similar to theirs and to help bring new insights into being. The use of bibliotherapy traditionally has been associated with psychiatric treatment, often as an adjunct to psychotherapy. Readings that are selected for the client contain characters with problems related to the client's problems. The client will then supposedly identify with the characters and project himself or herself into the story. This process results in an emotional reaction that can then be discussed with a helping professional. (Carson et al., 2000; Eisenberg & Delaney, 1986). Research findings have shown bibliotherapy to be an effective treatment, particularly for persons dealing with depression (Scogin, 1998).

Recreational therapist Laurie Jake (2001) has indicated that many types of literature can be used in bibliotherapy, including self-help books, fiction, and poetry. Such literature can be used in a variety of settings. According to Jake, bibliotherapy "can alleviate feelings of alienation when readers recognize characters with feelings, thoughts, and circumstances similar to their own. This can be especially therapeutic for someone who is in the process of recovery or rehabilitation from a disabling condition" (p. 1).

Bibliotherapy can be conducted with individual clients on their personal issues or with groups whose members are dealing with common themes. Typically, adults read the book, or other piece of literature, before a therapy session. They then discuss it with their therapist or members of their bibliotherapy group. Questions are asked by the therapist during the discussion to assist the client, or clients, to analyze, interpret, and apply concepts found in the reading.

With young children, the therapist may read a book to a single child or to a small group. Sometimes children who can read take turns reading pages of a children's book. Warm-up questions about the story may be posed before the reading begins. While the story is being read, the therapist facilitates discussion by asking the children questions. For example, the therapist might ask if the child (or children) have experienced something similar to what happened to the character in the book. Or the child (or children) can be asked what they think will happen next. A period for the sharing of thoughts and feelings about the story may also be provided once the book has been finished. For instance, the therapist may ask, What was your favorite part? Least favorite part? Would you change the story? Would you want to read it again? (Beland, 2001) Therapists may also work with parents to train them to read books with their children.

Jake (2001) has listed the following as possible goals of bibliotherapy to (a) develop self-concept, (b) increase understandings of human behavior or motivations, (c) foster self-appraisal, (d) provide a means for an individual to find interests outside of himself or herself, (e) relieve emotional or mental pressure, (f) show an individual that he or she is not the first person to encounter such a problem, (g) display that there is more than one way to solve a problem, (h) help a person to more freely discuss a problem, and (i) assist an individual to plan a constructive course of action to solve a problem (p. 1).

Beland (2001) has listed the following as benefits of bibliotherapy for hospitalized children: (a) offering enjoyment, (b) building rapport, (c) giving a break for parents, (d) gaining therapeutic insights about children, (e) providing cognitive stimulation, (f) allowing emotional involvement, (g) enhancing language development, and (h) providing social interaction.

Implications for Recreational Therapy

The availability of empirical studies to support the use of bibliotherapy has been limited. Yet meta-analysis has revealed "that bibliotherapy has the potential to be a powerful technique to achieve emotional and behavioral change," according to Jack and Ronan (2008, p. 177).

Bibliotherapy has become increasingly used by recreational therapists. Scogin (1998) has suggested that bibliotherapy can play a role in not only the treatment but also the prevention of depression in clients who are elderly. Both Scogin (1998) and Jake (2001) have suggested that bibliotherapy may be effectively employed in outpatient settings.

Bibliotherapy reinforces the importance of structuring ways for clients to help themselves. Clients can engage in self-help activities without direct assistance from recreational therapists if proper structures are provided.

Cinematherapy

Cinematherapy, cinema therapy, film therapy, movie therapy, and video work are all expressions that have been employed to describe the viewing of movies for therapeutic purposes. I have selected the term *cinematherapy* simply because it seems to best capture today's practice of having clients watch films that they later discuss with a therapist.

Cinematherapy grew out of bibliotherapy (Fleming & Bohnel, 2009) and is similar to bibliotherapy but uses movies rather than literature as its vehicle. At least part of the rationale for video therapy is that it takes far less time to watch a movie than to read a book. Movies also may have a great impact on individuals.

Aproberts (2000) has suggested that the huge popularity of movies portraying psychological problems "suggests many of us are more inclined to experience intense feelings and garner psychological insights from the screen than elsewhere" (p. D1).

Birgit Wolz (2005), who facilitates cinematherapy groups, wrote:

> Movies affect us powerfully because the synergistic impact of music, dialogue, lighting, camera angles, and sound effects enables a film to bypass ordinary defensive censors in us....Movies draw us into the viewing experience, but at the same time—often more easily than in real life—afford a unique opportunity to retain a perspective outside the experience, the observer's view.

Sharp, Smith, and Cole (2002) explained, "Cinematherapy is a therapeutic technique that involves careful selection and assignment of movies for clients to watch with follow-up processing of their experiences during therapy sessions" (p. 270). Brown (2005) has described the use of films in therapy. She has written that "the purpose of cinematherapy is not to entertain nor to make the client laugh or cry. The purpose is for the client to identify with situations and characters, and look for ways to solve their problems, as well as to encourage insight and personal growth through discussion in therapy" (p. 20).

Hesley and Hesley (2001) have explained that cinematherapy is "a therapeutic process in which clients and therapists discuss themes and characters in popular films to relate to core issues of ongoing therapy." They go on to write, "...we use films to facilitate self-understanding, to introduce options for action plans, and to seed future therapeutic interventions" (pp. 4, 5). Hesley and Hesley further explain that video therapy involves far more than just having clients watch movies. They make clear that cinematherapy, like other therapeutic approaches, needs to be provided by a skilled clinician when they state, "A film offers a wide range of interpretations determined by the specific needs of a client, by the directions a clinician gives for viewing, and by the connections that a therapist helps a client draw" (p. 7).

Hesley and Hesley (2001) have outlined seven ways that films benefit clients. These include (a) providing hope and encouragement; (b) reframing problems; (c) providing role models; (d) identifying and reinforcing internal strengths; (e) triggering emotions that otherwise might not be felt; (f) improving communications by offering metaphors that open up feelings that clients have a hard time putting into words; and (g) transmitting values that clients can examine, and perhaps, embrace (pp. 17-25).

In order to assist clients to achieve these benefits, Hesley and Hesley (2001) begin the discussion of movies with open-ended questions such as, "What did you find useful about the film?" "How did the film strike you?" "Of what value would this particular film be for someone in your situation?" (p. 70) Questions suggested by Hesley and Hesley to follow up on a client's identification with characters in a film include (a) "In what ways was the character you identified with similar to or different from you?"; (b) What attributes would you like to take from that character?" "What aspects of that character would you avoid?"; (c) "Are there other characters in the film who present positive options?; In what ways?"; (d) "Who were the antagonists, and what obstacles did they present?" How are they similar to people or situations in your own world?"; (e) "How did the protagonist succeed in overcoming the challenges?"; and (f) "How can you use a similar strategy to overcome your own challenges?" (p. 73)

Finally, in order to connect ideas gained from the film to the client's life, Hesley and Hesley (2001) suggest a final phase. Within this phase, clients (a) identify the central problem of the film and determine how it was resolved, (b) articulate and modify the client's basic concerns about using that approach, and (c) develop action steps that incorporate lessons learned from the film to the client's personal situation (p. 74).

Within their book, *Rent Two Films and Let's Talk in the Morning*, Hesley and Hesley (2001) offer an anthology of films that can be used in cinematherapy. For example, under the topic of "Transition to Adulthood," they list *Breaking Away* and *The Graduate*, and under "Inspirational" are *Field of Dreams, It's a Wonderful Life, Rudy*, and *The Shawshank Redemption*. This anthology offers a highly useful tool for those doing cinematherapy.

Another source of movie titles has been provided by Lampropoulos, Kazantzis, and Deane (2004). These researchers surveyed counseling psychologists to develop a list of the most highly rated cinematherapy pictures. Among the top 10 movies (with the main subject) were: *Ordinary People* (multigenerational issues, loss); *Philadelphia* (AIDS and prejudice); *The Great Santini* (father/son relationship, abuse); *On Golden Pond* (aging and relationships); *Trip to Bountiful* (age and ageism); *My Life* (terminal illness and dying); *Kramer vs. Kramer* (divorce and custody); *Dad* (aging and family); *Dead Poets Society* (adolescence, family issues); and *When a Man Loves a Woman* (alcoholism).

While Hesley and Hesley's (2001) book is directed toward therapists, Solman (1995, 2000) has authored self-help books that encourage readers to view movies on their own. These books provide readers with descriptions of scores of movies that hold the potential for producing therapeutic insights.

There are also a number of websites that offer information on cinematherapy. Cinematherapy.com is a particularly rich source of information. Resources covered on Cinematherapy.com include: guidelines for selecting films; guidelines for watching films; descriptions of films; and an index of films listed under categories such as inspiration, family issues, mental and emotional illness, and physical illness/medical issues.

Implications for Recreational Therapy

A study by Lampropoulos, Kazantzis, and Deane (2004) revealed that 88% of counseling psychologists surveyed saw films as effective in helping clients to achieve positive therapeutic outcomes. Yet, there exists a paucity of research on the efficacy of cinematherapy (Fleming & Bohnel, 2009; Lampropoulos, Kazantzis, & Deane, 2004).

Cinematherapy has not yet become a popular technique within recreational therapy. However, the potential for the use of movies in recreational therapy appears to be obvious. Because movies are a highly popular form of recreation, cinematherapy would likely be engaging for many clients. Of course, those conducting cinematherapy need to be trained in using this technique as an intervention. Due to the relative newness of this approach, recreational therapists will need to gain training in doing cinematherapy through courses or by serving as a co-therapist with a clinician skilled in this technique.

Fleming and Bohnel (2009) have proposed using films as a part of the assessment of psychiatric clients. Instead of assigning a specific film to clients as is done in cinematherapy, clients are given the lead role by asking them to identify personally significant films (i.e., their favorite films). Their strengths-based approach puts clients in charge by letting them suggest a film to the clinician that relates to themes or characters that they identify with. This approach would seem to have much in common with traditions of recreational therapy of using a nonthreatening approach in which clients retain as much control as possible.

Horticulture Therapy

"**Horticulture therapy** (HT) is a process through which plants, gardening activities, and innate closeness to nature are used as vehicles in therapy and rehabilitation programs," according to horticulture therapist Wichrowski and his colleagues (2005, p. 270). A horticulture therapy program can be simple or complex. It can range from simply growing plants indoors under lights, or having plants on a window sill, to extensive outdoor gardens or a complete greenhouse. A sampling of projects includes tending a moveable garden on wheels for wheelchair users; starting seeds in flats; rooting house plants; making corsages; constructing pine cone turkeys; Halloween pumpkin painting; constructing grapevine wreaths; using dried flowers to make picture frames and other crafts; making soda bottle terrariums; making orange juice, grapefruit juice, and lemonade; and cooking, using harvest from a vegetable garden (Asher, 1998; Smith, 1998). Haller and Kramer's (2006) *Horticultural Therapy Methods* also provides a number of activity ideas.

Horticulture activities can be used as a means to develop therapeutic relationships "for the dual purpose of helping with the problem of adjustment, and motivating a broader interest in the client's surroundings as a result of increased knowledge of the plant world," according to Rothert and Daubert (1981, p. 2). Horticulture therapy has been reported to provide the following benefits:

- Enhance life satisfaction, morale, and interaction with the environment.
- Obtain peace and quiet and renewed spirit by visiting gardens.
- Increase socialization, peer support, and self-esteem.
- Alleviate anxiety and reduce depression.
- Help improve brain functioning.
- Provide sensory stimulation.
- Improve mood state and reduce stress.
- Decrease agitation and aggression in persons with dementia.
- Establish commitment to a goal, a sense of responsibility, and feelings of control.
- Provide mild to moderate exercise through gardening, leading to improved functioning and gains in overall health.
- Bring about physical therapy benefits during participation in personally meaningful activity.
- Improve tactile abilities (e.g., for persons with arthritic hands).
- Stimulate contact with concrete reality and nature by working hands in soil.
- Develop appreciation for other living things, life cycles, growth, and development.
- Instill a sense of purpose and of being needed.
- Develop horticulture skills that may lead to employment.
- Develop a wholesome leisure activity that may be carried on following treatment and rehabilitation

(Asher, 1998; Austin, Johnston, & Morgan, 2006; Collins & O'Callaghan, 2008; Edinberg,1985; Elings, 2006; Friedman, 1985; Gonzalez et al., 2010, 2011, 2011a; Jarrott, Kwack, & Relf, 2002; Mizuno-Matsumoto et al., 2008; Rappe, Kivela, & Rita, 2006; Rothert & Daubert, 1981; Smith, 1998; Wichrowski et al., 2005).

It should be mentioned that horticulture therapy is gaining increased use within programs that serve clients with physical disabilities. Because of this, more attention is being given to creating environments that are conducive to gardening for persons such as those who use wheelchairs, have had strokes, or have visual impairments. For example, elevated areas can be constructed to allow clients using wheelchairs to do gardening (Smith, Austin, Kennedy, Lee, & Hutchison, 2005). Long-handled tools reduce the need to bend or stretch for those who have had strokes (Growing Confidence, 1993). A variety of ideas to facilitate horticulture activities for persons with disabilities (including the use of cut-and-grab scissors, one-handed wheelbarrows, and vertical planters) appear in a wonderfully illustrated booklet published by the Perkins School for the Blind (n.d.). Web-based sources of information on gardening for persons with disabilities are "Gardening from a Wheelchair" by LoBello (nd) and "Gardening" by the National Center on Physical Activity and Disability (2005).

Finally, related to horticulture therapy are "passive therapy gardens" or "healing gardens" (Femal, 2012; Stigsdotter & Grahn, 2003). These are gardens built by health care facilities to allow patients and staff to experience peace and solitude and to observe the constant growth and renewal of plant life (Davis, 1997). The development of a hospital garden at the Shriners Hospital for Children in Chicago has been chronicled in an article by Johnson, Bland, and Rathsam (2002).

Implications for Recreational Therapy

Clinical results hold promise that clients may receive therapeutic benefits through work with plants although scientific validity for horticulture therapy has not been well established (Elings, 2006; Pachana & Arathoon, 2003). There is, however, an emerging body of research suggesting the efficacy of horticulture therapy in the reduction of depression (e.g., Gonzalez, et al., 2010, 2011, 2011a; Rappe & Kivela, 2005; Wilson, 2012). A particularly interesting study on depression was completed by McCaffrey, Hanson, and McCaffrey (2010). These researchers combined walking and reflective writing in a garden setting to bring about depression reduction and mood enhancement.

Another interesting study that may have ramifications for recreational therapy practice was completed by Collins and O'Callaghan (2008). These researchers modeled their research after the classic study by Langer and Rodin (1976) on personal responsibility and found elderly residents who were given the responsibility to take care of plants significantly increased indicators of health and self-rated happiness.

Therapists must possess knowledge of plants and gardening, and be able to relate this knowledge to clients' problems or concerns in order to conduct horticulture therapy programs. The requirement of a high degree of facility with the medium employed in therapy or rehabilitation is, of course, a fundamental prerequisite to the application of any therapeutic approach, as is the ability to apply the medium to meet client needs. Some colleges and universities do offer a master's degree in horticulture therapy, although many horticulture therapy programs are conducted by therapists without such specialized preparation.

Therapeutic Community

Englishmen Tom Main and Maxwell Jones originated the term *therapeutic community*, which has typically been employed to describe a way of operating a relatively small unit within a general hospital, a large psychiatric hospital, or other institution. Therapeutic communities have been used primarily on psychiatric services and with nursing home residents in the treatment of emotional and behavioral problems. Most recently, the concept has been applied in community-based transitional living facilities for homeless, severe, and persistently mentally ill persons (Kennard, 1998; Murray & Baier, 1993).

Attributes of democratic therapeutic communities have been outlined by Kennard (1998). They are (a) an informal and communal atmosphere that is homelike, rather than institutional; (b) regularly held group meetings focus on issues that come up in the daily life of the community; (c) the work of maintaining and running the community is shared by clients and staff; (d) clients play a therapeutic role as auxiliary therapists by influencing each other's behavior; (e) authority is shared by staff and clients in organizing sports, social events, and outings; and (f) there exist shared beliefs within the community. Beliefs include that clients' difficulties are largely in relation with others, therapy involves a learning process in which clients learn about themselves and others to gain interpersonal skills, and there is an equality among all members of the community.

These therapeutic communities are based on the concept that the entire social milieu may be used as an intervention because clients change and grow as a result of involvement in interpersonal relationships. It is reasoned that since client problems have resulted from faulty social learning, positive social learning can build the individual's ability to cope. The goal is for persons to help themselves by helping others, ultimately learning to be responsible for themselves. In the therapeutic community, staff and clients interact freely in work and recreation within an understanding atmosphere designed to utilize the total impact of group processes. The Director and Assistant Director of Nursing at Menninger Foundation have noted that one of the main areas where learning is needed is in regard to leisure activities and the use of unstructured time on the unit (Benfer & Schroder, 1985, p. 454). The concept of therapeutic community stands in contrast to the hierarchical, authoritarian organization often associated with hospitals and institutions. The student of recreational therapy may recognize that the therapeutic community has much in common with the moral therapy of the nineteenth century (Barnes, Sack, & Shore, 1973; Kennard, 1998).

In the United States, the expression "therapeutic community" has also been used to describe user-run, drug-free communities for persons who have abused substances. These therapeutic communities are, in contrast to those that originated in Britain, not democratic but are hierarchical structures that employ rewards systems and encounter groups (Camping, 2001). It is the original concept of therapeutic communities from the U.K. that has application to recreational therapy.

Implications for Recreational Therapy

Even though there are problems related to the therapeutic community concept, including its abstractness and staff role blurring, the approach has implications for recreational therapists. A major one is the importance of all staff in facilitating change, because all client experiences have therapeutic value and all transactions between clients and staff are seen as having therapeutic potential.

The therapeutic community approach also shows that recreational therapists must learn to function harmoniously in a team effort with staff and clients in order to create a positive social structure to enhance treatment. Such an approach can transcend institutional care. The principles of the therapeutic community can have application in community-based treatment. As we move from institutional care to community care, we should not lose what was learned from the innovation of the therapeutic community more than 50 years ago in Britain.

Humor

Laughter results from **humor**, which develops out of incongruity. Things that appear funny are generally unexpected, ambiguous, inappropriate, or illogical (Adler, 1989). Laughter and humor have been associated with both being healthy and becoming healthy. Healthy persons are generally perceived to have a sense of humor and are able to laugh with others and at themselves.

Wooten (2013) has identified three types of therapeutic humor: hoping humor, coping humor, and gallows humor. She wrote:

Hoping humor gives the individual the courage to face challenges. Coping humor offers a release for physical and emotional tension. Gallows humor provides protection from the emotional impact of witnessing tragedy, death, and disfigurement. (p. 309)

The notion that laughter and humor have therapeutic value has long enjoyed popular support. All of us have no doubt used the phrase, "Laughter is the best medicine," on more than one occasion. Provine (2000) has suggested, "Laughter seems an ideal treatment that makes us feel good, is free, has no bad side effects, and is even contagious, bursting forth in a noisy and benevolent chain reaction" (p. 189). Even so, the concept of using laughter and humor as therapeutic interventions to a degree remains controversial (Fry & Salameh, 1993; Lumsden,1986); this may well be attributed to a previous lack of scientific evidence to support the use of humor in treatment.

Scientific Documentation

Interest in the therapeutic potential of humor was largely triggered by Norman Cousins (1979, 1983), who widely wrote about his personal use of humor in recovering from Collagen disease (a crippling illness) and a myocardial infarction. Scientific evidence on the value of humor in therapy was lacking at the time but recently has been developing. Scholl and Ragan (2003) have written, "Whereas members of the medical community know intuitively that humor can accelerate the healing process, scholars and medical experts only recently have begun to explore humor systematically in an attempt to understand it's therapeutic potential" (p. 319).

There are signs that systematic research has been accomplished to support the use of humor to bring about positive health outcomes. Vagnoli and colleagues (2005) wrote: "Multiple studies, beginning in the 1970s, have shown that humor has many positive effects on physical and mental health and well-being" (p. e563). This positive view of the empirical evidence supporting the use of humor has however been challenged by some scholars (e.g., Bennett, 2003; Martin, 2001).

The exact state of research on the healing power of humor is difficult to assess due to mixed conclusions by authors of reviews of the research literature related to humor therapy. Some authors of research reviews have been laudatory about the research in the area. Schor (2010), for example, following his review of the literature wrote, "In summary, the scientific literature demonstrates that the effects of humor and laughter on health are far-ranging and numerous" (p. 3). Paulose (2011) concluded his review of the research on the healing power of well-being by stating that "positive affective states provide health benefits by maintaining and improving the normal neuronal and hormonal functional balance. Also, it enhances chemicals such as endorphins In the brain and provides a state of euphoria" (p. 152). Berk (2001) concluded his review of 30 years of research by stating: "This review indicated that the psychophysiological benefits and risks of human are significant to the health and well-being of all humans, but especially to older adults" (p. 335).

Berk's research review reported eight psychological and seven physiological benefits of humor and laughter. Psychological benefits were reduced anxiety, reduced tension, reduced stress, reduced depression, reduced loneliness, improved self-esteem, restored hope and energy, and an increased sense of empowerment and control (p. 334). Physiological benefits included improved mental functioning, muscle relaxation, improved respiration, circulation stimulation, decreased stress hormones, increased immune system defenses, increased production of endorphins, and destroyed common viruses and bacteria (p. 335).

Other authors of research reviews however have found the research on humor and laughter to be woefully lacking. Martin (2001), for instance, determined that "taken together, the empirical studies reviewed…provide little evidence for unique positive effects of humor and laughter on health-related variables" (p. 514). He ended his review with the statement, "In conclusion, despite the popularity of the idea that humor and laughter have significant health benefits, the current empirical evidence is generally weak and inconclusive" (p. 516). Pressman and Cohen (2005) expressed "serious conceptual and methodological reservations" (p. 925) of research completed on the influence of positive affect on physical health. Bennett (2003) in his review article of humor in medicine wrote: "Despite statements about the health benefits of humor, current research is insufficient to validate such claims" (p. 1257). Likewise, two reviews of humor in mental illness both found a dearth of empirical evidence. Taber, Redden, and Hurley (2007) wrote, "Although the beneficial effects of humor and laughter have been a part of 'common wisdom' for many centuries, there is comparatively little solid scientific research in this potentially quite important area" (p. 359). Gelkopf (2011) concluded that "empirical studies are still lacking, the studies that do exist have major methodological shortcomings, and the field is in dire need of further investigation" (p. 1).

Gervais and Wilson (2005) perhaps best assessed the state of empirical studies on the effects laughter and humor on health. In their synthesis of laughter and humor evidence they found "myriad empirical advances" but concluded, "Nevertheless, the scientific study of laughter and humor is still in its infancy relative to other comparable subjects in emotions and communication research" (p. 396). Thus, while research evidence of the effects of laughter and humor on health is emerging, it is far from complete.

Humorous Movies and Videos

An area of inquiry that has consistently produced favorable research results has been the use of humorous movies or videos. An example is a study by Adams and McGuire (1986) in which these researchers tested the following hypotheses:

1. Individuals viewing humorous movies will experience more reduction in perceived pain than individuals viewing non-humorous movies.
2. Individuals viewing humorous movies will experience more improvement in affect than individuals viewing non-humorous movies. (pp. 160–161)

Subjects in the study were persons residing in a long-term care facility who viewed movies for 30 minutes three times each week for six weeks. Both self-report and decreases in the use of pain medications confirmed the positive impact of the humorous movies on the subjects' pain. Support was also found for hypothesis 2. Affect Balance Scale scores indicated that the subjects who viewed the humorous movies had significantly higher affect scores than those who saw the non-humorous movies.

Gelkopf and his associates have completed a series of studies on the effect of humorous movies with patients with chronic schizophrenia. Results from these studies have shown a lowering of anxiety and depression and less aggression (Gelkopf et al., 1993), increases in social support (Gelkopf et al., 1994), and reductions in psychopathology, anger, anxiety, and depression symptoms (Gelkopf et al., 2006), Weisenberg, Raz, and Hener (1998) studied 200 participants to investigate the effect of watching a humorous film on pain tolerance. They found significant increases in pain tolerance after patients viewed the film. Similarly, humorous videos have been found by researchers to bring about a number of positive health outcomes with a variety of populations. Bennett et al. (2003) reported humorous videos decreased stress and brought about increased immune function in healthy women. Hayashi et al. (2007) found the viewing of a comic video by those in an inpatient diabetes educational program resulted in positive effects on blood glucose regulation. Stuber et al.

(2009) discovered that children who watched funny videos better tolerated painful medical procedures.

Additional Studies

Other studies have likewise reported promising outcomes with the use of humor as an intervention. For instance, humor can reduce or alleviate pain (Smith & Oliver, 1998), free us from shame and guilt (Fry, 1993), reduce stress (Argyle, 2001; Kuhlman, 1993; Simon, 1988), liberate us from inhibitions (Yorukoglu, 1993), assist us in social bonding (Mosak & Maniacci, 1993), help us in establishing helping relationships (Kennedy, 1995; Kidd et al., 2009; Scholl & Ragan, 2003), effect postprandial glucose levels of patients with diabetes (Hayashi & Murakami, 2009), reduce hyperinflation in patients with severe COPD (Brutsche et al., 2008), produce feelings of mastery (Schimel, 1993), provide a sense of control or power when one can make light of a serious situation, and offer a break from stressors (Seaward, 2002). Additionally, Prerost's (1987) research findings indicate humor can diffuse both anger and anxiety. Deep laughter can increase heart rate and oxygenation to the lungs, stimulate the adrenal glands, and temporarily increase blood pressure, creating a state of relaxation (Hill & Smith, 1990). Laughter can stimulate the endocrine system, causing the release of natural painkillers, and to lead to reductions in muscle tension (Lumsden, 1986).

Research reviews have reported that there is research evidence that humor may bring about any number of therapeutic effects. Antai-Otong (2007) and Bennett et al. (2003) found research evidence that humor was helpful in dealing with stress, improving mood state, providing muscle tension reduction, and improving immune functioning. Bennett and Lengacher (2008) have reviewed evidence that suggests laughter reduces stress and muscle tension and improves cardiorespiratory functioning. Graham-Pole (2002) has stated that research has shown sustained laughter, in particular, can lead to tension reduction and decreases in anxiety and depression, as well as bringing about beneficial cardiovascular effects. Panksepp (2000) has written that "support has emerged to affirm that humor and laughter may ameliorate pain, alleviate stress, and promote functioning of the immune system" (p. 185). While the amount of humor research remains modest, these and other findings lend growing support for the use of humor in treatment (Paulose, 2011).

One voice advocating the use of humor and laughter has William B. Strean (2009) who wrote a commentary supporting what he termed the "laughter prescription." He stated that more scientific evidence is needed on using humor to reach health related outcomes but nevertheless he believed:

> There are, however, several good reasons to conclude that laughter is effective as an intervention. Although the evidence…demonstrating laughter's benefits could be stronger, virtually all studies of laughter and health indicate positive results. Similarly, there are almost no negative side effects or undesirable ramifications associated with laughter as an intervention. This is a case in which appropriate logic might be akin to the perspective of 'innocent until proven guilty.' (p. 965)

Implications for Recreational Therapy

According to the editors of *Advances in Humor and Psychotherapy* (Fry & Salameh, 1993), humor is becoming an accepted element in mental health care. The use of humor is also becoming accepted within physical medicine (Kennedy, 1995). Humor is seen by many as no longer being a questionable treatment modality but as a "powerful tool" (Mosak & Maniacci, 1993).

Although it may be premature for recreational therapists to open comedy clubs in their facilities, there is evidence to support the use of humor in treatment programs. Perhaps the first thing to gain from the recent interest in humor as therapy is that none of us should take ourselves too seriously. We all need to learn to laugh at ourselves and the situations we find ourselves in. Beyond modeling a sense of humor, we may wish to initiate humor in interactions with clients who display a sense of humor. To determine how a client may react to the use of humor, it is wise to conduct a humor assessment. Questions you may ask include the following: What makes you laugh? With whom do you laugh the most? When and where do you laugh most? Can you recall using humor in the past during stressful or painful experiences? (Erdman, 1991; Smith & Oliver, 1998).

We may help clients to experience humor by showing humorous movies, as was done by Adams and McGuire (1986), or by helping them to select something humorous to read. Some health facilities have "humor carts," "comedy carts," or "humor baskets." The carts and baskets have the obvious advantage that they can be taken to the clients' rooms. Baskets can even be checked out by clients. Clever names are often applied to the carts, such as "Laughmobile," "Jokes on Spokes," "Humor on a Roll," or "Humor a la Cart" (Wooden, 2013). Typically, items found in carts include CDs, DVDs, and listening and viewing devices. Media may contain humorous movies, situation comedies, and stand-up comedy acts. Also on the carts may be humorous magazines, joke and comic books, and even playful items such as soap bubbles, toys, games, play dough, and puppets. (Smith & Oliver, 1998).

Wooten (2013, pp. 321-322) has suggested the following for starting a humor program:

- Create a scrapbook of cartoons. Try to find humor about situations your clients will face.
- Develop a file of funny jokes, stories, cards, bumper stickers, poems, and songs.
- Collect or borrow funny books and audiobooks and CDs and DVDs of comedy routines.
- Keep a file of local clowns, magicians, storytellers, and puppeteers and invite them to perform.
- Collect toys, interactive games, noisemakers, and costume items and keep them available for play.
- Create a humor journal or log to record funny encounters or humorous discoveries to bring out on days when you really need a laugh but can't seem to find anything funny.
- Establish a bulletin board at your facility. Post cartoons, bumper stickers, and funny signs (always avoiding ageist, sexist, or ethnic material).
- Subscribe to a humorous newsletter or journal to collect new ideas and inspirations.
- Educate yourself about therapeutic humor by attending conferences and workshops and by staying up with the literature.

Other ideas are "laughter libraries," "humor rooms," and "bedside clowning." Humorous books, and DVDs can compose a "laughter library" collection from which clients can check out materials. "Humor rooms" are comfortable facilities where clients, with one another or with their families, can gather around game tables or other areas for sharing fun. One hospital named its humor room the "Happy Room." In "bedside clowning," clowns go into patient rooms to provide diversions to help patients forget their pain or burdens (Dossey, Keegan, & Guzzetta, 2000). The *Happiness Clown Newsletter* offers information to enhance bedside clowning (Wooten, 2013). Finally, Simon (1988) and Kuhlman (1993) have suggested that the use of humor can be taught within stress management programs as a coping skill that leads to relaxation and feelings of well-being.

Therapeutic Use of Touch

The use of touch as a therapeutic tool has a long history. Cave paintings in the Pyrenees some 15,000 years ago attest to the ancient use of the laying on of hands. Written history of healing by touch goes back 5,000 years. Both the Old and New Testaments of the Bible contain descriptions of its use. The terms "King's touch" and "Royal touch" came from early France and England, where kings used touch to cure goiter and other diseases of the throat. Numerous accounts of healing by the laying on of hands appeared in church histories of the Middle Ages. While these events make it clear that the therapeutic use of hands had been employed widely throughout history, with the arrival of the scientific age, such practices fell from favor. Only relatively recently has touch begun to be reexamined for its possible therapeutic value (Cohen, 1987; Krieger, 1979).

Some may use the term *therapeutic touch* in a very broad way to mean the therapeutic use of touch in general. The expression should however be reserved for a specific type of therapy developed by Professor Delores Krieger.

The term **therapeutic touch** (TT) was coined in the 1970s by Professor Krieger, then a nursing professor at New York University (Sayre-Adams & Wright, 2001). Ironically, TT is a non-touch technique that involves the therapist passing his or her hands two to six inches above the client's body in order to transfer healing energy (Childs, 2000). TT sessions may run up to 30 minutes and can be conducted with the patient fully clothed and either sitting or lying down (Fontaine & Kaszubski, 2004). While research on therapeutic touch has been criticized (Freeman, 2001b), Krieger and others have conducted studies on therapeutic touch that produced positive results, particularly in bringing about dramatic increases in subjects' hemoglobin counts (Krieger, 1979; Lawrence & Harrison, 1983; Meehan, 1999).

Scientific Evidence on the General Use of Touch

While scientific evidence supporting the general use of touch as a medium is not abundant, some exists. Aguilera (1967) reported increases in verbal interaction on the part of psychiatric patients who received touch from a nurse. Whitcher and Fisher (1979) found touch from a nurse prior to an operation lowered anxiety and blood pressure for female patients both before and following surgery. Touch for male patients, however, produced an opposite effect. It was speculated that touch for the men may have been interpreted as a sign of dependency that was a threatening reminder of their vulnerability. Elderly patients were found to eat more healthful foods following touch (Eaton et al., 1989). A study completed at the Harvard Medical School has been reported by Maxwell-Hudson (1988). Researchers there found that patients who received touch from an anesthetist, as part of a warm approach prior to surgery, required only about one-half the amount of drugs as the control group and, on an average, were dismissed three days earlier than the controls. Both Horton et al. (1995) and Willison and Masson (1986) found clients touched by their psychotherapists tended to open up more and perceived their therapists as more caring and trustworthy. Pinson (2002) reported psychotherapy patients viewed touch as providing safety, offering support, and promoting growth. A survey study of clients receiving psychotherapy by Horton, Chance, Sterk-Elifson and Emshoff (1995) found touch enhanced the therapeutic alliance. Clients used words and phases such as "bond," "closeness," "deepened trust," and "my therapist really cares about me" in describing their feelings about the use of touch by the therapist. The study further revealed that the increased closeness the clients felt toward the therapist allowed them to open up to the therapist and take more risks during therapy.

Social Barriers

Touch has been called the "most ancient" (Patterson, 2012, 485), "most important" (Colton, 1983, p. 14; Davidhizar & Giger, 1997, p. 203), and "most fundamental" (Cohen, 1987, p. 1) of all our senses. As a means to establish and continue contact with others, touch has been termed "an integral part of communication" (Davidhizar & Giger, 1997, p. 204) and "central to human social life" (App et al., 2006, p. 528). It has been called "an essential ingredient in the development of a well-adjusted being" (Voner, 2005, p. 16). Infants have been found to need touch for normal development (Field, 2010; Huss, 1977; McNeil-Haber, 2004). Adults become depressed and irritable without it (Maxwell-Hudson, 1988). Psychologist Stephen Thayer (1988) has termed touch "the most powerful of all communication channels" (p. 31). Gallace and Spence (2008) said that touch "provides a very powerful means of eliciting and modulating human emotion" (p. 247) and Lemmens et al. (2010) stated, "A simple touch can result in a profound and deep experience" (p. 11). Morrison et al. (2011) wrote, "Touch can act as a conductor of emotion between people, sparking positive feelings that forge attachments and strengthen social bonds" (p. 9554). Haans and IJsselsteijn (2009) have stated, "Touching is an important part of our social interaction repertoire. Physical contact, perhaps more than any other means of communication, bears the capacity for very intimate interpersonal interaction" (p. 136). Finally, in 2006, Haans and IJsselsteijn wrote, "Not surprisingly, people use touch when providing encouragement or emotional support, or when expressing intimacy or tenderness" (p. 149).

Yet, while the beneficial and powerful effects of touch have been acknowledged in the scientific and professional literature, many people are hesitant about touching others. Perhaps this is due to our Puritan heritage that has frowned on touching and because of connections we have drawn between touch and sex (Colton, 1983; Huss, 1977; Maxwell-Hudson, 1988; Zur & Nordmarken, 2004). Also, today in the United States, some health care professionals are fearful and confused about regulations, laws, and mores concerning touch in what has become a litigious society (Field, 2010; Young, 2005, 2007). There are signs, however, that touch is growing in acceptance. Indicators include books on the therapeutic use of touch (e.g., Cohen, 1987; Ford, 1992; Macrae, 1993) and articles on using touch therapeutically (e.g., Bonitz, 2008; Cassetta, 1993; Patterson, 2012; Phelan, 2008; Vortherms, 1991; Young, 2007; Zur & Nordmarken, 2004).

Implications for Recreational Therapy

Touch is a powerful form of communication (Field, 2010). But as a nonverbal form of communication, it is open to misunderstanding. While touch may be meant to be warm and caring, it may be interpreted as invading personal space or as being demeaning or seductive. Caution needs to be exercised when using touch. It is important to consider the appropriateness of the use of touch. Factors that should be appraised include the following:

- The environment in which touch takes place;
- Whether others are present;
- The relationship with the person being touched;
- The gender of the person;
- The body part being touched (e.g., handshake, hand on shoulder, or hug);
- Whether the person is in a mood to be touched;
- The cultural background of the person; and
- The history of the individual.

Jackson and Latini (2013) have indicated particular attention should be given to the cultural background of the client as attitudes toward touch will vary greatly among cultural groups. Persons from one culture may welcome touch, while those from another may view touch as forbidden. Kunstler and Stavola Daly (2010) have stated that cultural practices and meanings related to the use of touch with children must be taken into account and that recreational therapists working with children need to be well versed on the literature related to the use of touch with children.

The history of the individual should also be a particular concern. A person who is depressed or grieving may react to a touch as a gesture of concern. In contrast, a sexually promiscuous person may regard touch as a sexual advance. A child who has been abused may reject a touch meant to be comforting, while a person who is dying may feel a great deal of comfort from having his or her hand held (Shives, 1998).

Because touch can be misinterpreted, many therapists avoid it in order to protect themselves from legal or ethical charges from clients (Thayer, 1988). There are, however, times when words are not sufficient to express feelings. At these times, clients may need caring touch (Bolander & Manville, 2008; Zur & Nordmarken, 2004). Additionally, many individuals are starving to be touched (Ornstein & Sobel, 1989). Davidhizar and Giger (1997) have written, "Therapeutic use of touch can link professional caregivers with the patient and help promote a satisfying interpersonal bond during the time the patient is there. Touch can reassure and reduce anxiety, can increase self-esteem and worth, and can communicate warmth and support" (p. 206).

Young (2007) has suggested that not using touch can be perceived negatively because it is the human thing to do. She has written:

> There are also situations where it may be inappropriate not to touch, and doing so could be seen as being cold, remote, distant, inaccessible, unfeeling, or contraindicative to the person's psychotherapeutic process, etc. We are human beings, and touch is important and significant to us. 'Touching is not a technique; not-touching is a technique.' (p. 4).

Should recreational therapists risk using touch with clients? Davidhizar and Giger (1997), Durana (1998), Thayer (1988), Young (2007), Zur (2007), and Zur and Nordmarken (2004) have urged therapists and counselors to consider the use of touch as a part of their therapeutic repertoire. This would seem to be good advice. Of course, each individual must engage in self-examination in order to determine if he or she will take the risks involved with touch. Huss (1977) has suggested that first becoming aware of one's feelings about touch is a good place to begin this self-examination and has recommended participation in Gestalt therapy awareness exercises such as those found in Stevens' (1988) *Awareness Exploring, Experimenting, and Experiencing.*

Relaxation Techniques/Stress Management

Stress, with ensuing tension, is a normal part of everyday life. It has been reported that 67% of adults experience "great stress" at least once a week. There exists an obvious connection between stress and health, because stress is associated with between 50% and 70% of all illnesses (Corbin, Lindsey, Welk, & Corbin, 2001). "Many clients receiving TR services face innumerable challenges to maintaining well-being in the face of persistent and acute stressors associated with their health or social condition," according to Hutchinson,

Bland and Kleiber (2008). Health psychologists Hadjistavropoulos and Asmundson (2009) have written, "There are very few patients with health problems who cannot benefit from stress management. This is, in our opinion, a topic that is appropriate to address with all patients, including those with and without significant health problems" (p. 365).

Relaxation techniques are a means to deal with excess tension brought about by stress. The National Center for Complementary and Alternative Medicine (NCCAM; 2012b) has explained, "Relaxation is more than a state of mind; it physically changes the way your body functions. When your body is relaxed breathing slows, blood pressure and oxygen consumption decrease, and some people report an increased sense of well-being" (p. 1).

In addition to stress, the NCCMA (2012b) has reported there is research evidence that relaxation techniques can be effective in treating anxiety, depression, headaches, and pain. The New York University Langone Medical Center (2012) has also cited empirical evidence that relaxation therapy has been successfully used to treat insomnia, asthma, and hypertension. Potter and Perry (2009) have indicated that, additionally, relaxation has been used to facilitate burn care and improve cognition in older adults. Potter and Perry have cautioned however that even though relaxation techniques may help a number of different types of clients, they need to be applied judiciously as some require energy for clients with advanced diseases or those with low energy reserves.

It would be easy if we could tell ourselves to "just relax" but typically that does not work. Bourne, Brownstein, and Garano (2004) wrote:

> The truth is that to achieve real relaxation, it helps to master certain skills. In this way relaxation is closer to an active exercise like playing the piano than a passive one like sleeping. If you were taking piano lessons, you would have to commit to a certain amount of time for daily practice. The same is true for learning relaxation skills. (p. 5)

Thus, as Neven (2006) indicated, "Relaxation is a skill. The ability to relax can be developed in much the same ways as interpersonal skills can be developed—with practice" (p. 280). In the section that follows, several methods for eliciting a state of relaxation are described. Covered are deep breathing, progressive relaxation training, autogenic training, imagery, meditation, yoga, laughter yoga, biofeedback, massage, stretching, and physical exercise. Step-by-step instructions for many of these techniques can be found in Appendix B: Relaxation Techniques (p. 142). Breathing and progressive relaxation training are given the most attention because these approaches are commonly employed by recreational therapists.

Deep Breathing

Seaward (2002) has proclaimed that "Diaphragmatic breathing is unequivocally the easiest method of relaxation to practice" (p. 319). Mason (2001) has exclaimed that "Learning to breathe deeply . . . is the first step in learning to relax . . . ." (p. 27). Certainly learning **breathing techniques** is a skill crucial to most relaxation therapy techniques. This is not surprising when we consider how fundamental breathing is to our feeling of emotional states. Our breathing becomes shallow and irregular and our heart races when we become upset. When relaxed, our breathing becomes deeper and slower and our heart rate decreases. If we can develop the ability to control our breathing so we can breathe deeply, we can trigger the relaxation response (Mason, 2001).

Girdano, Everly, and Dusek (1997) have described how breathing leads to relaxation. They have written:

The breathing centers in the brain have a facilitating relationship with the arousal centers; therefore, constant, steady, restful breathing promotes relaxation. It is almost impossible to be tense and have slow, relaxed, deep breaths. Thus, control breathing and you control tension. Condition breathing and you condition your system to be more tranquil. (p. 197)

Authorities (Bourne, Brownstein, & Garano, 2004; Eshref, 1999; Girdano, et al., 1997; Lynch, 1989; Mason, 2001; Payne, 1995; Sachs, 1997; Stuart, 2006; Townsend, 2009) offer the following suggestions toward helping individuals to learn deep breathing:

1. Breathe in through the nose since the nasal passages filter and warm the air.
2. Inhale very slowly and deeply through the nose into the bottom of the lungs.
3. Breathing should be viewed as "letting the air in" rather than "taking a breath."
4. Let there be a smooth transition between inhalation and exhalation.
5. When letting air in, remember to breathe from the diaphragm. The abdomen should rise as if it were a balloon expanding when breathing in, and fall as if it were a balloon deflating with the exhale. When breathing well, we are using diaphragmatic breathing.
6. Lowering the diaphragm should occur with the jaw and throat relaxed, the stomach free, the hip joints permitting free leg movements and flexibility in the lower back.
7. Once the abdomen achieves full extension, the shoulders should draw back and the head should rise as the upper part of the lungs are filled.
8. The breath should normally be held for approximately three to five seconds.
9. Exhale slowly and fully, letting the air gently flow from the nostrils or mouth. In doing so, draw in the abdomen and drop the shoulders slightly.
10. Exhale deeply to get out the stale air and let in fresh air.
11. Once exhaling has occurred, wait two seconds before drawing the next breath.
12. Avoid abrupt transitions. Respirations should always be rhythmic and gentle.
13. Continue to practice abdominal breathing for 5 to 10 minutes. Stop for 30 seconds if you feel light headed or breathless and then start up again.
14. Avoid breathing practice after meals when the stomach is full as it presses against your diaphragm and constricts your lungs.
15. A guideline is to practice deep breathing for a few minutes 3 or 4 times each day or when tense.

Among specific breathing exercises that Mason (2001) has offered are "Three-Part Breathing" and "Alternate-Nostril Breathing." Descriptions of these techniques can be found in Appendix B: Relaxation Techniques (p. 141). When completing these or any deep-breathing exercises, it is important that they are done in a quiet environment in order to remove distractions and that the individual be in a comfortable position. Many clients will wish to close their eyes while they perform the exercises.

A variation on the alternate-nostril breathing exercise may be attempted once the person is comfortable with the alternate-nostril breathing. The more advanced technique calls for the individual to close off each nostril through visualization, rather than actually placing the finger over the nostril (Mason, 2001).

Deep breathing can be a helpful relaxation technique for many clients. In addition to stress reduction, it has been shown to be effective in reducing anxiety, depression, muscle tension, irritability, and fatigue (Townsend, 2009). Once learned, deep breathing may be used at any time stress is felt or anticipated. For some others, deep breathing, in itself, may not be enough to bring about complete relaxation, but it may be used in combination with other relaxation techniques such as yoga, tai chi, autogenic training, imagery, and progressive relaxation training (Seaward, 2002).

Progressive Relaxation Training

Progressive relaxation training (PRT) is "a stress-reduction intervention that consists of systematically tensing and relaxing various muscle groups from head to feet while focusing on the contrasting sensations of tension and relaxation" (Dolbier & Rush, 2012, p. 50). PRT is also known as progressive muscle relaxation or PMR (Seaward, 2002). It is a technique by which helping professionals train clients in achieving relaxation. Edmund Jacobson's name is usually associated with relaxation training. His progressive relaxation is based on becoming aware of the amount of tension in the body. By having people tense and release their muscles and attend to the resulting sensation of tension and relaxation, Jacobson discovered that a feeling of deep relaxation could be achieved. (Bourne, Brownstein, & Garano, 2004). Joseph Wolpe, the noted behaviorist, later further refined Jacobson's original relaxation procedure.

Systematic reviews of the research have found progressive relaxation training to be a validated clinical intervention to reduce negative stress responses (e.g., Carlson & Hoyle, 1993; Dolbier & Rush, 2012). From their research review, McCallie, Blum, and Hood (2008) concluded that the empirical evidence supports the use of PMR in "reducing tension headaches, insomnia, adjunct treatment in cancer, chronic pain management in inflammatory arthritis and irritable bowel syndrome" (p. 51). Results of their extensive review led Conrad and Roth (2007) to write, "In conclusion, a considerable number of published studies have succeed in showing that muscle relaxation is beneficial in a variety of medical conditions and in several psychiatric disorders, particularly anxiety disorders... "(p. 248). Studies (Chen et al., 2009; Vancampfort et al., 2011; Vancampfort et al., 2012) have also found progressive muscle relaxation to be effective in reducing feelings of stress and anxiety in people with schizophrenia. In addition, progressive relaxation training has been successfully applied with patients with multiple sclerosis (Ghafari et al., 2009), chronic obstructive pulmonary disease (COPD; Lolak et al., 2008), atopic dermatitis (Bae, 2012), and Alzheimer's disease (Suhr, Anderson, & Tranel, 1999). Finally, progressive muscle relaxation has been found to benefit high-stress college students (Dolbier & Rush, 2012).

Anselmo (2013) has suggested:

> Progressive muscle relaxation is particularly effective for clients who are feeling physically tense, anxious, and perhaps agitated. Because it is an active intervention, it may be preferable to other passive exercises, especially early in client training. It should be used with caution for clients with ischemic myocardial disease, hypertension, and back pain, however. (p. 340)

Progressive muscle relaxation is generally done with clients who are experiencing high levels of stress and tension. It takes place in a quiet room in which the windows and doors have been shut and the blinds or drapes drawn. This removes distracting stimuli. To create further a tranquil environment, lights in the room are kept dim. Clients assume a comfortable position in a chair or on a couch, or they may lie on their backs on blankets or mats on the floor. Comfortable, nonbinding clothing is worn by clients. Glasses, jewelry, belts, shoes, and other such items are taken off, and clients are instructed to close their eyes during the actual relaxation exercises.

The helping professional's voice is also used to create the proper atmosphere in which to bring about relaxation. Voice volume and tone are instrumental in the process. An initial conversational level gives way to progressive reductions in volume as the session continues. Likewise, the pace of presentation is reduced or slowed as the session goes on. Although the tone of voice is not hypnotic or seductive, it remains smooth and even.

The basic procedure is to move the client through the tensing and relaxing of a series of muscle groups. A similar five-step sequence is suggested by Bernstein and Carlson (1993) for relaxing each group of muscles. First, the client is told to focus attention on the muscle group. On signal, the muscle group is tensed. Tension is held for five to seven seconds. Tension is then released on the cue of the helping professional. Finally, the client's attention is focused on the muscle group as it is relaxed. Clients should take care however not to tense the muscles too hard. All that needs to be done is to tighten the muscles enough to feel the contrast with the relaxed state (Andrews, 2005).

Girdano et al., (1997) suggest that as each gross movement relaxation exercise is completed, the client breathe in during muscle contraction and out during muscle relaxation. Appendix B: Relaxation Techniques (p. 141) provides other specific instructions that may be employed in the teaching of progressive relaxation training skills.

Learning relaxation skills is similar to learning any new behavior. In order to get better at it, practice is necessary. There really is nothing particularly magical or mysterious about it. And, as with any new skill, some will pick it up quicker than others.

For detailed information on progressive muscle relaxation procedures, interested readers are referred to *Progressive Relaxation Training: A Manual for the Helping Professions* by Bernstein and Borkovec (1973); *Stress Power!* by Anderson (1978); *Teach Yourself Relaxation* by Hewitt (1985); *A Holistic Approach* by Girdano, Everly, and Dusek (1997); *Guide to Stress Reduction* by Mason (2001); *Managing Stress* by Seaward (2002); *Principles and Practice of Stress Management Natural Relief for Anxiety* by Bourne, Brownstein, and Garano (2004); *Stress Control for Peace of Mind* by Andrews (2005); and *The Relaxation and Stress Reduction Workbook* by Davis, Eshelman, and McKay (2008). *Relaxation, Meditation, and Mindfulness* by Smith (2005) contains an audio CD. An audio CD titled *Progressive Relaxation and Breathing* is by McKay and Fanning (2008). Other resources are Payne's (2005) chapter in *Relaxation Techniques;* and Townsend's (2009) chapter on relaxation therapy in *Psychiatric Mental Health Nursing*. These publications and resources were major sources for this section and the specific directions for "Progressive Relaxation Training" found in Appendix B: Relaxation Techniques (p. 141).

Autogenic Training

Autogenic means self-regulation or self-generation. Originated by German neurologist Johannes H. Schultz, autogenic training (or autogenics) is similar to progressive relaxation training in that both deal with inducing a state of muscular relaxation. Kanji, White, and Ernst (2005) wrote, "Autogenic training now a popular method, particularly in Europe, advocated for controlling stress, anxiety, phobias, depression, sleep disorders, headache, premenstrual problems, pain, asthma, hypertension, and other conditions" (p. K1). Like progressive relaxation training, it can be self-taught by reading books, although it is usually taught by a physician or psychiatrist. Unlike progressive relaxation training, autogenic training involves vasomotor and cognitive processes to teach an individual to exert control over physiological processes through a series of mental exercises involving sensations of heaviness and warmth (Hoeger & Hoeger, 2011; Hewitt, 1985; Kanji, White & Ernst, 2004; Marcer, 1986). As Brenneke (2001) has stated, "Autogenic training is based on the fact that the autonomic nervous system can be voluntarily controlled, and stress therefore reduced at command" (p. 39). Mason (2001) has explained, "In autogenic training you attempt to induce specific physical sensations that are associated with relaxation" (p. 37). Today there exists a body of scientific findings to support the effectiveness of autogenic training (Shealy, 1999; Stetter & Kupper, 2002).

Autogenic training is a form of voluntary self-regulation in which the trainee concentrates on certain physiological functions normally regulated by the autonomic nervous system. The trainee maintains passive concentration while repeating a self-instruction (e.g., "my left arm is heavy") several times. He or she then observes the sensation that follows (such as heaviness) (Hoeger & Hoeger, 2011; Hewitt, 1985; Titlebaum, 1988). Linden (1993) has clearly described the overall process that involves a series of six "formulas" (phrases that are repeated in the mind of the trainee) that produce self-hypnosis. The first formula is an exercise for muscular relaxation (The Heaviness Experience) in which the trainee thinks "My right (or left) arm is very heavy" six times; then once thinks to himself or herself, "I am very quiet." Other exercises involve "Arms and legs are very warm" six times and "quiet" once (Second Exercise: Experience of Warmth); "The heart is beating quietly and strongly" six times and "quiet" once (Third Exercise: Regulation of the Heart); "It breathes me" six times and "quiet" once (Fourth Exercise: Regulation of Breathing); "Sun rays are streaming quiet and warm" six times and "quiet" once (Fifth Exercise: Regulation of Visceral Organs); and "The forehead is cool" six times and "quiet" once (Sixth Exercise: Regulation of the Head). Linden's chapter offers the interested reader a complete introduction to autogenic training. Authors (Haber, 1997a; Kermani, 1996) have indicated that autogenic training is not generally recommended for children under the age of five or for persons with psychotic disorders, epilepsy, diabetes, or drug or alcohol addiction.

Imagery

"**Imagery** can be broadly defined as the mental generation of sensory experience, in the absence of perceptual input," according to Arbuthnott, Arbuthnott, and Rossiter (2001, p. 124). Guided imagery refers to the use of positive suggestions to create mental representations of things we know or can fantasize. Imagery has been described as "the oldest and greatest healing resource" (Acterberg, 1985, p. 3) having been used for centuries (Schaub & Burt, 2013). It is still however not widely used by Western medicine (Hoeger & Hoeger, 2011).

While largely associated with **visualization** (mental "pictures"), imagery can involve mental representations of other senses as well. We have the capacity to hear a voice, taste a lemon, recall a pleasant smell, or feel ourselves lounging in a warm bath or swimming in a cool stream (Smith, 1992; Zahourek, 1988). Guided mental imagery involves having images suggested by another person (Seaward, 2002).

While the process is not fully understood, we know that our mental images can affect us physiologically and, thus, may be used to bring about relaxation. The theory is that imagery is brought about when messages are sent from the higher centers of the brain, where the images are stored, to lower centers of the brain which control physiological functions (such as breathing, heart rate, and temperature) (Andrews, Angone, Cray, Lewis, & Johnson,1999). Mason (2001) has explained, "When you create a mental picture, your body can actually respond to the visualization as if it were a real experience. This technique can aid in relaxation…." (p. 79). Zahourek (1988) has provided a specific application of how to use images to promote relaxation. "Zahourek's Application of Imagery" is included in Appendix B: Relaxation Techniques (p. 141). An example of a relaxation exercise has been provided by Flynn (1980, p. 182). It is termed the "Lightness Relaxation Exercise" and is also in Appendix B (p. 141).

While information available on imagery is not as extensive as for some of the other relaxation techniques, resources are available. For example, guidelines for guided imagery are found in Andrews et al.'s (1999) book on alternative and complementary therapies, in Bourne, Brownstein, and Garano's (2004) book on natural relief from anxiety, in Snyder and Lindquist (2006) on complementary and alternative therapies, and in Mascott's (2004) *The Therapeutic Recreation Stress Management Primer*. Recreational therapist Vincent Bonadies (2009) has authored an article on using guided imagery to reduce pain and anxiety in recreational therapy.

Empirical support for the use of imagery as an intervention is evident in the literature. Arbuthnott, Arbuthnott, and Rossiter (2001) reviewed research on imagery and concluded, "Empirical evidence that imagery is effective in promoting change covers an impressive range" (p. 123). They list a wide variety of conditions for which imagery intervention have been successfully employed including: healing from surgery and serious illness; reducing infectious illness; managing chronic pain; treating stress, panic disorders, and posttraumatic stress disorders; and bulimia nervosa. Schaub and Burt's (2013) review of the literature found empirical evidence for using imagery in the treatment of cancer, migraine headaches, irritable bowel syndrome, hypertension, anxiety and depression, fibromyalgia, immune system disorders, and asthma. Synder and Lindquist (2006) have indicated imagery to be particularly valuable in alleviating muscle tension pain, such as from headaches and migraines. Studies (e.g., Huth, Broome, & Good, 2004; Kline et al., 2010; Polkki et al., 2008; Tusek, Church, & Fizio, 1997) have shown that guided imagery provides at least temporary beneficial results for pediatric patients undergoing surgery. A study by Apostolo and Kolcaba (2009), completed with hospitalized patients experiencing depression, found guided imagery significantly improved patients' comfort and decreased depression, anxiety, and stress. In general, a benefit of imagery is the relative absence of complications found with using it as an intervention. It should be noted however that imagery has been contraindicated for use with some psychiatric patients (Andrews et al., 1999).

Meditation

Many Americans have some knowledge of **meditation.** This is largely because the transcendental meditation (TM) of one time Beatles' guru Maharishi Mahesh Yogi received much media attention in the 1960s (Castleman, 2000; Marcer, 1986). Because TM is controlled by an organization that does not allow clinicians to practice it unless they are trained TM teachers, mental health professionals have developed their own modern meditation techniques. These techniques include Carrington's *clinically standardized meditation* (CSM), Benson's *respiratory one method* (ROM), and *mindfulness meditation,* a Buddhist form of meditation. Such methods of meditation are easily learned and have produced excellent results, according to Carrington (1993) and Freeman (2001a).

No matter the technique, meditation follows a relatively simple approach that involves sitting comfortably in a quiet place for 15-20 minutes one or two times each day, while passively dwelling on a single word or sound (Carrington, 1993; Marcer, 1986). The person meditating is told to concentrate only on the meditation object (sometimes termed mantra). Mantra are typically calming sounds that end in nasal consonants "m" or "n" and have no meanings. Examples are "Abnam" and "Shi-rim." When learning to meditate, the trainee first repeats the mantra, then whispers it and, finally, just silently thinks of it with his or her eyes closed. Any other thoughts, sensations, or images that might be distracting are allowed to pass through the consciousness (Carrington, 1993). This is typical of all meditation as the individual narrows his or her focus to only one thing at a time in order to reach an altered state of awareness (Mason, 2001).

Meditation stands in opposition to thinking about a topic. It transcends thought. As Andrews (2005) indicates, "Meditation offers a brief sabbatical from the busyness of thinking" (p. 42). As Hewitt (1985) states, "It aims at becoming detached from thoughts and images and opening up silent gaps between them" (p. 117). Seaward (2002) writes, "Meditation is the quintessential respite to calm the mind from sensory overload." He goes on to say that "meditation is an increased concentration and awareness; a process of living in the present moment to produce an enjoy a tranquil state of mind" (p. 327).

In his best-selling book, *The Relaxation Response*, Herbert Benson (1975) listed four elements basic to most meditation:

• A quiet place to meditate
• A comfortable or poised posture
• An object for attention-awareness to dwell upon
• A passive attitude

Meditation may be self-taught or may be learned from a teacher. According to Fontaine and Kaszubski (2004), those who teach meditation should have some years of meditation practice before teaching others. Among books that provide meditation exercises are those by Bourne, Brownstein, and Garano (2004), Jacobs (1996), Leshan (1999), and Nathan and Mirviss (1998). With these exercises, clients likely will find they can induce meditative states.

Freeman (2001a) has warned that clients who fear loss of control are not good candidates for meditation. Neither may be persons with schizophrenia since they have been known to experience acute episodes following meditation. Meditation may also be contraindicated for those with strong feelings of losing control, attention deficit disorders, anger, hostility, or those with obsessive thoughts, because these individuals may not be able to get into a meditative state (Andrews et al, 1999; Fontaine & Kaszubski, 2004; Potter & Perry, 2009).

Fortney and Taylor (2010) provided this rationale for the use of meditation:

Prescribed meditation practice can elicit physical ease and mental stability, which provide a foundation for health and wellness as they directly influence one's ability to meet the challenges resulting from stress, burnout, and illness for patient and practitioners alike. For most people, illness brings out feelings of confusion, anxiety, fear, and anger. Shock, isolation, depression, fear, and helplessness are some common experiences patients face when dealing with chronic disease. Feeling out of control or losing one's ground can give rise to reactivity of the mind and body that leads to increased pain and suffering. Applying the simple practice of nonjudgmental present-moment awareness and experiencing how this process influences one's relationship with life stressors is one way that meditation practice addresses the epidemic of mind-body afflictions that are expressed physically, such as acid reflux, migraine headache, low back pain, restless legs, fibromyalgia, chronic fatigue, irritable bowel, and many other conditions....Meditation is an inward-orienting, self-empowering practice that can stimulate the healing process and help patients and health care practitioners navigate through unsettling and turbulent experiences. (p. 82)

A variety of reported research studies have supported the use of meditation. For example, research found measurable effects for meditation in reducing physiological arousal and decreasing muscle tension to bring about deep relaxation (Benson, 1975; Titlebaum, 1988). Brain wave studies have displayed that the fullest relaxation occurs when there is an absence of thought or thoughts are few in number or of little importance. The meditator's conscious information-processing mechanisms seem to be temporarily shut off, providing a reprieve from stressful stimuli, resulting in a low level of arousal (Hewitt, 1985). A TM program for university students at risk for hypertension was found to decrease blood pressure and psychological distress and increase coping abilities (Nidich, et al., 2009). TM programs have been reported to reduce stress for older African Americans with hypertension (Schneider et al., 1995) and blood pressure for African American youth at risk for the development of hypertension (Barnes, Treiber, & Johnson, 2004). Anderson, Liu, and Kryscio (2008) and Barnes et al. (1999) have also reported reductions in blood pressure following meditation. Pace and colleagues (2009) discovered a significant correlation between the amount of meditation practice and innate immune and behavioral responses to stress. A mindfulness meditation program led to reductions in acute respiratory infection (ARI; Barrett et al., 2012). Meditation practice has been found to improve cognitive functioning (Kam-Tim & Orme-Johnson, 2001; Moore & Malinowski, 2009). Finally, two studies by Watson and his colleagues, published in 2004, have reported positive effects with the use of meditation for treating stress in patients with cardiovascular disease.

Research reviews however have cautioned that more evidence needs to be collected on the effects of meditation as an intervention. Manocha (2000), for instance, concluded, "…while meditation does appear to have therapeutic potential, there is a great need for further research before definitive conclusions can be made" (p. 1135). From their review of the research, Fortney and Taylor (2010) determined, "Evidence pointing to the medical benefits of meditation has been widely documented….However, research is only beginning to elucidate how the mind-body connection affects health in promoting wellness and managing and preventing disease" (p. 82). The National Center for Complementary and Alternative Medicine (NCCAM; 2012a) has indicated that while a 2007 NCCAM funded review of the research on meditation found some evidence of health benefits, the data were not definitive. The NCCAM stated that "the overall evidence was inclusive." Thus, while there is a substantial amount of empirical evidence supporting the use of meditation, it would seem that additional research is needed before a definitive statement can be made on the health benefits of meditation.

Benson's Technique

Benson's technique may be thought of as a type of meditation. He developed his technique after extensively studying the physiological effects of meditation and reported it in his book, *The Relaxation Response*. Benson's research led him to believe that there was no single, unique method to creating a relaxation response. Instead, he identified four common components of meditation, whatever technique was used. These were: (1) a calm, quiet environment with few distractions; (2) a mind shift to a mental device or constant stimulus (such as a word, sound, phrase, or fixed gazing at an object); (3) a passive attitude in which people do not worry about how well they are performing the technique and let distracting thoughts pass through; and (4) a comfortable position so there is no undue muscle tension (Benson, 1975).

Benson's technique involves all four of the elements. It is described by Benson (1975) in the six-step process that appears in Appendix B: Relaxation Techniques (p. 145). Benson views the relaxation response as the body's natural means to counteract the stress response (fight or flight response), the body's involuntary response to threat. The body uses the relaxation response as a protection from stress. He believes that regularly eliciting the relaxation response can be a means to prevent or counteract diseases in which increased sympathetic nervous system activity is involved (Marcer, 1986; Titlebaum, 1988).

Yoga

The word **yoga** means a union of the mind, body, and spirit (Heavey, 2002; Seaward, 2002). Yoga dates back to 3,000 B.C. in India, where it was used as a means to unify the mind and body. While there are many branches of yoga, hatha (pronounced ha-ta) yoga is the type most commonly found in the United States and Canada (Fontaine & Kaszubski, 2004). Yoga has been termed "an innate pattern of movement" (Girdano, Everly, & Dusek,1997, p. 226) because humans (like their pet cats and dogs) naturally stretch when arising from sleep or from sitting for a prolonged period.

Yoga requires little in the way of equipment because it is done barefoot on a thin mat or blanket. It emphasizes exercise postures, breathing, and meditation that together bring about relaxation and deep tension reduction in the body. Exercise postures (or poses) focus on contracting a group of muscles accompanied by the stretching or relaxing of an opposite muscle group.

These postures are designed to gradually improve strength and flexibility. A yoga session features a series of postures that focus on different parts of the body in sequence and concludes with directed physical relaxation. A number of books, including those by Girdano, Everly, and Dusek (1997), Mascott (2004), and Seaward (2002) offer excellent illustrations of postures. Mascott even provides photographs of yoga poses that can be done seated in a wheelchair.

Breathing is a second component of yoga. Breathing is a means to self-regulation and mental control. Meditation is the final part. In meditation, there is a narrowing of the focus of attention to an object chosen by the individual. The object can be a sound, word, or image. Those beginning yoga are not likely to attain the meditative state without some amount of practice.

Yoga has been termed "an excellent stress-coping technique" (Hoeger & Hoeger, 2009, p. 408). The ability of yoga to target stress brought about by chronic disorders such as depression, anxiety, obesity, diabetes, and insomnia has been displayed in an extensive review by Khalsa (2004) of yoga's use as a therapeutic intervention. Khalsa wrote about the yoga interventions he reviewed:

> A general feature of these practices is their capability of inducing a coordinated psychophysiological response, which is the antithesis of the stress response. This "relaxation response" consists of a generalized reduction in both cognitive and somatic arousal as observed In the modified activity of the hypothalamic pituitary axis and the autonomic nervous system. (p. 270).

Similarly, Streeter et al. (2012) have discussed how yoga can combat the stress that exacerbates the "symptoms of epilepsy, depression, PTSD, chronic pain and other disorders that are impacted by stress reactive systems." They have explained, "The therapeutic effects of yoga can be understood in part through its direct effects on the autonomic nervous system and indirect effects on the GABA system" (p. 7). Froeliger et al. (2012) have reviewed research that has shown yoga may positively affect brain patterns. Andrews et al. (1999) reported research has shown yoga to be effective in bringing about relaxation as well as "lowering blood pressure and respiratory rate, relieving pain, improving motor skills, increasing auditory and visual perception, (and) improving metabolic and respiratory function..." (pp. 183–184). NCCAM (2012c) has indicated studies show yoga may "improve quality of life; reduce stress; lower heart rate and blood pressure; help relieve anxiety, depression and insomnia; and improve overall physical fitness, strength, and flexibility."

Dr. Marieke Van Puymbroeck, while a professor of recreational therapy at Indiana University, conducted a series of studies on the positive effects of yoga programs. Among the findings of Van Puymbroeck and her colleagues (Schmid et al., 2012) were that people with chronic stroke made significant improvements in balance as a result of an 8-week yoga program. Research on a 12-week yoga program for seniors by Schmid, Van Puymbroeck, and Koceja (2010) found improvement in their balance, thereby reducing the risk of falling for these older adults. Another report on research from an 8-week yoga program by Van Puymbroeck et al. (2012), for individuals with chronic stroke, revealed improved activity, participation, and quality of life for participants. A study of veterans with chronic stroke by Van Puymbroeck and her colleagues (Miller et al., 2011) of an 8-week yoga program resulted in improvements in levels of pain, flexibility, and strength. In another study, Van Puymbroeck, Smith, and Schmid (2011) found yoga to be a means by which middle-aged and older adults overcome constraints on participation in physical activity. Finally, Van Puymbroeck, Payne, and Hiseh (2007) indicated an 8-week yoga program for informal caregivers increased their strength, flexibility, and endurance, as well as their coping abilities.

A number of other researchers have also reported on the benefits of yoga. Yoga has been found to be effective in bringing about better sleep quality for adults (Vera et al, 2009), improved sleep quality and decreased depression for persons in assisted living facilities (Chen et al., 2010a), improved physical fitness for frail elders (Chen et al., 2010b), improvements in the ability of older adults to transfer from the floor (Tatum, Igel, & Bradley, 2009), improved sleep, mood, blood pressure, and perceived stress in older women with restless legs syndrome (Innes & Selfe, 2012), improvements in body fat percentage, systolic blood pressure, balance, and range of motion on shoulder flexion and abduction for older women (Chen & Tseng, 2008), reduced pain and stiffness for seniors with arthritis (Hansen, 2010), reductions in symptoms and improved self-efficacy for persons with arthritis (Haaz & Bartlett, 2011), reductions in body weight, blood pressure, glucose level, and high cholesterol for those with chronic diseases (Yang, 2007), improved respiratory functioning and perceptions of well-being for adults with severe traumatic brain injury (Silverthorne, et al., 2012), increases in positive affect and physical vitality, and reduction in symptoms for those with post-traumatic stress disorders (Emerson et al., 2009), improved upper-extremity function for persons with hyperkyphosis (Wang et al., 2012), improvements in balance, strength, posture, and gait for people with Parkinson's Disease (Colgrove et al., 2012), improved balance, leg strength, and muscle control for young adults (Hart & Tracy, 2008), improved balance and ability for adolescent girls (Bal, Singh, & Vaz, 2011), improvements in mood and anxiety in healthy subjects (Streeter et al., 2010), reductions In distress, anxiety, depression, and fatigue and increases in general quality of life for patients with breast cancer (Buffart et al., 2012; Danhauer et al., 2009), enhancement of mood and emotional and social well-being of breast cancer survivors (Moadel et al., 2007), prevention of premature ejaculation (Dhikav, et al., 2007; Makwana & Patil, 2012), improvements in all domains of sexual functioning for males (Dhikav et al., 2010), reduced pain levels, better pain acceptance, and increased coping abilities for patients with chronic neck pain (Cramer, 2011), and pain reduction for obese patients with osteoarthritis of the knees (Kolasinski et al., 2005). The National Center for Complementary and Alternative Medicine (NCCAM; 2012c) has additionally reported that studies in persons with chronic low-back pain suggest yoga can help reduce pain and improve function. In support of the assertion by NCCAM, studies published in *Current Concepts and Treatment Strategies* (Danesh, Serban, & Herrera,

2011), the *Annals of Internal Medicine* (Tilbrook et al., 2011), and *Pain* (Williams et al., 2005) all have reported positive effects for yoga as an intervention for low back pain.

Research also indicates yoga has been successfully employed as an intervention in mental health. Psychiatric inpatients who participated in yoga experienced improved mood and stress reduction (Lavey et al., 2005). Yoga has been found to be effective as a complementary treatment of depression with participants experiencing improvement in mood and reductions in depression, anger, anxiety, neurotic symptoms, and low frequency of heart rate variability (Shapiro et al., 2007). Yoga therapy has been successfully employed as an adjunctive treatment to produce improvements in psychopathology and quality of life for patients with schizophrenia (Visceglia & Lewis, 2011). Panesar and Valachova (2011) have reviewed studies showing yoga as being effective in not only elevating moods and reducing psychopathology but also in treating patients with depression, as well as those with eating disorders. Further, Chen et al. (2010) reported a 6-month yoga program for residents in assisted living facilities produced significant improvements in sleep quality and significant decreases in depression. Additionally, Granath et al. (2006) found yoga to reduce self-rated stress and stress behavior in a nonclinical population of adults. In an American Psychological Association article, Novotney (2009) summarized the psychological benefits of yoga stating that: "there is a growing body of research documenting yoga's psychological benefits. Several recent studies suggest that yoga may help strengthen social attachments, reduce stress and relieve anxiety, depression and insomnia" (p. 40).

Even with the growing body of research evidence to support the use of yoga, authors (e.g., Bussing et al., 2012; Cabral, Meyer, & Ames, 2011) have cautioned that yoga research is still in its infancy. Bussing and colleagues have warned that more research is required to firmly establish yoga as a stand-alone therapeutic intervention. They indicate, however, that "currently it is safe to suggest that yoga can be a beneficial supportive add-on or adjunct therapy" (p. 6).

It is important to note that persons with back or neck problems should consult with their health provider before beginning yoga classes (Haber, 1997; Sachs, 1997). For those who wish more information on yoga, Becker's (2000) chapter in *Complementary and Alternative Medicine and Psychiatry* is an excellent resource. Another resource is Barnes & Noble's (2007) Quamut *How-to-Guide on Yoga* which offers yoga fundamentals, breathing techniques, and yoga postures with photographs. A final resource is *Yoga for Nurses* (Kollak, 2009). While designed to assist nurses to use yoga to care for themselves, the book contains many photographs of yoga exercises and descriptions for each. The National Center on Health, Physical Activity, and Disability (NCHPAD) offers a website on Yoga for Individuals with Disabilities at www.ncpad.org/295/1834/Yoga-for-Individuals-with-Disabilities

Laughter Yoga

Laughter yoga is a relaxation technique that combines laughter exercises with yoga breathing and stretching. It was first introduced in 1995 by Madan Kataria, a medical doctor from India. Laughter Yoga has been described as "a physically oriented technique that uses a perfect blend of playful empowering and otherwise 'tension-releasing' simple laughing exercises, interspersed with gentle breathing and stretching exercises, rhythmic clapping and chanting of Ho Ho Ha Ha Ha in unison" (Dvorak, nd).

Thus, Laughter Yoga is based on the idea that if people go through the motions of laughing, real laughter will follow. It takes advantage of the fact that our bodies cannot tell the difference between fake and real laughter. Contrived laughter soon turns to real laughter with ensuring positive emotion. Using this approach with groups almost always results in real laughter during sessions that last from 20 to 30 minutes. Two research studies have shown promise for the use of Laughter Yoga. Beckman, Regier, and Young (2007) found increases in personal efficacy beliefs (e.g., self-regulation, optimism, positive emotions) following a 15-day aerobic laughter program for employees in the workplace. Shahidi et al. (2011) reported Laughter Yoga to be as effective as group exercise in bringing about improvements in depression and life satisfaction of elderly women who were depressed. While such scientific studies to support its use is just emerging and is extremely limited to date, clinical reports indicate that Laughter Yoga to be a promising technique (Laughter Medicine, nd; Woods, nd). Outcomes that have been observed include improving blood circulation, increasing oxygen delivery, increasing muscle movement, enhancing inter-personal relationships, improving self-esteem, boosting the immune system, and generally contributing to a higher quality of life (Appleton, 2012; Weiss, 2012).

Biofeedback

Biofeedback is "instrumentation to become aware of processes in your body that you usually do not notice and to help bring them under voluntary control" (Townsend, 2009, p. 226). Devices are used to monitor physiological activities and provide a measurement of them to assist individuals to learn to control specific autonomic nervous system responses. For instance, heart rate may be measured with the monitoring device producing a graph of the heartbeat. Once the individual is given information about a process, such as heart rate, he or she can learn to consciously alter its functioning. In the case of heart rate, the person can affect it by controlling breathing. Mental states can also produce effects on physiological processes during biofeedback sessions. Just thinking about an anxiety-arousing happening can increase heart rate. Heart rate can be decreased when an individual imagines a restful scene (Mason, 2001).

The goal of biofeedback training is for the client to gain awareness of and control over physiological functions. This skill is then used in daily life to increase relaxation and manage stress (Gilkey, 1986; Titlebaum, 1988). Heart rate, skin temperature (blood flow), blood pressure, brain waves, sweat gland activity, and muscle tension may be monitored through biofeedback. Once the person knows what is occurring within the body, he or she can learn to regulate his or her biological responses since the mind can have a powerful influence over the body (Corbin & Mental-Corbin, 1983).

Biofeedback can be used to monitor progress toward relaxation. It is usually employed in conjunction with other relaxation techniques such as deep breathing exercises, progressive relaxation training, and imagery (Townsend, 2009). It has been used to treat a variety of health problems including pain, insomnia, tension and migraine headaches, anxiety, depression, stroke, hypertension, teeth grinding, attention deficit disorder, alcoholism and addictions, and gastrointestinal and urinary tract disorders (Moss, 2002; Potter & Perry, 2009; Russoniello, 2001; Titlebaum, 1988). It should be mentioned that biofeedback has the added advantage of helping clients to feel a sense of control and confidence in their abilities to cope with stressors (Stoyva & Budzynski, 1993).

Health care professionals from a wide variety of fields, including recreational therapy, may employ biofeedback. Those using biofeedback must hold certification from the Biofeedback Certification Institute of America (Fontaine & Kaszubski, 2004).

Massage

Thousands of years ago, people of the Mediterranean nations realized the importance of **massage** not only as an approach to release tension in the muscles but as a means to pleasurable feelings of relaxation (Cohen, 1987). Today massage is enjoying renewed acceptance within the health care community (Cassetta, 1993; West, 1990). Because it directly relaxes the muscles, massage is one of the best means of stress reduction (Eshref, 1999).

Research has shown that massage produces a relaxation response (Snyder & Lindquist, 2006). It should also be mentioned that research has shown that massage can produce therapeutic outcomes in addition to stress reduction. For example, McKechnie, Wilson, Watson, and Scott (1983) completed a study with subjects who had chronic muscle tension, aches, and pains. Following a treatment of 10 deep massage sessions, these subjects not only displayed decreased muscle tension, but they had slower heart rates, lower arousal, and even were reported to be more verbal during psychotherapy. Reader, Young, and Connor's (2005) research found massage reduced respiration and Alcohol Withdrawal Scale scores of those in a detoxification program. Other studies (Field, 1998; Field, Hernandez-Reif, Hart, Quintino, Drose, Field, Kuhn, & Schanberg, 1997) have found that massage therapy brought about decreases in both anxiety and depression and had positive effects on the immune system.

Extensive research reviews have also found positive effects for massage. A research review by Field (2011) additionally revealed massage has been successfully used to reduce pain and elevate mood in cancer patients, reduce back pain, migraine headaches, fibromyalgia, and juvenile rheumatoid arthritis in adults and brought about lower levels of pain discomfort, depression, and anxiety in children. Massage also has been found to enhance immune function. Moyer, Rounds, and Hannum (2004) concluded from their meta-analysis of 37 studies that massage therapy is generally effective. Single applications of massage therapy were found to reduce state anxiety, blood pressure and heart rate. Multiple applications reduced pain, trait anxiety, and depression. Tsao's (2007) research review focused specifically on the effect of massage therapy on chronic pain conditions. She reported strong support for the use of massage with low back pain, modest support for effects on shoulder pain and headache pain, and modest, preliminary support for the treatment of fibromyalgia, neck pain, carpal tunnel syndrome, and mixed chronic pain conditions.

Similarly to Moyer, Rounds, and Hannum (2004), NCCAM (2010a) has come to a general conclusion that massage therapy is effective. NCCAM cites research that has displayed the effect of massage therapy on state and trait anxiety, blood pressure, heart rate, anxiety, depression, and pain. The NCCAM report on massage therapy also cites evidence of the effectiveness of massage in reducing chronic low-back pain, pain reduction and mood elevation of patients with cancer, and symptom relief and improved functioning for those receiving massage for chronic neck pain.

Little research on self-massage is apparent in the scientific literature. Moraska and Chandler (2008) have reported self-massage has been effective for patients in reducing the pain of tension-type headaches. Field et al. (2004) in their research combined massage therapy group sessions with home self-massage to relieve symptoms of carpal tunnel syndrome (CTS). In another study Field et al. (2007) again combined massage therapy group sessions with home self-massage with the result of less pain and greater strength for those with hand arthritis pain.

Swedish Massage and Japanese Shiatsu

The **Swedish massage** is a smooth and flowing massage that leads to a feeling of total relaxation. The masseuse or masseur employs kneading movements in giving the massage. It is usually given in a warm, darkened room on a massage table, but may be given with the person lying on the floor (Cohen, 1987). Another popular method of massage is **Japanese Shiatsu**. Many massage therapists follow eclectic approaches, borrowing techniques from various sources (West, 1990). The problem with any type of full body massage is it takes an hour to an hour and one-half (Maxwell-Hudson, 1988), and, of course, it requires another person with training in massage therapy in order to give the massage. There is also a cost factor, unless a spouse or friend knows massage techniques. **Self-massage** provides an alternative means to relaxation when time, money, or a massage therapist is not available. As the name implies, in self-massage the individual learns to massage himself or herself.

Self-Massage

Experts generally agree (e.g., Brown, 1999; Dowing, 1972; Lidell, 1984; Maxwell-Hudson, 1988) that **self-massage** does not offer the potential for the same level of enjoyment and relaxation as traditional massage. Self-massage can nevertheless produce relief from tension. It can also offer an opportunity for clients who may not be aware of certain body parts and related problems to get in touch with their bodies (Fontaine & Kaszubski, 2004). Some self-massage exercises are ones many people do instinctively to reduce tension. For example, in the neck squeeze, the hand is placed over the back of the neck near the shoulders. The neck is squeezed moving from the shoulders to the area where the neck meets the head. In the shoulder tension release, the shoulder is stroked with the opposite hand, molding the hand to grasp the top of the shoulder. The hand then squeezes the shoulder as far down on the back as can be reached. Another self-massage is to use the fingertips on the scalp, pressing lightly and making small circles so that the top layer of the scalp is moving over the underlying layers. The fingertips can also be applied to make slow, firm circles at the temples on the side of the head. This technique involves working upward toward the area just forward of the top of the ears. A final fingertip self-massage is to place the fingertips on the forehead above the eyebrows. Inch up toward the hairline, moving the fingertips up and down and pressing in slightly.

The teaching of self-massage in recreational therapy would appear to hold great promise. Most self-massage techniques are relatively easy to learn, and many books on massage contain sections on self-massage. For example, D. W. Brown's (1999), Eshref's (1999), Jacobs' (1996), Maxwell-Hudson's (1996), Shealy's (1999), Smith's (1999), Stuart's (2006), Voner's (2005), and West's (1990) books offer self-massage sections. Atkinson (2005) has authored a book titled, *A Practical Guide to Self-Massage*, that contains 50 self-massage movements.

Stretching

Stretching is a means to loosen up muscles and eliminate muscle tension. Stretching also helps maintain flexibility and promotes mobility of the joints (Payne, 2005). It can be done about anywhere and does not require any special skills, equipment, or clothing (Andrews, 2005). Some individuals prefer to combine stretching exercises with self-massage. Stretching is a sustained effort in which the person stretching should not bounce up and down or back and forth (Eshref, 1999). Mascott (2004) and Payne (2005) offer a series of stretching exercises in their books. Lysycia's (2008) book, *Superstretch*, provides stretching routines for all ages and fitness levels. Another ready source is Barnes & Noble's (2007) *Quamut How-to-Guide on Stretching*, which contains photos and descriptions of a number of stretching exercises. A free source is provided in the National Institute on Aging's (2008) *Exercise: A Guide from the National Institute on Aging*. Chapter 4 of this online publication presents a number of stretching exercises with diagrams. Descriptions of various stretching exercises also appear in the appendix of this chapter (See Appendix B: Relaxation Techniques, p. 141).

Physical Activity and Stress Reduction

Perhaps the most natural way to bring about the control of stress is through physical activity. Physical activity may be conceived to be nature's tranquilizer. The importance of physical activity and exercise has been emphasized in an article by Jayson (2012) that termed the high prevalence of stress in America as the "new normal." Jayson quoted Michael Balme, Clinical Professor of Medicine at the University of Pennsylvania, as stating the "most successfully used stress management tool is still exercise." The professor went on to state, "Exercise doesn't just give people a break from their stress, like watching TV, it undoes some of the harmful biological effects of stress and helps the body to restore" (p. 2D).

While the terms physical activity and exercise are commonly used interchangeably and are employed as general terms in this section, some authors do define the terms as being distinctive. For example, Edelman and Mandle (2006) define physical activity broadly and exercise more narrowly. Physical activity is seen as bodily movement involving muscle contractions that produces energy expenditure and exercise is a structured type of physical activity to maintain or enhance a specific area of fitness.

The overall value of exercise and physical activity has been explained by Fillingim and Blumenthal (1993):

> Exercise has become an increasingly popular leisure-time activity in recent years, perhaps largely because of its potential health benefits, such as improved weight control and reduced risk of cardiovascular disease. In addition, there has been considerable interest in the potential psychological benefits of physical activity. Anecdotally, many individuals report "feeling better" following physical activity, and many health care professionals recommend exercise as a stress management technique. (p. 443)

Conflicts, frustration, threats, and insults may bring about psychological stress. In reaction to stress, the body activates itself for the occurrence of an anticipated "fight or flight" response. That is, the body becomes physiologically mobilized in anticipation of protective actions to deal with or remove danger. As a result, a widespread physical reaction is brought about. There is a general overall increase in arousal level to heighten alertness. The cardiovascular system shows increased activation, and respiration is increased. Adrenal cells secrete hormones into the blood, and the flow of blood is increased to the brain, heart, and skeletal muscles (Sundeen, Stuart, Rankin, & Cohen, 1998, Dusek-Girdano, 1979). In short, the body becomes ready for a physical reaction to stress.

Hadjistavropoulos and Asmundson (2009) have indicated that the stress response can affect health both indirectly and directly. They go on to explain: "Stress has indirect effects on health in that it often results in an increase in unhealthy behaviors and a decrease in healthy behaviors." Examples of unhealthy behaviors include people overeating to comfort themselves or drinking too much, and working long hours rather than taking time out for enjoyable leisure activities. Finally, these authors discussed direct effects of stress: "Directly, stress results in physiological changes that, when persistent or chronic, increase vulnerability to many disorders, including cancer, heart disease, diabetes, arthritis, headaches, asthma, digestive disorders, and anxiety and depression" (p. 365).

When the stress reaction occurs, Dusek-Girdano (1979) has proposed that physical activity can help handle stress by alleviating the stress state. She has written:

> This is not a time to sit and feel all of these sensations tearing away at the body's systems and eroding good health. This is the time to move, to use up the products,

to relieve the body of the destructive forces of stress on a sedentary system. Appropriate activity in this case would be total body exercise such as swimming, running, dancing, biking, or an active individual, dual, or team sport that lasts at least an hour. . .Such activities will use up the stress products that might otherwise be harmful and that are likely to play a part in a degenerative disease process such as cardiovascular disease or ulcers. (p. 222)

Evidence exists that stress is reduced by physical activity (e.g., Berger, 1994; Salmon, 2001). Research (e.g., Berger, 1987; Harper, 1984; Ismail & Trachtman, 1973; Muller & Armstrong, 1975; Palmer & Sadler, 1979; Smith, 1993) holds promise that running and jogging, in particular, may help many people by reducing stress and fostering positive psychological effects. (Treatment programs using these forms of exercise are sometimes referred to as "running therapy.") It might be speculated that the high level of interest in running in recent years may be correlated to people's need to cope with the stress of modern life. Some tips on "Running for Relaxation" and "Runners Stretches" have appeared in the literature. They are included in Appendix B: Relaxation Techniques (p. 141).

Some clients may wish to enter into a walking program because walking offers the benefits of running without a great amount of strain on tendons, muscles, and joints. Exercise walking (sustained brisk walking) is a natural form of exercise that offers a particularly good option for older adults, those with medical limitations, and those who have been inactive. Ekkekakis et al. (2000) found that participants, following walking 10 to 15 minutes, experienced feelings of calmness and relaxation. Corbin and Mental-Corbin (1983) and Getchell (1994) have made a number of suggestions on "Walking for Relaxation," which are included in Appendix B: Relaxation Techniques (p. 141).

A third area for stress reduction is that of engaging in a moderate to vigorous exercise program. Muscles that are exerted through exercise must respond with relaxation. Also, participation in a systematic exercise program requires concentration that focuses a person's thoughts away from stressful concerns. An exercise program may be a wise choice for older people who may not desire to run or walk, as well as for those individuals who have physical limitations that do not permit them to participate in a running or walking program. These individuals may particularly profit from water exercise, where the buoyancy of the water provides therapeutic value.

Implications for Recreational Therapy

Recreational therapists will find the relaxation techniques covered in this section to be helpful with tense clients. Progressive relaxation training, in particular, is a simple skill to learn and possesses few hazards for clients. Progressive relaxation training and deep breathing perhaps have been the techniques most used by recreational therapists. Young (2001) has outlined procedures for breathing training to be used in RT programs.

Clark (2009) has suggested using imagery to help group members to relax during the early stages of group formulation when anxiety is high or following an upsetting situation within the group. She has provided the following instructions to use with a group:

Ask the members to close their eyes and take a trip to a relaxing, comforting place. It can be a place they have been before or someplace they have never been. Encouraging the group to smell the smells associated with the peaceful and relaxing place; hear the sounds associated with the peaceful and relaxing place; taste the tastes and experience the sensations associated with the peaceful and relaxing place. Be silent for 2 to 3 minutes as the group totally immerses itself in the peaceful and relaxing place. After several minutes, ask the participants to come back through time and space to the group, keeping the relaxation and comfort with them. Remind group members that they can become more relaxed and comfortable at any time by closing their eyes and returning briefly to their peaceful and relaxing place. (p. 38)

Bonadies (2009) has provided an article on the use of imagery by recreational therapists. His article contains information to assist recreational therapists in learning the basic techniques of guided imagery. In it he first reviews research support for using imagery to bring about the reduction of pain and anxiety. He then illustrates how imagery might be used, offers guidelines for the provision of imagery, and provides a format for a guided imagery session. He even includes suggested scripts for guided imagery.

Brownlee and Dattilo (2011) have written that recreational therapists who have become certified massage therapists can employ basic therapeutic massage techniques with clients. If a recreational therapist has not become a certified massage therapist he or she can refer clients to a certified massage therapist. Self-massage is an emerging approach to relaxation. Its techniques may be taught by recreational therapists and offer clients an excellent means for stress reduction. Stretching exercises may also be combined with self-massage.

Because studies have revealed yoga to be effective in treatment, it is regularly prescribed by medical doctors as a complementary therapy (Andrews, 2005). Yoga, as a complementary treatment, has been termed to be "cost-effective and easy to implement" (Shapiro et al., 2007, p. 493). Although the small sample size makes findings tentative, research on a yoga therapy program run by a recreational therapist found the program was effective in reducing AIDS-related stress and anxiety (Bonadies, 2004). In India, yoga has been used extensively for stress reduction with persons with epilepsy (Indian Epilepsy Association, 1996). Yoga has the potential to be used within psychiatric programs as it has been found to successfully reduce stress in psychiatric patients (Cabral, Meyer, & Ames, 2011; Lavey et al., 2005). Beyond stress reduction, yoga has many potential applications within recreational therapy. Empirical evidence exists that indicates yoga programs can help to bring about a variety of health benefits for any number of populations served by recreational therapists.

The emergence of running on the American scene, along with the increasing amount of attention being given to "running therapy," has brought newfound recognition of the psychological benefits to be gained from physical exercise. Running would seem to have particular promise for recreational therapy, since it is not a costly activity and can be done almost anywhere.

Walking can be applied in recreational therapy as an alternative to running. Walking offers a low risk of injury and it is a natural activity that can be done by most people. It should be noted that there is a growing body of literature (e.g., Bowler et al., 2010; Hansmann, Hug, & Seeland, 2007; Maas & Verheij, 2007) that suggests that since most walking is done outside at least some of the tension-releasing properties of walking come from the enjoyment of being outdoors in a pleasant setting or in walking with others in a relaxed social atmosphere. Walking should be an excellent stress-reduction activity. After all, Greek physician Hippocrates deemed walking "man's best medicine" (Spilner, 2002).

Exercise programs offer still another approach to stress reduction through physical activity. Such programs offer an alternative to running and walking for older adults and persons with disabilities. Other physical activities such as swimming, boating, biking, and hiking seem to be particularly well suited to helping people handle stress because they are not normally approached on a competitive basis, which might lead to further threat, conflict, and frustration for participants. Heywood (1978) found a number of years ago that stress reduction occurs to a greater extent when the activity engaged in is perceived to be a recreative experience.

In closing this section on stress and relaxation, it should be noted that the therapeutic potentials of exercise and other forms of physical activity extend beyond stress reduction. As discussed in the section that follows, participation in physical activity can lead to a plethora of positive health outcomes.

Physical Activity

Physical activity may be defined as "any bodily movement produced by the skeletal muscle that results in an increase in metabolic rate over resting energy expenditure," according to Bouchard, Blair, and Haskin (2012, p. 12). Thus physical activity can take place in many ways and places, including activities such as home gardening or walking in one's neighborhood. It certainly is not restricted to workouts at the gym.

Exercise is a type of leisure-time physical activity. Exercise has been defined being "performed repeatedly over an extended period of time (exercise training) with a specific external objective such as the improvement of fitness, physical performance, or health" (Bouchard, Blair, & Haskell, 2012, pp. 12-13). A similar definition of exercise has been provided by Banks et al. (2012) who defined exercise "as planned and repetitive bodily movements with the aim to improve or maintain physical fitness and mobility."

Unfortunately, studies completed in several countries have shown that only about 15% of the adults take part in leisure-time physical activity for at least 20 minutes three or more days per week. From 15% to 40% were found to be sedentary (Phillips, Kiernan, & King, 2001). In America, the level of inactivity appears to be even higher. Herbert (2008) has written, "According to the surgeon general, more than 60% of American adults do not exercise regularly and 25% aren't active at all" (p. 13) The alarming nature of physical inactivity is reflected by this statement by Cronan, Shinew, and Stodolska (2008) who have written, "Physical inactivity has reached epidemic proportions across all age, social, ethnic, and economic categories in the United States" (p. 63). They go on to state, "However, it is most prevalent among ethnic and racial minority groups" (p. 63).

Disparities have been reported among other population groups as well. For example, persons with lower educational levels and lower socioeconomic levels are the least physically active. Persons who are disabled or have chronic health conditions are similarly less likely to take part in physical activity (U.S. Department of Health and Human Services, 2000). Approximately 60% to 70% of persons over 65 years of age are sedentary (Brandon, 1999). This information is particularly troubling for those in recreational therapy (RT) because many RT clients have low levels of education and income. Many also have disabilities, chronic health problems, or are elderly.

Almost anyone can benefit from participation in regular physical activity. There are many good reasons for individuals to be physically active. For one, those who are active live longer than those who are inactive (LaMonte & Blair, 2012; Manini et al., 2006). The U.S. Department of Health and Human Services (2000) has stated that "…moderate physical activity can reduce substantially the risk of developing or dying from heart disease, diabetes, colon cancer, and high blood pressure" (pp. 22-23). The same agency has stipulated that regular physical activity "…also helps to maintain the functional independence of older adults and enhances the quality of life for people of all ages" (pp. 22-23). Physical activity is particularly important for elderly persons who are in hospitals, nursing homes, or assisted living facilities as "inactivity delays recovery, reduces ability to function, and promotes deterioration of almost every body system" (Ferrini & Ferrini, 2000, p. 95). Physical activity programs are likewise important for all children, including those with disabilities. As Monsen (2002) has stated, "By giving every child a chance to enjoy physical activity, we can lower the risks for chronic illness and disability among our adult and older generations during this century" (p. 137). From the previous section, we know that physical activity has been shown to produce tension reduction and relaxation. In addition, physical activity has the potential to bring about a great number of other psychological and physical health benefits to persons throughout the lifespan.

Evidence At-A-Glance: The Benefits of Physical Activity to Mental and Physical Health

A substantial number of articles have called attention to the benefits to be derived from physical activity. The following are a sampling of titles of articles that reflect the benefits of physical activity that should catch the attention of those in recreational therapy:

- Alzheimer's Risk Falls with Activity (*USA Today,* 2012)
- Another Reason to Break a Sweat: In Addition to Boosting Your Brainpower, Exercise may Fend Off and Even Alleviate Cognitive Ills, Including Alzheimer's Disease, Research Suggests (*Monitor on Psychology,* 2010)
- Study: People Who Spend Most Leisure Time Sitting Die Soonest (*WebMD,* 2010)
- Fitness Key to Longevity (*MedPageToday,* 2011)
- Exercise Enhances and Protects Brain Function (*Sport Sciences Reviews,* 2002)
- Exercise is Brain Food: The Effects of Physical Activity on Cognitive Function (*Developmental Neurorehabilitation,* 2008)
- Exercise Training Increases Size of Hippocampus and Improves Memory (*Proceedings of the National Academy of Sciences,* 2011)
- Exercise Boosts School Performance for Kids with ADHD (*Psych Central,* 2012)
- Exercise and Mental Health: Many Reasons to Move (*Neuropsycholobiology,* 2009)
- Physical Activity Reduces the Risk of Subsequent Depression for Older Adults (*American Journal of Epidemiology,* 2002)
- Aerobic Exercise is Good for Asthma Patients (*MedPageToday,* 2011)
- Add a Mile to Walk Off Diabetes Risk (*MedPageToday,* 2011)
- Exercise Benefit in Diabetes Upheld (*MedPageToday,* 2012)
- Physical Activity is Essential to Healthy Aging (*Centers for Disease Control and Prevention,* 2010)
- The Bottom Line is that the Health Benefits of Physical Activity far Outweigh the Risks of Adverse Events for Almost Everyone (*Physical Activity Guidelines for Americans,* 2008)

In a fact sheet for professionals, the U.S. Department of Health and Human Services (2008) included the following review of the strength of scientific evidence of health benefits of physical activity:

Strong Evidence for Adults and Older Adults:
- Prevention of weight gain
- Weight loss when combined with diet
- Improved cardiorespiratory and muscular fitness
- Prevention of falls

- Reduced depression
- Better cognitive function (older adults)
- Lower risk of early death, heart disease, stroke, type 2 diabetes, high blood pressure, adverse blood lipid profile, metabolic syndrome, colon and breast cancers

Moderate to Strong Evidence for Adults and Older Adults:
- Better functional health (older adults)
- Reduced abdominal obesity

Moderate Evidence for Adults and Older Adults:
- Weight maintenance after weight loss
- Lower risk of hip fracture
- Increased bond density
- Improved sleep quality
- Lower risk of lung and endometrial cancers

Strong Evidence for Children and Adolescents:
- Improved cardiorespiratory endurance and muscular fitness
- Favorable body composition
- Improved bone health
- Improved cardiovascular and metabolic health biomarkers

Moderate Evidence for Children and Adults
- Reduced symptoms of anxiety and depression

Yet, even with the vast amount of evidence that displays significant relationships between physical activity and health, calls by authors for recreational therapy to give increased attention to physical activity have largely gone unheard (Austin, 2002b; Mobily, 2009), although Mobily (2011) has indicated a recent increase in interest by recreational therapists in the use of physical activities as interventions. At a time when physical inactivity has been termed "the biggest public health problem of the 21st century" (Human Kinetics Webinars, 2011), it would appear that the profession of recreational therapy is in a wonderful position to rise to the occasion in order to provide leadership in the delivery of physical activity programs that bring health benefits to clients.

Scientific Research on the Benefits of Physical Activity to Mental and Physical Health
In the book *Running as Therapy*, Buffone (1997) assessed the research on the positive effects of physical activity on mental health. He indicated that running and other forms of physical activity positively impact on persons who suffer from anxiety or depression. Reviews of the research literature by Barbour, Edenfield, and Blumenthal (2007), Callaghan (2004), Deslandes et al. (2009), Donaghy (2007), Paluska and Schwenk (2000), Phillips et al., (2001), Richardson et al. (2005), and Raglin and Wilson (2012) have found growing evidence to support Buffone's assertions. These research reviews showed that those suffering from anxiety benefit most from physical activity if they have lower levels of fitness to begin with or have higher levels of anxiety. Physical activity was likewise found to be beneficial for adults who were clinically depressed and those who were not clinically depressed but suffered from symptoms of depression. Barbour, Edenfield and Blumenthal (2007) have concluded, "It does appear that exercise is a viable treatment option for individuals with depression" (p. 360). Similarly, Donaghy (2007) commented: "There is evidence that exercise

protects against depression and is an effective intervention and adjunctive intervention for the treatment of mild to moderate depression" (p. 76). It has been suggested that at least part of the improvement with depressed clients taking part in group classes may be due to simply getting out and interacting with other people (Pilu et al., 2007). Finally, following her review of the literature, Hays (1999) concluded: "With exercise, negative moods, labeled Tension, Depression, Anger, Fatigue, and Confusion diminish" (p. 8).

"Green exercise" is physical activity that takes place in the presence of nature (Barton & Pretty, 2010, p. 3947). Maas and Verheij (2007) have suggested that the combination of physical activity and the natural environment has "synergic health effects" (p. 230). Mitchell's (2012) research has supported the notion of synergy when physical activity takes place in the natural environment. A meta-analysis found that exercising in greenspaces can have mental health benefits that include improved self-esteem and mood. The authors of the study (Barton & Petty, 2010) concluded "attention should be given to developing the use of green exercise as a therapeutic intervention…"(p. 3953). While more research Is needed on the exact type of nature from which clients will find the most benefit, green exercise holds promise for producing therapeutic outcomes.

It should be mentioned that there are other psychological benefits associated with physical activity. Donaghy (2007) reported positive results in the use of physical activities in treating those in substance misuse programs. Donaghy, along with Raglin and Wilson (2012), presented evidence that participation in physical activities can positively affect self-perceptions such as body image and self-esteem. The reviews by Donaghy and by Ragin and Wilson also revealed that physical activities may be effective in reducing symptoms, such as anxiety and depression, in those suffering from schizophrenia. Additionally, a meta-analysis of intervention studies by Netz et al. (2005) found physical activities had a strong effect on self-efficacy among older adults without clinical disorders.

A growing body of literature relates to exercise and the brain. As a result of their research review, Deslandes and his colleagues (2009) exclaimed, "The overwhelming evidence present in the literature today suggests that exercise ensures successful brain functioning" (p. 191). Penedo and Dahn (2005) reviewed studies showing that physical activity can buffer age-related cognitive decline. Hillman, Erickson, and Kramer (2008), in their review of research on the effects of exercise on the brain and cognition, found that aerobic exercise can improve a variety of aspects of cognition. Voss et al. (2011) conducted an extensive review of the relationship between physical activity and cognitive or brain health throughout the life span. They concluded while research has focused on the benefits of aerobic exercise for youth and young adults, there is a growing body of evidence of the positive effects of both aerobic and resistance training in maintaining cognitive and brain health in old age. Weuve et al. (2004) reported that physical activity, including walking, produced better cognitive function and less cognitive decline in older women. Hillman, Erickson and Kramer's (2008) research review covered studies of aerobic exercise. They reported positive effects of aerobic physical activity on cognition and brain function. Cotman and Berchtold (2002) concluded from their research review, "It is now clear that voluntary exercise can increase levels of brain-derived neurotrophic factor (BDNF) and other growth factors, stimulate neurogenesis, increase resistance to brain insult and improve learning and mental performance" (p. 295). Erickson and his colleagues (2011) conducted research which found aerobic exercise increased the size of the anterior hippocampus, which leads to improvements in spatial memory. The researchers concluded aerobic exercise may help older adults improve their memories. Such reports by Cotman and Berchtold (2002) and findings such as those of Erickson et al. (2011) lead one author to refer to exercise as "Miracle-Gro for brains" (Snider, 2008).

Two studies, reviewed by Penedo and Dahn (2005), found exercise to be instrumental in improving sexual functioning. In one study men being treated for localized prostate cancer reported better sexual functioning after increasing their levels of physical activity. In another study, a program for obese men, that involved reducing caloric intake and increasing physical activity, brought reductions in erectile dysfunction.

In what must certainly be considered to be an understatement, Phillips, Schneider, and Mercer (2004) stated that "most elders are not physically active" (p. S52). Fitzhugh, Klein, and Hayes (2008), in an article in the *Annual of Therapeutic Recreation*, reported that over 60% of older adults participate in little or no physical activity and that less than 30% engage in physical activity sufficient to gain health benefits. Ashe, Miller, Eng, and Noreau (2009) have reported similar findings for older Canadians.

Yet, the potential benefits of physical activity for aging persons are clear. Conn and her colleagues (2003), from their review of research, concluded, "Physical and psychological benefits of increased physical activity have been widely documented in healthy and chronically ill older adults" (p. 1159). Bean, Vora, and Frontera (2004) succinctly indicated the value of physical activity for older persons. They wrote that "perhaps the most universal and effective treatment for chronic illness and disability in late life is physical exercise. Reductions in physical activity are associated with significant impairments and limitations in function, augmenting disablement and chronic Illness. Exercise can reduce morbidity, reverse physiologic impairments, ameliorate functional loss, and are important means of both preventing and treating chronic disease" (p. S31).

Likewise, in her extensive chapter on physical activity and aging, DiPietro (2012) wrote this about the consequences of sedentary behavior:

> Disuse and a sedentary lifestyle are especially detrimental to older people. For example low levels of physical activity and cardiorespiratory fitness are primary determinants of the decline in metabolic and functional reserve observed in older age. Sedentary behavior has consistently demonstrated a relationship with the development of chronic disease, premature mortality, poor quality of life, and loss of function and Independence with aging. Sedentary behavior accumulated over a lifetime may be the risk condition with the biggest global public health impact that is faced by older people. Indeed, population risk estimates for heart disease attributed to low activity or low fitness levels in middle aged or older people are comparable to, or even greater than, those attributed to other well-known predictors of morbidity and mortality, such as hypertension, smoking, dyslipidemia, and obesity. (p. 312)

A number of studies of older adults have shown the positive effects of physical activity. For example, physical activity has been found to: improve health related quality of life (Wang, 2008); improve activity levels, energy, and lessen hospitalizations for primary care patients (Kerse, Elley, Robinson, & Arroll, 2005); increase cognitive functioning (Churchill et al., 2002); reduce depression (Sjosten & Kivela, 2005); increase social relationships (Bronikowska, Bronikowski, & Schott, 2011), and increase muscle strength and aerobic capacity and reduce functional limitations (Keysor, 2003). Even the risk of elderly individuals falling has been reduced by exercise programs that improve balance and increase mobility (Ferrini & Ferrini, 2000).

Of course, elderly people often encounter chronic conditions or disabilities. Having a chronic condition or disability has been found to reduce the level of physical activity (Saebu, 2010; Warburton, Nicol, & Bredin, 2006). It is a shame that those with chronic diseases and disabilities tend to be inactive because empirical evidence regarding the benefits of physical activity for those with chronic conditions or disabilities is abundant. As DiPietro (2012) has stated, "There is now substantial evidence demonstrating the benefits of physical activity in attenuating aging-related functional decline, even among older people with established chronic disease and frailty" (p. 315). Further, DiPietro wrote, "Physical activity and fitness have been associated with as much as a 40% reduction in morbidity and mortality from a number of major chronic diseases affecting older people." She went on to state that, "The psychological benefits or regular physical activity have also been well documented" (p. 312). Evidence of these benefits for those with specific chronic conditions and disabilities is reviewed in the following segment, beginning with the role of physical activity in arthritis.

Research on Physical Activity for Chronic Conditions and Disabilities

Arthritis. Abell et al. (2005) termed arthritis to be "the leading cause of disability." Happily, Abell and her colleagues have written that "Regular physical activity can reduce arthritis related pain, improve function, and delay disability without promoting disease progression among persons with disabilities"(p. 389). While declaring, "Arthritis is one of the most common and debilitating conditions experienced in later life,"in their research review Penedo and Dahn (2005) cited research on physical activity that combated the effects of arthritis. They wrote that a water-exercise program brought about"significant improvements in physical function and reductions in the perception of pain...."(p. 191). Feinglass et al. (2005) reported their research found physical activity brought about functional improvements in older middle-age adults with arthritis. Findings of interviews with patients with rheumatoid arthritis indicated physical activity produced increases in joint flexibility and their general conditions, as well as decreases in pain (Kamwendo, Askenbom, & Wahlgren, 1999). A study by Minor et al. (1989) of 12-week aerobic walking and aerobic aquatics programs found both were effective in bringing about improvements in aerobic capacity, walking times, anxiety and depression among patients with arthritis and osteoarthritis. Plasqui (2008), in his review article on the role of physical activity in rheumatoid arthritis, acknowledged the effect of physical activity in maintaining muscle strength and endurance, range of motion, and the ability to perform activities of daily living. Further, he declared physical activity "plays a central role" in the management of rheumatoid arthritis (p. 270). Finally, the Centers for Disease Control and Prevention (2011) concluded that "Scientific studies have shown that physical activity can reduce pain and improve function, mood, and quality of life for adults with arthritis."

Multiple sclerosis. Persons with multiple sclerosis (MS) tend to be less physically active than others (Motl, McAuley, & Snook, 2005). Yet, research has shown that those with MS can benefit from participation in physical activity. For instance, Kileff and Ashburn (2005) reported their research using bi-weekly, 30-minute cycling sessions on stationary bikes resulted in increased endurance and significant improvement in overall disability levels for persons with moderate disability multiple sclerosis. Mostert and Kesselring (2002) reported a four-week aerobic exercise program resulted in improvements in fitness, less fatigue, increases in levels of physical activity, and perceptions of improved health status in subjects with MS. A five-year study involving self-reports of persons with MS found physical activities decreased functional limitations and enhanced quality of life ratings (Stuifbergen, Blozis, Harrison, & Becker, 2008). In a research review, White and Dressendorfer (2004) reported regular physical activity to not only enhance quality of life but to alleviate fatigue, increase muscle strength, and enhance lifestyle activity, as well as to reduce the risk of secondary disorders. A meta-analysis of quality of life research for individuals with MS found evidence that exercise is associated with statistically significant improvements in quality of life (Motl & Gosney, 2008). Another meta-analysis on MS and physical activity by Motl, McAuley, and Snook (2005) found both aerobic and resistance exercise training as being beneficial for symptom management and general health, as well as the quality of life of those with MS. These authors concluded that physical activity "is crucial for long-term health in this population" (p. 461). Finally, following their review of the literature, Dalgas, Stenager, and Ingermann-Hansen (2008) wrote, "Physical exercise is an important non-pharmacological tool for MS rehabilitation" (p. 50).

Obesity. More than one-third (35.7%) of adults in the United States (over 72 million people) and 17% of children may be classified as being obese (Centers for Disease Control and Prevention, 2011a, 2011e). Wyatt, Winters, and Dubbert (2006), in an *American Journal of the Medical Sciences* article, wrote, "The prevalence of overweight and obesity now exceeds 60% among U.S. adults, and the rate is rapidly increasing among children and adolescents" (p. 166). For Canada, it has been reported that 59% of adults are overweight and 23% obese (Lau, 2007). Because of its prevalence, obesity has been termed an "epidemic"(Foster et al., 2003; Rimmer & Yamaki, 2006), as well as a "major health threat"(Wyatt, Winters, & Dubbert, 2006).

Both the terms *overweight* and *obesity* are labels for weight that is above what is considered healthy for a given height. The Body Mass Index (BMI) is used as a measure of how much a person's weight departs from what would be expected as being normal for a person of his or her height. An adult with a BMI ranging between 25 and 29.9 is considered to be overweight. Having a BMI of 30 or higher is considered obese. For example, someone 5'9" weighing 169 to 202 pounds would have a BMI between 25 and 29.9 and be considered overweight. If they weighed 203 or more, they would be considered to be obese (CDC; Centers for Disease Control and Prevention, 2012d). The BMI for children is similar but has its own scales. For children, overweight is defined as being at or above the 85th percentile on the BMI for children of the same age and sex. Obesity is defined as being at or above the 95th percentile for children of the same age and sex (CDC, 2012c).

There are a number of adverse consequences of being obese. Obesity is a prominent risk factor for premature mortality and for a number of chronic conditions that can negatively affect quality of life (Ross & Janssen, 2012). Among the chronic conditions are hypertension, diabetes, heart disease, liver and gallbladder disease, some types of cancer, arthritis, osteoarthritis, stroke, sleep apnea, high cholesterol, stress, depression, respiratory diseases, and reproductive health complications such as infertility (CDC, 2011e; Rimmer & Yamaki, 2006). Additionally, Chen and Guo (2008) found that for older people obesity is associated with functional disabilities independent of chronic conditions. Likewise, childhood obesity can lead to risk factors for (a) cardiovascular disease (e.g., high blood pressure, high cholesterol): (b) breathing problems (e,g., sleep apnea, asthma); (c) impaired glucose tolerance, insulin resistance and type 2 diabetes; (d) joint problems and musculoskeletal discomfort; and (e) fatty liver disease, gallstones, and gastro-esophageal reflux (i.e., heartburn). In addition, obese children and adolescents are at greater risk for social and psychological problems (e.g., discrimination, poor self-esteem). Finally, obese children are more likely to become obese adults (CDC, 2012a).

Behavior has much to do with being obese or overweight. While various factors influence weight (e.g., genes, metabolism, environment, culture, socioeconomic status), being obese or overweight generally results from an energy imbalance. That is, being obese or overweight is caused by eating too many calories and not getting enough physical exercise (CDC, 2012b). Supporting this notion is research by Foster et al. (2003) in which primary care physicians identified physical inactivity as the primary cause of obesity.

Thus, it is clear that physical activity is important for maintaining a healthy weight. As stated by Ross and Janssen (2012), "Obesity (or being overweight) results from a chronic energy imbalance whereby intake exceeds expenditure" (p. 204). It has been suggested by Ross and Janssen that, for most people, an additional 60 minutes of daily physical activity is required to bring about weight loss. Yet, these authors reported weight loss has resulted from as little as 200 minutes of physical activity per week. The American College of Sports Medicine (2001) recommends that adults who are obese or overweight should exercise 200-300 minutes per week.

Cardiovascular diseases. The research showing the benefits of physical activity for cardiovascular disease (i.e., diseases involving the heart or blood vessels; American Heart Association, 2011) has been termed "overwhelming" (Ford, 2012). It has been reported by the U.S. Department of Health and Human Services (2000) that those who are inactive are almost twice as likely to contract coronary heart disease (CHD) than those who are physically active. In fact, inactivity is now considered an independent risk factor for CHD. Happily, those who have CHD traditional risk factors, such as those who smoke or have high blood pressure, are particularly good candidates to benefit from regular physical activity. Thompson et al. (2003) stated that regular physical activity "prevents the development of coronary artery disease (CAD) and reduces symptoms in patients with established cardiovascular disease" (p. e42). Following Warburton, Nicol and Bredin's (2006) review of the empirical evidence, they concluded that "regular physical activity is clearly effective In the secondary prevention of cardiovascular disease and is effective in attenuating the risk of premature death among men and women" (p. 802).

Strokes. A stroke, or cerebrovascular accident (CVA), is sometimes referred to as a "brain attack" (Centers for Disease Control and Prevention, 2012d). A stroke occurs when there is damage to part of the brain caused by a blood clot that blocks the blood supply to the brain or when a blood vessel in the brain leaks blood outside the vessel walls. The damage done to the affected part of the brain leads to impairment of sensations, movements, or functions controlled by the damaged area. Resulting may be difficulties in talking or eating, the inability to move a limb or one side of the body (which may cause difficulty in daily activities such as walking or dressing), pain or numbness in parts of the body, the inability to see one side of the visual field, or memory loss or difficulty in thinking. After a stroke, people may also become less social, more withdrawn, and more impulsive (Janssen, 2012; Mayo Clinic, 2012). A transient ischemic attack (TIA) is a mini stroke when blood flow is cut off from the brain for a shot period (IU Health, 2013).

According to the CDC (2012d), 795,000 people in the United States have strokes each year and a total of 130,000 die from strokes each year. Factors that can raise the risk of having a stroke include high blood pressure, high cholesterol, heart disease, diabetes, being overweight or obese, and having had a previous stroke or TIA. It has been found that there is a reduction of risk for strokes by those who practice regular physical activity (Alzahrani et al., 2012; Deplanque et al., 2012).

A meta-analysis on physical training for patients with stroke by Brazzelli and her colleagues (2012) resulted in guarded conclusions. While they found beneficial results for walking programs that produced improvements in cardiorespiratory fitness and resistance training that brought improved muscle strength, they generally found the effects of exercise following stroke to be unclear.

Other research reviews however hold more promise for the use of exercise after stroke. Mead, Bernhardt, and Kwakkel (2012) wrote, "There is now an increasing body of evidence that suggests that exercise after stroke has a number of benefits and may help address common post-stroke problems including fatigue." Following a discussion of how task-oriented exercise has been found to be effective in helping clients attain optimal motor function and independence, Langhammer and Lindmark (2012) stated, "The importance of exercise and training after stroke has also been documented. Studies have shown that persons with stroke, given the opportunity to exercise in the year after the stroke, maintain their functional status after the initial rehabilitation and improve function."

An interesting longitudinal study by Langhammer and Lindmark (2012) found that exercise training following stroke produced gains that allowed those with better physical conditioning going into the program to function at a high level with few difficulties in motor function, balance, mobility, or activities of daily living. Those with lower physical conditioning, while not reaching the levels of independence as those in the high function group, also made significant gains as a result of the exercise program, thus establishing a need for a rehabilitation program for those with lower functioning levels after stroke. The researchers concluded, "The persons gaining most function from rehabilitation does not seem to be the ones that will gain independence but the ones that will still need some assistance."

In another research study, Alzahrani et al. (2012) have shown that mood and balance for clients after stroke can be improved by regular participation in everyday physical activities. Bringing about improvement in balance is important for stroke survivors because falls are a common complication after having a stroke (van Duijnhoven et al., 2012).

Factors have been identified as important in determining the extent of participation in physical activity for those who have had a stroke. These have been found to be persons' feelings of self-efficacy, beliefs about physical activity, and their level of social support for participation (Mead, Bernhardt, & Kwakkel, 2012).

Cancer. Leisure physical activity has been found to reduce the cancer-specific and overall mortality of those diagnosed with stages I to III colorectal cancer (Meyerhardt et al., 2008). For women with breast cancer, physical activity has reduced the risk of death (Holmes, et al., 2005). Obesity and physical inactivity are common among cancer survivors. For this population, physical activity interventions can reduce weight gain and decrease the risk of recurrence and death (Irwin, 2008). Following Warburton, Nicol and Bredin's (2006) review of the empirical evidence, they concluded that "there is compelling evidence that routine physical activity is associated with reductions in the incidence of specific cancers, in particular breast and colon cancer" (p. 803).

Diabetes. In an extensive article highlighting research on diabetes and physical activity, Zisser and colleagues (2012) summarized the value of physical activities in the prevention and treatment of diabetes when they wrote:

Regular physical activity increases insulin sensitivity, improves pharmacotherapy, Lowers blood sugar concentrations, reduces body fat content, builds muscle and improves cardiovascular fitness and function. A number of recent studies have demonstrated the effectiveness of regular exercise in improving metabolic control and overall health in persons with diabetes, although the clinical management of physical activity patients with type 1 diabetes (TID) remains a challenge. (p. 62)

In a brief but complete review of the research on physical activity and type 2 diabetes, Colberg (2012) termed physical activity to be the "forgotten tool for type 2 diabetes" (p.

1). In her article, Colberg cautioned that research suggests all with type 2 diabetes need to engage in at least minimal daily movement to better manage their diabetes and even low levels of physical activity can positively impact on insulin action and glucose control. She reported that modest amounts of exercise, even without weight loss, can positively affect markers of glucose and fat metabolism in sedentary adults with type 2 diabetes. Physical activity does not have to be intense to be beneficial. Physical activity of any intensity can improve glucose control but prolonged or intense activity enhances acute insulin action for longer periods. Colberg concluded her research review by indicating that getting sedentary individuals with type 2 diabetes activated with even low intensity activity will provide them with the confidence to enter into more structured types of physical activities, such as aerobic exercises and resistance training. She concluded such activities for those with type 2 diabetes "can greatly enhance their health and diabetes management" (p. 4).

A meta-analysis reported aerobic exercises, resistance training, or a combination of both, has been found to result in blood glucose control for those with type 2 diabetes (Umpierre et al., 2011). Based on such findings, the American Diabetes Association (ADA) has recommended both aerobic and resistance exercise for people with type 2 diabetes (Sigal et al., 2006). In fact, the ADA (2003), in a position statement, has portrayed physical activity "as a vital component of the prevention as well as the management of type 2 diabetes... (p. 577). The ADA position statement also spoke to physical activity and type 1 diabetes. ADA stated that with type 1 diabetes physical activity regimens must be adjusted to provide safe participation. The ADA stated: All levels of physical activity, including leisure activities, recreational sports, and competitive professional performance, can be performed by people with type 1 diabetes who do not have complications and are in good blood glucose control" (p. 576).

Asthma. While persons with asthma often have negative attitudes toward exercise (Christopher & Cochrane, 1999; Ford, Heath, Mannino, & Redd, 2003), research has shown they can benefit from physical activity. For instance, two published research reviews (Ram, Robinson, & Black, 2000; Ram, Robinson, Black, & Picot, 2005) reported physical activity programs for persons with asthma improved cardiopulmonary fitness without adverse effects on lung function.

Much of the research on asthma and physical activity seems to have been completed with children and adolescents. In an extensive review article, Welsh, Kemp, and Roberts (2005) reported on research effectively showing how physical training improved aerobic fitness in children and adolescents with asthma. This lead them to conclude "the overwhelming weight of evidence indicates that aerobic exercise training is of benefit in improving aerobic fitness in children and adolescents with asthma of mild to moderate severity" (p. 136). A number of studies also reported improvements in quality of life measures for children and adolescents who participated in physical conditioning programs.

Swimming programs are sometimes provided for children and adolescents with asthma. In two well designed swimming studies reviewed by Welsh, Kemp, and Roberts (2005), children with asthma improved their aerobic efficiency, leading to the author to note "there is considerable evidence that the indoor swimming pool environment, providing a warm and moist air inspirate, is much less asthmagenic for a given exercise ventilator stimulus than other modes of exercise (e.g., running, cycling)"(p. 134).

Welsh, Kemp, and Roberts noted, however, that in general, researchers in the studies they reviewed did not find that physical activity produced changes in lung function. Nevertheless, these authors concluded "an asthmatic child or adolescent with an increased level of aerobic fitness is likely to have improvements in maximum exercise breathing capacity" (p. 140).

Adults with asthma who participated in a physical training program experienced improvements in cardiovascular conditioning and reported less anxiety about exercising at a high intensity level following their 10 week program (Emtner, Herala, & Stalenheim, 1996). Adult outpatients with mild asthma improved aerobic fitness and ventilation efficiency, as well as decreased hyperpnea following exercise as a result of a 10-week aerobic conditioning program (Hallstrand, Bates, & Schoene, 2000).

Thus studies suggest physical activity has beneficial effects in the clinical management of persons with asthma. While exercise-induced asthma may prevent some individuals with asthma from taking part in intense physical activity, most persons with asthma should be able to fully participate in physical activities (Ford et al., 2003).

Other chronic conditions. Additionally, physical activity has been shown to bring health benefits to those with any number of chronic conditions. For instance, regular physical activity has been found to reduce hospital admissions and mortality for those with chronic obstructive pulmonary disease (COPD; Garcia-Aymerich, 2006). Exercise has also been found to reduce pain, as well as increase psychological well-being, for individuals with spinal cord injuries (Ditor et al., 2003). Research has shown that recreational physical activities (e.g., walking and swimming) produce positive results for clients suffering from low back pain (Hurwitz, Morgenstern, & Chiao, 2005). Physical exercise has brought about physical benefits for persons with Parkinson's Disease, including improvements in balance, flexibility, axial rotation, functional reach, mobility, and muscle strength (Crizzle & Newhouse, 2006). Clinical evidence has shown a positive relationship between exercise and Alzheimer's Disease and Parkinson's Disease (Deslandes et al., 2009). Research completed by Larson et al. (2006), with participants over age 65, demonstrated those who exercise three or more times per week are less likely to develop Alzheimer's Disease and other types of dementia. Both aerobic and resistance training have been shown to ameliorate the effects of osteroarthritis by reducing pain and improving physical functioning, mental health, and quality of life (Hootman, 2012). For persons with muscular dystrophy, studies have shown physical activity can improve strength and activities of daily living (Green, 2011). Physical activities have been found to prevent loss of bone mineral density and osteoporosis (Hootman, 2012; Warburton, Nicol, & Bredin, 2006). Not only can physical activity be instrumental in bringing about weight loss, it also can serve as a buffer against the risks (e.g., mobility difficulties) associated with being obese or overweight. Physical activity can also help buffer against cognitive decline in older people (Penedo & Dahn, 2005).

Does Physical Activity Have to be Vigorous?

A misconception has existed that physical activity must be vigorous in order to produce health benefits when, in fact, data support that health benefits can result from activities of moderate intensity. The U.S. Department of Health and Human Services (2000) has summed up this research in the following statement:

Although vigorous physical activity is recommended for improved cardiorespiratory fitness, increasing evidence suggests that moderate physical activity also can have significant health benefits, including a decreased risk of CHD. For people who are inactive, even small increases in physical activity are associated with measurable health benefits. (p. 22–24)

What are guidelines for physical activity? Following the *2008 Physical Activity Guidelines for Americans,* the Centers for Disease Control and Prevention (CDC; 2011b) recommend children and adolescents get 60 minutes or more of physical exercise each day. CDC (2011c) has suggested that adults need one of three types of physical activity each week. The first of these involves 150 minutes of moderate intensity aerobic activity (e.g., brisk walking), as well as muscle strengthening activities on two or more days per week to work all major muscle groups. The second is 75 minutes of vigorous intensity aerobic activity (e.g., jogging or running) each week and muscle strengthening activities on two or more days per week to work all major muscle groups. The third (also for 75 minutes) is for an equivalent mix of moderate and vigorous intensity aerobic activity, along with two or more days a week doing muscle strengthening activities working all major muscle groups. For even greater benefit, adults should increase their activity level to 300 minutes each week of moderate intensity aerobic activity, with muscle strengthening activities two or more days a week or 150 minutes of vigorous intensity aerobic activity (or an equivalent mix of moderate and vigorous aerobic activity) and two or more days a week of muscle strengthening activities.

For those 65 years of age and older, who are generally fit and have no limiting health conditions, the same general guidelines as for other adults have been published by CDC. In the CDC publication on physical activity and healthy aging, it is emphasized that aerobic activities (or "cardio") are any that make a person breath harder or increase heart rate. Even dancing, biking, or walking can count as aerobic activities as long as they are done at a moderate to vigorous intensity for at least 10 minutes at a time. There are a number of muscle strengthening activities for older people including lifting weights, working with resistance bands, doing exercises that use body weight for resistance (e.g., push ups, sit ups), heavy gardening (e.g., digging, shoveling), and yoga. For health benefits muscle strengthening activities need to be completed to the point where it is hard to do another repetition (such as lifting a weight or doing another sit up). (CDC, 2011d).

As explained by Phillips and his colleagues (2001), there has been a "paradigm shift" from vigorous exercise training to produce fitness to moderate physical activity for health benefit. The benefits of everyday activities such as walking, bicycling, gardening, and stair climbing have become recognized and are now encouraged as a part of a moderate physical activity program.

Implications for Recreational Therapy

It is clear that there are a number of mental health and physical health benefits to be gained through clients' participation in a variety of physical activities. As Bouchard, Blair, and Haskell (2012) have proclaimed, in their major work titled *Physical Activity and Health,* "Physical activity is associated with health benefits" (p. 16). On the other hand, LeMonte and Blair (2012) have warned, "Sedentary habits and low cardiorespiratory fitness are among the strongest predictors of premature morality…." (p. 168).

It seems obvious that recreational therapists need to develop educational programs (e.g., leisure education and leisure counseling) to share information on the benefits of physical activity that will positively alter client attitudes and beliefs about the value of being active. This education can begin during the initial assessment completed with each new client. Fitzhugh, Klein, and Hayes (2008), in an article in the *Annual in Therapeutic Recreation,* have suggested attention should be given to assessing the leisure physical activity participation of older clients. It would seem that this recommendation should be extended to all clients being assessed by recreational therapists. The physical activity history of each new RT client should be taken during each client's initial assessment and information should be shared with the client about the benefits to be gained from physical activity and opportunities for participation available through the recreational therapy program.

Of course, recreational therapists need to develop and offer physical activity programs (e.g., aerobic dance, aerobic exercise, resistance training, walking, swimming, and gardening programs) for client participation. Mobily (2009) has written that recreational therapy "is in the best position to deliver an ongoing lifetime program of regular physical activity that promotes and maintains functional ability and health among many persons with disabilities and chronic conditions" (p. 9).

Particular attention should be given to the needs of persons with disabilities and older clients. It has been reported that approximately 56% of persons with disabilities do not engage in any form of physical activity, as compared to 36% of people without disabilities. Further, those with disabilities are almost three times as likely to be sedentary as individuals without disabilities (Lakowski & Long, 2011). Like persons with disabilities, older people tend to be sedentary and, yet, they can benefit from physical activity in order to help prevent functional and cognitive decline and to cope with chronic conditions (DiPietro, 2012). DiPietro has stated that "physical activity and exercise have demonstrated effectiveness in improving function across the aging spectrum--from the very healthy to the most frail— and should be encouraged among all older people" (p. 313). For older people, Bronikowska, Bronikowski, and Scott (2011) have recommended that physical recreational activities (e.g., horseshoes, croquet, bocce) be provided because older persons are not drawn to highly structured exercise programs.

Early research on exercise and Alzheimer's disease (e.g., Desalandes et al., 2009; Larson et al., 2006) has shown enough promise that the U.S. government has initiated a five-year research program to examine the effect of drugs and exercise for patients with early stage disease (Preidt, 2013). Such efforts should signal to recreational therapists the possible potential exercise may have for their clients with early stage Alzheimer's disease.

A number of publications (e.g., Callaghan, 2004; Netz, Wu, & Tenenbaum, 2005; Richardson et al., 2005) have called for increased use of physical activities in the treatment of clients dealing with problems in mental health. Recreational therapists need to educate psychiatrists and other mental health professionals about the benefits of physical activity as in the past they have not commonly recommended physical activities for their clients. As new physical activities are initiated in mental health programs, recreational therapists do need to be cautioned that psychiatric clients need to perceive physical activity programs as therapy and not simply as leisure activities. Otherwise these clients likely will not readily engage in the programs or adhere to physical activities following the initial intervention (Burbach, 1997).

There seems to be an emerging consensus that physical activity in the natural environment can be particularly effective in bringing about mental health benefits. Therefore, recreational therapists should give consideration to providing opportunities for outdoor physical activities.

It should be noted that motivation to take part in physical activity programs can be heightened if clients enjoy their experiences. Recreational therapy researchers Porter, Shank, and Iwasaki (2012) have reported multiple studies that displayed the importance of enjoyment as a powerful force for physical activity engagement. Both listening to music during exercise and clients enjoying socially supportive interactions with the leader and other clients can greatly enhance the activity experience (Cox, 2002). The social element in group participation can play an enormous role in adding to client enjoyment (Herbert, 2008). Adapted physical educator, Georgia Frye (personal communication, 7/13/2006) of

Indiana University has indicated that social outcomes are the largest motivator for physical activity.

Herbert (2008) has warned that once clients complete a physical activity program they may stop exercising independently if they are not prepared to continue their activities after the structured program is no longer available. This is because clients are prone to use professionals as "proxy-agents," rather than assuming responsibility for themselves, according to Herbert. Therefore, it is important for recreational therapists to help clients to build self-confidence in their abilities to exercise on their own.

There are a number of resources that contain information on organizing and conducting physical activity programs. Specifically designed for older clients is an excellent book published by the National Institute on Aging (2010) titled *Exercise & Physical Activity.* This book provides a number of illustrated exercises for strength, flexibility, balance, and endurance. Brandon (1999) offers activities for elderly persons that can be completed either in a chair or standing. Eldercise (Penner, 1989) outlines a comprehensive exercise program for the frail elderly. In Dattilo and McKenney's (2011) *Facilitation Techniques in Therapeutic Recreation* are physical activities (e.g. exercises, sports, tai chi) to improve various aspects of health including cardiovascular endurance, strength, muscular endurance, body composition, and flexibility. Silver and Morin's (2008) *Understanding Fitness* covers how different exercises may be used to prevent and treat disease. Three specific types of physical activity (i.e., Pilates, qigong, tai chi) are covered in the following segment of this chapter.

Whenever an individual contemplates initiating a program of physical activities, it is always best for that person to check with his or her physician before beginning. Once the individual has received medical clearance, his or her program should start slowly and build from that point as greater fitness is developed.

Pilates

The term **Pilates** (pi-lah-teez) comes from the founder Joseph Hubertus Pilates who developed his exercise system more than 90 years ago (Adams, Caldwell, Atkins, & Quin, 2012). Born in Germany, Pilates was a sickly child who used physical exercise to become a healthy adult (Lange, Unnithan, Larkam, & Latta, 2000). He brought his exercise program to the United States in 1923 (Kloubec, 2010).

Pilates involves a system of low-impact exercises that allow participants to take control of their minds and bodies. It has the goal of toning and conditioning the body, while developing correct breathing and posture and increasing focus and mental concentration. Pilates believed his exercises would produce complete coordination of mind, body, and spirit by employing six principles: centering, concentration, control, precision, flow, and breath (Caldwell, Harrison, Adams, & Triplett, 2009; Cruz-Ferreira et al., 2011). In the words of Rogers and Gibson (2009), "Pilates offers a 'core' workout in which the fitness components of muscular strength, endurance, flexibility, balance, and cardiorespiratory endurance are anticipated benefits" (p. 569).

Pilates designed his exercise program with the objective of augmenting the neuromuscular system by increasing muscle strength, endurance, and flexibility, while stabilizing the spine. His method is based on the concept of stabilization of the spine while completing exercises (Emery, De Serres, McMillan, & Cote, 2010; Phrompaet, Paungmali, Pirunsan, & Sifilertpisan, 2011).

Pilates exercises are smooth, flowing movements designed to place as little stress on the body as is possible. Therefore, most people can do Pilates because it does not require a high level of fitness. Pilates exercises can be practiced two or three times a week beginning with sessions as brief as 10 minutes. (*Complete Guide to Pilates, Yoga, Meditation, Stress Relief,* 2006).

Pilates exercises work multiple muscle groups at the same time. They may be performed on a floor mat or on machines, although the use of mats is most employed. The exercises are directed toward building strength without "bulking up" the muscles. Descriptions of the Pilates modality typically mention that exercises develop a strong "core," the center of the body involving the abdominal muscles and back muscles (Reddy, 2006).

Any number of sources (e.g., Bernardo, 2007; Lange, Unnithan, Larkam, & Latta, 2000; Tierney, 2011) have commented on the growing popularity of Pilates. Cruz-Ferreira et al. (2011) wrote, "It is estimated that over 10 million people are now practicing Pilates in the United States alone, and the numbers are growing every year" (p. 251).

Claims have been made that Pilates programs can enhance physiological functioning (flexibility, range of motion, muscular strength, muscular endurance, muscular power, cardiorespiratory fitness); psychological functioning (mood, motivational state, focus of attention, enjoyment of life, energy and zest); and motor learning (core control, static and dynamic posture, intralimb and interlimb coordination, aesthetically pleasing movement form, body awareness, static and dynamic balance) (Lange, Unnithan, Larkam, & Latta, 2000). Unfortunately, research reviews of Pilates programs completed early or in the middle of the first decade of the 21st century (Bernardo, 2007; Lange, Unnithan, Larkam, & Latta, 2000; Shedden & Kravitz, 2006) were critical of the research that had been completed to substantiate these claims. A constant theme of these reviews was that the research lacked rigor and every review expressed a need for more well controlled empirical studies.

Some support for the claims for positive effects from Pilates' programs can be found however in more recent research. While the effects of Pilates programs have not been extensively researched, we know that Pilates exercises can improve abdominal strength and endurance (Emery, De Serres, McMillan, & Cote, 2010; Herrington & Davies, 2005; Kloubec, 2010; Sekendiz, Altun, Korkusuz, & Akin, 2007; Wang et al., 2012); improve dynamic balance (Irez et al., 2011; Johnson et al., 2007); improve flexibility (Bernardo, 2007; Cruz-Ferreira et al., 2011); improve lower back muscle strength and posterior trunk flexibility (Sekendiz, Altun, Korkusuz, & Akin, 2007); improve dynamic postural stability (Wang et al., 2012); improve range of motion, shoulder abduction, and upper extremities function (Keays, Harris, Lucyshyn, & MacIntyre, 2008); improve body balance (Coriolano Appell, Perez, de Maio Nascimento, & Appeli Coriolano, 2012; Cruz-Ferreira et al, 2011); increase upper-body muscular endurance (Kloubec, 2010); enhance lumbo-pelvic stability (Phrompaet, Paungmali, Pirunsan, Sifilertpisan, 2011); improve sleep quality (Caldwell, Harrison, Adams, & Triplet, 2009; Leopoldino et al., 2013), decrease the propensity to fall (Irez et al., 2011), increase life satisfaction, physical self-concept, and perception of health status (Cruz-Ferreira et al., 2011); enhance self-efficacy and mood (Caldwell, Harrison, Adams, & Triplett, 2009); increase body awareness, concentration, and confidence and improve stress management and relaxation (Adams, Caldwell, Atkins, & Quin, 2012); improve londosis, an exaggerated lumbar curve in the spine (Rezaeei & Ghofrani, 2012); improve pain, depression, and the evaluation of physical appearance by others in patients with fibromyalgia syndrome (Korkmaz, 2010); and improve the physical capacity of ankylosing spondylitis patients (Altan, Korkmaz, Dizdar, & Yurtkuran, 2011).

The benefits of Pilates are covered in a website, Pilates for Individuals with Spinal Cord Injury, provided by the National Center for Health, Physical Activity, and Disability (NCHPAD) at www.ncpad.org/240/1582/Pilates-for-Individuals-with-Spinal-Cord-Injury The website also offers information on adapted Pilates. Another website on adapted Pilates is offered by eHow (www.ehow.com/videos-on_7401_adaptive-pilates.html). On the website are 18 videos to help people with disabilities to do Pilates.

Implications for Recreational Therapy

Pilates seems to be an excellent exercise modality for older persons because it tones and strengthens muscles without impact on joints (Reddy, 2006; Smith & Smith, 2005). Laura Covert, is a master's prepared Certified Therapeutic Recreation Specialist and personal trainer at WellBound Health and Fitness in Omaha. There she instructs Pilates classes with a wide variety of clients, including not only older clients but persons with disabilities. According to Covert (personal communication, February 5, 2008), it is important for current and emerging recreational therapists to understand "how they can apply Pilates in any setting and how to adapt each exercise so any person, regardless of ability level, can do it." Of course, as is true with any intervention, those who instruct Pilates need to have extensive training. This involves several hundred hours in order to become certified. Once people have had instruction from a qualified instructor they can do Pilates exercises on their own (Teen Health, 2007).

Qigong

Qigong is a branch of traditional Chinese medicine that has been practiced for well over 5000 years (Jahnke et al, 2010). Pronounced "chee goong," qigong is sometimes called chi kung (Birdee et al., 2009). *Qi* means life force, the energy of life, or biological energy. Qigong expert Gin Foon Mark (2001) has written, "Qi is the continuous flow of energy that links the various tissues, organs, and brain functions that result in a whole, unified person" (p. 1). *Gong* means the development of skill through work. According to Mokone (2000), "Qigong literally means working to cultivate biological energy" (p. 217). Mokone has explained, "The goal of an individual studying qigong is to learn to sense the energy, develop it, and control it." She has gone on to state, "The subtle energies circulate throughout the entire body in energy channels, known as meridians" (p. 218). According to Mark (2001), "Too much or too little energy in one part of the body results in disease to that part and stresses the entire body….qigong exercises can cure such imbalances by awakening the Qi, or vital energy, and circulating it to the needed area" (p. 4). Shealy (1999) has described qigong as being a

> …system of simple exercises, breathing techniques, and meditation with visualization (that) improves the circulation of Qi, thereby maintaining or restoring physical or mental health to optimum levels. Qigong exercises are slow, gentle, and rhythmical. They are not meant to strengthen the body in any way, but to stimulate the flow of energy from one area to another (p. 44).

Students in qigong classes wear loose-fitting clothing and flexible shoes while participating in slow, controlled movements to regulate the mind, breath, and body. These movements, or exercises, are practiced until they become natural, producing feelings of tranquility and relaxation. Practice sessions are held in a quiet area to avoid distractions. Students are warned not to practice when they are aroused or excited. As a result of the relaxed movements, theory underlying qigong holds that latent energy is activated which, in turn, strengthens the internal organs of the body and produces resistance against disease.

In what has been perhaps the most complete research review of qigong, Jahnke and his colleagues (2010) proclaimed that a strong body of research is emerging to support the use of qigong. Several research reviews have reported qigong has been found to provide a wide range of health benefits. It has been particularly effective in relieving stress and stress-related illnesses such as anxiety, depression, headaches, migraines, chronic fatigue, ulcers, hypertension, high blood pressure, and chronic constipation. Other studies of qigong have found it produced reductions in BMI, improved balance, enhanced the immune system, improved cardiopulmonary function, improved self-efficacy, and improved quality of life. (Jahnke et al., 2010; Lake, 2002; Mark, 2001; Mokone, 2000; Ng & Tsang, 2009; Sancier, 1996,1999, 2004; Shealy, 1999). Studies have even indicated the value of reducing stress and enhancing the well-being of seventh graders in Sweden (Terjestam, Jouper, & Johansson, 2010) and shortening the detoxification period and reducing the discomfort of detoxification of heroin addicts (Li, Chen & Mo, 2002). Chinese researchers have reported successfully using qigong in the treatment of asthma, insomnia, anxiety, pain, diabetes, hypertension, spinal cord injuries, multiple sclerosis, cerebral palsy, joint disease, and cancer (Andrews, Angone, Cray, Lewis, & Johnson, 1999; Fontaine & Kaszubski, 2004).

Implications for Recreational Therapy

According to Sancier (1996, 2004), qigong exercises are not difficult to learn and are appropriate for almost everyone. They are particularly recommended for older adults, including the frail elderly (Ng & Tsang, 2009; Rogers, Larkey & Keller, 2009). Shealy has warned, however, that qigong is not appropriate for those with severe psychological problems. Thus, qigong could be employed with many recreational therapy clients. It could also be employed with clinicians as research by Griffith et al. (2008) has also shown qigong can be effective in bringing about stress reduction in hospital staff.

Unfortunately, there are a limited number of qualified qigong teachers outside of China from which recreational therapist might learn and even among those who claim to be qigong masters there are charlatans (Zixin, Li, Zhengyi, Zhenyu, Honglin & Tongling, 2000). One source of written information on qigong is Mark's (2001) book, which provides an introduction to the topic and contains numerous pictures that illustrate qigong exercises. Another book is *Qigong: Chinese Medicine or Pseudoscience?* (Zixin et al., 2000). Fontaine and Kaszubski (2004) have warned however that both ligong and tai chi are difficult to learn from books. Tai chi, covered in the following section, may be perceived to be a form of qigong since it also uses purposeful breathing along with slow, controlled movements and involves qi or human energy (Andrews, 2005; Mokone, 2000). Because health oriented qigong and tai chi share the same philosophy, principles and practices, Jahnke et al. (2010) have referred to them collectively using the term meditative movement.

Tai Chi

Tai chi (sometimes referred to as tai chi chuan) is an ancient form of exercise that originated some 800 years ago in China and which is now widely practiced not only in Asia but throughout Europe, Australia, Canada, and the United States. In the U.S. as many as 2.5 million persons use tai chi to improve their health and well-being (Birdee et al., 2009). According to Snyder and Lindquist (2006), tai chi "is one of the interventions widely recommended across different professions, including nurses, physicians, occupational therapists, physical therapists, and recreational therapists" (p. 313).

Tai chi (pronounced "tie-chee") uses smooth, continuous, nonstressful motions that resemble a fluent dance (Du & King, 1998; Sachs, 1997). The harmonious actions of tai chi have been described in the *Encyclopedia of Alternative Medicine* (Smalheiser, 1996) as "graceful, slow, liquid movements that look like a ballet underwater" (p. 276). Du and King (1998) have described tai chi as "swimming in the air." MoraMarco (2000) has portrayed tai chi movements as being "slow, fluid, captivating motions" (p. 47) in which the body bends gently like "bamboo in the wind" (p. 48). Hill, et al. (2001) have explained, "The basis of every style of tai chi is the practice of 'the form.' A form is a set of slow-moving, graceful exercises performed in a definite pattern" (p. 130). Hill and her colleagues go on to state, "The movements of the form are essentially self-defense movements....They are practiced in a slow, flowing sequence in order to encourage general relaxation and harmony between the mind, body and spirit" (p. 131). Seaward (2002) has termed tai chi "egoless activity," because those doing it are not to compare their movements against others because "There is no right or wrong, there only is" (p. 414).

Research has provided evidence that practicing tai chi can produce beneficial physical, mental, and emotional therapeutic outcomes. Physically, tai chi holds the potential to improve physical function, enhance endurance, build strength, improve coordination, increase flexibility, improve balance, decrease plain, enhance immune responses, increase circulation, improve kinesthetic sense, lower blood pressure, slow heart rate, reduce tension, and reduce falls for older persons. Mentally, it can produce a sense of calm and well-being. Emotionally, it can reduce stress, anxiety, and depression, and promote positive feelings. Tai chi has also been found to improve health-related quality of life (Du & King, 1998; Eliopoulos, 2005; Klein & Adams, 2004; Jahnke et al., 2010; Sachs, 1997; S. Silverman, 1998). Additional benefits of tai chi identified in the research literature have included: improved sleep quality for older adults (Irwin, Olmstead, & Motivia, 2008); improved social functioning of frail elders (Chen, Hsu, Chen, & Tseng, 2007); increased perceptions of social support (Taylor-Piliae, Haskell, Waters, & Froelicher, 2006); produced less stiffness in the joints of women with osteoarthritis (Song, Lee, Lam, & Bae, 2003); favorably influenced of self-efficacy in the elderly (Li et al., 2001); produced benefits on lower extremity range of motion for patients with arthritis (Han et al., 2004); increased exercise tolerance for elderly patients with chronic heart failure (Caminiti et al., 2011); improved ambulation for frail elderly (Greenspan, Wolf, Kelley, & O'Grady, 2007); improved symptoms for patients with fibromyalgia (Wang et al., 2010); increased glucose control for individuals with type 2 diabetes (Song, 2009); and improved exercise capacity for patients with chronic obstructive pulmonary disease (COPD) (Leung, Alison, McKeough, & Peters, 2011).

The potential for beneficial outcomes from tai chi is reflected the list of National Center for Complementary and Alternative Medicine (NCCAM; 2010b) funded research. NCCAM has funded research of tai chi's effects on bone loss in postmenopausal women; cancer survivors; depression in elderly patients; fibromyalgia symptoms (e.g., muscle pain, fatigue, insomnia); osteoarthritis of the knee; patients with chronic heart failure; and rheumatoid arthritis.

A number of studies have been conducted on older adults. This population seems particularly to benefit from practicing tai chi (Sandlund & Norlander, 2000; S. Silverman, 1998; Snyder & Lindquest, 2006).

While tai chi has become a meditation art, it was created as a martial art-based on the philosophy represented in the symbol of the yin and the yang. The yin and yang stand for opposites that interact with one another to create harmony and balance. Tai chi harmonizes participants' bodies with their mental, emotional, and spiritual elements. Lee (1993) has explained that in tai chi "the body is moving; however, the mind is still. This mental stillness in the midst of movement leads to the experience of meditation in action. By concentrating on the movement and postures, one's mind becomes calm and tranquil..." (p. 1). Sachs (1997) has written in regard to tai chi that "There can be no yin without yang, no yang without yin. Tai chi is based on circular patterns that mimic the cycling of human energy with that of the cosmos" (p. 418).

Implications for Recreational Therapy

Because of its low intensity, tai chi appears to be an excellent to use with older adults. It should be warned that learning tai chi is not necessarily easy, although it appears to be simple when watching those skilled in its practice. To learn the movements in order to be comfortable and relaxed with them takes time. Clients may, however, enjoy the challenge of learning tai chi movements (Smalheiser, 1996). Advantages of tai chi are that it is noncompetitive, requires no equipment, perfection in form is not required, and there are different styles and levels from which to choose (Dattilo & Wingate, 2011).

A growing number of recreational therapists teach tai chi as a self-help strategy, and instruction in tai chi for recreational therapists is becoming available. For example, Professor of Recreational Therapy Glenn Kastrinos at Western Carolina University, regularly teaches tai chi courses. Tai chi movements can also be learned from videos and DVDs that are commercially available. Any number of publications provide illustrations of tai chi movements (e.g., Dattilo & Wingate, 2011; Mascott, 2004; Seaward, 2002; Shealy, 1999). Perhaps the best single source for recreational therapists is Crider and Klinger's (2001) book on tai chi. This book offers many photographs to illustrate regular and adaptive exercises from the yang style of tai chi. Barnes and Noble (2007) also has published a Quamut how-to guide on tai chi, which contains basic fundamentals of tai chi and offers photos and descriptions of 24 forms of tai chi.

Aromatherapy

Aromatherapy means "treatment using scents" (Hill, Vowles, Craig, & Fyson, 2001, p. 70). It is the use of aromatic, or odorous, plant oils (termed essential oils) for health purposes (Campbell & Jones, 2000). d'Angelo (2002) explained:

> Aromatherapy, also known as aromatic medicine, is the art and science of using plant oils for health, well-being, and medical treatment. The oil is volatile because it evaporates in air. It is called an essential oil because the oil is the very essence, the lifeblood if you will, of the plant. (p. 72)

Aromatherapy is a holistic approach that seeks to help people to maintain a balance of mental, physical, and spiritual health. Although it has recently regained popularity, aromatherapy was practiced for medicinal purposes by the Egyptians 3,000 years before Christ. So, too, did the Greeks and Romans. The "Father of Medicine," Hippocrates, wrote of using a number of medicinal plants. The term *aromatherapy* was coined in 1928 by French chemist Rene Maurice Gattefosse after he applied lavender to successfully treat burns on his hands, suffered during a laboratory explosion (Buckle, 2013; Herz, 2009; Sachs, 1997; Tillett & Ames, 2010). Today aromatherapy is one of the most popular alternative therapies (Hill, et al., 2001; Tillett & Ames, 2010; Yim, Ng, Tsang, & Leung, 2009).

While aromatherapy has gained a level of popularity, critical assessment of the research literature has shown a lack of empirical data to support its use. Several research reviews (Cooke & Ernst, 2000; Tillett & Ames, 2010; Yin, Ng, Tsang, & Leung, 2009; van der Watt & Janca, 2008) have indicated there exists a paucity of methodologically sound research. Even those who strongly support it admit the scarcity of research on the clinical use of aromatherapy (Campbell & Jones, 2000). Buckle (1997) has pointed out, however, that the lack of a large body of research on aromatherapy must be kept in perspective as only 15% of all medical interventions are supported by scientific studies.

Essential oils are almost always diluted before use. They are combined with base or carrier oils, such as sweet almond oil, wheat germ oil, grapeseed oil, avocado oil, jojoba oil, peach/apricot kernel oil, soya oil, or semane oil. While sweet almond oil is probably most commonly used, any good quality nut, seed, or vegetable oil can be used. Mineral oil is not easily absorbed and should not be used. (D. W. Brown, 1999; Sachs, 1997; Walters, 1998). Strong-smelling carrier oils, such as olive oil, are to be avoided because their scents can interfere with the scents of the essential oils. While carrier oils are preferred, it is possible to combine essential oils with creams, lotions, and gels that do not contain perfume (Taylor, 2000).

There are two primary means to administer essential oils: topically and inhalation. Topical application involves essential oils being absorbed through the skin via diffusion. Eventually the oils are absorbed by the blood stream. Massage may first come to mind as is a means of topical administration of essential oils and is often associated with relief from stress and anxiety. Davis has exclaimed, "Essential oils exert a subtle influence on the mind and, combined with the loving care of a sensitive therapist, offer a truly holistic, gentle, and natural alternative to psychotropic drugs" (p. 7). In preparing message oil, a safe amount of essential oil should be used. The essential oil is blended with a base or carrier material with a dilution of 1 to 2 drops of essential oil to every teaspoon (5 ml) of carrier oil (Atkinson, 2005) or 2 to 3 drops of essential oil to 100 drops of carrier oil (Beale, 2003).

Message may not be appropriate, however, because the person receiving the aromatherapy is too fragile or the therapist is not trained in message. In these instances, the "M technique" may be employed. This registered method involves very gentle structured stroking of the hand or foot to enhance the absorption of essential oils (Buckle, 2013). Information is available on the M technique at www.rjbuckle.com

Another common aromatherapy application of essential oils is in aromatic baths, where essential oils combine with the therapeutic properties of warm water. For adults, adding 6 to 10 drops of essential oils to warm (not hot) bath water is recommended (Taylor, 2000). Other uses of essential oils are in hot or cold compresses (used with physical conditions) and skin preparations (mixed in crèmes, lotions, and water to treat skin diseases or to enhance the skin's complexion).

Olfaction is the most rapid way to get an effect from aromatherapy. Aroma can be powerful due to the way they trigger responses in the limbic system of the brain. It has been suggested that aromas or fragrances act on the brain to produce outcomes such as depression reduction, pain relief, improved sleep patterns, relaxation, or the bringing forth of deep seated memories (Keville, 2009). For example, studies have shown depressed residents in long-term care can reduce their depression with the aroma of familiar fruits or flowers (Buckle, 2013). To dispense fragrances into a room, an electric diffuser can be used. Another way to do this is to place a few drops of essential oil into a gently steaming pan of water. Still another means is to put a drop or two of essential oil on a special ring that rests over a light bulb (but not on a hot light bulb, as the bulb may burst) (Buckle, 2013). Another means is to simply add several drops of oil to a room humidifier.

What are examples of essential oils are used in aromatherapy? One example is the use of oil of lavender, employed for its soothing, uplifting and antidepressant properties. Lavender is also used to reduce stress, anxiety, and insomnia. Sandalwood aroma is also beneficial for treating anxiety, depression, and insomnia due to its calming and sedating properties. Rosemary is used for clearing the mind and stimulating memory. Sweet marjoram is known for being calming and for relieving negative emotional feelings such as anxiety, irritability, and loneliness. Clary sage has been used for its uplifting and relaxing properties, as well as reducing depression anxiety, fatigue, and calming irritable children (Herz, 2009). Other examples have been provided by Buckle (2007) who indicated studies have found inhaled peppermint reduced daytime sleepiness, lemon balm has been effectively applied topically for dementia, and lavender and thyme have been used topically for alopecia.

Implications for Recreational Therapy

Some recreational therapists have become skilled in using aromatherapy. In 1997, a recreational therapist from a nursing home in New York told the author how she had used hand lotion with lavender oil with a resident who had been highly aggressive. This use of lavender had a calming effect and seemed to relieve the resident's anger. The application of aromatherapy has been studied by recreational therapists working with residents in a skilled nursing facility. Kunstler, Greenblatt, and Moreno (2004) found that participants reported increased relaxation, pain relief, and improvement in sleep following aromatherapy. While isolated, these reports of the effective use of aromatherapy suggest that it may hold promise for application by recreational therapists, although there is an absence of a body of empirical evidence to support the use of aromatherapy. If applying aromatherapy recreational therapists need to keep in mind that certain medications can be affected by essential oils so consultation with a nurse or doctor may be called for. Those who do not wish to do aromatherapy may simply borrow concepts from aromatherapy, such as using a holistic approach to treatment that includes caring human touch exemplified by the topical application of essential oils. It would also appear that within recreational therapy programs, therapists could help clients to identify certain smells that they associate with past pleasant or relaxing times so that recalling this smell, or actually smelling the odor, may contribute to positive emotional reactions or to feelings of relaxation.

Adventure Therapy

Since the 1990s, a growing area of recreational therapy has been adventure therapy. Reflecting the swift acceptance of adventure therapy were a number of books published in the decade of the 1990s. Among these were Gass' (1993) *Adventure Therapy*; Nadler and Luckner's (1997) *Processing the Adventure Experience*; and Smith, Roland, Havens, and Hoyt's (1992) *The Theory and Practice of Challenge Education*.

The origins of adventure therapy can be traced to the Outward Bound movement in England in the 1940s, which was begun to satisfy youths' desire for adventure (Richards & Myers, 1987). Winn (1982) has reported that the original components of Outward Bound included "an unfamiliar environment, physical activity, a controlled amount of stress, a collaborative small group context, and the use of newly acquired knowledge and skills" (p.163). Outward Bound programs emphasized the development of each participant's inner resources through meeting physical and mental challenges (Sugarman, 1988).

Today, adventure therapy is employed with a variety of client groups including persons with a full range of disabilities and at-risk youth. It is enjoying particularly wide use with clients undergoing psychiatric treatment, including emotionally disturbed adolescents and teens with substance abuse problems (Autry, 2001; Ewert, McCormick, & Voight, 2001; Harper, Russell, Cooley, & Cuppies, 2007; Russell, 2006; Shanahan, McAllister, & Curtin, 2009; Witman, 1987).

In order to understand **adventure therapy**, it is necessary to comprehend the nature of adventure experiences. Sugarman (1988) has listed the values inherent in adventure activities. Included are the following:

- The activities tend to be noncompetitive.
- Successful completion of a specifically designed sequence of activities results in a sense of accomplishment.
- The activities promote cooperation and trust among participants. The entire group must communicate and work together to achieve specific goals.
- The activities can be implemented at the level of participants, which enhances the opportunity for improvement of self-concept.
- The activities can be used as a metaphor for situations which occur in the participants' daily life.
- Participants have fun while improving flexibility, strength, coordination and endurance.
- Activities require cooperation with the elements of nature, which leads to a greater respect and appreciation of the natural environment (pp. 27–28).

Several terms have been used to describe adventure therapy. Among these are experiential challenge program (Roland et al., 1987), adventure education (Sugarman, 1988), adventure programming (Witman, 1987), adventure/challenge therapy (Smith, 1987), wilderness therapy (Russell, 2000), wilderness adventure therapy, outdoor recreation therapy (Beriger & Martin, 2003), therapeutic outdoor programming (Ewert, Voight, & Harnishfeger, 2002), and adventure therapy (Alvarez & Stauffer, 2001; Ewert, et al., 2001; Gass, 1993; Groff & Dattilo, 2011; Itin, 2001; Newes & Bandoroff, 2004).

Likewise, many definitions have been set forth by authors in the area. Groff and Dattilo (2011) seem to best capture the essence of this approach to therapy. They have defined adventure therapy as:

> an action-centered approach to treatment that is used within the field of therapeutic recreation (TR). As opposed to other more verbally based therapies, adventure therapy encourages individuals to become mentally and physically engaged in adventure activities. The unfamiliar nature of these activities, combined with the sense of community developed during participation in activities, creates a climate in which individuals can challenge their current perceptions and behaviors, and affords them an opportunity to modify those behaviors (p. 15).

The most evident component reflected in the definitions of this modality is *active engagement* in a *risk or adventure activity* (i.e., an unusual experience with apparent danger) through which *individuals seek change*. Typically this is in an outdoor activity that participants *perceive as challenging*, although Alvarez and Stauffer (2001) have stated risk is not always a part of adventure therapy as some participants may prefer to stay in their "comfort zones."

Elements in adventure therapy that have been emphasized by Groff and Dattilo (2011) include (a) the novel nature of the activity that produces a sense of disequilibrium; (b) an environment that emphasizes community and cooperation; (c) the demand of problem solving; (d) feelings of accomplishment; (e) changes in behaviors, thoughts, or feelings resulting from participation and processing.

When the new or *novel nature* of adventure activities is emphasized it signals that this therapy is different from anything the clients have done before. This alone may provide clients with hope that this unique approach may lead to different outcomes than they have previously encountered in other forms of treatment. Doing something not previously experienced may also produce feelings of disequilibrium (i.e., discomfort) that will likely motivate the client to change in order to reduce these feelings. The novel situation forces clients to think and act in new ways (Ewert et al., 2001). The *sense of community and cooperation* comes from an environment that stresses interdependence and group cohesion. This environment results out of the nature of the activities and the atmosphere created by the leader facilitating the group. Most adventure activities demand group *problem solving*. Success in problem solving results in *feelings of accomplishment* that may lead to feelings of pride and enhanced self-esteem. *Changes occur* in clients as they transfer or generalize insights gained from their participation in adventure activities into other parts of their lives. Discussing thoughts and feelings stimulated by their participation often helps clients to gain insights that may not otherwise be apparent to them. This is termed *processing* on their experiences. Processing usually involves debriefing following taking part in the activity.

Adventure Therapy Program Benefits

A number of benefits resulting from adventure therapy programs have been identified by researchers. These include: enhanced self-confidence and self-esteem; increased feelings of self-efficacy and empowerment; enhanced social skills and greater trust, teamwork, and cooperation; improved problem-solving skills; better coping skills; increased locus of control; enhanced academic performance; increased muscular strength and cardiovascular efficiency; more realistic perception of self; reduced obsessive-compulsive behavior; decreased anxiety and depression; less disorganized thinking; recognition of personal values; reduced recidivism among adjudicated adolescents; and reduced deviant behavior (Autry, 2001; Caldwell, 2001; Chakravorty, Trunnell, & Ellis, 1995; Dattilo & Murphy, 1987; Ewert, 1987; Ewert, McCormick, & Voight, 2001; Gillis & Simpson, 1993; Winn, 1982; Witman, 1987; Witman & Munson, 1992).

Following their review of the literature, Groff and Dattilo (2011) concluded:

A considerable amount of research has been conducted to investigate effects of adventure therapy. The application of meta-analyses and longitudinal surveys in recent years provides evidence to support adventure therapy as an empirically based facilitation technique. The two consistently substantiated treatment outcomes are improved self-concept and internal locus of control. (p. 33)

Processing

The term **processing** is sometimes used to describe the procedure of debriefing groups following participation in an activity. However, authors such as Gass (1993) and Hutchinson and Dattilo (2001) have taken a broader perspective of processing that covers all techniques used, not only following the activity but before and during it, to enhance the therapeutic qualities found in the adventure experience. Hutchinson and Dattilo have written that "the traditional group discussion (following an activity) is but one of a myriad of strategies, activities, and techniques that are intentionally used to provide participants opportunities to reflect on, interpret, and make inferences about their experiences" (p. 44). The term processing then may be employed as a general expression to encompass any number of techniques including frontloading or framing, debriefing, providing feedback, and using metaphors that help clients to learn about themselves or gain personal insights from engaging in activities.

Helping clients focus their awareness on relevant therapy issues prior to the activity so they can work on changing their behavior during the activity is a type of processing referred to as frontloading (Hutchinson & Dattilo, 2001) or framing (Gass, 1993). Priest and Gass (1997) have also employed the term *prebriefing* to describe this technique of providing clients with a "heads up" prior to the activity so that they become aware of issues or experiences they may encounter.

Roland, Keene, Dubois, and Lentini (1988), Roland et al. (1987), Luckner and Nadler (1995), Nadler and Luckner (1997), Smith (1987), and Witman (1987) have all stressed the critical nature of **debriefing** following activities in order for clients to achieve benefit from adventure therapy. Roland and his colleagues (1987) emphasized that activities serve as a bridge or address important client issues. Debriefing permits participants to express their feelings, such as being supported or being pressured by the group. Being able to talk things out provides group members with opportunities to express their perceptions and to raise and resolve conflicts.

The leader can and should participate in the debriefing, but the group members must take primary responsibility for the discussion. It is only when the group's discussion bogs down that the leader should step in. Even when it is appropriate to assert himself or herself into the discussion, it should be to stimulate the group members to come to understandings on their own. The leader does not resolve dilemmas for the group but raises questions or makes statements aimed at stimulating discussion within a group.

In Witman's (1987) program for adolescent psychiatric patients, the following three questions were used to stimulate discussion and insights: "How was the session for you?" "What did you most/least enjoy?", and "What were some of your feelings during the activities?" (p. 25). Smith (1987) has suggested that leaders may wish to structure activities, such as candle ceremonies, to promote processing and bring closure to the session. It would seem that processing could be enhanced if activities were chosen that might lead to the discussion of issues with which the group as a whole or individual members were dealing.

The books *Cowstails and Cobras II* (Rohnke, 1989) and *Islands of Healing: A Guide to Adventure-Based Counseling* (Schoel, Prouty, & Radcliffe, 1988) both emphasize the importance of sequencing in debriefing because group members need to warm up before they are ready to deal with difficult issues. Borrowing from earlier work by Terry Borton, authors of these books propose the use of the sequence of the questions, "What?", "So What?", and "Now What?" This sequencing approach to debriefing is detailed in the section on Group Processing found in Chapter 7. Also found in the group processing discussion in Chapter 7 are approaches to processing during the activity (i.e., stop-action and reframing) as well as the use of metaphors.

Types of Adventure Activities

What specific activities are found in adventure therapy programs? While many different activities may be used, among the most popular have been trust activities (e.g., trust walks and falls); cooperative activities (e.g., "lap sit"); group problem-solving tasks (e.g., "human knot"); initiative games (e.g., "electric fence" and "wall"); low ropes courses (which involve maintaining balance while moving across a course made of rope, wire, and wooden beams that has been constructed a few feet off the ground); and high-adventure activities (e.g., rappelling, caving, high ropes courses, zip lines, tree climbs, kayaking, and wilderness camping) (Robb, 1980; Robb, Leslie, & McGowan, n.d.; Roland et al., 1987; Sugarman, 1988; Winn, 1982; Witman, 1987).

Havens' (1992) *Bridges to Accessibility* and Ellmo and Graser's (1995) *Adapted Adventure Activities* provide suggested program adaptations for persons with disabilities. These books cover the analysis and modification of a wide variety of adventure activities.

Implications for Recreational Therapy

Some of the early leading advocates for adventure therapy were from the recreational therapy profession. Two pioneers in the area were Gary Robb and Jeff Witman. Robb and his staff at Indiana University's Bradford Woods had extensive experience in using adventure activities as interventions and in training others on how to utilize the approach. Witman, while he was a practitioner in New Hampshire, conducted and researched adventure therapy programs in a psychiatric facility.

Work by Robb, Witman, and others has shown great promise for the use of adventure therapy, particularly with adolescents. However, the use of adventure therapy should be approached with caution by those without extensive training and experience in its application. Recreational therapists should seek consultation and training from those with expertise in the practice of adventure therapy before initiating programs.

Principles that guide adventure therapy can be applied with groups in other types of therapeutic activities. One is that activities are focused on providing challenges that lead to the achievement of positive outcomes. Providing activities that offer a challenge but are still within reach of clients is a principle that can be applied throughout recreational therapy programming. A related principle is that clients, and children in particular, find a great deal of interest in new and unusual activities, such as those employed in adventure therapy (Street, Gold, & Manning, 1997).

Another principle is that, while the leader's role is critical, the emphasis remains on the participants who are seen as agents for their own change and who assume increasing levels of responsibility for their treatment as time goes on. The focus in recreational therapy always remains on the clients, who are expected to be responsible for bringing about changes in themselves while taking greater responsibility for change throughout the treatment process.

A third principle from adventure therapy is that processing is a critical part of the clients' total experience. Learning from experiences gained during recreational therapy programs can be enhanced by processing the activities. Gains can be reinforced and feelings, behaviors, and cognitions that need to be altered can be brought to the attention of clients as a result of group processing. In fact, without processing, there is the danger that recreational therapy activities may become purely divisional.

Assertiveness Training

Assertiveness training is an offshoot of behavioral therapy that helps people to become more assertive in social relationships, sexual expression, work-related interactions, or other social situations. Assertiveness training helps persons to change habits or behaviors, allowing them to stand up for their legitimate rights and the rights of others. This new assertiveness, in turn, purportedly makes people feel better about themselves, thus increasing feelings of self-esteem.

Nonassertive behaviors are usually reflected by a passive or aggressive manner. Passive persons display submissive actions, inability to communicate in social situations, difficulty in maintaining eye contact, and fear of rejection. Those who are aggressive lash out at others to meet their own needs while having little concern for others. Assertive individuals stand up for themselves, while at the same time being considerate of the needs of others (Waughfield & Burckhalter, 2002). Milne (1999), a British author, has written, "Assertive behavior is neither aggressive or passive, but it is concerned with clear, honest, direct communication" (p. 92). Learning to respond in an assertive fashion begins with the client identifying situations in which he or she wishes to respond more assertively.

The helper then assists the client to examine irrational beliefs behind timid or aggressive behavior and to identify more rational beliefs. Once this is completed, the helper and client identify proper assertive responses that may be made. Role playing with feedback, video examples, rehearsal modeling, and reinforcement are some of the techniques used to establish new assertive responses. A regularly used strategy in assertiveness training is to help an individual learn to stand up for their rights without infringing on the rights of others by having them use "I messages" rather than "you messages" in order for the person to take responsibility for their own feelings and not cast blame on others. When the client has demonstrated assertive responses repeatedly within assertiveness training sessions, he or she is encouraged to try out his or her behavior in real-life situations. Successful clients put aside their inhibitions about responding assertively in all types of circumstances as newly learned behavioral tendencies generalize to other situations (Eisenberg & Delaney, 1986; Cormier & Hackney, 1999; Hutchins, 2011).

While a comprehensive research review on assertiveness training was not found, studies have reported assertiveness training being successfully employed with clinical populations such as patients being treated for alcoholism (Adinolfi, McCount & Geoghegan, 1976; Hirsch, Rosenberg, Phelan, & Dudley, 1978), persons with disabilities (Glueckauf & Quittner, 1993), persons with eating disorders (Shiina et al., 2005), hospitalized psychiatric patients (Lin et al., 2008), nursing home residents with depression (Segal, 2005), and patients who were both depressed and sub-assertive (Sanchez, Lewinsohn, & Larson, 2012).

Implications for Recreational Therapy

Assertiveness training provides a model for helping people reduce anxiety by developing responses that will enable them to responsibly say and do what they wish. Recreational therapists can easily allow for opportunities for clients to practice healthy assertiveness and can encourage and reinforce this behavior. Hutchins (2011) has indicated assertiveness skills can be of value to clients who: (a) have difficulty expressing their needs; (b) could benefit from increased self-esteem; (c) have difficulty with interpersonal relations; (d) have anxiety levels that limit their satisfaction with social situations; and (e) lack skills in other areas of social interaction (p. 242). Recreational therapists may also wish to gain skills to conduct assertiveness training. Assertiveness training has been suggested as a technique to be used in leisure counseling (Connolly, 1977).

Social Skills Training

Michael Argyle, British social psychologist, is most commonly associated with the beginnings of **social skills training** (SST). The origins of SST came from the emergence of the behavioral approach, research on the connection between social competence and psychiatric problems, and social psychology research on verbal and nonverbal communication (Hollin & Trower, 1986).

Strong support exists for the efficacy of SST. As early as 1988, it was reported: "A large body of research supports the efficacy of social skills training for schizophrenia and other serious and persistent mental disorders" (Liberman & Martin, 1988, p. 149). A 2006 article by Kopelowicz, Liberman, and Zarate, reported SST "has been empirically validated for a broad range of mental disorders and other psychological problems" (p. S12). Further, these authors indicated that the SST generalized to everyday life when opportunities were given to practice the skills and encouragement and reinforcement were provided. Results from a meta-analysis of research on SST for schizophrenia by Kurtz and Mueser (2008) were found to "support the efficacy of social skills training for Improving psychosocial functioning in schizophrenia" (p. 491).

Many people receiving recreational therapy (RT) services display deficits in social skills. Sneegas (1989) listed the following types of RT clients who often have social skills deficiencies: those who are chemically dependent; persons with intellectual disabilities; residents in long-term care facilities; individuals experiencing problems in mental health (particularly depression or schizophrenia); and children with learning disabilities. Such clients may profit from social skills training. In addition, social skills training has been used with managers, teachers, social workers, medical doctors, and other professionals (Harré & Lamb, 1986), as well as with those experiencing developmental difficulties through the life span. Adolescents and young adults anxious about heterosexual relationships and elderly persons making adjustments to aging are examples of such populations (Hollin & Trower, 1986).

Definitions of Social Skills and Reasons for Deficits

What are social skills? Lecroy and Archer (2001) have defined social skills "as socially acceptable behaviors that enable a person to engage in effective interactions with others and to avoid socially unacceptable responses from others" (p. 331). Social skills may be clustered under the headings of (a) attending and listening, (b) conversation, (c) supporting others, (d) problem solving, and (e) self-control (Stein & Cutler, 1998). Whether for children or adults, social skills are then those competencies employed in relating effectively to others. Social skills are interpersonal or interactive skills.

Hewitt (1988) listed five characteristics of social skills. First, social skills behaviors are goal directed or are performed in order to achieve a specific purpose (e.g., smiling and moving closer are directed toward the goal of achieving friendship). Second, each social behavior relates to a goal and, therefore, should be interrelated and synchronized with other behaviors (e.g., the smile and moving closer together are seen to relate to the common goal of achieving friendship). Third, social skills, similar to motor skills, may be broken down into parts (e.g., the social skill of making friends is composed of smaller elements ranging from making eye contact to asking personal questions). Fourth, social skills are learned behaviors that are reinforced in ways that motivate the individual to choose the most appropriate social response (e.g., some behaviors are more appropriate in making friends with someone of the same sex than someone of the opposite sex). Fifth, social skills are under the control of the individual (e.g., the individual does not apply social skills to form friendships in situations where friendship would not be appropriate).

What are reasons for social skills deficits? Anxiety, depression, confusion, and psychotic reactions may contribute to diminished social skills for clients who have undergone psychiatric difficulties. For some individuals, the skills may simply have never been learned (Birrell & Henderson, 1986). Still others have social skills, but negative experiences have convinced them that they lack these skills (Myers, 1996).

Social Skill Instruction

Social skills training is directed toward the correction of problems encountered in performing social skills with the aim of improvement both in social functioning and the way the person feels about himself or herself (Duck, 1998). SST involves the teaching of skills of social interaction through a planned and systematic method that reflects social psychology, Bandura's (1986) social learning theory, and contemporary pedagogic procedures.

SST consists of using *modeling* or *demonstrations* by competent persons, *role playing* by group members acting out previously modeled behaviors, *feedback* from others or from video recordings, *instruction* in the form of comments to improve performance, *social reinforcement* to provide positive feedback for achieving established standards, and *homework* to practice new skills in real-life situations (Birrell & Henderson, 1986). Steps in the SST approach have been identified by Sneegas (1989) as

1. assessment of the problem area,
2. task analysis of the behavioral components necessary to achieve the social skill,
3. introduction to the social skill and a rationale for the learning of the social skill are given to the client,
4. demonstration and modeling of specific social behaviors,
5. practice and rehearsal of the new behavior,
6. provision of feedback and reinforcement of the behavior, and
7. generalization to a variety of situations.

In a chapter on social skills training, Stumbo and Wardlaw (2011), drawning on the work of Stephens (1978), detailed an eight-step model for conducting social skills training. The eight steps are as follows: (1) Target appropriate individuals (e.g., adults with mental illness, children with ASD); (2) Identify behaviors for SST (e.g., social skills problems such as withdrawal, aggression or socially unacceptable deviant behaviors); (3) Task-analyze the identified behaviors (i.e., determine components of the behaviors and set criteria for successful completion); (4) Assess skill levels possessed by clients (i.e., evaluate if clients possess skills at the level of accepted criteria); (5) Where skill levels are not attained, select a strategy to teach the skill (e.g., demonstration, role playing, using social reinforcement); (6) Implement the strategy (i.e., teach the skill to the clients using the strategy selected); (7) Reassess the clients' skill levels (i.e., reassess following instruction to determine clients' achievement levels and reformulate teaching strategies if needed); and (8) Once clients succeed with a skill, another is chosen for instruction. Stumbo and Wardlaw's presentation provides examples of worksheets that can be used in implementation of the eight-step model.

Witman and Lee (1988) have provided a detailed description of a psychiatric hospital social skills group operated by an occupational therapy/therapeutic recreation department. Schleien and Wehman (1986) have discussed how social skills may be facilitated for children with severe disabilities through leisure skill programs. In their book, *Game Play: Therapeutic Use of Childhood Games,* Schaefer and Reid (2001) suggest that games are a highly effective means to teach social skills to children. They have described in detail the *Social Skills Game* through which children can learn social skills while they play.

Implications for Recreational Therapy

The use of social skills training has become widespread in recreational therapy (Kinney, Kinney, & Witman, 2004). Articles by Schleien and Wehman (1986), Sneegas (1989), and Witman and Lee (1988) display that SST may be successfully used as a technique to help people receiving recreational therapy.

The tradition of recreational therapy shares much in common with social skills training. The development of social competence has long been seen as an important goal of recreational therapists who have attempted to develop social skills in their clients through various means (although not formally utilizing the SST model). The development of social skills has been viewed by both recreational therapy and SST as a means to enhance self-esteem as clients take pride in their abilities to gain new skills and receive social reinforcement during social interactions.

Cognitive Rehabilitation

Cognitive rehabilitation is an approach employed with clients with acquired brain injury (ABI), particularly traumatic brain injury (TBI), to assist in their neuropsychological recovery. Sohlberg and Mateer (2001) have commented that impairments caused by brain injury "can profoundly affect an individual's daily functioning" (p. 7). Those with brain injury commonly experience impairments in attention and memory, as well as their abilities to initiate, plan, organize, and regulate their behaviors. *Executive functions* is the term used to capture this behavioral aspect. Sohlberg and Mateer (2001) have explained that executive functions

> constitute a superordinate system that mediates self-initiated behavior and governs the efficiency and appropriateness of task performance. Executive function deficits emerge most clearly in circumstances where strong response sets are developed and appropriate set shifting depends on the monitoring of outcomes. Executive functions are also stressed when successful performance requires maintenance of attention over time, prevention of distraction, and organization of information.... It incorporates basic capabilities, such as working memory and inhibitory control, as well as complex overarching abilities, such as planning, organizing, and self-monitoring. (p. 111)

No single occupational group has the comprehensive training to conduct cognitive rehabilitation so it is provided as a team effort by a number of disciplines, including recreational therapists. All professionals doing cognitive rehabilitation use the principle of empowerment. As Sohlberg and Mateer have stated, "Interventions should have as their ultimate goal an increase in skill or knowledge, a belief, a change in behavior, and/or the use of a compensatory strategy that will increase or improve some aspect of independent function (p. 7).

Toglia and Golisz (1990) have emphasized that brain injury is particularly disruptive to interpersonal or social functioning. Individuals with head injuries often have a difficult time processing all the relatively subtle cues that are part of the social situation. Their book, *Cognitive Rehabilitation: Group Games and Activities,* contains many group games and activities that can be used with brain-injured individuals to help them to function socially. Of the use of games, they have written, "Games stimulate motivation and interest while providing a meaningful context in which behaviors can be tried out and practiced. Life situations and problems can be confronted in a nonthreatening environment" (p. 17). They go on to stress that games and activities also allow clients to gain insights regarding their strengths and weaknesses, overcome the self-centered behavior that sometimes accompanies brain injury, build ability to control behavior, and develop more flexible thinking. One particularly interesting portion of Toglia and Golisz's book for recreational therapists is an eight-session leisure education module that contains several work sheets for client use.

Recreational therapists doing cognitive rehabilitation typically employ a functional approach involving everyday activities, such as games and community recreational outings. As Sohlberg and Mateer (2001) have explained, "Combining therapeutic cognitive and motor activities may approximate the demands of everyday life more closely than artificially separating them in separate therapy sessions" (p. 9).

Research reviews have shown there is clear evidence of the effectiveness multidisciplinary cognitive rehabilitation interventions (McCabe et al., 2007; Rees et al., 2007; Turner-Stokes,

2008). All reviews however reported that there continues to be a need for well-designed efficacy studies on the effect of cognitive rehabilitation. Research reviews (Limond & Leeke, 2005; Laatsch et al., 2007) focusing on cognitive rehabilitation for children with acquired brain injury have indicated the need for additional efficacy research is particularly apparent to examine cognitive rehabilitation programs for children with acquired brain injury.

Implications for Recreational Therapy

Recreational therapists who work with clients with traumatic brain injuries will apply cognitive rehabilitation methods with the aim of improving the functional abilities of those they serve. As members of the rehabilitation team, it is likely that recreational therapists will take the lead in the application of games and activities to enhance clients' leisure awareness and social functioning and in conducting community reintegration programs.

Animal-Assisted Therapy

The first use of animals in therapy occurred in a hospital in Belgian in the 11th century where patients cared for birds. From there it spread throughout Europe (Grandgeorge & Hausberger, 2011). The most documented example of the early use of animals in therapy is the Quaker Society of Friends York Retreat in England where, in 1792, animals such as birds and rabbits were used in the humane treatment of psychiatric patients (Hooker, Freeman, & Stewart, 2002; Velde, Cipriani, & Fisher, 2005). Two instances of the use of animals in therapy occurred In Germany in the 1800s. One was in a home for people with epilepsy (Brodie & Riley, 1999). The other, in 1867, was at the Bethel Institute, in Bielefeld, where not only dogs, cats, and birds were used in therapy but farm activities and an equestrian center were available (Grandgeorge & Hausberger, 2011). Even Florence Nightingale, the mother of nursing, is mentioned in history as having recognized the value of pets In the treatment of chronically ill patients (Pichot, 2012).

The history of the use of pets in therapy in the United States began in 1919 when dogs were used with psychiatric patients at St. Elizabeth's Hospital in Washington, DC (Hooker, Freeman, & Stewart, 2002). In the 1940s, the Pawling Army Air Force Hospital in New York used horseback riding and the caring for farm animals in the treatment of WWII veterans (Grandgeorge & Hausberger, 2011; Hooker, Freeman, & Stewart, 2002). Scientific investigation of the therapeutic use of animals awaited until American psychiatrist Boris Levinson began his work in the second half of the 20th century. Levinson, who is known as the father of animal-assisted therapy, employed dogs in his therapy. Levinson's contributions gave legitimacy to the therapeutic use of pets and inspired American psychiatrists Samuel and Elizabeth Corson who furthered Levinson's work in their investigations of the use of pets in their hospital practice. Their research included finding a decreased need for psychotropic drugs following the introduction of pet therapy (Grandgeorge & Hausberger, 2011; Hooker, Freeman, & Stewart, 2002).

More recently, in the 1990s, Dr. William Thomas used animals as a part of the long-term care program at the well-known Eden Alternative. Also, in the 1990s, the American Medical Association brought forth the benefits of animal-assisted therapy found in the treatment of health care facilities in Chicago, including Schwab Rehabilitation Hospital, Grant Hospital, the Shriner's Hospital, and the Rehabilitation Institute of Chicago (Velde, Cipriani & Fisher, 2005). **Animal-assisted therapy** (AAT) today is enjoying a rise in popularity (Palley, O'Rourke, & Niemi, 2010). It is being employed with clients of all ages in a variety of settings including hospitals, rehabilitation institutes, assisted living facilities, nursing facilities, group homes, special schools, and day care programs for elders. Occasionally, the terms *animal-facilitated therapy* or *pet-facilitated therapy* will be used to describe animal-assisted therapy. Nevertheless, animal-assisted therapy seems to be the most widely used in the literature and in practice.

The term animal-assisted therapy (AAT) connotes it is a goal-directed intervention that is employed as a part of the client's overall intervention plan. It facilitates the client's progress toward a specific therapeutic goal. In contrast, animal-assisted activities (AAA) are not directed toward meeting a specific treatment objective for an individual client. There are no specific treatment goals and programs are spontaneous (DeCourcey, Russell, & Keister, 2010; Kruger & Serpell, 2010).

Because animal-assisted therapy has been found to be effective in working with clients who have not been able to establish satisfying social relationships, it has been used extensively as a means to reach persons who are lonely, isolated, or withdrawn (Jessee, 1982; Robb, Boyd, & Pristash, 1980). The accepting, nonthreatening tendencies of pets are ideal to meet the needs of nonsocial clients.

Pets tend to seek attention, eagerly respond to attention, and are very accepting. McCandless, McCready, and Knight (1985) have explained, "Animals naturally respond to their caretakers with a trusting innocence, unconditional love, affection and acceptance without judgment, criticism or unreasonable demands" (p. 56). Perhaps animals, with their nonjudgmental natures, represent the ultimate in Rogerian therapy!

Goals of animal-assisted therapy include the following:

- forming bonds with a loving pet;
- reducing hospital stays;
- increasing social interaction and communications;
- improving social skills;
- heightening emotional expression, particularly joy and pleasure;
- decreasing depression, anxiety, and confusion;
- decreasing pain;
- enhancing self-confidence and self-esteem;
- maintaining contact with reality;
- developing attitudes toward birth and death;
- reducing feelings of alienation;
- decreasing feelings of loneliness;
- providing diversional activity;
- learning responsibility, cooperation, and social skills;
- experiencing self-expression and trust;
- maintaining responsibility and impulse control;
- increasing memory recall;
- providing sensory stimulation;
- reducing tension and stress;
- inducing calm;
- increasing attention/concentration;
- increasing range of motion;
- lowering blood pressure, pulse, and heart rate; and
- increasing strength, mobility, coordination, and balance.

(Beck, 2000; Brokie & Biley, 1999; Buettner, Fitzsimmons, & Barba, 2011; Center for Pet Therapy, n.d.; DeCourcey, Russell, & Keister, 2010; Fontaine & Kaszubski, 2004; Frisch, 2002; Geist, 2011; Kruger & Serpell, 2010; Pichot, 2012; Snyder & Lindquist, 2006; Stanley-Hermanns & Miller, 2002; Velde, Cipriani, & Fisher, 2005.)

A growing number of investigations have been conducted on animal-assisted therapy (AAT). Several research reviews of AAT have reported positive findings. Nimer and Lundahl (2007) reported from their review that there was support for AAT showing Improvement in "autism spectrum symptoms, medical difficulties, behavioral problems, and emotional well-being" (p. 225). Brodie and Biley (1999) concluded from their review of the research that the positive benefits of AAT "are considerable" (p. 329). Grandgeorge and Hausberger (2011) wrote after their review of AAT studies that "The literature is now abundant and multidisciplinary" (p. 400). Finally, DeCourcey, Russell, and Keister wrote in their research review that: "Currently, no evidence that refutes the benefits of AAT could be found" (p. 212).

A number of studies have been conducted on elderly populations in long-term care facilities. A study of nursing home patients with dementia found animal-assisted therapy brought about improvements in levels of mood and alertness, along with higher levels of enjoyment, reality orientation, and patient-staff interactions (Furstenburg, Rhodes, Powell, & Dunlop, 1984). Fick (1993) reported the presence of a dog increased verbal interactions of nursing home residents. Clay (1997) reported on another nursing home study where statistically significant decreases in depression, anxiety, and confusion resulted from twice-weekly visits by animals. Results from still another nursing home study by Richeson and McCullough (2003) revealed residents experienced significant increases in their overall satisfaction with life and on feelings of being interested, excited, attentive, and inspired. Banks and Banks (2002) reported AAT decreased loneliness and Le Roux and Kemp (2009) found positive effects of companion dogs on depression among elderly residents in long-term care facilities. In a veterans' home study, Kongable, Buckwalter, and Stolley (1989) found that the social behaviors of Alzheimer's residents increased due to the presence of a dog.

Studies by recreational therapy researchers have also revealed the effectiveness of animal-assisted therapy. A study was conducted by Barker and Dawson (1998) on AAT sessions as a part of a recreational therapy program with hospitalized clients. These researchers found significantly significant reductions in anxiety for clients with a variety of psychiatric disorders. Richeson (2003) reported decreases in agitated behaviors and increases in social interactions by nursing home residents with dementia. Petterson and Loy (2008) found a calming response from AAT for individuals with Alzheimer's disease. Buettner and her research team (2011) indicated perceived benefits of AAT in an oncology waiting room included helping time to more quickly pass, feeling more comfortable at the cancer center, cognitive stimulation, and reductions in pain and anxiety. In a case study on therapeutic horseback riding for an adolescent girl with traumatic brain injury, Malkin, Lloyd, and Gerstenberger (2011) reported increases in attention and memory.

AAT programs using specific types of animals are found in the literature. For example, McKinney, Dustin, and Wolff (2001) summarized the results of research done on dolphin-assisted therapy. They stated, "...dolphin-assisted therapy aids in reducing stress and increasing relaxation, alleviating depression, boosting production of infection fighting T-cells, stimulating production of endorphins and hormones, enhancing recovery, and reducing pain" (p. 49). Those conducting therapeutic riding programs for children with disabilities have found physical benefits such as improvements in strength, balance, and mobility. Gains in hand coordination, muscle function, and ambulatory skills have been reported for clients working with dogs (Beck, 2000). The attracting and viewing of wildlife may have a positive effect on the morale of clients (Cable & Udd, 1988). Even birds have been known to have a calming effect on people (Beck, 2000).

An emerging area is the use of robotic animals in animal-assisted therapy. Will robotic therapy provide an alternative to traditional animal-assisted treatments? That question is addressed in a later segment in this chapter on intervening with technology.

In their chapter in Dattilo and McKenney's book on facilitation techniques, Cory, McKenney, and Marsden (2011) offer considerations that can be employed to structure programs involving the therapeutic use of animals. Included are the selection and care of the animals and the training of group facilitators. For those wishing to do animal-assisted activities, the book *Starting a Visiting-Animal Group* (Howie, 2000) provides a step-by-step approach for volunteers who wish to implement a visiting-animal program. Another resource is the Delta Society, proclaimed by Cole (1993) to be "the most progressive nonprofit organization advocating the use of animals to help people promote their health, increase independence, and improve quality of life...." (p. 509). Cole has recommended consulting with a Delta-certified animal evaluator when initiating a program.

Implications for Recreational Therapy

Animal-assisted therapy has direct implications for recreational therapists who may employ it with a wide variety of clients. It is a relatively inexpensive program that has shown promise of bringing about therapeutic outcomes. As Damon and May (1986) have remarked with "tongue in cheek": "The use of pets for therapeutic purpose represents an interactional therapy that draws upon an abundant resource. Unwanted dogs and cats can be made available for more hours at a much lower cost and in greater numbers than psychiatrists, nurses, poets, and others. . ." (p. 130).

Aquatic Therapy

Aquatic therapy uses the environment of water for treatment and rehabilitation. This therapy involves far more than just swimming. It is an intervention by which treatment and rehabilitation goals are reached through passive and active motor activities in pools. Benefits of aquatic therapy include both improved physical and psychosocial functioning. Physical benefits that may be derived are increased pulmonary functioning, muscle strength, endurance, energy, agility, aerobic capacity, flexibility, relaxation, range of motion, mobility, balance, and coordination. Psychological benefits that have been identified are decreased depression, enhanced mood, greater locus of control, enhanced self-concept, enhanced self-esteem, greater confidence, socialization, decreased perceptions of pain, decreased perceptions of fatigue, and improved body image (Becker, 2009; Broach & Dattilo, 1996; Broach & Dattilo, 2011; Broach & Dattilo, 2001; Broach & Dattilo, 2003; Broach & Dattilo, 2011a; Broach, Dattilo, & McKenney, 2007; Kelly, 2005; Moon, 2010; Veenstra, Brasile, & Stewart, 2003; Yurcicin, 1995; Zych, Yang, & Malkin, 2011). Additionally, Eveik et al. (2008) and Yurcicin (1995) have claimed that clients often have greater motivation to actively engage in their treatment programs when they begin to experience functional gains and enjoyment through participation in aquatic therapy.

Aquatic therapy has been used to treat chronic pain, arthritis, fibromyalgia, multiple sclerosis, heart disease, high blood pressure, asthma, obesity, diabetes, chronic fatigue, and depression. It is also used in the rehabilitation of clients who have had strokes, amputations, spinal cord injuries, brain injuries, mastectomies, multiple sclerosis, bone loss, hip or knee replacements, and athletic injuries (Becker, 2009; Broach & Dattilo, 2001; Broach & Dattilo, 2003; Broach & Dattilo, 2011a; Broach, Dattilo, & McKenney, 2007; Driver et al., 2004; Sova, 2000; Veenstra, Brasile, & Stewart, 2003). Becker (2009), in his extensive review of the research, has indicated the effectiveness of aquatic exercise has been studied extensively with individuals with arthritis and fibromyalgia and is especially firmly established in treating these populations. He has also stated that aquatic exercise is particularly appropriate for obese persons as it is safe, effective, and minimizes the risk of joint injury.

While many can benefit from aquatic therapy, recreational therapists need to be aware of contraindications and precautions. Broach and Dattilo (2011a) have written:

> Water activity is contraindicated for individuals with open wounds, unstabilized bowel incontinence, a disease transmissible by water, hepatitis A, certain skin conditions, open tracheotomies, and unstable blood pressure. In addition, TR specialists conducting aquatic therapy must closely monitor participants with cardiac conditions, high/low blood pressure, loss of sensation, epilepsy, body temperature regulation problems, urinary tract infections, bladder incontinence, fear of the water, intravenous lines, vital lung capacity of less than one-third of nominal for the individual, and those who are subject to fatigue. (p. 72)

Elements that are often mentioned (Becker, 2009; Kelly, 2005; Moon, 2010; Veenstra, Brasile, & Stewart, 2003) as being particularly helpful to the success of aquatic therapy are the warmth of the water, the water's natural buoyancy, and uniform resistance offered clients by the water. The warmth of the water (typically 33.5–35.5 C) decreases sensitivity and perceptions of pain and reduces muscle tone, which allows more efficient movement. The buoyancy of water reduces the force of gravity that clients encounter on land, allowing them to function in ways that they could not on land. The buoyancy of individuals in water has great therapeutic utility. Buoyancy permits participants to take the weight and pressure off of their joints and other parts of their bodies, thus permitting them to stand, walk, jog, and generally move with a maximum of independence and a minimum of pain or discomfort. Water also offers clients a "constant, uniform resistance, which stimulates the body to gain added strength and endurance by performing specific exercises" (Yurcicin, 1995, p. 50).

Aquatic therapy sessions may be one-on-one or in a group. A suggested format for aquatic therapy sessions has been presented by Beaudouin and Keller (1994):

> All treatment interventions begin and end with warm-up and cool-down periods (approximately five minutes each) consisting of simple stretching, toning, and flexibility exercises. Main workouts commonly start with range of motion exercises, followed by strength and/or endurance training (15-35 minutes). All activities focus on individuals' physical and psychosocial needs and goals. (p. 197)

A continuing trend exists to use community facilities for aquatic therapy (Sova, 2000). In this day of health care cost containment, it makes sense to use existing community aquatic facilities for therapeutic programs (Becker & Cole, 1997). Such facilities can be full-service health and wellness centers, as they serve a full spectrum of clients ranging from those who need very specific treatment for musculoskeletal injuries to those along the continuum of services who can use the pool for health maintenance. Because community aquatic facilities are often underused, they offer an opportunity for recreational therapists to provide aquatic therapy services that otherwise might not be provided. It is fortunate that, due to the Americans with Disabilities Act, many community-based aquatic facilities have been made accessible to persons with disabilities.

Implications for Recreational Therapy

Aquatic therapy has an extensive research base but, according to Becker (2009), it is "vastly underused despite its recent increase in popularity" (p. 867). Greater use of aquatic therapy by recreational therapists has been suggested. For example, Moon (2010) has advocated for the use of aquatic exercise for those with mental illnesses. Funderburk and Callis (2010) have proposed using aquatic interventions with individuals who are obese. As with any intervention that is gaining popularity, recreational therapists should not initiate aquatic therapy programs simply because they are becoming more widely adopted. If it is determined that an agency's clients can benefit from the introduction of aquatic therapy, then it is important that staff acquire proper training in order to gain the skills necessary to deliver quality programs. Many professional organizations offer workshops and short courses in aquatic therapy. An excellent source of information on aquatic therapy is the chapter by Broach and Dattilo (2011a) in Dattilo and McKenney's book on facilitation techniques.

Intervening With Technology

As science and technology change, so will recreational therapy practice. While it is highly unlikely that technology will ever replace recreational therapists, it is likely to significantly influence what they do. The therapeutic use of technology is an emerging area of recreational therapy. Innovations covered in this section involve the use of video games, video productions, computers, Snoezelen rooms, robotic therapy, and assistive technology.

Video Games

"Wiihabilitation" is a term coined to describe the use of Nintendo's Wii™ (pronounced "we") video game system. The Wii wireless remote control lets players generate a large number of motions, just as they would in real-life actions in playing games such as bowling, baseball, tennis, and golf. The interactive controller device permits those playing to manipulate on-screen actions. For instance, when playing golf the participant swings the controller in a fashion similar to using a real golf club (Grohol, 2008). This "real-life" element of the motion-sensitive controller allows players to really become engrossed in the game, often competing against others. In the spring of 2008, Nintendo introduced its Wii Fit bundle that included software and a pressure-sensitive Wii Balance Board. About the size of a bathroom scale, the Balance Board is a wireless battery-operated device that measures both the player's weight and center of balance. Wii Fit™ has over 40 activities including aerobic exercises, yoga, strength training, and balance games of various types. Features of the Wii Fit system allow participants to create a personal profile and to track daily progress. It also permits participants to check their Body Mass Index (BMI) (Lammers, 2008; Nintendo, 2008).

According to Tanner (2008a), use of the Wii video system "is fast becoming a craze in rehab therapy for patients recovering from strokes, broken bones, surgery, and even combat injuries." "Wiihab" programs are, in fact, found in rehabilitation centers, general hospitals, psychiatric hospitals, assisted living facilities, Veterans' Hospitals, and even at Walter Reed Army Medical Center (Ames, 2007; Grohol, 2008; Tanner, 2008b). At Walter Reed Army Medical Center, the Wii video games are naturally popular with patients in the 19-to-25-year range due to this age group being "into" playing video games. Reported gains by these patients included improved endurance, strength, and coordination (Tanner, 2008a).

A positive in employing video games is that they are entertaining and fun to play but offer therapeutic outcomes (Baranowski et al., 2008). Lt. Col Stephanie Daugherty of Walter Reed Army Medical Center commented that her veterans really enjoy playing video games. She said, "They think it's for entertainment, but we know it's for therapy" (Tanner, 2008). Kata (2010) has discussed that video games have the ability to engage and motivate patients undergoing painful, aversive, or boring procedures in a medical setting. Games hold the potential to make potentially monotonous, repetitive tasks appealing.

There are limitations inherent in the research completed thus far on the effects of video games on health (e.g., a lack of randomized controlled trails (RCTs) exists and more rigorous examination of reliability and validity are needed) and thus as Baranowski and his colleagues (2011) have stated, "We are in the earliest stages of understanding how serious video games can influence health-related behaviors" (p. 232). Yet, Primack et al. (2012), in perhaps the most extensive research review of video games and health-related outcomes, wrote, "Despite these limitations, this comprehensive systematic review demonstrates that video games may have potential for improving health in a wide variety of areas" (pp. 635-636).

A number of research reviews (Baranowski et al., 2008; Barlett, 2009; Kato, 2010; Gamberini et al., 2008; Peng, Crouse, & Lin, 2012; Primack et al., 2012; Wilkinson, Ang, & Goh, 2008) have indicated a multitude of therapeutic outcomes from video games. Among those reported have been physical outcomes such as improved balance, enhanced muscle strength, recovery from stroke, improved unilateral upper limb function, pain reduction, less nausea, lower blood pressure, better eye-hand coordination, vestibular normalization, enhanced kinesthetic awareness, improved flexion and extension, and increased range of motion. Psychological outcomes have included mood enhancement, decreased anxiety, stress reduction, phobia reduction, decreased aggression, improved cognitive functioning, improved attention capacity, improved executive control skills, improved self-efficacy, better concentration, greater social-support, and increased feelings of mastery and control. Other reported outcomes have been: improved motivation for participation in physical activity, increased prosocial behavior, and improved self-management of diabetes, asthma, and cancer.

Additional research studies of video games have found improved dexterity, fine motor skills, and balance in patients with Parkinson's disease and enhanced mental well-being in all patients (Sugumaran & Prakash, 2011); improvements in sensorimotor functions for children with Down syndrome (Wuang et al., 2011); improved self-concept and quality of life for elderly persons (Torres, 2008); and attenuated cognitive decline in older adults (Basak et al., 2008).

Still an additional area of research has been in using active video games to promote physical activity. So extensive has been development in this area that the term "exergames" has been coined to describe it (Sallis, 2011). Active video games are seen as a good alternative to sedentary activities often engaged in by many clients. An extensive research review by Peng, Crouse, and Lin (2013) found all laboratory studies demonstrated active video games (AVGs) produced increases in physical activity. Only however 3 of 13 intervention studies produced increases in physical activity, leading these authors to call for additional research to determine how best to employ AVGs to increase physical activity. In contrast, from their review of the research, Chamberlin and Gallagher (2008) reported that most studies of AVGs demonstrated a positive effect in promoting physical activity. Perhaps this discrepancy is because Peng, Crouse, and Lin had access to more studies because their review was published four years after that of Chamberlin and Gallagher. Certainly a number of studies have displayed that active video games, such as the Nintendo Wii™, promote increases in energy expenditure in any number of populations including children, adolescents, young adults, and older adults (Graf et al., 2009; Graves et al., 2010; Lanningham-Foster et al., 2009; Leatherdale, Woodruff, & Manske, 2010). A study of adults with cerebral palsy, who played Wii™ sports, also found increases in energy expenditure (Hurkmans, van den Berg-Emons, & Stam, 2010).

Recreational therapy professor and researcher Carmen Russoniello runs the Psychophysiology and Biofeedback Laboratory at East Carolina University. In his research lab, Russoniello studies the effects video games have on reducing stress and the improving mood of participants who play them (Russoniello, 2009). Preliminary results from Russoniello's work have revealed players of the video games *Bejeweled 2, Bookworm Adventures,* and *Peggle* reported less fatigue, less mental confusion, more vigor, less anger, decreased depression, and less mental stress as a result of their play. Peggle had the most effect on the reduction of mental stress (Begley, 2008). Russoniello has been quoted as stating, "I believe there is a wide range of therapeutic applications of casual games in mood-related disorders such as depression and in stress-related disorders including diabetes and cardivascular disease" (James, 2008). While the use of video games has not been widely reported in recreational therapy, video game virtual reality has been suggested as a technology for use in recreational therapy. This technology, which employs computer graphics to place the participant in a virtual environment, is currently used in mental health and physical rehabilitation settings (Yang & Poff, 2001). Conyers, Malkin, and Yang (2011) have reported on the effects of a recreational therapy program using the Nintendo Wii Fit™ balance board on balance and body mass Index (BMI) of adolescents with traumatic brain injury. In an article in the *Therapeutic Recreation Journal,* Weybright, Dattilo, and Rusch (2010) reported women with mild cognitive impairment who participated in an interactive video game made significant gains in attention to task and displayed higher levels of positive affect.

Video Production

The Director of a Child Life Program and her colleagues (Rode, Fishman, Capitulo, & Holden, 1998) related how a 10-year-old from Africa by the name of Valerie discovered in a New York City hospital that a video camera could enable her to cope with a terminal condition. Valerie was brought from Africa to New York City for treatment of a tumor in her neck. The tumor proved to be malignant, and the little girl eventually died, but not before developing an interest in video recording that provided a focal point for her during her hospitalization. Enthusiastic reactions to Valerie's video productions resulted from both staff and fellow patients. She not only gained friends through the experience, but emerged as a leader among her peers due to their admiration for her video work.

The staff of the Child Life Program at Mount Sinai Medical Center has evolved a video production project titled "Through Our Eyes Productions." Chronically ill children document their experiences in the hospital on video to create videos that tell their stories about living with illness. In their roles as both producers and performers of videos these young patients educate other patients, their families, and healthcare workers about their feelings, questions, and coping strategies as they deal with illness and hospitalization (Child Life Program, 2007).

A video production program at Kosair Children's Hospital in Louisville, Kentucky, is similar to that of the Mount Sinai Medical Center. Patients at Kosair's have access to an iMac computer with a webcam and video editing software in order to make videos where they discuss overcoming their fears and anxieties brought on by their diseases or medical procedures. New patients can then watch the videos to learn how other children dealt with their illnesses and hospitalizations. Several of the videos have even been uploaded onto a website so patients around the world can access them. It has been reported that children making the videos have benefited from feelings of accomplishment in producing and editing their videos. A doctor at the hospital commented, "They're getting therapy for themselves by helping other kids cope" (Novotney, 2010, p. 60).

Computer Applications

"STARBRIGHT World" is an online computer network for children across the United States and Canada who are hospitalized. The system allows children at one hospital to interact online with children at other hospitals. Thus, it permits children with even rare medical disorders to link to other children with the same disorder. One study with children with sickle cell disease or asthma found that "STARBRIGHT World" was effective in increasing health knowledge, decreasing negative coping, and building peer social support. Additionally, the children rated "STARBRIGHT World" as the recreation activity in which they most frequently participated and they ranked it third among the "best things about being in the hospital," only behind playing in the recreational therapy playroom and playing Nintendo™ (Hazzard, Celano, Collins, & Markov, 2002). For information about Starbright World see http://www.starbrightworld.org/default_login.aspx?ReturnURL=%2fhome. aspx

Within the research literature of recreational therapy, have been studies using computers in teaching social skills. McKenney, Dattilo, Cory, and Williams (2004) employed a computerized program to teach social skills to youth with emotional and behavioral problems. Results from their research displayed improvement in the participants' social skills as a result of the computer-assisted instruction. A prior study by Dattilo, Williams, and Cory (2003), this time with boys with intellectual disabilities, also found improvement in social skills as a result of a computerized leisure education program. It would appear that computer created virtual environments would also be a useful mechanism to employ in teaching social skills. Computers can be used to simulate virtual environments where clients can experience highly realistic sights and sounds (and even smells) (DeAngelis, 2012).

Finally, with mobile devices so widely used by Americans and Canadians, the popularity of software applications, or apps, will almost certainly grow. Already, apps are being employed in treatment by clinicians in areas such as speech and language pathology (Dunham, 2011).While reports of the use of apps are not yet plentiful in the recreational therapy (RT) literature, their use would appear to hold great promise for RT practice. A review of the literature on apps for students with communication needs (Menard, 2011) has appeared in the *American Journal of Recreation Therapy*. Temple University has developed a resource blog for iPad and app technology for recreational therapists. The address is http:// tripstu.wordpress.com/

Snoezelen Rooms

Another use of technology in therapy is the **Snoezelen room**. The Snoezelen room is a multisensory environment involving "music, lighting effects, gentle vibrations, tactile sensations, and aromatherapy to create a unique sensory experience" (What on Earth is a Snoezelen Room? 2002, p. 38). The room was developed to provide adults and children with developmental disabilities and sensory impairments with pleasant sensory experiences with the intent of producing a relaxing learning environment that promotes exploration and self-expression. It has been claimed that the rooms are particularly effective with older persons with confusion and with children who are autistic (What on Earth is a Snoezelen Room?, 2002).

Patterson (2004) has indicted that while beneficial client outcomes from the Snoezelen experience have been reported in the literature (e.g., pain reduction, increased concentration, relaxation), he cautions that some conflicting results have also been published. According to identified research reviews (Chan et al., 2010; Lai, 2003; Lancioni, Cuvo, & O'Reilly, 2002; Letts et al., 2011; Lotan & Gold, 2009; Yeap, Leow, & Ng, 2008), a great deal of caution is called for due to a lack of empirical evidence to support the use of multi-sensory environments. All reviews cited methodological issues that raised questions about the validity of the research. Yet, Snoezelen remains a popular approach, particularly among those working with people with developmental disabilities and dementia (Lancioni, Cuvo, & O'Reilly, 2002). The acceptance of the approach, according to Carter and Stephenson (2012), seems to rest on an inherent belief in the benefit of sensory stimulation "despite the absence of a plausible theoretical mechanism and weak supporting empirical evidence" (p. 108).

Robotic Therapy

Robotic therapy is an emerging field that uses robotic pets built to mimic animals. As has been revealed in the discussion of animal-assisted therapy (AAT) and animal-assisted activities (AAAs), interactions with animals have long been known to be beneficial for people. Some healthcare facilities, however, have turned to robotic therapy as a substitute for AAT and AAAs due to possible negative effects of animals such as allergies, infections, bites, and scratches. An early robotic animal has been a seal-like animal named Paro, who was designed for use at pediatric wards and in residential institutions for elderly persons (Wada, Shibata, Musha, & Kimura, 2008).

Studies have shown interactions with Paro with elderly residential patients increased social interactions (Wada & Shibata, 2008) and decreased stress levels for both residents and nursing staff (Wada, Shibata, Saito, & Tanie, 2004). A research review found that the seal robot has similar effects on elderly people undergoing mental healthcare as AAT (Shibata & Wada, 2010). Another study revealed interactions with robotic dogs reduced feelings of loneliness in residents in long-term care facilities (Banks, Willoughby, & Banks, 2008). A study of the use of a robotic dog with children with autism reported more social interactions and fewer autistic behaviors by the children (Stanton et al., 2008). Studies of the robotic dog, AIBO, however suggest caution in assuming that robotic pets will effectively substitute for living animals (Melson, Kahn, Beck, & Friedman, 2009). A comprehensive research review (Bemelmans, Gelderblom, Junker, & de White, 2012) reported positive effects for the use of robots in the care of elderly patients but cautioned the methodological quality of the studies reviewed was low. Thus, it is far too early in the research on use of robotic therapy to know to what extent robotic pets may be used to replace animals in bringing about therapeutic benefits to clients.

Assistive Technologies

Any number of **assistive technology** devices may be applied to help people with physical disabilities to increase their functional abilities. At times, recreational therapist may teach persons with disabilities simply how to use such devices to assist them in participating in daily recreation activities. At other times, recreational therapists and clients may employ these devices as aids in rehabilitation.

Robitaille (2010) has explained that "assistive technology can be 'no-tech,' such as Velcro for fastening your shirt; 'low-tech,' such as a walking cane; or 'high-tech,' such as screen-reading software" (p. 4). Examples of low-tech devices include playing card holders and card shufflers for those who have use of only one hand, mobile bridges for holding the ends of pool cues off of pool tables, and ramps on which to place bowling balls for release toward the pins. An example of the application of a more high-tech assistive technology is an adapted pinball machine that has paddles controlled by puff-and-sip or other switches (Cook & Hussey, 2002).

People with severe physical or cognitive impairments may benefit from the use of switches. Various actions (e.g., pull, push, depress, squeeze, sip/puff, eye blink) are used to activate switches that can be used to control any electronic device (such as the previously mentioned pinball machine, a battery-operated toy, or a computer). Broach and Dattilo's (2011b) review of the literature on the use of switches revealed an abundance of research to support the therapeutic use of switches. The authors reported, "Switches influence attention to task and task completion, purposeful movement, reaction times, opportunities for an expression of preferences of activities, request for social attention, hierarchy of preferences, adherence to activities, and duration in activity participation" (p. 134).

Implications for Recreational Therapy

It is likely that this section on therapy through technology will have direct implications for recreational therapists who are apt to employ technology to intervene with a wide variety of clients. The use of video games, in particular, would seem to hold great promise. Commercial games can be applied by recreational therapists now. Tailor-made games to reach specific therapy goals are becoming available. It would seem that collaboration between recreational therapists and developers is called for to produce tailor made games for use in recreational therapy.

There are implications for the role of the recreational therapist (RT) in the use of video games. RTs are involved in many tasks related to the effective use of video games. Other than selecting an appropriate game, or helping the client to select a game to meet his or her goals, the RT has to assist the client to get started, to offer feedback and emotional support to the client during play, and to assess the client's performance (Annema et al., 2010). At least some of the time, it will be necessary to do debriefing with the client as it cannot be assumed that the client will understand the transfer of learning to his or her life without a discussion of the game (Thompson et al., 2010).

And why should clients have all the fun with video games? Video games are now beginning to be used in the training of healthcare professionals (Kato, 2010). Should not video games be used in the training of recreational therapists?

RTs should keep in mind that clients' preferences need to be taken into account when applying any type of technology. For example, while the latest technology may appeal to a young recreational therapist, older clients may prefer more traditional therapy approaches (Jung et al., 2009; Laver et al., 2011).

Technology seems to hold great promise as an innovative means to bring about positive health-related outcomes. While there has been much research published, recreational therapists must scrutinize it closely to determine the clinical usefulness before introducing new technologies into practice.

It is surprising that the use of some technologies is not apparent in the literature of recreational therapy. The use of "e-therapy" electronic technologies, such as e-mail, chat, and videoconferencing, has been described in the counseling literature (e.g., Gross & Anthony, 2003; Lavallee, 2006). Even though these electronic technologies would seem to have direct application in aspects of recreational therapy (such as leisure counseling and leisure education) the use of such electronic technologies by recreational therapists does not appear to be widespread.

It is anticipated that in addition to the application of the technologies described in this section, "e-therapy" technologies now used in counseling, and others yet unknown, will grow in use in recreational therapy practice once they become more widely known among recreational therapists. It is safe to say most possibilities for the use of technology in recreational therapy have only begun to be explored.

Creative Arts

Nathan and Mirviss (1998) stated in their book, *Therapy Techniques Using the Creative Arts*, that "the creative process can be a means of both reconciling emotional conflicts and fostering self-awareness and personal growth" (p. 7). Today research studies that document the therapeutic value of creative arts appear in the literature. For example, researchers have reported studies resulting in decreased agitated behaviors, improvement in verbal memory and focused attention, and enhancement in mood from listening to music (Gerdner, 1997; Kemper & Danhauer, 2005; McCoffrey & Locsin, 2002; Sarkamo, et al., 2008), reduced stress and improvements in physical and mental well-being following writing about emotional experiences (Carpenter, 2001; Pennebaker, 1997), and the increases in positive growth as a result of journaling (Ulrich & Lutgendorf, 2002).

Music listening seems to offer a particularly beneficial intervention for many clients, including those who are elderly. Research reviews on music listening (Biley, 2000; Kemper & Danhauer, 2005; McCaffrey & Locsin, 2002) have reported therapeutic outcomes including reductions in stress, anxiety, tension, fatigue, hostility, and perceptions of pain, as well as decreases in blood pressure and heart rate, and feelings of increased general well-being. It should be noted that the type of music listened to is important. Most studies used classical music or preferred music selected by the clients or clients' families. Kemper and Danhauer (2005) reported that listening to grunge rock actually increased hostility, fatigue, tension, and sadness, in contrast to the relaxing properties of classical, new age, or designer music. Mitchell et al. (2007) found that the personal importance of music played a significant role when listening to music to help with the reduction of chronic pain.

A heavily researched area has been music listening with older people with dementia. Findings indicate that music listening decreases agitated behavior for residents with dementia. It has been suggested that relaxing music or personally preferred music best sooths agitation (Chang, 2005; Garland et al., 2007; Lou, 2001; Remington, 2001; Sung et al., 2006). Music listening has also been shown to affect mood. Knobloch and Zillman (2002) found that those needing "mood repair" from bad moods chose to listen to energetic-joyful music for longer periods of time than those in good moods. For patients recovering from stroke, music listening has been found to enhance mood, as well as verbal memory and focused attention (Forsblom et al., 2009; Sarkamo et al., 2008).

Clarity in the use terms related to *writing therapy* appears to be lacking. As Wright and Chung (2001) commented, "Defining 'writing therapy' is difficult" (p. 279). Ultimately accepted by these authors was the definition of writing therapy as "client expressive and reflective writing, whether self-generated or suggested by a therapist/researcher" (italics removed, p. 279). This definition encompasses both expressive writing and journaling (two approaches that are sometimes not differentiated in the literature). *Expressive writing* typically involves a structured writing paradigm where participants are asked to write about assigned topics (which often focus on negative events that have been traumatic, stressful, or emotional) for 15-20 minutes at a time over 3-5 occasions (Baikie & Wilhelm, 2005; Smyth, Nazarian, & Arigo, 2008). The term expressive writing is typically used in conjunction with traditional psychotherapy (Esterling, L'Abate, Murry, & Pennebaker, 1999) and is associated with Pennebaker (1997, 2004) who is a leading authority and researcher on expressive writing. *Journaling* is a daily writing intervention, typically in a bound booklet, to write "about emotions, reactions to situations, and thoughts experienced that day" (Smith et al., p. 173). Journaling is not simply recording what has occurred as would be done in keeping a log of events. Instead, journaling is "a valuable tool for self-understanding" (Kelly & Mosher-Ashley, 2001, p. 40) that helps to record and clarify thoughts and feelings, manage stress, and evolve insights (Scott, 2011b). Journaling does not have to focus on negative events. A type of journaling is maintaining a gratitude journal in which the focus is on positive aspects in life (Scott, 2011a).

Adding to the confusion between expressive writing and journaling are interpretations of research found in the literature. Those writing about journaling (e.g., Smith et al., 2000; Scott, 2011b) when heralding beneficial outcomes (e.g., reductions in health center visits; reductions in anxiety, stress, and depression; enhanced mood; improved lung function for those with asthma; improved sleep quality; improved immune system responses) often cite benefits from articles of Pennebaker (1997) and others (e.g., Baikie & Wilhelm, 2005; Smyth, Nazarian, & Arigo, 2008) that pertain to research on expressive writing rather than findings from journaling research. And even with expressive writing, the benefits of are not as clear as researchers would like (Pennebaker, 2004), Thus recreational therapists must be cautious when consuming information about research findings related to journaling.

While intensive work with expressive therapies is usually reserved for trained music therapists and art therapists, other helping professionals can use creative activities in therapy. For example, two nurses (McGarry & Prince, 1998) reported developing a successful "Creativity Group" for patients receiving care at a Veterans Affairs (VA) psychiatric facility. The nurses used poetry, storytelling, music, drawing, and painting as modalities for creative expression. For those in the program, group poetry and group storytelling were their favorite activities because, as the patients explained, they particularly enjoyed the experience of working together to create poetry and develop stories. According to Nathan and Mirviss (1998), creative arts groups, such as the one at the VA, are effective, because people have opportunities to learn by doing; express themselves both verbally and nonverbally; purge unconscious tensions and anxiety; enhance self-esteem; develop self-awareness; and find enjoyment, insight, and knowledge.

The types of creative arts activities available are almost endless. Creative arts activities covered in Nathan and Mirviss' (1998) book include drawing, painting, sculpting with clay, making masks, drama, theater games, music, clowning, dance/movement, poetry, and creative writing. To this list could be added scrapbooking, where people put together photos, newspaper and magazine articles, and other memorabilia into albums that they decorate. Karaoke has been used with patients in a mental health program in China promote social interaction (Leung et al., 1998). Even a trip to a museum can have potential therapeutic benefits. Benefits reported from a pilot study by Silverman (1998) of organized visits to museums by clients in mental health programs included "(enhanced) self-esteem and heightened self-awareness, community integration/decreased social isolation, and increased personal knowledge and skills" (p. 21).

Implications for Recreational Therapy

Creative arts modalities can be used in interventions by recreational therapists. Music listening may provide a simple and effective method to promote a variety of therapeutic outcomes. A particularly good use of music listening would seem to be with those with dementia.

Writing therapy has been shown to be beneficial for at least some people in some circumstances, Wright and Chung (2001) concluded from their review of the literature. Researchers (Smith et al., 2000) have recommended journaling as a low cost approach that warrants its use, particularly to reduce depression. Murray (1997) has furnished an account of how recreational therapists can establish journaling programs. Seaward (2002) has similarly offered steps to initiate journal writing. Martin and Wilhite (2003) have described a writing intervention for clients who wish to examine the relevance of recreation and leisure participation in their lives.

Others within the recreational therapy profession have added to the literature of creative arts therapy. Within their book titled *Therapy Techniques Using the Creative Arts*, recreational therapists Ann Nathan and Suzanne Mirviss (1998) have offered a wealth of information directed to those who are initiating creative arts groups. Included are over 200 creative arts activities and a chapter that deals specifically with planning for a creative arts group. Carter and Messerly (2001) have provided basic information on using arts and crafts as a RT intervention. Linda Madori, a Certified Therapeutic Recreation Specialist, has authored the (2007) book *Therapeutic Thematic Arts for Older Adults*. In it she presents a nine-step process to promote creativity and to encourage older adults to use their strengths and abilities. Madori's book explores a number of areas of expressive art including music, dance, poetry, sculpture, and photography. Devine (2011) has elaborated on specific visual arts, music, dance, drama, and poetry activities that may be employed within RT.

Retail Therapy

A shopping trip-a-day may keep the doctor away, according to those who study retail therapy. Today there is an emerging body of research literature on retail therapy, although it remains relatively small (Kang & Johnson, 2011).

Pratt (2004) has raised the question as to whether retail therapy is a valid therapeutic approach or simply an avoidance mechanism, or distraction, to escape from confronting a problem. The answer to this question depends to some degree on whether the compensatory consumption view of retail therapy, adopted by Pratt, is taken or the mood regularity device concept of retail therapy is accepted. The mood regulation perspective has been argued by Kang and Johnson (2011) to be the best explanation of retail therapy. These researchers have indicated that the compensatory compensation view that sees shopping as a means to combat a number of psychological difficulties (e.g., low self-esteem or feelings of boredom or anger) is too broad and that retail therapy from a mood repair perspective is a more direct perspective to adopt. Thus, Kang and Johnson (2011) define retail therapy as "consumptive behavior, including shopping and buying, that individuals engage in to alleviate their negative moods" (p. 4).

The idea that retail therapy is a means to improve mood has been assumed by retail therapy researchers Atalay and Meloy (2011). Their research found that people buying themselves small-treats results in cheering them up or making them feel better. In short, retail therapy improved the moods of participants. Atalay and Meloy have however added the caveat that their research only investigated the effect of therapeutic treats on those who had mildly negative, temporary moods but did not include those with chronic negative conditions (e.g., feelings of loneliness). They also pointed out that in their research no distinctions between specific negative emotions (e.g., fear, anger, sadness) were made when examining the effects of retail therapy on mood.

Rick, Pereira, and Burson's (2012) research investigated the benefits of retail therapy specifically on reducing residual sadness. Their perspective to retail therapy, supported by two experimental studies, is that buying reduces sadness due to increased feelings of control produced by exercising choice while shopping. Thus, Rick, Pereira, and Burson concluded from their research that the benefits derived from retail therapy come from people choosing to buy items in order to gain increased feelings of control.

Implications for Recreational Therapy

Due to the differing theoretical perspectives and the relatively small number of empirical studies now available, it would seem prudent for recreational therapists to further examine retail therapy before adopting it as an intervention. While early research is promising, retail therapy seems to offer a limited basis on which to rest practice.

Cognitive Stimulation Therapy

Cognitive Stimulation Therapy (CST) can be traced back to Reality Orientation (RO) which originated in the 1960s. RO was developed to reorientate persons with dementia by constantly offering repetitive orientation to the environment (O'Connell et al., 2007). RO involved the technique of regular repetition of basic facts and constant orientation to time, place, names, events of the day, and things in the environment (Clark, 2003). The use of RO reached its peak in the early 1980s. Research studies on Reality Orientation "had all but dried up by the mid-1980s" (Woods, 2002, p. 155), at which time RO came under fire for being applied in a rigid, demeaning, confrontational, and impersonal manner (Spector, Orrell, Davies, Woods, 2001; Woods, 2002).

Clark (2003) had written, "There has been some criticism of this approach, with some fear that it has been applied in a mechanical fashion that could be insensitive to the needs of individual group members" (p. 211). Patton (2006) had echoed Clark's concern by being critical of staff that do not orientate clients in a way that is appropriate for them, such as talking to clients in a "child-like" manner. Finally, Clark criticized RO programs for reducing clients' self-esteem by constantly asking them to relearn material regarding time, place, and person orientation.

A New Approach

A new approach that was delivered in a "sensitive, respectful, and person-centered manner" (Woods, Aguirre, Spector, & Orrell, 2012) was called for in order to treat people with dementia. The notion that cognitive decline is related to a lack of cognitive activity formed the basis for a new approach termed Cognitive Stimulation Therapy (CST). While CST attempted to avoid the depersonalization and confrontation for which RO had been criticized, it turned to RO (along with Reminiscence Therapy, Validation Therapy, and memory training) to draw key elements for the new intervention (Spector, Orrell, Davies, & Woods, 2001).

Cognitive Stimulation Therapy, as described in a Cochran Review by Woods, Aguirre, Spector, & Orrell (2012), "is an intervention for people with dementia which offers a range of enjoyable activities providing general stimulation for thinking, concentration and memory usually in a social setting, such as a small group." Further, the Cochran Review stated the program "involves a wide range of activities that aim to stimulate thinking and memory generally, including discussion of past and present events and topics of interest, word games, puzzles, music, and practical activities such as baking or indoor gardening." Cognitive Stimulation Therapy sessions generally last 45 minutes and are conducted in small groups of four or five participants at least two times per week for seven weeks. Within the sessions multisensory stimulation is used when possible and the focus is on information processing instead of factual knowledge (Spector et al., 2003).

The cognitive approaches employed in CST are implemented in a sensitive and respectful manner to avoid frustration and distress on the part of participants. Respecting patients' "personhood" or treating each person with dementia as an individual adult is an important feature of CST. As Spector, Orrell, Davies, and Woods (2001) explained, the focus of the program "is on harnessing implicit memory, emphasizing active engagement with materials and the plentiful provision of retrieval cues. This minimises conscious memorisation, with the danger of overt failure and promotes general cognitive stimulation and individual well-being" (p. 393).

Five general principles guide CST according to Spector, Orrell, Davies, and Woods (2001). These include the following:

1. Experiential learning involving the use of all five senses to promote cognitive stimulation and memory process.
2. Focused psychological interventions which address the difficulties of everyday living.
3. Acknowledgment of the emotional lives and enhancement of the cognitive skills of people with dementia.
4. Implicit learning (familiarity and "intuition"), rather than explicit "teaching." Extensive rehearsal and consolidation of essential information about themselves and their world are thought to be most beneficial.
5. The reciprocal, psychological process (involving cognitive and emotional states) in which people with dementia and those who care for them learn more about each other's capabilities and vulnerabilities. (p. 384)

Each CST session begins with a similar warm-up activity. Spector, Orrell, Davies, and Woods (2001) described the beginning of each session as consisting of the following:

1. Five minute warm-up, such as a softball game. When throwing the ball, people may either state their own name or (for the more able) the name of the person they are throwing the ball to.
2. Discuss the day, month, year, season, time, name, and address of home.
3. Short-term memory prompts, such as asking people what they had for breakfast/lunch, what they thought of yesterday's weather.
4. Discuss something that is currently in the news. (p. 396)

Four phases are featured in CST: (1) *the senses* (in which sensory experiences are provided that are separate from usual group activities and sensory elements are used to assess abilities of the group and establish a sense of community); (2) *remembering the past* (where clients gain enjoyment through chronological remembering); (3) *people and objects* (involving recognizing people from the past, people in the group, family, and staff, and familiar and modern objects like mobile phones); and (4) *everyday practical issues* (on the use of money, the clients knowing their way around the facility, and a final summing up session ending with a tea party). (Spector, Orrell, Davies, & Woods, 2001, pp. 388-389)

The 14 specific sessions used in CST have been presented in detail by Spector, Orrell, Davies, and Woods (2001). They are as follows:

1. **Physical game**, such as rollaball or indoor boules (i.e., rolling a ball such as boules in France, or bocce in Italy, or bowling with plastic pins in North America), which involves teamwork. This should be relatively relaxed activity for the first session, incorporating movement, touch and score calculations.

2. **Sound:** Sound effects tapes, which include different categories, such as "indoor sounds" and "outdoor sounds," to be matched with the correct picture. This provides people with both visual and auditory stimulation, making the task easier. Percussion instruments given to each person In the group, to be played with music (such as popular 1940s music).

3. **Childhood:** Activities include people filling out a sheet asking their name, father's name, mother's name, schools attended, etc.; construction of their childhood bedroom or home on a board; and demonstrating the use of old-fashioned childhood toys.

4. **Food:** Using miniature grocery replicas which have been priced, give people a budget and a scenario, e.g., dinner for four. Alternatively, eat food with reminiscent or personal meaning, and brainstorm food categories on the whiteboard.

5. **Current affairs:** Discuss issues from a selection of the day's national and local newspapers, and picture magazines. Use cue cards to evoke conversation on news, views, attitudes, dreams and aspirations.

6. **Faces/scenes:** To reduce the attentional problem of only one person being able to look at each picture at a time, multiple sets of the famous faces cards (added to more modern pictures) have been created. Give people four cards. Ask them to identify named person/scene. Ask opinions, e.g., most beautiful, oldest. Attempt to use opinions to generate memories for names.

7. **Associated works/discussion:** Sentence completion task. Includes amounts (e.g., a cup of...), famous couples (e.g., Laurel and ...), famous places (e.g., Westminister...). Use "Golden Expression" cards to stimulate discussion, e.g., "What do you think of medicine today?".

8. **Using objects:** Creative session, such as cookery. Multiple tasks enable all to participate (e.g., greasing bowl, mixing ingredients, making crumble mixture, peeling and slicing apples).

9. **Categorizing objects:** People think of words beginning with a particular letter (picked from a card) in a particular category (picked from a card). Alternatively, brainstorm categories on board.

10. **Orientation:** Construct map of England (or the USA or Canada), local area or home on whiteboard. Fill in the "map" by asking the group to suggest different places or landmarks, such as the post office, and draw them in the appropriate position.

11. **Using money:** Use laminated cut-outs of common objects from a catalogue, with prices on the back. Tasks could involve guessing the prices, adding prices (how much will the bill be?), or matching the pricetag with the object.

12. **Number game:** involving the recognition and use of numbers.

13. **Word identification game** ("Hangman"): involving the recognition and use of letters and words. Draw a number of dashes for each letter or word, and ask the group to guess the letters. Incorrect letters contribute to the drawing of a "hangman" and losing the game. The group is required to guess the word.

14. **Team games:** divide the group Into two teams, ask them to choose a team name, and play trivia quiz. Give prizes to all the group, and say farewells. (pp. 396-397)

According to the Cochran Review by Woods and his colleagues (2012), results of Cognitive Stimulation Therapy show a "clear consistent benefit on cognitive function was associated with cognitive stimulation." Self-reports also indicated improvements in quality of life and well-being as a result of CST.

Implications for Recreational Therapy

It seems that existing empirical evidence supports the replacement of Reality Orientation (RO) with Cognitive Stimulation Therapy (CST). CST contains many elements of RO but is delivered in a less rigid, more person-centered manner using enjoyable activities, much as Austin (2011a) has described are typically used in recreational therapy. Thus, CST may be seen to have a good fit with recreational therapy and may be an intervention for recreational therapists to employ with people with dementia. Minimizing social deprivation and increasing stimulation for older people can promote improvement in persons who otherwise might be termed "demented" and simply be forgotten. The too-common, stereotyped "bingo and birthday party" programming that prevails in some facilities becomes just another part of the monotonous institutional atmosphere. Such programming should not be tolerated. It must be replaced by creative programs that offer small group social interaction and put variety into the residents' lives.

Validation Therapy

Validation therapy was developed by Naomi Feil in the 1970s from her experience in working with very old persons with Alzheimer's-type dementia (Feil, 2002). Feil's experiences led her away from the use of reality orientation (RO), to which residents often reacted with withdrawal or hostility. Instead of orienting them to reality, Feil empathized with residents and "validated" the feelings and needs underlying their perceptions. Hartz and Splain (1997) have proclaimed, "The greatest value of validation therapy may lie in its providing a healthy corrective to the traditional emphasis upon reality orientation, in which staff constantly correct disoriented residents in order to ground them in present reality" (p. 80). In contrast to reality orientation (RO), validation therapy does not emphasize orientation to name, date, and time but, instead, uses a series of techniques in order to communicate effectively with disoriented "old-old" clients (those over 85) who need help in resolving their pasts. These are individuals who have not resolved key developmental tasks and must return to the past in order to resolve their unfinished life tasks. People who have met their developmental tasks at various life stages are able to achieve integrity and have no need for validation, according to Feil (2002).

The basic premise for validation therapy is that there is a sense of reality or logic that underlies the behavior of even the most disoriented individuals. These persons have certain unmet social and psychological needs: to express suppressed feelings, to regain equilibrium following physical losses, to restore formal social roles, to resolve past relationships that have not been satisfactory, and to resolve life tasks that remain unfinished. Validation therapy uses empathetic communication to help clients to "regain dignity, reduce anxiety, and prevent withdrawal to vegetation" (Feil, 2002, p. 12). While other types of clients may benefit from validation therapy, it has been primarily directed toward very old people with Alzheimer's-type dementia (Robb, Stegman, & Wolanin, 1986). Validation therapy is not appropriate for old persons who are chronically mentally ill, intellectually disabled, or have alcoholism (Feil, 2002).

Feil (2002) has listed the following principles on which validation therapy is based:

(1) Painful feelings that are expressed, acknowledged, and validated by a trusted listener will diminish. (2) Painful feelings that are ignored or suppressed will gain strength and can become "toxic." (3) Early, well-established, emotional memories remain on some level into old-old age. (4) When more recent memory fails, older

adults try to restore balance to their lives by retrieving earlier memories. (5) When eyesight fails, they use the mind's eye to see. When hearing goes, they listen to sounds of the past. (6) Human beings have many levels of awareness. (7) When present reality becomes painful, some old-old survive by retreating and stimulating memories of the past. (8) Emotions felt in present time can trigger similar emotions felt in the past. (p. 30)

Validation therapy can be used by anyone properly trained in its relatively simple techniques. The main qualities needed by a validation therapist are having the ability to accept people who are disoriented and being empathetic toward them. Feil (2002) lists 14 techniques to be employed by therapists. Some of these are merely widely accepted counseling techniques, such as maintaining eye contact, employing rephrasing in responding, speaking with a caring tone of voice, using appropriate touch, and avoiding "why" questions. Other techniques, such as mirroring motions and emotions and employing extreme examples of client complaints, are unique to validation therapy. All 14 techniques are covered by Feil (2002) in her book, *The Validation Breakthrough*.

In her book, Feil also discussed conducting a validation group meeting. Validation meetings for groups of seven or eight members usually are conducted for 20 to 60 minutes at least weekly. There are four phases. *Phase One* is titled *Birth of the Group: Creating Energy* and lasts 5 to 15 minutes. The therapist initially greets each group member in the circle. Care is given to greeting each person by his or her last name (e.g., Mr. Jones), while using touch and eye contact. At this time members are also reminded about their assigned roles in the group, such as the welcomer (who opens and closes the meeting), song leader, prayer leader, or chair arranger. Members are encouraged to hold hands during the meeting. The therapist helps the welcomer to rise and open the meeting and then asks the song leader to begin a song and, finally, the poet or prayer leader to recite a poem or lead a prayer. *Phase Two* has the title *Life of the Group: Verbal Interactions*. During this phase lasting 5 to 10 minutes, the therapist introduces a topic (such as how to help overcome loneliness or what makes a happy person) and encourages each group member to respond at some level. The therapist then summarizes the discussion and gives praise to the group members for addressing the topic. *Phase Three* is termed *Movement and Rhythms*. This lasts 3 to 20 minutes. The therapist helps the group leader and other members of the group to engage in the movement activity, which might involve passing a ball, throwing a bean bag, completing arts and crafts projects, taking part in a rhythm band, or dancing (e.g., "The Hokey Pokey"). The final phase is *Phase Four: Closing of the Group, with Anticipation for the Next Meeting*. This lasts 5 to 15 minutes. The therapist asks the song leader to lead the closing song. After this, the assigned host or hostess passes out the refreshments. Following refreshments, the group member who is the welcomer says good-bye to the members and reminds them of the next meeting. Then an upbeat song is led by the song leader with members holding hands. Finally, the therapist wishes each of the members good-bye while using touch and telling them he or she looks forward to the next meeting of the group.

According to Feil (2002), validation therapy restores self-worth; reduces the need for chemical and physical restraints; minimizes the degree to which they withdraw from the outside world, promotes communication and interaction, reduces stress and anxiety, stimulates dormant potential, helps resolve unfinished life tasks, and facilitates independent living for as long as possible. Potential adopters of Feil's program should, however, be aware that research findings on validation therapy have not been strong. For example, systematic research reviews (Livingston et al., 2005; Scott & Clare, 2003) have concluded there is a lack of high-quality research evidence to support the efficacy of validation therapy. A Cochrane review abstract by Neal and Barton Wright (2003) similarly reported a lack of evidence to draw any conclusions regarding the efficacy of validation therapy for those with dementia or cognitive impairment.

Implications for Recreational Therapy

While lacking research support, validation therapy offers an approach that has been used with "old-old" confused or disoriented clients, particularly those with Alzheimer's disease. Practitioners working with disoriented clients who do not wish to adopt validation therapy may well benefit from a review of Feil's (2002) techniques, as well as her suggested structures for groups.

It is apparent that there is a real need to conduct empirical investigations on validation therapy and other means of working with confused elderly persons since well-grounded interventions are increasingly needed. Today one in eight older Americans has Alzheimer's disease. Almost half of those persons age 85 and older have the disease and projections call for rapid growth in the numbers of persons having Alzheimer's disease. It is projected that as many as 16 million Americans could have the disease by 2050 (Alzheimer's Association, 2012).

Remotivation Therapy

Professor Dorothy Smith originated **Remotivation Therapy (RmT)** while volunteering at the Pennsylvania State Hospital in the 1950s. Following the successful employment of RmT with withdrawn elderly patients there, its use spread throughout America's state psychiatric hospitals.

Remotivation therapy initially grew rapidly. It flourished in the 1960s and peaked in the early 1970s. The decline In RmT was largely due to the closure of many state psychiatric hospitals due to the deinstitutionalization movement. Then, in the 1980s and 1990s, remotivation therapy began to find its way into alternative settings.

Today remotivation therapy is being employed with all age groups with various clinical populations including clients in physical rehabilitation and community-based mental health programs, as well as with individuals with intellectual disabilities, and persons in substance abuse programs. Most recently, remotivation therapy has been conducted in long-term care facilities and with persons with dementia (Meixsell, 2005; Williams, 2005).

Remotivation therapy is a group approach in which the leader attempts to stimulate mental processes, encourage conversation, facilitate socialization, enhance self-esteem, increase self-awareness, improve quality of life, increase participation in planned activities, and get participants interested in their environments (Capuzzi, Gross, & Friel, 1990; Herlihy-Chevalier, 2005; Sullivan, Bird, Alpay, & Cha, 2001).

Remotivation therapy sessions are designed to motivate individuals who have withdrawn into themselves and lack interest in either the present or future. Herlihy-Chevlier (2005) has specifically identified individuals who may profit from RmT to include "those who may be withdrawn, isolated, depressed, bored, or in need of environmental stimulation" (p. 15).

Remotivation therapy's emphasis is on identifying the strengths of individuals and then concentrating on them rather than deficits. As Bierma (1998) has indicated, "Remotivation differs from other therapies because it focuses on the patients' abilities rather than on their disabilities. The major endeavor is to discuss and develop the patients' healthy aspects no matter how regressed they may be" (p. 9).

RmT sessions are typically held once a week, from 30 to 60 minutes for groups of six participants. Leadership for groups is provided by certified group leaders, termed remotivators (Herlihy-Chevalier, 2005). Group discussion is the primary method used within group meetings. Participants are encouraged to take a renewed interest in their environment through a series of carefully planned conversations that stress simple, objective features of everyday life not related to the participants' emotional difficulties. The leader chooses a topic to discuss during each meeting of the group. Topics chosen may be wide ranging from baseball to gardening; the only restriction is that controversial subjects such as sex, politics, religion, or marital relations may not be discussed.

Each meeting features a specific topic and includes five steps, each lasting about 10 minutes. The first and fifth steps may be shorter (e.g., 5 minutes), while the second, third, and fourth steps may occasionally be longer (e.g., 15 minutes). The five steps are as follows:

1. **The Climate of Acceptance** begins each session in order to establish a nonthreatening, warm, and friendly atmosphere. The leader warmly greets each participant (usually with a handshake) while addressing the person by name and making some comment in regard to the individual's appearance.
2. **A Bridge to Reality** is when the leader introduces a topic relative to the group in order to facilitate group discussion. The bridge to reality is built by the leader (or sometimes a participant) reading a poem, story, or article that relates theme for the day in order to stimulate thought.
3. **Sharing the World We Live In** is a time for the leader to ask broad questions to encourage the recalling and sharing of ideas and events related to the topic. Visual aids are often used to encourage clients to share personal experiences related to the topic.
4. **An Appreciation of the Work of the World** is a phase in which to get clients to think about positive aspects of work, to think about work world activities, or think about work in relation to themselves. Participants may be encouraged to rediscover past occupations or hobbies that they are reminded of as a result of the discussion. Projections into the future may also be encouraged.
5. **The Climate of Appreciation** concludes each session. The leader summarizes what has been said, comments about the participation of each individual, personally thanks them for attending, and then informs the group about plans for the next meeting (Herlihy-Chevalier, 2005).

The interested reader may wish to refer to Leitner and Leitner's (1985) article, "Recreation Leadership Principles," which appeared in Volume 7 of *Activities, Adaptation, & Aging*, in order to obtain examples of remotivation sessions. In addition to Leitner and Leitner, other resources on RmT include Teague and MacNeil's (1992) book on aging and leisure and Dyer and Stotts' (2005) *Handbook of Remotivation Therapy.*

Research on remotivation therapy began to emerge as early as the 1960s. Beard and Bidus' 1968 study of remotivation therapy with psychiatric patients reported improved social interest on the part of participants. More recent research has shown positive results for RmT. Sullivan, Bird, Alpay and Cha's (2001) RmT program, with patients with Huntington's disease, showed increases in self-awareness and self-esteem, as well as improvement in quality of life. A abstract by Ng, Lo, and Chan (2009), on RmT with adult psychiatric patients in China, reported significant improvements in memory recall, speech, comprehension, and interpersonal relationships, leading to increases in the patients motivation to participate in treatment. No comprehensive research reviews on remotivation therapy could be located.

Implications for Recreational Therapy

The concepts expressed in remotivation therapy of establishing a warm, accepting atmosphere, dealing with the well parts of clients, and encouraging the rediscovery of interests have obvious merit in the provision of strength-based recreational therapy programming for older persons. For recreational therapists who wish to conduct RmT, they may complete a training course to become certified remotivators.

Resocialization

Resocialization is a group treatment that is used to decrease the confusion and increase the social functioning of confused residents in geriatric settings. This modality was developed to use reminiscence and sensory stimulation to target clients' cognitive capabilities. Through group meetings, resocialization attempts to increase awareness of self and others by forming relationships, establishing friendships, and discovering new interests.

Resocialization groups are conducted by a staff member for groups of 5 to 17 residents, depending on the mental and physical abilities of the participants. Refreshments are served at group meetings, which take place three times a week. Sessions usually last 30 to 60 minutes. The leader serves as a role model by showing acceptance of participants, making nonjudgmental comments, displaying flexibility, and raising discussion questions (Barnes, Sack, & Shore, 1973). Resocialization groups have a less rigid structure than remotivation therapy groups. McCrone (1991) has explained that resocialization groups are organized around topics chosen by the leader who uses props to stimulate clients' senses and promote reminiscence. Group discussions are focused on having participants express their thoughts and opinions with the intent of having them learn to listen to one another and to respond to one another. The leader attempts to maintain a free and accepting group atmosphere where participants will feel at liberty to discuss interpersonal problems (Barnes, Sack, & Shore, 1973).

Research on resocialization groups is sparse but a well-designed controlled study, completed by McCrone in 1991, did demonstrate the efficacy of resocialization with mildly confused nursing home residents. A six-week program resulted in decreasing confusion; although gains were short-term as they were lost one month after the resocialization treatment was terminated.

Implications for Recreational Therapy

The decreasing of confusion and restoring of social functioning through group processes are common goals of recreational therapists working with older clients who exhibit symptoms of confusion. Many recreational therapy programs for older people follow structures and objectives similar to those of the resocialization technique.

Sensory Training

Originally developed to work with children with perceptual-motor problems, **sensory training** has been used extensively with regressed and disoriented older persons in psychiatric facilities and nursing homes. Sensory training attempts to maintain and improve the functioning of regressed patients through a program of stimulus bombardment directed toward all five senses. Its goal is to improve the individual's perception and alertness in responding to the environment.

Carter et al., (1995) described the sensory training effects in the following way:

The overall effect of sensory training is similar to the effects of physical exercise. When you exercise, you overload or stress certain muscle groups to strengthen and develop those muscles. So too, when a person participates in a systematic sensory stimulation program, his or her neurological function is effectively increased. (p. 103)

In group sensory training, clients meet with a leader in groups of four to seven for sessions lasting 30 to 60 minutes. Each session begins with the group sitting in a circle. The leader introduces himself or herself and asks the participants to introduce themselves. The purposes of the session are explained, perhaps using a blackboard or bulletin board to note major points; then the leader conducts a series of activities requiring use of all the senses. At the conclusion of the session, the leader thanks each participant for taking part and reminds each individual when the following session will be held.

Actual activities include kinesthetic awareness exercises (in which participants name, flex, and extend part of their bodies from a sitting position); tactile stimulation activities (in which patients feel objects such as balls, sponges, or pieces of wood while being asked questions about the sensations received, preferences, and feelings); smelling activities (in which participants smell sharp or distinct-smelling substances and are questioned about feelings regarding them and uses the substances have); listening activities (providing a number of sounds through media such as recordings, simple instruments, clapping, and singing); tasting activities (using different foods such as candy and pickles to establish contrasts); and visual activities (employing mirrors and colorful objects) (Barnes, Sack, & Shore, 1973; Kraus, Carpenter, & Bates,1989).

Not to be confused with sensory training is the technique **sensory stimulation**. Sensory stimulation has been used as a treatment for brain-injury patients who are in prolonged coma. Two types of sensory stimulation have been described in the literature, multimodal and unimodal stimulation. In multimodal stimulation, all of the senses are stimulated in every treatment session. Using this technique, each of the senses (visual, auditory, tactile, gustatory, olfactory) is stimulated to the highest degree a response can be achieved. For example, for the sense of smell, smelling salts are first tried, and if a reaction occurs, then more pleasant strong odors (e.g., cooking spices) may be used. Unimodal stimulation follows a similar pattern but involves treating just one sense in any single session. Selecting the senses is done on a random basis (Wilson, Powell, Elliot, & Thwaites, 1993). With either technique, therapists observe patient responses to stimulation to determine which are the most effective in producing consistent responses such as hand or head movement or an eye gaze. While limited, research (Doman, Wilkinson, Dimancescu, & Pelligra, 1993; Wilson & McMillan, 1993) suggests that sensory stimulation can affect behavior in unconscious patients and can reduce the depth and duration of coma. A Cochrane systematic review (Lombardi et al., 2002), however, reported no evidence was found to support the effectiveness of sensory stimulation programs for patients in coma or vegative state and recommended randomized control trails should be conducted on sensory stimulation.

Also differing from sensory training is *multisensory stimulation* provided by multisensory rooms that have become increasingly employed with older people with dementia, as well as with those with problems in mental health and patients in pain clinics and pediatric settings (Baker et al., 2003; Hope, 1997). Snoezelen multisensory rooms are discussed in this chapter under the section on intervening with technology.

Implications for Recreational Therapy

Sensory training provides input to activate perception and increase alertness. It is important to recognize that older people can become more functional if they receive the proper stimuli to activate their senses. Recreational therapists can conduct sensory training as well as recreation programs that emphasize the use of the senses. Through sensory programming, aging clients may be able to reactivate senses that have not received adequate stimulation from the dull, routine environments that exist in many long-term care facilities. Recreational therapists also may be directly involved as members of sensory stimulation treatment teams and use multi-sensory stimulation.

Reminiscence Therapy

Reminiscence has been broadly defined as "the act of relating personally significant past experiences" (Koffman, 2000, p. 29). Today **reminiscence therapy** has become widely accepted (Watt & Cappeliez, 2000) and is among the most popular psychosocial interventions applied with clients with dementia (Woods, Spector, Jones, Orrell, & Davies, 2005). It has long been used by recreational therapists, beginning at least in the 1980s.

Within recreational therapy, Caroline Weiss was an early advocate for reminiscence therapy while a professor at the University of Minnesota. Weiss (1989) termed reminiscing "the excursion into one's memory of the past" (p. 7). Weiss explained that people recall objects, places, other people, and their own self-reflections while reminiscing. She saw reminiscence as a normal and healthy process that should be experienced by old people and suggested that old people who engage in reminiscence are not indulging themselves in idle ramblings but, instead, are taking part in a positive process that should be encouraged.

The employment of the terms *reminiscence therapy* and *life review* can be confusing because the terms are sometimes used interchangeably in the literature (Lee, Henningfeld, & Taboure, 2012). While related, reminiscence therapy and life review differ. Based on the work of pioneering gerontologist Robert Butler, Kast-Godley and Gatz (2000) have made a distinction between reminiscence and life review. They explain: "Life review involves the evaluation and re-synthesis of past experiences precipitated by the need to resolve conflicts and achieve a sense of meaning to one's life before one dies, whereas reminiscence is the act or process of recalling the past" (p. 760). Thus life review uses reminiscence as a tool to use in reviewing and evaluating an individual's life.

This helpful distinction is congruent with the definition of reminiscence therapy proposed by Woods, Spector, Jones, Orrell, and Davies (2005). They have written:

Reminiscence therapy (RT) involves the discussion of past activities, events, and experiences with another person or group of people, usually with the aid of tangible prompts such as photographs, household and other familiar items from the past, music, and archive sound recordings. Reminiscence groups typically involve group meetings in which participants are encouraged to talk about past events at least once a week. Life review typically involves individual sessions, in which the person is guided chronologically through life experiences, encouraged to evaluate them, and may produce a life story book.

Life review is often done individually on a one-to-one basis, rather than in a group, as is typical for reminiscence therapy. The goals of life review, for those who are nearing the end of their lives, are "to facilitate the inevitable life review process and minimize distress by providing support, understanding and acceptance" (Kasl-Godley & Gatz, 2000, p. 760).

Although literature on exactly how to conduct life review therapy is limited, various methods may be used to engage participants. These include preparing a verbal or written summary of life work; reviewing written or audio autobiographies; going on pilgrimages (in person or via correspondence); attending reunions; constructing a genealogy; and reviewing memorabilia in the form of scrapbooks, photo albums, or collections of old letters (Kasl-Godley & Gatz, 2000). Recreational therapy researchers Lee, Henningfeld, and Tabourne (2012) have described the life review protocol they employed in their study conducted in Korea with persons with Alzheimer's disease. Those wishing to conduct life review programs may find the protocols provided by Burnside and Haight (1995) to be helpful.

According to Lee, Henningfeld, and Tabourne (2012), there is "considerable research" (p. 59) that documents the benefits of life review programs. Lee, Tabourne, and Yoon (2008) have written, "Life review has been found to be a highly effective and efficient therapeutic process that reduces behavioral problems, promotes self-control, and prevents further deterioration" (p. 172). They went on to also cite research that showed life review to be effective in decreasing depression. In their own research on life review, Lee and colleagues reported positive outcomes including decreases in emotional disturbance and increases in self-esteem and life satisfaction.

Reminiscence therapy is typically conducted in small groups that meet at least once a week. Sessions usually last 30-60 minutes with most participants taking part in 6 to 10 sessions. Within sessions participants are encouraged to talk about past positive or happy events in their lives. Typical topics include pets, school, friends, and family. Rather than focusing on intrapersonal functions (as life review therapy does), the focus in reminiscence therapy is more on interpersonal functions (Clark, 2003; Kast-Godley & Gatz, 2000; Liu, Lin, Chen, & Huang, 2007). In addition to providing social interaction, numerous benefits of reminiscence have been extolled in the literature.

Reminiscing may do the following:

- enhance self-esteem as people review their history of competence and productivity;
- positively affect life satisfaction;
- reaffirm an individual's sense of identity;
- bring pleasure from relating the past to others;
- create joy or mood enhancement in sharing with others who have lived through similar times;
- help to overcome loneliness and separation;
- stimulate cognitive processes that might otherwise atrophy;
- increase orientation for time, person, and space;
- provide feelings of cognitive competence as persons draw on their long-term memories;
- allow for the expression of feelings, producing a positive effect from fond memories or release of pent-up anger;
- reduce feelings of depression as individuals recall their lives as worthwhile;
- increase individuals' respect by being able to express themselves clearly in front of others;
- comfort those who feel that their lives were in the past;
- provide opportunity for persons to "improve" their past lives by "redesigning" them to enhance self-images or public impressions;
- serve to enable persons to come to terms with old disappointments in order to gain a balanced perspective on their lives;
- allow persons to see that others have the same problems they do;

- encourage people to discover similarities with others, creating a common bond;
- reduce fear and anxiety as individuals learn to share experiences with others who are accepting;
- offer enjoyment by sharing old jokes and humorous events;
- improve behavioral and cognitive functioning;
- resolve grief;
- serve to disrupt the feeling of pain;
- provide opportunity for individuals to gain insights into themselves because listening to others' lives is a means to obtaining new personal perspectives into one's own life; and
- create self-awareness about leisure.

(Chiang et al., 2009; Deig, 1989; Edinberg, 1985; Field, 1989; Gayle, 1989; Johnson, 1999; Koffman, 2000; Liu, Lin, Chen, & Huang, 2007; Teague & MacNeil, 1992; Tabourne, 1995; Wang, 2007; Weiss, 1989; Weiss & Kronberg, 1986; Weiss & Thurn, 1987)

Randomized controlled trails (RCT) research completed in recent years would seem to collaborate many of the claims made for reminiscence therapy. Liu, Lin, Chen, and Huang's (2007) study of elderly people living alone found participation in a reminiscence therapy group resulted in increases in self-esteem and life satisfaction and decreases In loneliness and depression. Wang (2007), who conducted group reminiscence therapy with patients with dementia in Taiwan, reported increases in cognitive function and diminished depression following the intervention. Chiang et al. (2009) examined the effects of reminiscence therapy on institutionalized elderly people. These researchers reported improved socialization, induced feelings of accomplishment in participants, and decreased depression.

Research reviews (Johnson, 1999; Livingston et al., 2005; Nugent, 1995; Scott & Clare, 2003; Thornton & Brotchie, 1987; Woods, Spector, Jones, Orrell, & Davies, 2005) have warned, however, that formal research studies on reminiscence therapy remain sparse and those published have produced mixed results. It appears that many more empirical studies are needed to explore key variables represented in reminiscence. For example, varying social contexts (e.g., widowed men, widowed women, single women) may produce inconsistent findings (David, 1990), as may the lack of a standard model or approach to reminiscence (Soltys & Coats, 1995).

Watt and Cappeliez (2000) have amplified on the lack of standardization in models or approaches to reminiscence. They have proposed that a possible reason for inconclusive research findings may be because there appear to be up to six different types of reminiscing. These researchers have suggested the type of reminiscing emphasized can have a large affect on results.

For example, those who successfully age tend to engage in integrative and instrumental reminiscing. In integrative reminiscence participants are provided a sense of meaning and purpose for their lives. This approach involves attempting to accept or resolve past negative experiences, engaging in positive evaluation of how the person lives up to his or her ideals, and demonstrating some level of continuity between the person's past sense of self and his or her current self-beliefs.

The focus in instrumental reminiscing is on recollections of past problem-solving with the result that this process can positively impact current coping practices by influencing the selection of successful coping strategies. Remembering past problem-solving includes recalling memories of past plans, activities to reach goals, attainment of goals, assisting others to deal with their problems, and attempts to overcome difficulties.

Research conducted by Watt and Cappeliez (2000) employed one group that used an integrative reminiscing approach and a second group that used an instrumental reminiscing approach. They found both reminiscing approaches decreased levels of depression in older adults. It may be that one procedure researchers may wish to employ is that of more sharply defining the type of reminiscing approach they emphasize in their reminiscing groups. Planning specifically what type of reminiscing will be emphasized would allow more precision in conducting the intervention and in measuring results.

The lack of specificity in the reminiscing approach used in research perhaps reflects the technique of reminiscence therapy in general. In contrast to approaches such as remotivation therapy, reminiscence therapy does not have a formalized set of structures or procedures. Nevertheless, several authors have provided guidelines and suggestions for conducting reminiscing groups.

For instance, it has been suggested that group members should be approached individually about being in the group so that they may be given a choice regarding their participation and that they may know in advance who the other group members will be. They should also be briefed that the purpose of the group is simply not to talk about "the old days" but to review life experiences to learn to better appreciate themselves.

The size of the group should be kept under 10 to 12 members, with some groups as small as five or six, depending on the type of client. It is important to allow time for each individual to interact within the group session, which is typically an hour or less. Normally, groups meet at the same time and place once each week, with the flexibility to meet more often if desired. At times, however, sessions may be held in special locations in order to stimulate the reminiscing process. Sessions may be organized around a specific topic (e.g., most enjoyable vacation, favorite games, first playmate, first pet, school days), a topical area (e.g., historical event, holidays, seasons), or developmental stage (e.g., childhood, adolescence). The group may be long or short term, depending on the purpose of the group and the length of stay within a facility (Deig, 1989; Edinberg, 1985; Field, 1989; Johnson, 1999).

Weiss (1989), in a *Therapeutic Recreation Journal* article, suggested a one-on-one approach to reminiscing for those who do not have the capacity to interact successfully in a group setting. Staff, volunteers, and family members may be trained to facilitate reminiscing with individual clients during one-on-one contacts.

Any number of approaches have proven effective as means to trigger memories of the past. Weiss and Kronberg (1986) used a "lifeline" in order to facilitate reminiscence about leisure. Various formats, ranging from paper and pencil to verbal interactions, were used to consecutively (by dates) present major historical events (i.e., political, social, scientific events) of the past hundred years. Weiss, this time writing with Thurn (1987), has also described the use of mapping to stimulate reminiscence. Maps and mapping activities were successfully used with people residing in nursing homes who were mildly to moderately confused.

Other aids or props that have been employed to encourage reminiscing include visual aids (e.g., antiques, old photographs, scrap-books, vintage clothing, artworks), food (to stimulate recall of experiences related to taste or smell), scents (spices, flowers, perfumes), videos and slides (of old news, political speeches, etc.), and music (to arouse memories and feelings) (Edinberg, 1985; Field, 1989; Karras, 1987).

An interesting approach from Japan allowed participants to guide staff in the use of old-style tools, in contrast to having them verbally describe their memories. Participants were reported to be eager to take part and displayed increased concentration and improved mood. Another unique aspect of this approach was the occurrence of a "role reversal" as participants taught staff how to use tools with which the staff were not familiar (Yamagami, Oosawa, Ito, & Yamaguchi, 2007). Whatever means are used to facilitate reminiscing about a chosen topic, it is important that the leader be an empathetic listener who displays acceptance and appreciation for each member of the group.

Implications for Recreational Therapy

Recreational therapists need to understand that reminiscing is not simply an idle activity to fill time, but the process of reminiscing is a natural phenomenon that may provide valuable benefits for old people. Recreational therapists who serve elders may conduct reminiscence therapy groups or may wish to train other staff, volunteers, and relatives of clients to conduct one-on-one reminiscing sessions for clients for whom a group is not appropriate. Reminiscence may also be actively encouraged during various recreational therapy programs. Art and music programs, in particular, would seem to offer opportunities for facilitating reminiscence on the part of clients. Reminiscing may also be used by recreational therapists as a tool in completing life review.

Chapter Summary

Recreational therapy is diverse in the types of populations it serves and the nature of the settings in which it is delivered. Diversity is therefore demanded in its methods. In this chapter, a wide variety of facilitation techniques have been reviewed that have implications for, or direct application in, the practice of recreational therapy. It is up to each recreational therapist engaged in evidence-based practice to assess research findings and other reliable evidence, along with his or her talents and abilities, to determine which facilitation techniques are most appropriate to use.

Several of the facilitation techniques covered in this chapter (e.g., meditation, therapeutic touch, biofeedback, imagery) could be referred to as *alternative therapies*. These are techniques not traditionally embraced by the medical community and, therefore, fall outside the mainstream of medical practice. Another term for such treatment approaches is *complementary therapies*, suggesting these therapies are to be employed in conjunction with conventional treatment approaches (Swackhamer, 1995).

Recreational therapists have generally remained open-minded toward complementary and alternative therapies. Their holistic underpinnings provide a basis for practice that is accepting of means to treat the whole person in order to meet psychosocial, intellectual, and spiritual needs, as well as physical needs. It is likely that complementary and alternative therapies will continue to be developed and will be used within recreational therapy.

No matter what techniques are used, it is wise to keep in mind that recreational therapy is a very human enterprise. Any helping interaction must begin with the building of a person-to-person relationship based on mutual respect and a shared confidence in the abilities of both persons to meet the client's problems or needs. Good person-to-person relationships remain at the heart of recreational therapy, regardless of which particular approach is used.

Reading Comprehension Questions

1. What are the components of leisure education/counseling?
2. Do you personally favor using values clarification exercises as a major part of leisure education or leisure counseling?

3. Why do you think bibliotherapy is enjoying increased popularity within TR?
4. Are there advantages of cinematherapy over bibliotherapy? Explain.
5. Are there films you believe could be useful tools for cinematherapy? Please describe.
6. Can you suggest applications of horticulture therapy in therapeutic recreation?
7. Do you see therapeutic recreation as playing a critical role in the therapeutic community? Please explain.
8. Have you ever observed the use of humor in therapy? Explain.
9. Do you believe it is "risky" to use touch in therapy? Explain.
10. Should progressive relaxation training be used by therapeutic recreation specialists?
11. Do you agree that diaphragmatic breathing is the first step to relaxation? Explain.
12. Do you agree that physical activity is nature's tranquilizer? Explain.
13. At what level do people need to exercise to gain benefits from physical activity?
14. List potential health benefits to be derived from physical activity.
15. What are means to use essential oils in aromatherapy?
16. Describe qigong and tai chi.
17. What types of preparation do recreational therapists need before leading adventure therapy?
18. Explain processing. Why is processing important in producing therapeutic outcomes?
19. How does assertiveness differ from aggression?
20. What is social skills training?
21. What is cognitive rehabilitation?
22. Do you believe animal-assisted therapy should be done by recreational therapists? If so, with which client groups?
23. For what purposes might aquatic therapy be used?
24. Can you suggest any uses of technology in RT interventions?
25. Should recreational therapists use creative arts or should they be only used by music therapists and art therapists?
26. What is your opinion of retail therapy?
27. What is your evaluation of validation therapy? Can it or principles from it be used in recreational therapy? Explain.
28. Compare and contrast Cognitive Stimulation Therapy, Remotivation Therapy, Resocialization, Sensory Training, and Reminiscence Therapy.

Appendix A: 20 Things You Love to Do Activity

Twenty Things You Love to Do

The procedure for 20 Things involves each participant writing the numbers 1 to 20 down the middle of a sheet of paper. To the right of each number, participants are asked to "make a list of 20 things in life that you love to do." Sometimes the leader will encourage participants by telling them the things can be "big" or "little" and may give an example or two of things that bring him or her happiness or enjoyment. The leader also constructs a personal list and, when finished, he or she should tell the participants that it is fine if they have over or under 20 things listed.

Then the leader asks the participants to use the left side of their papers to review their list and code each behavior in the following way:

1. A dollar sign ($) is to be placed beside any item that costs more than $3 each time it is done. (The amount could vary, depending on the group.)
2. The letter A is to be placed beside those items the student (participant) really prefers to do alone; the letter P next to those activities he (or she) prefers to do with other people; and the letters A-P next to activities he (or she) enjoys doing equally alone or with other people.
3. The letters PL are to be placed beside those items that require planning.
4. The coding N5 is to be placed next to those items that would not have been listed five years ago.
5. The numbers 1 through 5 are to be placed beside the five most important items. The best-loved activity should be numbered 1; the second best, 2; and so on.
6. The participant is to indicate next to each activity when (day, date) it was last engaged in.

The list may be used in any number of ways. For instance, participants can discuss within a group what they learned from the exercise; they may describe to a partner how they like to do their No. 1-rated activity; or, they may use the sheet to develop a plan to engage more frequently in enjoyable activities.

Appendix B: Relaxation Techniques

Three-Part Breathing

Take a deep, diaphragmatic breath. Imagine that your lungs are divided into three parts. Visualize the lowest part of your lungs filling with air. Use only your diaphragm; your chest should remain relatively still. Imagine the middle part of your lungs filling, and as you visualize the expansion, allow your rib cage to move slightly forward. Visualize the upper part filling with air and your lungs becoming completely full. Your shoulders will rise slightly and move backward. Exhale fully and completely. As you empty your upper lungs, drop your shoulders slightly. Visualize the air leaving the middle portion of your lungs, and feel your rib cage contract. Pull in your abdomen to force out the last bit of air from the bottom of your lungs. Repeat the exercise four times (Mason, 2001).

Alternate-Nostril Breathing

Place your right forefinger over your right nostril, pressing lightly to close off the nostril. Take a deep, full breath, inhaling with your left nostril. Visualize your lungs filling fully and expanding completely. Remove your finger from the right nostril and lightly close off the left nostril. Exhale slowly through the now open right nostril. Be certain to exhale fully and completely. Inhale through the right nostril. Close off the right nostril and exhale fully and completely through the left nostril. Repeat slowly and rhythmically for three more breaths (Mason, 2001).

Introduction to Progressive Relaxation Training

(Here is what might typically be provided as an introduction to progressive relaxation training. Naturally, the therapist should adjust the presentation for his or her own style.)

1. Start by making sure you are comfortable, whether you are sitting or lying down. You should remove any item that might constrain you. You may wish to take off your watch or glasses or slip out of your shoes.
2. Please refrain from talking during the session. You can nod or give a hand signal to communicate. I will dim the lights in the room to cut down on external stimuli (and, perhaps, turn on soft background music).
3. We will tense each muscle, or muscle group, for five to seven seconds; then relax for 10 to 12 seconds. As we do this, remember to pay attention to the feelings of tension as you contract your muscles and the relaxation feeling once you release the tension.
4. Release the tension immediately upon my cue. Release it immediately, rather than gradually. Once you've relaxed a group of muscles, don't use them unnecessarily, except to move to make yourself more comfortable.
5. Let's begin by closing your eyes gently, keeping them closed throughout the session. Get into a comfortable position. Take a deep breath from your diaphragm. Slowly and easily take deep breaths through your nose. Fill up your lungs as much as you can. Hold it briefly, being aware of the contractions of the back and chest muscles. (pause) Now breathe more slowly. (pause) Keep this slow breathing going. Breathe deeply in (pause) and deeply out. (pause) Let the tension go from your body. (pause) As the air leaves your lungs, say to yourself, "relax," and notice how your muscles relax.

(In the section that follows, the actual relaxation training begins.)

Progressive Relaxation Exercises

By making a tight fist, tense the muscles in your dominant hand. Now (pause) concentrate your attention on the muscles of your hand and lower arm. Feel the tension in these muscles as they pull hard and tight (for 5-7 seconds). OK, relax. (pause) Notice how it feels to have those muscles limp and loose. (pause) Take a deep breath, feel the relaxation as the tension flows out as you exhale. Notice how the muscle group becomes more and more relaxed. (Some authors suggest repeating each exercise a second time. Do so, if you wish.)

Now tense your bicep in your dominant arm as much as possible by pushing down with your elbow. If you have trouble getting the amount of tension you want, pull your elbow inward toward the body as you press down. Hold it. (pause) Concentrate on the tension. (pause) Now, relax. Just let yourself relax. Note the difference between the tension you felt and the relaxation you feel now as you allow the bicep to become limp. (pause) Take a deep breath, then feel the relaxation as the air flows out of your body. Breathe deeply and fully as you allow the tension to flow away. (Once again, you may wish to repeat this exercise.)

Now let's repeat for the nondominant hand and lower arm. Ready, make a fist. (pause) Hold it. Feel the tension, (pause) notice the tension. (pause) OK, relax. (pause) Think of your hand going loose and limp. Be aware of the contrast between your feeling of relaxation and the prior tension. (pause) Breathe deeply and relax. (You may or may not wish to ask participants to do deep breathing with each exercise. Deep breathing is not included in each exercise in Appendix B but you may include it if you wish.)

Now tense your bicep for the nondominant arm.

Push down with your elbow, putting tension on your bicep as much as possible. Concentrate on the tension. (pause) Hold it. (pause) OK, now relax. (pause) Try to be aware of the feelings in your arm. It really doesn't matter how it feels, just learn to pay close attention to those feelings.

Just allow the muscles to go on relaxing while you shift attention to the next muscle group, the face and neck. We'll begin with the forehead. Use an exaggerated frown to do this—or lift the eyebrows as high as you can. Notice where your forehead feels particularly tense. (pause) OK, relax. Take a few seconds to notice your forehead as it relaxes; let it feel smooth and fully relaxed.

Let's do the central part of the face. Close your eyes very tightly and focus on your slow, calm breathing. (pause) Now with your eyes still tightly closed, wrinkle your nose. Hold the position. (pause) Now relax, letting tension out. (pause) Feel the relaxation in and around your eyes and nose.

Next, tense the muscles in the lower part of your face.

To do this, bring your upper and lower teeth together lightly and curl up your tongue hard against the roof of your mouth. (pause) Hold it. (pause) Relax, letting your tongue fall to the floor of your mouth. Notice how it feels to have those muscles loosen and relax.

Clench your teeth firmly. Bite your teeth together and pull the corners of your mouth back. Notice the tension. (pause) *Let go* of the tension, so your jaw relaxes and your teeth and lips part slightly. Notice the difference in the way it feels. Notice the absence of tension in the jaw right up to your temples.

Pucker your lips. Keep up the pressure, noting where it feels tense. (pause) Now, let the lips go free and loose. (pause) Notice the difference in the way it feels.

Ok, good, now let's go to the neck muscles. To tense the neck muscles, pull your chin down toward your chest, but keep it from touching. Do you feel just a bit of trembling? OK, relax. (pause) Notice how you feel with the neck muscles loosened.

Fine. Next we'll move to the chest and abdomen. Tense the chest by taking a deep breath, holding it, and at the same time pulling the shoulder blades together—try to get the shoulder blades to touch. Go ahead, deep breath, hold it with your shoulder blades pulled together. Do you feel tension in the chest, shoulders, and upper back? OK, relax. (pause) Let your arms go loose. (pause) Notice the feeling as those muscles loosen.

Tighten your abdomen. Hold the tension by pulling it in and making it hard. Pull your muscles in even more. (pause) Hold it. (pause) Now, relax. (pause) Breathe calmly, releasing tension. As you exhale, let out even more tension.

Now we'll move to the legs and feet. Begin with the upper right leg. Try to make the large muscle on your upper leg get hard. Lift the leg slightly if you have difficulty hardening the muscle. Now, let your muscles go slack. (pause) Let go of the tension. Observe the relaxation.

Now let's do your lower right leg. Tense these muscles by pulling your toes toward your head or pointing your toes away from your head. Be aware of the tension. (pause) OK, relax. (pause) Let your leg go back to a relaxed position. Take note of the relaxation.

Now let's do your right foot. Turn your foot inward and at the same time curl your toes. Ready, begin. Not too hard, just enough to feel the tension. Feel the tension in the foot. (pause) OK, fine, relax. (pause) Notice the relaxation when the foot and toes are released to take their most restful position.

We'll now shift to the left leg, starting with the upper left leg.

Make the large muscle on your upper left leg get hard now. (pause) Hold it. (pause) OK, good, relax.

Now for your lower left leg, create tension by pulling your toes toward your head, now. Put tension on the calf of your leg. (pause) Hold it. (pause) OK, relax. (pause) The calf now feels loose and floppy. Be aware of that feeling in your calf.

Turn your left foot inward and, at the same time, curl your toes. Ready, begin. (pause) Hold it for just a second. (pause) Now, relax. (pause) Notice the relaxation when the foot and toes are released to a restful position.

Try to be aware of the feelings in your legs. Do they feel relaxed? Whatever they feel like is fine, what's important is that you learn to pay close attention to these feelings.

Now slowly and easily, take a *deep breath.* Be sure to fill up the bottom part of your lungs as well as the top. Now exhale fully and completely, releasing even more tension with the exhalation. Feel your rib cage relax as you exhale. Keep this slow, deep breathing going.

With each in-breath, whisper a thin "re." With each out-breath, whisper or think "lax." No rush. (pause) Pause between breaths. Remember "re" as you breathe in and "lax" as you breathe out. (pause) Go ahead, try it now. (pause) Relax.

Don't force your breathing. Just let it flow, easy and slow.

(pause) Re-lax. (pause) Try it now on your own for the next minute or so.

We've now relaxed the muscles of the whole body. Just allow them to continue relaxing. (pause) Let your whole body lie limp. Feel the relaxation spread throughout your body. (pause) If you feel any tension in any muscle group, let go of it. Let go of any tension anywhere. (pause) Relax, loose and easy. (pause) Just relax.

Enjoy your state of relaxation. (pause) Focus on the pleasant feelings of relaxation. (pause) Enjoy your relaxation.

Now before you get up, stretch yourself slowly and gently. Don't rush. (pause) Open your eyes slowly, feeling calm and relaxed, just as if you had a brief nap. (pause) Get up slowly, feeling relaxed and refreshed.

Zahourek's Application of Imagery

A person might be encouraged to experience a visit to a favorite vacation spot, the mountains, a fantasy place, or his or her most relaxing spot at home. Drawing on a past positive experience or reminding a patient that he or she has experienced previous relaxing times vivifies the scene. If a beach is visualized (a popular image for many people), instruct the patient to "see" the color of the water and the sky, to notice the "smell" of the salt air, and to "hear" the birds singing and the surf hitting the shore. A sense of relaxation is encouraged and other bodily sensations are mentioned, such as "feel the warm sun on your back and how the sand feels as it slips through your toes." Using words such as *relax, comfort, peace,* and *soft* all develop sensory responses to the images (Zahourek, 1988, p.76).

Lightness Relaxation Exercise

Get into a comfortable, relaxed position. . .
Allow your mind-body to relax. . .
As you gently allow your eyes to close
Take some relaxing breaths and notice your body
Relaxing even further. . .
And your mind becoming still and peaceful. . .
And your feelings calm. . .
As you remain in this peaceful state of relaxation
Concentrate your attention on your right arm
Just notice your right arm and a sensation of lightness
Your right arm is feeling lighter and lighter
It is so light as it begins to float higher and higher

You notice two helium balloons attached to your wrist
You notice the colors of the two light balloons pulling your
arm up even higher.
Repeat to yourself. . .
My right arm is light. . .
I feel it floating. . .
The balloons are lifting my arm up even higher. . .
Just allow your arm to float without any effort . . . higher and
higher
Fine. . .
And now let your arm gently float down to its resting position
and take the balloons from your wrist.
Let them float up to the ceiling or to the sky. . .
Take an energizing breath, open your eyes, stretch, and smile.
Notice how relaxed and refreshed you feel.
Go about the rest of your day calmly active
And actively calm. (Flynn, 1980, p. 182)

Benson's Techniques

1. Sit quietly in a comfortable position.
2. Close your eyes.
3. Deeply relax all your muscles, beginning at your feet and progressing up to your face. Keep them relaxed.
4. Breathe through your nose. Become aware of your breathing. As you breathe out, say the word "One" silently to yourself. For example, breathe IN. . .OUT, "ONE"; IN. . .OUT, "ONE"; etc. Breathe easily and naturally.
5. Continue for 10 to 20 minutes. You may open your eyes to check the time, but do not use an alarm. When you finish, sit quietly for several minutes, at first with your eyes closed and later with your eyes opened. Do not stand up for a few minutes.
6. Do not worry about whether you are successful in achieving a deep level of relaxation. Maintain a passive attitude and permit relaxation to occur at its own pace. When distracting thoughts occur, try to ignore them by not dwelling upon them and return to repeating "ONE." With practice, the response should come with little effort. Practice the technique once or twice daily, but not within two hours after any meal, since the digestive processes seem to interfere with the elicitation of the Relaxation Response. (Benson, 1975, pp. 162, 163; italics removed)

Running for Relaxation

- Loosen the face and drop the jaw, with the idea that if the face is relaxed the rest of the body will follow.
- Run upright, keeping the body perpendicular to the ground.
- Pull the shoulders back slightly and push the buttocks forward.
- Carry the arms low and slightly away from the body with the shoulders loose and relaxed, yet stable.
- Keep the hands softly closed and relaxed.
- Keep the stride at a comfortable length that allows for smooth striding, not too short and no overstriding.

- To move faster, keep the stride fluid, focusing on relaxation rather than power. (Lynch, 1989)

Runners Stretches

Each position is held for 10 to 15 seconds, unless otherwise noted. The *total body stretch* is a good one to use to begin and end stretching. The runner lies on his or her back with arms and legs fully extended. Fingers and toes are pointed and stretched as far as possible for five seconds, three to five times.

The *foot lift* involves standing on one foot while grasping the opposite ankle and slowly pulling the heel toward the buttocks, where it is held during the stretch. Balance is maintained by supporting the other hand and arm against an object such as a wall or tree. The exercise is done for both legs.

The *toe touch* is done to prevent hamstring pulls, back pain, and pulled muscles. With the feet spread about shoulder width apart, the runner bends slowly from the waist until he or she can feel a pull in the back of the legs and then holds the position.

The *wall lean* is performed for the Achilles tendon, calf, and shin muscles. With the runner facing the wall and a couple of feet away from it, both hands are placed against the wall at about shoulder to eye level. Starting from the position of having the legs about shoulder width apart, one leg is placed forward of the other, bending the front leg and slightly bending the rear leg, while attempting to keep the heels flat on the ground. From this position, the person pushes his or her hips forward until the stretch is felt on the inside of the leg and in the Achilles. After holding the position for the usual 10 to 15 seconds, the legs are switched and the stretch is repeated for the other leg.

The *spinal twist* is completed while sitting with the right leg straight and the left leg bent so it crosses over the right leg with the foot resting to the outside of the right knee. The right elbow is bent slightly so it rests on the outside of the upper left thigh. The left hand and arm rest on the floor behind the person to provide support. From this position, the head is turned to look over the left shoulder while rotating the upper body toward the left hand and arm. After stretching, the same position is repeated for the other side of the body.

The final stretch is the *groin stretch*, which is used to relax the body and prevent groin pulls. Here the individual lies on his or her back with the soles of the feet together. The knees fall apart, and as this occurs, the hips are relaxed. The position is held for about 40 seconds. (Coats, 1989)

Stretching Exercises

- neck stretch (drawing the head down toward the chest); neck turn (looking over the left and then right shoulder);
- shoulder shrug (drawing the shoulders up toward the ears);
- elbow waggle (with the hands behind the head, drawing the elbows backward);
- wraparound (extending the arms out to the sides from the shoulders parallel to the floor, then drawing the hands backward as though attempting to touch the back, and finally, bringing the arms across in front of the body to give yourself a hug);
- palms down (sitting on the floor with legs in front on the floor, bending forward from the waist in an attempt to touch the palms of the hands on the floor);
- shin clasp (sitting on the floor with legs in front, raising one knee while clasping the shin of the leg with both hands trying to pull the kneecap so the head rests on it. Repeat for other leg.) ;

- shoe stretch (sitting on the floor with legs in front, extending both legs while sliding both hands forward in an attempt to reach the shoe. Repeat for the other shoe.); and
- leg left (sitting in a chair with the back against the back of the chair, raising one leg so it is parallel to the floor, curling the toes toward the body as much as possible—then raise the leg upward. Repeat for the other leg.)

In presenting these stretches in "Unstress Your Life (1987), the editors of *Prevention* magazine suggest that slow, deliberate movements should be used until a tug is felt and, at that time, the position should be held. At first, it should be held for 10 seconds; then increased to 30 seconds with practice. The editors recommend each exercise be done while seated and repeated two or three times.

Walking for Relaxation

1. Walk at a natural, comfortable pace that is brisk enough to increase heart rate and cause breathing to have greater depth than normal;
2. let the arms swing loosely and naturally with a rhythm in the walk;
3. walk upright with the head high, back straight, and abdomen flat;
4. lean forward slightly on hills or when walking rapidly;
5. land on the heel first and roll on to the ball of the foot;
6. swing the legs forward freely from the hips, taking long easy strides, but do not overstride;
7. take deeper breaths than normal while not becoming breathless;
8. pace and distance should increase as physical fitness improves;
9. the pace should always be brisk, challenging the cardiorespiratory system.

Walking requires a minimum of equipment; the choice of shoes and clothing needs to be given some thought. Shoes may range from running shoes to hiking boots (depending on walking style and terrain). The main criteria for the selection of any shoe are comfort and good support. Clothing should be comfortable and suitable for weather conditions.

Chapter 4

The Recreational Therapy Process

■ Chapter Purpose

It is critical that recreational therapists become aware of basic philosophical beliefs that prevail in recreational therapy. Beliefs affect theoretical notions that, in turn, affect the principles on which professionals operate. It is equally important that a thorough understanding of the recreational therapy process be gained, since this process underlies the delivery of all recreational therapy services. This chapter will help the student to develop a more comprehensive and systematic perspective on these fundamental concerns that will ultimately pervade the delivery of services to clients.

■ Key Terms

- Humanistic perspective
- Holistic medicine
- Actualizing tendency
- Functional interventions
- Prescriptive activity
- Recreation
- Leisure
- Diagnosis
- Skilled observation
- Specific goal observation
- Reliability
- Maslow's hierarchy
- Strengths list
- Goals set
- RT individual intervention plan
- Activity analysis
- Referrals
- Theory

- Stabilizing tendency
- Health Protection
- Health Promotion
- Recreational therapy process
- Intrinsic motivation
- Assessment
- High-level wellness
- Naturalistic observations
- Standardized observations
- Validity
- Goals/General objectives
- Needs list
- Specific objectives
- Evaluation
- Conceptual models
- Discharge planning
- Philosophy
- Evidence-Based Practice

◼ Objectives

- Understand the humanistic perspective as it relates to recreational therapy.
- Recognize the relationship between recreational therapy and high-level wellness.
- Appreciate the need to employ a systematic method of problem solving known as the recreational therapy process.
- Reduce the recreational therapy process to a series of logical steps, defining each in terms of its role in the total process.
- Explain methods of client assessment, including strength-based assessment.
- Describe the setting of priorities to meet client needs.
- Relate guidelines for formulating client goals and objectives.
- Describe the elements of an individual (customized) recreational therapy intervention (care) plan.
- Know the importance of clearly defined implementation procedures.
- Recognize approaches to evaluation.
- State a rationale for involvement of clients in the entire recreational therapy process.
- Understand the process of making referrals.
- Have basic understandings of discharge planning.
- Define the terms philosophy and theory.
- Understand the relationship of theory to practice.
- Understand how theory from conceptual models affects the recreational therapy process.
- Describe major recreational therapy conceptual therapy models.
- Describe the place of evidence-based practice in recreational therapy.

The Humanistic Perspective

Components of the humanistic psychology perspective are outlined in Table 4-1. The humanistic perspective is the perspective of Carl Rogers and Abraham Maslow (Austin, 2011a).

Table 4.1

The Humanistic Approach

Those embracing a humanistic approach:

- take a holistic view of the person;
- hold that both children and adults are capable of growth and change;
- view each person as being unique and possessing dignity and worth who should be treated with positive regard;
- see people as being in dynamic interaction with the environment, not just reacting to the external world;
- hold that people have a need to find meaning in their lives;
- view people as primarily social beings who have a need to belong and feel valued;
- perceive people as healthy who strive for personal satisfaction, yet go beyond their own needs to understand and care about others;
- believe that people express a tendency toward self-actualization;

Table 4.1 (cont.)

- believe therapists should display positive, warm, and accepting attitudes toward clients;
- believe therapists should be genuine and display empathetic understanding of clients;
- see the therapeutic relationship as a means to promote client growth so that clients can deal not only with their presenting problems but prepare to deal with problems they encounter in the future as well.

Sources: Austin, D. R. (2011). *Lessons Learned: An Open Letter to Recreational Therapy Students and Practitioners.* Urbana, IL: Sagamore Publishing; Cain, D. J. (2002). Defining characteristics, history, and evolution of humanistic psychotherapies. In D. J. Cain & J. Seeman (Eds.). *Humanistic Psychotherapies: Handbook of Research and Practice.* Washington, D.C.: American Psychological Association; Kunstler, R., & Stavola Daly, F. (2010). *Therapeutic Recreation Leadership and Programming,* Champaign, IL: Human Kinetics.; Sundeen, S. J., Stuart, G. W., Rankin, E. A. D., & Cohen, S. A. (1998). *Nurse-Client Interaction: Implementing the Nursing Process* (6th ed.). St. Louis, MO: Mosby.

Recreational therapy seems to epitomize the humanistic psychology perspective (Austin, 2011a, 2011b; Kunstler & Stavola Daly, 2010). O'Morrow (1980) stated that recreational therapists "emphasize the concept that the 'whole person' is involved" (p. 151). Recreational therapists take a holistic approach with their clients. They see each client as an individual possessing a unique biological, psychological, and social background from which to react to the environment as a total person or whole being.

Also central to the humanistic orientation of recreational therapy are the beliefs that people have the freedom to change, make decisions, and assume responsibility for their own actions—particularly in regard to leisure. This "freedom to become" or ability to develop oneself more fully is in keeping with the provision of recreational therapy activities. Through activities, clients express their natural motivation toward stimulus-seeking in positive recreative experiences in contrast to waiting passively for the environment to act on them. Within the accepting atmosphere provided in recreational therapy, clients have the opportunity to reach unexplored potentials.

Finally, recreational therapy is interested in helping people feel good about themselves through personal satisfaction gained in recreation and leisure. The recreational therapist assumes a caring, understanding attitude toward the client and attempts to create a free and open recreational environment where the client can experience positive interactions with others. Good person-to-person relationships are at the heart of recreational therapy, as are opportunities for self-expression and creative accomplishment. Through such experiences, persons may enhance positive self-concepts and learn to grow beyond themselves to care about others.

Positive Psychology as an Extension of Humanistic Psychology

This affirming approach that flows out of humanistic psychology shares the optimistic view of human nature assumed by positive psychology. Both humanistic psychology and positive psychology maintain humans possess a self-actualizing tendency. (Please see Chapter 2 for more complete information on humanistic psychology and positive psychology.) Like humanistic psychology, the focus of positive psychology is the development of human strengths and potentials (Jorgensen & Nafstad, 2004). In fact, there are so many similarities between humanistic psychology and positive psychology that some see positive psychology simply as an extension of humanistic psychology (Austin, 2011b).

Certainly positive psychology's *Broaden-and-Build Theory of Positive Emotion* (Fredrickson, 2001, 2009) supports the longstanding approach by recreational therapists of helping clients to experience positive emotions that negate negative emotions, thus opening up clients to try new ways of behaving, thinking, or feeling. Recreational therapists have also long followed the positive psychology approach of developing clients' strengths and abilities, typically using client strengths and abilities to overcome client problems. Another major principle of positive psychology is providing positive environments that promote change. This principle is one that recreational therapists embraced long prior to the advent of positive psychology. Over years of practice, recreational therapists have striven to provide clients with safe, warm, and supportive recreational environments that support client change.

Finally, those applying positive psychology "promote optimal functioning across the full range of human functioning, from disorder and distress to health and fulfillment" (Linley & Joseph, 2004, p. 4). It is generally agreed that recreational therapists take a holistic approach that spans the spectrum of treating illness to promoting well-being—or simultaneously relieving suffering and promoting well-being. Thus the philosophical underpinnings of positive psychology join philosophical beliefs from humanistic psychology as another basis for recreational therapy practice.

High-Level Wellness

The humanistic perspective has also helped to bring about the concept of **high-level wellness** first championed by Dunn (1961) and Ardell (1977). High-level wellness is defined by Dunn (1961) as ". . . an integrated method of functioning which is oriented toward maximizing the potential of which the individual is capable" (p. 4). Dunn's approach, which centers on the wholeness of the individual, calls for not only an absence of physical illness, but also implies a psychological and environmental wellness. Thus the physical well-being of the total person is joined by mental and social well-being in forming the concept of health under the notion of high-level wellness.

High-level wellness is gained, according to Dunn (1961), when we exist in a "very favorable environment" and enjoy "peak wellness" (where illness and wellness are conceived along a continuum, with death on one end and peak wellness at the other). When limitations hinder the attainment of peak wellness, an optimal level of high-level wellness may be achieved by making the individual's environment as conducive to growth as possible. For example, intellectual potentials are difficult to alter, but we may enhance the opportunity for intellectual growth by providing a deprived child with a stimulating play environment.

Holistic Medicine

The **holistic medicine** proposed under the banner of high-level wellness treats the person, not the disease. Like recreational therapy, holistic medicine is concerned with the "whole person" and with allowing individuals to assume responsibility for their own health and well-being. According to Ardell (1977), the ultimate aim of "well medicine" (in contrast to the "traditional medicine" normally practiced by the medical community) is moving clients toward self-actualization and, therefore, the achievement of high-level wellness. While traditional medicine deals solely with illness according to Ardell, well medicine deals with wellness or health enhancement. This is not to criticize those who follow the traditional medical model where disease is eliminated by treatment without concern for the entire person. The medical model has been highly successful in developing specific treatments for diseases. The concept of wellness simply extends beyond traditional medical practices to encompass all aspects of the person—mind, body, spirit, and environment—rather than dealing with isolated parts and symptoms.

Recreational Therapy and Wellness

The similarity between **recreational therapy** and the concepts expressed by Dunn (1961) and Ardell (1977) in their separate works titled *High-Level Wellness* is striking. Both have health enhancement and self-actualization as major goals, and both have seemingly been heavily influenced by the humanistic viewpoint.

Recreational therapy, like traditional medical practice, has long dealt with the problem of illness. Unlike traditional medicine, however, recreational therapy has not dealt exclusively with illness. Recreational therapy has historically promoted the goal of self-actualization, or the facilitation of the fullest possible growth and development of the client.

Therefore, recreational therapy may be conceived to be much like traditional, medically oriented, allied health professions in its concern for preventing and alleviating illness. At the same time, recreational therapists join physicians practicing "well medicine" in their desire to bring about the self-actualization of their clients. Thus recreational therapists may be perceived to have concern for the full range of the illness-wellness continuum (Figure 4.1).

It may be seen by observing Figure 4.1 that the recreational therapist may assume several different functions, depending on the needs and desires of the client. At one point, the function of the recreational therapist may be to join with other clinical staff to help a client alleviate illness. For example, the recreational therapist may function as a member of an interdisciplinary team in a psychiatric hospital. Moving along the continuum toward wellness, we may find the recreational therapist conducting a leisure counseling program at a comprehensive behavioral health center for clients who reside in the community.

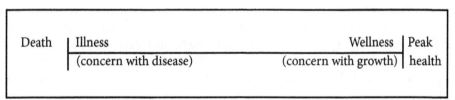

Figure 4.1. Illness-Wellness Continuum

Even further along the continuum, the recreational therapist might be found working with a community-based recreator on a community recreation program aimed at bringing about stress reduction for health enhancement.

Similar examples may be provided in all areas of recreational therapy service. For instance, the recreational therapist may initially assist the patient undergoing physical rehabilitation to prevent, curtail, or reverse secondary disabilities such as muscle atrophy or decubitus ulcers, which may be caused by inadequate care, neglect, or disuse (Avedon, 1974). This programming usually occurs within the hospital or rehabilitation center. Later, as the patient moves along the wellness continuum, the recreational therapist may provide a reintegration program to begin to foster social and leisure skills necessary for community living. Still later, the patient may be introduced to organized, community-based recreation programs as a part of a leisure counseling program.

Finally, recreational therapy and high-level wellness are similar in that they both hold that each of us is responsible for our own health. We cannot simply entrust our health to medical staff, letting them "take care of us." We may use resources outside of ourselves to improve our health but the primary responsibility is ours. As Ridenour (1983) has stated, "No one else hurts when you are sick; no one else is left out when you can't keep up in the Sunday volleyball game. No one else dies when you do. Of course, others care, but the experience is yours alone" (p. 1). Their clients are active partners with recreational therapists, rather than being passive recipients of treatment.

The recreational therapist recognizes that helping clients strive toward health promotion is the main goal of recreational therapy. This belief rests on the right of all persons to achieve their highest state of well-being, or optimal health. It is based on a philosophy that encourages clients to endeavor to achieve maximum health, rather than just conquering illness. Recreational therapy is directed toward not only the provision of treatment and rehabilitation but the dynamic process of health promotion.

Stabilizing and Actualizing Tendencies

Recreational therapists, then, assist clients in both their quests for health protection (overcoming illness) and health promotion (the achievement of the highest level of wellness possible). Two central human motivational forces underlie health protection and health promotion: the **stabilizing tendency** and the **actualizing tendency** (Pender, Murdaugh, & Parsons, 2002).

The stability tendency is directed toward maintaining the "steady state" of the organism. It is responsible for helping us adapt in order to keep stress in a manageable range and protect us from possible biophysical and psychosocial harm. It is the force behind health protection. The actualization tendency is the growth enhancement force brought to the forefront by humanistic psychologists. It is this tendency that is the motivational force behind the achievement of health promotion (Pender, Murdaugh, & Parsons, 2002).

King and Pender, among others, have offered definitions of health that emphasize the stability and actualization tendencies. King (1971) defined health as "a dynamic state in the life cycle of an organism which implies continuous adaptation to stress in the internal and external environment through optimum use of one's resources to achieve maximum potential for daily living" (p. 24). Pender, Murdaugh, and Parsons (2002) defined health this way: "Health is defined as the actualization of inherent and acquired human potential through goal-directed behavior, competent self-care, and satisfying relationships with others, while adjustments are made as needed to maintain structural integrity and harmony with relevant environments" (p. 22).

Health is a complex concept that encompasses coping adaptively, as well as growing and becoming. Healthy persons are able to cope with life's stressors, as well as develop themselves to the fullest. The healthy individual is free of barriers to actualization so he or she may actively pursue personal growth and development. Recreational therapists contribute to health by assisting clients to fulfill their needs for stability and actualization. Recreational therapy is a means to regain stability or equilibrium following a threat to health (health protection); and it is a way to achieve high-level wellness (health promotion).

Further Defining Recreational Therapy

Recreational therapy employs purposeful, goal-directed interventions that involve clients in activities that have the potential to produce recreational and leisure experiences that lead them to experiencing what are the optimal levels of health for them as individuals. For some clients, the optimal level of health may be restoring health to what was normal for the individual prior to illness. For others, it may be improving health so the person enjoys a high level of wellness. The optimal level of health for individuals coping adaptively with chronic illnesses or disabilities may be gaining the highest quality of life that is possible for them. To accomplish these ends recreational therapists employ a systematic four-step process termed the *recreational therapy process.*

The recreational therapy process is a systematic approach employed by credentialed recreational therapists to help clients who are dealing with health related concerns. It provides an organizational framework in which recreational therapists can use their knowledge and skills to assist clients to restore, maintain, or improve their levels of health, as well as to adaptively cope with chronic illnesses and disabilities in order to enjoy as high a quality of life as possible. In short, the recreational therapy process is a means by which recreational therapists can identify the status of a client's health and then assist that person to meet their health needs. It is the structure that provides a foundation for the practice of recreational therapy (Austin, 2002a).

Why the Recreational Therapy Process is Important

A long list of reasons why the recreational therapy process is important to both clients and recreational therapists can be constructed. The RT process

- provides a problem-solving structure to accomplish the delivery of effective, customized care;
- involves orderly step-by-step actions directed to achieve stated goals;
- promotes customized care by providing a system to meet specific, unique client needs;
- tailors interventions directed to the individual (not to the disease or disability);
- increases client participation in care by collaboration between the client and recreational therapist during each phase of the RT process;
- offers an efficient, systematic approach where the focus is always on the client;
- allows the delivery of care that is organized, continuous, and systematic;
- leads to a goal directed approach and outcomes that may be reached through recreational therapy interventions;
- assures accountability by including the evaluation of sought outcomes;
- through its cyclical nature, establishes interrelationships among and between its phases which assures all of its parts work together;
- provides systematic and logical sequence through which recreational therapists can apply knowledge, skills, and critical thinking to deliver quality care;
- may be universally applied as a framework in all settings in which recreational therapy transpires; and
- offers a means to interpret to others how recreational therapy contributes to client care.

History of the Recreational Therapy Process

In their early book, *Therapeutic Recreation: Its Theory, Philosophy, and Practice,* Frye and Peters (1972) referred to the delivery of recreational therapy as "a process through which purposeful efforts are directed toward achieving or maximizing desired concomitant effects of a recreative experience" (p. 44). Yet, these authors did not present the process we today we refer to as the recreational therapy process. That would come in 1976 with the publication of O'Morrow's book, titled *Therapeutic Recreation: A Helping Profession,* in which the author presented what initially was known as the therapeutic recreation process and later has been termed the recreational therapy process.

A process, O'Morrow (1976) explained, was a type of action where a goal was obtained as a result of moving from one point to another. Further, he stated that in order for a process to reach its sought ends, "Conscious and deliberate effort must be exerted...." (p. 178). O'Morrow deemed what was then referred to as the therapeutic recreation process to be "a systematic and complex planning process." He went on to spell out that its "essential characteristics" were "that it is planned, it is person-centered, and it is goal-directed" (p. 178).

The four phases of the process outlined by O'Morrow (1976, pp. 178-201) were

- assessment,
- planning,
- implementation, and
- evaluation.

The beginning letters of each word are often used as an acronym to remember the four phases. The acronym is APIE (pronounced "a-pie"). In everyday language, many students and practitioners refer to the recreational therapy process as the "a-pie process."

It has been mentioned that O'Morrow would sometimes jokingly refer to the APIE process as being "A-pie in the sky," when questioning whether the process was actually being followed by some practitioners (Austin, 2011a). On a serious note, the critical place of the recreational therapy process has been emphasized in the book *Lessons Learned*:

It is my view that a recreational therapist who does not follow the recreational therapy process should not claim to be doing recreational therapy. Without the use of the systematic problem-solving process termed the recreational therapy process, no therapeutic intent can exist. (Austin, 2011a, p.7)

Through the orderly phases of the recreational therapy process, the client's problems or concerns and strengths and needs are determined (assessment), plans are made to meet the problems or concerns (planning), the plan is initiated (implementation), and an evaluation is conducted to determine how effective the intervention has been (evaluation). Each of the phases of the recreational therapy process is dependent on the other. No phase stands alone. It is a cyclical process (Figure 4.2) that can be repeated as often as necessary in order to meet client needs.

The four parts of the recreational therapy process are presented in Figure 4.2.

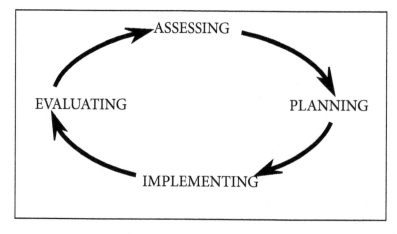

Figure 4.2. Cyclical Nature of Recreational Therapy Process

Assessment. An accurate assessment is basic to providing an individualized, comprehensive intervention plan. In the assessment phrase recreational therapists collect, organize, validate, record, and analyze data about the client. This first step in the recreational therapy process is to determine the status of the client in order to initiate a starting place in working with the client.

Planning. Planning follows assessment and is based on the analysis of assessment data. Planning involves examination of the client's needs and strengths to determine priorities, formulate goals, and develop an intervention or care plan that will stipulate specific interventions. In most settings the recreational therapist's customized care plan will become a part of an overall plan, often termed a master treatment plan or interdisciplinary treatment plan.

Implementation. The planning phase is set into motion during the implementation phase. This step in the recreational therapy process involves the actual actions necessary for carrying out the treatment, rehabilitation, care, or wellness plan (sometimes referred to as the intervention plan). The sought end of the actions is to assist the client's attainment of the treatment goals by providing interventions that are conducive to reaching the goals stipulated in the care plan.

Evaluation. Evaluation is the last step in the recreational therapy process. Both quantitative and qualitative data are collected and examined during evaluation. This phase deals with measuring the effectiveness of the client's treatment, rehabilitation, care, or wellness program. In short, evaluation answers the question: Were the sought outcomes achieved as a result of the program or intervention?

While the recreational therapy process truly provides a cornerstone for the practice of recreational therapy, it needs to be made clear that the helping process is a complex one. While guided by the recreational therapy process, recreational therapists must continually employ recreational therapy theory (e.g., conceptual models), professional knowledge and skills, and critical thinking, in designing, carrying out, and evaluating their programs. The recreational therapy process is not a "lock step" process in which the recreational therapists mechanistically design and carry out care programs. Recreational therapists must ever strive to be critical thinkers who constantly reflect on what is occurring and then decide on what course of action to pursue.

It has been stated (Austin, 2011a) that recreational therapists must be reflective (not habitual) practitioners who examine what they do and why. It is this ability to think critically by monitoring their thoughts and actions that produces reflective practitioners who employ the recreational therapy process as a means to guide them in their quest of the achievement of therapeutic outcomes for their clients.

Before discussing each of the four phases in detail, it is important to establish that the client and recreational therapist should work together throughout the entire recreational therapy process to the greatest extent to which the client is capable. The importance of this cooperation is perhaps best illustrated when considering the planning phase. Inherent in a plan is a systematic effort to reach certain goals. If the client has not been included in the planning, the client's goals could differ from those developed by the recreational therapist. Also, the likelihood is small that commitment and motivation will spring forth from the client to achieve aims he or she has not been involved in formulating. Duchene (2008) has emphasized that client involvement is a key element in developing an optimal recreational therapy plan.

Client Assessment

The first step in the recreational therapy process, **assessment**, is concerned with data collection and analysis in order to determine the status of the client. Once baseline assessment information is available, the recreational therapist can help identify and define the client's concerns and strengths. Assessment provides a beginning point so the recreational therapists can find out "where the client is," in order to determine a starting place in working with the client.

Complete assessment is a *sin quo non* for meaningful recreational therapy intervention. Witman and Ligon (2011a) found in their survey of Certified Therapeutic Recreation Specialists (CTRSs) that assessment was seen to be the top priority for collective action by RT professionals in order to improve the recreational therapy process.

Gathering Information

The purpose of recreational therapy assessment must remain clear. Assessment is *not* conducted in order to label or categorize the client. Instead, we assess to gain information that is useful in helping the client to profit from our services. Assessment should aid us to determine client strengths, interests, and expectations and to identify the nature and extent of problems or concerns. Determining client strengths and interests will allow us during the planning phase to construct a strengths list on which to base interventions. Identifying client expectations helps us to determine treatment, rehabilitation, care, or wellness goals. Evolving from the exploration of client problems will come a needs list, since a problem reflects an individual's inability to meet a need (O'Morrow & Reynolds, 1989).

Many of the different needs that may arise and become the focus for planning include the following:

- increasing confidence,
- feeling a sense of belonging,
- learning social or leisure skills,
- managing stress,
- reducing anxiety,
- reducing depression,
- reducing feelings of isolation,
- developing a wholesome body image,
- developing coping mechanisms,
- improving physical fitness,
- improving motor skills,
- becoming aware of values,
- developing a sense of humor,
- enhancing self-esteem,
- building self-efficacy,
- developing social support,
- establishing a sense of control,
- increasing leisure awareness,
- increasing leisure satisfaction,
- experiencing fun and enjoyment,
- decreasing confusion,
- improving memory, and
- increasing functional skills (e.g., ADL skills).

It should be noted that the conceptual model that predominates within a given agency will influence the focus of the treatment, rehabilitation, care, or wellness program and accordingly will have an effect on the nature of the assessment conducted. For example, agencies that subscribe to the Health Protection/Health Promotion Model will likely focus more on assessment of health concerns. Those that follow the Leisure Ability Model will necessarily emphasize leisure concerns, and so on.

The primary source of information is usually the client. Secondary sources are, however, almost always used as well. Secondary sources include medical or educational records, results of testing (e.g., psychological testing), interviews with family or friends, the social history (usually taken by a social worker), case recordings or progress notes that staff have charted, and conferences and team meetings with other staff. Occasionally, recreational therapists also assess the client's home and community to determine leisure patterns of the client, or to survey for recreation opportunities. Knowledge of the potential recreation environment found in the client's home and community are useful in understanding the client and in future planning with the client.

Recreational Therapy Diagnosis

A **diagnosis** is derived from the assessment by the recreational therapist. This diagnosis is very different from a medical diagnosis that identifies a specific disease from the patient's symptoms and involves a classification system adopted by the medical profession. O'Morrow and Reynolds (1989) lamented that once diagnosis was "a forbidden word" in recreational therapy. They wrote about the term, diagnosis:

> A literal definition of the word, with no qualifier preceding it, suggests it is a good term to use when conveying the idea that we are seeking knowledge or information about what needs to be improved, what is causing the difficulty, or what is interfering with normal functioning. (p. 142)

O'Morrow and Reynolds stated that recreational therapists can, and should, use the word "diagnosis" to describe their efforts to analyze each client's case in order to determine if recreational therapy is required and, if so, what is required. Recreational therapy diagnosis involves clinical judgments or conclusions that are made following a complete analysis and interpretation of assessment data. Recreational therapy diagnoses identify issues or problems that can appropriately be addressed by recreational therapy and form a basis for the selection of interventions and outcomes that will benefit the client. Just as nurses or doctors talk about nursing diagnosis or medical diagnosis, recreational therapists can think in terms of recreational therapy diagnosis.

The recreational therapy diagnosis may relate to the medical diagnosis but pertains strictly to those needs and strengths that the recreational therapist is able to diagnose and leads to the intervention plan that the recreational therapist will implement. Recreational therapy diagnoses deal with maintaining or restoring the client's health (i.e., health protection) or improving the client's health or health-seeking actions (i.e., health promotion).

Examples of areas where recreational therapy diagnosis deals with maintaining or restoring health for geriatric clients might consist of cognitive deficits, including memory, suspiciousness, and disorientation, or feelings of isolation and a desire for contact with others. Clients in mental health agencies may experience anxiety in social situations, a lack of self-esteem, or poor impulse control. Clients in physical medicine and rehabilitation facilities may experience pain or discomfort, or a desire for reintegration into the community. All are areas where recreational therapy can be used an as intervention.

Health promotion or wellness recreational therapy diagnoses focus on the clients' progress toward healthier behaviors, rather than a problem or issue. The recreational therapy wellness diagnosis portrays the readiness of the client to move to a higher level of health.

While recreational therapists regularly go through the process of deriving a recreational therapy diagnosis, in the field the term "diagnosis" has not usually been employed. More typically the RT diagnosis is simply presented as the end result of the assessment and is not labeled a diagnosis. For example, in the RT individualized intervention plan (see Table 4.3) in this chapter listed under "Assessment" are what may be considered diagnoses of: limited social skills, lack of self-confidence, limited leisure repertoire, and poor leisure-related problem solving skills. Thus the recreational therapy process (i.e., Assessment, Implementation, Planning, Evaluation or APIE) has not included a separate step of diagnosis. Instead, diagnosis has been subsumed under the first step of assessment.

What Are Methods of Assessing Clients?

Observing and interviewing are the two most frequently used methods of client assessment. Both observations and interviews offer a number of perspectives from which to approach client assessment. Schulman (1991) has outlined several methods of observation. Among these are what he has termed casual observation, naturalistic observation, specific goal observation, and standardized observation.

Casual observation versus skilled observations. Casual observation is the type of nonsystematic observation in which we engage on a daily basis. It is responding to our environment in a somewhat random fashion and out of our personal bias and background. It is not "skilled observation" in that it is not directed or purposeful.

Skilled observations are carefully completed in an organized manner and are as free as possible from personal bias. Skilled observers learn to disregard irrelevant material in order to become selective in their observations. Knowing what to look for and what to expect in terms of normal behavior is important to doing clinical observation, as is the ability to describe observations in objective, factual terms (O'Morrow & Reynolds, 1989). Skilled observers also are unobtrusive so as not to alter or change clients' behaviors (Wilkinson & Canter, 1982).

Naturalistic observation. In naturalistic observation there is no attempt to manipulate or change the natural environment. This method calls for keeping an ongoing account of the client's behavior through written anecdotal notes, photographs, video, or a combination of these techniques. In recreational therapy, naturalistic observation might be accomplished while watching the hospitalized client interact during unstructured recreation on the ward or by observing children with disabilities on the playground in a free play situation. Hutchinson, LeBlanc, and Booth (2002) have outlined the importance of this type of assessment. They have written that therapists they studied often used:

> ...activity engagement (e.g., community outings, activity groups, individual skill development sessions) as a context for further assessing patients' needs, personal motivations, and feelings about their illness or injury. More importantly, activity engagement afforded the therapists opportunities to move *quickly* from assessing needs and abilities to acting on this assessment by initiating involvement in the type of activity that might be instrumental in sustaining patients' engagement (in recreational therapy).... (p. 28)

Specific goal observation. Specific goal observation requires precision in planning, since the observer sets definite goals for observation to meet a particular purpose or to assess a well-defined behavior. Here the recreational therapist may observe how cooperative the client is in a co-recreational game situation or the client's response to frustration in an athletic contest.

With children, the recreational therapist may confirm other information concerning the child while viewing the child at play. Takata (1974) has provided a list of questions to guide such observation:

- With what does the child play?
- How does the child play?
- What type of play is avoided or liked the least?
- With whom does the child play?
- How does the child play with others?
- What body posture does the child use during play?
- How long does the child play?
- Where does the child play?
- When does the child play?

Examples of goal observations calling for specific behaviors might include observing an adult playing a card game, such as bridge, or observing an adolescent square dancing. These activities make certain cognitive, psychomotor, or social demands on the client. The recreational therapist observes to determine how the client responds to these specific demands and records this information.

A closely related assessment that might be categorized as a specific goal observation is *role playing*. The basis for role playing can be a standard social situation or a particular situation in which the client has experienced difficulty in the past. The client is told to act as though he or she normally would in the situation. Props (e.g., tables and chairs) may be used and the therapist may prompt that role playing either verbally or nonverbally.

Standardized observation. Standardized observations take two major forms (Schulman, 1991). One is the standardized or norm-referenced instrument. The other involves the use of time-interval observations. Norm-referenced tests provide a measure of how an individual performs in relation to others who are from the same classification of persons. In contrast, criterion-referenced assessments do not compare people.

Criterion-referenced tests measure achievement toward some established standard (Hogg & Raynes, 1987). An example of a standardized test that a recreational therapist might apply is the Leisure Diagnostic Battery (LDB) developed by Witt and Ellis (1987).

Determinations regarding the choice of standardized assessments are influenced by two major considerations, reliability and validity. **Reliability** deals with the question of whether an instrument yields reproducible results. A reliable instrument produces consistent results over time. It reflects consistency (Cone, 2001). A reliable assessment also demonstrates internal consistency within items contained in the instrument and equivalency between various forms of the instrument, if more than one form is available (Dunn, 1989).

Validity answers the question of whether "the measure really assesses what it is supposed to assess. Does it tap the behavior or construct as intended by its developer?" (Cone, 2001, p. 154). Or, can the results be interpreted as an accurate representation of the phenomenon being assessed? Or, does it test what it sets out to test. A minimum requirement for any clinical assessment is that it has content validity, or that it makes intuitive sense. Another type of validity is criterion-related validity that is derived from a statistical comparison of the instrument against some previously established criterion. A third type, construct validity, deals with how well an instrument reflects the construct that underlies the assessment (Dunn, 1989). Information on reliability and validity should be provided in the manual that accompanies any assessment instrument.

Dunn (1989), Zabriskie (2003), and Stokes (2011) have supplied a number of useful guidelines for the selection and application of standardized assessments. These guidelines are listed in Table 4.2.

A type of assessment related to standardized instruments is the self-rating form that has not been normed. Self-ratings are, of course, completed by the client and then are later reviewed by the therapist. Most agencies have leisure interest instruments on which clients are asked to designate hobbies and other recreation interests by checking them on a checklist or by indicating a level of interest (e.g., high, moderate, none) or frequency of participation (e.g., often, rarely, never).

Table 4.2

Guidelines for Using Standarized Assessments

Assessing the Quality of the Instrument

1. The instrument has been published in a peer-reviewed journal.
2. Standardization procedures are clear for every part of the instrument.
3. Clear scoring procedures are provided.

Guidelines for Selection of Assessment Procedures

1. The assessment measures what you intend to measure.
2. The assessment instrument rests on a strong theory base.
3. The assessment should provide evidence of validity.
   a. The assessment should be validated on a representative sample of sufficient size.
   b. The assessment should be valid for its intended use.
   c. There should be evidence of the relationship of subscores to total scores of those measures which produce subscores.
4. The assessment must provide evidence of reliability.
5. The manual and test materials should be complete and of appropriate quality.
6. A test user should demonstrate relevance for the assessment selection.
   a. The assessment should be relevant to the clients served by the agency.
   b. The assessment should be relevant to the decisions made based on assessment results (i.e., It measures the specific behaviors or constructs you hope to influence).

Table 4.2 (cont.)

___

Guidelines for Assessment Use

1. An assessment should be revalidated when any changes are made in procedures, or materials, or when it is used for a purpose or with a population group for which it has not been validated.
2. The assessment should be selected and used by qualified individuals.
3. The assessment should be used in the intended way.
4. Published assessments should be used in combination with other methods.
5. The assessment should be usable with your population in your situation (e.g., it is not too difficult for your clients. It may be completed in the time available).

Guidelines for Administering, Scoring, and Reporting

1. The administration and scoring of an assessment should follow standardized procedures.
   a. During the administration of an assessment, care should be taken in providing a comfortable environment with minimal distractions.
   b. During the administration of assessments, the administrator should be aware of the importance and effect of rapport with the client.

2. It is the responsibility of the test user to protect the security of materials.

Guidelines for Protecting the Rights of Clients

1. Test results should not be released without informed consent.
2. Data regarding a client's assessment results should be kept in a designated client's file.

___

Sources: Dunn., J. D. (1989). Guidelines for using published assessment procedures. *Therapeutic Recreation Journal*, 23(2), 59°69; Stokes, E. M. (2011). *Rehabilitation Outcome Measures*. New York: Churchill Livingstone; Zabriskie, R. B. (2003). Measurements basics: A must for TR professionals today. *Therapeutic Recreation Journal*, 37(4), 330–338.

Some agencies have goal lists. Clients use these to check the goals on which they wish to work while in the program. Others have self-rating scales where clients may check problematic behaviors (e.g., to stop drinking too much, to feel at ease talking in a group, to stop swearing at other people). Willson (1987) has offered these rules to guide those who might desire to design self-report questionnaires:

1. Be clear about what information is to be obtained and why it is needed.
2. Choose a format that will be most easily understood.
3. Construct the questions avoiding unnecessary words or ambiguities.
4. Try it out on a sample of its intended respondents to see if it can be administered easily and if the results can be processed in a meaningful way. (pp. 119–120)

Time-interval observation. Time-interval observations are standardized observations in which clients are observed at predetermined times during the day. These observations may last for 15 minutes, 30 minutes, or any period of time. During the observation, the recreational therapist looks for a specific behavior and records frequency counts when that behavior occurs. For instance, the number of verbal interactions with other clients or the number of times a client behaves in an aggressive manner could be recorded. Besides time-interval observations, Dattilo and Wolfe (2002) have presented several behaviorally orientated types of observations. The interested reader is referred to this excellent resource for detailed information on these observational methods.

Assessment Instruments

Extensive reviews of assessment instruments suitable for application in recreational therapy have been completed by Stumbo (1991) and burlingame and Blaschko (2002). Now in its third edition, burlingame and Blaschko (2002) have authored an entire book on assessment tools titled *Assessment Tools for Recreational Therapy and Related Fields*. It contains extensive chapters on instruments that deal with measuring leisure attributes, functional skills, specific skills, and multidimensional aspects.

RT assessment instruments. In the remainder of this section a sampling of some of the most commonly applied and more readily available assessment instruments for recreational therapy is provided. Covered are the Leisure Diagnostic Battery, the Comprehensive Evaluation in Recreation Therapy Scale, and the Functional Assessment of Characteristics for Therapeutic Recreation Scale.

Leisure Diagnostic Battery. The Leisure Diagnostic Battery (LDB) (Witt & Ellis, 1987) contains a group of instruments that have been designed to assess the leisure functioning of both disabled and nondisabled individuals. Long and short forms are available for most of the instruments in the LDB for both adults and adolescents.

Witt and Ellis have described the purposes of the LDB as (a) to enable users to assess their clients' functioning; (b) to enable users to determine areas In which improvement of current leisure functioning is needed; (c) to enable users to determine the impact of offered services on leisure functioning; and (d) to facilitate research on the structure of leisure to enable a better understanding of the value, purpose, and outcomes of leisure experiences. (p. 7)

Comprehensive Evaluation of Recreation Therapy Scale (CERT). The CERT is one of the more established assessment instruments. It was developed by Parker and his colleagues (1975) for therapists to apply when assessing clients in psychiatric settings. The CERT contains three areas of assessment: general, individual performance, and group performance.

A second CERT has been developed for use with clients who have physical disabilities. It has eight clusters of items. These include (1) gross muscular function, (2) fine movement, (3) locomotion, (4) motor skills, (5) sensory, (6) cognition, (7) communication, and (8) behavior. Both forms of the CERT are available from Idyll Arbor, Inc.

Functional Assessment of Characteristics for Therapeutic Recreation (FACTR). The FACTR is designed to identify client needs related to basic functional skills and behaviors used in leisure participation. It covers functional skills in three domains. These are the physical, cognitive, and social/emotional domains. Under each are 11 items for a total of 33 items. The FACTR is available through Idyll Arbor, Inc.

Final thoughts on the use of standardized instruments. Howe (1984) has discussed that, as well as those factors outlined in Table 4.2, the actual selection of assessment instruments is based on the therapist's philosophy, education, and past experience. A major practical influence on instrument selection is, of course, the availability of the instruments and background information to support their use.

The Interview Method

The recreational therapist will generally attempt to conduct at least one interview with every new client. The interview usually has three purposes. First, the interview provides an opportunity to gain information from the client and to observe the client. Second, the recreational therapist wishes to begin to develop a relationship, or gain rapport, with the client. Third, orientation to the program or programs available to the client may be provided. Additional information on the process of conducting interviews is contained in Chapter 6.

A prime purpose of the interview is, of course, to gather information regarding the client and to provide the client with an opportunity to begin to identify his or her needs and how these may be met. This may be accomplished by talking with the client and observing the client's condition and behavior.

The client's leisure behaviors and interests are regularly a focus of discussion during the interview. The recreational therapist will likely ask the client about past leisure patterns, including the amount of time given to leisure, the activities in which he or she has participated, and who has taken part in recreation with the client. Additionally, an attempt is usually made to help the client identify recreational interests for possible future participation.

Open-Ended Questions and Leisure Interest Instruments

Common techniques to facilitate the interview are using a list of open-ended questions related to leisure patterns and using leisure interest instruments. Typically, the open-ended questions appear on an interview form with a brief space following each one in which the client's response may be recorded. Leisure interest instruments are normally in a checklist format so that the client may complete them with the help of a recreational therapist, or the recreational therapist may read the items to the client and check the appropriate place on the forms.

An innovative field-based study by Canadian researchers (Pedlar, Hornibrook, & Haasen, 2001) discovered five open-ended questions that best achieved the assessment data. These questions were: (a) What do you enjoy (past/present leisure interests); (b) What about that do you enjoy? (characteristics of pursuits that are enjoyed); (c) Recently, what has brought enjoyment/happiness to your day? (current leisure status); (d) What is stopping you from enjoying _____? (or some of those activities/i.e., barriers); (e) Is there something that you have always wanted to do? (dreams). Additional examples of open-ended questions appear in Appendix A: Open-Ended Questions. Long, Higgins, and Brady (1988, p. 52) have suggested "Open-Ended Questions for Adults" and "Open-Ended Questions for Older Adults" that are also included in Appendix A: Open-Ended Questions (see p. 221).

It is important that these or similar questions be used only to form a guideline for interviewing and not be strictly adhered to. Instead the interviewer should feel free to deviate from any set of questions in order to follow up on a client's statement or probe more deeply into a particular area.

Most agencies or institutions offering recreational therapy services will adopt or develop some type of leisure interest instrument appropriate for use with their clients. Whatever the approach, clients should be given the opportunity to express themselves in regard to their perceptions of strengths, weaknesses, and problems. Knowing how each client views himself or herself, the environment, and his or her place in that environment is necessary to completely understand the client's behavior.

Children and the Questioning Process

For children, traditional interview methods may not be appropriate. When feasible, the recreational therapist may begin assessment procedures with an interview with each child's parents. Stanley and Kasson (n.d.) have produced materials to be used by those faced with the task of interviewing parents of children with disabilities. These materials contain a series of questions that may be directed toward the parents regarding their child's play and social patterns. Questions based on those posed by Stanley and Kasson appear as "Open-Ended Questions for Parents" in Appendix A: Open-Ended Questions (see p. 221).

When interviewing children, conduct the interview in an area conducive to creating a relaxed, friendly environment. A play area may help create this atmosphere and has the added feature of allowing for possible observation of the child at play. The interviewer should make sure that various age-appropriate playthings are available so the child may play in a variety of modes during the interview. If the interviewer invites the child to play, this should always be done in a friendly and sincere manner so that the child is not given the impression of being tested.

For the shy child or the child who has difficulty with verbal expression, Stanley and Kasson propose the use of pictures illustrating children taking part in various play or recreation activities. The child can be asked to choose those that he or she likes or would enjoy exploring. With all clients, nonverbal language is often the best indicator of the client's true feelings. Clues provided by bodily movement, gestures, and posture can prove to be more revealing than verbal expression. Most people would agree that the child's smile is a good indicator that he or she likes something.

Relationship Development

A second purpose of the interview is to develop a relationship with the client. Developing rapport is not usually a major hurdle for the recreational therapist, who is customarily seen by clients as a nonthreatening person. In highly clinical settings, clients may feel particularly alienated by the surroundings and too frightened to approach the doctor or nurse. In such situations the unique role of the recreational therapist often comes to the forefront. With the recreational therapists, clients usually feel that they can relax, "drop their guards," and "be themselves." In the clinical atmosphere a recreational therapist may become a "professional friend," since he or she is viewed as someone who enters into a mutual participation with clients instead of as someone who does something to clients.

Orientation to the Program

The interview is sometimes also used to acquaint the client with the program or services provided by the recreational therapy service. Even though this orientation is often limited and necessarily brief, the interview allows the opportunity to inform the client of basic program offerings. The recreational therapist must exercise judgment in determining how extensive an orientation is appropriate for the individual client. This may range from a few general statements regarding the availability of selected programs to a review of the complete recreational therapy offerings provided by the agency or institution.

Secondary Sources of Information

There are many sources from which to obtain the different types of information that you will find useful when working with your clients. A discussion of a few such secondary sources follows.

Medical records include the results of the physician's examination report, along with information on the client's medical history, physical assessment, and diagnostic studies. Also contained in the medical record is the medical diagnosis, a prognosis, a plan for medical treatment, physician's orders, progress reports, and other relevant medical information.

In educational settings, *educational records* may be a basis for client assessment. Assessment information for children with learning disabilities or behavioral disorders should include an assessment of academic skills, a determination of which sensory modes are most effective in learning, and an evaluation of the level of social skills. Other information that might be found in educational records includes educational diagnoses and teacher and physician reports.

Testing provides objective data about the client. Results from tests administered by psychologists or staff from other allied disciplines can be useful to recreational therapy assessment.

Much can be learned about the client and his or her relationships with others by *interviewing family or friends* who may possess knowledge about the client's past leisure interests and behaviors. Information may also be gained in regard to future expectations and anticipated resources for the client's leisure participation.

The *social history* is normally completed by the social worker. It contains information on where the client was born, raised, and educated, the client's home and family, past occupations, family income, recreational pursuits, and religious affiliation.

Progress notes written by various staff contain objective comments regarding the client's behaviors as they deviate from normal. Charting is commonly accomplished daily in treatment and rehabilitation facilities by staff members, including nursing services and rehabilitation therapy personnel. Where *interdisciplinary teams* exist, the recreational therapist will likely be an integral part of the team. In this capacity he or she will confer regularly with other staff, both within and outside of formal team meetings. The formal and informal sharing of information with other staff will provide information that may be applied in recreational therapy assessment.

A great deal may be learned by *visiting the client's home and community*. What are the social and recreational opportunities accessible to the client? What specific recreational outlets are evident in the home? Are parks, community centers, libraries, or other recreational facilities available in the client's neighborhood or community? Some treatment facilities maintain an up-to-date inventory of recreational programs and facilities available in the communities they serve.

Assessment Information

Initial Information

General information that the recreational therapist might wish to have on hand as soon as possible would include the following:
- client's full name, address, and telephone number;
- sex, age, and marital or family status;
- date admitted;
- education completed;
- language(s) spoken;
- occupation;
- leisure interests briefly noted;
- limitations or precautions (e.g., physical restrictions, suicidal);

- medications; and
- why the client is seeking service.

In a clinically oriented facility, it would also be appropriate to note the names of the client's physician, social worker, and case manager when recording initial assessment information. In a community-based program, it would be advantageous to list with whom the client is living and who should be contacted in case of emergency. This ensures that the information is readily available when required.

Factors Affecting the Assessment Process

Beyond general information, exactly what assessment data should be collected by the recreational therapist? The answer to this question will vary depending on the setting in which recreational therapy services are being delivered and the personal preferences and theoretical perspectives of the therapist. The following section discusses settings and personal preferences and theoretical perspectives as they affect assessment and then conclude with observations that reveal biases toward assessment.

Setting. Variables within the *setting* that affect assessment include the type of client being served and the prevailing treatment, rehabilitation, care, or wellness orientation of the agency. Data collected on psychiatric clients will differ from those needed in physical rehabilitation centers or centers for persons with developmental disabilities. The age of the client will obviously play a role. Different developmental information will be needed about children than adolescent or geriatric populations. The overall model adopted by the agency will likely affect assessment as well. For instance, does a medical model prevail where other health professionals serve under the direction of a physician? Or, does an educational model apply where the program is centered on children's educational needs? Goals, and therefore assessment procedures, will differ markedly according to the prevailing orientation of the agency. In sum, the recreational therapist will have to adapt assessment procedures to take into account the setting in which his or her program is located, as well as the prevailing orientation of the particular agency.

Therapists' preferences and perspectives. Therapists will likely collect data using assessment procedures with which they are most familiar. Therefore, past training and experiences will affect assessment practices. Students need to be particularly aware of the biases toward various assessment approaches present in their university instructors and clinical supervisors. Personal theoretical perspectives held by therapists also affect choices in the types of assessment data collected.

For instance, psychiatric recreational therapists who favor the psychodynamic approach are apt to explore tensions underlying disorders, whereas those who are behaviorally orientated are likely to examine directly observable behavior (Ellis, 1987). Similarly, recreational therapists who adopt the Leisure Ability Model are likely to focus assessment on independent leisure functioning, while those following the Health Protection/Health Promotion Model are apt to be more concerned with issues related to health and wellness.

General guidelines for assessment. No matter the setting or the therapist's preferences and perspectives, the following general guidelines for recreational therapy assessment have been suggested by Bullock, Mahon, and Killingsworth (2010):

1. Seek as much input as possible from the individual.
2. Assess the physical and human environment as well as the individual's skills and needs.
3. Remain focused upon the individual's long-term goals.
4. Assess strengths, abilities, and desires as well as deficits and needs. (pp. 363-364)

Holistic approach. I believe in taking a **holistic approach** to assessment. A person is a unified entity. One part of a person affects another. Clients' physical problems almost always have a psychological component and a social impact. Psychological difficulties inevitably involve a physical response, and so on (Yura & Walsh, 1988). Therefore, the total person needs to be assessed, taking into account all the parts that come together to make each of us a unique individual.

Complete assessment will also encompass the client's developmental level, a sometimes neglected area of recreational therapy assessment. It is important that the recreational therapist has knowledge of human development throughout the life span and of developmental issues so that he or she may complete a thorough assessment in order to identify developmental problems with which the client may need help.

Data gathered by the recreational therapist deals largely with psychosocial aspects of the person (i.e., emotional, behavioral, mental, environmental, and interactional processes) in an effort to identify past and current levels of functioning. Recreational therapy assessment may also involve the physical domain, depending on the client population being assessed. Even when physical assessment is accomplished by another health professional (e.g. physician or nurse), information from that assessment is integrated into the overall recreational therapy assessment.

Areas for recreational therapy assessment include the following:

1. Client's general perceptions about their present health status, how they are dealing with their health problems or concerns, and how their health problems/concerns may be impacting on regular recreation and leisure patterns.
2. Sensory or motor impairments, cognitive deficits, limitations in activities of daily living, and any precautions (e.g., heart problems) are noted.
3. Leisure values, interests, and pursuits are explored, along with client attitudes toward participation in recreational therapy programs.
4. The developmental level of the client is appraised to determine developmental tasks or issues with which the client may be dealing.
5. Problems or concerns are explored in order to reveal needs (e.g., need to belong, for self-esteem) in order to establish a needs list.
6. Strengths (e.g., abilities, virtues, support from family and friends) are identified in order to build a strengths list.
7. Client expectations and goals are identified.

Strengths-oriented assessment. Particular attention should be devoted to item 6, assessment of client strengths, or what Glicken (2004, p. 4) has termed an "asset review." Traditionally, clinical assessment has had symptoms, disorders, and deficits as its focus. Deficits-oriented assessment however provides an incomplete picture of clients. Client assessment can, and should, also incorporate strengths (Feeley & Cottlieb, 2000). As Rashid and Ottermann (2009) stated, strength-based assessment involves: "Exploring *what's strong* to supplement traditional digging for *what's wrong*" (p. 490).

With the rise of positive psychology, the topic of strength-based assessment has emerged within the clinical literature (e.g., Peterson, Park, & Seligman, 2006). It was, however, humanistic psychology that initiated the assessment of client strengths. Those taking the growth orientation of the humanistic perspective have had a long history of advocating the examination of client strengths and on focusing on the development of client strengths (Rashid & Ostermann, 2009). It is written elsewhere (Austin, 2011b) that "the humanistic approach indicates a focus on client strengths rather than pathology" (p. 21).

Recreational therapy, having been strongly influenced by the humanistic perspective, has likewise long identified clients' strengths in order to both use these strengths to help clients overcome health issues and to amplify client strengths to build clients' capacities to deal with future situations (Austin, 2011a, 2011b), Therefore recreational therapy intervention goals include enhancing strengths and the facilitation of protective processes for the future in addition to attacking client symptoms or concerns.

Thus, a high level of attention to the assessment of client strengths is in keeping with the traditional practice of recreational therapy of emphasizing clients' positive traits and abilities. I can recall when I was a young recreational therapist working in a psychiatric hospital in the 1960s, that we strove to work with the intact parts of our patients, focusing on them as strengths clients could use to overcome problems in mental health. A claim could certainly be made that recreational therapy was in the forefront of advocating a strengths-based approach (Austin, 2011b). Today there is a growing emphasis on acknowledging the strengths perspective within recreational therapy. A case in point is the title of Anderson and Heyne's (2013) book titled, *Therapeutic Recreation Practice: A Strengths Approach.*

Rashid and Ostermann (2009) have suggested a strength-based assessment should take a four-pronged approach. While provided to give direction to those doing strength-oriented assessment in clinical psychology, these four areas of assessment would seem to have application with most populations served by recreational therapists. They propose attention be given to:

> (a) deficiencies and undermining characteristics of the person (what deficiencies does the client contribute to her/his problems; (b) strengths and assets of the person (what strengths does bring to deal effectively with his or her life; (c) deficits and destructive factors in the environment (what environmental factors thwart clients' development; (d) resources and opportunities in the environment (what environmental resources facilitate positive human functioning. (p. 491)

Rashid and Ostermann went on to illustrate how two of the most common mental health problems, depression and anxiety, can be analyzed using strength-based assessment. They wrote:

> For example, depression may not just be a cluster of symptoms described in the *DSM-IV*, but it could also be a lack of positive emotions and meaning in a client's life. Strengths, from this standpoint, serve us best not when life is easy, but when life is tough. With a depressed client, the clinician can explore and work on strengths like perspective, zest, and gratitude. Shoring up social strengths of the client such as teamwork, social intelligence, and kindness could be a viable way of counteracting depression. Similarly, anxiety may not only represent worrying, feeling restless, fidgety and impulsive behaviour, and lacking focus, but it could be a lack of purposeful goals, actions, and habits that utilize clients' strengths and absorb him or her immensely. (p. 491)

Recreational talents and abilities as strengths. Within recreational therapy we have long perceived recreational talents and abilities to be strengths for our clients. For instance, our clients may possess exceptional skills in a particular sport or physical activity, such as tennis or swimming. Some have developed creative skills in art or writing. Others have musical or performing abilities. Still others may have developed proficiencies in activities such as yoga or Pilates. All of these, and many other recreational abilities, are strengths that have the potential to be used by clients to bring about therapeutic benefits within recreational therapy.

Virtues or personality traits as strengths. The literature of positive psychology can be helpful to recreational therapists in identifying and assessing client strengths of character. You may recall from the discussion of positive psychology in Chapter 2 that an extensive list of strengths or virtues (i.e., personality traits) include those under the following six categories: (a) wisdom and knowledge, (b) courage, (c) love, (d) justice, (e) temperance, and (f) transcendance.

Wisdom strengths are curiosity, interest, love of learning, judgment, critical thinking, open-mindedness intelligence, creativity, originality, ingenuity, and perspective. *Courage strengths* include valor, industry, perseverance, integrity, honesty, authenticity, zest, and enthusiasm. Under *love* fall intimacy, reciprocal attachment, kindness, generosity, nurturance, social intelligence, personal intelligence, and emotional intelligence. Strengths listed under the category of *justice* include citizenship, duty, loyalty, teamwork, equity, fairness, and leadership. Under temperance are forgiveness, mercy, modesty, humility, prudence, caution, self-control, and self-regulation. Finally, under *transcendence* are the strengths of awe, wonder, appreciation of beauty and excellence, gratitude, hope, optimism, future-mindedness, playfulness, humor, spirituality, sense of purpose, faith, and religiousness. It is probably best to think of the strengths delineated as examples of strengths, rather than as an exhaustive list (Seligman, 2000; Seligman & Peterson, 2003).

Glicken's areas of strength. A list of client strengths presented by Glicken (2004, pp. 21–28) may also prove helpful in recreational therapy strengths assessment. Glicken has outlined 45 areas of strength. Some of Glicken's strength areas that appear to be particularly relevant to recreational therapy assessment include the following:

- *Coping skills.* Do clients have "habits" they have successfully used in dealing with past difficulties? An example might be how they have dealt with stress in the past by adopting the habit of running or doing yoga to bring about stress reduction.
- *Support network.* Do clients have a network of people who can be called upon in times of need? Do clients understand the need for friends and work to maintain friendships?
- *Prior life successes.* What have clients successfully achieved in the past in areas such as work, leisure, family life, and community life? Do clients recognize their own past achievements?
- *Educational success.* Have clients achieved educational success? Are clients interested in new ideas, particularly if they are relevant to their problems?
- *Interpersonal skills.* Do clients relate to others in a positive and effective way? Do they have the ability to communicate well with staff in order to build therapeutic relationships?
- *Communication skills.* Do clients use clear and precise language? Can they convey difficult emotions?

- *Relationships with significant others.* Are clients able to seek healthy and constructive relationships? Do clients have warm, positive relationships with their extended family, love interests, or close friends?
- *Healthy personal habits.* Are clients interested in good diet, exercise, not abusing drugs, and so forth to make changes in their lifestyles?
- *Locus of control.* Do clients believe they have the capacity to make changes (i.e., have an internal locus of control)?
- *Self-concept.* Do clients think positively about themselves? Are they able to provide a realistic list of positive attributions?
- *Creativity.* Do clients use creative expression (e.g., art, writing, sculpting, gardening) to deal with life stresses? Do they get enjoyment from going to the theater, exhibits, poetry readings, or other creative experiences?
- *Intimacy.* Do they desire physical and emotional closeness? Are they comfortable with being touched? Praised?
- *Fun.* Do clients know how to laugh? Enjoy having fun? Have a good sense of humor?
- *Trust.* Are clients able to trust others? When the right people reach out to them, do they permit those people to influence them?
- *Risk taking.* Are clients able to take chances to improve their lives?
- *Resilience.* Are they able to come back from adversity? Can they gain success despite their environment?
- *Passion.* Are clients passionate about many things (e.g., recreational activities)?
- *Persistence.* Are clients able to stay with things?
- *Determination.* Do clients hold strong positive notions that they will be able to master most life situations?
- *Variety.* Are clients able to change behaviors to prevent repetition and boredom? Are they willing to change personal interests to avoid rigidity and isolation?
- *Insight.* Do clients have the ability to see a situation as it really exists?

External resources as strengths. Another area of strength for clients may be external resources they possess. Examples of such resources identified by Glicken (2004) were support networks and relationships with significant others. Having support networks of family and friends offers clients social support. Another resource that can be a strength for clients is their community. For example, a client's community may offer activities that can be accessed by the client such as yoga or aquatic programs at the YMCA or inclusive or special recreation programs within the park and recreation department.

Completing strengths assessment in recreational therapy. Two means of strengths assessment are often employed in recreational therapy. One means is the initial assessment interview where recreational interest surveys or inventories are typically employed with clients and clients' recreation and leisure pursuits are discussed. Opportunities for observations of clients and verbal interactions with clients during their participation in recreational activities offers a second means for strength-oriented assessment.

Because people are generally interested in activities in which they have enjoyed success, indications of leisure interests often reveal clients' recreational skills and abilities. Good swimmers tend to express interest in swimming. Those proficient at tennis, are interested in tennis, and so on. Therefore, in the process of completing a leisure interest indicator, clients may likely reveal strengths. Such revelations are especially anticipated to occur when recreational therapists ask follow-up or probing questions about clients' recreational interests.

Even when interest inventories are not used, interviews can be used to assess client strengths. Interview questions might include, "Tell me what you are good at." "Let's pause here and talk about what you are good at." (Rashid & Ostermann, 2009, p. 492) "What are some of the things you think you are best at?" "What do you like to do In your free time?" "What does your family think you are best at?" "What activities and interests do you share with your family? With friends?" (Deschenes, Clark, Herrygers, Blase, & Wagner, 2010, p. 35).

When there are opportunities to talk with family and friends of clients, recreational therapists can also pursue strengths assessment with them. For example, the recreational therapist might ask family members or friends of a young person, "What are the young person's interests?" "What are some of the things you think the young person is best at?" "What do you like or respect about the young person's friends? Why?" (Deschenes, Clark, Herrygers, Blase, & Wagner, 2010, p. 39).

Family nurses Feeley and Gottlieb (2000) have suggested that individuals and families should explicitly be asked to identify strengths with such questions as: "What do you think you do well?" and "Do other people ever tell you that you are good at doing something?" Further, these authors recommended the following questions when listening to or observing families: "What are the strengths and competencies of the individual family members and the family unit?" and "What are they able to accomplish and why?" (p. 13).

A second means for recreational therapists to assess client strengths is during recreational activities. Here clients may display strengths through their actions. For example, during an informal volleyball game, clients may exhibit exceptional motor abilities or character strengths such as enthusiasm or teamwork. Recreational activities also provide relaxed environments in which clients "let their hair down." Particularly once rapport has been established by recreational therapists, within the informal atmosphere of a recreational activity clients often open up to recreational therapists in a way that they might with a friend. Questions such as those suggested for client interviews can be used by recreational therapists to draw out client strengths.

Additional strength assessment techniques have appeared in the psychology literature. These include strengths measures such as the Values in Action Inventory of Strengths (VIA-IS) (Peterson & Seligman, 2004) that uses 240 self-report items to measure 24 character strengths. Other strengths measures include the Authentic Happiness Inventory, Fordyce Emotions Questionnaire, General Happiness Questionnaire, Gratitude Questionnaire, and Grit Survey, most of which are available online without charge (Rashid & Ostermann, 2009). Hershberger (2005) suggested an alternative to the identification of a person's signature strengths (i.e., top strengths) through testing would be to have the individual simply review a list of strengths and identify those they perceive to be their best strengths.

An innovative strategy is to help clients to identify their strengths through discussions of icons (e.g., Mother Theresa, Martin Luther King, Jr., Nelson Mandela) or characters from popular films (e.g., *Pay it Forward, Forrest Gump, My Left Foot*) that possess certain strengths. By discussing strengths displayed by icons or film characters, the clinician can determine how fully clients identify with the icons or characters, under what conditions would clients envision themselves displaying the specified strengths, and what might result. Another innovative approach is a narrative strategy that can elicit strengths. In this strategy, termed Positive Introduction, the client is encouraged to introduce himself or herself by means of a real-life story of about 300 words containing a beginning, middle, and having a positive ending. The story is then reviewed with the client to identify strengths found in the story and to discuss if they reflect descriptions of the client's present functioning (Rashid & Ostermann, 2009).

In addition to completing assessment focusing specifically on strengths, additional data on strengths may be acquired as the recreational therapist completes a thorough leisure assessment. Areas for a total leisure assessment have been suggested by Kunstler and Stavola Daly (2010). They include the following:

- attitudes and beliefs about leisure and its meaning, value, and significance in one's life;
- needs that can be met through recreation participation, such as needs for socialization, physical activity, intellectual stimulation, fun, accomplishment, community involvement, development of interests, and challenge;
- participation in recreation activities, both current and hoped for future participation, and reactions to and feelings about these activities;
- recreation participation patterns (when, where, with whom, with how many, how often) and what has influenced the formation of these patterns (such as family social networks, cost, availability);
- recreation activity skills and skills in developing, utilizing, and evaluating recreation resources, including financial resources, transportation, accessibility, and social skills; and
- barriers to satisfying leisure experiences. (p. 59)

Some Final Thoughts on the Strengths-Based Approach and Assessment

Clients may have untapped resources (i.e., strengths) that can be drawn upon. Often, however, these are unknown to the individual client. Therefore, assessment can play a role in helping clients to realize their own strengths. The self-realization of knowing they possess strengths they may not have previously recognized, in itself, may be therapeutic for clients.

A key concept in recognizing the importance of assessing strengths is that skills from one area of life can be transferred to another (Glicken, 2004). For instance, strengths often employed at work (e.g., persistence, determination) can be used in outside of work as well, such as in rehabilitation or therapy. Thus, learning to realize and apply strengths can be critical in overcoming difficulties.

Another key concept is that assessment of strengths can lead to discovering potentials for building strengths. Once potentials are identified, recreational therapy interventions can be used to assist clients to develop strengths that can lead to overcoming problems or reaching potentials.

Concluding Statement on Assessment

The total recreational therapy assessment provides the recreational therapist with data to determine where the client is along the illness-wellness continuum so appropriate interventions can be designed. By assembling all available assessment data, the recreational therapist will gain an overall picture of the client from which a statement of a problem (i.e., recreational therapy diagnosis) may be made. The overall purpose of recreational therapy assessment is to gain information that will be useful in the provision of interventions (assuming it is determined recreational therapy interventions are needed), although recreational therapy assessment data are likely to be helpful to other members of the interdisciplinary team as well. For instance, the assessment of client strengths by recreational therapists will allow the entire interdisciplinary team to support identified client strengths.

Adequate assessment is a prerequisite to the provision of individual program planning. However, assessment is a continuing process that does not end after the initial work-up on the client. Clients, like all human beings, are in a dynamic state of change, necessitating that ongoing assessment be conducted with every client.

Both objective data from various sources and subjective information gained directly from the client are usually required in order to formulate a clear definition of the client's problem and to identify client strengths. *Objective information* includes data from medical records, educational records, results of standardized testing, interviews with family and friends, social history, case recordings or progress notes, information from staff conferences or team meetings, community survey information, systematic observations, and general client information, including demographic data.

Subjective assessment data are gathered directly from the client. Narrow and Buschle (1987) wrote, "*Subjective data* include information which can be provided only by the patient (or client), such as his [or her] perception of what he [or she] is experiencing or his [or her] attitudes, desires, feelings, and needs" (p. 253).

Client assessment employing objective and subjective data allows the recreational therapist to assess both client strengths and weaknesses and then identify client needs that flow from the client's problem or concern. Such assessment data also permits the analysis of client readiness for health-seeking actions to bring about health maintenance or enhancement. An excellent resource for understanding clients' readiness for change is Prochaska and DiClemente's (1982) Transtheoretical Model (TTM) of client change that is discussed in Chapter 8. Once the initial assessment procedures have been completed, the recreational therapist has formed the basis for individual, customized program planning and can move to the second step in the recreational therapy process, the planning phase.

What Constitutes the Planning Phase?

After identifying the client's needs, the needs are examined to determine priorities, goals are formulated, and a plan of action is determined. As a result of this planning phase, the client's customized recreational therapy program emerges.

A four-step procedure may be conceptualized for the planning phase: (1) setting priorities following examination of the client's needs, (2) formulating goals or general objectives, (3) determining strategies or actions to meet the goals, and (4) selecting methods to assess progress made toward the goals.

Setting Priorities

After the client's needs have been identified, the recreational therapist should examine them carefully to determine if recreational therapy services can be helpful and to set priorities for dealing with the client's needs. Marriner (1983) suggests that for nursing plans it should be determined which needs the client can handle independently, which require professional help and what kind of help is indicated, and which needs are most urgent. She goes on to recommend that Maslow's needs hierarchy may serve as a guide to setting priorities. It would seem that Marriner's thoughts translate well to recreational therapy planning.

Maslow, considered by some to be the father of humanistic psychology, pictured humans as constantly striving toward self-actualization, or self-fulfillment, the highest level of need. Maslow's (1970) hierarchy contains five basic needs. At the lower levels are physiological needs (thirst, hunger, etc.) and safety needs (security, protection from threat of danger, freedom from fear). Next are social needs (belongingness and love needs) and self-esteem or ego needs (for self-respect, status, recognition). At the top of **Maslow's hierarchy** is the need for self-actualization (or the need to fulfill one's potentials). (See Chapter 5 for a more thorough explanation of Maslow's hierarchy.)

Once a need has been met, it no longer evokes behavior. Satisfaction of lower-level physiological and safety needs provides a firm foundation from which the individual can move forward, developing his or her potentials. Generally, there are fewer problems with these lower-levels needs than with the other needs, although physiological and safety needs certainly must be considered by the recreational therapists. One area where this is particularly true is in dealing with the client's need for psychological safety. Psychological safety may be a problem if the client does not feel free from the fear of being labeled or discriminated against because of a disability or illness (Ringness, 1975). Neurotic anxieties also may threaten psychological safety (Maslow, 1970).

Recreation and leisure offer natural means by which the client's higher-level needs for belonging, self-esteem, and self-actualization may be met. Through gratifying recreation experiences, clients gain acceptance, validate their personal worth, and grow toward their potentials.

Employing Maslow's hierarchy, the recreational therapist can analyze the client's needs and set priorities for the needs that require professional help. The client should be included in this planning if at all possible, although physical or mental conditions may prohibit the client's participation at times. Nevertheless, it is desirable to seek this involvement as soon as the client is ready to join the recreational therapist in the planning process. Like all of us, clients are apt to become more committed to plans that they have helped to form. In recreation, where self-direction and independent decision making are hallmarks, client involvement becomes paramount.

Formulating Goals and Objectives

Having goals and objectives gives direction to the recreational therapist and allows others to know what outcomes are intended. When goals and objectives are clearly spelled out, the client knows just what is expected and will likely feel a real sense of accomplishment when they are achieved. Goals and objectives also provide a sound basis for selecting interventions or programs appropriate for client needs. Further, goals and objectives are useful to evaluation, since they represent clear statements of sought outcomes.

It should be clear that goals and objectives reflect sought outcomes that are directed toward satisfaction of our client's needs. Therefore, goals and objectives are written in terms of the client's behavior and not to reflect the activities or processes of the recreational therapist. Of course, goals and objectives need to be realistic and attainable for the client (Biswas-Diener & Dean, 2007).

The critical nature of clearly formed goals and objectives in recreational therapy planning is reflected in a statement by O'Morrow and Reynolds (1989). They have written, "Without goals or objectives, the plan has lost its therapeutic value" (p. 144).

Short-term and long-term goals and objectives. Today, recreational therapists need to consider both short- and long-term outcomes when writing goals and objectives. In settings with short-term client stays, it may be appropriate to write only short-term goals and objectives. In other settings both short- and long-term goals and objectives may be prepared. Timelines should be indicated for both short- and long-term outcomes. This can be done by stipulating a time for attainment within each goal or objective (e.g., "within 90 days") or by listing goals and objectives under headings such as "short-term (within one week)" and "long-term (within one month).

Of course, these illustrations of "within one week" (for short-term) and "within one month" (for long-term) are only examples. The actual length of what constitutes "short-term" or "long-term" will be decided by each agency. For instance, in an acute care facility, "long-term" may be one week. In an assisted-living facility, "long-term" may be six months.

Goals and objectives defined. Goals (also known as general objectives) and objectives (also known as specific behavioral objectives) describe proposed changes in the individual client or in the client's environment. Within this discussion, the terms *goal* and *general objective* are used interchangeably. Goals or general objectives are outcome statements that are broad in nature and may be contrasted with objectives. Objectives, or specific behavioral objectives as they are also known, are narrowly written and deal with very specific, objective, and measurable behaviors.

Goals, or general objectives, are written at the level of specificity needed to direct action but not be overly restricting. Gronlund (1985) speaks of goals in terms of educational outcomes and likens objectives to the training level. Goals provide direction toward a general type or class of behavior, while objectives deal with a narrow band of behavior.

In fact, one way to conceptualize the difference between a goal and objective is to think in terms of having to realize several specific objectives in order to reach one goal. Therefore, we may evaluate progress toward goals by sampling from a number of specific objectives that fall under the broader, more general goal.

Use of goals and objectives in agency intervention planning. There is a great deal of variance in the use of the terms *goals* and *objectives* by agencies. Certain agencies will use both terms in individualized intervention planning (also termed *treatment planning, care planning*, or *wellness planning*). In some instances when both terms are used, goals (i.e., general objectives) will not only be written at a more general level but will be concerned with long-term outcomes. Objectives used by these agencies are not only more narrowly written than goals but deal with short-term outcomes. Other agencies will employ only broad goals. They will not stipulate objectives under the goals but will apply interventions toward achieving the broad goals. Still other agencies will refer only to the term, objectives, having three to five very specific objectives for each client.

Within this chapter, we will use both terms, goals and objectives. *Goals* are conceived to be broad in nature (e.g., "Increases social interaction with others.") with *objectives* being more narrow and supporting the goals (e.g., "Initiates conversations with others during social recreation activities without staff prompting."). It may be noted that the examples of the goal and specific behavioral objective provided here do not contain timelines. Therefore, it can be assumed that they would appear in the customized intervention plan (also known as a treatment plan or care plan or wellness plan) or recreational therapy plan listed under the heading of short-term or long-term outcomes.

Characteristics of useful objectives. For the sake of brevity, in this section we will refer to both goals (also known as general objectives) and specific behavioral objectives by the term "objectives." The chief characteristic of the useful objective (whether a goal or specific behavioral objective) is that it states what the client will do, or, said another way, it identifies the kind of behavior expected. The lone exception to this would be the objectives having to do with changing the client's environment instead of seeking changes from within the client. Even with environmental goals, however, we should remain cognizant of the need to be explicit. But, in the main, the recreational therapist will be working with behavioral changes; therefore, the discussion of objectives will stress measurable behavioral objectives. Some rules for stating objectives, drawn primarily from Gronlund (1985), follow:

- *Begin with an action verb* instead of with a phrase such as, "The client will. . . " By placing the verb first, the focus of the reader is placed on the sought outcome from the beginning.
- *State the objective to reflect client behavior* instead of mixing client objectives with process objectives you may have for yourself in helping the client to reach goal satisfaction.
- *Only state one terminal behavior per objective* instead of placing several behaviors in the same objective. This allows you to tell more easily if the objective has been fully realized. Putting two or more behaviors in the same objective is confusing and creates problems in evaluation when one behavior has been achieved, but the other has not.
- *Aim the objective at the appropriate level of specificity* instead of being too broad or too narrow. This is a difficult rule to follow, since it involves a certain amount of "feeling" or "intuitiveness" to stipulate objectives at the proper level. General objectives should be definable by stating specific types of behaviors that fall under them. Specific objectives should be relevant to a more general objective.

Table 4.3

Examples of Verbs for Specific Behavioral Objectives

Accepts	Identifies
Cooperates	Informs
Describes	Initiates
Demonstrates	Lists
Discloses	Participates
Displays	Performs
Expresses	Shares
Explains	States

Writing specific behavioral objectives. Mager (1997) has suggested that specific behavioral objectives may also stipulate conditions under which the behavior is to be performed and criteria for performance. To use Mager's terms, a **condition** is a "given" or a "restriction." These further define terminal behaviors by stipulating exact conditions imposed on the individual who is striving for the objective. **Criteria**, on the other hand, state a standard, or "how well" the individual is to perform.

Shank and Coyle (2002) have offered sample phrases of *conditions* that may appear in behavioral objectives. These include: "Upon request...;" "When asked...;" "After two weeks...;" "With visual cues...;" "With verbal prompts...;" "During treatment sessions...;" "Given a list of resources...;" and "Following group discussion..." (p. 139).

Shank and Coyle (2002) have also provided useful illustrations of *criteria* that may appear in behavioral objectives. Illustrations include: amount of time (within five minutes); degree of accuracy (within two feet of the target); number of trails (four out of five times); percentages or fractions (50% of the time); and therapist judgment (as judged by the CTRS to be appropriate to the situation) (p. 138).

Some brief examples may help clarify the concepts of criteria and conditions. Say you have a specific objective that reads like this:

- "Locate the show times for films playing at local theaters."

You could begin by imposing a condition of the source information. So the specific objective might now read as follows:

- *Given a copy of the Herald-Telephone* daily newspaper, locate the show times for films playing at local theaters.

In addition to this given, you might add another condition to the objective. This could be a restriction such as this:

- *Without the help of the recreational therapist*, and given a copy of the *Herald-Telephone* daily newspaper, locate the show times for films playing at local theaters.

If you really want to become specific about your objective, you might add a criterion. The objective might then read like this:

- Without the help of the recreational therapist, and given a copy of the *Herald-Telephone* daily newspaper, *locate within a three-minute period of time* the show times for films playing at local theaters.

By now you may be thinking, "Come on, let's not overdo it." Perhaps the example is overstated, perhaps not. Just how detailed should you be in writing specific behavioral objectives? Mager (1997) answered the question when stating the following:

> Simply put, a usefully stated objective is one that succeeds in communicating an intended instructional result to the reader. It is useful to the extent that it conveys to others a picture of what a successful learner will be able to do; and to the extent that the picture it conveys is *identical to the picture the objective writer has in mind.* (p. 43)

Mager (1997) has gone on to stipulate three characteristics of useful objectives:

1. **Performance.** It describes what the learner is expected to be able to do.
2. **Conditions.** It describes the conditions under which the performance is expected to occur.
3. **Criterion.** It describes the level of competence that must be reached or surpassed. (p. 51)

As a help in writing specific behavioral objectives, Diswas-Diener and Dean (2007) have suggested using the acronoym SMART, which stands for:

- **Specific** (Every objective is in behavioral terms, states only one behavior, and lists any conditions or criteria.)
- **Measurable** (Objectives provide specific ways to measure behaviors so it is clear the objective is accomplished.)

- **Attainable** (Objectives are realistic. They are not established just to have something for which to strive.)
- **Relevant** (Objectives are relevant to the individual and that individual's needs.)
- **Timelined** (Objectives provide specific deadlines by which they can be achieved.)

Still another system for writing behavioral objectives was developed by the American Occupational Therapy Association. It is RHUMBA, and stands for something other than Latin dance music. According to Sames (2005) RHUMBA stands for the following:

- **Relevant/relates:** The objective must relate to the area the client hopes to improve or maintain.
- **How long:** What is the timeframe or when will the objective be met?
- **Understandable:** Anyone reading the objective will know what it means.
- **Measurable:** There must be a way to measure or put the outcome into quantitative terms.
- **Behavioral:** The objective must express a behavior that is observed, not inferred.
- **Achievable:** The objective must be realistic.

Stating outcomes. To summarize this section, it is important to state outcomes in terms of clearly written goals and objectives. These outcomes should (a) be individually based or written for an individual client; (b) indicate a change in the client's condition (or the client's environment); (c) stipulate short-term or long-term outcomes with timelines; and (d) be realistic, attainable, and measurable.

Recreational Therapy Individualized Intervention Plan

While terms such as *treatment plan, rehabilitation plan,* and *care plan* are employed in the literature, the term *individualized intervention plan* is used in this book to describe the client's personalized plan of care customized to meet the client's specific needs. This useage is consistent with the definition of individualized intervention plan presented by the National Council for Therapeutic Recreation Certification (NCTRC) in its *2007 Job Analysis Report.* NCTRC defined individual intervention plan as "an individualized plan of care or intervention for a person served by a qualified TR/RT professional (CTRS) based on assessed strengths and needs, and includes goals, objectives and intervention strategies aimed at fostering desirable and necessary outcomes" (p. 6).

The recreational therapy individualized intervention plan is a written document stating what the client and recreational therapist intend to accomplish. This customized plan flows from the client's previously established goals set. The therapeutic goals set must fit, of course, into any overall master plan or interdisciplinary treatment plan.

Many settings employ goal-directed recreational therapy planning, but the terms used to describe the recreational therapy individualized intervention plan vary. For example, in many clinical facilities it has been referred to as a "recreational therapy treatment plan." Likewise, the exact nature of individualized intervention plans will necessarily differ from setting to setting. Common elements that are likely to transcend all RT individualized intervention plans regardless of setting are as follows:

- an indication of the client's problems and needs, in order to formulate a **needs list** (Problems represent obstacles to meeting needs. Therefore, the identification of problems leads to needs);

- an identification of client strengths (e.g., abilities, virtues, family support) to formulate a **strengths list**;
- a prioritized **goals set** appropriate to guide the delivery of recreational therapy services;
- a listing of **specific objectives** for each goal;
- a **plan** of interventions or programs indicated for participation by the client, approaches to be utilized by staff, and the proper environment in which to facilitate change; and
- a brief description of procedures by which client progress will be periodically evaluated, or a plan for **evaluation**.

The *needs list* will lead directly to the development of the *goals set* because goals are derived out of client needs. The *strengths list* will be useful in the determination of the *plan* of activities or programs because recreational therapy interventions use client strengths to reach specific outcomes through the use of therapeutically designed programs. *Specific objectives* will flow directly out of the *goals* because specific behavioral objectives break down each goal into observable, measurable parts. The *evaluation* plan will provide information regarding the success of the planned interventions toward reaching the stated goals.

By constructing a plan containing these six elements, the client will have an individualized intervention plan based on sought behavioral changes, the needs and strengths of the client, and the anticipated impact of the client, environment, and staff on behavioral change. The strategies formulated for the plan should meet the established goals and consider each client's unique background, psychological makeup, and personal needs and expectations. By doing so, each properly prepared plan will be distinctive and customized. An example of an individualized intervention plan is shown in Table 4.4.

Master Treatment Plan (MTP) or Interdisciplinary Treatment Plan (ITP)

In most settings, there will exist an overall plan to manage the comprehensive care of each client. This plan provides overall direction for the client's care and indicates the responsibilities of various members of the team of professionals assigned to the client's care. In the clinical settings in which recreational therapy regularly transpires, this documentation system is commonly called the **master treatment plan (MTP) or the interdisciplinary treatment** plan (ITP) (Farnsworth & Biglow, 1997). Other similar terms may be employed in nonclinical settings. An example would be in educational settings where the expression individualized education program (IEP) is used.

The MTP or ITP is usually based on a medical or psychiatric diagnosis-related group (DRG). This type of MTP or ITP is referred to as clinical pathways, critical paths, clinical practice guidelines, patient care protocols, or integrated plans of care. Whatever term is used (and in this discussion, the term *clinical pathways* will be used) the plan's function is to provide interdisciplinary practice guidelines with predetermined standards of care with the aim of providing the most effective and efficient way to approach a diagnosis.

A number of definitions of clinical pathways have appeared in the literature. It may be helpful to review some of these. Clinical pathways "delineate a predetermined written plan of care for a particular health problem," according to Cherry and Bridges (2005). They go on to state: "Clinical pathways specify the desired outcomes and interdisciplinary interventions required within a specified time period for a specified diagnosis or health problem" (p. 460). In the words of Stuart (2001b), a clinical pathway "is a written plan that serves as a map or timetable for the effective delivery of health care" (p. 80). Another definition has been provided by Pilon (1998), who defines critical pathways as "multidisciplinary care management plans that organize, sequence, and guide the patient care tasks and interventions for an episode of care" (p. 92). According to burlingame and Skalko (1997),

Table 4.4

RT/TR Individual Intervention Plan

Data Line:
Who:

Rose E. Mullins

Why admitted:

Suicide attempt by overdose of over-the-counter sleeping pills and alcohol.

Subjective:

She stated that she "gets along" well with her children and "OK" with her mother. Ms. Mullins stated "not missing work" as her only personal strength. She stated that her life seems "out of control" and "too difficult." Although she does have a boyfriend, they rarely go out socially. She reported that her rotating shifts at the glass factory make it difficult to find other people to do activities with. Ms. Mullins stated that she has become increasingly depressed over the course of the past year, and has no close friends. She stated that when she was younger she had a few close friends with whom she regularly "partied."

Objective:

Ms. Mullins is a divorced mother of two elementary school-aged children. She presents as a socially withdrawn and quiet adult female. She does not initiate interactions with other clients or with staff. Affect is sad most of the time. She is unable to identify with any currently satisfying leisure activities. She stated that she used to camp and fish with her ex-husband, but is uncertain if she would like to resume participating in these activities. When presented with a barrier to a desired leisure activity, she was unable to identify strategies to negotiate the barrier.

Assessment:

Ms. Mullins shows limited social skills and self-confidence. Ms. Mullins appears to desire an expanded social network, but has limited ability to act on this desire. She has an extremely limited leisure repertoire. Leisure-related problem-solving skills are poor.

Strengths:

1. Family support.
2. Able to form intimate interpersonal relationships.
3. Stable employment.

Needs:

1. Improved self-esteem.
2. Improved social interaction.
3. Stress management skills.
4. Expanded leisure repertoire.
5. Exploration of potential problems related to alcohol consumption.

Table 4.4 (cont.)

Goals (within one month):
Upon completion of specified plan, the client:

1. Increases self-esteem.
2. Expands supportive social network.
3. Reports less stress in her daily life.
4. Expands repertoire of leisure activities.

Specific Objectives:
Over the course of intervention, the client:

1. Increases self-esteem:
   a. Makes at least one verbal or written positive comment about herself when asked by the group leader within each self-esteem group session.
   b. Employs two or more strategies she has developed to become accepted by members of the group within each self-esteem group session,.
   b. Verbally identifies at least one successful outcome she has had from her participation in activities, when prompted by the recreational therapist.
   c. Verbally identifies daily to staff and/or other clients at least one explanation (attribution) for her successful outcomes while participating in activities.
   d. Regularly displays acceptance of complementary feedback from others by saying "thank you" or making some other appropriate response, as judged by the recreational therapist.

2. Expands supportive social network:
   a. Discloses at least one fact about self during each social competence class session.
   b. Initiates at least one conversation during each social competence class session.
   c. Identifies a plan for seeking increased social interaction in her community.

3. Reports less stress in her life:
   a. Verbally identifies two or more sources of stress in her life during the stress and anger management class.
   b. Verbally informs the recreational therapist and fellow members of the stress and anger management class of one or more strategies she has developed to cope with identified sources of stress.
   c. Performs one or more tension reduction exercises when feeling stressed and reports on her experience about completing the exercise(s) in the stress and anger management class.

Table 4.4 (cont.)

d.   At the conclusion of each week, tells the recreational therapist and fellow members of the stress and anger management class her feelings about whether she is decreasing stress in her life.

4.   Expands repertoire of leisure activities:
   a.   Identifies verbally to fellow members of the leisure education group at least three leisure activities that interest her.
   b.   Identifies verbally to fellow members of the leisure education group one or more barriers to her leisure activity participation.
   c.   Each week, verbally reports her intent to engage in one new leisure activity within the leisure education group.
   d.   Each week, verbally reports whether she engaged in the one new leisure activity of her choice.
   d.   As a homework assignment for the leisure education group, constructs a one-page written plan for managing personal time.
   e.   Within one to two weeks of constructing her plan for managing personal time, reports verbally within the leisure education group on how effective the plan was.

Plans:
Interventions
- Client to attend self-awareness/self-esteem group twice weekly for one-hour sessions.
- Clients to attend leisure education group twice weekly for two-hour sessions.
- Client to attend social competence class twice weekly for one-hour sessions.
- Client to attend stress and anger management class twice weekly for one-hour sessions.

Therapeutic Approaches
Self-esteem
- Encourage participation in success-oriented activities.
- Process activities with client.
- Facilitate client's identification of attributions for activity outcomes.
- Dispute attributions indicating helplessness.

Social Interaction
- Remind and reinforce social interaction goals.
- Teach client assertiveness skills.
- Teach client to identify barriers to social interaction.

Stress Management
- Facilitate client's identification of sources and symptoms of stress.
- Instruct client in tension reduction exercises (physical).

Table 4.4 (cont.)

- Teach client time-management and cognitive coping techniques.
- Use role playing to practice skills.

Leisure Repertoire
- Teach client strategies for negotiating leisure barriers.
- Teach client time-management strategies.
- Use behavioral contracting for developing new leisure activities.
- Use homework.

Evaluation:
- Use time-interval observations to monitor 1a, 1b, 2a, 2b.
- Maintain progress notes of behavior in intervention sessions to monitor 1c, 1d, 2c, 3a, 3b, 4a-d.
- Monitor nursing staff notes for behavior related to 3b.

March 19, 2013	Bryan P. McCormick, CTRS
(date)	(signature)

---

a clinical pathway is a "clinical guide to care using a systematic sequence of treatments and interventions delivered within an established length of stay ... by having a preestablished method of approaching a specific patient problem and using previously identified successful intervention strategies, the treatment team can better predict the patterns of treatment and allocate resources appropriately" (p. 82). Finally, *Charting Made Incredibly Easy!* (2010) has stated, "A critical pathway is an interdisciplinary plan of care that describes assessment criteria, interventions, treatments, and outcomes for specific health-related conditions (usually based on a DRG) across a designated timeline" (p. 54).

From these definitions, it can be derived that clinical pathways are "road maps" for the provision of multidisciplinary clinical services that stipulate expected time frames and resources needed to treat a specific diagnosis. They are plans that identify critical interventions and sequence them along a timeline with the intent of achieving specified outcomes. In short, clinical paths (a) state what is to be done and who is to do it in order to achieve expected outcomes for clients from a specific group; (b) establish timelines for procedures, interventions, and outcomes; and (c) serve as communication tools that all disciplines can use to coordinate client care.

Expert clinicians from professions that routinely treat a particular diagnostic group form multidisciplinary teams to develop clinical pathways. Their collaborative efforts determine what might be the best way to treat the average client within a diagnostic group. Thus the experts agree on the best practices to use, and the practices are organized and sequenced along a timeline. Completed clinical paths identify (a) care provider interventions, (b) expected client outcomes, and (c) timelines or the expected treatment time. Timelines are important because they organize and sequence care. Units of time vary tremendously from minutes in hospital emergency departments to weeks in rehabilitative centers.

Depending on the nature of the diagnosis, the actual critical care document itself can be as brief as a page or as long as several pages. An example has been provided by Farnsworth and Biglow (1997, p. 325). It is a one-page clinical pathway for major depression. Across the top of the page are columns that chart six time periods (0-8 hours, 8-24 hours, day 2, day 3, day 4, day 5). Within each time-period column is listed the procedures, interventions, and expected outcomes for each specific time frame.

Clinical pathways offer the capacity to capture variance data. Variances are deviations from the pathway. Variances occur when clients do not achieve their expected outcomes within the stipulated time frame (i.e., negative variances) or when outcomes are achieved earlier than anticipated (i.e., positive variances). Variances also include instances when interventions need to be changed. Variance reports are typically written as narrative notes. In some agencies, the critical path and variance reports are not part of the chart because of the fear of possible legal repercussions. In others, both the pathway and variance report are regular parts of the medical record (Forkner, 1996). The communication of variance is, of course, important to members of the treatment team. Variance data also provides clinicians with a powerful tool for continuous quality improvement (Pilon, 1998).

Clinical pathways work best in facilities where there are a large number of clients with the same problem and where predictable outcomes are expected. They are less useful with complex situations. For instance, they are less effective with clients who have several diagnoses or who encounter complications (*Charting Made Incredibly Easy!*, 2010).

In the end, like all documentation systems, clinical pathways "are only as sound as their design and the judgment of the providers who use them" (Forkner, 1996, p. 2). Clinical pathways simply provide guidelines. They are not absolute because clinicians can change them to meet their clients' unique needs. Nor does the use of clinical pathways preclude the use of a recreational therapy individual intervention plan.

Recreational Therapy Individual Intervention Plan

An example of a *recreational therapy individual intervention plan* appears in Table 4.4 The following case is a hypothetical client that has been created as a composite of a number of actual clients. The therapist in this case is working with the client in a day hospital setting, and expects to work with the client over the period of at least one month. The client has already completed a 5-day in-patient psychiatric treatment. The client is a 34-year-old divorced mother of two children who was admitted to the in-patient psychiatric unit of the local general hospital following a suicide attempt.

Ms. Mullins' plan covers a number of needs. The list of needs represents a prioritized list in the sense that unless more primary needs are met, lower order needs may not be relevant. For example, until Ms. Mullins can cope with her apparent depression and low self-esteem, it is unlikely that she will be motivated to work on stress management or expanding her leisure repertoire. If the therapist were working with Ms. Mullins at a time in which she had a shorter length of stay (one week, for example), he or she would probably only be able to begin to work on the first and second areas of need. With a longer length of contact with Ms. Mullins, the therapist would be able to work on all areas of need.

Unfortunately, the strengths assessment revealed Ms. Mullins possesses virtually no recreationally related strengths. In fact, she lacks a repertoire of leisure activities. Therefore, one of the goals in her plan is to expand her leisure repertoire. Ms. Mullins' identified strengths do include having support from her family, an ability to develop intimate relationships, and stability in her employment. The plan particularly builds on her potential to develop intimate relationships by helping her with learning how to expand her social network.

Another aspect of this plan is that there is a great deal of "overlap" in the types of interventions and goals. For example, both leisure repertoire and social interaction goals can be worked on simultaneously. Since many leisure activities are social in nature, the therapist could be helping Ms. Mullins to expand her leisure repertoire through participation in activity clubs. This could expand her leisure repertoire and social network at the same time. Also, issues related to time management have been identified under the leisure repertoire goal; however, they also address the issue of stress reduction. Ms. Mullins is likely to feel less stressed if she is able to have more control over her time.

Finally, it should be noted that this individualized intervention plan uses an intervention-specific approach (Thompson, 1996) in which individual interventions, such as leisure education and social competence training, are identified in the plan. In addition, the intervention section of the plan specifies frequency and duration of interventions. Although these interventions may appear to be written in terms similar to objectives given that there is a performance (attend specified intervention) and criteria (two times a week for one hour sessions), it should be remembered that these interventions specify the *process* of treatment, and not the *outcomes* of treatment.

In general, this plan is based on a cognitive-behavioral approach to intervention. For example, the plans related to self-esteem are based on Martin Seligman's theory of Learned Optimism (1998). Seligman's theory takes a cognitive-behavioral approach to helplessness and resultant depression. In general, the intervention plans are intended to assist Ms. Mullins in identifying her patterns of thought and the resulting behavioral problems they create. By assisting her to reframe the way she thinks about her life and its challenges, the therapist helps her to negotiate barriers and live a more satisfying life.

Activity Analysis

Once goals and objectives have been specified in the customized RT individualized intervention plan, the recreational therapist must select activities to apply in the intervention process. The activities used in intervention must be thoroughly understood in order to help assure optimal therapeutic benefit for the client. The name given the procedure for systematically achieving a precise and complete understanding of activities is *activity analysis*. The *Glossary of Recreation Therapy and Occupational Therapy*, has defined **activity analysis** as a "process of systematically appraising what behaviors and skills are required for participation in a given activity" (Austin, 2001a, p. 2).

Activity analysis permits the practitioner to break down an activity into its component parts. Requirements that are inherent for successful participation are identified and understood in order to assure that the activity is an appropriate vehicle to employ to derive client outcomes. A total comprehension of a given activity is acquired so that the activity may be properly used to meet the goals and objectives of the RT individual intervention plan. Or, as Stumbo and Peterson (2009) have stated, the recreational therapist "makes sure that the activities are the best possible choices to help clients achieve their intended goals" (p. 176).

Nonadapted activities. In some instances, the activity will be employed "as is." That is, no alterations will be required in order for clients to gain maximum benefit from participation. For example, a dance for clients would be planned and conducted in much the same way as a dance for any group. At other times, the recreational therapist may manipulate the activity to bring about therapeutic intents. In so doing, opportunities are created for the activity to contribute directly toward sought behavioral objectives. For example, cooperation might be emphasized in a particular sports activity in order to reinforce cooperative behaviors on the part of a certain client or clients.

Adapted activities. In still other cases, activities will need to be adapted or modified to accommodate clients with limitations. Assistive devices may be employed, such as audible softballs for visually impaired clients or a handle grip bowling ball for those who have difficulty gripping. Games may be modified by reducing the dimensions of the playing area, simplifying rules, or through other similar means. Whatever the modification, it is important that the recreational therapist has a detailed understanding of the activity so that artificial or unnecessary modifications are not made. As a general principle, the best modification is the least modification.

Behavioral domains. Activity analysis includes three behavioral domains (i.e., psychomotor, cognitive, affective), as well as social or interactional skills. It is the task of the recreational therapist to examine the demands placed on participants by the activity in regard to specificities. Each of the four components must be appraised to determine what behaviors and skills are required by those who take part in the activity. Examples of aspects for possible consideration follow under each of the four major components.

Psychomotor (physical) domain:
- Is the full body involved or only part of the body?
- What types of manipulative movements are required (throwing, hitting, catching, kicking, bouncing, pulling, pushing, grasping, lifting)?
- What types of locomotor movements are required (crawling, walking, running, climbing, jumping, hopping, rolling, skipping)?
- What kinds of non-locomotor movements are required (twisting, turning, stretching, extending, bending, swinging, hanging, landing)?
- What level of exertion is required?
- What degree of fitness is necessary?
- What degree of strength is needed?
- Is a high level of skill development required (e.g., hand-eye coordination, balance)?
- Is rhythm required?
- How much endurance is necessary?
- How much flexibility is needed?
- How much repetitiveness in movement is required?
- What sensory demands are made?

Cognitive (intellectual) domain:
- Is the level of complexity appropriate for the clients?
- Is there a high degree of repetitiveness in the activity?
- Are academic skills required (e.g., spelling, reading, or math)?
- How much recall (i.e., memory) is involved? For example, are there many rules to remember? Is recognition of persons or objects called for?
- What level of concentration is needed? Attention span?
- What level of analysis (i.e., breaking down material) and synthesis (i.e., putting parts together) is required?
- Is the sequencing of actions or information called for?
- What level of verbal skill is needed?
- Are participants called on to think quickly and make rapid decisions?
- Is abstract thinking called for?

Affective (psychological) domain:

- Does the activity release tension (stress)?
- Does the activity allow the client to communicate feelings?
- Does the activity generally lead to fun?
- To what degree is it possible to display creativity?
- Does frustration commonly arise from participation?
- How much control (over the environment) can the client experience?
- Does the activity have potential for enhancement of self-esteem?
- Is teamwork emphasized? Sharing? Helping others?
- Is self-discipline necessary? Listening skills?
- Are democratic processes followed?
- Is the activity stimulating? Exciting?
- Are values apparent in the activity? If so, what values?

Social (Interactional) Skills:

- Is cooperation emphasized? Competition?
- Do structures (rules) reinforce prosocial behavior?
- Is the activity individual? Small-group oriented?
- How many persons may participate?
- How much leadership must be provided?
- How structured is the activity?
- May all ages take part? All sizes?
- Are traditional sex roles emphasized?
- What types of interaction patterns occur?
- What amount of initiative is required?
- Is a high level of interaction called for?
- Is verbal communication necessary?
- What noise level will likely be generated?
- Does the space dictate being close to others? Physically touching?

The recreational therapist will also necessarily need to analyze activities for other aspects in addition to social skills and the psychomotor, cognitive, and affective domains. Elements for consideration, drawn primarily from the classic work of Fidler and Fidler (1954) and from Lamport, Coffey, and Hersch's (1996) *Activity Analysis & Application*, include the following aspects.

Several question for assessing an activity's *adaptability* and *variability* follow:

- How much time is required for participation?
- Does the activity have a sequence of steps to complete it? If so, what is the time required to complete each step?
- Is the activity adaptable to various chronological and mental age levels? To various educational levels?
- Does the activity have cultural relevance?
- How much is speed emphasized in completing tasks within the activity, and to what degree can this be controlled?
- How much variety is possible in selection of tasks or projects within an activity (e.g., how many types and levels of leather-tooling projects would be available)?

Asking the following questions can help determine an activity's *usefulness:*

- Is the cost of the activity within the means of clients?
- Will materials or supplies be available to clients?
- Does the activity have any carryover value in terms of participating in it outside of the clinical setting?
- Do products made have any useful value to clients (i.e., to use themselves or give as gifts)?

Answers to the following questions may help determine whether an activity is *practical:*
- What are the space and environmental requirements for the activity (e.g., size of room or outdoor space needed, requirements for light, equipment readily adjusted to the needs of clients)?
- Is the activity practical for bed patients when factors such as noise and equipment are considered?
- Is the activity too expensive for the agency in terms of equipment and supplies?
- How much staffing is required to conduct the activity?
- Do staff have the leadership skills needed to conduct the activity?
- Are there precautions that need to be taken?
- When would the activity be contraindicated for particular types of clients?

A word of caution is in order here. The recreational therapist must remember that for each individual client, his or her perception of an activity may differ greatly from others. Individuals may view the same activity very differently. It is the individual's particular approach to the activity that defines his or her experience. *How* the client takes part in the activity has a primary impact on the experience. For example, those who are hard driven and competitive will approach an activity very differently from persons who have more relaxed dispositions.

Therefore, it is not entirely the activity itself but also the way someone approaches the activity that affects the experience. The recreational therapist must be aware that, although understanding behavioral requirements of the activity is important, employing activities with clients is a complex task that should not be started on a simplistic level in which prescribed outcomes are expected by simply having clients participate in a given activity.

Progress Assessment

It was previously mentioned that the last step in the planning process is to determine methods of assessing client progress. In the case of Ms. Mullins, assessment took the form of observations and progress notes. In long-term care, there are likely to be three actual stages in planning:

1. The initial plan to deal with essential interventions while full assessment is being completed.
2. The total assessment plan based on a complete assessment utilizing the techniques mentioned earlier in this chapter and from which the major intervention strategies are evolved.
3. The revised plan based on new data that leads to altered actions either to bring about revisions in unproductive change strategies or to meet newly identified needs.

Therefore, each client will likely have several RT individualized intervention plans developed as a result of the ongoing assessment process.

The Implementation Phase

Implementation is the actual provision of the program. It is the action phase in which the strategies developed in the planning phase are put into motion.

Perhaps the most important item to be considered in the implementation of the master treatment plan is consistency. A well-formed plan allows all those involved to strive for similar goals following agreed-on approaches. Such planning also contributes to the continuity of care provided by establishing short-term and long-term goals.

Often an interdisciplinary team effort will be utilized in implementing the plan with recreational therapists carrying out their portion of the plan. In other instances, the recreational therapy individualized intervention plan will be carried out by one or more recreational therapists. The setting and needs of the client dictate the particular procedures to be pursued. In any case, it is necessary to determine who has the authority and responsibility for coordinating the client's activities. Without clear delineation as to who is in control of the plan, problems will likely arise, since much coordination is necessary in maintaining client plans.

Usually some type of written communication is sent to all appropriate staff members informing them of the individual plan to be implemented. Additionally, in settings such as hospitals and residential centers where clients are in various types of activities throughout the day (e.g., recreational therapy, psychotherapy, physical therapy), an activity schedule is often provided for each client. This schedule usually lists the days of the week and the hours of each day so that the activities planned for the client may be recorded. Written communications, such as the interdisciplinary treatment plan and activity schedule, provide sources of reference and serve as reminders of the client's program for all staff. By following a systematic routine and using written communication, misunderstandings are avoided and consistency is promoted in the carrying out of the plan.

Most agencies with recreational therapy programs have written descriptions that detail each program offered. These are generally referred to as *protocols*. "A protocol is simply a written description of how intervention and routine procedures are conducted," according to Munson (2002, p. 297). *Program protocols* provide concrete information to illustrate the contributions of recreational therapy to therapeutic outcomes. While there is no single standard format for protocol development, Table 4.5 provides an example of an outline for protocols.

The recreational therapist who is conducting a program should make sure he or she is familiar with the protocol information and that his or her actions are consistent with it. The recreational therapist should likewise be certain his or her approach with the client is consistent with the approach directed in the client's plan. Finally, the recreational therapist implementing a program needs to continually assess the results of the program on clients, as well as the reactions of clients to the program. This data provides information for the final phase of the recreational therapy process—evaluation.

The Evaluation Phase

Evaluation is the final step in the recreational therapy process. Through evaluation, the effectiveness of the client's program is examined.

Table 4.5

Outline for Program Protocols

Program Title
Time and Place of Program
Target Population/ Size of Group
Client Referral Criteria
Contraindicated Criteria
General Program Purpose
Program Description
Problems or Deficits the Program Might Address
Interventions or Facilitation Techniques to be Employed
Staff Program Responsibilities
Training Requirements for Staff
Risk Management Considerations
Expected Program Outcomes
Program Evaluation Methods/Frequency

Sources: Cole, M. B. (1993). *Group dynamics in occupational therapy: The theoretical basis and practice application of group treatment.* Thorofare, NJ: SLACK Incorporated; Kelland, J. (Ed.). (1995). Protocols for recreation therapy programs. State College, PA: Venture; O'Morrow, G. S. & Carter, M. J. (1997). *Effective management in therapeutic recreation service.* State College, PA: Venture; Stumbo, N. J., & Peterson, C. A. (2009). *Therapeutic recreation program design* (5th ed.). San Francisco: Pearson.

In recreational therapy, we are concerned with individual client evaluation and program evaluation. Both are important, and each is difficult to separate from the other, since programs are the vehicles by which we in recreational therapy help individual clients to meet needs and to grow as persons. In individual client evaluation, the client is central to our purpose. In program evaluation, we target our concern on the program itself. In either case, distinctions may be conceived to be somewhat arbitrary and difficult to maintain.

The terms *formative evaluation* and *summative evaluation* are used to describe two types of program evaluation. *Formative evaluation* occurs while the program is being conducted and leads to immediate program modifications if they are needed. *Summative evaluation* takes place at the conclusion of a program (e.g., at the end of fall programs or the end of a semester) and is used to revise the program the next time it is provided. Kunstler and Stavola Daly (2010) have stated about summative evaluation, "It may result in changing the time, location, format, leadership style, or content of a program" (p. 67).

For the purpose of this chapter, however, the focus will remain with the individual client. Therefore, discussion will center on completing client evaluation. Individual client evaluation is closely tied to the planning process because part of the planning process is determining methods to assess client progress. The actual carrying out of these methods is client evaluation. Staff should not limit their analysis only to "measurable" or quantitative items. Staff can and should use qualitative approaches such as naturalistic observations, observations of behaviors related to specific objectives (i.e., specific goal observation) and subjective feelings. Nevertheless, the emerging recreational therapist will be more apt to rely on more quantitative means, such as norm-referenced tests and time-interval observations, since it requires some experience to develop observational skills and to learn to place trust in feelings.

In addition to the observational methods that have been mentioned, other methods used in initial client assessment are appropriate for evaluation. For example, the interview method offers an opportunity for clients to respond retrospectively as to how they perceive themselves after participation in therapeutic activities compared to their perceptions prior to beginning the program. Secondary sources of information offer another means for client evaluation. For instance, pretest and posttest scores on standardized tests given by a psychologist may be contrasted to measure gains on a variable such as self-esteem. Family and friends may be interviewed following a home visit by a hospitalized client. Information may be gained from other staff at a team meeting, or progress notes may be reviewed.

If several different sources of information agree on the progress of the client, it can be said that congruence exists among them. Generally, the recreational therapist should attempt to structure evaluation procedures to retrieve data from several independent sources to see if the data stand up to the test of congruence (i.e., the information is consistent).

Of course, all methods of client evaluation exist to determine if the anticipated results transpired as a consequence of whatever recreational therapy intervention was applied. In other words, evaluation answers the question, "Were sought outcomes achieved as a result of the program?" If evaluation is not completed, the recreational therapist has no basis on which to judge the effectiveness of the program in bringing about the objectives stated in the client's individualized RT intervention plan or interdisciplinary treatment plan.

Making Referrals

There are instances when evaluation data reveal that the client has succeeded in reaching his or her goals. In such instances, where the client has done well and is ready for the next step, it may be that a referral is appropriate. For instance, a client from a rehabilitation agency might be referred to a community-based wheelchair sports program.

There are other instances where an initial assessment, or even a prolonged evaluation, reveals that, for one reason or another, the client can be better served by another individual. According to authorities (George & Cristiani, 1995; Purtilo, Haddad, & Doherty, 2014), it is appropriate to make a referral when

- the client's needs exceed the boundaries of your training and capabilities;
- you lack the equipment for providing the proper services for the client;
- you just have not been able to make progress with a particular client;
- there are irresolvable personality differences between you and the client;
- you hold a negative bias toward the client or group to which the client belongs that interferes with you providing competent care;
- the client is a personal friend or relative; or
- for some reason, the client is not willing to discuss problems with you.

No matter the reason, therapists will occasionally be called upon to make referrals. What should you do on such occasions? Conventional wisdom might lead you to place the responsibility for making the contact with the client, once you are certain the referral is appropriate. Leaving the responsibility with the client may be wise if he or she is ready to function independently. However, Miller and Rollnick (1991) have presented empirical evidence to suggest that referral success rates were much higher when counselors placed referral calls for their clients, in contrast to giving the number to their clients to make their own calls. Miller and Rollnick have suggested that it is preferable for the therapist to err on the side of taking the responsibility for the client who may find it difficult to follow up.

These authors have written, "If a simple caring letter or telephone call can double, triple, or quadruple the chances of a client's continuing with counseling and change efforts, in what way does this constitute harm to the client?" (p. 28) There obviously is not one "right answer" when it comes to making referrals. You, as a helper, must assess the situation and then exercise your own best professional judgment.

There are some general guidelines that can be followed to make referrals more effective. It is a good idea to contact a specific person at the potential referral agency if you think there is a possibility of making a referral. This step will prepare an individual professional and the agency, should urgent action become necessary. You should become familiar with potential professionals to whom you may refer so you can match the client's needs with the specific professional's competencies. When explaining to clients the types of services available from the referral agency, be accurate about the potentialities of the program so clients' expectations are not unrealistically high.

Information about the clients being referred should not be given to the new agency without permission from the clients, or their parents in the case of minors. This permission should be in the form of a signed release (Brammer & MacDonald, 2002; George & Cristiani, 1995).

Discharge Planning

Discharge planning involves making plans for the transition of clients being released from the care of an agency or rehabilitation center or from a hospital or institution. If the client is moving from a hospital or institution, the transition may be back to the client's home or into a setting such as a group home or long-term care facility. Those being discharged from the care of a community agency will likely remain in their homes, but their discharge planning could involve a referral to a community agency or an individual healthcare professional. For example, in the case of clients needing further rehabilitation, they might be referred to a physical therapy clinic or to an aquatic therapy program. In the case of clients who have received psychiatric care, they might be referred to an individual therapist or a community support group, The intent of any discharge planning is to assist the client to enjoy as high a quality of life as possible when leaving the care of an agency or facility.

As explained by Kunstler and Stavola Daly (2010), the recreational therapist considers what will be important and useful in the client's transition and "helps the client prepare for discharge, identifying the specific skills and behaviors that will facilitate the next placement, and then helps the client to acquire or improve these skills and behaviors." These authors go on to state it is natural for anyone going into a new situation to be fearful and anxious so that the recreational therapist who does not assist in a client's transition "is doing a disservice to the client" (p. 65). It is likely that the recreational therapist will refer some clients to another agency as a part of discharge planning. In those instances the information in the prior segment on making referrals will be helpful.

Theoretical Thinking and the Recreational Therapy Process

It has been stated that the recreational therapy process provides a cornerstone for practice in recreational therapy. The recreational therapy process is *the* mechanism through which recreational therapy services are delivered. So it may be said that the recreational therapy process and practice are inextricably tied together.

But there has to be more to form the basis for recreational therapy practice than the four steps of the recreational therapy process. What else is there? The answer is *theory*.

The Relationship of Theory to Recreational Therapy Practice

Because nursing has had a longer concern for theory than has recreational therapy, it is to nursing that we turn for understandings of the relationship of theory to practice. Nursing theorists McEwen and Wills (2011) wrote, "In a practice discipline such as nursing, theory and practice are inseparable" (p. 375). Certainly the same can be said for recreational therapy. Recreational therapy, like nursing, is a practice discipline in which theory and practice are integrally related.

McEwen and Willis (2011) have gone on to explain the strong relationship between theory and nursing practice when they stated, "Theory provides the basis for understanding the reality of nursing; it enables the nurse to understand why an event happens" (p. 375). Further, these authors have stated that nurses must not conceive theory as simply an intellectual exercise but, instead, they need to think of theory as the basis for practice.

The notion that theory should guide practice has also been prevalent in the literature of our sister discipline of occupational therapy (e.g., Parham, 1987; Kielhofner, 2007; Krefting, 1985). Haglund, Ekbladh, Thorell, and Hallberg (2000) have written for practicing occupational therapists that "it is essential to have theoretical knowledge of models and to be able to assess their relevance in relation to daily practice" (p. 107).

Similarly, we need to acknowledge that theory provides us with a means to understand why events occur within recreational therapy. And, like nurses and occupational therapists, recreational therapists need to embrace the notion that theory furnishes them with the basis for their clinical practice. McEwen and Wills' (2011) words ring true when they state that "…practice without theory becomes rote performance of activities based on tradition, common sense, and following orders" (p. 377). Similarly, I have indicted elsewhere:

> It is critical that recreational therapists are reflective practitioners who examine what they are doing and why they are doing it. This keeps us from doing things simply because "that's the way we've always done it," which is a trap the unthinking recreational therapist can fall into. The best recreational therapists are thoughtful, not habitual, in their practice. (Austin, 2011a, p. 13)

Means by Which Theory Influences Practice

What specifically are the means by which theory influences practice? The nursing literature offers insights that may be translated into recreational therapy to capture how theory impacts on practice in recreational therapy. McEwen and Wills (2011) have examined the work of other nursing scholars in order to construct a list of ways in which theory influences nursing practice. Items on their list range from the identification of clients of nursing care and the clarification of objectives for practice to the differentiation of nursing practice from the practice of other health disciplines and the identification of areas for research. In Table 4.6, McEwen and Wills' (2011) list of ways in which theory influences nursing practice has been adapted for use in recreational therapy.

Table 4.6

Ways in Which Theory Influences RT Practice

- Identifies clients of recreational therapy care
- Describes settings in which practice occurs
- Defines which data to collect for assessment and evaluation
- Outlines actual and potential problems for consideration

Table 4.6 (cont.)

- Assists in analyzing and understanding health situations
- Guides formulation of recreational therapy diagnosis
- Clarifies objectives and establishes expected outcomes
- Specifies interventions that are provided
- Differentiates RT practice from that of other health disciplines
- Identifies areas for research

Adapted from McEwen, M., & Wills, E.M. (2011), *Theoretical basis for nursing* (3rd ed.). Philadelphia, PA: Wolters Kluwer Health/Lippincott Williams & Wilkins, p. 376.

A Potential Theory-Practice Gap

Even though the relationship between theory and practice is emphasized in this book, unfortunately there remains the potential for a gap between theory and practice. To begin, a hindrance to practitioners linking theory to practice is a lack of exposure to theory as a part of their professional preparation. Practitioners who have not been steeped in theory cannot be expected to understand how to draw on theory as a basis for practice. Those who have not studied conceptual models and the theoretical perspectives which accompany them are not prepared to comprehend linkages between theory and practice. Neither is it likely that practitioners, whose studies did not prepare them to apply theory, will gain insights into the application of theory when there is little contact between theorists and those "in the trenches." Theorists tend to be faculty at universities while practitioners are out on "the firing lines" (McEwen & Wills, 2011).

It can only be hoped that the potential for the existence of a theory-practice gap will be lessened as students gain understandings of how theory and practice interrelate and those already in the field receive continuing education to make them aware of the potentialities for improved service delivery that occur when theory and practice are linked.

Kiehofner (2005) has suggested that within occupational therapy the theory-practice gap can be reduced if academics and practitioners collaborate with theory emerging out of this partnership. This kind of academic/practitioner teamwork would seem to be a valid approach that could be applied in recreational therapy as well.

Levels of Abstraction

Often theory and philosophy are confused, and this is understandable because they are closely related. What is the difference between theory and philosophy? Smith and Liehr's (2008) "Ladder of Abstraction" is a useful paradigm in comprehending how theory and philosophy relate to one another. They envision a ladder with three rungs. At the highest rung is found the philosophical, on the middle rung is the theoretical, and positioned on the lowest rung the empirical.

In this formulation, the philosophical level, being the most elevated level, represents the beliefs (in the form of assumptions and perspectives) upon which theory rests. This highest level of abstraction contains beliefs that underlie theories. The step below the philosophical rung is the theoretical. The theoretical level represents abstract ideas or concepts. On the bottom step, or lowest rung, is the empirical level, which is the most concrete level of abstraction.

The empirical level is a much more pragmatic. It is defined by direct experiences, in contrast to the higher level abstractions represented by the philosophical and theoretical levels. The empirical level is where theory meets practice. Or, said another way, it is the level in which theory influences what the therapist actually does in his or her practice. We can employ Smith and Liehr's hierarchal ladder to understand how, in recreational therapy, philosophy influences theory which, in turn, affects practice.

Philosophy

Our professional philosophies are made up of the values we hold and the beliefs we have about human nature (Austin, 2011a). Values have been defined as "ideals, beliefs, customs, modes of conduct, qualities, or goals that are highly prized or preferred by individuals, groups, or society..."(Burkhardt & Nathaniel , 2008, p. 83). Values then represent strongly held principles to which we subscribe. Examples of values that may be held by recreational therapists include (a) valuing the therapeutic role in helping clients to reach optimal levels of health; (b) desiring that clients maintain as much autonomy and control as possible over their lives; (c) valuing the importance of the therapist-client relationship in fostering change; (d) valuing a strength-based approach to health enhancement; (e) valuing fun, enjoyment, and pleasure as important aspects in therapy; (f) viewing clients and what is happening to them, rather than the activity, as the focus of practice; (g) valuing recreational therapy as a purposeful and goal-directed enterprise; (h) valuing every client as a person of worth who should be treated with dignity and respect; and (i) valuing the therapist's responsibility to deliver competent and ethical care (Austin, 2011a).

Representative of philosophical beliefs in recreational therapy are those proposed by Austin (2011a). Austin's list draws on a list of beliefs originally set for forth by Brill and Levine (2002). These include believing that (a) humans are social animals who have a need to interact with other human beings; (b) both the welfare of the group, as well as the individual, need to be given consideration by the therapist; (c) relationships involve the understanding that mutual rights and responsibilities are both given and received; (d) all living things, including humans, possess intrinsic worth; (e) people possess a drive toward the achievement of self-realization; (f) individuals and society as a whole can be understood; and (g) each individual possesses the capacity for change.

Concepts and Theoretical Thinking

Concepts have been purported to be the "first unit to consider in the language of theoretical thinking," according to George (2011, p. 3), who has gone on to describe a concept as "an idea, thought, or notion conceived in the mind" (p. 3). Blais and Hayes (2011) termed concepts "words that bring forth mental pictures of the properties and meanings of objects, events, or things" (p. 98). Fawcett (1995) similarly defined concepts as "words that describe mental images of phenomena" (p. 2).

The importance of concepts in theories is that within theories they are identified and then used to describe the phenomenon, their interrelationships are explained, and they together provide the structure for the theory. In short, "concepts are the elements used to generate theories" (George, 2011, p. 4). Due to their importance in theory construction, concepts have been termed "the building blocks of theories" (Blais & Hayes, 2011, p. 98).

Theory

Theory refers to the thoughtful and rigorous structuring of interrelated concepts derived from philosophical beliefs in order to produce a systematic view of some phenomenon. Theory organizes concepts in such a way that relationships between concepts are specified so as to produce an explanation and understanding of a phenomenon. McEwen and Wills (2011) wrote that "theory has been called a set of interpretative assumptions, principles, or propositions that help explain or guide action" (p. 23). Each theory contains a number of parts. These include a stated purpose, concepts and their definitions, theoretical propositions, theoretical linkages, structures, and assumptions.

Theories embraced by members of a discipline reflect the assumptions and values held by its members and define the profession's nature and the purpose of its practice. Theory becomes the lens through which practice is viewed. That lens then affects what those in the profession see. It colors how the discipline and clients are perceived. (Wilkinson, 2007).

Theories are often represented by conceptual models that provide diagrammatic representations of the theories (McEwen & Wills, 2011). Conceptual models may be perceived to be components of theory development that help to clarify concepts and display relationships among concepts. Conceptual models do this by employing graphic representations or diagrams designed to demonstrate how the component parts of a theory work together. Thus conceptual models may also be termed theoretical models since they interpret theory (McEwen & Wills, 2011).

Conceptual Models Provide Recreational Therapy Theory

To understand the derivation of recreational therapy theory, it is useful again to borrow from the literature of nursing. Authorities on nursing theories (Allgood & Marriner-Tomey, 1997; McEwen & Wills, 2011) have explained that conceptual models for a practice discipline are the sources of theory.

According to Allgood and Marriner-Tomey (1997), conceptual models serve the dual roles of first addressing the central phenomena that define a discipline and, secondly, offering theories reflected in them to guide what information is obtained on clients, how to understand dynamics affecting clients, and how to approach clients, as well as determining the actions of practitioners in delivering care. McEwen and Wills (2011) have termed theories the narratives that accompany conceptual models. Further, these authors have declared that theories define and clarify the nature of the profession and its purpose, distinguishing it from other helping profession by marking professional boundaries.

If conceptual models represent theories that help distinguish a profession and determine the actions of its practitioners, the next logical question is, "Does recreational therapy have conceptual models from which to draw?" Happily, the answer is yes.

The Advent of Conceptual Models in Recreational Therapy

It is no secret that during its history recreational therapy has struggled with its professional identity. In order to remedy the situation, theorists developed conceptual models; each of which offers those in the profession a comprehensive view of the purpose and scope of recreational therapy and proposes to guide practice in the field. Formal conceptual models for recreational therapy initially appeared in the period beginning around the 1980s and extending into the early 1990s. Peterson and Gunn's Leisure Ability Model was the first. It was followed by Austin's Health Protection/Health Promotion Model (Austin, 2003).

McEwen and Wills (2011) indicated that professions emerge as distinct disciplines when they have an identifiable philosophy and at least one conceptual model that define them. At least seven additional conceptual models have been proposed since those presented by Peterson and Gunn and by Austin. Yet no single conceptual model has received universal acceptance in recreational therapy.

What Exactly are Conceptual Models for Recreational Therapy?

Thus far, the notion of conceptual models has been introduced but the term *conceptual model* has been used without a definition being provided. Then what is a conceptual model? Previously we presented *concepts* as "words that bring forth mental pictures of the properties and meanings of objects, events, or things" (Blais & Hayes, 2011, p. 98) or as "words that describe mental images of phenomena" (Fawcett,1995, p. 2). A *model* is a representation of something. It is not the real thing but it represents reality. For example, it is not theory but it represents theory. Morgan (1996) has defined a model as "a simplified representation of reality that explains the relationship of different concepts" (p. 29). Models are typically presented in the form of schematic diagrams.

Applying these definitions, it may be said that a **conceptual model** is a device that represents theory by providing an image or a picture of the concepts contained in it and how these concepts relate to one another. A conceptual model for a discipline presents "basic assumptions, boundaries, content, and context associated with the substantive focuses of the discipline" (Reed, 1998, p. 385). So **conceptual models in recreational therapy** "offer an image or visualization of the component parts that make up the discipline ... and then describe how these parts relate to one another. Conceptual models outline the purpose and scope of practice (of recreational therapy)" (Austin, 2002c, p. 4).

A New Era in Recreational Therapy

In the past it seems that recreational therapy conceptual models have been used primarily to define and describe the profession. In this era, the value of conceptual models to the recreational therapy profession was largely their use in understanding who we were (e.g., a health profession or a leisure profession).

Today there seems to be a new era on the horizon in which conceptual models for recreational therapy will be used to do more than define and describe the discipline. Recreational therapy conceptual models, and the theories that accompany them, are beginning to be acknowledged to have practical utility. This utilization of theory as a basis for practice properly places emphasis where it should be for a practice discipline, on practice. Theory, in this new era, informs practice.

Conceptual models may then be conceived as sources of theoretical perspectives to guide practice. They can be seen as frameworks for substantive approaches to recreational therapy practice. Recreational therapy theories represented by conceptual models provide guiding structures for reasoning about clients and determining the types of activities carried out in recreational therapy. In short, theory from conceptual models can be used to guide the critical thinking of recreational therapists in decision-making throughout the recreational therapy process.

Theoretical Concepts from Conceptual Models Govern Steps in the Recreational Therapy Process

Conceptual models are somewhat abstract but the theoretical concepts represented in them become real or operational through the recreational therapy process. Each step in the recreational therapy process is governed by the particular conceptual model that is subscribed to and its accompanying theory.

You will recall that the four steps in the recreational therapy process (aka APIE process) are assessment, planning, implementation, and evaluation. To provide an initial illustration of the implications of conceptual models, in the paragraphs that follow the impact of theoretical concepts from the Leisure Ability Model (Peterson & Gunn, 1984; Stumbo & Peterson, 2009) and the Health Protection/Health Promotion Model (Austin, 1991,1998, 2009, 2011b) are used to illustrate how theoretical perspectives from the two different models influence practice within each of the four phases of the recreational therapy process.

Assessment. The specific assessment data collected are influenced by the theory inherent in the conceptual model being followed. For example, if the Leisure Ability Model is followed, then the focus of the assessment would be on leisure behavior because the mission of the Leisure Ability Model is to improve leisure functioning. On the other hand, to be in harmony with the Health Protection/Health Promotion Model assessment must primarily be concentrated on the client's health and well-being.

Planning. Likewise, planning is directly governed by the conceptual model adopted. Goals and objectives need to fit with the conceptual model being followed. This is true for both the planned outcomes and the process by which they are derived. For instance, goals and objectives under the Leisure Ability Model would deal with the improvement of leisure functioning. Under the Health Protection/Health Promotion Model, goals and objectives would be concerned with returning the client to health, assisting the client to cope with illness or disability, or increasing the client's level of wellness. In terms of process, the Health Protection/Health Promotion Model calls for a strong partnership between the client and therapist in arriving at the plan.

Implementation. Implementing the planned intervention is also is governed by the theory represented in the conceptual model being followed by the therapist. The theory influences the recreational therapy intervention and how it is carried out. Implementation, for instance, following Austin's Health Protection/Health Promotion Model would be instructed by the level of direction provided by the therapist depending on whether the intervention was a prescribed activity, a recreation activity, or a leisure pursuit. The implementation of programs under the Leisure Ability Model depends on whether the client requires functional interventions to improve leisure functioning, leisure education to develop leisure or social skills, or simply opportunities to participate in recreation.

Evaluation. Depending on the conceptual model, the goals and objectives being assessed will be different. Leisure functioning will be what is being assessed under the Leisure Ability Model. In contrast, health behaviors will become the focus of evaluation under the Health Protection/Health Promotion Model.

Conclusion: Conceptual Models and Practice

It can be seen that there is a direct and significant relationship between the theoretical perspectives represented in the conceptual model being subscribed to and actual practice carried out through the recreational therapy process. Thus, a critical attribute of any conceptual model is whether its theoretical concepts can be operationalized and employed by recreational therapists using the recreational therapy process.

Hopefully the brief examples provided of how actual practice may be affected by theoretical perspectives offer clear illustrations of how theory and practice are interrelated in recreational therapy. This introduction to the relationship on how theory impacts on practice, through the lens of the recreational therapy process, is however just a beginning point in the examination of how the theory represented in conceptual models impacts recreational therapy practice.

In order to more fully comprehend the dynamics involved in moving from recreational therapy theory to recreational therapy practice, we first need to examine how to go about critically reviewing theory represented in conceptual models. By applying a systematic method for our critical review of theory found in conceptual models we can be in a position to more thoroughly understand theoretical notions from conceptual models as they relate to practice.

Systematically Evaluating Theory Contained in Conceptual Models in Recreational Therapy

McEwen and Wills (2011) synthesized nine different methods of evaluation for nursing theories in order to construct their well-conceived Synthesized Method for Theory Evaluation. In their book titled *Theoretical Basis for Nursing*, these authors have successfully applied their systematic method of evaluation in the examination of a variety of nursing theories. This proven approach of McEwen and Wills (2011) is outlined in the following segment of this chapter.

McEwen and Wills' Synthesized Method for Theory Evaluation uses a series of evaluation questions under three categories: theory description, theory analysis, and theory evaluation. Their questions have largely been taken directly as they posed them, although in some instances, wording has been changed to reflect recreational therapy concepts. What follows is a brief review of the three major parts of the McEwen and Wills' method.

Theory Description

Evaluation questions formed by McEwen and Wills under theory description include What are the origins of the theory? What is the purpose of the theory? What is the scope of the theory? What are the major concepts? What are the major theoretical propositions? What are the major assumptions? Is the context for use described?

Theory Analysis

In order to analyze theory, the following questions are posed by McEwen and Wills: Are concepts theoretically and operationally defined? Are statements theoretically and operationally defined? Are linkages explicit? Is there a model/diagram? Does the model contribute to clarifying the theory? Are the concepts, statements, and assumptions used consistently? Are outcomes or consequences stated or predicted?

Theory Evaluation

From McEwen and Wills' evaluation model come the following theory evaluation questions: Is the theory congruent with current standards? Is the theory congruent with current interventions? Has the theory been tested empirically? Is it supported by research? Does it appear to be accurate/valid? Is there evidence that the theory has been used? Is the theory socially relevant? Is the theory relevant cross-culturally? Does the theory contribute to the discipline of recreational therapy? What are implications for recreational therapy related to implementation of the theory?

While the evaluation model will be applied to the theory of the Health Protection/ Health Promotion Model, it could be used to critically review theories represented in other recreational therapy conceptual models as well. Critiquing theory, of course, is a necessary process prerequisite to selecting any theory for research or practice.

Application of the Synthesized Method for Theory Evaluation

The following portion of this chapter offers an in depth illustration of the relationship of theory to practice. First a recreational therapy conceptual model, the Health Protection/ Health Protection Model (Austin, 1991, 1998, 2009), as reformulated (2011b), will be critically reviewed through the application of the systematic evaluation method just described. Understandings derived from the evaluation will hopefully provide a foundation for the demonstration which follows on how theory from the Health Protection/Health Promotion Conceptual Model influences practice during the application of the recreational therapy process.

Theory Description

The following offers a description of the Health Protection/Health Promotion Model following the format of McEwen and Wills (2011).

Background of the theorist. David R. Austin is the developer of the Health Protection/Health Promotion Model (Austin, 1991, 1998, 2009, 2011b). Austin was a professor of recreational therapy at Indiana University for many years. He earned his PhD in recreational therapy from the University of Illinois where he completed his cognate area in social psychology. Prior to his academic career he worked as a recreational therapist in mental health (Smith, 2002).

The origins of the Health Protection/Health Promotion Model. The historical context for his Health Protection/Health Promotion Model was Austin's view that the profession needed a conceptual model to describe and direct practice in health care. Austin (2002c) has noted that his Health Protection/Health Promotion Model extended the clinical approach championed by the National Association of Recreational Therapists (NART) in the 1950s. NART saw recreation to be a "tool" used as a means to health restoration. At the time the Health Protection/Health Promotion Model appeared the major formal conceptual model was the Leisure Ability Model that had leisure functioning as its mission. In contrast, Austin's model was an attempt to describe and direct recreational therapy practice that had the attainment of optimal health as its goal (Austin, 1991, 1991a, 2009, 2011b).

The purpose. The overall mission of the Health Protection/Health Promotion Model is to help people to enjoy the highest levels of health possible for them. Under this mission are two purposes. One is the purpose of health protection. This purpose has two parts. One is meeting threats to health by helping people to return to their steady state or regain their equilibrium following illness or disability. The second is assisting persons with chronic illnesses and long-term disabilities to cope with their conditions and to maintain their health to the highest level possible. The purpose of the health promotion part of the model is to help people to enjoy the highest or optimal levels of health and well-being that they can achieve. High-level wellness implies a level of optimal health in which the person enjoys physical, psychological, and environmental wellness. (Austin, 2011b)

Scope of the theory. The Health Protection/Health Promotion Model is an attempt to capture the full spectrum of practice within recreational therapy ranging, at one extreme, from health restoration for persons experiencing threats to health in unfavorable environments to, at the other end of the spectrum, high-level wellness experienced by those in optimal health within favorable environments. The name of the conceptual model attempts to reflect a full range of recreational therapy services running from protection from threats to health to health enhancement through health promotion.

Major concepts. The Health Protection/Health Promotion Model is illustrated in Figure 4.3. At the top are three interventions: prescriptive activities, recreation, and leisure. These fall along the illness-wellness continuum that ranges from poor to optimal health and from unfavorable to favorable environments. Clients may enter into recreational therapy at any point along the continuum that corresponds to their level of health within the environment that they exist. Thus any persons wishing to restore, maintain, or improve their level of health may become a candidate to receive recreational therapy services. The model indicates that clients choices enlarge and the control of the recreational therapist narrows as clients move along the continuum toward independent functioning and optimal health.

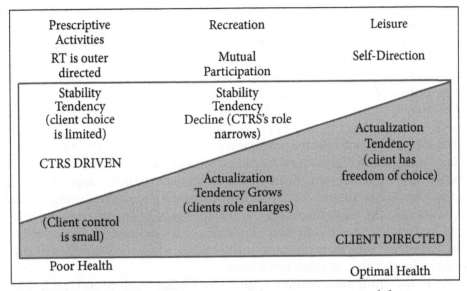

Figure 4.3. Health Protection/Health Promotion Model. TR continuum from Austin, D. R., & Crawford, M. E. *Therapeutic recreation: An introduction.* By permission of Allyn & Bacon, Needham Heights, MA 02194 ©1996.

The three types of *interventions* are found under the Health Protection/Health Promotion Model (i.e., prescriptive activities, recreation, and leisure) are used by recreational therapists to help people to meet problems that cause barriers to health (i.e., health protection) and then to assist them to achieve the highest levels of health possible for them (i.e., health promotion).

Prescriptive activities are employed under the direction of the recreational therapist to activate clients suffering demoralization arising from poor health. Prescriptive activities offer means to stir emotions such as pleasure and fun, thus motivating clients to regain a sense of power to change themselves or their environments. Once actively engaged in activity, clients begin to perceive of themselves as having the capacity for successful interaction with their environment, for making improvement, and for regaining a sense of control. As clients begin to become energized and gain confidence in themselves as a result of their successful participation, recreational therapists gradually decrease the degree of client dependency with the intent of entering into a full partnership with clients during the recreation portion of the continuum.

Recreation is the second type of intervention. The term *recreation* is used in this model to help people to "re-create" themselves or to restore or refresh their minds, bodies, and spirits. In recreation, clients are motivated by the fun and enjoyment of participation. At the stage that recreation activities are a part of the treatment or rehabilitation milieu, clients are exercising choice and control. Clients are taking responsibility for change and the role of the recreational therapist is that of being a partner with the client in goal setting and activity selection. The focus remains positive with recreational therapists providing social support and affirmative feedback. Because recreational therapists view all clients as having intact strengths (Austin, 1998), emphasis in concentrated on client strengths. Strengths include things such as inherent abilities, highly developed recreational skills, or a good sense of humor. By means of exercising their strengths during recreation, clients make gains that move them toward the achievement of their goals.

In recreation, clients are afforded opportunities to experience control over their environments within a supportive, nonthreatening atmosphere. Through participation in activities that allow mastery experiences and build a sense of accomplishment, clients learn they are able to be successful in their interactions with the world. They learn new skills, new ways of behaving, new means to approach interactions with others, new values and philosophies, and new ways to think about themselves. Their personal evaluations of their abilities, or feelings of self-efficacy are enhanced.

In the initial formulation of the Health Promotion/Health Protection Model recreation was seen solely as a means to regaining or restoring health (Austin, 1991). In the reformulated version (Austin, 2011b) however the model was expanded to using recreation to help clients to maintain health to the highest level possible for them, or at least help them to cope with their health concerns. This reformation permits the model to be better applied to clients with chronic illnesses or disabilities. For these clients, regaining health by curing the condition may not be realistic. But these clients may be able to engage in recreation in order to reduce or prevent further deterioration in their conditions or to improve the quality of their lives by coping adaptively with their illnesses or disabilities when their illnesses or disabilities produce discomfort, stress, or other symptoms.

Leisure is the third intervention under the Health Protection/Health Promotion Model. Leisure is seen as a means to health promotion within the Health Protection/Health Promotion Model. Leisure provides clients with self-determined experiences that are health enhancing and move clients toward optimal health and wellness. The role of the recreational therapist is a supportive one in helping clients to engage in a leisure pursuit and engendering positive attitudes in clients so they develop an "I can" approach to the chosen leisure activity. Once clients are skilled and confident in their abilities, it may be that the help of the recreational therapist will no longer be required.

The three types of interventions employed with clients are delivered according to the individual client's needs using an *illness-wellness continuum* as a guide. At the left end of the continuum is poor health in an unfavorable environment (This end of the continuum is exemplified by death as the most extreme point; see Figure 4.1). On the right end of the continuum is optimal health in a favorable environment (which represents high-level wellness). Clients may enter into recreational therapy at any point along the illness-wellness continuum. Those who are most ill will be likely candidates to engage in prescriptive activities. Farther along the continuum clients are apt to enter into recreation experiences jointly selected by them and their recreational therapist. Still farther along, toward the wellness end of the continuum, clients seeking health promotion enter into leisure pursuits with the intent of seeking a more optimal level of health (Austin, 2011b).

Major theoretical propositions. Austin (2011a) has termed Carl Rogers the "grandfather of recreational therapy" due to the strong influence his *humanistic perspective* has had on recreational therapy. Rogers' humanistic theory emphasized a holistic approach to clients he viewed to be social beings who possess a strong desire to belong and to be valued by others. Rogers' therapeutic approach was a positive, accepting, and nonjudgmental one which reflected an empathetic and genuine relationship with clients in a safe, caring environment. The humanistic perspective of Rogers also sees people as possessing an overriding drive for health and wellness which is a central concept in the Health Protection/Health Promotion Model (Austin, 2011b).

The drive for health is reflected in two tendencies termed the *stabilizing tendency* and the *actualizing tendency* (Pender, Murdaugh, & Parsons, 2002). The stabilizing tendency is that motive that pushes us toward maintaining our "steady state." It is the part that moves us to attempt to minimize stress and to protect us from biophysical and psychosocial harm. It is what stands behind the Health Protection part of the model. The actualization tendency is the need we all have for growth and development. Or the need we have to fulfill our potentials. This tendency provides the motivational drive that underlies the Health Promotion portion of the model.

The term *health* has been employed a number of times in describing the Health Protection/Health Promotion Model. Yet, it has not been defined. The views of health that follow represent health according to the Health Protection/Health Promotion Conceptual Model. Jones (2000) wrote:

Health is a positive balanced, state of being characterized by the best available physical, psychological, emotional, social, spiritual, and intellectual levels of functioning at a given time, the absence of disease or the optimal management of chronic disease, and the control of both internal and external risk factors for both disease and negative health conditions. (p. 15)

Pender, Murdaugh, and Parsons (2002) wrote:

Health is defined as the actualization of inherent and acquired human potential through goal-directed behavior, competent self-care, and satisfying relationships with others, while adjustments are made as needed to maintain structural integrity and harmony with relevant environments. (p. 22)

Thus, health is a complex concept that encompasses coping adaptively, as well as growing and becoming. Healthy persons are able to cope with life's stressors, as well as develop themselves to the fullest. The healthy individual is free from barriers to actualization so he or she may actively pursue personal growth and development. Recreational therapists contribute to health by assisting clients to fulfill their needs for stability and actualization.

Positive psychology has been added as a theoretical element underlying the Health Protection/Health Promotion Model in the reformulated version of the model. Because positive psychology can be perceived to be an extension of humanistic psychology, it fits well in joining humanistic psychology to provide theoretical underpinnings for the Health Protection/Health Promotion Model (Austin, 2011b).

Positive psychology is discussed in depth in Chapter 2, so it will be described only briefly in this evaluation of the Health Protection/Health Promotion Model. Austin (2011b) has provided this introduction to positive psychology:

The focus of positive psychology is on the positive side of human beings rather than the negative. Instead of concentrating on pathology, positive psychology emphasizes human strengths and optimal functioning (Austin, 2009). As Biswas-Diener and Dean (2007) have expressed, "(positive psychology) focuses on what is going right, rather than what is going wrong with people. " Similarly to capture the approach of positive psychology, Duckworth et al. (2005) have coined the terms "build-what's-strong" and "fix-what's-wrong" to contrast positive psychology (i.e., building on strengths) with the approach often found in traditional medical practice (i.e., "fixing" the person). (p. 24)

The three major components of positive psychology are positive emotions, positive traits and abilities, and positive environments are certainly congruent with recreational therapy practice under the Health Protection/Health Promotion Model. Recreational therapists help clients to enjoy positive emotions. They assist clients to take advantage of and develop their strengths (i.e., traits and abilities). And they attempt to provide a positive environment for recreational therapy activities, as well as to assist clients to develop a positive environment in which to live.

Specific theoretical propositions that may be drawn from the Health Protection/Health Promotion Model include the following:

- Persons are motivated toward health through the stability and actualization tendencies.
- Recreational therapy involves planned interventions that are purposeful and goal-directed.
- Recreational therapy can assist a wide spectrum of clients along the illness-wellness continuum, including those with chronic illnesses and disabilities, as well as those with acute conditions.
- People have social needs that include belonging and feeling valued.
- Social support often plays a prominent role in the maintenance and improvement of health.
- Positive emotions, such as pleasure and fun, are means to the achievement of optimistic views that open people up to new experiences.
- Prescriptive activities have the potential to energize clients and motivate them to take action to restore their health.
- Recreation experiences allow clients choice and control, as well as help clients to maintain or restore their health.
- Leisure experiences, which contain the elements of intrinsic motivation, self-determination, and mastery, produce feelings of self-efficacy, empowerment, and enjoyment that, in turn, move participants toward the achievement of optimal health.
- Successful participation in prescriptive activities, recreation, and leisure enhances self-efficacy.
- A strength-based approach provides clients means to both health protection and health promotion.
- A strength-based approach helps clients to identify their strengths and to use their strengths to live empowered lives.
- Strength-based practice pays attention to identifying strengths and what works, rather than just using deficits to guide interventions.
- A holistic approach to health goes beyond concern for the illness, disease, or disability and extends its concern to biological, psychological, and social aspects of health.
- The client/therapist relationship plays a key role in bringing about changes in health status.
- Being genuine, nonjudgmental, and empathetic toward clients promotes therapeutic relationships and create a safe, caring environment.
- Warm, positive, accepting, and hopeful atmospheres in programs promote client change.
- Persons strive to maintain control over their lives and to function independently, so recreational therapists are not manipulative or controlling.
- Different roles are assumed by recreational therapists who, depending on the needs of clients, may serve as guides providing clients with direction (during prescribed

activities), partners in mutual relationships with clients (in recreation), or as facilitators of leisure experiences (during leisure).

- Clients who are experiencing very poor health are the most dependent on recreational therapists but recreational therapists encourage client choice and control for these and all clients.
- Clients' preferences and perceptions are important in all phases of the recreational therapy process.

Major assumptions. It was previously indicated that major assumptions that underlie theories come from the philosophical foundations upon which it rests. Assumptions take the form of values and beliefs. As previously indicated in this chapter, values represent strongly held principles to which we subscribe. Several of the values previously employed to illustrate examples of values do in fact serve as values that underlie theory represented by the Health Protection/Health Promotion Model. While Austin (2009) did not directly include a listing of values in his description of this model, in his 2009 book he did present values related to recreational therapy. These include (a) valuing the therapeutic role in helping clients to reach optimal levels of health; (b) desiring that clients maintain as much autonomy and control as possible over their lives; (c) valuing the importance of the therapist-client relationship in fostering change; (d) valuing a strength-based approach to health enhancement; (e) valuing fun, enjoyment, and pleasure as important aspects in therapy; (f) viewing clients and what is happening to them, rather than the activity, as the focus of practice; and (g) valuing recreational therapy as a purposeful and goal-directed enterprise.

The second set of assumptions underlying the theory represented in the Health Protection/Health Promotion Model involves beliefs held about human nature. As with values, Austin (2009) has discussed beliefs underlying recreational therapy practice but did not include them in the section of his book where he describes his Health Promotion/Health Protection Model. These philosophical beliefs include believing that (a) humans are social animals who have a need to interact with other human beings; (b) people's social needs include feeling they belong and feeling valued; (c) relationships involve the understanding that mutual rights and responsibilities are both given and received; (d) people are motivated to take part in activities they find to be fun and enjoyable; (e)people possess a drive toward the achievement of self-actualization; (f) the stability and actualization tendencies move people toward better health; (g) individuals and society as a whole can be understood; (h) each individual possesses strengths in the form of virtues, abilities, and resources; and (i) each individual possesses the capacity for change.

Context for use. An individual does not have to be labeled ill or disabled to benefit from recreational therapy. Clients are self-defined in that a candidate for recreational therapy can be anyone wishing to maintain or improve his or her health. The recreational therapy process composed of assessment, planning, implementation, and evaluation is employed with all clients in order to provide them with the therapeutic benefits to be found in recreational therapy.

Theory Analysis

The following provides an analysis of the Health Protection/Health Promotion Model following the format of McEwen and Wills (2011).

Theoretical and operational definitions of concepts. Theoretical definitions of concepts appear within the description analysis of the Health Protection/Health Promotion Model. Included are major concepts such as health protection, health promotion, prescriptive activities, recreation, leisure, illness-wellness continuum, stability tendency, actualization tendency, and health. Operational definitions are not provided for the concepts.

Statements theoretically and operationally defined. Within the description analysis, statements of theoretical propositions are explicably stated but not defined. Major concepts such as the humanistic approach, views of positive psychology, stability and actualization tendencies, and health are defined. However, no operational definitions are provided.

Linkages explicit. Linkages between concepts are described and are explicated in the model. Included are linkages between health status, interventions, client choice, and the stability and actualization tendencies.

Model/diagram. A diagram is a part of the presentation of the Health Protection/ Health Promotion Model. This diagram clearly portrays and clarifies the linkages between the parts of the model.

Consistent use of concepts, statements, and assumptions. Concepts, statements, and assumptions are consistently applied within the presentation of the Health Protection/ Health Protection Model.

Predicted outcomes and consequences. Outcomes and consequences from the Health Protection/Health Promotion Model are stated. Major outcomes are maintaining or improving health and functioning as independently as possible.

Theory Evaluation

What follows is an evaluation of the Health Protection/Health Promotion Model following the format of McEwen and Wills (2011).

Congruence with recreational therapy standards. Theoretical perspectives represented by the Health Protection/Health Promotion Model subscribe to all standards of practice the American Therapeutic Recreation Association (2000).

Congruence with current recreational therapy intervention. The use of prescriptive activities, recreation activities, and leisure experiences portrayed by the Health Protection/ Health Promotion Model appears to be in accord with current approaches to recreational therapy intervention represented in the literature. For instance, they are in accord with both clinical and personal growth approaches to programming that appeared in Kunstler and Stavola Daly's (2010) book on leadership and programming. The emphasis on the achievement of fun, enjoyment, and pleasure through recreation and leisure participation has long been a stable of recreational therapy and has been recently reflected in the literature of the profession (e.g., Austin, 2011). The continuum of services to match clients' needs, the strength-based approach, the increasing of client self-determination, and the use of progressively decreasing therapist control within interventions are elements reflected in the Health Protection/Health Promotion Model that are commonly found in other recreational therapy conceptual models that have appeared in the literature of the profession (Bullock, Mahon, & Killingsworth, 2010).

Evidence of empirical testing/research support/validity. The theory reflected by the Health Protection/Health Promotion Model was derived from a review of the literature that included numerous research studies. Certainly the writings of Dunn (1961) and Ardell (1977), two champions of high-level wellness, highly influenced the theory reflected in the model. The structure for the spectrum of interventions along the illness-wellness continuum was modeled after continua presented by early authors of recreational therapy literature (Ball, 1970; Frye & Peters, 1972). Influential in the formulation of prescriptive activities was work on client demoralization and hope by psychologists Frank and Frank (1991) and recreational therapy scholars Shank and Kinney (1987). The writings of Pender (1982) and Pender, Murdaugh, and Parsons (2002) played a significant role in the conceptualization of parts of the model related to client motivation and health. Research by Deci and Ryan (1985) on self-determination, by Bandura (1986, 1997) on self-efficacy, and by Seligman (1980) on helplessness had major impacts on the theory of the Health Protection/Health Promotion Model. No direct testing of theory drawn from the Health Protection/Health Protection Model has been found in the literature of recreational therapy.

Use by educators, researchers, or administrators. The Health Promotion/Health Protection Model has appeared in any number of textbooks (e.g., Austin, 2009; Austin & Crawford, 2001; Bullock, Mahon, & Killingsworth, 2010; Kunstler & Stavola Daly, 2010; Sylvester, Ellis, & Voelkl, 2001), so it is likely that theory from the model is being taught by educators to students studying recreational therapy. Application of theory from the Health Protection/Health Promotion by researchers and administrators has not been apparent in the recreational therapy literature.

Social relevance. Theory from the Health Protection/Health Promotion Model is relevant to individuals no matter their health status, age, or socioeconomic status.

Cross-cultural relevance. The theory is potentially relevant across cultures, but with the goal of independent functioning being a featured concept of the model, it may not be relevant to cultures that stress cooperation, rather than independence.

Contribution to recreational therapy. Theory from the Health Protection/Health Promotion Model has perhaps contributed to recreational therapy through three major means. First, it offered an alternative health-orientated approach to the Leisure Ability Model. Second, it helped move concern for health promotion into the forefront of discussions on the benefits of recreational therapists. Third, it served as a forerunner for other health related recreational therapy conceptual models that would follow.

Implications for recreational therapy related to the implementation of the theory. Theory from the Health Protection/Health Promotion Model is useful to recreational therapists practicing in an array of settings. It would seem that a case could be made that the successful application of any theory in actual practice is perhaps the best test available to confirm its validity. The next segment of this chapter is directed at an examination of how theory from the Health Protection/Health Promotion Model influences practice during each stage or phase of the recreational therapy process.

Ramifications of Theory from the Health Protection/ Health Promotion Model for Practice

As previously indicated, conceptual models become operational through the recreational therapy process because each of the four steps in the recreational therapy process is governed by the theory that is a part of each conceptual model. In the following segment of this chapter the four steps in the recreational therapy process provide the focus for implications of theoretical perspectives from the Health Protection/Health Promotion Model.

Assessment

In following theoretical perspectives from the Health Protection/Health Promotion Model, health concerns become the focus of assessment. Sensory or motor impairments, cognitive deficits, limitations in activities of daily living, and any precautions (e.g., heart problems) are noted. Following a holistic approach to assessment, clients' general perceptions about their present health status are appraised, as are clients' expectations they may have for their care, treatment, rehabilitation, or wellness program.

Both a needs list and a strengths list should arise as a result of the assessment phase. The needs list will guide the development of goals and the strengths list will assist in determining the type of activities and approaches used as interventions.

The development of the client/recreational therapist relationship begins during the assessment phase. It is important that the client and recreational therapist establish a good relationship as they will work closely together to recognize and define facts related to the client's needs so that the client's initially expressed "felt needs" are clarified. Problems are explored in order to reveal needs (e.g., need to belong, for self-esteem enhancement) as a means of establishing items for a needs list.

Clients typically require the recreational therapist's help in identifying their strengths because their health concerns or a lack of self-awareness may interfere with the ability of a client to fully appreciate the strengths they possess. Clients often have untapped strengths that the recreational therapist can help them to identify. Strengths include a multitude of characteristics (e.g., persistence, determination, creativity, interpersonal skills, prior life successes), as well as social support (e.g., support networks, environmental resources) and recreational abilities (e.g., skills possessed in recreational activities). Clients' recreational interests need to be explored during assessment as interests are closely tied to client abilities. Clients' leisure values are typically explored, along with their attitudes toward participation in recreational therapy programs.

Both objective assessment data from sources other than the client (e.g., the social history, information from staff team meetings, systematic observations, progress notes) and subjective assessment data obtained directly from the client (e.g., perceptions about what he or she is experiencing or attitudes, desires, and feelings) are used by recreational therapists. Such a holistic assessment assists the recreational therapist to arrive at a statement of the problem (i.e., recreational therapy "diagnosis"), as well as to determine where the client may be on the illness-wellness continuum and, therefore, what activities and approaches may be most helpful to the client. Please see Table 4.7 for a summary of the areas for holistic assessment under the Health Protection/Health Promotion Model.

Table 4.7

Areas for Holistic Assessment Under the Health Protection/Health Promotion Model

- Client's general perceptions about his or her present health status.
- Sensory or motor impairments, cognitive deficits, limitations in activities of daily living, and any precautions (e.g., heart problems).
- Leisure values, interests, and pursuits are explored, along with client attitudes toward participation in recreational therapy programs.
- The developmental level of the client is appraised to determine developmental tasks or issues with which the client may be dealing.
- Problems are explored to identify needs (e.g., need to belong, for self-esteem enhancement) in order to establish a needs list.
- Strengths (e.g., abilities, virtues, support from family and friends) are identified in order to build a strengths list.
- Client expectations and goals are identified.
- The client's environment is assessed to determine if changes in the environment are needed or if there is potential support for the client within the environment.

Planning

Following the identification of the client's needs and strengths, these are examined to decide priorities and client goals. Based on this information a plan of action is formulated. As a result the client's customized recreational therapy program is formed.

In the traditions of the humanistic perspective of the Health Protection/Health Promotion Model, Maslow's Needs Hierarchy is typically employed in setting priorities. It may be recalled that Maslow's Hierarchy ranges from basic physiological and safety needs at the bottom to social needs (belonging and love) and self-esteem needs (status, self-respect), to self-actualization at the top. Of course, the determination of where the client falls on the illness-wellness continuum weighs heavily on where the focus is placed for each individual client.

Client goals are derived from the needs list developed during assessment. Typical of goals in recreational therapy planning under the Health Protection/Health Promotion Model are managing stress and reducing anxiety, reducing depression, reducing feelings of isolation, developing social skills (including leisure skills), enhancing self-esteem, building self-efficacy, establishing a sense of control, developing social support, learning to experience fun and enjoyment, decreasing confusion, improving memory, improving mobility, and increasing functional skills (e.g., ADL skills). Examples of outcomes specifically for clients with chronic conditions or disabilities to assist them in coping adaptively include managing stress, reducing pain or discomfort, increasing feelings of control, building social networks, making accommodations to continue past leisure interests, and finding new interests.

Following the strength-based approach found in the Health Protection/Health Promotion Model, client strengths form the basis for the selection of strategies or actions to meet identified goals. Rather than focusing on client deficits, client strengths are built upon in the selection of activities and the approaches to be employed by the recreational therapist with each client. To the greatest extent possible, clients are engaged in selecting the activities in which they will take part as the Health Protection/Health Promotion Model encourages client choice and control and acknowledges the self-responsibility clients have in their care, treatment, rehabilitation, or wellness programs.

Implementation

The implementation phase of the recreational therapy process involves the actual provision of the client's program. During implementation the client's plan is put into action. The intent of this phase is a successful outcome leading to termination of the relationship between the client and recreational therapist.

During the implementation phase, recreational therapists nurture the human drive for the achievement of health and wellness by providing their clients with support and encouragement in their commitment to carry out the plan of action. A strong therapeutic relationship between the client and the recreational therapist is a critical element to the success of the plan. The therapeutic relationship has been well characterized by Arnold and Boggs (1989) who wrote that:

> ...it is the goal-directed, helping focus that characterizes a relationship as "therapeutic." In this type of relationship, two separately existing individuals come together for the sole purpose of helping one of them, the client, achieve maximum levels of self-care functioning and well-being. (p. 130)

The relationship between the recreational therapist and client lies at the heart of recreational therapy interventions due to the assistance provided to the client by the recreational therapist and the understandings the therapist has of "client needs, feelings, and motivations" (Austin, 2002e, p. 116). Lyons, Sullivan, Ritvo, and Coyne (1995) have suggested that a "special kind of bond" (p.128) exists between the client and therapist because both have shared knowledge of the client's experiences with his or her health concerns and this emotional connection produces an atmosphere of trust and caring.

To help foster the therapeutic relationship, recreational therapists are genuine, nonjudgmental, and empathetic toward their clients. Recreational therapists strive to create an emotional environment that is warm, positive, accepting, and hopeful while at the same time, assisting clients to assume greater levels of independence. Those clients who are in the poorest health are most dependent on the recreational therapist. As Shank and Kinney (1987) have indicated, when clients are not ready to assume control the premature assumption of control can be counterproductive, bringing on stress and anxiety. Clients at this time are engaged in prescriptive activities by the recreational therapist in order to help them to become energized and motivated. Farther along the illness-wellness continuum, as clients begin to maintain or restore their health, they become less dependent on the recreational therapist as they take on increasing responsibility for their own health, exercising choice and control while enjoying recreation experiences. At this time there exists a working partnership between clients and the recreational therapist. Still farther along the illness-wellness continuum, clients assume even more responsibility for their own health, fostering health enhancement through their participation in leisure pursuits. Eventually, it is hoped, that clients will take complete responsibility for themselves and no longer require the services of a recreational therapist.

Evaluation

Evaluation is the final step or phase of the recreational therapy process. It is concerned with assessing client progress toward goals established in the client's plan and evaluating the effectiveness of the plan.

Under the Health Protection/Health Promotion Model, client goals will be health related. Examination of progress toward the achievement of goals such as developing social skills, enhancing self-esteem, building of feelings of self-efficacy, improving memory, improving mobility, and increasing functional skills. No matter what evaluation methods are used, the Health Protection/Health Promotion Model calls for clients to be directly involved by sharing their perceptions of how they have progressed from the beginning of their program to the end. Clients' views should also be sought to assist staff in evaluating the plan of action designed to help the client to reach their goals.

Theory Informs Practice

Hopefully the presentation of the manner in which each of the four phases in the recreational therapy process is influenced by theory from the Health Protection/Health Promotion Model provides convincing evidence of how theory informs clinical practice. Of course, in actual clinical practice recreational therapists may combine theory, the best current evidence on which to base practice, and personal clinical knowledge with critical thinking in order to make informed decisions and, in doing so, produce the highest level of practice possible.

Conclusion Regarding Theory-Based Practice

In conclusion, there seem to be two primary reasons for recreational therapists to engage in theory-based practice. The first is that theory is required to describe the purpose and scope of recreational therapy practice. Therefore, the recreational therapists who are theory-based in their practice will be able to describe and interpret what they do in their work to others. This is a critical skill needed to inform colleagues, administrators, policy makers, and not the least, clients, as to what recreational therapy is.

The second, and perhaps the foremost reason for recreational therapists to engage in theory-based practice, is that without theory, practice "becomes rote performance of activities base on tradition, common sense, and following orders" (McEwen & Wills, 2011, p. 377). Austin (2011a) similarly stated, "It is critical that recreational therapists are reflective practitioners who examine what they are doing and why they are doing it" (p. 13). In short, theory provides recreational therapists a basis for what they do in their clinical practice. Of course, it is the recreational therapy process that provides the framework or vehicle for the application of recreational therapy theory in practice.

Conceptual Models Developed for Recreational Therapy

A number of conceptual models have been developed to offer theoretical bases for the practice of recreational therapy (or therapeutic recreation, the expression commonly used by authors of the conceptual models reviewed). Because the models serve as underpinnings for the practice of recreational therapy, they are sometimes referred to as **practice models** as well as conceptual models.

According to research by Witman and Ligon (2011c), the four models most often used by Certified Therapeutic Recreation Specialists (CTRSs) are the TR Service Delivery Model, the Leisure and Well-Being Model, the Leisure Ability Model, and the Health Protection/ Health Promotion Model. In the sections which follow the contents of these models, as well as others, are briefly outlined.

Leisure Ability Model

Already briefly discussed in this chapter has been the Leisure Ability Model that was initially introduced in 1978 by Gunn and Peterson. This was the first and is perhaps the best-known conceptual model. The Leisure Ability Model has been revised through the years with the most recent revision appearing in Stumbo and Peterson's book in 2009. The model holds that recreation and leisure are necessary experiences that all should enjoy, including those with limitations. The purpose of services delivered under the model to help the client develop "a satisfying leisure lifestyle, the independent functioning of the client in leisure experiences and activities of his or her choice" (p. 29).

The model contains three components: functional intervention, leisure education, and recreation participation. These components exist along a continuum running from client-orientated therapy a one end to special recreation programs at the other. The functional intervention component is directed primarily toward therapy or rehabilitation to assist clients to gain the basic functional abilities necessary for leisure involvement. The leisure education component deals with the development of activity skills and social interaction skills, as well as issues for leisure counseling to assist clients gain leisure awareness and information on leisure resources. Recreation participation concerns the provision of recreation programs for individuals with disabilities or illnesses.

Health Protection/Health Promotion Model

The Health Protection/Health Promotion was reformulated in 2011 by Austin (2011b) in order to include theoretical perspectives from positive psychology and to fully encompass the entire spectrum of clients, including those with chronic illnesses and disabilities. The overall mission of the model is to help people to enjoy the highest levels of health possible for them. Under this mission are two purposes. Health protection is the first. This purpose has two parts. One is meeting threats to health by helping people to return to their steady state or regain their equilibrium following illness or disability. The second is assisting persons with chronic illnesses and long-term disabilities to adaptively cope with their conditions and to maintain their health to the highest level possible. The purpose of the health promotion part of the model is to help people to enjoy the highest or optimal levels of health and well-being that they can achieve. High-level wellness implies a level of optimal health in which the person enjoys physical, psychological, and environmental wellness. Thus, recreational therapists assist clients to maintain, restore, and promote health, as well as help clients to cope adaptively with chronic conditions and disabilities.

The Health Protection/Health Promotion Model (see Figure 4.3) has three major components of prescriptive activities, recreation, and leisure that fall along an illness-wellness continuum that ranges from poor health to optimal health. Prescriptive activities are employed when clients experience poor health (often in a poor environment). Activities prescribed by the recreational therapist to activate and motivate clients. Recreation (or "re-creation) activities are mutually selected by clients and their recreational therapists in order to maintain or restore the clients' health. Leisure involves self-determination in the selection of growth producing activities on the part of clients who are seeking to optimize their levels of health or to enjoy high levels of wellness. A complete analysis of the Health Protection/Health Promotion Model appears earlier in this chapter.

Therapeutic Recreation Service Delivery and Therapeutic Recreation Outcome Models

The Therapeutic Recreation Service Delivery and Therapeutic Recreation Outcome Models, developed by Glen Van Andel, first appeared in Carter, Van Andel, and Robb's book in 1995. The purposes of the two models are to assist clients to attain their optimal levels of health, well-being, and quality of life.

The Therapeutic Recreation Service Delivery Model describes the scope of services that range along a continuum that begins with diagnosis/needs assessment and is followed by treatment/rehabilitation, education, and, finally, prevention/health promotion. During the first phase of diagnosis/needs assessment, client abilities, strengths, and limitations are assessed. The treatment/rehabilitation phase involves the application of interventions to ameliorate the effects of disease or disability. In the education phase, interventions are provided in order to build client knowledge and skills leading to enhanced health and well-being. The final phase of prevention/health promotion emphasizes the promotion and reinforcement of healthy lifestyles that will lead to healthy living habits after discharge.

The Therapeutic Recreation Outcome Model involves the relationship between the client's quality of life and his or her health status and functional abilities. The client's quality of life is enhanced as symptoms decrease, health improves, and functional capacity increases. The model recognizes six domains which constitute quality of life. The domains are cognitive, psychological, physical, spiritual, social, and leisure. Growth in functional abilities related to any one or all of these areas may bring about improvement in a client's quality of life (Carter, Van Andel, & Robb, 1995, 2003, 2011).

Self-Determination and Enjoyment Enhancement Model

The Self-Determination and Enjoyment Enhancement Model was developed by Dattilo, Kleiber, and Williams (1998). The purpose of this model is to bring about increases in self-determination and enjoyment in order that clients with disabilities may improve their functional capabilities. But the model purports to do more than bring about functional improvements. The authors of the model have written:

> …we hope to encourage not only functional improvements, but also the promotion of participants' self-determination associated with leisure participation, creation of leisure environments conducive to the development of intrinsic motivation, cultivation of perceptions of manageable leisure challenges, and fostering of investment in attention so that optimal experience and enjoyment will be abundant in their lives. (p. 268)

The basic premise behind the model is that people with disabilities often do not possess opportunities to develop and use self-determination, that they have a need to feel in control of their lives, and that self-determination is facilitated by enjoyment. Components of this psychologically grounded model include perception of intrinsic motivation, manageable challenges, self-determination, investment of attention, enjoyment, and functional improvement. The facilitation of self-determination, intrinsic motivation, perception of manageable challenge, and investment of attention in time result in enjoyment and functional improvement, according to the model. Self-determination is a key in the process leading to functional improvements as clients are encouraged to make decisions and choices, indicate their preferences, and set goals for themselves. Intrinsic motivation is tied to self-determination since it may be assumed that freely made choices about activities carry with them interest in the chosen activities. Intrinsic motivation, according to Kleiber, Walker, and Mannell (2011), "involves interest, enjoyment, and engagement in activities for their own sake" (p. 235). Interest then leads to involvement. Intrinsic motivation is also energizing as it leads people to attempt to meet realistic challenges and to gain success within activities they choose. Ultimately, if properly facilitated by recreational therapists, these experiences can result in enjoyment and functional improvements. Dattilo and his colleagues have explained:

> To increase the chance that participants consider the challenge of an activity to be manageable, they can be encouraged to assess their skills, make adaptations,

make realistic appraisals of challenges, and develop activity skills. Practitioners can recognize and avoid sending messages that undermine self-determination and creating conditions that are distracting. Teaching participants to make accurate attributions relative to their success and failures encourages investment of attention and enjoyment. In turn, generating enjoyment can help facilitate functional improvements. (p. 262)

Optimizing Lifelong Health Through Therapeutic Recreation Model

Wilhite, Keller, and Caldwell (1999) authored the Optimizing Lifelong Health Through Therapeutic Recreation (OLH-TR) Model. The purpose of the OLH-TR Model is the enhancement of health and well-being and the minimization of the effects of illness and disability across the lifespan. The end that is sought is to bring about optimal health through individuals engaging in a healthy leisure lifestyle involving well-chosen leisure activities that meet client needs.

The major components of the OLH-TR Model are four processes: selecting, optimizing, compensating, and evaluating. Selecting involves the client and recreational therapist selecting activities to address the client's needs. Optimizing refers to the client engaging in the selected activities. Compensating is using alternative activities to compensate for impaired abilities. Evaluating is assessing how effective the activities were in meeting the client's needs.

Leisure and Well-Being Model

Carruthers and Hood (2007) authored the Leisure and Well-Being Model (LBM), which is largely based on positive psychology. As such, it focuses on client strengths, rather than pathology. The authors have stated the purpose of their model is to produce "a state of successful, satisfying, and productive engagement with one's life and the realization of one's full physical, cognitive, and social-emotional potential" (p. 301).

The leisure experience and clients' reactions to disability are central features of the LBM. The model relies on the practitioner having understandings of the empirical and theoretical knowledge related to the leisure experience. The model's authors state that this knowledge provides "TR with the language and techniques required to effectively work with people who are experiencing difficulties in adjusting and adapting to disability and other limiting conditions" (p. 201).

Two dimensions of well-being provide the focus of services under the LBM. These are the use of positive emotions and the development of client strengths and resources. The emphasis on the development of clients' strengths and resources is reflected in the authors' statement that their model "explicitly identified a focus on both developing individual capacities, as well as developing contexts and resources that are outside of the individual, thus taking a more ecological perspective on the role of TR in the lives of clients" (p. 281) The authors have indicated that those with higher levels of well-being regularly experience positive emotions and possess strengths and resources that they know how to use in their lives.

The Flourishing Through Leisure: An Ecological Extension of the Leisure and Well-Being Model

Anderson and Heyne's (2012) Flourishing Through Leisure Model extends the Leisure and Well-Being Model (LWM). Like the LWM, the extended model has concern for helping individual clients with leisure enhancement and strengths development that will assist them in achieving their goals. But the model of Anderson and Heyne goes beyond the development of clients as individuals to include changing the environment in ways that will support clients in their quests to reach the ends to which they aspire. Thus the focus of the model is on the individual within his or her environment.

The purpose of the Flourishing Through Leisure Model, as stated by the authors, is helping clients to achieve "a flourishing life and well-being across several domains in enriched environments" (p. 148). The domains identified are (a) psychological and emotional, (b) cognitive, (c) social, (d) physical, and (e) spiritual. The environment is seen as multidimensional, consisting of not only other people and the physical environment but the cultures, policies, and norms found within society.

The model is grounded in the social model of disability that the authors have described as being "embedded in an ecological approach." They went on to explain that "the ecological approach is based on the concept of an interdependent system, where human beings are interreliant with each other and with their environments" (p. 132). Under the social model disability is seen as a social construct. The social model, in contrast to the medical model, views the social environment (i.e., society's attitudes and practices) as being disabling for persons with impairments. Disability is seen to be a social phenomenon that disadvantages people with disabilities. The disadvantages arise from society's lack of responding to the needs of people with disabilities, rather than the impairments possessed by individuals with disabilities. In short, people with disabilities are disabled by society, not their impairments. Thus disability is caused by the social environment, an environment that can be changed through actions that allow persons with impairments to enter fully into society.

Commonalities Among Conceptual Models for Recreational Therapy

As a footnote to this segment on conceptual models for recreational therapy, it is interesting to note that there seem to be a number of common themes that run through the majority of conceptual models that have been proposed. These include the following:

- Helping clients to both alleviate problems and to achieve optimal levels of health and well-being.
- Assisting clients to toward the achievement of independent functioning.
- Dealing with the entire spectrum of the illness-wellness continuum.
- Viewing self-determination and positive emotions as being integral to client success in recreational therapy.
- Prizing the positive consequences to be gained through meaningful recreation and leisure experiences.
- Following a systematic step-by-step approach with clients.
- Taking a strengths-based perspective.
- Acknowledging the importance of the client/recreational therapist relationship in the achievement of positive outcomes.
- Fostering positive, supportive environments that offer clients optimal opportunities for success.
- Assisting clients to develop healthy living habits that they will take with them once they are no longer in recreational therapy.
- Having a theory base (primarily resting on humanistic psychology and positive psychology).

Evidence-Based Practice

No matter which conceptual model is followed to direct clinical practice, it is important that practitioners engage in evidence–based practice (EBP). Yoder-Wise (2011) has defined EBP as follows:

Evidence-based practice (EBP) is a systematic approach to clinical decision making to provide the most consistent and best possible care to patients. EBP integrates current research findings that define best practices, clinical expertise, and patient values to optimize patient outcomes as well as their quality of life. (p. 211)

Similarly, Melnyk and her colleagues (2010) have given this description of evidence-based practice: "Evidence-based practice is a problem-solving approach to the delivery of health care that integrates the best evidence from well-designed studies (i.e., external evidence) with a clinician's expertise and a patient's preferences and values." (p. 302)

A third definition of evidence-based practice, by Johns Hopkins nurses (Dearholt & Dang, 2012), nicely summarizes the prior two definitions of EBP. They wrote, "EBP Is a problem-solving approach to clinical decision-making within a health care organization. It integrates the best available scientific evidence with the best available experiential (patient and practitioner) evidence" (p. 4). Thus EBP is a procedure by which practitioners base their clinical practice on the best available research evidence, while considering their own clinical expertise and client preferences.

Recreational therapy educators Lee and McCormick (2002) have remarked that the use of EBP does not at all negate therapists considering their clinical experience. They have written, "Instead, it (EBP) implies that good therapists use both individual clinical expertise and the best available research evidence, and neither alone is enough." They go on to conclude, "In short, it is not that therapists' experience and intuition are unimportant sources of information for clinical practice, but that experience should not overrule the evidence presented in research" (p. 168). The preferences of clients also need to be considered when following evidence-based practice, as well as determining if required resources are available (Amarsi, 2002; Berman, Snyder, Kozier, & Erb, 2008).

McHugh and Barlow (2010) indicated the broad support that has arisen for evidence-based practice treatments (EBPT), writing, "Motivated by the continued lack of widespread availability of EBPTs, both public and private funding mechanisms for dissemination and implementation efforts have emerged. Government agencies with a marked sense of urgency have created financial and regulatory incentives and mandates promoting a shift to evidence-based practice and driving these efforts with large financial commitments totaling several billion dollars" (p. 72).The National Institutes of Health (NIH) has created clinical and translational science awards in a high priority effort to improve the process by which basic science laboratory discovers are transformed into new interventions and products—a process called *translational research* (Knafl & Grey, 2008). This initiative should further emphasize the importance of EBP in health care.

The primary gain to be made by adopting evidence-based practice is to improve clinical practice and ensure that clinical decisions are based upon the best available information. It must be acknowledged that occasionally research evidence may not exist to tell the practitioner what to do. But research evidence may exist that warns what *not* to do. A secondary gain is that in developing evidence-based practice recreational therapy professionals are keeping pace with colleagues in medicine, nursing, and other allied health fields. These health professionals are leading the way in the implementation of EBP.

The concept of EBP implies that practitioners will not select an approach because "we have always done it that way here" or base their practice on out-of-date information. Instead, they will practice as reflective practitioners who will be thoughtful in their actions and who keep up-to-date with the latest research findings. Those committed to EBP "must emphasize the use of *theory*-derived research-based information over the use of evidence obtained through tradition, authority, trial and error, personal experience, and intuition whenever possible" (Schmidt & Brown, 2009).

Unfortunately, instead of basing practice on the best available evidence, current practices of recreational therapists too often remain mired in traditional practices, knowledge from their academic training gained years ago, and outdated organizational policies. Results from a master's thesis study conducted with Certified Therapeutic Recreation Specialists (CTRSs) from the southern region of the United States indicated that evidence-based practice "is not being used by most CTRS (*sic*) a majority of the time" (Mrkic, 2011, p. 58). Recreational therapists who have not adopted EBP are not alone. The prestigious Institute of Medicine (2001) once termed the disconnect between research and practice in health care to be "not just a gap, but a chasm" (p. 1). Hopefully, progress has been made over the years but it remains likely that many today do not fully embrace EBP.

EBP therefore demands that university professional preparation programs prepare emerging professionals with the latest clinical research information. Recreational therapy textbooks must use research as a foundation when discussing interventions—as I have attempted to do throughout this book and especially within Chapter 3, which covers facilitation techniques.

Also, as recreational therapy professors Lee and McCormick (2002) have indicated, research can no longer be just an "add on" in university professional preparation programs but must be a central feature of the curriculum. Further, universities must instill in their students the need for continuing education in order to stay current once they are in the field. Finally, universities have to teach students steps involved in doing evidence-based practice.

Based on the work of Brown (1999) and Rosenberg and Donald (1995), Lee and McCormick (2002) have suggested a five-step process for implementing evidence-based practice in recreational therapy. The first step is to formulate clinical questions concerning the client problem. An example would be: What interventions work best with this type of client? The second step is to search for research evidence. Current textbooks, professional journals, and databases, such as MEDLINE and PsychINFO, are potential sources. Additional databases include: CINAHL (Cumulative Index to Nursing & Allied Health), a general nursing database; Ovid, a database containing a collection of health sciences databases; and RehabDATA, a library and information center focusing on disability and rehabilitation, provided by the National Rehabilitation Information Center. Perhaps the best place to find systematic research reviews is the Cochrane Collaboration (www.cochrane.org). The Cambell Collaboration (http://www.cambellcollaboration.org/Index.asp) provides systematic reviews of the effects of interventions. (Craig & Smyth, 2007; Law & MacDermid, 2008; Larrabee, 2009). The third step is appraising the evidence. Skills in being a critical consumer of research are needed at this stage. The fourth step is implementing research findings in practice. Here the practitioner needs to use his or her clinical judgment and to consider client preferences. The final step is to evaluate the impact of the intervention. The major question is: Did the intervention work?

Evidence-based practice offers an opportunity for recreational therapy to enlighten its practice and to change the way many recreational therapists think about and approach their work. The critical nature of adopting EBP has been reflected in the words of Dearholt and Dang (2012) who stated, "A culture of critical thinking and ongoing learning creates an environment where evidence supports clinical and administrative decisions, assuring the highest quality of care by using evidence to promote optimal outcomes, reduce inappropriate variation in care, and promote patient and staff satisfaction" (p. 192). An even more direct rationale for adopting EBP has been provided by Law and MacDermid (2008) who wrote, "The argument for EBP is simple. If there is a better way to practice, therapists should find it" (p. 5).

Chapter Summary

The recreational therapy process has commonly been associated with highly clinical programs; however, its application goes far beyond the bounds of any clinical setting. The recreational therapy process of assessment, planning, implementation, and evaluation can be applied in any setting in which goal-directed programs are desired. Thus the recreational therapy process is not restricted to hospitals or rehabilitation or treatment centers. The systematic process outlined in this chapter can guide recreational therapists who practice professionally in community-based programs, corrections facilities, long-term care facilities, and all other settings where recreation is used with therapeutic intent. Conversely, if this process is not followed, recreational therapy services are not being provided, no matter what group is being served. The simple provision of recreation service for individuals who are ill or have disabilities does not constitute in itself the delivery of recreational therapy services. Recreation programs for persons who are ill or disabled that do not utilize the recreational therapy process should make no claims on the term "recreational therapy." They are better called special or inclusive recreation programs.

Reading Comprehension Questions

1. What is the humanistic perspective? Is it reflected in recreational therapy?
2. Describe the concept of high-level wellness.
3. Construct and interpret a continuum of service for recreational therapy.
4. What is a conceptual model? Why are conceptual models important for recreational therapy?
5. Do you have a favorite RT conceptual model? If so, why do you like it?
6. What is evidence-based practice?
7. Outline and describe briefly the phases in the recreational therapy process.
8. What is the purpose of recreational therapy assessment?
9. List methods that the recreational therapist might use in completing client assessment.
10. Would you approach an interview with a child in the same way as with an adult? If not, how might these interviews differ?
11. What secondary sources are used in assessment?
12. What basic general information the recreational therapist might wish to gain on the client as soon as possible?
13. What is objective assessment data? Subjective data?
14. What are four steps in the planning phase?
15. How may Maslow's needs hierarchy be used to assist in setting priorities?
16. How do goals, or general objectives, differ from specific objectives?
17. Why formulate goals? Specific objectives?
18. Outline rules useful in stating objectives.
19. Clarify what Mager means by conditions and criteria as applied to specific objectives.
20. What does SMART stand for?
21. What common elements are likely to be found in individualized intervention plans?
22. Why is it important that each client's RT individual intervention plan is customized for them?

23. Do you agree with the customized RT individualized intervention plan developed for the case presented in this chapter? Why or why not?
24. Can you apply activity analysis to a recreation activity of your choosing?
25. Outline considerations for the implementation phase.
26. With what types of evaluation are we concerned in recreational therapy?
27. Should the client be involved in decision making during the recreational therapy process? Why or why not?
28. What are referrals?
29. What is discharge planning?
30. What is the relationship of philosophy to theory?
31. Do you understand how conceptual models inform practice?
32. Can you name and briefly describe at least two conceptual models for recreational therapy?
33. Can you describe the concept of evidence-based practice?

Appendix A
Open-Ended Questions

Open-Ended Questions for Adults
- Do you think leisure is important?
- How much leisure time do you have?
- Do you like the balance between your work and recreation?
- What kinds of things do you do for fun in your spare time?
- What are some of your hobbies?
- What would you like to do?
- Do you own any recreational equipment such as golf clubs, a tennis racket, or canoe?
- Do you watch television, and, if so, what programs do you watch?
- What things do you do with your family (spouse, children)?
- With whom do you take part in recreation?
- When do you usually participate in recreation?
- Would you rather do things with others or alone?
- Of the things you do in your free time, which do you like best?
- Do you like outdoor activities such as fishing or camping?
- Do you take vacations, and, if so, what do you usually do on vacation?
- What would be your ideal vacation?
- Do you experience any problems with the expense involved in your recreation participation?
- Are there any other reasons for not participating in leisure activities?

Open-Ended Questions for Older Adults
- Are you retired? (Consider adjustment, future plans, time spent in leisure/pleasurable activities.)
- Do you feel safe going out during the day, evening? Why or why not?
- Is there someone to go with you?
- Do you have your own transportation? If not, what means do you have?
- Do you belong to retirement or senior groups? (Consider political activity, veterans' organizations, volunteer work.)
- Do you use a community or senior citizen center?
- How do you relax and unwind?
- Have your leisure activities changed?

Open-Ended Questions for Parents

- What kinds of things does (child's name) do after school? On the weekends?
- Who does (child's name) play with? Other children? Parents? By himself or herself?
- If (child's name) does play with other children in the neighborhood, do they invite him or her to play?
- Does (child's name) indicate a preference for certain activities, such as sports, art, or music?
- What recreation equipment does (child's name) have?
- What sorts of recreation equipment or toys does (child's name) like to buy?
- Does (child's name) get excited easily or is he or she calm and easygoing?
- Does (child's name) like to try new things?
- Does (child's name) stick to projects or give up easily?
- Does (child's name) tend to be a self-starter or does he or she rely on others to get things started?
- Is (child's name) outgoing or shy? Can you give examples of this behavior?
- Does (child's name) enjoy helping around the house?
- Does (child's name) like to make decisions?

Open-Ended Questions for Children

- What sorts of things does your family do together for fun?
- What sort of hobby would you like to learn?
- Tell me the best birthday or Christmas present you ever got. What made it so good?
- What things do you do after school? On the weekend? With whom do you play?
- Did you like your summer vacation? What was good about it?
- What are your three favorite things to do?
- If you get an allowance, what do you spend it on?

Chapter 5

Helping Others

█ Chapter Purpose

Professional helping relationships have much in common with social relationships. Nonetheless, there are distinctions between helping as a professional and helping as a friend. Being an effective helping professional requires certain characteristics. One of these is possessing self-awareness. This chapter will clarify the role of the professional helper and will discuss characteristics of professional helpers with particular attention to the development of self-awareness. The chapter also contains information on professional ethics, cultural diversity, and burnout as concerns for professional helpers.

█ Key Terms

- Self-awareness
- Physiological needs
- Love and belonging needs
- Self-actualization
- Value-free professional
- Client autonomy
- Privacy
- Professional competence
- Veracity
- Burnout
- Cultural diversity

- Self-concept
- Safety needs
- Self-esteem needs
- Metaneeds
- Professional ethics
- Confidentiality
- Socio-sexual relation
- Justice
- Fidelity
- Multiculturalism

█ Objectives

- Comprehend the nature of a professional helping relationship.
- Appreciate the qualities or characteristics necessary for those who desire to be effective professional helpers.
- Recognize characteristics that should be possessed by recreational therapists in order to practice as helping professionals.

- Appreciate the necessity for recreational therapists to increase and refine their level of self-awareness.
- Analyze self-conceptualizations.
- Analyze fundamental personal needs.
- Recognize how values help to define behaviors.
- Recognize some of your own values.
- Evaluate basic philosophical beliefs for practice as a recreational therapist.
- Know issues related to professional ethics in recreational therapy.
- Understand cultural diversity as a professional concern.
- Understand burnout as a problem for helping professionals.

Professional Helping

One of the most widely read books within the clinical psychology and psychiatric communities has been Schofield's (1964, 1986) *Psychotherapy: The Purchase of Friendship*. In this book, the author likened the role of some clinical psychologists, psychiatrists, and psychiatric social workers to that of a "professional friend." Schofield stated that the long-term relationships often provided to clients by these professionals were simply substitute friendships for those in need of someone to talk to about problems and concerns.

Helping relationships do share similarities with friendships; despite these similarities, however, they do differ. With friends we are regularly giving of ourselves, and we, in turn, are helped by our friends. There is mutuality in the relationship. There is a norm of reciprocity at work. If we find ourselves constantly giving and never receiving, in all likelihood we will end the relationship; and, in such cases, we may even claim we have been taken advantage of.

Professional helping relationships differ from social relationships in that the primary focus is always on one person: the client. The client has come for professional help with no intent of reciprocating. The mutuality existing in friendships is not present in the professional helping relationship because those involved have different roles. One role is to give help (the helper), and the other is to receive help (the client). The fundamental reality that the relationship exists to meet the needs of the client, not the helper, is basic to maintaining a healthy helping relationship (Brill & Levine, 2002).

This, of course, is not to say professional helpers, including recreational therapists, are not human. Helping others certainly does meet very real human needs. Through helping we gain satisfaction in seeing others succeed and we feel needed. Perhaps helping professionals need clients as much as clients need them; however, help is given by the helping professional without the expectation of personal gain. Mayeroff (1971) has presented the concept of helping in an insightful work titled *On Caring*, in which Mayeroff states, "To care for another person, in the most significant sense, is to help him grow and actualize himself. . . . Caring is the antithesis of simply using the other person to satisfy one's own needs" (p. 1). Through helping others, we help ourselves. We fulfill, or actualize, ourselves through caring for others.

The Aim of Helping Relationships

The helping relationship is, as stated previously, directed toward maximizing the client's growth potential and preventing or relieving problems. Helping is not resolving problems or handling crises *for* the client. Instead, in a helping relationship we *assist* clients to meet pressing needs and then help further in their preparation for the future. Therefore, the ultimate goal of the helping relationship is to facilitate growth, leading to independence and self-sufficiency.

Needed Professional Characteristics

What characteristics should the effective helper possess? Many answers have been given to this question. Carl Rogers has had a significant impact on the helping professionals who have followed him. In fact, the triad of elements originally stipulated by Rogers (1961, pp. 61-62) are reflected in all subsequent lists. His three elements are as follows:

- **Congruence (genuineness).** Helpers are themselves. They do not put up a false front or facade.
- **Unconditional positive regard.** A warm, positive, accepting attitude is displayed by the helper. The helper prizes the client as a person.
- **Empathetic understanding.** Helpers experience an accurate understanding of the client's private world.

Okun (2002, pp. 43-49) has provided a practical list of helping characteristics. Her list includes the following qualities:

- **Self-awareness.** Helpers who possess self-awareness have a basis for helping others in the development of self-awareness.
- **Honesty.** A crucial quality for helpers is to express themselves honestly and to develop trust.
- **Congruence.** Helpers who have congruence between their values and beliefs and their style of communication are seen as more credible and as more potent models.
- **Communication skills.** Helpers' behaviors involve the ability to communicate observations, feelings, and beliefs.
- **Knowledge.** Helpers know and interpret theories on which effective helping is based.
- **Ethical Integrity.** Helpers' behaviors are responsible, moral, and ethical.

Characteristics of effective helpers have been portrayed by Cormier and Cormier (1998, pp. 11-18) to be the following:

- **Intellectual competence.** Helpers need intelligence to learn the skill required of helping professionals and, once in the field, to search for data in order to make informed decisions about client treatment and progress.
- **Energy.** Helpers have the energy to meet both emotional and physical demands made on them.
- **Flexibility.** Helpers are flexible so they can adapt methods and technologies to meet the needs of individual clients.
- **Support.** Helpers are supportive of clients.
- **Good will.** Helpers have positive motives for helping clients and behave in ethical and responsible ways with clients.
- **Self-awareness.** Helpers are aware of personal feelings and attitudes as well as strengths and limitations.
- **Competence.** Helpers need to possess feelings of personal competence and adequacy.
- **Power.** Helpers must be comfortable with issues of power and control.
- **Intimacy.** Helpers need to have resolved their intimacy needs so they do not fear rejection or feel threatened by closeness.

Brammer and MacDonald (1999, pp. 36-44) listed the following helper characteristics:

- **Awareness of self and values.** By helpers knowing their needs, they can avoid the unethical use of helpers for their own needs satisfaction and they can be in a better position to protect against the tendency to project their values onto clients.
- **Awareness of cultural experiences.** Knowledge of cultural diversity assists helpers to confront ethnocentrism and stereotypic thinking.
- **Ability to analyze the helper's own feelings.** Helpers need to develop understandings of their own feelings that emerge during interactions with clients so they remain therapeutic agents for their clients and learn when they are becoming emotionally drained so they can "recharge their own batteries." (p. 35)
- **Ability to serve as model and influencer.** A great deal of social learning goes on with clients, so helpers need to realize the power of their modeling behaviors for their clients. Helpers also may exert strong social influences on clients.
- **Alertism.** Effective helpers value others and are altruistic, rather than narcissistic.
- **Strong sense of ethics.** Helpers are moral and ethical in their interactions with clients.
- **Responsibility.** Helpers assume responsibility for their own behavior. They also have a sense of shared responsibility for their clients.

Helping in Recreational Therapy

It can be seen from the lists of characteristics that the helper's self-awareness is a key theme. Effective helpers also need to possess more than good intentions. Okun (2002) has stated that communication skills, a knowledge base, and professional ethics are prime qualities for a helping professional to possess. Recreational therapists additionally need to project a strong belief in recreation and leisure experiences and the values inherent in these experiences. The following are proposed as characteristics of the effective recreational therapist:

- **Self-awareness.** Recreational therapists must know themselves; they must have a developed sense of self.
- **Ability to communicate.** The ability to communicate effectively is basic to the helping process.
- **Knowledge base.** Recreational therapists must possess special knowledge in recreational therapy to be effective.
- **Strong belief in recreation and leisure experiences.** Recreational therapists prize the positive consequences to be gained through meaningful recreation and leisure experiences.

These characteristics are a working list and so are not intended to be complete. However, these elements are, I believe, the *sin qua non* of the helping relationship in recreational therapy.

Self-Awareness

Recreational therapists should pursue self-awareness from a personal viewpoint and from a professional one. They must know themselves and feel reasonably satisfied with themselves as persons before entering into fully effective helping relationships.

Concern about Self

In a curriculum study completed at Indiana University (Austin & Binkley, 1977), practitioners were asked to rate competencies needed for practice as a master's degree-prepared recreational therapist. "To increase and refine self-knowledge" was one of the highest-rated competencies. It is logical that practitioners would rate this competency high because we must know ourselves in order to help others. If we are overly concerned about ourselves and our personal needs, we are apt to have a difficult time helping others. Chapman and Chapman (1975) have reported that beginning helping professionals are often concerned first about themselves and second about the client. Such preoccupation with the self is a part of the natural evolution in becoming an effective helping professional.

Knowing ourselves helps us to understand the client more quickly. Having a personal experience with any problem enables us to identify and relate more readily to similar problems in clients. This, in part, is the logic behind having those who have had drinking problems work with individuals diagnosed with alcoholism. By being aware of our personal value system, we can also monitor ourselves to make a conscious attempt not to force our values on our clients. Finally, professionals are also people and, like clients, have strengths and weaknesses. Knowing ourselves helps us to realize when we reach the limits of our helping abilities (Chapman & Chapman, 1975).

Introspection and Interpersonal Communication

Within the literature of recreational therapy, little mention has been made of the need to know ourselves or how to go about the critical task of gaining self-awareness. There are various ways to achieve self-knowledge. Brill and Levine (2002) have suggested we can get to know ourselves in two general ways: introspection (looking within ourselves) and interpersonal communication (interacting with others). In the remainder of the chapter, specific techniques employing these two methods will be discussed.

A word of warning should accompany this section. That is, it is often an anxious experience to learn or relearn things about ourselves. It may even be a painful experience when we discover things that we dislike. Although learning about ourselves is not an easy process, it should be kept in mind that none of us is perfect. Even the best helpers possess limitations in addition to strengths.

Some questions to be pondered by the reader as a means to self-learning follow. They were inspired by a similar list constructed by Brill and Levine (2002):

- What is my sense of self?
- How do I deal with my personal needs?
- What are my values?
- What is my basic philosophy?

What Is My Sense of Self?

Perhaps no other question is as central to knowing ourselves as this one: "What is my sense of self?" Our concept of self is composed of all of the information, perceptions, beliefs, and attitudes we have about ourselves. Our self-conception is viewed by many social scientists (e.g., Coopersmith, 1967; Gergen & Gordon, 1968; Gergen, 1971; Samuels, 1977) as a vital factor in determining what we do and what we become. For example, Eisenberg and Patterson (1977) propose that persons who feel inadequate and insecure see outside forces as controlling their lives. In contrast, secure individuals perceive themselves as maintaining control of their lives.

We do not have to be social scientists to understand that the images we have of ourselves can have considerable impact on our thinking and behavior. Can you remember days in which you have felt really good about yourself and imagined that you could tackle the whole world? You could do anything. On the other hand, have you ever felt, as my daughter would say, lower than a snake? When we do not feel good about ourselves, we avoid setting high goals and may literally stay in bed instead of facing what we perceive to be a dismal world.

We can see that our self-concept is perhaps more accurately referred to as our self-concepts. Our self-concepts are relatively stable, but we do hold differing opinions of ourselves at different times and in various situations. Likewise, self-concepts are not carved in stone. It is possible to change them.

Different authors hold varying views on exactly what core elements compose our self-concepts. Samuels (1977) states that the critical dimensions of **self-concept** are body image (feelings about your body), social self (your racial, ethnic, cultural, and religious self), your cognitive self (your perceptions about self), and self-esteem (your evaluation of self-worth). Eisenberg and Patterson (1977) propose the central elements of self-concept to be personal adequacy and worth ("I'm OK."), appraisal of one's abilities or competencies ("I can't do anything with my hands"), and interests and activities ("I like the solitude of walking in the woods"), along with self-attributions or explanations people provide for their own behavior ("I work hard to achieve, because success means a lot to me").

How do you see yourself? Are you obese, slim, weak, strong, young, old, handsome, pretty, or sexy? Are you able to reach personal goals? Do you meet personal standards or ideals you have set for yourself? What are your preferences for specific interests or activities? Do you like yourself? Do you feel worthy of being loved? A few of the suggested exercises found in Appendix A: Self-Concept Exercises deal with sense of self and personal needs, values, and basic philosophy, including the "Who Am I?" exercise (p. 248).

How Do I Deal with My Personal Needs?

One of the first steps to success as a helping professional is to gain an understanding of one's needs. The helper who is aware of his or her own personal needs can then examine the ways in which he or she meets them. By doing so, the helping professional can

- gain personally from this knowledge,
- better understand similar needs and expressions in clients, and
- avoid using helping relationships to meet personal needs rather than needs of clients.

As with most things, saying we should become aware of our personal needs is easier than doing it. A scheme useful in client assessment may prove helpful to self-assessment as well. Maslow's (1970) hierarchy of needs can serve as a means to self-understanding.

According to Maslow (1970), all people possess an innate tendency to become self-actualized, or to become what they have the potential to become. This need is the fifth, and highest, of the needs found on the hierarchy. Four other needs exist below that of self-actualization: (1) physiological needs, (2) safety needs, (3) belonging or love needs, and (4) self-esteem needs. Once a need has been met, it no longer evokes behavior; therefore, we know that a need has been at least partially satisfied before a higher need appears.

Let us review briefly the five needs in the hierarchy. We will begin with the lowest, physiological needs, and proceed to the highest need, self-actualization.

Physiological needs are basic for survival. Included are physical needs for food, water, air, and sleep for self-preservation, and sex for reproduction. Few recreational therapists have to be concerned about the satisfaction of survival needs.

The second set of needs is **safety needs**. Safety needs are concerned with psychological safety and security. Stability is needed in all of our lives, but so is some amount of risk-taking. In meeting our safety needs, we keep tension resulting from uncertainty in a range that is comfortable for us as individuals.

The third level of need is **love and belonging**. This social need has to do with feeling wanted and accepted by others and with the giving and receiving of friendship and love. This need may be met through belonging to clubs or organizations, family relations, friendships, and intimate relationships. If we feel lonely or isolated from others, we may resort to unproductive or attention-getting behaviors ranging from pouting and disruptive acts to severe depression and aggression. Scarf (1980) has suggested that promiscuous sexual behavior may result from depression brought on by feeling unloved and uncared for.

Emotional intelligence is the ability to understand our emotions and to be able to effectively react to our emotions (Williams & Davis, 2005). Recreational therapists need to learn to acknowledge and appropriately react to their emotions. For example, they need to resist sexual feelings toward clients or control impulsive displays of potentially harmful emotions, such as anger, that may be precipitated by feelings of being unloved or not accepted.

The fourth level of need is **self-esteem**. High self-esteem means having self-confidence, self-assurance, and a general feeling of adequacy and worth as a person. It means feeling good about ourselves. To achieve a genuine sense of self-esteem, we must be able to conduct valid self-evaluation. We have to know our own strengths and weaknesses. One of the paramount outcomes of our work as helping professionals is to assist our clients to develop positive self-esteem. A lack in our esteem or our clients' might be reflected by *having to* drive the latest model car or live in the "right neighborhood" to prove to others that we are persons of worth.

The highest-level need is **self-actualization**. This represents the growth drive that moves us toward meeting our highest potentials. In self-actualization, we have continued self-development, leading us to a rich, full, and meaningful life.

Schultz (1977) has provided an excellent interpretation of Maslow's theory. He discusses the concept that those who have reached the level of satisfaction of self-actualization are no longer in a state of becoming but, instead, are in a state of being. They are no longer attempting to remove deficiencies (the lower-level needs). Instead, these extremely healthy persons experience metamotivation (otherwise known as growth motivation, or being, or B-motivation). **Metaneeds** (also known as B-values) represent a state of growth for self-actualizers. Among the metaneeds are concepts such as truth, beauty, unity, aliveness, uniqueness, justice, order, simplicity, meaningfulness, and playfulness. For most of us, metaneeds remain in the realm of ideals for which we strive.

In a moment you will be asked to think about yourself. First, read the remainder of this paragraph, which will invite you to engage in specific types of self-reflection. Close your eyes and reflect on yourself for a few minutes, thinking about your personal needs. Which have been past concerns? Which are most pressing now? How are these expressed in your actions and thoughts? Stop at this point in your reading and, for the next few minutes, engage in self-reflection.

Now that you have thought about yourself for a few minutes, what did you discover or rediscover? Are your adjustments to meeting your needs satisfactory to you? Are you engaging in any attention-getting or self-defeating behaviors? What things made you feel good about yourself?

If, through your self-analysis, you find that you are not perfect, welcome to the club! Schultz (1977) states that Maslow found that even his self-actualizers could occasionally be irritating, temperamental, vain, stubborn, and thoughtless. Nor were they totally free from anxiety, guilt, and worry. Also, if you are young, it would be anticipated that you would be still evolving as a person and would not yet be expected to be self-actualizing.

A general characteristic of self-actualizers, reported by Schultz (1977), was that they were middle-aged or older. According to Schultz, Maslow assumed that younger persons had not yet had the necessary life experiences to enable them to develop a powerful sense of identity and independence. It follows that you, if you are a young person, are in a natural state of becoming and should be optimistic about your ability for future growth. In fact, we all should remain optimistic about our abilities to change because all of us possess the potential to grow and expand throughout our lives.

To stimulate further self-examination, I have constructed a list of questions. These "Self-Examination Questions" appear in this chapter's Appendix A (p. 248). It is not to be taken as an inclusive list, but the questions will reveal areas for exploration for you as an emerging, or even established, recreational therapist.

On Becoming a Helping Professional

One serious question that all recreational therapists must address at some point whether if they truly desire to become helping professionals. When students actually begin to gain field experience, they sometimes find that the helping relationship does not meet their personal needs. For example, they may learn that while they like being with other people, they do not enjoy participating in actual helping relationships. It is critical that students gain experiences in the real world of the helping professional in order to confirm or challenge their suppositions. It is also important that students gain exposure to several different client groups. Some people work well with children who have intellectual disabilities. Others find enjoyment in serving adults with problems in mental health, individuals undergoing physical rehabilitation, old people, or members of some other group. Professional exploration is essential for the helping professional. There is nothing wrong with students making alternative career choices. In fact, it reflects the development of self-awareness on their part.

What Are My Values?

When I began my professional career in recreational therapy, two myths existed. One was that professionals were value-free. That is, their personal values were not allowed to enter into their professional lives. The second was that even the beginning helping professionals held the highest of professional values. Young professionals presumably gained these through some unknown means because, to my knowledge, no college instructors ever helped us to develop them as students.

The myth of the value-free professional has passed. Professionals today are allowed personal values (i.e., values we hold as individuals). We have also come to understand that there is a place in professional preparation programs for examination of both personal and professional values (i.e., values accepted by our profession). Please see Table 5.1 for examples of professional values held by recreational therapists.

Values defined. Before proceeding further, it may be wise to make explicit exactly what is meant by values. To value something is to attribute worth to it. Beliefs that we prize form our value system and are one basis for determining our behavior. Burkhardt and Nathaniel (2008) have defined values. They have written:

> Values are ideals, beliefs, customs, modes of conduct, qualities, or goals that are highly prized or preferred by individuals, groups, or society....Values, which are learned

Table 5.1

Examples of the Professional Values of Recreational Therapists

1. **Health and Well-Being.** Recreational therapists value assisting persons to achieve their optimal levels of health whether these persons are in normal health, or have an illness, disorder, or disability. All possess the potential for change.

2. **Control and Choice.** Recreational therapists respect and promote the autonomy of clients so they may maintain control over their lives to the greatest degree possible and make informed choices.

3. **Client-Therapist Relationship.** The client-therapist relationship is valued as a critical element in recreational therapy. The essential role of the recreational therapist is that of a catalyst who works in partnership with clients in order to help them be as self-directed as possible.

4. **Client Abilities and Strengths.** Each client is seen as possessing abilities and intact strengths that may be used to meet client challenges. Clients can build strengths and abilities through participation in recreational therapy.

5. **Fun and Enjoyment.** Fun and enjoyment are valued as motivators for client participation. People are motivated to take part in activities that are fun or enjoyable. Fun and enjoyment are positive emotions that open clients up to try new behaviors.

6. **Emphasis on Client.** Recreational therapy is action oriented but the emphasis is always on the client as a person and not on the activity.

7. **Goal-Directed.** Recreational therapy is valued for being purposeful and goal-directed. Being purposeful means having a plan, which implies choice making on the part of clients.

8. **Intrinsic Worth.** Every client is valued as an individual possessing intrinsic worth who should be treated with dignity.

9. **Competent and Ethical Care.** Recreational therapists value the ability to offer competent and ethical care and therefore meet their professional obligations to clients.

Sources: Austin, D. R. (2002).This I Believe. In D. R. Austin, J. Dattilo, & B. P. McCormick (Eds.), Conceptual Foundations for Therapeutic Recreation (pp. 313–314). State College, PA: Venture.; Austin, D. R., & Crawford, M. E. (2001). *Therapeutic recreation: An introduction* (3rd ed.). Needham Heights, MA: Allyn & Bacon, pp. 12 – 13; Burkhardt, M. A. & Nathaniel, A. K. (2008). *Ethics and issues in contemporary nursing* (3rd ed.). Clifton Park, NJ: Thomson Delmar Learning, pp. 523–535.

in both conscious and unconscious ways, become part of a person's makeup....Our values influence choices and behavior whether or not we are conscious that the values are guiding the choices. Values provide direction and meaning to life and a frame of reference for integrating, explaining, and evaluating new experiences, thoughts, and relationships. (p. 83)

Values are then critically important to us. They are the principles by which we live our lives. They affect our life choices and our behaviors (Purtilo, Haddad, & Doherty, 2014; Reilly, 1978). Therefore, as Burkhardt and Nathaniel (2008) have exclaimed: "Becoming more aware of one's values is an important step in being able to make clear and thoughtful decisions" (p. 85).

Values knowledge. Simon and Olds (1977) have discussed the ways by which we learn values. Included are "The Three Misleading Ms." These are moralizing, manipulating, and modeling. These authors recommend none of these three methods. Few readers need convincing regarding the problems with moralizing. Manipulation limits choices and does not teach us how to think through conflicts. And, although modeling can be a potent force, learning by example does not afford the opportunity to make personal choices or wrestle with issues. Instead, Simon and Olds recommend the values clarification process developed by Raths. Values clarification "refers to the process of becoming more conscious of and naming what we value or consider worthy. It is an ongoing process that is grounded in our capacity for reflective, intelligent, self-directed behavior" (Burkhardt & Nathaniel, 2008, p. 85).Through analysis of our choosing, accepting, and acting on values, the values clarification process helps us to determine our values for ourselves.

Values clarification strategies. Perhaps the most noted book on values clarification and values clarification strategies is *Values Clarification: A Handbook of Practical Strategies for Teachers and Students* (Simon et al., 1995). Because Simon and his colleagues have prepared this book and several others, values clarification will not be discussed in detail in this section. Instead, the reader is encouraged to seek out works on values clarification. The exercises, or strategies, found in these books offer enjoyment and insights to those who complete them. They are highly recommended. Among the topics covered are work, sex, friendship, family, ethics, authority, material possession, self, culture, and leisure. (See Chapter 2 for a listing of specific values clarification exercises on leisure.)

Other ways of clarifying our values have been proposed by Reilly (1978). Among them are reading and discussing values found in good literature, such as Shakespeare's sonnets. A second method is listening to popular music and analyzing it to determine the values it reflects. Role-playing value-laden situations is a third method. Another is taking field trips to unfamiliar environments in order to broaden understandings of values represented in other lifestyles, cultures, and socioeconomic strata.

Through the process of examining your own values, you will learn to aid clients in clarifying their value systems, because exercises and experiences useful to you may be equally valuable to clients. A note of caution should, however, be sounded if you do deal with client values. Clients have the right not to have your values imposed on them. Avoid placing on them your personal values toward achievement, sexual behavior, conformity, work, leisure, and other issues (Brill & Levine, 2002).

What Is My Basic Philosophy?

It is important that we become aware of our basic philosophical beliefs, because these influence our theoretical notions, which, in turn, affect the principles by which we operate. Or, as Frye and Peters (1972) wrote in the first book on recreational therapy, "philosophy is the rudder that gives guidance and direction" (p. 32).

Brill and Levine (2002, p. 35) have listed the following seven beliefs that form their overall philosophical base for human service:

- The individual is a social animal.
- The individual exists in interrelationship with other people and with all other life forms
- This relationship may be defined as one of mutual rights and responsibilities.
- The welfare of the individual and of the group cannot be considered apart from each other.
- Each person, and all living things, possess intrinsic worth.
- Each person, and all living things, are characterized by a need to grow and develop toward the realization of a unique potential.
- The individual and the society can be understood.

- The individual and the society possess the capacity for change as a part of their intrinsic natures.

Do you subscribe to these philosophical beliefs? If not, with which ones do you disagree? It might be anticipated that beliefs such as the necessity for play in the developmental process, the importance of recreation and leisure as means to attainment of basic human needs, and the fundamental right of all people to engage in the pursuit of happiness might be added by recreational therapists. Do you agree with these? Can you add others?

Obviously, philosophical beliefs are required to direct our practice. For some time, we in recreational therapy struggled with the development of a philosophical statement to represent our field. It is important for the evolution of recreational therapy that such a process occurred, but it is more critical that budding recreational therapists develop personal philosophies. The emergence of newer, creative philosophies will cause us to examine continually past beliefs and will ultimately strengthen the profession.

Resources for Self-Examination

There are many resources from which to draw in order to facilitate development of self-awareness. Some have been mentioned previously. Others are listed here.

- **Audio recordings.** You may listen to audio recordings of interactions you have had with friends or actual clients. My students record an interview tape with a person with whom they are not in a close relationship. Then they critique it with a classmate, discussing needs, values, and behaviors that reveal themselves. The information on communications in Chapter 6 may be helpful in such an evaluation.
- **Videos.** You may video the role-playing of various situations typical of practice in recreational therapy and then review them. Students in my classes have videoed roleplaying situations of interviews and recreational groups and then reviewed and discussed them to gain insights.
- **Diaries.** Keeping a diary in which you express feelings about your self-concepts, values, and beliefs may be helpful. Students completing internships may find this technique particularly valuable in gaining self-awareness.
- **Small-group discussions.** Self-disclosure in small groups offers the opportunity to share information and insights. It is important to foster an open atmosphere conducive to such dialogue. Of course, confidentiality should be maintained.

Reporting on her innovative course dedicated to the development of students as reflective practitioners, Gilbert (2010) employed many of the self-awareness techniques mentioned in this chapter. She found her students benefited from a variety of experiences, including role-playing, journaling, self-reflection papers, life story papers, and papers on their personal and professional philosophies. During role-playing, two students served as co-leaders of recreational therapy groups composed of eight students who took the roles of clients. The students in the class who were not directly involved served as observers and provided feedback to the two group leaders. According to Gilbert, students gained many insights as a result of the course experiences and were "unanimously positive about the structure of the course and assignments" (p. 308).

Other Characteristics

The helping characteristics previously listed for recreational therapists included the ability to communicate, possession of a knowledge base, and a strong belief in recreation and leisure experiences. So important are communications that a separate chapter (Chapter 6) has been devoted to this topic. Hopefully, a knowledge base for practice will be built from many sources. Throughout this book, specific information on theoretical approaches and practical techniques utilized in recreational therapy will be found. The recreational therapist, in developing a personal and professional philosophy, will arrive at a belief in the values to be found in recreation and leisure.

Additional characteristics for recreational therapists include developing a strong sense of ethics, gaining understandings of cultural diversity, and learning about burnout and how to avoid or react to it. These topics are covered in the remainder of this chapter.

Ethical Issues

Capable recreational therapists believe in ethical principles and are moral and ethical in their interactions with clients and colleagues. **Professional ethics** comprise a system of principles or standards of behavior that govern conduct in terms of right and wrong in the performance of professional responsibilities. The term **ethics** comes from the Greek word *ethos,* which translates to our word "custom." Custom, in this sense, has to do with established duties and obligations instituted by common consent to insure uniform practice in a profession in order to protect human rights (Potter & Perry, 1995). According to Burkhardt and Nathaniel (2008), ethics provides structured guidelines to answer the question, "What should I do in this situation?" (p. 29).

A **code of ethics** is a written document listing the values held by a profession and expected standards of conduct for members of a profession (Jacobson & James, 2001). The American Therapeutic Recreation Association (ATRA), and the Canadian Therapeutic Recreation Association (CTRA) have published codes of ethics. Their codes of ethics appear on the websites of these organizations. Within this segment, ethical issues central to recreational therapy practice are discussed. Client autonomy, confidentiality, social-sexual relations, professional competence and training, veracity, fidelity, and justice are ethical issues covered in this chapter on helping others.

Client Autonomy

As professionals who have strongly cherished the ideal of freedom of choice in recreation and leisure, the issue of **client autonomy** is one to which recreational therapists can easily relate. According to Burkhardt and Nathaniel (2008), "The word *autonomy* literally means self-governing" (p. 53). "The autonomous person," stated Sylvester (1985), "is one who is self-governing, being morally free to make the choices that direct the course of his or her life" (p. 13). Dahnke and Dreher (2006) have written autonomy is the "right to self-determination: being one's own person without constraints by another's actions or psychological and physical limitations" (p. 12).

The **principle of autonomy** "recognizes that clients have authority over their lives" (Jacobson & James, 2001, p. 240). Autonomy deals with the client expressing his or her freedom to make choices. A part of client autonomy concerns *informed consent.* Clients need to know what the therapist plans to do and why. As Sylvester (1985) has stipulated, "Informed consent provides that the client has the right to know, in adequate detail and comprehensible terms, what is likely to occur during and as a result of professional intervention" (p. 15). But what happens when after you have explained the program, there is a conflict between what you believe in your best professional opinion to be good for the client, and what the client wishes?

Should clients be allowed to refuse to take part in therapy programs that are part of their individual intervention plan or treatment plan? This type of ethical dilemma related to client autonomy is one with which the recreational therapist must learn to deal.

As is the case with all ethical problems, it is not easily solved. It is, however, within the therapist's prerogative to ask reluctant clients to participate if such participation is clearly seen to be in their best interests. As Shank (1985) has explained, "the use of recreation as a therapeutic modality, especially in a health care setting, may necessitate action which restricts or reduces the autonomy of the patient" (p. 33). What about clients who express values that stand in opposition to yours? What if you know their values are "wrong"?

Sylvester (1985) has raised some interesting questions regarding leisure values. He asks:

Is astrology an appropriate form of leisure, even when clients use it to make major life decisions? What about witchcraft or satanic worship? How should professionals deal with clients who neglect their families by devoting all their discretionary time to religious activity? What about clients who claim to receive "meaning and enjoyment" from child pornography, or who use their free time to support white supremacist causes? (p. 14)

Thank goodness we do not regularly encounter clients who hold the values reflected in Sylvester's questions! Nevertheless, we do encounter clients with values that may differ from those we hold. What should we do when this occurs? Should we ignore the obvious conflict out of respect for the client's right to autonomy? Should we tell them how wrong they are and how they need to change their values?

Most authorities probably agree with Corey's (1985) and Corey and Corey's (1987) thoughts regarding handling value conflicts. First, the Coreys stated it is unreasonable to believe that we can divorce our values from our professional practice: "Your values are a fundamental part of the person you are. Thus, they cannot help but influence how you lead a therapeutic group" (p. 63).

They go on to say that every therapist must first address possible values conflict by knowing himself or herself. If you are to be an effective leader, you must become aware of your own values and the direct and indirect ways in which you may try to influence your clients. It is suggested that once this is done, you may choose to resolve conflicts between your values and those of a client's by *expressing* your views so the client may have the advantage of a new way of thinking about something. But you need to let the client discover what is right for her or him and *not impose* your values. To use Corey and Corey's terms, you need to *expose* but not *impose*.

Confidentiality

According to Burkhardt and Nathaniel (2008): "The terms *confidentiality* and *privacy* are interrelated. Privacy refers to the right of an individual to control the personal information or secrets that are disclosed to others. Privacy is a fundamental right of individuals" (p. 67). They go on to comment: "The ethical principle of *confidentiality* demands nondisclosure of private or secret information about another person with which one is entrusted. That is, confidentiality requires that one maintain the privacy of another" (p. 68). Shank (1985) explained that the concern of **privacy** deals with a person's right to control personal information, while confidentiality has to do with an individual's right to control *access to information* that others have gained about him.

Confidentiality may present a problem for young professionals who are naturally extremely interested in their work and may be anxious to share their excitement for what they are doing by relating details of their on-the-job experiences with family, friends, or even fellow staff members. The impulse to tell a good story must be held in check if client confidentiality is to have meaning.

Are there times when confidentiality may be broken? Yes, there are occasions when confidentiality may be broken when harm may befall either the client or others. If a client indicates she is planning to commit suicide, for example, this information should be reported. Or if a client informs you that he is going to harm another individual, this intent needs to be made known. Authorities (Corey, 1985; Corey & Corey, 1987; Okun, 2002) agree that therapists need to inform clients of these instances when confidentiality will not be honored as a part of initial informed-consent procedures.

Confidentiality within group leadership situations presents complexities not encountered with individuals. Corey and Corey (1987) have explained:

> One of the central ethical issues in group work is confidentiality. It is especially important because the group leader must not only keep the confidences of members but also get the members to keep one another's confidences. (p. 55)

It is important for group leaders to initially raise the issue of confidentiality with the group and then to remind clients from time to time of the necessity of maintaining confidentiality. While there is no way to ensure confidentiality when working with groups, some suggestions to the groups may prove helpful. Besides raising the need to avoid malicious gossip, the therapist can provide pointers for the group members regarding talking about their experiences with significant others outside the group. These should include that it is permissible to talk about what therapeutic gains they have made as a result of their group participation but not discuss specifics about interacting with other group members (Corey & Corey, 1987).

It is critical that recreational therapists are clear about their positions with regard to confidentiality. Recreational therapists will interact with clients in recreational settings marked by informality and an accepting atmosphere. Additionally, many clients perceive recreational therapists to be less threatening than other staff, and some will view them as friends. For these reasons, clients have a tendency to share much personal information with recreational therapists.

Social-Sexual Relations

It is generally accepted that sexual relationships between helping professionals and their clients are unethical. Nevertheless, sexual relations between therapists and clients do occasionally occur (Sylvester, 1985), although the prevalence of such practices in recreational therapy is unknown due to a lack of research on sexual behaviors of recreational therapists.

Recreational therapists encounter many occasions when warm, accepting gestures may be taken as sexual overtures by clients. Examples are hugs to demonstrate pleasure with a client's performance or embraces following success within an activity. It is therefore important that therapists monitor their own behaviors in order to (1) minimize misunderstandings with clients, and (2) become aware of any romantic feelings that they might possess toward a client (Austin, 2011a; Sylvester, 1985).

Social relationships with clients should not be encouraged by recreational therapists. The bounds of the role of "professional friend" should not be exceeded by the recreational therapist while the client is in the dependent position that is a natural part of the helping relationship. Professionals need to enter into close self-examination before pursuing a social relationship with a client even after the professional relationship has ended (Sylvester,

1985). Some agencies have personnel policies prohibiting social relationships with former clients. It is important that professionals become aware of any such ethical policies that may govern their behaviors.

Professional Competence

It is critical that recreational therapists know their levels of **professional competence** and that they do not exceed them. Corey and Corey (1987) have suggested the following to leaders of therapy groups. Their sentiments have application to recreational therapists. They have written:

> Group leaders must provide only services and use techniques for which they are qualified by training and experience. Leaders have the responsibility of accurately representing their competence to the participants in their groups. (p. 42)

Okun (2002) has stated that helping professionals tread on unsafe ethical grounds when they administer or interpret tests without sufficient training and supervision. Similarly, those without extensive training and experience in conducting programs that may involve potential psychological or physical risks to clients (which would include most recreational therapy programs) should not assume responsibility to lead those programs. For example, those leading adventure therapy need to have had sound training and adequate clinical supervision before leading this clinical program. The need for recreational therapists to upgrade their clinical skills becomes apparent whenever they contemplate initiating a new technique or program area. Equally evident should be the need for recreational therapists to continually update themselves in order to remain current in the program areas that they regularly apply as clinical modalities.

A second area related to competency deals with guarding against impaired performance on the part of the helping professional. Professionals need to seek help when they themselves encounter personal problems that may interfere with professional performance. For example, a professional who is under an exceptional amount of personal stress may need to seek counseling, or a professional who is abusing substances may need to enter a drug rehabilitation program.

The ethical principle that underlies the concept of performing with competence is the *principle of nonmaleficence*, which means "do no harm." Nonmaleficence is a basic ethical principle in that all professionals should wish to prevent harming any client. Jacobson and James (2001) have explained: "The principle of nonmaleficence directs practitioners to provide only services that can be delivered with competence. Sometimes (in ethics literature) competency is listed as a separate principle, underlying the need to have acquired the skills in any intervention undertaken" (p. 240).

The "twin" ethical principle to the principle on nonmaleficence is the *principle of beneficence* which "proposes that a health professional's duty is to promote the well-being of clients" (Jacobson & James, 2001, p. 240). Beneficence, of course, is an ethical foundation for the very existence of recreational therapy, which has as its mission promoting the well-being of clients.

Veracity. "The term *veracity* relates to the practice of telling the truth" (p. 65), according to Burkhartdt and Nathaniel (2008). Telling the truth is a basic ethical principle promoted by almost all professionals groups in their codes of ethics. Clients should not be deceived, nor should the truth be concealed from them. Not telling the truth to clients will likely result in a feeling on the part of the client that the professional cannot be relied upon. Conversely, veracity fosters respect and trust on the part of clients (Maville & Huerta, 2008).

Fidelity. "The ethical principle of *fidelity* relates to the concept of faithfulness and the practice of keeping promises" (p. 74), according to Burkhartdt and Nathaniel (2008). Because recreational therapists do have standing as certified or licensed professionals, they have responsibility to their clients, employers, society, and themselves to be faithful to their professional codes of ethics. On an everyday level, recreational therapists need to live up to their promises when they make promises to clients such as "I'll find out for you and get back to you on that" (Berman, Snyder, Kozier, & Erb, 2008).

Justice. A basic ethical principle is the *principle of justice*. According to Jacobson and James (2001):

> The principle of justice in clinical ethics focuses on fairness in the distribution of service. Justice commits the professional to distribute time and effort on the basis of client need. The client's values, disposition, race, or gender should not factor into the decision. The principle of justice encourages equitable treatment to the least-likeable client. (p. 240)

This principle of justice is reflected in the codes of ethics of the American Therapeutic Recreation Association (ATRA) and Canadian Therapeutic Recreation Association (CTRA). The ATRA *Code of Ethics* (2009) reads:

> Recreational Therapy personnel are responsible for ensuring that individuals are served fairly and that there is equity in the distribution of services. Individuals receive service without regard to race, color, creed, gender, sexual orientation, age, disability/disease, social and financial status.

Table 5.2

Ethical Principles

Principle	Meaning
Autonomy	Self-governing
Confidentiality	Right to control access to information
Social-Sexual Relations	Need to avoid social/sexual involvements with clients
Professional Competence	Do not exceed levels of competence
Nonmaleficence	Obligation not to harm others
Beneficence	Promote well-being
Veracity	Telling the truth
Fidelity	Faithfulness; keeping promises
Justice	Fairness in distributing services

The principle of justice serves as a foundation for much of the discussion that follows on cultural diversity. A growing concern facing all helping professionals is that of offering quality care to clients of ever increasing cultural diversity. Unfortunately, cultural bias on the part of helping professionals has become more apparent as demographics have changed (Peregoy, Schliebner, & Dieser, 1997).

Cultural Diversity

America has become the most racially and culturally diverse nation in the world and will continue to become even more so. It is projected by 2030 racial and ethnic minorities will constitute 42% of the U.S. population (Rand, 2010). And, by 2050, it is anticipated that in the U.S. there will be a "majority minority" where racial and ethnic minorities will be in the majority (Malveaux, 2012). Canada likewise is a truly multicultural country and is becoming even more diverse. According to Statistics Canada (2005), Canada could have between 11.4 and 14.4 million persons belonging to a visible minority group by 2031. This would be more than double the 5.3 million reported for 2006. The rest of the population, in contrast, is projected to increase by less than 12%.

Of course, persons from racial and ethnic minority groups represent only a part of the diversity found in society. Others, such as those defined by age, gender, affectional orientation, class, religion, and disability, have too regularly been marginalized, in a similar fashion to those from racial or ethnic minorities.

It is important to clarify terms related to cultural diversity. **Culture** refers to the total, integrated "set of values and beliefs, norms and customs, rules and codes, that socially define groups of people, binding them to one another and giving them a sense of commonality" (Trenholm & Jensen, 2000, p. 363). All of us are the products of cultural backgrounds. We have been influenced by values and understanding gained from our cultures.

Diversity has been defined by Getz (2002) as "simply difference or variety" (p. 153) typically represented by those from different races, classes, ethnicities, affectional orientations, and so on. The term **cultural competence** has been defined by Antai-Otong (2007) as "A set of knowledge, skills, behaviors, and policies that help clinicians to form therapeutic relationships, convey empathy and sensitivity, and collaborate and work effectively with diverse populations" (p. 154). Getz (2002) has explained: "Cultural competence is a lifelong pursuit of increasing personal awareness of other cultures. This is a conscious effort of working toward the goal of gaining a working knowledge of all cultures represented within one's personal and professional life" (p. 154).

Finally, **multiculturalism** is a "social-intellectual movement that promotes the value of diversity. . . and insists that all cultural groups be treated with respect and as equals" (Flowers & Richardson, 1996, p. 609). Multiculturalism is centrally concerned with the dignity and rights of persons from marginalized groups who have been given lower status or have not been fully accepted into the mainstream of society (Sheldon & Dattilo, 1997).

It is critical that professionals avoid thinking and acting according to their own monocultural orientation in a society that is becoming more and more multicultural. Those who recognize only their own ways as being the acceptable modes to think and act need to learn to recognize and respect diversity. Otherwise, there can arise unintended bias resulting from recognizing only one's own cultural background. In fact, it has been suggested within the counseling literature (Ivey et al., 1997) that it is unethical for helping professionals not to be competent in the provision of services to clients from culturally diverse populations.

Multicultural aspects enter into any helping relationship where the helper and client(s) have different perceptions of their social worlds. Professionals employing a multicultural orientation are sensitive to how issues such as race, ethnicity, age, gender, disability, affectional orientation, class, and religion can affect the provision of professional services to persons with culturally diverse backgrounds (Corey, 2012). They understand that their clients often possess views, attitudes, and values that differ from those they hold. They do not assume their ways of thinking and behaving are the only "right" ones and that any others are "wrong." All of us learn our perceptions of the world, and it is only logical that individuals coming from different cultural backgrounds will have different perceptions of the world. Those embracing multiculturalism recognize and value diversity.

Kim and Van Puymbroeck (2011) indicated that since Shelton and Dattilo's (1997) and Peregoy and Dieser's (1997) seminal articles on multicultural awareness there has been a recognition of the vital importance of recreational therapists to educate themselves so that they are competent to serve clients with different cultural backgrounds. This is especially important in the United States, where Anglocentric and middle-class values tend to predominate. To do so requires maintaining freedom from bias, becoming aware of and welcoming diversity, learning about various cultures, developing empathy for others who are culturally different, seeing individuals as individuals and not just members of a particular group, having contacts with clients from a variety of cultural backgrounds, and completing clinical affiliations with clients from minority groups (Bernard & Goodyear, 1998; Flowers & Davidov, 2006). It is reasonable to assume that each of us will wish to gain cultural understandings of those specific client groups that we will most likely encounter in our practice.

Authors (e.g., Blair & Coyle, 2005; Flowers & Davidov, 2006) writing about cultural competence often suggest three necessary components in training professionals in cultural competence. These are (a) self-awareness, (b) knowledge, and (c) skill.

The first component of *self-awareness* begins with each professional becoming aware of his or her own values, biases, and preconceived notions. In this process, Flowers and Davidov (2006) have emphasized that openness is key because prior socialization may bring about faulty thinking. They have written: "Racism, ethnocentrism, chauvinism, and other ingroup biases are commonly internalized as individuals are enculturated into cultural, racial, religious, and other well-established groups" (p. 584). Sue and Sue (2003) have stated, "Culturally competent therapists accept responsibility for their own racism, sexism, and so forth and attempt to deal with them in a nondefensive, guilt-free manner" (pp. 18–19).

The second component deals with *knowledge* of two types. One is a general knowledge of understanding how cultural bias has lead to discrimination, prejudice, and oppression of minorities. The other is specific knowledge about the cultural groups the therapist frequently serves. Following their review of the literature, Flowers and Davidov (2006) stated, "It is clear from this extensive literature that culturally competent practice is crucially dependent on general and specific knowledge about culture" (p. 587).

The third component is the *skills* component of cultural competence. This component has to do with putting cultural sensitivities gained through awareness and knowledge into action by skillfully applying interventions and interacting with clients to produce a therapeutic relationship.

The findings of Blair and Coyle (2005) regarding the cultural competence of recreational therapists are interesting and provide some insights regarding training in cultural competence. These researchers surveyed Certified Therapeutic Recreation Specialists (CTRSs) regarding their multicultural competence (MC). They found that while the CTRSs felt they had skills competence, including skills in forming therapeutic relationships, other findings revealed this self-perception may have been faulty. Blair and Coyle wrote:

> However, contradictory findings were observed with regards to MC competencies related to MC knowledge and MC awareness. These areas, which are hypothetically supposed to be pre-requisites for having MC counseling relationship skills, were areas which CTRSs reported the lowest level of self-perceived competence in the current study and in Stone's (2003) research. (pp. 151–152)

Blair and Coyle propose that the relatively low scores on awareness and knowledge on the part of the CTRSs show a lack of information about different cultures and that these recreational therapists may not have been comfortable with cultural belief systems different from their own beliefs. Further, the researchers suggest the recreational therapists may lack of awareness of their personal beliefs, values, and biases and how these may affect clients from minority groups. Blair and Coyle concluded that these recreational therapists "may be operating, as Stone (2003) suggested, at an 'unconsciously incompetent' level, meaning they lack the awareness to determine if in fact they are practicing in a culturally sensitive manner" (p. 152).

Thus findings from Blair and Coyle's (2005) research, as well as those reported in a separate study by Stone (2003), seriously question whether today's recreational therapists truly possess cultural competence. Both in-service and pre-service training seem to be called for. A study by Stumbo, Carter, and Kim (2004) indicated more and better multicultural training is needed in university recreational therapy curricula.

In closing, it should be acknowledged that there are those who are critical of multiculturalism, believing that to single out groups of people is divisive. For example, Flowers and Richardson (1996) have written that "to the extent that multiculturalism promotes separatism and self-protection, it loses sight of the continual dialogue between subcultures and larger cultures and the ways that this dialogue inescapably defines us" (p. 614). Conversely, those who endorse multiculturalism believe "behaving as if culture is irrelevant is counter-therapeutic" (Ridley, Mendoza, Kanitz, Angermeier, & Zenk, 1994) and that such thinking ignores the necessity to be culturally sensitive with clients who are cultural beings. It would appear that those on each extreme of the question of multiculturalism need to recognize that all of us, as humans, share a great many commonalities, while, at the same time, we are affected by varying cultural differences. As Corey (2012) has reminded us, we need to acknowledge that there are ties that bind all of us, regardless of cultural differences. We will always wish to maintain the understanding that our clients are individuals, as well as members of a specific cultural group.

Burnout

"Staff burnout is a critical problem for the human service professions. It is debilitating to workers, costly to agencies, and detrimental to clients," according to psychologists Shinn, Rosario, Morch, and Chestnut (1984, p. 864). Organizations have to deal with problems caused by staff who have burned out and have to replace those who resign. Clients suffer due to reductions in the quality of services performed by staff who are burned out (Szymanski, 1989). Thus, in order for organizations to function optimally, for staff to be at their best, and for clients to receive the services they deserve, employees must be engaged, enthusiastic, and energetic, not burned out.

The first mention of burnout occurred in the literature in the 1970s (Morse et al., 2012). Unfortunately, at present burnout continues to exist at a high rate of incidence (Jenaro, Flores, & Arias, 2007) or "at an alarming level," as Shanafelt and his colleagues (2012) have indicated. Today burnout is perceived to be a "serious problem" (Rupert, Stevanovic, & Hunley, 2009) whose consequences can be "severe and far-reaching" (Morse et al., 2012, p. 343) Thus, it is obvious that burnout is a major current concern for healthcare professionals and organizations.

Emerging healthcare professionals are especially susceptible to burnout. In fact, the prevalence of burnout is greatest for young professionals. This is likely because their still-developing skills do not yet match their high expectations, producing feelings of incompetence and uncertainty which ultimately lead them to burnout (Ilhan, Durukan, Taner, Maral, & Bumin, 2007; Lim, Kim, Kim, Yang & Lee, 2010). Thus, it is particularly important for emerging professionals to gain an understanding of the phenomenon of burnout.

What is Burnout?

Freudenberger (1975) originated the term *burnout* to describe the emotional and physical exhaustion experienced by professionals working in healthcare agencies. Cherniss (1980), an early burnout researcher, termed burnout "a process in which the professional's attitudes and behavior change in negative ways in response to job strain" (p. 5). His contemporaries, Edelwich and Brodsky (1980) defined burnout as a "progressive loss of idealism, energy, purpose, and concern as a result of conditions of work" (p. 14). More recently, Lee, Lim, Yang, and Lee (2011) stated: "Burnout is a specific kind of work-related strain that results from job demands…(and) correlates with negative occupational indicators, including poor job performance, absenteeism, and high turnover" (p. 252). Elsewhere (Austin, 2011a) I have written:

> Burnout occurs when the prolonged mental stress of the job results in a gradual loss of positive feelings about serving as a helping professional. Positive feelings are replaced by negative attitudes and behaviors. Burnout may result in an employee who has blunted emotions, lacks motivation for the job, and quits caring about clients. At its extreme, burnout may even produce feelings of hopelessness, helplessness, and depression. (p. 64)

Maslach (1982) introduced the framework of a three-phase process to describe the burnout syndrome. The initial phase of the process starts when a person experiences **emotional exhaustion.** A burned-out individual lacks the energy to face another day. During the second phase, an individual begins to reduce client contact and treats clients in a **depersonalized** fashion. In the final phase, an individual feels a **reduced sense of personal accomplishment** resulting from his or her work. The three dimensions approach taken by Maslach of emotional exhaustion, depersonalization, and a feeling of reduced personal accomplishment has been widely adopted by today's burnout researchers (e.g., Lee, Lim, Yang, & Lee, 2011; Lim et al., 2010; Morse et al., 2012; Rupert & Morgan, 2005).

Candidates for Burnout

Who are candidates for burnout? First, only good people burnout. "The employees most likely to develop burnout are your best employees. Your superstar employees are more likely to feel burnout because they usually put more of themselves into their job, spend more time at work, and take work more seriously and personal," burnout expert Vikesland (2006) indicated.

According to Mayo Clinic staff (2006), those prone to burnout

- identify so strongly with work they lack a reasonable balance between work and their personal lives;
- try to be everything to everyone;
- work in a helping profession, such as healthcare, where their roles are generally defined as "givers," a requirement that may not always result in a sense of reward or satisfaction; and/or
- have feelings of boredom and stasis because job responsibilities or duties may be monotonous.

Do recreational therapists encounter any of these job characteristics in their roles as health care professionals? Of course they do. Especially common are the first three of the foregoing characteristics. Unfortunately, some people may also encounter job monotony in positions where they are not allowed to enlarge or enrich their responsibilities.

Signs or Symptoms of Burnout

If recreational therapists are at risk for burnout, for what signs or symptoms should they be alert? Patrick (1981, pp. 18-22) has listed the following objective signs of manifestations of burnout:

- Overtime work increases as it becomes more difficult to get work accomplished during normal hours;
- Rest breaks and lunch are skipped to get work done;
- Vacations are delayed or canceled;
- People lose their sense of humor, often being overly serious and, perhaps, effectively flat;
- Physical fatigue occurs;
- People become more irritable;
- Susceptibility to illness increases;
- Physical complaints of muscle tension, headaches, low back pain, and gastrointestinal irritability increase;
- Social withdrawal occurs in the form of pulling away from coworkers, peers, and family or taking part in life activities but without true participation;
- Job performance declines, as reflected in absenteeism, tardiness, use of sick days, accidents, and decreased efficiency and productivity; and
- Self-medication begins or increases.

Subjective signs of burnout include the following, according to Patrick (1981, pp. 23-29):

- Emotional exhaustion occurs as people experience emotional emptiness and drained inner resources;
- Self-esteem declines;
- People feel trapped in their jobs;
- Emotional withdrawal occurs;
- Depression commonly appears;
- People experience increasing difficulty receiving support from others;
- Boredom and apathy occur;

- Helpers shift from understanding clients to blaming clients for their dysfunctions;
- Feelings of frustration increase;
- Feelings of anger appear; and
- Feelings of aloneness and isolation occur.

Austin and Szymanski (1985) conducted a research study with counselors in a residential camp serving campers with disabilities. Staff experiencing burnout reported

- a lack of control over their environment;
- little support from fellow staff members;
- a lack of recognition from camp administrators;
- focusing on finishing tasks rather than long-term goals;
- viewing the schedule as being without flexibility; and
- experiencing a lack of self-fulfillment from their roles as camp staff.

Such findings are, no doubt, very representative of those that might be reported by helping professionals who encounter burnout in other settings. Smith, Jaffe-Gill, Segal, and Segal (2007) indicated that signs of burnout tend to be more mental than physical and include feelings of powerlessness, hopelessness, emotional exhaustion, detachment, isolation, irritability, frustration, being trapped, failure, despair, cynicism, and apathy. They wrote:

> If you're burning out and the burnout expresses itself as irritability, you might find yourself always snapping at people or making snide remarks about them. If the burnout manifests as depression, you might want to sleep all the time or feel "too tired" to socialize. You might turn to escapist behaviors such as sex, drinking, drugs, partying, or shopping binges to try to escape from your negative feelings. Your relationships at work and in your personal life may begin to fall apart. You may lose your trust in others, believing that people act out of selfishness and nothing can be done about it.

Distinction Between Stress and Burnout

Smith and her colleagues (2007) have made a distinction between stress and burnout. They wrote:

> Burnout may be the result of unrelenting stress, but it isn't the same as too much stress. Stress, by and large, involves *too much*: too many pressures that demand too much of you physically and psychologically. Stressed people can still imagine, though, that if they can just get everything under control, they'll feel better.

Burnout, on the other hand, is about *not enough*. Being burned out means feeling empty, devoid of motivation, and beyond caring. People experiencing burnout often don't see any hope of positive change in their situations. If excessive stress is like drowning in responsibilities, burnout is being all dried up.

Further, Smith and her colleagues (2007) draw several contrasts between stress and burnout. Chief among these is that stress is characterized by over engagement, while burnout is characterized by disengagement. Also, in stress emotions are overactive, while in burnout emotions are blunted. Additionally, stress produces urgency and hyperactivity, while burnout produces helplessness and hopelessness.

Factors Leading to Burnout

There are any number of contributing factors to burnout. Among them are inadequate social support, lack of autonomy and clarity, work pressure, and a work environment that is not a healthy one. Those who burn out repeatedly report that they do not receive adequate social support from fellow workers or supervisors or reinforcement from clients. They often feel a lack of control over their work activities. They regularly experience difficulty with role ambiguity and a lack of encouragement to be self-sufficient, along with problems related to not knowing what to expect in their daily routines, and rules and policies not being explicitly communicated. Work pressure results when people are overloaded with long hours, large amounts of time doing administrative and paperwork tasks, excessive responsibility, or have inadequate preparation to do the job. Finally, staff often have to work in environments that are less than attractive and comfortable (Austin & Voelkl, 1986; Constable & Russell, 1986; Lee et al, 2011; Lin et al., 2010; Paris & Hoge, 2010; Rosenthal, Teague, Retish, West, & Vessell, 1983).

Results, from acclaimed burnout researchers Maslach and Leiter (2008), have indicated that burnout also arises from feelings of being disrespected when people perceive themselves as not being treated fairly. Unfair treatment is seen by these individuals as not valuing them and their contributions and, in turn, produces insecurity, anger and cynicism on their part. Thus, it is apparent that the variable of fairness is an additional contributing factor in burnout.

Preventing Burnout

Now that we have reviewed what burnout is, its signs and its causes, the obvious question is, "Can burnout be prevented or is it a malady that helping professionals cannot escape?" The answer is happily, yes, burnout can be prevented. McBride (1983, pp. 228, 229) has offered an extensive list of actions that individuals can use to reduce stress and prevent burnout.

- **Development of a support system.** It is very important to have people who care about you and what you do. A close relationship with at least one other person is vitally important.
- **Take responsibility for what you do with your own body.** Exercise regularly, eat properly, limit the use of tobacco, alcohol, and drugs.
- **Learn how to manage time effectively.** Prioritize what needs to be done—do high-priority items first.
- **Know and respect your own limits, skills, energy, and level of commitment.** Do those things that are your responsibility—learn to say no.
- **Spend time out of your usual role.** Develop a hobby. Don't compete—just enjoy yourself.
- **Look upon life as a challenge.** Take risks.
- **Take time off.** "Mental health" days, vacations, planning periods during the day. Use relaxation techniques, self-hypnosis, or other ways to "escape" daily pressures for a few minutes every day.
- **Seek professional help.** Career or personal counseling may be appropriate.
- **Learn to cry "uncle" when you need to.** Realizing that stress is affecting you adversely is the first step in dealing with it.
- **Enjoy "strokes" when they occur.** Get thanks, recognition, and validation from all available sources.

- **Stack the deck in your favor.** Take on assignments, when possible, at which you will be successful.
- **Learn to laugh at yourself and the absurdities of life.** Learn to live life with a sense of humor. Angels can fly because they take themselves lightly.

Of all the items on McBride's list, the first, involving social support, is one of the most crucial. We need a support system made up of people who care about us. Social support can be emotional, as others reinforce us as being accepted and valued as persons. It can be informational, as others provide us with advice on how to cope with stressful events. It can be instrumental, as we are supported in the form of tangible items such as money or assistance. Finally, social support can offer companionship or belongingness as we participate with others in leisure pursuits (Spacapan & Oskamp, 1988). It has been reported that those who enjoy collegial support are less likely to exhibit depersonalization (Paris & Hoge, 2009). Research (Azar, 1997; Rupert, Stevanovic & Hunley, 2009) has shown that social support from the family can reduce stress on the job. Having a good relationship at home can dramatically decrease distress at work. Likewise, good work experiences can serve as a buffer from home stress. Therefore, employers should not pit work and families against one another but understand that each can positively impact on the other.

Of course, the relaxation techniques mentioned previously in Chapter 3 can be applied as "self-help" methods in order to reduce feelings of tension. These techniques can prove to be very helpful to emerging professionals who are subject to burnout. Emerging professionals, who are the most susceptible to burnout (Bedini, Williams, & Thompson, 1995; Ilhan, Durukan, Taner, Maral, & Bumin, 2007; Lim, Kim, Kim, Yang & Lee, 2010), should also have concern for gaining the highest degree of professional competence they can achieve through their higher education preparation. While certainly not assuring the prevention of burnout, having the necessary competencies to meet job expectations can reduce the probability of burnout occurring. Once in the field, the importance of keeping up with recent developments through continuing education opportunities needs to be underscored. Finally, it should be emphasized that recreational therapists need to "practice what they preach" in terms of restoring themselves through recreational pursuits and expanding themselves through leisure experiences (Horner, 1993; McGuire, Boyd, & Tedrick, 1995).

Organizational Approaches to Combat Burnout

Maslach and Leiter (2005) have pointed out that there are two means to combating burnout. In addition to the steps individuals can take, organizations too can take approaches to maintain their employees' engagement in their jobs, rather than allowing them to burn out. In fact, Maslach and Leiter (1997) have suggested that organizations must be involved in the prevention and reduction of burnout in the workplace. Organizations can do this by both reducing the negatives and increasing the positives in the work environment. Maslach and Leiter proposed a five-step strategy for employee/management cooperation in fighting burnout:

- **Step one.** An individual must take the lead. One employee must prompt a work group to organize to consider the problem of burnout.
- **Step two.** Group momentum needs to follow. A group in the workplace must then get involved to work to maintain the momentum for change.
- **Step three.** The organization must become involved. The agency or organization must become involved because solutions cannot be implemented in a vacuum.

- **Step four.** Assessment and action need to follow. Areas to assess are (1) employee workload; (2) feelings of choice and control; (3) the recognition and reward system; (4) the sense of community or social support (or lack thereof); (5) employee treatment in terms of fairness, respect, and justice; and (6) how meaningful and valued the work is.
- **Step five.** It is an ongoing process. Fighting burnout is a continual process that is ever evolving within the organization.

In their 2005 article on reversing burnout, Maslach and Leiter, have amplified on the six areas listed in Step Four of their strategy for fighting burnout. These include the following:

- **Workload:** too much work, not enough resources;
- **Control:** micromanagement, lack of influence, accountability without power;
- **Reward:** not enough pay, acknowledgment, or satisfaction;
- **Community:** isolation, conflict, disrespect;
- **Fairness:** discrimination, favoritism; and
- **Values:** ethical conflicts, meaningless tasks.

In what they term their six-category framework they indicate that it is likely that at the heart of burnout is a mismatch between the individual and the workplace that needs to be addressed. They propose that by assessing the six areas mentioned in Step Four that the mismatches can be identified and a customized solution can be tailored to bring about engagement and avoid burnout.

It would seem that two additional categories mentioned by Ilhan, Duruckan, Taner, Maral, and Burnin (2007) might be added to those of Maslach and Leiter in order to form an "eight-category framework." These two categories are: (a) physical conditions of the workplace; and (b) dissatisfaction with relations with colleagues and superiors. Certainly being provided with a clean and attractive work environment that contains up-to-date technological devices (e.g., computers and hand held devices) is something that employees need. The other category related to dissatisfaction with relationships should be assessed in order to enhance the level of social support that comes from good relations with colleagues and superiors.

One could make an argument that dissatisfaction with relationships could be subsumed under Maslach and Leiter's (2005) categories of community and fairness. But however the area is categorized, the point is that relationships need to be examined to determine any determinable effects of workplace relationships.

Maslach and Leiter's (2005) words provide an excellent conclusion for this section on burnout. They wrote:

Burnout is not a problem of individuals but of the social environment in which they work. Workplaces shape how people interact with one another and how they carry out their jobs. When the workplace does not recognize the human side of work, and there are major mismatches between the nature of the job and the nature of people, there will be a greater risk of burnout. A good understanding of burnout, its dynamics, and what to do to overcome it is therefore an essential part of staying true to the pursuit of a noble cause, and keeping the flame of compassion and dedication burning brightly.

Chapter Summary

Helping others is a very human enterprise aimed toward the development of independence and self-reliance on the part of our clients. Certain characteristics are required of recreational therapists in order to function as effective helping professionals. The characteristic receiving primary attention in this chapter was self-awareness. It is clear that we, as helping professionals, have a responsibility to know ourselves so we know what we bring to the helping relationship and what we have to offer clients. We must also be responsible for understanding issues in professional ethics and cultural diversity. Finally, it is clear that we must learn to recognize burnout and how to prevent it.

Reading Comprehension Questions

1. How do professional helping relationships differ from social relationships?
2. Explain how helping others is a very human enterprise that meets the helper's needs.
3. What is the ultimate goal of the helping relationship?
4. Analyze the lists of characteristics of effective helpers. With which do you most fully agree?
5. Do you concur with the list of primary helping characteristics of recreational therapists? If not, how would your list differ?
6. Explain why we need to know ourselves in order to serve effectively as helping professionals.
7. Do you agree that gaining self-awareness may be a painful experience?
8. Review the list of questions posed for self-examination. Are there others that you might add? If so, think about yourself in regard to these questions.
9. Does self-concept influence our behavior and expectations? How?
10. Do you agree with Eisenberg and Patterson that those with high self-esteem are more likely to feel they have control over their lives?
11. Did you participate in the "Who Am I?" activity? Did it help you to examine yourself? How do you see yourself?
12. Why might it be important to become aware of your needs?
13. Can you outline Maslow's hierarchy? Do you recognize any of these needs in yourself?
14. Why might it be assumed that the majority of students are in a state of becoming?
15. Have you had firsthand experiences in helping relationships in recreational therapy? Were they what you thought they would be?
16. Why are values important? Can you recognize some of the values you hold in regard to work? Leisure? Other areas?
17. Do you agree with Brill's list of philosophical beliefs? Would you add or subtract any beliefs to form your own list of beliefs as a philosophical base for practice in therapeutic recreation?
18. Have you tried any of the resources suggested for self-examination?
19. Name issues related to professional ethics.
20. Describe the principles of nonmaleficence and beneficence.
21. Do you believe in the importance of recreational therapists developing multicultural orientations?
22. Have you observed health professionals experiencing burnout? What behaviors did they exhibit?

23. Have you experienced burnout as a student? What steps have you taken to deal with it?
24. What are actions individuals can take to prevent burnout? Are there things organizations can do to help prevent burnout from occurring?

Appendix A

Self-Concept Exercises

Who Am I?

Eisenberg and Patterson (1977) suggest that most of us are not fully aware of our beliefs about self. They submit that the "Who Am I?" exercise, often used to bring about self-learning, causes difficulty for all but a few people. This activity requires two people. One simply repeats the question, "Who are you?" To each inquiry the other person must respond by providing a new description of self. Eisenberg and Patterson claim most people do not go beyond their roles (e.g., wife, husband) and cannot respond to more than 10 inquiries.

Collage

A self-awareness exercise that many students enjoy is completing a two-sided collage. [This exercise was adapted from Borden & Stone (1976)]. On one side of a piece of poster paper, a collage is prepared to represent how you think people see you. On the reverse side, a collage is constructed representing the way you see yourself (the "real you"). The collages can be made out of pictures, advertisements, cartoons, or words from headlines from old newspapers and magazines. These can be cut out and pasted or taped to the paper. Or, you may draw or write things that represent you. The poster paper should be covered with collages on both sides in about an hour's time. Once your artwork is completed, you may get together with another person to describe your artwork and have the other person describe his or hers to you. After this, you may wish to display your collage for all to see. If done as a part of a class, you may desire to share information about your collages with your classmates and instructor.

Self-Examination Questions
On Physical Contact
- Do you enjoy being touched?
- Do you feel comfortable in touching others?
- Do you feel touching has sexual connotations?

On Giving and Receiving Compliments
- Can you receive compliments without discounting them?
- Are you comfortable with issuing compliments?

On Self-Esteem
- Do you have a feeling of being esteemed by others?
- Do you continually seek support or reassurance from others?
- Do you have a need to boast about exploits?

On Being Assertive
- Are you able to reveal what you think or feel within a group?
- Do you attempt to make things happen instead of waiting for someone else to do it?

On Social Relationships
- Are you free to let friends expand themselves or are you possessive or jealous when close friends make new acquaintances?
- Can you enter into intimate, honest relationships with others?

On Leadership Style
- Are you people-oriented?
- Are you task-oriented?

On Play
- Are you playful?
- Are you competitive, placing a priority on winning?

On Sharing Yourself
- Are you willing to transcend your own needs in order to facilitate growth in others?

Chapter 6

Communication Skills

▌ Chapter Purpose

Recreational therapy is action oriented, not talk oriented. Even though recreational therapists regularly interview clients and may engage in leisure counseling, the thrust of recreational therapy is toward active participation instead of purely the discussion of client problems and concerns. Nevertheless, the ability to maintain effective interpersonal communication is important and is a basic competency the recreational therapist needs to perform as a viable helping professional. If the recreational therapist cannot communicate with his or her clients, the recreational therapy process is almost certainly doomed to failure. This chapter will help you to develop a fundamental understanding of communication processes and refine specific communication skills.

▌ Key Terms

- Communication skills
- Nonverbal communication
- Medium
- Feedback
- Paraphrasing
- Checking out
- Probing
- Interpreting
- Informing
- Focusing
- Facilitative questions
- Facilitative statements

- Effective listening
- Message
- Receiver
- Mental set
- Minimal verbal responses
- Clarifying
- Reflecting
- Confronting
- Summarizing
- Closed questions
- Making observations
- Barriers to therapeutic communication

▌ Objectives

- Comprehend the pragmatic approach (i.e., practical approach) to communication taken in this chapter.
- Know determinants of successful verbal communication.

- Translate theoretical knowledge of effective listening into practice.
- Demonstrate knowledge of verbal responses that may be used to facilitate client self-understanding.
- Understand barriers that can interfere with therapeutic communication.
- Use feedback principles appropriate in learning and performance situations.
- Appreciate the importance of studying nonverbal communication.
- Analyze specific cues in nonverbal communication.
- Know examples of how cultural differences can affect nonverbal communication.
- Know how to communicate with clients with specific needs.
- Apply basic interview skills.

One day a student of mine excitedly exclaimed as she entered the classroom, "I used some of those verbal responses we've been practicing in class with my friends, and they really worked!"

Students are often surprised when they initially find that the interpersonal communication skills taught in their classes are useful in their everyday lives. Such skills have application because the skills you use to be an effective communicator in your everyday encounters with others are the same skills you need to be a capable helping professional.

Effective Interpersonal Communication

It is important to recognize nothing is particularly esoteric about the interpersonal communication skills you employ in your relationships with clients. They are the skills used practically every day of your life and are not the exclusive domain of recreational therapists or any other group of helping professionals. As difficult as it may be to admit, recreational therapists possess no magical means by which to relate to clients.

All of this is not to detract from the communication process, but it underscores that the business of helping is a human enterprise that employs communication skills used in day-to-day life. It follows that the higher your level of personal communication skills, the higher your potential will be to perform successfully as a helping professional. This chapter emphasizes the communication skills necessary for effective listening, interviewing, counseling, and activity leadership.

What Is Communication?

There are several frames of reference from which to view communication, including syntactics (information theory), semantics (dealing with meanings), and pragmatics (behavior; Waltzlawick, Beavin, & Jackson, 1967). In this chapter, all three will be discussed, but the primary concern will be pragmatics, or the behavioral effects of interpersonal communication. This practical approach will concentrate on basic communication processes in interacting with clients.

Because there are several perspectives from which to approach communication, there is no single definition of communication that is appropriate to all. For the purpose of the pragmatic approach, communication may be defined as the verbal and nonverbal transmission of ideas, feelings, beliefs, and attitudes that permits a common understanding between the sender of the *message* and the *receiver* or *recipient*. Some authors (e.g., Antai-Otong, 2007; MTD Training, 2010a) referred to the sender as the *encoder* and the receiver or recipient as the *decoder*.

Thus, communication implies the exchange of information and ideas between at least two people, resulting in a common understanding. The word *communication* is derived from a Latin word meaning common, or shared by all alike (Antai-Otong, 2007; Gibson, Ivancevich, & Donnelly, 2000). If, through verbal and nonverbal symbols, people achieve a common or shared understanding, communication has taken place.

The communication process has five elements:

- **communicator**—who,
- **message**—says what,
- **medium**—in what way,
- **receiver**—to whom, and
- **feedback**—with what effect (Gibson et al., 2000, p. 401).

Communication is clearly a two-way sharing of meaning in which a message is both sent and received. Russell (2005) defined communication as "a two-way process of interaction that is dependent on the reception of, and feedback in response to, information" (p. 2). Feedback provides assurance that the intended message has been received. Through feedback the receiver either verifies the message was understood or discovers the message was misunderstood. Because feedback may be subtle, it is important that the sender be alert and sensitive to those with whom he or she is communicating. Okun and Kantrowitz (2008) stipulated that effective helpers utilize verbal messages (containing cognitive and affective content) and nonverbal messages (including affective and behavioral content) and respond verbally and nonverbally to feedback.

To say that communication skills are important is an understatement. Noted therapist Virginia Satir (1972) long ago stated, in regard to the human being, "Communication is the largest single factor determining what kinds of relationships he or she makes with others and what happens to him or her in the world about him or her" (p. 4, italics removed).

Recreational therapy presents an environment conducive to the development of positive interpersonal communication. In the open, nonthreatening atmosphere of the recreation situation, clients often feel free to communicate with the recreational therapist. However, this openness is only one element in client–therapist interpersonal communications. Also critical is the appropriateness of the recreational therapist's responses. Unless the recreational therapist is prepared to respond appropriately, communications may break down. It follows that the recreational therapist must learn to develop effective communication skills.

Success in Verbal Communication

There are four factors that influence successful verbal communication, according to Purtilo, Haddad, and Doherty (2014):

- how material is presented in terms of vocabulary,
- the ability to speak with clarity,
- the voice tone and volume, and
- the speaker's attitude or feeling toward the client.

Vocabulary

Failure to choose the right words will produce an unclear message. Acquiring an adequate professional vocabulary will allow recreational therapists to avoid using inappropriate words or giving rambling descriptions to clients or other staff. This does not mean that you should use large, technical words in conversations with clients. Although a certain amount of professional jargon is necessary in staff communication, problems arise when highly technical terms are used when speaking with clients.

Once a colleague of mine jokingly remarked, "I never use a two-syllable word when an eight-syllable one will do as well." This man was noted across campus for his eloquent utterances. In the academic community, where a command of language is valued, my colleague succeeded as a communicator because he knew how to gear his message to that particular audience. He knew that presenting material that was too simple would fail and throwing in a few eight-syllable words here and there might earn him some amount of credibility! But being a good communicator, he also knew that presenting a message that was too complex would be equally bad. As all effective communicators know, failure to assess properly the receiver's ability to comprehend will severely hinder communication.

A good rule to follow is to state your ideas in simple terms in as few words as possible. Although my colleague was an apparent exception to this rule, you are better off using everyday words, even when communicating with highly intelligent and well-schooled persons. In short, you should "be yourself" and use your regular vocabulary.

Clarity

Articulation is important in getting a message across. A clearly spoken sentence is neither spoken too softly nor rushed. Professionals who are regularly asked by clients to repeat instructions are probably speaking too softly or too fast. The rate of speaking must always keep pace with the listener's ability to comprehend. Therefore, you should monitor yourself to make certain you are communicating with your clients. For example, you may find you are speaking too softly to be understood by older people who may have difficulty hearing or you may be speaking too rapidly to effectively get your message across to children. It is also important to be clear about the purpose of each therapist–client interaction. You should let the client know the goal of the interaction from the beginning and about how long the interaction may take.

Another part of clarity is to avoid lengthy, rambling conversations. Chartier (1981) presented several communication guidelines to avoid rambling communications:

- Have a clear picture of what the sender wants the other person to understand. It is particularly imperative that the communicator holds a clear conception of what he or she wishes to say when dealing with complex or ambiguous topics.
- Define terms before discussing them and explain concepts before amplifying them. New terms and concepts cause problems for those not acquainted with them and thus require explanation before they are utilized.
- Organize messages into a series of sequential stages so that only one idea is developed at a time and it leads to the next idea.
- Redundancy leads to clarity. Repetition is a good form of learning and is helpful in communication. Summarizing at the end of the message is a common form of repetition. As Chartier (1981) said, "Repetition is important. Very important" (p. 45). •
Relate new concepts and ideas to old ones. The rationale is that an individual can better understand a new idea if he or she has been able to relate it to a previously held one.
- Determine which ideas in the message need special emphasis. Underscored ideas have increased impact. For example, Chartier (1981) stated, *"This last principle is an important one—remember it and use it"* [emphasis added] (p. 45).

Voice Tone and Volume

Have you ever had persons remark to you, "You didn't say it like you meant it"? They were probably indicating they detected a lack of commitment in the tone of your voice. Voice inflection can be more important in projecting understandings than the actual choice of words. For instance, uncertainty reflected in the voice may communicate "yes" even though the speaker says "no."

The tone of voice can express attitudes and emotions ranging from pleasure and exuberance to dejection and depression. When clinical psychologists refer to the client as having a "flat affect," they are no doubt basing this observation at least partly on the client's tone of voice. Occasionally, a speaker will not realize the emotion accompanying his or her speech until another person makes an observation regarding it. When leading activities, the recreational therapist needs to monitor his or her voice to make certain that it is projecting excitement, enthusiasm, or whatever the appropriate feeling.

Closely related to voice inflection is volume. Volume can be used to control others. Speaking loudly will keep people at a distance, and a whisper may draw others closer. In recreational therapy leadership, the attention of a group is usually better gained by speaking at a relatively moderate volume instead of using a loud voice. If you speak at a moderate volume, the group must become quiet to understand you. This technique also has an added advantage in that clients feel irritated if you shout at them. As with tone of voice, the volume of the voice has implications of which you should be aware. *How* you say things makes a difference.

Attitudes and Emotions

One of Purtilo et al.'s (2014) determinants of successful verbal communication deals with the communicator's attitudes or feelings toward the client. When the sender and receiver have high regard for one another, the effectiveness of communication is aided. Displaying genuine concern for the client through a warm, caring attitude enhances the prospect for successful communication. Williams and Davis (2005) correctly stated, "A key element of therapeutic communication is having an *attitude of respect* for the client" (p. 18).

On the other hand, the recreational therapist who is not honest with clients will run into difficulties with interpersonal transactions. Confronting a client about his or her behavior may be difficult. However, displaying an accepting attitude toward inappropriate behavior is not an honest or helpful response; in the long run, the nonconfrontational professional runs the risk of destroying the helping relationship. It is also wise for the professional not to admit anger on the rare occasions when he or she is obviously feeling anger toward a client. Providing the client with an understanding of why the anger arose displays an open, honest attitude.

An often overlooked area for the recreational therapist to become familiar with is the client's attitudes and mental state. For instance, client fear and anger may complicate communication and the management of his or her condition. Purtilo et al. (2014) illustrated this point when they wrote:

Fear may present itself as stony silence, clenched fists, or an angry outburst. Patients may not recognize the emotion that they are experiencing as fear, so you must be watchful for the signs of fear and do your best to help reassure the patient. (p. 171)

Problems With Directives

Directives are a form of verbal communication that recreational therapists sometimes employ. Directives are phrases that instruct people to do certain things. For example, instructions given to clients or other staff are directives. A problem with directives is that sometimes clients can take them more literally than they are intended.

I can recall an experience during my first summer of working as a recreational therapist at a state hospital in Indiana. At the time, I conducted an afternoon program for a group of older male patients at a park on the hospital grounds. Each day I would scurry around, beginning one activity and then another in an effort to get as many of the men active as possible. I began one afternoon program by tossing a playground ball with two of the men. As soon as I was sure they were thoroughly engaged in tossing and catching the ball, I withdrew to try to interest others in activities. When I returned a full half hour later, much to my dismay I found the two men (who were now obviously tired and totally bored) still dutifully tossing the ball to one another! Of course, I did not wish for them to keep up the activity to the point of exhaustion. I had no idea they would interpret my communications to mean they should continue until I instructed them to stop.

Professionals in clinical settings must be particularly alert to problems with interpretation of directives. Clients may place a great deal of credence in instructions given by staff, perhaps feeling they will become well if they do exactly what they are told. In such settings, miscommunication can lead to false expectations, disappointment, and loss of trust.

On Listening

To improve communication, recreational therapists must seek not only to be understood but also to listen. It is also important they understand listening from the client's vantage point.

Anyone who has ever had fun playing the gossip game knows that listening can be difficult. This is a game in which everyone sits in a circle. The leader whispers a tidbit of information to the next person in the circle, who in turn passes on the gossip. The gossip continues to be passed from person to person until it gets back to the leader. Rarely, if ever, are the original and final versions of the gossip even slightly related.

Distortion may occur with the sender, with the message itself, or with the receiver. Primary factors influencing the sender are the physical ability to produce sound and motivation. Disease processes affecting the client's teeth, mouth, nose, or throat may impair speech, as may conditions such as aphasia. Motives such as fear or embarrassment may also cause the sender to distort or conceal information. For example, negative information may be forgotten for fear it may be upsetting to someone or information may be slightly altered to give a more positive picture of an event.

The message itself may also become distorted. Words or phrases may be interpreted in several ways, causing semantic difficulties. For example, the phrase "go jump in the lake" may be taken as either a helpful suggestion to beat the heat on a hot day or a derogatory remark.

Finally, communication may break down with the receiver. As with the sender, the receiver has physical problems that may be a factor in message distortion. A hearing problem can drastically alter the message's meaning. Additionally, there are several other ways in which the listener may distort what he or she hears. Chief among these are the listener's mental set, perceptual defenses that may lead to distortions, and sensory overloading.

Mental Set

The listener's **mental set**, or frame of reference resulting from previous experiences, often brings about unintentional distortions of communication. One author listed stereotypes, fixed beliefs, negative attitude, lack of interest, and lack of facts as pitfalls that may lead to distorted messages (Killen, 1977):

- Stereotypes are widely held generalizations about people or things. Although stereotypes may contain a grain of truth, they rarely hold when applied to a particular person or thing. It is a pitfall to engage in closed-minded, stereotyped-based thinking instead of being open to new perceptions.

- Fixed beliefs are barriers to listening somewhat akin to stereotypes. The accurate listener does not filter out or automatically dismiss information because it is not congruent with his or her own beliefs.
- A negative attitude toward the sender may interfere with listening. If the sender is not liked or trusted, the result will be a lack of credibility that will negatively affect how the receiver perceives the message.
- A lack of interest in the communication will cause the receiver to tune out the sender. The attention of others is aroused when people see how the message relates to them.
- A lack of facts causes people to complete information gaps with their own ideas because people do not like incomplete information. Thus, the listener must be aware of information gaps and seek to obtain all necessary facts rather than fill them in as he or she wishes them to be.

Perceptual Defenses

Another barrier to communication is to ignore aspects of a message or to distort material so it is congruent with the self-conceptions of the receiver or listener. Perceptual defenses may particularly be a barrier to client listening. For instance, it may be expected that the client whose self-concept is threatened by an illness or disorder will experience difficulty in accepting information that might further threaten self-image.

Sensory Overloading

Sometimes people cannot absorb or adequately respond to the information directed toward them. At such times, they are experiencing sensory overload. Limitations in the receiver's capacity to hear and comprehend all incoming stimuli cause barriers to communication. It was mentioned previously that talking too fast may cause problems for the receiver. The presentation of too many ideas or too much complexity may also cause difficulties. To prevent sensory overloading, the recreational therapist must attempt to speak at a rate that the client can understand.

Preparing to Listen: External Barriers to Listening

Bateman (2000) listed a number of external barriers to effective listening. One external barrier is the *environment in which the listening occurs*. For example, the room may be too crowded and noisy, the temperature may be too hot or too cold, or the area may be dirty or smelly. *Interruptions* are a second external barrier. Phone calls, deliveries, and colleagues dropping in are examples of interruptions. *Distractions* are a third category of external barriers. Overheard outside conversations, music playing, or items on a desk may be distracting. A final category of external barriers is *concentrating on something other than listening*, that is, concentrating on the client's clothing, physical appearance, or unusual expressions or ways of speaking. A related barrier may be the listener concentrating on his or her own appearance rather than the message being communicated.

Happily, recreational therapists can take a number of simple measures to remove external barriers to listening. For instance, they can select a meeting place that is pleasant and provides privacy. If there is a phone in the area, calls can be diverted. Distractions can be anticipated and avoided, for example, by meeting at a time when others will not be nearby engaged in conversations. Finally, practitioners can prepare themselves mentally to concentrate on listening both at the beginning and throughout the interview or activity.

Listening Skills Development

Listening may seem to involve just remaining quiet and hearing what others have to say. This is a false perception of what it means to be an effective listener. Becoming an effective listener involves the development of listening skills. In fact, Purtilo et al. (2014) exclaimed that the majority of people do not have the skills to be effective listeners. Most helping professionals need to learn to listen effectively.

Effective listening is sometimes referred to as *empathetic listening* because the helper is not judgmental or critical while attempting to gain an empathetic understanding of the client's thoughts and feelings. Another term commonly used when referring to effective listening is *reflective listening*. When listening reflectively, the helper responds in a way that reflects back to the client that the helper is interested in understanding his or her perceptions and feelings (Miller & Rollnick, 2002). Still another term to describe effective listening is *active listening*. It implies active participation as a listener, as opposed to passive listening that is often without any response or with an inaccurate response (Duxbury, 2000; MTD Training, 2010b).

Effective listening is an *active process*. It begins with four basic skills that involve both nonverbal and verbal responses. These are *attending, paraphrasing, clarifying, and perception checking* (Brammer & MacDonald, 2002).

Attending

Attending behaviors let the client know you are interested in him or her and are paying attention to what he or she has to say. In my years of going to the inevitable receptions held at conferences, I have had the opportunity to view a number of humans behaving. One type of behavior I have regularly observed at these events is that of the person who I initially think wishes to speak with me, but who turns out to be more interested in looking past me to see whether he or she can spot anyone with whom he or she would rather be talking. That person does not attend to me or my conversation because he or she is too preoccupied with his or her own hunting expedition. I usually feel as though I am being used as nothing more than a prop and start looking around myself for a more stimulating, or at least more attentive, person with whom to share a conversation.

Attention is something most people appreciate. Clients are no different. If anything, attending behaviors have even greater impact with clients, particularly those who are insecure and easily experience feelings of rejection. Attending skills should be basic to your interpersonal transactions if you hope to develop and maintain positive helping relationships.

Attending is accomplished through four primary means:

- eye contact,
- posture,
- gestures, and
- verbal behavior.

Eye contact. You have heard the expression, "he (or she) gave her (or him) the eye," meaning that one person was indicating a particularly high level of interest in another person. Eyes offer an expressive mode of communication. Frequent eye contact is one way by which you can indicate you are attending to clients.

Eye contact with clients should occur on a regular basis when communicating. Of course, this does not mean staring at the client. You do not continually fix your eyes on friends during social interactions. Clients also dislike being stared at, but they find frequent eye contact reinforcing.

Posture. As with eye contact, extremes should be avoided in posture. Appearing too tense or too relaxed is not good. You should neither sit or stand in a rigid or stiff position with arms crossed nor present yourself in a slouching fashion. Instead, sitting or standing in a relaxed and open body position, in which you lean forward slightly, should help the client feel comfortable and indicate that you are interested in what he or she is saying.

Gestures. When speaking with friends, you may occasionally nod your head as if to say nonverbally, "Yes, I see." This is a type of body movement that indicates interest in what the other person is saying. Other bodily movements, such as hand gesturing, can also be used to suggest that attention is being extended to the client. Nonverbal behaviors involving eye contact, posture, and gestures are captured in the acronym SOLER (see Table 6.1).

Table 6.1

Attentive Listening Using Acronyms " SOLER"

S   Sit squarely facing the client. (This gives the message that   the therapist is there to listen and is interested in what the client has to say.)

O   Observe an open posture. (Posture is considered "open" when arms and legs remain uncrossed.)

L   Lean forward toward the client. (This conveys that you are involved in the interaction.)

E   Establish eye contact. (Ensure that eye contact conveys warmth and is accompanied by smiling and intermittent nodding of the head, and that it does not come across as staring or glaring, which can create intense discomfort in the client.)

R   Relax. (Communicate a sense of being relaxed and comfortable with the client. Use normal gestures. Restlessness and fidgetiness communicate a lack of interest and a feeling of discomfort that is likely to be transferred to the client.)

Adapted from Egan, G. (2009). *The skilled helper: A problem management approach to helping* (9th ed.). Pacific Grove, CA: Brooks/Cole Publishing Company; Townsend, M. C. (2000). *Psychiatric mental health nursing: Concepts of care* (3rd ed.). Philadelphia: F. A. Davis Company.

Verbal behavior. The fourth attending channel is verbal behavior. What you say as well as what you do indicates how attentive you are. Refraining from interruptions, questions, and topic-jumping displays that you are interested in listening to what the client has to say. Cormier and Hackney (2005) suggested that minimal verbal responses such as "ah," "I see," "mm-hmm," and "mm-mm" can effectively indicate you are listening yet do not interfere with the client's verbal expressions. They also stated that using animation in facial expression, such as an occasional smile, can create the feeling that you are attending to the client's communication.

Paraphrasing

A second listening skill is *paraphrasing*. In paraphrasing, the client's basic communication is restated in similar, but ordinarily fewer, words. This tells the client that you are listening. It also gives feedback to confirm your understanding of the client's central message.

Brammer and MacDonald (2002) outlined a three-step process for paraphrasing: (1) listen for the basic idea or ideas expressed; (2) restate these in a brief way, summarizing what the client said; and (3) note the client's response to your restatement to determine the accuracy and helpfulness of your paraphrasing.

An example of paraphrasing follows:

Client: I really think it's neat to go out to the beach; it's so nice with the sand and all. It's fun. I could spend days there.
Helper: You really do enjoy going to the beach.
Client: Yes, I like it a whole lot.

Clarifying

The clarifying response is admitting to the client that you are confused about what was said and wish to clarify its meaning. When you are confused by an ambiguous or cryptic message, you can simply request the client to rephrase what was said or you can ask the client to respond to your interpretation of what he or she said.

In the first instance, you might say, "I'm confused. Would you go over that again for me?" or "I'm afraid I don't follow you. Could you describe your feeling in another way?" When using the second clarifying technique, you are actually using a form of paraphrasing. This response might begin, "I think I got lost there. Let me try to restate what I thought you said."

Perception Checking

Perception checking, sometimes referred to as *checking out,* is similar to clarifying. You are checking on the accuracy of your perceptions of what the client said. You are validating your understanding of the client's communication. You might say, "You seem to be happy. Is that right?" Another example would be, "You really seem to care about attending the dance. Did I understand you correctly?"

Brammer and MacDonald (2002) provided a three-step process for perception checking:

- paraphrasing what you think you heard,
- asking for the client to confirm or disconfirm your understanding, and
- permitting the client to correct inaccurate misperceptions.

Listening Exercises in Appendix A provide an opportunity to try out the four major listening skills: attending, paraphrasing, clarifying, and perception checking (p. 282).

Additional Verbal Techniques

Effective listening begins with nonverbal attending skills and verbal techniques such as minimal verbal responses, paraphrasing, perception checking, and clarifying. These are basic skills. But to hear and communicate at a deeper level, helping professionals need to employ additional verbal techniques. A number of verbal techniques for helping professionals to employ in therapeutic communication have appeared in the literature (e.g., Corey, 2012; Frisch & Frisch, 2002; Haber, 1997b; Okun & Kantrowitz, 2008; Sundeen, Stuart, Rankin, & Cohen, 1998; Townsend, 2000). The following are included:

- probing,
- reflecting,
- interpreting,
- confronting,
- informing,

- summarizing,
- self-disclosing,
- focusing,
- making observations,
- suggesting,
- closed questions, and
- facilitative questions and statements.

A review of the list of verbal techniques (see Table 6.2) may bring to mind visions of formal interviews or counseling sessions in which a recreational therapist helps a client to gain self-understanding. Recreational therapists conduct interviews and engage in leisure counseling, but these structures account for only one segment of the total delivery of their services. As with listening skills, these verbal techniques likely will be a part of day-to-day contacts with clients. Thus, although particularly helpful in facilitating client self-understanding during interviews and leisure counseling, the effective use of these verbal techniques has much wider application.

Two final comments are necessary before reviewing specific verbal techniques. First, another response that can be made is no response, or the *use of silence*. Brief periods of silence provide clients with a chance to consider what they said and to prepare to speak again. For clients who are not verbal, silence may also provoke anxiety on their part and cause them to become more verbal. When silence is used, the helper must be aware of his or her nonverbal communication to indicate interest in what the client has to say. Second, the verbal techniques presented do not constitute the universe of verbal responses that the recreational therapist can employ.

Table 6.2

Verbal Techniques

- **Minimal Verbal Responses** are verbal cues such as "mmmm," "yes," "I see," and "uh-huh." Their purpose is to indicate interest without disrupting the client's communication.
- **Paraphrasing** involves rephrasing the content of the client's message in slightly different words. It is used to assist the helper in understanding the client's statements and to provide support and clarification.
- **Checking Out** provides the helper with a chance to confirm or correct perceptions or understandings. It is used to clear up confusion about perceptions of the client's behavior or to try out a hunch.
- **Clarifying** facilitates understanding the basic nature of the client's statement. Its purpose is to help the client sort out conflicting and confused thoughts and feelings and to assist the helper to understand what is being communicated.
- **Probing** involves searching for additional information with such statements as "Tell me more" or "Let's talk about that." It is used to obtain more information.
- **Reflecting** is rephrasing the affective part of the client's message. Its purpose is to help the client to understand his or her feelings.
- **Interpreting** involves offering possible explanation for certain behaviors, thoughts, or feelings. Its purpose is to add new perspectives to the client's understanding of his or her behaviors, thoughts, or feelings.

Table 6.2 (cont.)

- **Confronting** challenges clients to examine discrepancies between their words and actions. Its purpose is to encourage honest self-examination.
- **Informing** transpires when objective and factual information is shared with the client. Its purpose is to convey information and not to advise the client.
- **Summarizing** pulls together and condenses the important elements of the session. It is used to avoid fragmentation and give direction. Often, it is employed as a means to draw a session to a close.
- **Self-disclosing** is sharing personal information with the client about the helper's experiences, attitudes, or feelings. Such information is disclosed when it appears it will help the client.
- **Focusing** assists clients in setting priorities in dealing with problems. It helps clients to determine which problems are most important.
- **Making observations** is verbalizing what is observed or perceived.
- **Suggesting** encourages clients to consider alternatives. It is not telling clients what to do.
- **Closed questions** are those that can be answered "yes" or "no" or with factual information. Because they do not encourage flow of information, they have very restricted use as verbal responses.
- **Facilitative questions and statements** are open-ended questions and broad openings. They encourage clients to express ideas and feelings.

Probing

A probe is a question that is directed toward yielding information to gain empathetic understanding. Probes are open-ended questions requiring more than a "yes" or "no" reply. Okun and Kantrowitz (2008) suggested probes such as "Tell me more," "Let's talk about that," and "I'm wondering about...." A brief example of a probe in a client–helper interaction follows:

Client: There are lots of things I like about hiking.
Helper: Tell me some of them.
Reflecting

The reflection response is a statement to reflect feelings received from the client through verbal or nonverbal means. Its aim is to mirror the *feelings or emotions* of the client so that they may be recognized and accepted. An example is, "It sounds as if you were really pleased to learn the outcome." An example of a client–helper exchange follows:

Client: I was mad as hell that they didn't ask me to join the team.
Helper: It seems you were feeling very angry about not being chosen.

Interpreting

Through interpretation, something is added to the statement of the client. The helper tries to help the client understand his or her underlying feelings. These responses are based on direct observation of what the client does and says, not on deep psychology. After the interpretation has been given, immediate feedback is sought from the client to see if the interpretation is correct. An example of a client–helper exchange follows:

Client: I just can't seem to get my act together to join the club.
             I tend to put it off even though I really want to do it.
Helper: You seem to be frightened to take the first step in joining.

Confronting

The purpose of the confronting response is to assist the client to achieve congruency in what he or she says and does or to help him or her be fully aware and honest in gaining self-understanding. Confrontation involves "telling it like it is," without being accusatory or judgmental. If the client does not seem to be genuine in his or her communications, this should be pointed out. Okun (2002) gave these examples: "I feel you really don't want to talk about this," "It seems to me that you're playing games with her," and "I'm wondering why you feel you always have to take the blame. What do you get out of it?" (p. 82). In raising discrepancies, the helper expresses contradictions in the client's comments or behavior. The following are examples of pointing out discrepancies: "You say you're angry, yet you're smiling" or "On the one hand, you seem to be hurt by not getting that job, but on the other hand you seem sort of relieved, too."

It has been suggested that confrontation should not be used until rapport has been fully established and a positive helping relationship has developed (Egan, 2009). Schulman (1991) mentioned that the wise helper limits confrontations to *strengths* instead of picking on the client's imperfections.

An example of a confronting verbal response follows:

Client: I don't want to be around any girls.
Helper: You say you don't want to associate with girls, yet I saw you dancing with
             both Sharron and Jen last night and you seemed to be having a very
             good time.

Informing

Informing transpires when objective and factual information is shared with the client. Informing is providing factual information to the client. Its purpose is to convey information only, not to advise the client. In recreational therapy this might be describing types of programs available to the client. Informing is *not* telling the client what to do. The following is an example of informing:

Client: I don't know what activity to get into.
Helper: Let me describe the choices you have here at the center.

Summarizing

Summarizing pulls together and condenses the important elements after a length of time. It is used to avoid fragmentation and give direction. It may be helpful to summarize at intervals during a session to pull together themes of what the client has said. Often, it is employed as a means to draw a session to a close. Summarizing brings together the client's central ideas, feelings, or both. The summary synthesizes what the client communicated so he or she can see significant patterns. It is normally applied at the conclusion of a counseling session or after several sessions. An example of a summarizing response follows:

Client: A lot of time I'd rather stay home and watch a game on TV,
             or read the paper or something like that. My wife always
             wants to go out and I don't think I should have to go just
             because she wants to.

> *Helper:*   You would prefer to stay home, while your wife wishes for
> you to go out with her.

Self-Disclosing

Self-disclosing allows personal disclosures on the part of the helper with the intent of providing the client with an opportunity to perceive the helper as another human being who has encountered situations, thoughts, or feelings similar to those the client has faced. Revealed may be personal experiences, thoughts, attitudes, or feelings. In so doing, the helper not only reveals his or her reactions but also creates trust and presents a model of how to reveal oneself to others (Corey, 2012). The use of limited self-disclosure has been suggested to be particularly effective during the beginning phase of the therapeutic relationship, at which time the client may seek information about the helper such as hometown, marital status, and years in his or her profession (Sundeen et al., 1998). An example of self-disclosure follows:

> *Client:*   This is my cat, Plato. I don't know what I would do without
> him. He is like a friend.
> *Helper:*   I love my cat, Sam, too. He greets me every evening when I
> get home and sleeps on the bottom of my bed at night.
> I guess he is like a friend to me also.

Focusing

By means of focusing, priorities are formed. The client is assisted in establishing the relative importance of his or her problems. Once it has been determined which problems are most important, the client has a place to begin in dealing with them.

> *Client:*   And the last thing, from the many I've discussed, is that I
> can't stand up for myself. I let other people walk all over me.
> *Helper:*   You've talked about a number of problems. These appear to include
> being dissatisfied with your school work, obesity, loneliness, and an inability
> to be assertive. Which one seems the most important, and which do
> you want to work on first?

Making Observations

Verbal statements are made on what the helper observes or perceives. These encourage the client to recognize specific behaviors and to compare perceptions with the helper.

> *Observation:* The helper notices the client's hands are drawn together,
> forming tight fists.
> *Helper:*   You seem tense.

Suggesting

Suggesting is a response the helper can use to encourage the client to consider a new idea as an alternative option to a situation. It is raising ideas for the client to ponder, not telling the client what to do. The client's decisions always rest with him or her, not the recreational therapist.

> *Helper:*   Have you considered joining the wheelchair basketball team
> as a means to get exercise?

Closed Questions

Closed-ended questions are those that may be answered "yes" or "no" or call for factual information. Their use is limited in therapeutic communication to occasions when asking for specific information is appropriate.

Helper: What is your hometown?
Client: I'm from Bloomington.

Facilitative Questions and Statements

Formative questions and statements provide open-ended questions or broad openings to encourage clients to discuss their thoughts, feelings, and experiences from their perspective. These are in contrast to closed-ended questions. Examples of facilitative questions and statements appear in Table 6.4.

To close this section, it should be mentioned that the verbal techniques presented here may seem to be similar in nature. They are actually distinctive types of responses among which the emerging helping professional should learn to discriminate. Once familiar with them, the helping professional will use them more naturally. Just as word processors differentiate among the keys on a keyboard without having to think about striking a particular letter, helping professionals learn to use the verbal responses without consciously defining the type of response before employing it.

It should also be reiterated that the verbal techniques outlined bring about an expanded understanding of self and others. Although these responses are often employed in formal interviewing and counseling sessions, they may also be appropriately applied in less structured interpersonal communications that typify recreational therapy. With the knowledge of these responses also comes the responsibility to resist temptation to become a pseudo psychotherapist. Appendix B, Verbal Response Identification Exercise, is a verbal technique exercise (see p. 283). Okun and Kantrowitz (2008) provided eight general guidelines for using the major verbal techniques. These are listed in Table 6.3.

Table 6.3

General Guidelines for Using Major Verbal Techniques

1. Phrase your response in the same vocabulary that the client uses.
2. Speak slowly enough that the client will understand each word.
3. Use concise rather than rambling statements.
4. Relate the topic introduced by the client to the identified cognitive theme that is of most importance.
5. Talk directly to the client, not about him or her.
6. Send "I" statements to "own" your feelings, and allow the client to reject, accept, or modify your messages.
7. Encourage the client to talk about his or her feelings.
8. Time your responses to facilitate, not block, communication.

Adapted from Okun, B. F. (2002). *Effective helping: Interviewing and counseling techniques* (6th ed.). Pacific Grove, CA: Brooks/Cole.

Table 6.4

Facilitative Questions and Statements

Type	Example
Observe—to notice what went on or what goes on.	"Tell me about yourself." "Tell me every detail from the beginning." "To what degree do you feel that way?"
Describe—to stimulate recall and details of a specific event or experience.	"What did you feel at the time?" "What happened just before?" "How did he respond to your comment?"
Analyze—to review that information for greater understanding.	"What is the importance of the event? "What do you see as the reason?" "What was your part in it?"
Formulate—to restate in a clear, direct way the relationship between thoughts, feelings, and experiences.	"Tell me again." "What would you say was the problem?" "Can you tell me the essence of it?
Test—to try out new thoughts, feelings, or behaviors.	"What would you do if a situation like that came up again?" "In what way will this understanding help you in the future?"

Adapted from Haber, J. (1997). Therapeutic communication. In J. Haber, B. Krainovich-Miller, A. L., McMahon & P. Price-Hoskins (Eds.), *Comprehensive psychiatric nursing* (5th ed.). (pp. 121-142). St. Louis, MO: Mosby.

Barriers to Therapeutic Communication

There are a number of barriers to therapeutic communication. Some are simply old habits that you need to break so they do not become roadblocks to therapeutic communication with clients. You may find yourself using other barriers when you are uncomfortable with issues the client raises. For instance, Creasia and Friberg (2010) explained that when clients bring up difficult subjects in an indirect way or hesitantly, the therapist may find it easy to avoid the subject by moving on to a more comfortable topic. Barriers to therapeutic communication are summarized in Table 6.5.

Communication in Success–Failure Situations

Recreational therapists spend a great deal of time interacting with clients while the clients take part in recreation activities. Therefore, it is important to explore communications between leaders and clients so that an understanding of effective feedback patterns can be gained. In the following section, feedback patterns and their effects are discussed.

Table 6.5

Barriers to Therapeutic Communication

Barriers	Nontherapeutic Examples
Giving advice	"If I were you...."
Giving false reassurance	"Don't worry—everything will OK."
Topic jumping (changing the subject)	"Let's wait on that and talk about . . ."
Interrupting	"Hold it, hold it!"
Being judgmental	"You're wrong."
Blaming	"It is all your fault."
Giving directions	"Just do what I say."
Excessive questioning	"What is the real reason?"
Challenging	"You can't really hear the devil speaking."
Expressing disapproval	"I don't approve of that." (or frowning)
Hurried approaches	"Will you please hurry up?"
Closed-mindedness	"That's the only way to see it."
Stereotyped responses	"Keep your chin up; it won't be responses much longer."
Double messages	"Tell me more." (While nonverbals show lack of interest.)
Defending or defensive responses	"Don't blame me; you're the one with problems."
Self-preoccupation or daydreaming	"Oh, excuse me; could you repeat that?" I didn't hear what you said."
Patronizing	"Now, Honey, it will work out."

Adapted from Antai-Otong, D. (2007). *Nurse-client communication: A life-span approach.* Boston: Jones and Bartlett Publishers (p. 59-60); Creasia, J. L., & Parker, B. (1996). *Conceptual foundations of professional nursing practice* (2nd ed.). St. Louis, MO: Mosby (p. 390); Haber, J. (1997). Therapeutic communication. In J. Haber, B. Krainovich-Miller, A.L. McMahon, & P. Price-Hoskins (Eds.), *Comprehensive psychiatric nursing* (5th ed.) (pp 136-140). St. Louis, MO: Mosby.

Feedback

Research strongly has suggested that recreational therapists need to develop both an awareness of the messages given to their clients during recreation participation and a working knowledge of the types of effective **feedback** that may be applied in leader–client communication. In a study completed at a camp for children with disabilities, Bullock, Austin, and Lewko (1980) examined the nature of feedback counselors provided to campers. Bullock et al. (1980) found that no feedback was supplied in more than 20% of the interactions where campers experienced success on a task. They pointed out the child may interpret lack of feedback as an indication of failure.

Furthermore, Bullock et al. (1980) commented that for feedback to be most useful in failure situations, it should be specifically related to the task at hand (i.e., contingent), should give the participant information to make corrections in performance (i.e., informational), and should give some amount of encouragement (i.e., motivational). In situations where the campers did not succeed, the researchers found that less than 50% of campers were furnished this type of feedback. In approximately 16% of the failure situations, no feedback was provided.

Attribution Theory

Bullock et al. (1980) considered the attributional nature of feedback. The theoretical basis for this portion of the study was Weiner's (1974) *attribution theory*, which theorizes that people formulate explanations for their own and others' successes and failures. Basically, these explanations involve two dimensions: stability (stable, unstable) and locus of control (internal, external). Four determinants of success or failure are also involved: ability (a stable internal factor), effort (an unstable internal factor), task difficulty (a stable external factor), and luck (an unstable external factor).

Therefore, a camp counselor might judge that a camper is successful because he or she has a high level of ability (a stable internal attribution), because he or she tries hard (an unstable internal attribution), because it is an easy task (a stable external attribution), or because of chance (an unstable external attribution). On the other hand, the counselor could stereotype the child with a disability and, therefore, reason that any failure is due to a low ability ascribed to the disability. This would result in the expectation that the child cannot succeed unless the task is made easier. If, instead, the failure is judged to be because of an unstable factor (low effort or bad luck), a more optimistic expectation will follow.

Guidelines for Feedback

Bullock et al. (1980) presented several explicit guidelines for providing feedback in leadership situations in recreational therapy:

- Feedback should be given in nearly all, if not all, performance situations.
- In successful outcomes, the feedback should be contingent, informational, and positive and/or motivational.
- Attributional statements should be made more frequently.
- Attributional information must be explicitly stated for the client to have a clear understanding.
- Success should be reinforced with internal stable attributional statements such as "Nice shot, I knew you could do it!"
- The child should be encouraged with unstable attributional statements following unsuccessful attempts, for example, "Bad luck. Try again." (pp. 147–148)

Findings by sports psychologists have confirmed the work of Bullock et al. (1980). Smith and Smoll's (1997) research was with youth coaches, but it appeared to generalize to recreational therapy. Their research revealed "that the most positive outcomes occurred when children played for coaches who engaged in high levels of positive reinforcement and technical instruction, and who emphasized the importance of fun and personal improvement over winning" (p. 17). Appendix C is an exercise on feedback (see p. 285).

Nonverbal Communication

Although communication usually involves verbal behavior, words represent only a small part of interpersonal communication patterns. The vast majority of communicating is done on a nonverbal level (Sundeen et al., 1998). One source stated that in face-to-face communication, only one third of communicating is verbal and two thirds is nonverbal (Brill & Levine, 2002). Furthermore, it has been found that people are more apt to believe nonverbal behavior than verbal behavior when contradiction exists between the two forms of communication (MTD Training, 2010a).

When the nonverbal and verbal messages match, they are congruent. Writing for nurses, Williams and Davis (2005) provided this illustration of the concept of congruence that applies to recreational therapists as well:

> For example, congruence is present when the nurse admits that he or she is frustrated or irritated rather than denying these feelings. If the nurse denies feelings, nonverbal responses such as muscle tension and facial expression will communicate the feeling to the client anyway and create confusion. Incongruence is present when the nurse denies anger but says it with clenched fists. Incongruence appears dishonest or "not ringing true." (p. 31)

Nonverbal communications are, of course, the messages that pass between a sender and a receiver that do not rely on the spoken word, such as tone of voice or body language. Touch, eye movements, and facial expressions are other examples of nonverbal communications (Berman & Snyder, 2012).

It has been specified that nonverbal communication is expressed continuously in human interactions. With or without accompanying verbal behavior, nonverbal communication is continuous in the presence of others because all nonverbal behavior has potential message value (Brill & Levine, 2002). Waltzlawick et al. (1967) wrote in their classic work, from this perspective:

> It follows that no matter how one may try, one must communicate. Activity or inactivity, words or silence all have message value: they influence others and these others, in turn, cannot *not* respond to these communications and are thus themselves communicating. (p. 49)

For example, even silence or inactivity in the company of others may carry a message that a person is sad, bored, or perhaps depressed. Nonverbal communication is always occurring, making it impossible not to communicate.

Nonverbal communication is obviously of great importance in interpersonal transactions. Recreational therapists must become aware of nonverbal communication to pick up nonverbal cues from clients and staff and be aware of possible effects of their own nonverbal communication on others.

Nonverbal communication is also important in recreational therapy because it can be particularly effective as an outlet for expressing feelings and attitudes that clients cannot express or do not wish to express verbally. Expressive recreation pursuits such as music, physical movement, and creative writing allow for the manifestation of feelings and attitudes through nonverbal means.

Specific Examples of Nonverbal Behaviors

Tubbs and Moss (2010) classified nonverbal behaviors into three categories: visual cues, vocal cues, and spatial and temporal cues.

Visual cues. Some visual cues to nonverbal communication have been mentioned as a part of the discussion on listening skills. Nevertheless, information on facial expressions, eye contact, body movement, and gestures is important and is repeated in the visual cues that follow.

Facial expression. A person's face expresses numerous feelings and emotions. A friendly smile invites further interaction. A frown may indicate sadness. Grimaces may be a sign of anger. Blushing often indicates embarrassment. An animated face may show excitement and vigor, and a "poker face" may project the image of a bland person.

Eye contact. It is reinforcing to receive eye contact. When someone does not look you in the eye, you may feel they are shifty or they are hiding something. Of course, you must be aware there are cultural differences in the use of eye contact and remain sensitive to these.

Body movements. A person's body is used to signal others in various ways. Biting your nails may indicate nervousness. Physical touch may be used to demonstrate caring and support. Fidgeting may distract from other messages.

Hand gestures. The peace sign and the hitchhiker's raised thumb are two gestures most people recognize. Most people would also recognize the drumming of fingers on a table as a sign of impatience. Hand gestures may substitute substantially for verbal behavior, as in the case of sign language for those who are hearing impaired.

Physical appearance and the use of objects. Rightly or wrongly, as documented by the classic social psychology study of Kelley (1950), first impressions have a potent effect. Therefore, it is important to realize that you may project a negative impression through extremes in clothing or jewelry. Equally important is that you guard against the pitfall of stereotyping that may result from generalizations made about clients after only brief contact.

The term *object language* is used to denote the message value in physical objects. How people dress, how they decorate their homes and offices, their choices of magazines, the car they drive, and many other physical objects communicate nonverbal messages about them. Bumper stickers and T-shirts are popular means today for passing along nonverbal messages. A bumper sticker stating "I'm a Leisure Lover" or a T-shirt reading "Let's park and recreate" brings certain connotations to mind.

Vocal cues. Earlier in this chapter, vocal cues such as tone of voice and volume and rate of speech were discussed. These and voice pitch and quality constitute vocal phenomena that accompany speech and are sometimes termed *paralinguistics.* Various vocal cues are briefly reviewed here.

An old adage:

It's not what you say, it's how you say it that counts

Volume. Speaking too loudly is likely to offend others. Speaking too softly also can be irritating. However, what is an appropriate level of volume to one group of people may not be for another group coming from a different cultural background. Therefore, it is best to test which volume works best in each situation.

Rate and fluency. Others may take a person's rate of speech as evidence of his or her mood. People often speak rapidly when they are excited and exhibit slower speech when depressed. When a person is speaking too rapidly or too slowly, tension may be revealed in the listener. Fluency has to do with the continuity of speech. Pausing frequently and inserting "ah" or "er" distracts from the central message.

Pitch. The unvarying use of one level of voice pitch can be monotonous. An expressive person will vary voice pitch to reflect attitude or mood naturally.

Quality. Voice quality deals with how pleasant a person perceives a voice to be. For example, a harsh, piercing voice may be distracting.

Temporal and spatial cues. To be effective in your interpersonal communications, you should be aware of the factors of time and space and the possible effects they have on communications.

Time. The concept of time varies from culture to culture. Americans generally are aware of time and may react when normal customs regarding time are violated. For instance, arriving late for a social invitation or a business appointment may offend those who are expecting you. This behavior may say to them that you do not hold them in high regard.

Space. Human communication may be affected significantly by the way people position themselves in relation to others. Height is one aspect to consider. If a professional stands and looks down on a client who is in a bed or a wheelchair, this may communicate to the client that the professional is an authority figure. Therefore, in such instances it is best to sit down to be at the client's level.

The scientific study of human spatial behavior is termed *proxemics*. Within the proxemics literature, four zones for interactions have been identified. These distances are (a) *intimate*—close or touching when interacting with those with whom you are in intimate relationships; (b) *personal*—ranging from 12 or 18 in. to 4 ft for informal interactions with those you know well (e.g., casual friends); (c) *social*—ranging from 4 to 12 ft for more formal business and social interactions; and (d) *public*—ranging from 12 to 25 ft for interactions with the public in general or in making presentations before a group (Purtilo et al., 2014; Williams & Davis, 2005). These zones are generally maintained in human interactions. For example, you may likely stand or sit close to someone with whom you are in an intimate relationship. On the other hand, you may normally attempt to maintain the personal distance or social distance with clients so as not to infringe on their sense of personal space.

To summarize this section, nonverbal communication processes clearly are extensive. In face-to-face communication with clients, you must take advantage of the cues available to use. Therefore, developing skills in interpreting nonverbal communication is essential. Several excellent exercises related to perceiving and giving nonverbal cues are available. The exercises in Appendix D, Nonverbal Cue Exercises (p. 285), are drawn and adapted from Cormier and Hackney (2005), Okun and Kantrowitz (2008), and Stevens (1988).

Cultural Diversity in Nonverbal Communication

It should be recognized that cultural differences play a significant role in nonverbal communication. Professionals need to continually learn about the conventions of clients who come from backgrounds that are different from their own.

Eye Contact

Euro-Americans tend to use direct eye contact. In some cultures, this is construed to be rude, or at least intrusive. Native Americans and Latinos, in particular, prefer less eye contact. African Americans have a tendency to have eye contact patterns that are the opposite of Euro-Americans. African Americans tend to gaze at the person to whom they are speaking and avoid direct eye contact when they are listening.

Body Language

Body language may vary greatly from one culture to another. For example, whereas Americans and people from many countries turn their heads from side to side to indicate "no," Russians tend to shake their heads up and down to signify "no."

Personal Space

Although Americans may stand close to someone with whom they are in an intimate relationship, normally they keep about an arm's length of space between them when interacting. Those of Arab ancestry may prefer a closer distance of 6 to 12 in. Still, persons from other cultures, such as Australian aborigines, tend to like much more distance than Americans (Williams & Davis, 2005).

Gender Differences and Communications Patterns

Empirical research has shown that communication patterns of women and men differ. Arnold and Boggs (2007) summarized studies related to the differences between women and men. For example, studies have shown women, compared to men, tend to touch and smile more often. They also maintain eye contact more and use more facial expressions than men. Compared to men, women are more constrained in their use of gestures. Finally, women tend to use vocal tones more than men to signify emotions such as surprise and cheerfulness.

Studies have found that men want larger interpersonal distances between them and others than do women. Although men maintain less eye contact than women, they tend to maintain it longer in negative encounters. Men have been found to be more prone to initiate interactions, talk more, talk louder, interrupt others, disagree more, employ hostile verbs, and talk more about issues than women. Finally, men are more likely than women to use conversations as a contest to gain status.

Communication With Clients With Specific Needs

Recreational therapists often need to communicate with individuals with specific needs. The guidelines that appear in Table 6.6 can prove helpful to communicate with clients who have visual impairments. Table 6.7 concerns clients with hearing impairments and those who speak a foreign language. Table 6.8 covers clients who are wheelchair users. Table 6.9 provides guidelines to communicate with clients in cross-cultural communications. Table 6.10 offers suggestions to communicate with children. Table 6.11 gives guidelines to communicate with persons with cognitive impairments. Table 6.12 focuses on clients with intellectual disabilities and other learning impairments. Table 6.13 gives attention to communication with older clients. Table 6.14 deals with clients with problems in mental health.

Table 6.6

Communication With Clients With Visual Impairments

- Speak directly to the person who is visually impaired, not through an intermediary.
- Do not shout or speak louder than necessary. Having a visual impairment does not imply hearing loss.
- Do not worry about using words such as *look* and *see*. Persons with visual impairments desire that you speak to them as you would to anyone.
- Acknowledge your presence in a room and tell the client who else is present if anyone is with you. Identify yourself by name.
- If you need to leave an area, let him or her know you are leaving.
- Assist with the initiation of social interactions with other participants.
- If the person uses a guide dog, do not touch or speak to the dog unless you first ask permission from the dog's owner.
- When you first meet someone who has a visual impairment, feel free to shake hands. If the other person has not extended his or her hand, say, "How do you do? Let me shake your hand." Of course, the process of aligning and making contact is up to you.
- Describe the environment, people, and events in the area to increase the client's understanding.
- Provide orientation to the area by helping the person to use all senses to become oriented. If the individual tends to rely on one sense more than others, the dominant sense should be emphasized.
- Use consistent language and terminology when orienting a client, as well as the reference system. Use compass directions, or identify boundaries (of the room, playground, etc.) by permanent landmarks.
- Prior to participation in an activity, encourage individuals to walk around the area with a guide so they become comfortable with the surroundings.
- Use tactile maps and signs to help persons to orient themselves to new surroundings.
- When offering assistance, do so directly, asking, "May I be of help?"
- When walking with a person who has blindness or low vision and needs assistance, ask how he or she wishes to be guided. One preferred method, known as *sighted guide*, is for the person to hold on to your elbow and walk to your side and slightly behind. Verbal cues can be used to avoid obstacles.
- Use clear, concise, and consistent directions. Use directional words such as *left* and *right*. Provide specific feedback for tasks to facilitate activities.
- Use tactile, hands-on demonstrations along with verbal instructions. The client should be near enough to see or touch when demonstrations are provided.
- Use verbal instructions to create mental images for persons with adventitious visual impairments.
- Use sighted peers or volunteers to provide individual attention to maximize participation.
- Glare and other lighting conditions may create difficulties for some clients with visual impairments. Consult with clients to determine the correct type and amount of lighting to provide because optimal conditions for vision vary from person to person.
- Never leave the client without a way to secure help by means of a signal of some kind.
- Never leave the client in an open area. Lead the client to the side of a room, to a chair, or to some landmark.

Table 6.6 (cont.)

- To assist a client to a chair, simply place his or her hand on the back or arm of the chair. Remember that a client with a visual impairment may not have the ability to use nonverbal cues to interpret messages.
- Use large print, audio-recorded information, or Braille.

Sources: Austin, D. R., & Lee, Y. (2013). *Inclusive & special recreation: Opportunities for persons from diverse populations to flourish.* Urbana, IL: Sagamore; Boggs, K. U. (2007). Communicating with clients experiencing communication deficits. In E. C. Arnold & K. U. Boggs (Eds.), *Interpersonal relationships: Professional communications skills for nurses* (5th ed.) (pp. 382-394). St. Louis: Saunders Elsevier; Hogan, M. A. (2008). *Nursing fundamentals.* Upper Saddle River, NJ: Pearson Education, Inc.; Kelley, J. (Ed.). (1981). *Recreation programming for visually impaired children and youth.* New York: American Foundation for the Blind; Maloff, C., & Wood, S. M. (1988). *Business and social etiquette with disabled people.* Springfield, IL: Charles C. Thomas Publishers. Murray, R. B., & Huelskoetter, M. M. W. (1991). *Psychiatric/mental health nursing* (3rd ed.). Norwalk, CT: Appleton & Lange; Taylor, C., Littis, C., & LeMone, P. (2008). *Fundamentals of nursing* (6th ed.). Philadelphia: J. B. Lippincott Company; Toseland, R. W., & Rivas, R. F. (2005). *An introduction to group work practice* (5th ed.). Boston: Pearson.

Table 6.7

Communication With Clients With Hearing Impairments and Those Who Have Limited Knowledge of English

---

Clients With Hearing Impairments

- Alert the client to your presence before starting a conversation. This may be done by gently touching him or her on the arm or shoulder or by moving so you can be seen.
- When using speech to communicate with a client who has hearing loss, always face him or her so you are in full view of the person in a clearly lighted area so the client can see your lips move.
- Speak distinctly but naturally. Speak moderately loudly, but do not shout. Do not exaggerate your speech or speak slowly. On the other hand, do not speak too rapidly.
- Do not let any object (e.g., hand, cigarette) cover your mouth. Men cause difficulty for the client if they wear big mustaches that obscure the lips.
- Look for cues (e.g., facial expression and inappropriate responses) that indicate the individual has misunderstood.
- When coming to the end of a sentence, do not drop your voice because the last two or three words can be important to understanding. Pause slightly at the end of a sentence to allow the client to comprehend the message.
- When conveying a lengthy message, get intermediate feedback along the way to make sure you are communicating.
- If someone is having difficulty understanding you, do not simply repeat what you have said but substitute synonyms.
- If the person has an unaffected ear, stand or sit on that side of the individual when you speak.
- Always have a writing pad available. If you are having a difficult time communicating, write key words on the pad of paper. Of course, you do not have to restrict yourself to words. A map, picture, or diagram may be a better idea.
- Any written instructions should be short, using clear and simple sentences.

Table 6.7 (cont.)

- Use text messaging on client's cell phones or e-mail at his or her computer.
- Present games and activities with straightforward rules and instructions. Avoid verbal cues during the activity. No new rules should be added before the activity.
- Learn basic signs (e.g., good, okay, better, start, line up, stop, thank you) and use them in activities.
- Demonstrations are the most effective way to help persons with hearing impairments to develop or improve skills.
- Consider building a "buddy system" to help clients with hearing impairments understand instructions and know when a phase of an activity is complete.
- Supply a visual schedule to clients with hearing impairments; it will help them predict what is coming and to prepare for it.
- Have an interpreter with sign language skills available for large group presentations.

Clients Who Have Limited Knowledge of English
- Use an interpreter if one is available.
- Avoid slang terms, medical terms, and abbreviations.
- Speak slowly in a respectful manner.
- Use a dictionary that translates foreign words so you can speak a few words in the client's language.
- Use a normal tone of voice (do not speak loudly).
- Demonstrate or pantomime ideas you wish to convey, as appropriate.
- Use pictures or environmental cues to communicate.
- Be aware of nonverbal communication. Many nonverbal cues are universal.
- Validate the client's understandings of what is being communicated, but do not assume the client's smiling and nodding mean he or she understands, as the client may be attempting to please you.

Sources: Arnold, E. C., & Boggs, K. U. (2007). *Interpersonal relationships* (5th ed.). St. Louis: Saunders Elsevier; Austin, D. R., & Lee, Y. (In press). *Inclusive & special recreation: Opportunities for persons from diverse populations to flourish.* Urbana, IL: Sagamore Publishing; Boggs, K. U. (2007). Communicating with clients experiencing communication deficits. In E. C. Arnold & K. U. Boggs (Eds.), *Interpersonal relationships: Professional communications skills for nurses* (5th ed.) (pp. 382-394). St. Louis: Saunders Elsevier; Berman, A., & Snyder, S. (2012). *Fundamentals of Nursing* (9th ed.). Upper Saddle River, NJ: Pearson.) Hogan, M. A. (2008). *Nursing fundamentals.* Upper Saddle River, NJ: Pearson Education, Inc.; Kelley, J. (Ed.). (1981). *Recreation programming for visually impaired children and youth.* New York: American Foundation for the Blind; Maloff, C., & Wood, S. M. (1988). *Business and social etiquette with disabled people.* Springfield, IL: Charles C. Thomas Publishers. Murray, R. B., & Huelskoetter, M. M. W. (1991). *Psychiatric/mental health nursing* (3rd ed.). Norwalk, CT: Appleton & Lange; Taylor, C., Littis, C., & LeMone, P. (2008). *Fundamentals of nursing* (6th ed.). Philadelphia: J. B. Lippincott Company; Toseland, R. W., & Rivas, R. F. (2005). *An introduction to group work practice* (5th ed.). Boston: Pearson.

Table 6.8

Communication With Clients Who Use Wheelchairs

- If a conversation lasts more than a few minutes, conduct your conversation at eye level with the person who uses a wheelchair. Make an effort to position yourself so that it will not be uncomfortable for him or her to look at you. This often means simply sitting in a chair beside the person in a wheelchair.
- Offer assistance, but do not insist. Ask whether help is wanted before beginning to assist the person. This includes pushing the person in the chair. Realize that many individuals who use wheelchairs are independent.

- Do not hang or lean on a person's wheelchair because it is part of the wheelchair user's personal body space.

Source: Austin, D. R., & Lee, Y. (2013). *Inclusive & special recreation: Opportunities for persons from diverse populations to flourish*. Urbana, IL: Sagamore.

Table 6.9

Cross-Cultural Communication

- Do not assume all cultures are similar to yours.
- Be aware of your personal cultural beliefs and biases (ethnocentric values/beliefs).
- Be open to learning about the communication styles of those from other cultures.
- Practice cross-cultural communication.
- Listen actively during cross-cultural communications.
- Respect others' decisions to engage in communications with you.
- Become aware of speech patterns of cultural groups you serve.
- Become aware of nonverbal communication expressed by those from other cultures.
- When needed, clarify messages.
- Do not assume communication breakdowns are due to others' errors.
- Be aware communication occurs in context.

Note. Adapted from Williams, C. L., & Davis, C. M. (2005). *Therapeutic interaction in nursing* (p. 56). Boston, MA: Jones and Bartlett.

Table 6.10

Communication With Children

- Do not "get in the middle" of a child and a parent, especially in front of the child.
- Know the child's developmental level.
- Become familiar with the child's interests by observing him or her.
- Talk at the child's level with vocabulary he or she will understand.
- "Level the playing field" by sharing your thoughts or observations about what is happening to the child.
- Take an approach that is calm, unhurried, caring, and gentle.
- Employ concrete examples or link information to activities of daily living versus abstractions.
- Allow the child to express his or her opinions.
- Be an active listener.

Note. Adapted from Williams, C. L., & Davis, C. M. (2005). *Therapeutic interaction in nursing* (p. 70). Boston, MA: Jones and Bartlett.

Table 6.11

Communication With Persons With Cognitive Impairments

- Simplify your message (as aphasia limits the ability to understand complex messages).
- Use common words and short sentences.
- Accept what the client says (even though clients may confuse the date or use one word when meaning another, so you are supportive and not always correcting the client).
- Allow the client extra time (due to slowed comprehension due to cognitive impairment).
- If a client does not respond, try repeating the message in different words and gestures.
- Break down tasks into simple steps, giving instructions one step at a time.
- Avoid the use of pronouns and repeat names to provide a clear message.
- Use an approach that is calming with a soothing tone and unhurried speech.
- Should the client become frustrated, try another approach at a later time.
- Strive to maintain a warm and supportive relationship.

Note. Adapted from Williams, C. L., & Davis, C. M. (2005). *Therapeutic interaction in nursing* (p. 79). Boston, MA: Jones and Bartlett.

Table 6.12

Communication With Clients With Intellectual Disabilities and Other Learning Impairments

---

- The wide range of behaviors and functional abilities of people with learning impairments necessitates careful consideration of each client's abilities. Assumptions about the individual based on a categorical designation should be avoided.
- Use verbal instructions that are clear and easy to understand.
- With individuals who have learning disabilities, reduce extraneous stimuli and limit the quantity of materials, directions, and verbal suggestions.
- Break tasks into small and simple steps for ease of communication.
- Praise clients when they do well.
- When possible, provide a demonstration so clients with learning impairments see the task to be performed.
- Avoid "multistep" commands when giving directions.
- Consider using colors or shapes in place of numbers or written words.
- Structure activities to provide positive feedback, especially when teaching social skills.
- For clients with learning disabilities, establish a positive working relationship with parents, teachers, and health care personnel. Through regular communications, gain and share information about the client's strengths, interests, and social relationships.

Source: Austin, D. R., & Lee, Y. (2013). *Inclusive & special recreation: Opportunities for persons from diverse populations to flourish.* Urbana, IL: Sagamore.

Table 6.13

Communication With Older Clients

- Do not use condescending language when working with older clients. Never treat an elderly client like a child no matter what kind of impairments he or she may have.
- Opportunities to socialize with age cohorts are important; flexible programs in a relaxed atmosphere should facilitate communications.
- Clients who are older are capable of learning new information and skills. Communicate with them on the same level you would with any adult learners.
- Be sensitive to life changes that affect older adults' ability to cope, such as hearing loss, memory problems, grief, and loss.
- To the extent that is possible, support diminished vision and hearing with appropriate lighting and acoustical design features.
- In general, visual, hearing, or motor impairments may accompany the aging process; therefore, be prepared to integrate tips and techniques related to these impairments as needed.

Source: Austin, D. R., & Lee, Y. (2013). *Inclusive & special recreation: Opportunities for persons from diverse populations to flourish.* Urbana, IL: Sagamore.

Table 6.14

Communication With Clients With Problems in Mental Health

- No single technique of behavior management has been found to be effective with all clients receiving mental health care. Regardless of the technique used, consistency and empathy are essential. Be specific and firm about expected behaviors and express expectations in a clear and calm manner. Refrain from expressing negative emotions. If it becomes necessary to express displeasure, do so calmly and clarify that the *behavior* (not the person) is the concern.
- Be respectful to the client. When someone feels respected and heard, they are more likely to return respect and consider what you have to say.
- Do not assume that clients are not smart and will believe anything you tell them. You should not assume that someone with problems in mental health has reduced intellectual functioning.
- Listen to the client and try to understand what he or she is communicating. Often, if you do not turn off your communication skills, you will be able to understand.
- Set, define, and post positively worded rules and expectations that are age appropriate.
- Consistently acknowledge and reward appropriate behaviors.

Source: Austin, D. R., & Lee, Y. (2013). *Inclusive & special recreation: Opportunities for persons from diverse populations to flourish.* Urbana, IL: Sagamore.

Interviewing: A Form of Communication

The interview is a structured, face-to-face method of communication directed toward a particular end. Intents for interviews in recreational therapy will vary, but probably the most common type is the initial assessment interview discussed in Chapter 4. Recreational therapists may additionally conduct interviews with clients' families and friends, during new client orientation programs, during leisure counseling, and for other purposes.

The Setting

Ideally, the interview setting should offer a quiet, relaxed atmosphere where privacy is assured. Too often, it seems recreational therapists are expected to conduct interviews on busy admissions wards or in active recreation areas. Do not trap yourself, or the client, into approaching the interview too casually because it concerns "only recreation." There is a great deal of difference between being relaxed and being careless in your approach.

Interviews can be structured to be formal or informal. Formal interviews are often conducted in an office or in a special room designed for interviewing. An informally structured interview might be conducted in a recreation area. In fact, some clients (and interviewers) feel most comfortable in an informal recreation setting. If this is the case, interviews might be conducted while shooting baskets in a gym, playing a table game, or having a soft drink in a quiet area of a snack bar. Psychological privacy, or feeling that you have a place to yourself, is perhaps as important as the actual physical setting that is chosen.

Whatever the area selected to conduct the interview, it should be free from interruptions. There is nothing more distracting than to have clients called away to take medication, see the social worker, or participate in a seemingly "more important" activity. Protect yourself by scheduling your interviews at times when competition for the client's time is at a minimum, and clearly inform other personnel of the need for an uninterrupted interview.

Phases

Most authorities agree that interviews have three phases: the beginning phase, the working phase, and the termination phase.

Beginning phase. In any interview, the first step is to help the client feel as comfortable as possible (Bernstein & Bernstein, 1985). Strive to create an atmosphere displaying openness, warmth, and respect for the client.

How the client should be greeted varies from interview to interview and person to person. It would be inappropriate to approach a small child with a strong handshake or to provide a depressed individual with a vigorous welcome (Schulman, 1991). It has been suggested that a good beginning may be simply welcoming the client with a smile, introducing yourself, and inviting the person to sit down. Early in the initial interview, you may indicate the length of time available for the session, your role, and the purpose of the interview. You may wish to inform the interviewee how you prefer to be addressed and also inquire as to how he or she would like to be addressed. Finally, you may want to talk with new clients about the confidentiality of the situation. Will the information be shared with anyone? If you are taking notes or audio recording, who will have access to these? Depending on your agency and situation, particular questions on confidentiality may or may not be important. You will have to determine which specific confidentiality issues are seen as important at your agency or institution (Cormier & Hackney, 2005).

Working phase. During this stage, both you and the client have settled into comfortable positions and are ready to begin work. At this time, you direct the interview toward the primary goal for the session. This might involve any number of general objectives, such as gaining information regarding a client's leisure interests or allowing the client to express how he or she would expect to profit from recreational therapy programming.

Termination phase. Toward the conclusion of the session, indicate that it is almost time to stop. This may be done with a short, clear statement ("It seems our time is almost up for today"); summarization; or mutual feedback. By briefly summarizing the information and/or feelings expressed, you and the client leave the interview with similar ideas about what has been communicated. Mutual feedback involves both the client and the helper. This termination strategy is recommended if a plan has been formed or specific decisions made. Both participants can clarify and verify what has been decided and what future steps to take (Cormier & Hackney, 2005). Of course, it is appropriate to use the last few seconds of the session to make arrangements for the time and place of the next session if additional interviews are necessary.

In Appendix E on page 287, you will find an interview exercise. Table 6.15 offers tips for conducting a productive interview.

Table 6.15

Techniques for the Productive Interview

- Establish rapport. Create a warm, accepting climate.
- Control the external environment. Minimize external distractions in a comfortable environment that offers privacy.
- Wear clothing that conveys the image of a professional and is appropriate for the situation. In some cases, clients will respond more readily to casual dress. With other clients, professional dress may inspire feelings of confidentiality.
- Begin by stating and validating with the client the purpose of the interview. You may begin with social conversation but should move relatively quickly into the purpose of the interview.
- Use a vocabulary on the level of awareness or understanding of the person. Avoid jargon and abstract words.
- Avoid preconceived ideas, prejudices, or biases. Do not impose your values on clients.
- Be precise in what you say, so the meaning is understood. Say as little as possible to keep the interview moving. Careful timing of your communications and allowing time for the client to understand and respond are important.
- Avoid asking questions in ways that get only socially acceptable answers. Otherwise, clients may tell you what they think you want to hear.
- Be gentle and tactful when asking questions about home life or personal matters. Things you may consider common information may be seen as being very private by some clients. You may inquire tactfully by asking indirect and peripheral questions.
- Be an attentive listener. Show interest by using attending behaviors such as eye contact, posture, gestures, and minimal verbal response.
- Carefully observe nonverbal messages for signs of anxiety, frustration, anger, loneliness, or guilt. Encourage the free expression of feelings and look for feelings of pressure hidden under attempts to be calm. Allow ventilation of feelings.
- Encourage spontaneity. Provide movement in the interview by picking up verbal leads, cues, bits of seemingly unrelated information, and nonverbal signals from the client.
- Ask questions beginning with "What..." "Where...?" "Who...?" and "When...?" to gain factual information. Words connoting moral judgments should be avoided because they are not conducive to feelings of acceptance and freedom of expression.

Table 6.15 (cont.)

- Keep data obtained in the interview confidential and share this information only with the appropriate and necessary health team members. The client should be told what information will be shared and with whom.
- Evaluate the interview. Was the purpose accomplished?

Source: Murray, R. B., & Huelskoetter, M. M. W. 1991. *Psychiatric/mental health nursing* (3rd ed.). Norwalk, CT: Appleton & Lange; pp.139-145.

Chapter Summary

Success in helping relationships depends to a large degree on the ability of the recreational therapist to communicate effectively with clients. The interpersonal communication skills employed in client transactions are basically the same skills used in everyday encounters. In social relationships, however, they may be casually employed. In contrast, in professional helping relationships, where the primary focus is always on the client, the communications are consciously directed toward meeting client needs.

Reading Comprehension Questions

1. Define the term *communication* in your own words.
2. Why are communication skills important to recreational therapists?
3. Is professional jargon appropriate in client communications?
4. What are some guidelines to avoid rambling communication?
5. How may attitudes enter into interpersonal communication?
6. How may voice tone and volume affect communication?
7. What things may cause the receiver to distort a message?
8. Explain why listening may be termed an active process.
9. What behaviors let the client know you are attending to what he or she is saying?
10. Explain the four major listening skills discussed in the chapter.
11. What does the acronym SOLER stand for?
12. Briefly explain each of the verbal responses or techniques outlined in the chapter.
13. Briefly explain each of the barriers to therapeutic communication.
14. Do you understand the rationale behind each of the guidelines for feedback?
15. How much of your face-to-face communication is transmitted through nonverbal means?
16. What is the importance of studying nonverbal communication?
17. Why might it be said that one cannot "not" communicate?
18. Give specific examples of nonverbal cues.
19. What does an "I'm a Leisure Lover" bumper sticker have to do with nonverbal communication?
20. Are there differences between women and men in their communication patterns? If so, what are examples?
21. What are guidelines for communicating with clients who are visually impaired? Hearing impaired?
22. What are guidelines for communicating with clients who are wheelchair users?
23. What are guidelines for communicating with clients who speak a foreign language?

24. What are guidelines to apply in cross-cultural communications?
25. What are guidelines to use when communicating with children?
26. What are guidelines to use when communicating with persons with cognitive impairments?
27. What are guidelines for communicating with older persons?
28. What are guidelines for communicating with persons experiencing problems in mental health?
29. Can you make any suggestions as to the setting for interviews?
30. What may be stipulated as the initial step in any interview?
31. Outline the phases of an interview.
32. List techniques for conducting a productive interview.

Appendix A

Listening Exercises

Attending Exercises

Eye contact, posture, gestures, and verbal behavior can have a powerful reinforcing effect on clients' communication. Although attending seems like a simple process to grasp and an easy thing to do, lack of attending in interpersonal relations is common (Egan, 2009).

One simple attending exercise you might try is nonresponsive. Get a partner and decide who will be A and who will be B. For 2 or 3 min, A should talk about any topic of his or her choice. B should not attend to A (e.g., avoid eye contact, look around the room). Discuss how this felt. Did A feel frustrated? What sort of attending behaviors would A have appreciated receiving? Did B wish he or she could have responded? How? When?

Now switch roles. A should assume the B role, and vice versa. At first, B should not attend to A as this person talks about something he or she likes very much. But after 2 min, B should try out his or her best attending skills. For the next 2 or 3 min, B should use eye contact, gestures, posture, and verbal responses to encourage A to talk. Stop after a total of 4 or 5 min and discuss the differences between minimal and appropriate attending behaviors.

Egan (2009) suggested an exercise that involves four persons. In this group of four, decide who is A, B, C, and D. A and B should spend 5 or 6 min discussing what they like or do not like about their styles of interpersonal communication. C and D should act as observers, with particular attention paid to nonverbal behavior, voice tone, pitch, volume, pacing, and so on (sometimes referred to as paralinguistic behavior). C and D should give feedback to A and B regarding their observations. Then the roles should be exchanged and the exercise repeated.

Paraphrasing Exercises

The following are client statements. Practice restating these by writing your restatement either in the space that follows each or on a separate piece of paper.

Client: I really have an awful time with trying to remember everyone's names.
Response:
Client: Probably the worst thing I have to do is see Dr. Smith.
Response:

Then, with a partner, practice using paraphrasing while a third person observes. After you have used this technique for 3 or 4 min, the observer should report his or her observations, and these should be discussed among the three of you. Following this discussion, you may wish to change roles and repeat the exercise.

In completing the exercise, keep in mind that trite phrases prefacing your remarks, such as "I hear you saying…," should generally be avoided (Brammer & MacDonald, 2002). Researchers have warned also that the overuse of paraphrasing can lead to a "parrotlike" effect (Cormier & Hackney, 2005), so attempt to interfuse other types of responses with the paraphrase. For instance, you may try some of the attending techniques.

Clarifying Exercise

College students have been exposed many times to clarifying in their classes when other students attempted to clarify what instructors said. Within a small group of students, discuss occasions when you or other students have sought clarification in class. Do you remember any particularly well-stated clarification responses? Have any sounded like criticisms of the instructor instead of requests for clarification? For example, a student seeking clarification may sound critical by saying, "I haven't understood one word you've said all day. What in the world are you talking about?"

Listening Exercise

To listen effectively, the four major types of responses must become a natural part of your behavior repertoire. Again, with a partner, try out perception checking, clarifying, paraphrasing, and attending listening skills. Discuss the importance of developing effective listening skills (or any other topic of your choice) while being observed by a third person. After 5 min, this person should present feedback to you and your partner on the use of listening skills. The observer may wish to jot down behaviors to aid the discussion.

Appendix B

Verbal Response Identification Exercise

Verbal Technique Exercise

Okun and Kantrowitz (2008) presented an exercise on identification and recognition of 10 major verbal techniques. This exercise is adapted from that of Okun and Kantrowitz. Each of the helper statements uses one of the 10 responses. Read the helper's response, and then identify it as one of the following: minimal verbal response, paraphrasing, checking out, clarifying, probing, reflecting, interpreting, confronting, informing, or summarizing. Record the responses you identify on a piece of paper. Then check them with the answers provided.

(1)
Client: I really felt good about being at the dance last night.
Helper: You were glad to be there.
(2)
Client: I don't even want to think about the swim team, let alone join it.
Helper: I saw you at the pool yesterday and you are an excellent swimmer, yet you always back off when the swim team is mentioned.

(3)
Client: I used to be really involved but during the last term I haven't done anything for recreation. I guess I've been too busy… but that's not it either… I just don't know exactly why I've gotten into this rut.

Helper: You have been active in recreation in the past but you have been inactive for the last few months, and you are unsure as to the cause for this.

(4)
Client: I can't really get with it.
Helper: I see.

(5)
Client: I really like being in a group.
Helper: Let's talk about that.

(6)
Client: Which program is the best for me?
Helper: I would advise you to look at three of the programs offered here at the center. Let me tell you about them.

(7)
Client: As I've said before, I just don't like it.
Helper: I want to check out with you what I'm hearing. You said that you really didn't enjoy it.

(8)
Client: At any rate, I just can't do it because it's too far away, and in addition, they aren't interested in helping me anyway.
Helper: I'm not sure I follow you. Could you tell me some more about it?

(9)
Client: I just don't know what to do. One time he tells me do this. The next time he says just the opposite.
Helper: He seems to confuse you.

(10)
Client: All they care about is themselves and not what happens to me.
Helper: It is tough when you don't feel people care about you.

Answers
(1)   Reflecting
(2)   Confronting
(3)   Summarizing
(4)   Minimal verbal response
(5)   Probing
(6)   Informing
(7)   Checking out
(8)   Clarifying

(9)   Paraphrasing
(10)   Interpreting

Now you may wish to get together with others who have independently completed the exercise to discuss the responses. Did all of you agree with the above answers? Did members of the group feel any of the helper's responses were inappropriate or poorly phrased? If you have time, half of the group should rewrite the helper's statements 1 to 5; the other half should rewrite 6 to 10. Share your statements and discuss which were most difficult to write.

Appendix C

Feedback Exercise

Feedback Exercise

This exercise involves three people. A should take the role of the leader and B the role of the client. The third person should serve as an observer. A and B should complete a 3- to 5-min role-play in which the client is learning or performing a task. This might include making a leather belt or taking part in archery. As B takes part in the activity, A should attempt to offer helpful feedback. The observer should review the guidelines for feedback stated in the chapter. He or she should then take notes regarding the feedback of A. At the conclusion of the role-play, all three members of the group should discuss these observations. If time is available, change roles and repeat the exercise.

Appendix D

Nonverbal Cue Exercises

Portraying Feelings

This exercise is done with a partner. A is the speaker and B assumes the role of the respondent. The idea of the exercise is to portray feelings exclusively through nonverbal means. A selects a feeling from the following list without identifying it to B. A then portrays it, and B should attempt to identify the feeling. After a feeling has been identified, another feeling should be chosen and the process repeated. A and B reverse roles so that B may portray the feelings. Choose feelings from the following:

- Contented or happy
- Puzzled and confused
- Angry
- Discouraged

Magazine Pictures

From magazines, cut out pictures of people, but leave out any captions. First, ask a partner what he or she believes to be the message in each picture. Then ask for the responses in a group of four to six people. After you have looked at several pictures, see whether your group can identify common patterns for the group members' identification of feelings expressed in the pictures. The exercise is designed to examine different responses to the same nonverbal stimuli. Was there agreement on rationale behind the identifications? Was there disagreement? If so, what was the basis for it? Can you explain the diversity in perceptions?

Identifying Feelings

This is similar to the portraying feelings exercise, but involves three or more people. In this exercise, A identifies a specific feeling or emotion and informs an observer of what it is. A then attempts to communicate the feeling or emotion nonverbally to a partner or to members of a small group. When it has been identified, another person should take the place of A, and the exercise should continue until all in the group who wish to participate have had an opportunity. When you finish, process your experience to determine reasons for agreements and disagreements in identifications.

Self-Analysis

Self-awareness is the purpose of this exercise, which asks you to list nonverbal behaviors used with each of the four major emotions: anger, fear, happiness, and sadness. For example, list what nonverbal behaviors you engage in when angry (such as frowning or clenching your fist). After recording these behaviors for each emotion, share your list in a small group, noting similarities and differences. As an alternative, you may share your list with a close friend. See whether the friend agrees with how you express yourself in the ways you have listed. If your friend disagrees, what is the basis for this?

Nonverbal Canceling

The object of this exercise is to become aware of possible nonverbal messages you or others provide. A should purposefully cancel out everything stated to B with an accompanying nonverbal cue. Whatever the spoken message, cancel it out with an opposite gesture, facial expression, body movement, eye contact, or any other nonverbal means of communication. A and B should switch the sender–receiver roles back and forth for 5 min. At the end of this time, each should sit quietly and reflect on the exercise before processing on it. Begin the processing by telling each other what you experienced during the exercise. How did you feel when canceling verbal messages? Did you recognize any of the canceling behaviors from previous personal experience? As an alternative, you might complete this exercise in a small group, allowing all members to take the sender and receiver roles.

Shoulder Massage

This is a group exercise in which a circle is formed by standing behind someone to whom you would like to give something. Once you are in a circle, you should face clockwise, sit down, and silently begin to massage or rub the shoulders, neck, and back of the person in front of you. Everyone should close his or her eyes and refrain from speaking. The only communication is with your hands. After several minutes, you may make noises (but do not use formal language) to let the person giving the massage know how it feels. Your noises should tell the person behind you what kind of things you like best. After 5 min, silently turn around in the other direction and give the massage to the person who has been massaging you. Again, communicate with noises to inform the person what feels good to you. Do this for 3 to 5 min more. Before beginning, the group leader should tell those in the group that the exercise may make them slightly uncomfortable and, if this happens, not to laugh and talk but to follow the directions. After you have finished, share your ideas on the experience with the person in front of you and the person behind you. How did you communicate? Was this nonverbal expression natural? Did you feel uncomfortable in touching others of the opposite sex or others of the same sex?

Appendix E

Interview Exercise

Cormier and Hackney (2005) outlined an exercise that involves videotaping two persons in an interview situation. The exercise that follows has been based on that of Cormier and Hackney.

In this exercise, A is the interviewer and B is the client. Their communications are videotaped for 4 or 5 min. During this time, A should try to accomplish the following:

1. welcome B appropriately,
2. set B at ease (less bodily tension, voice not tense),
3. project being at ease (relaxed, open posture),
4. use reinforcing attending behaviors (e.g., eye contact, gestures),
5. get B to start talking about anything, and
6. get B to identify a current concern or problem in regard to his or her leisure.

After this, A and B should reverse roles and repeat the exercise. Again, this segment should be videotaped. Once all parts have been videotaped, the tapes should be replayed and critiqued for strengths and weaknesses displayed in the interviewers' skills.

Chapter 7

Being a Leader

Chapter Purpose

Leadership is vital in recreational therapy. Even so, leadership has remained a relatively neglected area in literature of the profession. Few researchers have carefully examined the dynamics of leadership processes in recreational therapy, and professionals in the field have not written extensively of their own leadership experiences.

Nevertheless, all would probably agree that there is no substitute for effective leadership. In fact, many recreational therapists would propose that the effectiveness of the leader is the single most important factor affecting therapeutic outcomes with clients.

Happily, a great deal of research and literature on leadership is available from other disciplines (e.g., psychology) from which recreational therapists can borrow and apply. Thus, empirical evidence is available as a basis for leadership. This chapter will help you to develop a general understanding of leadership and to gain exposure to specific information applicable to leadership in recreational therapy.

Key Terms

- Expert power
- Legitimate power
- Coercive power
- Connection power
- Democratic leadership
- Overjustification effect
- Director
- Stimulator
- Advisor
- Enabler
- Social-emotive functions
- Self-disclosure
- Modeling
- Coleadership
- Termination
- Group processing

- Referent power
- Reward power
- Information power
- Autocratic leadership
- Laissez-faire leadership
- Controller
- Instigator
- Educator
- Observer
- Task functions
- Nonfunctional behavior
- Transference
- Countertransference
- Recreational therapy group phases
- Debriefing

◼ Objectives

- Define leadership in recreational therapy.
- Understand power and influence in leadership.
- Comprehend major leadership styles.
- Recognize factors influencing choice of leadership style.
- Identify possible leadership roles.
- Know ways to deal with dependency.
- Evaluate principles listed for the recreational therapy leader.
- Explain the function of the group leader.
- Distinguish between various group structures used in recreational therapy.
- Know advantages of recreational therapy groups.
- Know considerations in selecting activities for groups.
- Show awareness of what constitutes a sense of "groupness."
- Interpret stages of group development.
- Know elements in conducting evaluations.
- Distinguish between functional and nonfunctional behaviors in groups.
- Identify roles group members take.
- Recognize special leader concerns and strategies in group leadership.
- Understand how group climate is affected by environmental and emotional factors.
- Know concepts related to group processing.
- Know techniques for group processing.
- Interpret principles for group leadership.

Basic Leadership Components

In their book titled *ABC of Clinical Leadership,* Swanwick and McKimm (2011) stated, "Leadership is a process of *influence* to the attainment of some sort of goal" (p. 8). Effective leadership in recreational therapy then involves the ability to influence the activities of clients toward accomplishing sought outcomes. Therefore, at a specific level, a leader's effectiveness may be primarily measured by how well clients achieve specific objectives. More generally, the recreational therapist's success as a leader may be evaluated by his or her ability to facilitate the movement of clients toward achievement of optimal levels of health and well-being.

Basis for Leadership Power and Influence

The term *power* may carry with it negative connotations. For example, power may be abused to obtain personal gain. Such misuse of power is certainly negative, but power can be used positively as well (Kelly, 2009). For instance, recreational therapists can use positive power to help clients.

Bishop (2009) proclaimed, "Leadership without power is of little use in any environment..." (p. 14). It is advantageous for the recreational therapist to understand the basis for the leader's power. Various types of power have been proposed from classic studies by French and Raven (1959) and elaborated on by Toseland and Rivas (2005), including *legitimate power* (gained by being designated by those in control who bestow the right of the leader to be influential), *connection power* (gained from being able to call on influential people or resources), *information power* (gained by possessing information valuable to others), *reward power* (gained by being viewed as having the ability to give rewards), *coercive power* (gained by being perceived as being able to levy punishment), *expert power* (gained by being viewed as having knowledge or expertise), and *referent power* (gained by the identification or closeness others feel for the leader).

Recreational therapists are likely to have legitimate power because they are designated for leadership by those in authority. Recreational therapists are also likely to have connection power attributed to them because they have access to doctors, nurses, therapists, and others of influence. Clients may perceive recreational therapists to have information power due to the access staff have to health care information and to decisions about individual clients. Because of their positions of authority, recreational therapists will likely have reward and coercive power bestowed on them by clients. Depending on the particular situation, recreational therapists may also be attributed with expert power because they may have a high degree of skill or knowledge in a certain activity or in group leadership. Leaders who develop rapport with clients obtain referent power (See Table 7.1, Sources and Examples of Power for Recreational Therapists).

Research has shown that the development of referent power is particularly important for therapists. Nicholi (1988) concluded from the results of several studies that

> the therapist's ability to convey an intrinsic interest in the patient has been found to be more important than his [or her] position, appearance, reputation, clinical experience, training, and technical or theoretical knowledge.... Close, detailed attention must therefore be given to how, within the confines of a professional relationship and without patronizing or condescending, the therapist conveys genuine interest in the patient. (p. 8)

Recreational therapists are typically advantaged because clients tend to grow close to their recreational therapists (Austin, 2011a). First, recreational therapists do things *with* clients not *to* them (e.g., examining them or giving them injections as doctors or nurses might). The activities recreational therapists do with clients are generally enjoyable, even fun. Beyond this, however, is a reciprocity that develops between clients and recreational therapists. Recreational therapists are genuinely friendly toward clients. They display friendly demeanors that project openness and warmth, and they offer clients opportunities to make choices and be self-directed, opportunities often not available to clients in health care environments. This approach brings about feelings on the part of clients to reciprocate by returning the kindness and support shown to them by thinking favorably of recreational therapists or even expressing fondness for recreational therapists who they see as befriending them.

Haidt (2006) termed this affinity as the "automatic reciprocity reflex" (p. 49). Austin (2011a) discussed Haidt's explanation of reciprocity:

> Haidt has provided an everyday example of reciprocity that may help illustrate why recreational therapists develop reciprocated relationships with their clients. His example is that of the salesperson who, to get something from us, gives us something first. A good personal example of this was when I recently received a dollar bill in the mail from a company that asked me to complete a survey. I had been given something (i.e., $1.00), so I responded to the request to fill out the survey. (p. 67)

Think about yourself. If a friend who has done something for you asks you for a favor, are you likely to respond positively? You probably would be. Haidt (2006) termed the norm of reciprocity a "tit-for-tat" (p. 49) reaction in which the reactor responds in kind. It seems, in recreational therapy, recreational therapists are privileged to enjoy unique professional relationships with their clients that produce referent power, which allows them to positively influence clients and the outcomes they receive from recreational therapy interventions.

Table 7.1

Sources and Examples of Power for Recreational Therapists

Type	Source	Example
Legitimate	Power bestowed on the leader by those in places of authority.	Appointed by an authority (e.g., clinical director) or displaying symbols (e.g., pins, certificates) of professional standing such as holding licensure and certification (e.g., CTRS).
Connection	Power from relationships with those with influence.	Being a member of a care team composed of doctors, nurses, and others of influence.
Information	Having information valuable to others (such as clients).	Having knowledge of client cases and the evaluations and decisions of members of the care team.
Reward	Power that comes from having the ability to bestow awards.	Being seen by clients as having the authority to reward client behaviors.
Coercive	Power that comes from being able to levy punishment.	The ability to use the hospital's or agency's disciplinary system to alter behavior.
Expert	Power derived from the skills and knowledge one possesses.	Displaying valued personal characteristics by showing high levels of skill in recreational activities. Exhibiting expert knowledge as a clinician.
Referent	Grained by the closeness others feel for the leader.	Clients tend to like RTs. RTs do things *with* clients not *to* clients as medical personnel may do. RTs are seen as being open, warm, and friendly and typically allowing choice and self-direction on the part of clients. Because of this, clients tend to quickly develop an affinity for their RTs.

Note. RT = recreational therapist; CTRS = Certified Therapeutic Recreation Specialist. Adapted from *Essentials of Nursing Leadership and Management* (2nd ed.), by P. Kelly, 2009, Boston: Cengage Learning.

RTs also develop close relationships with clients by building trust. Table 7.2 lists means to build trust.

Yoder-Wise (2011) stated, "*Influence* is the process of using power" (p. 179). Leaders must use their influence (gained through referent power and other types of power) to help clients to reach their goals, thus helping clients to achieve their optimal levels of health and well-being. It is also important that leaders apply their understandings to the dynamics of power and influence to produce positive outcomes within the groups they lead.

To understand the atmosphere within a recreational therapy group, it is important that those in leadership positions be able to analyze the power structures that are present. Leaders should know who has power and how it is being employed; for example, they should know who in the group may enjoy expert power by means of being a good athlete or referent power due to having a charismatic personality.

Additionally, Toseland and Rivas (2005) stated that a positive group atmosphere generally exists when members see themselves as having some amount of power. Most persons want to feel that they have influence in relation to important others (such as the leader), and when they have some degree of influence, they feel more secure. Therefore, it is the wise recreational therapist who understands the issues of power within groups and uses his or her leadership position to create a positive social climate by encouraging feelings of influence among group members.

Table 7.2

Developing Closeness by Achieving Trust

- Communicating clearly in a way a layperson can understand
- Keeping promises
- Protecting confidentiality
- Avoiding negative communications (e.g., blocking, false reassurance)
- Being available to the client

Adapted from Sallee, A., & Forrest, S. (2005). Effective communication and conflict resolution. In B. Cherry, & S. R. Jocob (Eds.), *Contemporary nursing: Issues, trends, and management* (3rd ed.) (p. 397). St. Louis, MO: Elsevier Mosby.

Leadership Styles

Most discussions of leadership (e.g., Kelly, 2009; Kunstler & Stavola Daly, 2010; Posthuma, 2002) center on three leadership styles: autocratic, democratic, and laissez-faire.

Autocratic leadership is a directive style of leadership. The autocratic leader supposedly has superior knowledge and expertise. He or she makes all decisions and expects obedience from others. All authority and all responsibility remain with the leader. Autocratic leaders allow minimal group participation. There is never any question as to who is in charge.

Democratic leadership is a shared leadership style. It involves others in decision making. The leader draws on group members for ideas, thus creating a feeling of participation and teamwork. Authority is often delegated to others. Under democratic leadership, people sense that their participation is important.

Laissez-faire leadership is an open and permissive approach. The leader does not exercise authority. Instead, minimum control is used so that participants may take on responsibility for decision making. Laissez-faire leadership is participative and client centered.

Recreational therapy has no one best leadership style. A number of factors influence the best style for any given situation. These factors include

- the ability and personality of the leader,
- the characteristics and needs of clients, and
- the environment in which the leadership occurs (e.g., pediatrics unit, adult psychiatric unit, long-term care facility).

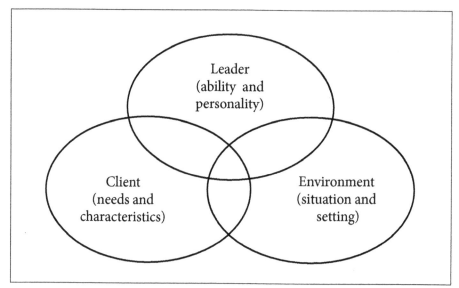

Figure 7.1. Factors Influencing Choice of Leadership Style

Leader Abilities and Personality

As discussed in Chapter 5, it is important that each recreational therapist gains self-knowledge. This includes becoming aware of which leadership style best suits the abilities and personality of the individual. Good leaders choose a style with which they feel comfortable most of the time, but remain flexible enough to deviate from it when clients or situations dictate another style.

Client Needs and Characteristics

The second factor to consider in selecting a leadership style under the interactional model of leadership is the type of client being served. No one style is the best overall style for the recreational therapist because the leader must match his or her style to fit the characteristics of the group members. Information in this section on matching leadership style with client needs has been drawn primarily from Higginbotham, West, and Forsyth's (1988) excellent presentation on the leader/therapist.

An autocratic approach may be the logical choice when working with a group of clients with severe psychological problems. Clients who are pathological, aggressive, or resistant will likely not respond to influences within groups, but instead need the leader to impose structure. Directive leadership might likewise be called for when working in a behavior modification program for clients with intellectual disabilities who have clearly defined tasks or behaviors to learn. Still another example where an autocratic style could be appropriate is with confused nursing home residents who, like some psychiatric clients, require a structured environment. With any population, an autocratic leadership style works best when group members respect the leader and are willing to accept the leader's recommendations. With directive leadership, the more status the leader has with the clients, the more influence he or she will exert over the group.

Directive leaders must maintain their status within the group to be effective. When French and Raven's (1959) bases of power are considered, it appears that the reward power and coercive power lead to influence on the part of the directive leader. The problem with these approaches is that they do not result in internal acceptance of behaviors and values that have been imposed through a system of reward and punishment. Anger and hostility can result when clients feel directive leaders are using coercive power to influence them. Reward power must be used with caution because rewards can undermine intrinsic motivation for behavioral change.

An **overjustification effect** may occur that changes the person's motivational system from internal motivation to external motivation. If extrinsic rewards are repeatedly given for a desired behavior, the individual may become personally less favorably disposed toward performing that behavior as the motivation becomes more extrinsically driven (Austin, 2011a). Consequently, leaders using an autocratic or directive approach need to attempt to base their influence on legitimate, expert, and referent power.

Democratic or laissez-faire leadership is best suited to groups in which members will accept social influence from others within the group, have group goals, and do not need or desire autocratic direction. Unlike clients in autocratic groups, clients operating under group-centered approaches can make decisions and can accept responsibility.

Leaders of groups in recreational therapy ideally strive to employ a group-centered style of leadership that allows as much control as the clients are willing and able to assume. While doing so, leaders of recreational therapy groups have to keep in mind that no one leadership approach is always effective in promoting client change.

Leadership Situation or Environment

The final factor to be considered under the interactional model of leadership is the situation or the environment in which leadership transpires. The situation will sometimes dictate the type of leadership style that will be effective. For example, when working with large groups, leaders will need a more directive, autocratic leadership style. Small, intimate groups will likely need a group-centered approach.

Generally, the environment is closely tied to client needs and characteristics because policies and practices of organizations are based largely on the type of clients being served. For example, confused psychiatric patients may be placed on a locked unit for their own safety and protection. The types of activities provided in such an environment are likely to be highly structured, allowing for a minimum of control by the clients.

The type of clients discussed in the prior example (confused psychiatric patients), coupled with the environment (a locked ward with a highly structured program), may dictate an autocratic style of leadership. If a recreational therapist is not comfortable with this style, he or she may be better suited to another client population or setting. It is important for emerging recreational therapists to realize that various types of leadership styles are needed because of the diversity of clients and the variety of settings in recreational therapy. There is no one best leadership style. A wide variety of persons with varying abilities and personalities may become successful practitioners in recreational therapy, each fitting into the type of leadership position for which he or she is most ideally suited.

Continuum of Leadership Styles

The three major leadership styles—autocratic, democratic, and laissez-faire—may be conceptualized to exist along a continuum, with autocratic leadership on one end and laissez-faire leadership at the other extreme. This continuum is represented in Figure 7.2.

Even though recreational therapists must initially be autocratic in leadership, it is important to remember that the ultimate goal is to help each client move away from dependency on the leader and thus gain greater self-dependence. Progressive movement along the continuum of leadership style from a controlling, autocratic style toward the client-centered, participative leadership style is the goal of all leadership in recreational therapy. The recreational therapist sincerely believes that all clients are first-class citizens who deserve the right to move toward the greatest possible level of independence.

Autocratic	Democratic	Laissez-faire
(leader centered)		(client centered)
Dependency		Independence

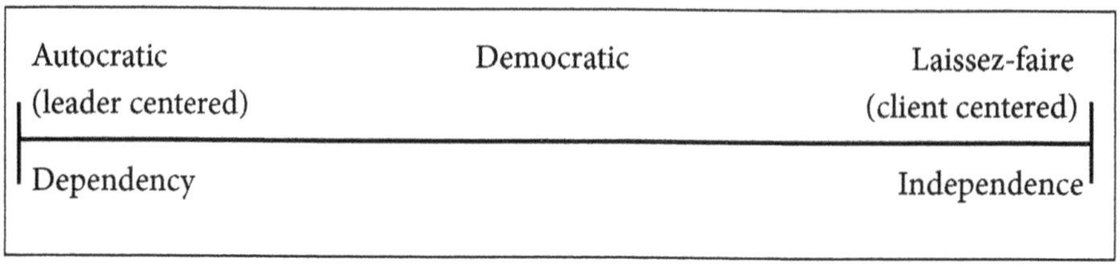

Figure 7-2. Continuum of Leadership Style

The process of allowing clients to move past planned activities to choosing their own leisure pursuits requires a supportive atmosphere that provides for—and fosters—the growth of the individual. The leader moves toward ultimately reaching the role of an enabler who promotes the greatest possible level of independence and self-determination on the part of clients.

Leadership Roles

Avedon (1974) listed eight diverse roles that the recreational therapist may assume as clients move from dependence to independence: controller, director, instigator, stimulator, educator, advisor, observer, and enabler.

The **controller** exercises a high level of control over clients, making all decisions regarding the activities of the group. The **director** still holds most of the power and leads the activities of the group, but allows clients latitude in decision making. The **instigator** incites action on the part of the group and then withdraws, leaving the group members in control. The **stimulator** begins activities by generating interest on the part of clients and then helps maintain this interest by encouraging participation. The **educator** instructs clients in activities and social skills. The **advisor** provides counseling and guidance to clients. The **observer** provides leadership by his or her presence and evaluates and reacts to clients' responses. The *enabler* role fits well into the laissez-faire style, where the leaders simply provide opportunities for participation in activities that clients determine.

The leadership styles and roles discussed in this section exist only as means by which to help clients move toward their optimal level of independence and healthful living. During this process of moving away from dependency, clients will need the recreational therapist's help with problems and feelings related to dependency.

Leadership and Dependency and Interdependence

Dependent clients rely on staff for psychological and social support. They accept a subordinate status in which they depend on others instead of acting independently.

Dealing with dependency is a concern in almost every recreational therapy setting. A certain amount of dependency is a natural part of successful rehabilitation because clients must give their consent to be influenced by those directing the treatment, rehabilitation, or care program (Kutner, 1971). However, some individuals may use their role as client as a means to gain excessive attention and/or escape personal responsibilities. If reinforced, such behavior can produce clients who learn to be "helpless," who rely on others instead of on their own initiative (Schmuck & Schmuck, 1997).

Haber, Leach-McMahon, Price-Hoskins, and Sideleau (1992) suggested various ways to deal with dependency. The following guidelines are based on their suggestions:

- Be conscious of demands for advice and answers to problems by clients who lack the confidence to make decisions for themselves.
- Show acceptance of clients, but do not give in to their demands if demands are excessive or irrational.
- Help clients become aware of their feelings of dependency and develop new ways to seek gratification of their needs through more independent means.
- Build the self-esteem of clients by making ability statements in which they are assured they have the ability to succeed.
- Provide opportunities for clients to make decisions and accept responsibility.

Although dependence can be a problem for those who become overly dependent, recreational therapists should not necessarily think of dependence as a negative attribute. Some people, particularly in the Japanese culture, believe dependence in social relationships is normal and positive (Creek, 2010). All people are interdependent to some degree. They depend on their families, friends, and neighbors every day. Even in their work lives, they must depend on colleagues to help them to be successful. Dependency, in this sense, is a natural part of life.

Authors such as Kunstler and Stavola Daly (2010) questioned the notion of declaring independence as an overriding goal in recreational therapy. It would seem that both independence and interdependence have their place in the lives of recreational therapists and should both be embraced. Kunstler and Stavola Daly stated, "While the ability to act independently is highly valued, the ability to be interdependent is equally important" (p. 303).

Function of Group Leaders

Much of the recreational therapist's time is spent working with groups of various types. Gordon (2001) stated that human beings participate in groups because they believe that their needs will be satisfied as a result. People accept the influence and direction of leaders to meet their individual needs.

Gordon provided a model as an explanation of group leadership. The model rests on the assumption that people are continually in the process of *satisfying needs* or *relieving tension*. To satisfy their needs, some means are necessary. Most needs in society are satisfied through *relationships with other individuals or groups*. Persons take part in groups because they anticipate that this participation will result in meeting their individual needs. Individuals accept direction from a leader because this behavior is considered to be a means to needs satisfaction. The relationship with the leader is seen as an avenue through which their needs will be met.

Posthuma (2002) agreed with Gordon that members join groups to meet personal needs. She expanded the discussion by adding that people join groups "because they like the others in the group, they like the activity or purpose of the group, (and) they want to experience feelings of belonging" (p. 14).

Frisch and Frisch (2006), Posthuma (2002), and Toseland and Rivas (2005) proposed a number of advantages for clients who take part in therapeutic groups as a means to meet their needs. These form the basis for a list of advantages of recreational therapy groups for clients (see Table 7.3). Perhaps the advantages particularly important to clients within recreational therapy groups are the hope being fostered through optimistic leadership, social skills being developed through group interactions, control being experienced within recreation participation, new behaviors being learned and tried out, and confidence being gained as a result of learning and developing skills in recreation.

In sum, clients join recreational therapy groups to satisfy needs, and groups offer special advantages to members in meeting their needs. Consequently, it is the function of the recreational therapist to organize the activities of client groups so that individuals may reach maximum needs satisfaction.

Recreational Therapy Groups and Structures

Austin (1987) extended Avedon's (1974) original outline of structures for group participation in recreational therapy to include the following: *clubs* (that are made up of clients who meet regularly to pursue common interests), *special interest groups* (that are for clients who share a special interest such as photography or improving self-awareness or self-esteem), *classes* (that offer opportunities for instruction ranging from yoga to art classes), *leisure counseling groups* (that provide small group counseling to help clients develop appropriate leisure attitudes and behaviors), and *adventure therapy groups* (that involve activities containing elements of perceived risk or danger in which client groups engage in natural outdoor settings). Other group structures identified by Austin (1987) and Avedon are not as therapeutically oriented, but offer opportunities for clients to try out skills gained in therapy groups, to develop activities of daily living skills, to build leisure skills, and to enjoy leisure experiences. These activities also offer staff occasions to observe clients' behaviors. These include *informal lounge programs* (which are casual programs of low organization in which a multipurpose area is open to clients on a drop-in basis to play cards, pool, video games, etc.); *special events* (which include occasions such as carnivals, dinner–dances, dining in restaurants, theater parties, and special tours); and *leagues, tournaments, and contests* (which include bowling leagues, card tournaments, and bingo nights).

Group Elements

Do the clients involved in the types of recreational therapy program structures outlined in the prior section really constitute groups? Think for a moment of the groups of which you are a member. What makes each of them a group? Is there a difference between a collection of individuals and a group?

You probably have a feeling about what constitutes a sense of "groupness." First, you want to be a part of the group. There is a conscious *identification* with the group, or a sense of belonging. You also have some sort of *interaction* with others in the group. You communicate with and react to others in your group. Finally, there is a sense of *shared purpose* or group goals or ideals that the members hold (Posthuma, 2002; Schwartzberg, Howe, & Barnes, 2008; Shoemaker & Lala, 2006).

Are recreational therapy "groups" really groups? It is perhaps best not to answer this question in absolute terms, but to recognize that most recreational therapy groups can be described as ranging somewhere along the previously identified dimensions of identification, interaction, and shared purpose by which groups may be defined. In some recreational situations, a sense of groupness exists; in others a complete sense of group does not form

Table 7.3

Advantages of Recreational Therapy Groups

Advantages for Clients:

- Group identity—Experience feelings of belonging
- Socialization—Build socialization skills
- Empathetic understanding—Receive caring, trust, and acceptance
- Social support—Receive support from others in the group
- Hope—Instillation of hope by seeing examples of members who have succeeded
- Control—Gain a sense of control by being able to experience control within recreation participation with others
- Vicarious learning—Learn by hearing about others' coping responses
- Modeling coping—Ability to observe new ways of behaving in terms of how others meet problems and struggles and model after these
- Role-Modeling—Ability to observe how others interact
- Practice new behaviors—Ability to try out new ways of behaving in a supportive environment
- Feedback—Gain feedback from multiple sources
- Sharing thoughts—Opportunity to exchange ideas and share problems
- Self-confidence—Increase self-confidence through successful participation
- Give and take—Learn the give and take involved in interacting with others
- Transcendence—See how others adapted to and compensated for disorders or disabilities
- Validation—Other group members confirming similar experiences, problems, concerns
- Self-awareness—Become aware of themselves (broader view of themselves)
- Helping others—Opportunity to help and support others may be therapeutic
- Recreation skills—Build recreational skills through group participation
- Cost saving—Save time and money compared to individual therapy

Advantages for Group Leaders:

- Cost saving—Cost and time effectiveness by serving several clients at once
- Provide added support—Ability to provide additional supportive interactions
- Resources of the group—Can draw on strengths and ideas from the groups
- Stimulating—Working with groups provides a stimulating challenge

---

Adapted from Frisch, N. C., & Frisch, L. E. (2006). *Psychiatric mental health nursing* (3rd ed.). Clifton Park, NY: Thomson Delmar Learning p. 758; Posthuma, B.W. (2002). *Small groups in counseling and therapy: Process and leadership* (4th ed.). Boston: Ally and Bacon, pp. 3-7; Toseland, R. W., & Rivas, R. F. (2005). *An introduction to group work practice* (5th ed.). Boston: Pearson, pp. 17-19.

because the members have not developed along one or more of the dimensions. This may occur in situations in which the membership continuously changes, in instances where the program itself is structured in a way that discourages client interaction (such as an art class in which clients engage in separate projects), or in cases where members are not ready to interact with others.

Selecting Activities

As emphasized in the discussion of the planning phase of the recreational therapy process in Chapter 4, before determining which activity is best to use with a group, the leader should systematically examine any potential activity. The process of appraising what behaviors and skills are required for participation and what possible outcomes may result from participation is termed *activity analysis*. (Activity analysis is covered in detail in Chapter 4.)

It is critical for the group leader to become completely familiar with any potential activity so its innate features are understood before implementing it. For example, it is important that the activity is appropriate for the functioning level of the group members. Do the members have the skills and abilities demanded by the activity? Will they likely feel achievement, mastery, or accomplishment as a result of their participation?

The group leader should also consider whether members will be positive about the activity. Will the members like the activity? Will they be interested in the activity? Does it fit within their cultural norms? Will they be given opportunities for making choices within the activity?

The group leader should also consider in activity selection whether he or she has firsthand knowledge of the activity. The leader not only should know demands of the activity and possible effects on participants but also should be comfortable with the activity to the point that it is second nature to him or her. Having this background allows the leader's focus to be on the members and their reactions within the activity, not on the rules or procedures of the activity itself.

In activity selection, the group leader must consider the therapeutic benefits that may be derived from activity participation. Posthuma (2002) stipulated that the leader needs to address the following questions:

1. What is the purpose in using the activity?
2. Is the purpose congruent with the goals of individual members and the goals of the group as a whole?
3. What outcomes can be expected? (p. 224)

These questions are a reminder that activities involve a therapeutic enterprise. It should be emphasized that *an activity should never be employed unless the purpose for using it is clear. Additionally, activities need to be related to the individual goals of members and the group goals. After all, the reason members are in activities is to reach their goals.* Therefore, it is imperative that group leaders be cognizant of likely outcomes from activities so the activity is conducted in a way to realize positive outcomes for the members.

Whitaker (1985) warned that the selection of activities for therapeutic purposes must be done in a careful and reasoned manner. Activities should always be chosen with the needs of the clients in mind rather than the needs of the leader. Some leaders, for instance, may be worried about filling the time for which the group is scheduled with activities and may select an activity as a time-filler only on the basis that they are familiar with it. This is a risky action because activities can be powerful devices, and therefore, leaders' choices need to be based on specific therapeutic needs of the group members with an awareness of the range of potential consequences that may ensue. All consequences of using the activity, including both intended and unintended likely consequences, need to be considered. Thought also has to be given to ways the activity could go wrong and, if it does, what the leader will do.

Finally, Schwartzberg, Howe, and Barnes (2008) provided a list of considerations when choosing an activity. Their list draws together and extends major points previously made in this section. Their considerations are as follows:

- The goals of the activity should have meaning for the group members. The meaning of any activity will vary, depending on the stages of development of the group. The activity should be useful to individual members and related to their culture, interests, life roles, and so forth. Of course, the goals of the activity need to directly relate to each individual client's goals.
- The group members should be able to participate in choosing or adapting the given activity, to promote a maximal level of self-initiated mental, social, or physical participation.
- The activity demands should enable members to take an active role in the group. The task should arouse member interest, and the demands of the task should elicit an adaptive response.
- The activity should be chosen according to members' skills, ages, and/or performance levels. This includes an awareness of individuals' extent of participation with, identification with, and relationship to the group, as well as the role of the group.

Stages of Group Development

Various authors have proposed different phases of group development (e.g., Kelly, 2010; Longo & Williams, 1986; Posthuma, 2002; Purtilo, Haddad, & Doherty, 2014; Schwartzberg et al., 2008). No matter which phase model is embraced, all portray groups as moving from dependency to interdependency, as Schwartzberg et al. (2008) indicated:

> What appears to be a commonality to understanding stages of group development regardless of the frame of reference, is that as the social and emotional needs of members emerge, a dynamic interplay unfolds as members work through their uncertainty and dependency to build toward interdependence and an ability to balance their individual needs with those of the group. As part of this developmental process, members come to terms with what they are capable of doing and gradually assume responsibility for their actions and interactions at the level to which their chronological age or personal abilities will allow. (p. 24)

Usually authors talk of four stages that groups encounter: (a) the orientation or forming stage, (b) the conflict stage, (c) the group cohesion stage, and (d) the performance or production stage. Students often find Tuckman's terms of *forming, storming, norming,* and *performing* (Tuckman & Jensen, 1977) useful when attempting to memorize the four stages.

Forming. During the *orientation stage* or forming stage, the natural insecurity and apprehension about being in a new group is paramount. The members' concern is largely with acceptance. Due to their fears, some members may initially resist fully participating. Thus the leader may wish to have members discuss any fears (Corey & Corey, 2006). Because of their anxious feelings, members' insecurities may come out. Posthuma (2002) stated, "Members may be overtalkative or withdrawn, display a self-centered unawareness and insensitivity to others, try to impress the group by talking about outside experiences, display attention-getting behaviors, and pressure others into taking responsibility" (p. 28). At this time, a great deal of reliance is on the leader because group members still feel dependent on the leader for direction. Group members will likely look at the person speaking and then shift their focus to the leader for his or her reaction.

Tasks for the group leader include *developing trust, fostering identification* with others in the group, and *gaining a commitment* to the group from members. The focus on *developing trust* "is on getting to know other group members; their interpersonal boundaries; and their basic orientation to the sharing of responsibility, collaborative decision making, and control" (Arnold, 2007, p. 275). At this time, the leader works with group members to help them feel accepted. This will likely involve inviting group members to introduce themselves at which time they may tell something about themselves or relate why they joined the group. The leader needs to attempt to reduce anxiety by clarifying how the group will be conducted to achieve its goals. Additionally, the leader needs to facilitate group interaction.

Fostering identification with the group involves helping members know they are not alone and others in the group likely share their same concerns. A leader technique at this point would be persuading members to talk about their expectations. This will promote mutual identification as members share information and provide the leader with an opportunity to correct misinformation.

Gaining a commitment to the group involves establishing a sort of contract or working agreement in regard to the time and place of the group meetings, types of interactions during the sessions, and behaviors expected. During this task, the leader reveals behavioral norms in regard to attendance, confidentiality, and mutual respect (Arnold, 2007).

Storming. In the second phase, a period of *conflict* is likely to occur. This has been termed the *griping* or *war* stage (Purtilo, Haddad, & Doherty, 2013). As people reveal more of themselves, their personalities, beliefs, or values may begin to clash. They may become hostile toward each other and toward the leader. This may be overt or covert. The leader may feel threatened by challenges to his or her role and may even become angry with members because they are not cooperating (Corey & Corey, 2006). Generally, groups work through this phase. The leader has a large role in this stage as he or she teaches members appropriate ways to disagree with others (Arnold, 2007). This involves modeling healthy behaviors by sharing feelings and thoughts about what is going on within the group, without blaming or criticizing (Corey & Corey, 2006).

Norming. In the norming phase, members become more relaxed in their interactions and assume more responsibility for group leadership. Group goals are agreed upon and members work together toward their achievement (Arnold, 2007). As they do, they resolve conflicts, develop sensitivity to one another, and begin to enter a stage of *group cohesion* (*Kelly, 2010*). During this stage, individuals begin to identify with the leader and other group members. Longo and Williams (1986), who referred to this as the "we stage," suggested members may find pleasure in the cohesiveness of the group and may even set aside their tasks to enjoy being part of the group.

Performing. In the fourth stage, *performance or productivity*, members become functional and devote themselves to achieving individual and group goals. The atmosphere is one of trust and give and take. The stage is characterized by members' commitment to gain from their experiences. Group members display maturity and work to maintain and improve interpersonal relationships. The leader in this phase is supportive of the members, promotes cohesive behaviors, and stays aware of therapeutic factors that produce change in the members (Corey & Corey, 2006; Kelly, 2010).

Authors sometimes add a fifth stage, the *termination stage*. In this stage, members look back to review their experience and look forward to transferring their learning to real-life situations. They also begin to dissolve their ties with the group as the closure process begins (Kelly, 2010; Posthuma, 2002). The leader needs to help members to deal with feelings about termination, to reinforce changes members have made, and assist members to see how they will apply specific skills in everyday life. The leader may also call upon the members to evaluate the group experience (Corey & Corey, 2006).

Although it is true that groups go through somewhat predictable stages, each individual group will be different from other groups. Groups vary in the amount of time spent in any stage and may move through several stages in the space of one meeting of the group. Groups also may not move precisely from one stage to the next in a sequential fashion. Instead, they may bypass a stage or may move backward to a previous phase. In fact, some groups may never move beyond the formative stage of development. This could be envisioned for open-membership groups that have frequent membership changes (Toseland & Rivas, 2005). Nevertheless, it is important for the leader to develop an understanding of the developmental stages so that he or she may better help members in their individual and group development.

Evaluation of the Group

Evaluating group dynamics and the progress of group members needs to be an ongoing process. Such evaluation helps the recreational therapist to examine what has occurred in order to know how to conduct subsequent sessions. One group evaluation strategy is to review each session with another therapist (who might or might not be a recreational therapist). Ideally, this can be done with a coleader. An alternative in the absence of a coleader is to audio or video record the session for later review with another therapist. If this strategy is used, the purpose of the recording needs to be explained to group members and consent needs to be obtained from them. Another group evaluation strategy for post-session evaluation is to take notes in a notebook. Written notes should be made available as soon as possible following each group session.

Whitaker (2001) warned that the therapist should avoid two common mistakes when writing notes. One is that the therapist sometimes condenses too much, so it is difficult for even the therapist who conducts the session to reconstruct what happened. The second is that the therapist may not differentiate between a simple description of what occurred and a personal interpretation of the situation.

No matter which strategy is adopted, it will be helpful to have identified areas of evaluation. For example, questions can be formulated to guide the review of a session with another therapist. In the case of keeping a notebook, a note-taking outline can be developed for ease of making observations. One area is to record basic information about *attendance* (i.e., members attending, absent, late).

Another area is in regard to *data* on each individual member of the group. Examples of evaluation questions are as follows: What were pertinent issues of members? Has my understanding of the person changed from my initial understanding? Was participation particularly meaningful to the individual? If the session was particularly meaningful to a member, in what respect was it meaningful? Was a member angered, attacked, or harmed by others? Was a member ignored by others? In addition to these evaluation questions, the therapist may use rating scales to assess the progress each member made toward reaching identified treatment or rehabilitation objectives. Additionally, the therapist may apply instruments (or request that a psychologist administer instruments) to measure pertinent variables such as perceived stress or quality of life.

A third area for evaluation is *group dynamics*. In this area, important group process issues are noted. Examples of evaluation questions include the following: In which developmental stage was the group operating? Was the group working productively, and if so, how? Were there shifts in topics or issues through the session, and if so, what prompted these shifts? Were group norms evident? What roles did members assume?

Both norms and group roles are covered in the next sections of this chapter. Questions regarding norms are listed in the Group Functions section that follows. These questions may be useful in evaluation. As a matter of fact, many of the questions raised for analysis of functional and nonfunctional behavior can be applied in evaluation of group dynamics in post-session evaluations. In the Group Roles section of this chapter, task roles, maintenance roles, and self-oriented roles are explained. An understanding of group roles will, of course, be helpful in answering the question, what roles did members assume?

A fourth area is in respect to *interactions between and among individuals*. Evaluation questions in this area include the following: What part did different members take on in developing the group theme or in altering the theme? Did one person become central within the group, what maintained this, and what consequences resulted for that person and the group as a whole? If one individual particularly benefited from the group dynamics, what processes led this to occur?

A fifth and final area for evaluation deals with the *feelings and actions of the leader or leaders*. The leader or leaders should ask questions such as the following: Did I have a grasp of what was going on in the group or was I confused? Was I comfortable or anxious and why? Was I angry or pleased by anything that occurred or by any individual? Was a critical leadership strategy used? What leadership strategies might work in the future? How might members respond in the next session? (Stuart, 2001a; Whitaker, 2001).

Creating mechanisms for monitoring and evaluating groups is a necessary responsibility of the group leader. In addition to post-session evaluations, it is also important for leaders to conduct periodic evaluations of long-term groups as well as to reflect on groups when they are ended. Beyond being a source for post-session evaluations, the following sections provide information on group functions and group roles that may help leaders with long-term evaluations of groups.

Group Functions

The activities of group members can be analyzed in terms of the functions the members perform. Two major functions are generally discussed in group dynamics literature: *task functions* (or content functions) and *social-emotive functions* (or maintenance functions). Task functions promote the work or task of the group. They are activities that help group members to achieve their goals. Social-emotive functions have to do with building the group or promoting group development. They include activities that produce a positive group atmosphere in which members can find satisfaction through their group participation. Longo and Williams (1986) used the term *nonfunctional behavior* to describe a third class of activities in which group members may engage. These activities interfere with the processes of the group.

In the section that follows, guidelines are offered to help the group leader to analyze functional and nonfunctional behaviors in groups. These guidelines have been drawn from several sources (Beal, Bohlen, & Raudabaugh, 1976; Jones & Pfeiffer, 1972; Knowles & Knowles, 1972; Longo & Williams, 1986; Posthuma, 2002).

Participation
- What percentage of the members actively take part?
- Which members are high participators?
- Which members are low participators?
- Do participation patterns shift? Why?
- Do those who participate too much realize this?
- How are quiet group members treated?
- Do certain members regularly withdraw?
- Who speaks to one another? Why does this interaction take place?
- Are members included in goal setting and major decisions, or does the leader set goals and make decisions without involving group members?
- Does the leader consciously try to involve members in the activities of the group?
- Are activities analyzed to bring about the type of participation desired?

Influence and Control
- Which members have a high amount of influence?
- Which members have a low level of influence?
- Is there rivalry or competition for leadership in the group? If so, between whom? How does this affect the group?
- Do any members seek recognition by drawing attention to themselves by presenting extreme ideas, by boasting, or through other behaviors?
- Are rewards or incentives used to influence others? How?
- Are formal and informal controls used to maintain group standards?
- Are members ever involved in deciding the means to enforce group standards?
- Are standards enforced relatively uniformly?
- Is the group self-directed?
- Is responsibility and leadership shared within the group?
- What is the relationship between the group and the leader? What type of rapport exists?
- What is the role of the leader within the group?

Norms
- Are members overly nice or polite? Do they agree too quickly? Do they express only positive feelings?
- Are norms of behavior made explicit to all?
- Are certain areas avoided (e.g., sex, feelings)?
- Does the leader reinforce avoidance of certain areas?
- Does the formal leader serve as a model by living up to group standards? What about informal leaders?
- How much variety is there in the types of activities that are done with the group? Little? Some? Considerable?
- Are members consulted regarding group standards?

Atmosphere

- Is the physical setting conducive to the group atmosphere (e.g., size of meeting room, furniture arrangement, lighting, ventilation)?
- Are new members helped to feel a part of the group?
- Do members seem involved and interested? Do they seem to gain satisfaction?
- Is there much disruptive behavior such as clowning around or making fun of others?
- Which members seem to prefer and encourage a friendly atmosphere?
- Which members prefer conflict and disagreement?
- Do members share and cooperate?
- Does the leader set a good example by projecting a warm, accepting attitude?
- Are basic needs for security, belonging, recognition, approval, and achievement met through the group?

Membership

- Do any subgroups exist? Do some people almost always agree and others consistently oppose one another?
- Are some members "outsiders" in the group? How are they treated?
- Does the body language of some members (i.e., leaning forward or backward) indicate moving in or out of the group?
- Is the size of the group about right for group involvement and participation?
- What is the degree of group unity, cohesion, or "we-ness"?

Feelings

- What signs of feelings of group members are observed (e.g., anger, frustration, warmth, boredom, defensiveness)?
- Do members attempt to block the expression of feelings?
- Do they stop discussion by blaming or insulting others?

Social-Emotive Functions

- Which members help others get involved? Which ones are friendly and encouraging?
- Which members cut off or interrupt others?
- Do members feel free to be themselves?
- How are disagreements resolved within the group?
- Do members attempt to mediate conflict by bringing about compromise or reconciling divergent ideas?
- Do members encourage others to express ideas and feelings?
- How are ideas rejected?
- Are members supportive of others by recognizing others' ideas and actions?
- Do members relieve tension through a healthy sense of humor?
- Do members assume follower positions by going along with the group and listening to others during discussions?
- How good are members about accepting new members?
- Do members really identify with the group?
- Is there really two-way communication with the leader?

Task Functions

- Do members initiate ideas and suggestions?
- Do members ask others for ideas and suggestions?
- Are there attempts to gain feedback and clarification?
- Are there attempts to elaborate on the thoughts of others?

- Does anyone attempt to summarize what has happened?
- Do members check out or evaluate the opinions of others in regard to making group decisions? Do they test for consensus?
- Who keeps the group on target?
- Does the leader underestimate or overestimate how much members really know and understand?

Group Roles

Another way to analyze groups is to examine the roles that members assume to (a) accomplish the work of the group and meet group goals (task roles); (b) promote the processes of group building or group development (maintenance roles); or (c) meet their own individual needs, as opposed to group needs (self-oriented roles). In the section that follows, the roles members may take are listed to help the group leader to analyze roles that members may perform. These have been drawn from Boyd (2008), Cole (1993), Posthuma (2002), Schwartzberg et al. (2008), and Sundeen, Stuart, Rankin, and Cohen (1998).

Task Roles

- **Initiator/contributor:** Proposes new ideas, tasks, methods, directions, and means to organize; suggests innovative solutions to problems.
- **Information seeker:** Requests clarification of suggestions; focuses on fact.
- **Information giver:** Offers facts, ideas, and information.
- **Opinion giver:** States opinions with emphasis on what should be the group's values.
- **Clarifier:** Seeks to clear up ideas, indicating definition of terms.
- **Elaborator:** Expands on existing suggestions; gives further meaning to the group's plan.
- **Coordinator:** Pulls together ideas; clarifies relationships among various ideas expressed.
- **Orienter:** Defines the position of the group in regard to its goals.
- **Explorer:** Explores alternatives and deeper meanings or ramifications related to alternatives.
- **Evaluator/critic:** Critically evaluates ideas, proposals, and plans; evaluates accomplishments of the group against some standard of group functioning.
- **Summarizer:** Pulls ideas together and restates suggestions following discussion.
- **Energizer:** Prods the group to take action or to make a decision.
- **Procedural technician:** Expedites the group by doing tasks such as distributing materials, arranging chairs, and so forth.
- **Recorder/record keeper:** Serves as the "group memory" by maintaining a record of the group's ideas, discussions, and decisions.

Maintenance Roles or Group Building Roles

- **Encourager:** Offers other members responsive praise and agreement for their contributions, especially nonverbally.
- **Harmonizer:** Reduces tension; mediates differences among members.
- **Compromiser:** Modifies his or her own position in the interest of group cohesiveness, growth, or productivity.
- **Standard setter:** Checks with the group members to see whether they are satisfied with how things are going; expresses ideal standards to which the group can aspire.
- **Supporter:** Actively supports ideas other group members present; acknowledges group task performance.
- **Follower:** Passively accepts ideas; goes along with the group.

- **Gatekeeper:** Facilitates the participation of all in the group; maintains the flow of communication.

Individual Roles or Self-Oriented Roles

- **Aggressor:** Acts negatively; shows hostility toward other members; denigrates others' contributions; attacks the group.
- **Arguer:** Needs to disagree; presents views opposing prior agreement by the group.
- **Blocker:** Is negative and stubbornly resistant; attempts to bring back previously rejected ideas.
- **Recognition seeker:** Calls attention to himself or herself by boasting or acting in unusual ways to remain in the limelight.
- **Self-confessor:** Uses the group as an audience to express non-group-oriented feelings, insights, or ideologies; may attempt to gain sympathy from the group.
- **Dominator:** Monopolizes the group through a number of means including manipulating other members, giving directions authoritatively, or interrupting others; wants to be in control.
- **Playboy/playgirl:** Does not take his or her involvement in the group seriously; jokes; is cynical; is nonchalant.
- **Self-protector:** Is defensive when responding.
- **Special interest pleader:** Speaks for a special interest (e.g., "grassroots"), often representing personal prejudices or biases.
- **Invisible man/woman:** Remains silent, nonparticipant.
- **Confused:** Never understands, so never has to carry the load.
- **Yes man:** Goes along with everything without commitment to anything or anyone.

Special Concerns and Strategies for Group Leaders

The following material discusses special challenges that confront group leaders, including dealing with anxiety new leaders feel, dealing with anxiety new group members experience, modeling behaviors for clients, using self-disclosure appropriately, handling conflict with group members, dealing with "difficult" group members, working with group members who only look toward the leader, dealing with members who monopolize, counteracting physical aggression, acknowledging transference and countertransference, using coleadership, and learning to work within a system.

Anxiety as a New Leader

Most people have some amount of anxiety when they try something new. Emerging recreational therapists are no exception. They may wonder about their abilities to lead a therapy group and commonly experience accompanying anxiety. It is important for beginning leaders to recognize and acknowledge that self-doubts and anxiety are common among practitioners at their stage of professional development. In fact, a moderate amount of anxiety can be good in that it can move the new leader toward self-appraisal. Of course, when anxiety becomes overwhelming, it may interfere with functioning. It is therefore important for students completing clinical experiences, and for those with limited experience, to discuss their feelings with other students or staff and with their clinical supervisors. Once the new leader admits feelings of anxiety, he or she will likely learn that other emerging leaders are experiencing similar anxiety or that more seasoned staff experienced it when they were emerging professionals. Unwarranted anxiety can be dissipated through such exchanges (Austin, 2011 a; Corey, 2012), and emerging leaders can learn strategies to help them to deal with being new leaders.

New Group Members

New members may want to be a part of a recreational therapy group, but, like most people, they are likely to find new situations threatening. When clients feel threatened, they will likely exhibit anxiety. Clark (2009) indicated that anxiety may be reflected by "restlessness, lack of eye contact, body tenseness, stiff or repetitive gestures, rapid shallow breathing, perspiration, rapid or unclear speech, changing the topic of conversation, silence, distorting or overreacting to others' comments, griping, daydreaming, or forgetfulness" (p. 35).

Naturally new members will be concerned about whether the leader and other clients will accept them and whether they will be able to perform to the expectations of the group. With such uncertainty, it is not surprising that the defense mechanisms of new clients may cause blocks to group participation. Persons may approach new situations by simply repeating old behaviors (Hansen, Warner, & Smith, 1980) even though these behaviors may not be functional.

The recreational therapist must understand fears of rejection or incompetence. He or she must not ridicule the client who attempts to adjust to a new experience by employing a nonfunctional defense mechanism. Understanding potential client problems will allow the leader to help clients to overcome fears that interfere with their adjustments. Instead of becoming angry with clients for their inappropriate behaviors, the recreational therapist must learn to ask the important question, why?

Thus, the first task of the group leader is to reduce threat to new members by helping them to become comfortable. This involves expressing a warm, accepting attitude toward new clients; interacting with them in an open, nonjudgmental way; and helping them become acquainted with other members of the group. In doing so, the leader creates a positive atmosphere for new members and functions as a model for all group members.

Clark (2009) indicated the introduction of a new member to a group that is highly cohesive may present problems for the existing group members. Members may become anxious that the new member may alter old patterns of doing things or may challenge existing power or leadership structures. The leader can ease the situation by meeting new members individually before they take part in the group. At this time, the leader can inform the new member about the goals of the group and rules the group has for behavior. The leader can also encourage the new member to ask questions about the group and offer expectations about what will occur in the group. Finally, the leader should consider preparing the group for accepting the new member. To reduce the potential for hostility toward a new member, the leader may wish to ask the current group members for their reactions to a new member joining the group. Once the new member is with the group, the leader may also have current members introduce themselves to the new person so they can talk about themselves and acquaint the newcomer with what has transpired in the group (Clark, 2009).

Modeling

One way for people to learn new behaviors or strengthen existing behaviors is to observe others who exhibit the desired behavior. Recall how your coaches and physical education teachers would model motor skills for you to imitate and then reinforce you for following their example, or remember how you learned a new dance step or some social behavior by watching older brothers and sisters and their friends. Clients also learn from imitation. Therefore, it behooves the recreational therapy group leader to consider the potentially potent effect of modeling.

Because modeling can play a large role in shaping clients' behaviors, the emerging recreational therapist particularly should engage in self-examination to become aware of the picture he or she is presenting to group members. First, he or she thinks in advance about which social-recreational behaviors are desired and therefore should be demonstrated, and second, he or she monitors his or her own behavior to ensure that appropriate behaviors are displayed. Of course, once appropriate social-recreational behaviors are imitated, the recreational therapist should reinforce clients for performing them (Schwartzberg et al., 2008).

Schwartzberg et al. (2008) offered the following leader tips to enhance the modeling process:

- Have the attention of the other person. If he or she is not aware of the leader's behavior, he or she cannot imitate it.
- If the other person thinks that imitating the leader's behavior will help to accomplish goals, he or she will likely imitate that behavior.
- If imitating leader behavior brought success in the past, there is a stronger possibility that leader behavior will be imitated in the present.
- If the other person values the leader's friendship, likes the leader, or seeks the leader's approval, he or she is more likely to imitate the leader's behavior.
- Others are more likely to imitate the leader's behavior when they are emotionally aroused.
- If the other person is unsure about what behavior is appropriate in a given situation and the leader is sure, that person will tend to imitate the leader. (p. 71)

Self-Disclosure

The question of *how much* self-disclosure is appropriate is a concern for both new and experienced group leaders, although more experienced leaders may have more comfort in the use of self-disclosure due to past experiences. Appropriate self-disclosure is a vital part of group leadership. Corey (2012), taking his lead from Yalom (1995), suggested that the leader should keep in mind that self-disclosure should only be used to benefit group members. Self-disclosure should provide group members with feelings of encouragement, acceptance, and support and help them to reach their goals. Corey believed the most productive use of self-disclosure relates to the dynamics of the group. For example, if group members are not actively participating and taking responsibility for the group, the leader may wish to disclose how he or she is affected by this lack of participation. Corey learned that much thought needs to be given before self-disclosure is employed. It cannot be assumed that it is always good to disclose. First, the leader must analyze the reasons for disclosure. Are they valid? Then, the leader needs to evaluate the readiness of the members of the group for the disclosure and what impact it is likely to have on those in the group. Finally, the leader needs to consider whether disclosure at this point in the life of the group is relevant and warranted.

Conflict With Clients

Clark (2009) stated, "*Conflict* is best viewed as a challenge and an inevitable part of human interaction" (p. 41). Perhaps as critical as any understanding of group leadership is the realization that the leader will occasionally encounter direct conflict and confrontation with group members. This may occur initially because the leader may not fit the preconceived stereotype of a leader formed in the mind of the client. As discussed by several authors (Knickerbocker, 1969; Hansen et al., 1980), people possess previously developed concepts of what a leader should be like based on prior experiences with significant others such as parents and teachers. If the leader refuses to fit this stereotype, conflict can arise and hostility may result. Another possible occasion for conflict is when the relationship between the group leader and members begins to change as a result of group members becoming less dependent on the leader. Conflict can develop if the members see the leader as being unwilling to play a reduced role in order for them to assume more leadership (Austin, 2011a). If conflict occurs in either case, the leader must handle any resulting personal attacks in a mature manner without retaliating against the attacking client or clients so that a positive example of dealing with aggression is provided for the group.

"Difficult" Group Members

Group members may meet the leader with resistance. For example, they may remain silent, try to monopolize the group, be overly dependent, or display hostility and aggression. When group members behave this way, leaders tend to label them as "difficult." Corey (2012) suggested that therapeutic group leaders need to understand that all people are subject to using avoidance or resistive strategies when they are attempting to change, and therefore, leaders must accept that such behaviors will occur within groups. Instead of labeling individuals as *problems* or *difficult*, leaders should consider that there is a reason for the member's behavior and try to understand the individual and the behaviors he or she exhibited. Duxbury (2000), a British professor, explained the dynamics of difficult group members by describing two distinct categories of difficult clients or patients:

> They are patients who are noticeably perceived as being uncooperative via manipulation and confrontation, this I have termed defensive behavior, and those who are more *self-protective*, including withdrawn and passive patients. The protective group incorporates patients who exhibit a general lack of cooperation, which may or may not be intentional. (pp. 19-20)

Duxbury went on to state:

> Difficult patients who are protective often present in a less hostile manner than those who are defensive and intent on being hostile by disrupting treatment or by posing a threat. While it can be problematic to pigeonhole all patients or their behaviors in such an objective way, or equally difficult to believe that some patients are intent on behaving in a threatening way, there will always exist a small minority of individuals who wish to inflict harm on their fellow humans, whomever they might be and whatever the setting. (p. 20)

Corey (2012) explained that leaders should not take resistance personally. Leaders are not bad leaders because group members engage in resistance. It may be that clients' "problem behaviors" that disturb leaders the most are those that "hit too close to home." In other words, they are ones that leaders see in themselves but would like to deny. They must be alert that they do not overreact to clients' behaviors because they may be reminded of themselves.

Members Only Looking Toward the Leader

Particularly early in the life of a group, some group members only look to the leader for direction or for help with personal issues. This may be because they think the leader is the most knowledgeable or most understanding. They also may be attempting to establish a relationship with the leader, trying to impress the leader with their involvement, or focusing on the leader because they do not know how others may react to them. There are techniques the leader can employ to avoid clients who overuse the one-to-one interaction pattern. First, the leader must think about the way he or she interacts with group members or the group process so he or she can prevent the occurrence of interacting with a single member or extricate himself or herself from interactions with just one member. A second technique is to break eye contact because people tend to want to talk with people who maintain contact with them. Without being rude, the leader should casually glance away from the member attempting to monopolize him or her. A third technique is to redirect the member who is in one-to-one interaction. The leader might say, "What do others think about what Bryan is saying?" or "Bryan, how about asking what other members of the group think about that." If the member is talking about another person in the group, the leader might say, "Bryan, I think it is important that you tell that directly to Judi." This request may be initially uncomfortable for the member, but he or she usually comes to understand the importance of speaking directly to others (Posthuma, 2002).

Group Members Who Monopolize

Clark (2009) suggested that monopolizing a group's conversation can occur when the overtalkative individual is allowed to talk as a means of protecting them from responsible participation in the group. Even so, those who engage in monopolizing behavior can cause irritation and frustration for other group members. Posthuma (2002) indicated there are some means a leader can employ to quiet the monopolizer without being hostile. One way is to praise the monopolizing individual for his or her input but move the focus to others. Posthuma (2002) suggested saying, "Mary, you have given us some very good ideas. Now let's hear what the others have to say?" (p. 192). While doing this, the leader should physically turn toward others to invite their involvement. Another way to avoid monopolizing behavior is to use an activity that demands that each group member take a turn, or a related approach is to go around the circle to hear from everyone. A third technique is to sit next to the monopolizing member. The leader can give the person nonverbal communications (e.g., a slight touch on the arm) to quiet his or her participation while others are talking. A final approach is to use confrontation. This is usually a last resort. Posthuma (2002) suggested saying, "John, I'm wondering if you are aware of how much you have been talking in group this morning. We appreciate your ideas, but it is important that others also have a chance to speak" (pp. 193–194). Clark (2009) suggested additional approaches. One is for the group leader to counsel the overtalkative member between group sessions. Another approach, if other techniques have not been successful in curtailing excessive talking, is to ask the overtalkative person to take a 5- to 10-min "time-out" from the group when their talking becomes excessive.

Nonparticipative Behavior

Posthuma (2002) offered techniques by which group leaders may encourage quiet members to join in the group. One technique is to use eye contact. People are more likely to respond if the speaker is looking directly at them. For example, the leader might look at the person and say, "How do people feel about that." Another technique is to simply ask the quiet person whether he or she agrees with what another group member has said. The person can respond with a brief answer, but it will be a response, and perhaps the individual will feel the leader values his or her opinion. A related technique is to ask the nonparticipating person to share his or her thoughts on the topic being discussed. This should be done in a caring tone because the person may feel he or she is being put on the spot. Still another approach is to go around the circle with each member taking a turn. A final technique is most appropriate when several in the group are not participating, that is, the use of silence. The leader should not fill in the silence but let a member end the silence. Should the leader observe that someone is about to speak, he or she should nod or say, "Yes, John," giving permission for the person to speak (Posthuma, 2002).

Clark (2009) suggested structured exercises that could easily be employed in recreational therapy groups to gain clients' participation. One approach is to have members record their answers on a card or piece of paper to these incomplete sentences posed by the leader:

- Today I feel…
- I wish someone would ask me about…
- The worst (best) thing that has happened to me since our last session was…
- I like (dislike) this group because…

Following this, the leader should collect and read group members' responses to stimulate discussion. Responses should be kept anonymous unless a group member wishes to volunteer that they made the remark. Another approach to stimulate discussion is to have group members draw pictures of themselves or their families or to bring in living or inanimate objects to serve as the focus for discussion. Clark explained,

> Objects could include a kitten, a loaf of freshly baked bread, a plant, some flowers, or a picture. Using a picture that contains one of more people, ask each group member to tell what the person in the picture is thinking, feeling, or doing; this may initiate discussions about attitudes, biases, and other barriers to working together or communicating with other people. (p. 155)

Physical Aggression

The group leader must display respect for himself or herself and others in the group by not allowing any physically aggressive behavior to occur, according to Clark (2009):

> The leader cannot allow any physically aggressive behavior among group members. This includes touching group members who do not wish to be touched, throwing restricted objects, and hitting or hurting oneself or others. Such behavior must be halted immediately, and firm limits must be set so that all group members will feel safe within the group setting. In many adult groups, the leader will decide before the first session that touching will not be allowed; this rule is often set so that people will be encouraged to express feelings verbally rather than through potentially dangerous actions. (p. 153)

Clark (2009) advised that at any indication of aggression, the leader should immediately say something such as the following:

- "No touching in this group."
- "Stop hitting me. I won't allow you to hurt me."
- "No throwing; somebody could get hurt." (p. 153)

If this does not work, Clark suggested the group leader restrain the aggressive member in a gentle but firm manner. An alternative is to request the person leave the group and return only when he or she is able to verbally express his or her feelings. Because physically aggressive members are often frightened, another approach is to have the person sit next to the leader (unless the leader is frightened by the aggressive individual). Clark also suggested asking members of the group what they think and feel about their fellow member's outburst. Such discussions can evoke strong reactions from members within the group. Finally, Clark wrote that when other alternatives do not work, if the leader feels comfortable doing it, he or she may say to the aggressor, "I want to help you but I can't do much about it when I'm frightened and can't use my energy to help" (p. 153).

With children, Clark advocated that the leader acknowledge the child's feelings by saying, "You're angry and you want to hit me." Then the leader should follow up with, "No hitting allowed here." An alternative Clark proposed is to redirect the child by saying, "Here, hit this pillow instead of me." or "Tell me in words what you are feeling." The final approach Clark put forth is to ask the child about being restricted by stating, "What do you think about not being able to hit me?"

For younger children, Clark advised the use of nonverbal approaches. She suggested:

> hovering over the child in a calm, protective manner or using your own arms or legs to restrain the child's arms or legs gently but firmly. When relaxed, the child may be able to cry (in relief) and/or share feelings. (p. 154)

Transference and Countertransference in Groups

Group members who unconsciously project feelings associated with a significant other from their past to the group leader or another group member are experiencing *transference*. These projections are sometimes hostile and sometimes affectionate (Austin, 2001a). Clark (2009) described transference as it occurs in groups:

> Group members tend to project aspects of former relationships onto current figures in the group setting. This transfer of feelings initially evoked by parents or other significant people in a person's life is called *transference*. Transference occurs when a group member reacts toward you (i.e., the group leader) as toward a parent, because both are identified as authority figures. If the person's parent was harsh and unloving, the group (member) will expect you to be the same, and warm, loving behavior will be discounted. If you remind a group member of a close aunt, this member may be extremely friendly toward you—far beyond what would be expected in a brief relationship. When you are quiet, those in the group who have had the silent treatment from parents or significant others may react with transference of their earlier feelings of resentment. Group members may transfer onto others in the group feelings of love, hate, competition, or even guilt that they feel (or felt) toward brothers, sisters, husbands, or other family members. (p. 151)

Clark warned that it may be compelling for leaders to take on the role group members associate with them. This, however, would not be an honest or therapeutic way to relate to the group members.

In *countertransference* group leaders unconsciously respond to group members as if they were significant others from the group leaders' own past (Austin, 2001a). Clark (2009) explained,

> If you (the group leader) respond to group members because they evoke reactions reminiscent of your own earlier relationships, you are engaging in *countertransference*. This occurs when a group member reminds the leader of past experiences with significant people who had acted similarly and were irritating, menacing, showed the need to be cared for, were of a different race or cultural group

(and therefore not completely understood), or, on the other hand, had attractive qualities. Because of these past experiences, you are apt to react with anxiety or a sense of immediate recognition when you meet group members who have styles of relating that tap memories of these past relationships. In such cases, you are likely to be unreasonably irritated by, fearful or overprotective of, underreactive to, or attracted to one or more group members. The effect on the group is to provoke anxiety and disruption of communication. (p. 152)

It is important for group leaders to acknowledge and recognize that they may experience countertransference so they become aware of overreactions to group members. It is healthy for group leaders to realize that they may experience countertransference and to be prepared to concede its occurrence when it does take place.

Termination

To avoid an abrupt ending to a group, Posthuma (2002) stated that termination should be viewed not as an end but as "a transition—a time to move on" (p. 197). This approach fits well in recreational therapy because recreational therapists often attempt to move clients toward increasing levels of independence. Posthuma provided tips on how to deal with the termination of a group member, the group itself, or the group leader. When an individual group member is known to be leaving the group, the leader should announce this to the group. If someone drops out of the group without the leader knowing, the leader should ask the group whether they know where the member is and whether anyone wishes to invite the person to return to the group. If the individual chooses not to return, the leader should allow the group to discuss the person's decision even if he or she is not there. In the case of the termination of the entire group, prior to the termination the leader should remind the members that the last session is going to occur so they are prepared.

Often members feel ambivalence as a group terminates. If so, the leader should facilitate a discussion of the group's ambivalence. Another approach is to allow members the opportunity to come to closure by holding a discussion of their overall experience in the group. The leader can also have a brief evaluation form for the members to complete during the last session. Finally, the termination of the group leader may be handled similarly to the termination of a member. As far in advance as possible, the group should be told the leader is leaving and the reason for this. Members should be assured the departure of the leader has nothing to do with them, as they may think the leader is leaving because they have not been a "good group." It may also be that the group may feel abandoned if the members have grown close to the leader over time. Acting out may even occur as a result. If there are abandonment issues, the leader should acknowledge these. Posthuma (2002) suggested the leader may comment, "I know it's hard when people we have come to depend on leave us," or "I know it's hard when things change and you have to get used to a new person" (p. 200). Posthuma further suggested that the leader follow up with a positive statement such as "You all try so hard; I know Margaret is going to enjoy working with you" (p. 200). It is generally not a good idea for a terminating leader to promise he or she will return to visit the group. It is best to make a "clean break" when terminating.

Coleadership

Many recreational therapy groups are led by a single recreational therapist. Yet, it is not uncommon for recreational therapy groups to have coleadership. Thus, the recreational therapy group leader may face the dilemma of whether to have a coleader join him or her in the leadership of a group. There are certainly advantages in having coleadership. Advantages reported by Clark (2009), Kunstler and Stavola Daly (2010), and Toseland and Rivas (2005) include the following:

1. Coleaders offer a ready source of support.
2. Coleaders provide a source of peer feedback.
3. Opportunity for professional development is available through the coleader.
4. The coleader can provide an alternative frame of reference.
5. A coleader can provide training for the novice group leader.
6. An inexperienced leader working with an experienced colleague can validate his or her perceptions of the group process.
7. Models are provided for members of appropriate communication, interactions, and resolution of disputes.
8. Coleaders can act in complementary roles such as one leading the group and the other being a nonverbal observer of the group process or one can focus on group process and the other on individual members of the group.
9. Assistance is available during interventions.
10. Leaders have help setting limits and structures for the group.
11. Group members may receive more attention with two leaders than they would with a single leader.
12. Coleaders from other disciplines can gain an understanding and appreciation for the purposes and processes of recreational therapy by working with a recreational therapist.

As might be expected, there are disadvantages attached to coleadership. Clark (2009) and Toseland and Rivas (2005) listed the following disadvantages of using coleadership:

1. It is likely to be more expensive than single leadership.
2. Leaders need to meet to coordinate between group meetings.
3. If the two leaders do not function well together, they will not be good role models.
4. Having to train new leaders may create conflict and tension on the part of experienced leaders.
5. If conflict exists between the leaders, negative group outcomes can occur.
6. Coleadership creates a more complex situation than having a single leader.
7. To succeed, the coleaders must be committed to working on their relationship.

From personal experience as a coleader, I can report a positive result from coleading a community-based social club (i.e., social recreation club) with a social worker. The purpose of the group was to assist members to be confident in their social encounters. Members either were referred by a therapist in the community or were recently released patients referred by the social work department of the local psychiatric hospital. We, as coleaders, helped develop leadership from the group, and the members determined the specific recreational activities in which they wished to take part. Activities they chose included attending concerts, going bowling, and taking ballroom dance classes. The female social worker and I functioned together well. She had a strong background in group dynamics, from which I profited, and I had recreational leadership skills that she appreciated. We liked one another and found the social club to be a satisfying and enjoyable leadership assignment that seemed to have a great deal of therapeutic value for our group members. Such a relationship is critical to success in coleadership. Of course, if we would have had conflicts, our personal experiences and our group's outcomes might have been negative instead of positive. Thus, each recreational therapist needs to determine whether it is wise to choose to use coleadership with recreational therapy groups.

Schwartzberg et al. (2008) suggested that coleaders must be clear about

- frames of reference and how they influence their actions and interpretations as group leaders;
- leadership style similarities or differences;
- how they will balance their leadership in the group sessions; and
- their conflict agenda, including personal levels of comfort with conflict and confrontation; ability to tolerate and address issues of transference and countertransference; and skills with, or approach to, setting limits. (p. 58)

Working Within a System

Whether within a community-based agency or an institution, the group leader must learn to cope within the system. For example, in an institutional environment the administrators may be more concerned with maintaining the status quo than with providing meaningful treatment or rehabilitation programs. Such administrators may also employ top-down, bureaucratic administrative styles that do not encourage or reward innovations by group leaders. Still another challenge within a system may be overworked staff who lack continuing education opportunities and thus have to use their own time and pay their own expenses to attend professional workshops and conferences. Even when faced with such challenges, group leaders need to find means to offer quality programs despite the systems in which they work. Professionals must not let the system "win," but must continue their efforts to remain competent and to offer therapeutic groups (Corey, 2012).

Group Development

A primary dimension that affects the growth and development of a group is the climate that is created by both *environmental* and *emotional factors*. Other dimensions that can influence the growth and development of a group are the interaction, involvement, cohesion, and productivity of its members (Posthuma, 2002).

Factors Affecting Group Climate

"The importance of the effects of the environment on the process and functioning of a group cannot be overemphasized," according to Posthuma (2002, p. 56). First, the leader needs to become familiar with *environmental factors* that may affect the group. Then, the leader needs to take steps to reduce group members' fears and anxieties by structuring elements in a way that will make the group setting as conducive as possible to achieving the outcomes its members seek. Is the room an appropriate size? It should not be so small that members feel closed in or so large that members feel insecure in an undefined space. Is the room a comfortable temperature? Any group will suffer if the room is too hot or too cold or if there is poor ventilation. Does the seating arrangement facilitate the outcomes the group seeks? For instance, if the leader wishes to downplay his or her role to encourage participant involvement, he or she needs to take a seat other than at the end of the table. With groups where verbal interaction is primary, it is important to place seats in a circle so participants can easily see each other. With task-related groups, a round table is a good selection because it provides workspace and still allows ease in interaction patterns among group members. In placing members in a rectangular configuration, or any seating arrangement other than a circle, the leader is in danger that the total group will not interact because the seating arrangement will encourage interactions only among subgroups.

Emotional Factors

Emotional factors can likewise affect the climate of a group. Posthuma (2002) stated,

> It is important to realize that the leader-therapist, by virtue of her (or his) status, has the power to influence the emotional climate of the group. If you are enthusiastic, open and caring, you have a better chance of eliciting these behaviors from the group members. (p. 49)

The group leader needs to ask himself or herself, "Am I aware of my own behavior and how it is affecting the group?" and "What is the mood of the group today?" The leader can alter his or her behavior to facilitate the group process. If members are not enthusiastic, the leader can encourage the members to discuss the mood of the group (Posthuma, 2002).

Interaction

"The more group members interact among themselves the more likely is the group to grow and develop," stated Posthuma (2002, p. 51). Of course, the activity in which participants take part will dictate interaction patterns. Some activities require a great deal of social interaction; others do not. The leader needs to be aware of the demands of potential activities and select those that will meet the needs of the group.

Based on Hall's (1966) early work in proxemics (the study of human spatial behavior), most authorities categorize space into four zones. With someone a person knows and likes, her or she interacts in the *intimate* zone, which is up to 18 in. apart. For casual friends or acquaintances, the personal zone runs from 18 in. to 4 ft. For other interpersonal encounters, the social zone is from 4 ft up to 12 ft. For public speaking, the public zone represents the 12 ft or more that the speaker stands away from the rest of the group (Duck, 1998). It is important for the leader to recognize these zones so members have enough personal space and do not feel as though it has been invaded.

Involvement

Posthuma (2002) stipulated, "The more members that are involved in a group the greater the probability of the group growing and developing" (p. 53). People are attracted to a group because they like the leader, others in the group, or the group's activities; believe the group can help them; or observe others gaining enjoyment and benefits from their participation. Once in the group, members' involvement can be encouraged by allowing them to make decisions about the group to build feelings of group "ownership" (Posthuma, 2002).

Cohesion and Productivity

Finally, positive outcomes may be expected from groups in which members feel a sense of group cohesion and believe the group is accomplishing its purposes. Group cohesion is experienced when a climate of openness and trust has been established. Feelings of productivity grow when members are able to integrate their individual goals into the group goals and gain a sense of accomplishment. The leader needs to continually monitor the group to maintain a positive climate and ensure therapeutic outcomes (Posthuma, 2002).

Phases in Conducting Recreational Therapy Groups

Kunstler and Stavola Daly (2010) identified three phases for recreational therapy groups: (1) the warm-up phase, (2) the experience phase, and (3) the wrap-up phase.

Warm-Up Phase

The *warm-up phase,* or orientation phase, is the beginning part of the session. Its intent is to establish a relaxed, welcoming atmosphere for the group; to begin to involve participants; and to describe what will occur in the program. As a result of receiving orientation information about the purpose of the group and group structures, members know what to expect and they begin to feel more comfortable being in the group. It is at this time that the leader should present any rules that group members will be expected to follow, such as not touching one another without permission and maintaining confidentiality. Hopefully, receiving this information will help participants to reduce their levels of anxiety and help them to feel secure in the group environment. Of course, a portion of the warm-up should be used to introduce all members and the leader or leaders.

Following the initial group session, the recreational therapist or therapists will want to use the warm-up to welcome participants and to review what occurred during the prior session. This may involve asking group members what they recall about the last session or what they have accomplished since the last meeting of the group. Normally leaders use warm-up activities or icebreakers so that members can have fun, get to know one another, and feel a part of the group.

Experience Phase

During the *experience phase*, group members strive to meet the goals and objectives that they hope to realize through their group experience. It is the recreational therapist's job to facilitate this occurrence through the provision of structured experiences for the group members. The recreational therapist must assess the needs of those in the group and then select an appropriate activity (perhaps with the involvement of group members in its selection) through which group members may receive therapeutic benefits. Then the recreational therapist must conduct the activity in such a way that all clients are effectively engaged and actively moving toward achieving the benefits from their participation. One responsibility the group leader has is to regularly scan the group to see who may need assistance in completing the activity, help in interacting with others within the group, or a supportive comment. During this experience phase, many of the understandings gained from the section earlier in this chapter on special concerns and strategies for group leaders can be applied to meet challenges such as nonparticipation, monopolization, and conflict or transference.

The final portion of the experience phase is devoted to group processing (sometimes referred to as debriefing). Group processing allows the members to reflect on what occurred during the group session, what was learned as a result, and how what was learned may be used in the future. An extensive section of this chapter, which follows, details group processing.

Wrap-Up Phase

The third phase is the wrap-up phase, which may also be referred to as the cooldown phase. Kunstler and Stavola Daly (2010) listed the following elements that should be covered to wrap-up or conclude a group session:

- summarize the key points of the session;
- identify homework or assignments for members to complete for the next session;
- provide comments on what to look forward to in the next session;
- provide feedback and one last opportunity for clients to discuss or ask questions about the experience;
- provide contact information so that group members can connect with the leader between sessions;
- have members assist with the room cleanup when appropriate;
- make sure all completed projects are labeled and placed in a safe location; and
- make sure there is a plan to escort clients to their next session, meal, or room or provide additional   transportation after the session if needed. (pp. 327–328)

Of course, the work of the recreational therapist is far from done once the three phases have been completed. Still remaining will be cleaning up and readying the area for the use of the next group, evaluating the group session (with the coleader if a coleader exists), and charting client progress.

Group Processing

A basic tenet in recreational therapy practice has long been that the emphasis is always on the client, not the activity. It is what happens to the client as a result of participating in an activity that is important (Austin, 2011a).

The activity may be perceived as simply a vehicle. It is a means through which clients can learn about themselves and their interactions with others. An activity is successful if clients derive therapeutic outcomes by making a connection between their participation in the activity and their lives outside of the activity. Group processing allows clients to engage in a discussion about their participation in an activity, with resulting self-awareness that extends beyond the activity into their everyday lives.

Examples of activities in which group processing is commonly accomplished include games, icebreakers, team-building exercises, and adventure/challenge experiences. Virtually any recreational activity has the potential to be processed.

Processing Involves Learning by Doing

All people, including clients, learn by doing. By engaging in an activity and analyzing (i.e., processing) that activity, participants gain self-knowledge as the discussion of what went on in the activity can lead them to insights into their attitudes, values, thought processes, and interaction patterns.

Clients are human. Because they are human, like all people, they do not always learn from their experiences, or said another way, their learning may not initially be evident to them. Because clients do not always immediately learn from their experiences, they sometimes need help to become better learners.

Recreational therapists employ group processing techniques to help clients transfer what they learned from the activity to their real-world lives. Processing is facilitating the action of "learning by doing." The term *experiential learning* (Biech, 2008) has been used to describe this phenomenon of learning through actively participating in an activity that the group leader processes with the members.

Processing is important because clients may not learn from their experiences unless they can link their learning from the activity to their individual lives. McKenzie (2000) offered a succinct definition of processing, stating that processing "can be defined as the 'sorting and ordering of information' that enables participants to internalize meaning from an (activity) experience and, therefore, contributes to program outcomes" (p. 22).

Fletcher and Scott (2002) listed examples of program outcomes for adventure experiences, including psychological benefits such as confidence building, increased risk taking, improved self-concept, enhanced leadership skills, increased logical reasoning, and greater reflective thinking. Examples of program outcomes in social skills include enhanced cooperation, better communication skills, more trust of others, improved problem solving, and greater conflict resolution skills. These examples of therapeutic outcomes are, of course, only for adventure activities.

The outcomes that may be gained through the transfer of what is learned during activities to everyday life are almost endless. Behaviors, cognitions, and feelings on which clients are working can be brought to the participants' attention. Processing also allows the leader to reinforce gains clients have made.

An expert in group dynamics rather than recreational therapy, Posthuma (2002) reinforced the importance of processing activities:

> Activity groups tend to be focused and topic-oriented. For example, if the chosen topic is how to handle anger, it is better to have the members make a collage, do a drawing, make a list, or choose symbols that represent how they handle anger than to start by saying, "Today we are going to talk about handling anger," and then wait for the group to begin. The concrete production of lists or pictures gives members something to talk about, and refer to, and will serve as departure points and comparisons for the discussion (when processing on the activity). (p. 229)

Processing is perhaps the most important part of any program and therefore needs to be skillfully and carefully accomplished. Unfortunately, in the recreational therapy literature, authors have given limited attention to the topic of processing. Thus, recreational therapists have had to borrow from the literature of education and adventure therapy for information on processing. The provision of this section in this chapter on being a leader will hopefully offer a basic foundation for recreational therapists who process groups and provide an impetus for further writings on group processing in the literature of recreational therapy.

The Term *Processing*

The term *processing* has often been limited to describing the procedure of debriefing group participants following an activity. It should be acknowledged that today's view of processing is more encompassing. Authors (e.g., Gass, 1993; Hutchinson & Dattilo, 2001) have taken a broad perspective of processing that covers all techniques recreational therapists may employ to enhance client self-knowledge—not only following the activity but also before and during it.

Therefore, *processing* is a generic term covering a number of techniques that can be applied to help participants to internalize experiences to enhance their self-knowledge. Specific techniques that can be employed in group processing are discussed in the following section.

Processing Techniques

The first processing technique is termed *no loading*. Ironically this means letting the activity speak for itself. It is letting participants figure out for themselves the meaning of the activity (Fletcher & Scott, 2002). No loading appears to be best used when meanings from activities are self-evident.

A second processing technique is referred to as *frontloading* (Hutchinson & Dattilo, 2001), which is also known as framing (Gass, 1993), briefing (Richardson, 1998), or prebriefing (Priest & Gass, 1997). During frontloading, the recreational therapist sets up the experience before the activity starts. Clients are helped to focus their awareness on relevant issues or experiences prior to beginning the activity. The intent of frontloading is to provide a "heads-up" so clients become aware of issues or experiences they will encounter. Hutchinson and Dattilo (2001) warned that frontloading should be used sparingly as overusing it can be overwhelming for clients, producing feelings that they are saturated with information.

A third processing technique is providing *feedback*. Often feedback is thought of as offering encouragement or support with statements such as "great," "nice going," or "way to go." This is one form of feedback. But such statements lose their impact when dispensed randomly. When attempting to reinforce behaviors, therapists leading groups need to be intentional in providing statements to clients. For instance, instead of just saying, "nice job," they need to tell clients precisely what was good about what they did (Hutchinson & Dattilo, 2001). Gass (1993) suggested other feedback techniques such as *stop-action* and *reframing* **that** can be employed during an activity. Stop-action involves actually stopping the activity to talk about something that just occurred. The leader says, "stop!" and then asks participants to describe what just happened. Reframing offers an alternative interpretation of something that has happened. Using reframing, the leader can provide the group with a different way to look at what has occurred.

Posthuma (2002) reminded that people vary as to the degree of feedback they wish to receive. Some seek feedback; others are not welcoming of it. People, in general, prefer positive feedback and tend to accept it much more than negative feedback, which will likely produce defensive behaviors. Posthuma offered seven tips for effective feedback. These are presented in Table 7.4.

A fourth technique in processing is the use of *metaphors*. "A metaphor is an idea or description used in place of a different idea or description to symbolize similarities between them," according to Hutchinson and Dattilo (2001, p. 47). They illustrated with this example: *"Climbing a ladder* can symbolize people's effort to move beyond their present state of emotional discontent or physical immobility through activity participation" (p. 47). The metaphor can then be used as a point of departure in talking about climbing the first rung of the ladder or asking how far up the ladder the person has progressed. Books by Bacon (1983) and Luckner and Nadler (1997) offer helpful approaches for using metaphors as a processing technique.

A major processing technique, *debriefing*, is perhaps the best known and most widely used. Debriefing takes place at the end of the session as group members reflect on their participation. Roland, Summers, Friedman, Barton, and McCarthy (1987) recommended using approximately one third of the time of the session on activities, with two thirds devoted to debriefing. They attached a warning that without this processing there is the risk that activities will become diversional.

During debriefing, clients draw upon their experiences during the activity for lessons learned. Participants may not see the effect of their actions until these are drawn out for them through group discussion. They also may not realize the link between their behaviors during the activity and their behaviors at other times of their lives unless a structure is provided for them to examine these through debriefing.

The recreational therapist, as group leader, helps direct the debriefing, but the members of the group should assume primary responsibility during discussion. Of course, the leader

Table 7.4

Guideliness for Giving Feedback

- **Be sensitive** to what information the group is ready to use. You may have valid observations to make but they should only be made when it will be helpful to the group to receive them.
- **Do not "avalanche"** the group with information. It can be overwhelming to the group to receive too much information at one time.
- **Do not overpraise the group.** The leader must be selective in giving praise, relating it to specific behaviors. Too much praise may not be taken seriously by group members or members may feel they have achieved so much they will let down.
- **Try not to punish, preach, or judge**. Feedback should be descriptive, not evaluative or judgmental.
- **Feedback should be immediate.** Research shows that feedback that is given when the behavior occurs is best, rather than waiting until the end of the session to give it.
- **Use confrontive feedback carefully.** Until rapport has been established, confrontation is not generally a good response because it can inhibit members from freely participating. Of course, disruptive behaviors should be confronted whenever they occur.
- **Act as a role model for giving and receiving feedback.** Using a positive approach will provide members with good role modeling. It is also important for leaders to accept feedback from members without becoming defensive.

Source: Posthuma, B. W. (2002). *Small groups in counseling and therapy: Process and leadership* (4th ed.). Boston: Allyn and Bacon, pp. 137-138.

will have to jump in when the group's discussion bogs down. But even then, this should be only for the purpose of stimulating members to come to understandings of their own. The leader should not tell the group how to resolve dilemmas, but rather raise questions or make statements that prompt further discussion by the group members. Rohnke (1989) stated,

It is not that you (i.e., the leader) shouldn't share your knowledge. But you need... to get participants to do the thinking as much as possible, to dig into their feelings, to build up their own collection of observations, and provide an atmosphere to act on them. (p. 23)

Dieleman and Huisingh (2006) described the process of debriefing:

The participants will always have an array of experiences, but they will need a context and some help to facilitate their clarification and expression of the emotive "learnings" they experienced. Also, of course, as they express their "learnings" and listen to the "learnings" of others, they will realize that people learn very different things from performing the same activities. Reflections on the differences in perceptions and emotions that are elicited via the games (or activities) are extremely valuable. Such debriefing sessions are essential to also help participants to reflect on how they may use the lessons they learned in their personal and professional lives. (p. 846)

Procedures for Processing

Many procedures are available for recreational therapists to use in group processing. Schwartzberg et al. (2008) outlined seven stages (modeled after Cole, 2005):

- *Introduction.* A warm-up activity may be used to bring the group together, followed by the leader outlining the purpose of the group, expectations, and plans for the activity and discussion.
- *Activity.* The activity that is conducted is chosen to meet therapeutic goals of members. It is designed to involve one third of the group session.
- *Sharing.* When a product results from the activity, members share the product of their work in the group with each other. Sometimes this process is highly structured by the leader after the activity is completed, whereas at other times it may be incorporated as part of the activity.
- *Processing (debriefing).* This stage elicits how members felt about the group and interactions within the group.
- *Generalizing.* The leader reviews what occurred and identifies general themes that emerged during the activity. Generalizing involves the leader reviewing commonalities group members discussed to present what was learned during the group session.
- *Applying.* This stage follows up on the generalizing stage by examining what was learned in the context of how it may be applied outside the group. Members are asked to talk about how they will use their new understandings.
- *Summary.* This stage focuses on the key points learned to help individuals understand how what they learned may be applied in their lives. Positive outcomes and members' participation are acknowledged. Members may be thanked for their participation. (p. 28)

Cowan and Gibson (2002) provided another example. They suggested four sequential stages in processing: (1) the briefing stage (also known as frontloading, framing, or prebriefing), (2) the experience stage, (3) the reflection stage, and (4) the debriefing stage. Briefing or frontloading is giving participants information about the activity and goals that may be achieved. The experience stage is actually doing the activity. The reflection stage immediately follows the experience stage and consists of participants looking back at what happened and expressing what it meant to them. The final stage of debriefing helps participants to look within themselves to discover what they learned as a result of participating.

Most processing procedures roughly follow the stages presented by Schwartzberg et al. (2008) and Cowan and Gibson (2002). Nevertheless, there often will be variation. For example, many who would prefer to let group members solely arrive at their own understandings consider the generalizing stage of Schwartzberg et al. to be too leader driven. Furthermore, the briefing stage discussed by Cowan and Gibson may or may not be used for the reason expressed by Hutchinson and Dattilo (2001) involving the potential for having clients overwhelmed with too much information. In this case, only directions for taking part in the activity would be provided. In many instances, the reflection stage Cowan and Gibson described would not be conceived as separate from the debriefing. Reflection would typically be blended into the debriefing session. The major point is that there is no one "right" way to conduct group processing.

The Basic Leadership Approach in Processing

Recreational therapists leading groups must keep in mind that they are not directly teaching clients who take part in their groups. As the leader responsible to conduct the group processing, the recreational therapist has to resist the temptation of imposing specific outcomes he or she desires from the activity. Thus, recreational therapists processing groups do not lecture their clients or tell them what they should have learned from their experiences. Instead, the leadership approach is one of helping clients to learn from their experiences. The recreational therapist's leadership style must reflect the belief that learning can best transpire from direct client experiences and that such personal experiential learning can have a lasting impact on clients (Jacobson & Ruddy, 2004).

Jacobson and Ruddy (2004) emphasized the nondirective approach used in processing. They believed that group leaders

> should be carefully observing participant behavior, guiding reflective conversation, and encouraging the application of what is learned. Beginning facilitators (i.e., leaders) may slip unknowingly into a teaching mode, telling the participants what they should have learned (e.g., "This exercise was about teamwork."). The goal should be to help participants uncover the learning that is paramount for them. (p. 4)

Biech's (2008) words were similar. She warned group leaders:

> Remember that your task is not to tell them, not to assign your learning on them, but—through a series of questions—to help them uncover the lesson themselves. The lesson they need to learn may not be the lesson you want to teach. This is called experiential learning. (p. 5)

On the other hand, Jacobson and Ruddy (2004) warned that group leaders have the responsibility to keep participants on track. Leaders must help those in their groups to not let their focus wander from the group experience. Otherwise, they may not learn from it.

Finally, recreational therapists must recognize that all approaches to group processing simply offer useful guidelines for leaders. Although approaches found in the literature can be extremely useful, they provide only general frameworks. The recreational therapist conducting group processing will need to ask additional questions to guide clients' learning.

General frameworks for debriefing groups follow: (a) What? So What? Now What?, (b) the 5 Question Model, and (c) the Experiential Learning Cycle."

What? So What? Now What?

One popular approach to debriefing appeared in the books *Cowstails and Cobras II* (Rohnke, 1989) and *Islands of Healing: A Guide to Adventure-Based Counseling* (Schoel, Prouty, & Radcliffe, 1988). Borrowing from the earlier work of Terry Borton, the authors of these books proposed the use of three sequential debriefing segments of what?, so what?, and now what?

In the initial *what? phase,* group members are asked to review what happened during the group activity with the intent of raising issues about positive behaviors and those behaviors that participants may wish to change. Examples of questions that the leader may raise are as follows: What happened during the activity? What was hard about the activity? What was easy? What did you like or dislike about the activity. What is everyone feeling right now? What one word summarizes your feelings? It looked like people were working well together; what do you think?

Once the group has identified issues and is talking, the leader should move the conversation toward the *so what? phase.* At this point, participants express what they have learned from the experience. They move from the descriptive (i.e., what?) to the interpretive (i.e., so what?). For example, the leader may encourage them to describe their feelings about the activity and their participation in it. The leader could also ask them to reflect on goals on which they have been working. Questions that might be used in this phase are as follows: So what does this teach us? Why would we take part in this activity? In what ways did the activity relate to your treatment goals?

Finally, the *now what? phase* provides opportunities to talk about what the group members will do with what they have learned as a result of their participation. It is the phase in which they generalize what they have learned from the group to other parts of their lives. Examples of questions that might be employed are as follows: What can you learn from that? How can you use what you learned in your life? What did you learn about yourself and your fellow participants? What does that make you think of? How can you use these skills in other situations?

5 Question Model

Jacobson and Ruddy (2004) suggested a more directed approach to debriefing. Five questions are featured in their approach:

1. Did you notice…?
2. Why did that happen?
3. Does that happen in life?
4. Why does that happen?
5. How can you use that?

Each question serves a specific purpose in facilitating learning. In fact, each question reflects a learning stage. In the first stage of description, participants are asked to clearly describe or identify what has happened, with the question, did you notice…? Examples of questions include the following: Did you notice any fear as you were climbing? Did you notice that a few people really took a leadership role? Did you notice how quickly you responded? Such questions are used to get participants to react to specific observations the group leader made. This requires the leader to carefully form observations for group members' reactions. This more directive approach of the 5 Question Model is in contrast with an open-ended question (e.g., What just happened here?).

In the second learning stage of interpretation the question is, why did that happen? In the first stage, participants acknowledged something about the activity. In this stage, they search for meaning behind what occurred. Jacobson and Ruddy (2004) supplied the example of following up on acknowledging that the group worked well together with the interpretation, "We worked so well because we have really gotten to know each other" (p. ?). In this stage, participants find meaning behind an observation they made.

The next stage of generalization involves both the third question, does that happen in real life?, and the fourth question, why does that happen? With these questions, the participants are asked to generalize their experiences to their lives. Question 3 is a closed-ended question that permits those answering to tie what they agree has occurred in their group to other parts of their lives. The question may be made more specific by asking, for example, "Does that happen at work?" Question 4 is a follow-up question that helps participants to address why the occurrence happened. Jacobson and Ruddy (2004) explained the value of Question 4 to participants: "Question 4 helps them tease out the patterns and causal relationships that underlie that connection" (p. 63). Understanding why the thing observed occurred sets up the fifth, and final, question, how can you use that?

The final stage is that of application, or as Jacobson and Ruddy (2004) stated, "Fundamentally, the final question of any experiential exercise is 'How will you be different in the future as a result of this experience'" (p. 64).

Readers who wish to learn more about the 5 Question Model may find Jacobson and Ruddy's (2004) brief book to be a useful resource. The title is *Open to Outcome: A Practical Guide for Facilitating & Teaching Experiential Reflection.*

Experiential Learning Cycle

Borrowing from the earlier work titled *Reference Guide to Handbooks and Annuals* (1999), Biech (2008) outlined the Experiential Learning Cycle. It employs five steps:

1. experiencing,
2. publishing,
3. processing,
4. generalizing, and
5. applying.

The *experiencing* step involves the actual participation in the activity selected. The intent is to actively engage the participants.

In the publishing step, group members talk about what occurred during the experience of taking part in the activity. Group members talk within the group about what they observed during the activity and what they experienced or felt. The leader starts with a general question (e.g., What happened? What did you observe?) and then asks more specific questions (e.g., What helped or hindered the process? Did anything surprise you? How did you feel about what happened?).

The *processing* step allows group members to interpret why something occurred. Biech (2008) explained in this step that "the key here is to allow participants to discover this for themselves, avoiding your desire to 'tell' them why" (p. 4). Questions Biech suggested include the following:

- "Why do you suppose that occurred?"
- "What did you learn about yourself?"
- "What did you learn about others?"
- "What can you glean from this activity?"
- "What principles might be true based on your experience?" (p. 4)

In the *generalizing* step, group members begin to make a connection from what they have learned to real life. This is similar to the so what? phase in the What? So What? Now What? model. Biech (2008) provided the following questions for this step:

- "How does this relate to your situation?"
- "What does this suggest to you?"
- "What patterns or similarities come to mind?"
- "How does this experience help you understand others like it?" (p. 5).

The final step is termed *applying*. This is the now what? phase of this debriefing model. This encourages group members to think about how they will change based on what they have learned. Recreational therapists can help participants apply what they have learned to their personal lives. Examples of questions Biech (2008) suggested for this step are as follows:

- "What will you do differently as a result of this experience?"
- "How and when will you apply your learning?"
- "How will this help you to be more effective in the future?"
- "What support would make this change easier to implement?"
- "What's next?" (p. 5).

Possible Questions or Statements for Debriefing

It has been mentioned that leaders conducting group processing will likely need to expand their questions beyond those provided in the descriptions of the three debriefing models. But what are some questions or statements recreational therapists might use in debriefing groups? Although not an exhaustive list, the following are possibilities drawn from Posthuma (2002) and two websites (Debriefing Cooperative Games, n.d.; Group Processing, n.d.).

To focus clients on feelings, the therapist might ask the following: How do you feel? What is everyone feeling right now? Use one word to summarize your feelings. What feelings were easiest to express? What feelings were the most difficult to express? How did you feel during the activity?

To gather reactions to the activity, the therapist might ask participants the following: What was easy? What was difficult?

To monitor verbal and nonverbal cues, the therapist might ask questions or statements such as the following: (1) It seems like people are not paying attention here. What is going on? (2) It appears to me that you are really enjoying this.

To check out perceptions, the therapist might use statements such as the following: (1) It looked like people were working well together. (2) During the activity it seemed like a lot of people were getting frustrated. Is that true?

To encourage self-disclosure, the therapist might say, "I'm confused. How do other people feel?"

To explore at a deeper level, the therapist might use the following: Can you say more about that? Keep talking. Tell me more. Give me an example if you can.

To look at decision making, the therapist might pose the following questions: How did the group make decisions for completing the tasks during the activity? Did one or several individuals make decisions? What did you like about the manner in which group decisions were made? What didn't you like about the manner in which group decisions were made?

To examine cooperation, **the therapist might offer** the following questions: What are some specific examples of when the group cooperated well? How did cooperation lead to the success of the group? What would you do to produce a cooperative atmosphere in the future?

To examine the effect on group process, the therapist might ask the following: What did you learn about others? How did members interact and react?

To focus on leadership, the therapist might ask the following: What were the behaviors that you would describe as demonstrating leadership? Was it difficult to assume a leadership role with this group? What are specific skills you need to develop to become a more effective leader?

To have clients think about what they gained from the activity, the therapist might ask the following: What did you learn about yourself? What did you learn about others in the group? What did you learn in this activity that you can apply in a life situation? What would you like to change? What did you learn in this activity that relates to your treatment goals?

The prior questions and statements are, of course, just examples of those recreational therapists may use in processing groups. There are many more questions or statements that recreational therapists can employ. The listening skills and verbal techniques covered in Chapter 6 of this book provide one ready source of information available to those exploring possible questions or statements to employ in processing groups.

Final Thoughts on Successful Group Processing

Clients may enjoy taking part in an activity, but what is the therapeutic value of participation if they do not take anything away from their experience? It should be clear that processing an activity allows participants to examine and discuss individual and group dynamics. This discussion ultimately leads to participants transferring their learning experiences from the activity to their everyday lives.

To be successful in this enterprise, two elements are essential. One essential element is that those leading group processing need to possess a strong background in group dynamics. Recreational therapists should be highly prepared to conduct group processing because their professional preparation provides them with a solid knowledge of group dynamics, as well as a developed set of abilities to lead groups. In fact, it is difficult to conceive of members of any other profession being better prepared to conduct group processing.

The other essential element to success in group processing is the provision of an environment that leads to an open discussion by clients. Recreational activities provide safe, warm, supportive environments where clients can gain fun and enjoyment. These attributes set a positive tone and provide a foundation for openness by group members. Recreational activities are also inherently less threatening because of their "nonserious," playful nature. Such a relaxed and positive atmosphere allows participants to "let their hair down" so they can freely engage in the activity and involve themselves in a discussion of the meaning of the activity to them. Additionally, as discussed in the section of Chapter 2 on positive psychology, successful participation in activities brings about positive emotional experiences that open people up to take risks that lead to growth. Thus, recreational activities are wonderful springboards for group processing. In short, recreational activities can be fun with a purpose.

Principles for Group Leadership

A fitting conclusion to a chapter on being a leader is to end with a brief discussion of principles for group leadership. Hansen et al. (1980, pp. 435–442) developed principles to guide the practice of leaders in groups. Although they were developed specifically for group counselors, many of their principles apply in recreational therapy group leadership. Selected principles of Hansen et al. have been stated here, followed by implications for recreational therapy practice.

Group leaders have a responsibility to develop a theoretical rationale for group practice that will enable them to identify goals of their activity.

Recreational therapy group leaders need to recognize that their practice must rest on a philosophical base. They must know the *why* underlying the goals for their groups, as well as the *how* of conducting the group. If they do not clearly articulate the purpose of the group, they will find it extremely difficult to set directions for the group's activities.

Group leaders have a responsibility to limit their group practice to developed levels of competence and skills and to reveal these limits to clients.

The principle holds in any type of recreational therapy programming, but has particular application in leisure counseling and adventure therapy groups. Leaders of leisure counseling groups must have the competencies called for to conduct the type of counseling in which they are engaged. Once that level has been determined, its limits should not be exceeded. Because adventure therapy involves psychological and physical risks, only recreational therapists with proper training and supervised leadership experiences should lead adventure therapy groups.

Group leaders should be relatively congruent and stable individuals free from gross pathology and with developed insight into their own unique characteristics and needs.

Leaders of recreational therapy groups must know themselves and feel reasonably satisfied with themselves as a person before they can help others. If they are overly concerned about their own ego, they will have a difficult time helping others because it takes ego strength to deal with the stresses of group leadership.

Every effort should be made to ensure the maximum privacy of participants in the group process by appropriate discussion of the principles, needs, and implications of the concept of confidentiality. Leaders should frankly confront the fact that they are able to guarantee only their own commitment to the privacy of discussions.

Professional ethics dictate that recreational therapists should maintain confidentiality in helping relationships. In one-to-one situations, this simply means that they must maintain discretion in the use of client information.

Group leaders face a different situation because others are involved. Particularly when dealing with the discussion of potentially sensitive topics—as might be discussed in some types of leisure counseling—leaders should discuss the issue of confidentiality with group members.

Individuals and institutions that offer and support group activities have the obligation to evaluate those activities periodically. Furthermore, those professionals and institutions have an obligation to participate in research activities designed to reform and refine practice and to determine the effectiveness of variations in practice.

Ongoing evaluation is necessary for the improvement of services offered in recreational therapy groups. Additionally, recreational therapists should feel an obligation to conduct research efforts themselves and/or cooperate with university faculty and others in carrying out research investigations.

Reading Comprehension Questions

1. Define leadership in your own words.
2. What are the major types of power? In what ways may therapeutic recreation specialists possess power?
3. How will the wise leader deal with power?
4. Explain autocratic, democratic, and laissez-faire leadership.
5. Is there one best leadership style for recreational therapy? Why or why not?
6. Describe the continuum of leadership styles outlined in this chapter.
7. Do you understand the eight leadership roles of Avedon?
8. What is dependency? Have you felt dependent? How can dependency be dealt with positively?
9. What is the overjustification effect?
10. What types of power should directive leaders employ? Why?
11. What is the function of the group leader?
12. What types of therapeutic groups can you identify?
13. What makes a collection of people into a group?
14. What are the stages of group development? Can you describe each?
15. Can you successfully employ the guidelines for group leader evaluations?
16. Can you identify major types of functions performed by group members?
17. Can you identify roles that group members may assume?
18. What are some things you might do as a leader to ease the entry of a new member into a recreational therapy group?
19. Why is the leader's example important to the group?
20. Do recreational therapists ever have to face conflicts with clients? If so, how should they be handled?
21. What are dimensions that can influence the growth and development of the group that the leader must consider?
22. Can you describe the three phases in conducting recreational therapy groups?
23. What is group processing?
24. What is the role of the leader in group processing?
25. What is debriefing?
26. Do you agree with Hansen's principles to guide the practice of group leaders? Which do you feel have particular application in recreational therapy practice?

Chapter 8

Specific Leadership Tasks and Concerns

■ Chapter Purpose

Critical to the success of recreational therapists is their development in terms of gaining understanding of several leadership tasks and concerns. This chapter offers information on a number of these tasks and concerns, including (1) individual client documentation; (2) incident reports; (3) the recreational therapist as teacher; (4) motivating clients; (5) teamwork; (6) advocacy; (7) the International Classification of Functioning, Disability and Health (ICF); and (8) understanding transactions. Areas covered within the section on understanding transactions are self-concept, learned helplessness, the self-fulfilling prophecy, labeling, loneliness, social support, social facilitation, self-efficacy, and attributional processes. Particularly within the discussion of understanding transactions, the reader will find many research studies by social psychologists that can be used to support evidence-based practice.

■ Key Terms

- Source-oriented records
- Problem lists
- Progress notes
- Problem-oriented-record (POR)
- Affective skills
- Incident reports
- Motivation
- Teamwork
- WHO
- Transtheoretical Model
- Self-concept
- Playing a role
- Self-esteem
- Self-reported handicap
- Reactance
- Loneliness

- Database
- Initial plan
- SOAP
- Cognitive skills
- Psychomotor skills
- Teaching/Learning Process
- Stages in change
- Advocacy
- ICF
- Motivational Interviewing
- Social comparisons
- Social distinctiveness
- Self-handicapping
- Learned helplessness
- Self-fulfilling prophecy
- Self-efficacy

- Attributional processes
- External attributions
- Fundamental attributional error

- Internal attributions
- Self-serving bias
- Social support

■ Objectives

- Justify charting.
- Analyze a progress note.
- Know categories of behavior for progress note writing.
- Understand major principles in the teaching/learning process.
- Understand the Transtheoretical Model and Motivational Interviewing.
- Understand advocacy as a professional activity.
- Understand the International Classification of Functioning, Disability and Health (ICF)
- Appreciate topics of concern in understanding leader transactions: self-concept, learned helplessness, the self-fulfilling prophecy, labeling, loneliness, social support, self-efficacy, and attributional processes.

The Client Documentation Task

An important function for recreational therapists is the documenting of the recreational therapy process (i.e., assessment, planning, implementation, evaluation) through charting. "Charting is the concise, accurate, factual, written documentation and communication of occurrences and situations pertaining to a particular client," as defined by Hoozer, Ruther, and Craft (1982, p. 13) in their book titled *Introduction to Charting.*

Charting is done in written form or is electronically created by health care professionals. It involves recording information on clients' conditions or status, their progress, the delivery of their treatment or care program and their responses to it, at a specific place on a given date and time (Wong, 2009).

While recreational therapists spend a significant amount of time completing documentation, it is time well spent as all members of the health care team depend on the information communicated in client charts. The quality of the client's care may be jeopardized if information is not successfully communicated because a critical occurrence is not recorded or a note is poorly written. The chart is also a legal document that can be subpoenaed for use in a court of law. Legal action can be taken against an individual who falsifies or helps to falsify a client's chart. Because of possible legal ramifications, "charting is one of the most significant responsibilities that the health care professional assumes," according to Hoozer, et al. (1982, p. 14). Therefore, the recreational therapist needs to be sensitive to how the client is responding to clinical interventions and to record both subtle and dramatic changes in clear charting. Finally, good charting practices help establish professional accountability for recreational therapy. Reasons for charting are found in Table 8.1.

Types of Records

Each setting will adopt a standard method of charting and will supply forms for the client's chart that reflect the particular type of system that is used by the agency. Common systems for charting include narrative notes, SOAP notes, PIE notes, focus charting, and charting by exception. No matter which system is used the major purpose of progress notes is to provide a documented record of the progress the client is making toward the achievement of expected outcomes (Taylor, Lillis, LeMone, & Lynn, 2008).

Table 8.1

Reasons for Charting

- It is a vital tool for communication among health care team members.
- It is a legal document admissible as evidence that can protect you.
- It establishes recreational therapy's professional accountability.
- It is a document for evaluation of changes in a client's condition.
- It is used to develop improvements in the quality of care.
- It aids in accreditation, licensing, and reimbursement.
- It serves an educational purpose as students read notes.
- It is used in research to identify researchable problems.

Narrative Charting

The traditional means of recording has been narrative charting, although today only a few facilities use narrative charting alone. Typically it is combined with other charting formats (*Complete Guide to Documentation*, 2008). Narrative charting provides a chronological account of the client's status, interventions performed, and the client's responses to the interventions. It is suggested that a narrative progress note should be written whenever the therapist observes: (a) a change in the client's condition; (b) a client's response to an intervention; (c) a lack of improvement in the client's condition; and (d) a client's or family member's response to teaching (*Charting Made Incredibly Easy!*, 2010).

A charting format termed AIR has been developed to simplify and structure narrative charting. AIR stands for Assessment, Intervention, and Response. Under assessment, the client's condition is not described but trends and the therapist's impression of the problem are documented. Under intervention, the actions of the therapist and other caregivers are summarized. Under Response, the client's response to the intervention is documented (*Charting Made Incredibly Easy!* 2010).

A type of narrative charting is source-oriented charting. In contrast to the problem-oriented record that groups information from all health care disciplines according to the client's specific problems, the source-oriented record separates recordings according to source or discipline. Sections of the chart are designated for medical notes, nursing notes, recreational therapy or rehabilitation therapy notes, and so on. Those favoring the source-oriented record state that it is easier for each discipline to record all its data in one section of the chart. Those opposing the approach claim that it places data in too many locations, making it fragmented and cumbersome to retrieve information.

Problem-Oriented Records

The problem-oriented record (POR), or problem-oriented medical record (POMR), was originated by Dr. Lawrence Weed in the 1960s as a means to improve the documentation of client care (Taylor et al., 2008). Today it is frequently used for documenting client care, with many agencies adapting the system to meet their particular needs.

The problem-oriented record is organized around the client's problems, rather than around the sources of information. It contains five basic parts. Those components are a defined database, a problem list, care plans, progress notes, and discharge summary.

All members of the interdisciplinary team contribute to the database. The database contains information collected during the assessment phase. Analysis of the database leads to the establishment of a comprehensive problems list. Problems are numbered in chronological order based on the date each was stipulated. The list of numbered problems appears in the front of the chart with the date each was identified and is used as a table of contents to be referred to when recordings are made. The initial plan outlines an approach to be used to meet each of the identified problems. Progress notes record the results of interventions and the client's progress. Frequently, the SOAP format is used to organize entries in the progress notes of the POR.

SOAP Notes

S stands for *subjective data*. Subjective data are those gathered from the client or the client's family. **O** stands for *objective data*, which are collected through observation, measurement, and sources such as documentation by other health care professionals. **A** represents *assessment*. Assessment answers the question, "What do the subjective and objective data mean?" The professional records his or her professional judgments or conclusions following a review of the subjective and objective data. **P** is for *plan*. Under this part of the progress note, the professional formulates a plan or approach that he or she believes will resolve the problem. This may mean following the initial plans, revising them, or developing new plans.

Variations of the original SOAP format have been developed. Some use the SOAPIE format that adds *Intervention* and *Evaluation*. The intervention segment contains the actions actually taken to achieve expected outcomes. The evaluation portion provides an analysis of the effectiveness of the intervention. The SOAPIER format adds a *Revision* section where any changes from the original plan of care are recorded (*Complete Guide to Documentation*, 2009).

"Soaping," as recreational therapists sometimes refer to completing progress notes using the SOAP format, has been widely accepted by numerous agencies in its original or an adapted form. Some staff, however, complain that the technique is too restrictive and too narrowly focuses on identified problems. They favor a return to the traditional narrative format (Taylor et al., 2008).

The following progress note, which employs the SOAP format, is based on an example provided by Shannon, Wahl, Rhea, and Dyehouse (1988, p. 159).

Date	Number	Title
3-8-13	2	Anxiety

S Stated feeling less anxiety: "I'm not feeling so nervous as I had been."

O Engaged in a table game for 45 minutes on the unit with two other clients and the recreational therapist without notable restlessness. Concentration and attention span were adequate to meet the demands of the game.

A Anxiety level is slowly decreasing. Still exhibits inability to express other emotional states.

P Continue care as outlined in initial plans.

The discharge summary is the last part of the POR. Within the discharge summary it is noted whether each problem on the problems list was met. *Within Charting Made Incredibly Easy!* (2010) it is explained: "This is the place in your SOAP or SOAPIE note to discuss any unresolved problems and to outline your plan for dealing with the problem after discharge. Also, record communications with other facilities, home health agencies, and the patient" (pp. 69, 71).

Other Charting Systems

PIE charting, focus charting, and *charting by exception* are other charting systems. *Problem-intervention-evaluation* (PIE) system charting is similar to the plan, implementation, and evaluation of the SOAPIE format. The PIE system eliminates the traditional care plan. Instead, client problems are identified by number and each is assessed at shift changes using flow sheets (preprinted fill-in-the-blank forms). *Focus Charting* has the purpose of making the client's concerns and strengths the focus of care. Client-centered topics, or foci, can include client concerns or behaviors, interventions and responses, changes in conditions, significant events such as management of activities in daily living, and assessment of functional behaviors. In the narrative portion, information is divided into the categories of data (D), action (A), and response (R). Data are information pertinent to the focus. Action includes immediate and future actions, including changes in the plan of care as necessary. The response category describes the client's response to the intervention. *Charting by exception* (CBE) is a charting system that requires documentation of only significant or abnormal occurrences. This system is often used in nursing, where well-defined standards or norms exist. When standards or norms are met, a simple check is made in a box. If an exception exists, then a narrative note is made. Thus there is relatively little note writing because the majority of areas assessed will be normal (Taylor, et al., 2008; Varcarolis, 2006).

Computer Charting

Comprehensive computer systems have revolutionized documentation in many health care settings. Computers are typically located throughout the facility for convenience in retrieval of information and ease in entry of documentation. Some agencies provide staff with small handheld computers. Automated speech technology, where available, permits staff to enter data by voice so it can be transformed into written documentation. To enter information, typically a special code, the client's name, or his or her account number is used to call up the client's electronic chart. Then the progress note can be completed. There are precautions that need to be taken when computer charting. For instance, for reasons of confidentiality and security, you should never leave the computer terminal or handheld devise unattended after you have called up the chart. You should never give your personal password to other personnel. Nor should you provide to anyone your computer "signature" that you use to sign notes (Berman, Snyder, Kozier, & Erb, 2008; *Charting Made Incredibly Easy!,* 2010; Taylor et al., 2008).

The phrase *electronic health record* (EHR) is often used to describe the client's computerized record. Other terms for the EHR are electronic clinical records, electronic patient records, and electronic medical records. While computerized charting facilitates the recording of progress notes, the electronic health record (EHR) is more than just the equivalent of putting paper records on the computer. The EHR allows members of the health care team access to many types of needed client information, including information on precautions and medication. Additionally, EHR systems have been found to reduce errors by forcing standardization in terminology and the use of abbreviations (Boggs, 2007). Kelly (2010) has indicated some of the major values of EHR systems: "The EHR eliminates paper record storage, improves access to patient records, controls legibility, and facilitates timely capture of data" (p. 332).

Effective Progress Note Writing

A number of specific guidelines for charting have appeared in the literature. Those that follow have been drawn from: *Charting Made Incredibly Easy!* (2010); College of Respiratory Therapists of Ontario (2005); *Complete Guide to Documentation* (2008); Narrow and Buschle (1987); Potter and Perry (1995); Lippincott Manual of Nursing Practice (2007); Ramont & Niedringhaus (2008); Sames (2005); Taylor et al., (2008); and Varcarolis (2006).

Conciseness

1. **Be brief.** Eliminate unnecessary words. The term "client" or "patient" is not usually required and may be omitted from progress notes. Incomplete sentences may be used, along with appropriate symbols and abbreviations. Avoid using long words when short ones will do. Write concise sentences.

2. **Be precise.** Attempt to be as precise as possible. For example, state "six times in one hour," not "often." Avoid such words as "bad," "good," "average," "normal," and "better" that may mean different things to different readers. Do not use vague phrases such as "seems to be" or "appears to." Avoid generalizations such as "seems uncomfortable today."

3. **Use simple descriptive terms.** Avoid the use of jargon as much as possible. The use of "big words" does not make a person an expert. For instance, in working with clients who have problems in mental health, avoid such terms as "psychotic," "schizophrenic," and "bizarre" to describe behavior. Instead, describe the specific event or activity that was seen or heard. If a particular professional term is used, define it or tell what you mean by it.

4. **Do not use the client's name.** Do not use the client's name when charting. Avoid the use of the words client, patient, or resident as they only add words and the reader knows who is being charted on. It is fine to use incomplete sentences when charting.

Appropriateness and Completeness

5. **Be informative.** Ask yourself, "Does the note contain the information I intended it to?"
6. **Avoid stereotypes.** Avoid the use of stereotypes or derogatory terms when charting.
7. **Any unusual events need to be documented.** Unusual occurrences need to be documented in the progress notes. Record when and where the event occurred and facts about it.
8. **Chart pertinent observations.** For example, symptoms related to the diagnosis or behaviors related to the diagnosis.
9. **Record only pertinent information.** Record only information that specifically pertains to the client's health problem and care.
10. **Record all pertinent information**. Record all assessments, interventions, client problems, responses to interventions, and progress toward goals.
11. **Use only accepted abbreviations, symbols, or terms**. Do not use abbreviations, symbols, or terms that are not specified by agency policy.

Accuracy

12. **Be sure you have the correct chart.** Before making any entry, check to make sure you have the correct chart by verifying the client's name and identification information.
13. **Be accurate.** Information must always be correct. Never falsify a client's chart. Discriminate in a clear fashion whether subjective or objective data are being presented.

Normally record only observations of behavior; when interpretations are made, differentiate these from behavioral observations.

14. **Use original source if possible.** Attempt to obtain firsthand information from the client. Write only what you know is correct, always verifying secondhand information. If you must report unsubstantiated information, label it as such and identify the source of the information.

15. **Document promptly.** Document as soon as possible. If you put off your documentation until the end of the day you will likely forget important Information.

16. **Quote the client directly.** Quote the client in the client's exact words, using quotation marks around the quote.

Sequence

17. **Employ a format.** Use a systematic format or logical order. For example, when recording observations about physical conditions, start with the head and go down the body.

18. **Document in order of events.** Documents events in the order in which they occur (e.g., interventions and then client's response).

Presentation

19. **Write neatly and legibly.** While notes are often entered directly on computers, many are still handwritten or printed. Use clear handwriting or printing and always write in ink. If others cannot read the note, it will not serve its intended purpose.

20. **Use present tense and correct grammar and spelling.** Write using present tense. Employ correct grammar. Look up words when you are unsure of their correct spelling.

21. **Use permanent, nonerasable ink.** When completing written chart entries, use permanent, nonerasable ink to assure the record is permanent and cannot be changed.

22. **Correct errors.** No erasures should appear in progress notes (because others would not know if you or someone else erased the information). Likewise, correction fluids should not be used. Errors should be corrected by drawing a line through the error and writing the word "error" over or next to the mistake.

23. **Never leave blank space.** Do not leave blank space in a note because another person can add incorrect information to the blank space. Draw a single line through blank spaces so no one may write in the space.

24. **Do not use ditto marks.** Ditto marks are not allowed in progress note writing.

25. **Chart entries chronologically on consecutive lines.** Do not skip lines.

Follow Agency Policies and Procedures

26. **Be familiar with agency policies.** Agencies have specified forms that should be used to make progress note entries. Agencies also have policies as to who may place information in the client's record, or they may require different staff (e.g., nurses, social workers, recreational therapists) to use a particular color of ink when writing notes.

27. **Determine frequency of recordings.** Follow agency policies to determine precisely how often entries are to be made (e.g., daily, weekly). This schedule should be strictly followed. As a rule, it is best to record as close to the time of the event as possible. Delaying charting is a dangerous practice because during a busy day it is easy to forget important details.

28. **Do not mention incident reports.** Incident reports are confidential and are kept separate from the chart. On the chart, document only the facts of the incident and do not indicate that you filed an incident report. When entering the factual account in the chart, include treatment and follow-up care and the client's response. Be certain that descriptions in the chart match those in the incident report.

Confidentiality

29. Consider confidentiality. Always preserve the dignity and privacy of every client. Progress notes should be used only as a means to improve client care and treatment.

Record Date and Time and Sign Each Entry

30. Date and time each entry. Be specific about the date and time you are charting. Agencies often use military time because it removes confusion about being a.m. or p.m. Never document ahead of time.

31. Sign each entry. Be certain to sign each progress note you write. You should normally sign with your first and last name, along with your certification (e.g., CTRS). Your employer may also require you to include your job title. Recreational therapists need to countersign the signatures of RT assistants or student interns. When charting by computer, the therapist will sign a statement that he or she alone will use the code for the computer key.

Examples of what *not* to do and what to do in writing progress notes follow. How NOT to Write a Progress Note:

The client often becomes angry when he plays basketball, and when he is not playing, he is always pacing the sidelines. He is uncooperative and more psychotic than before.

Obviously, the writer did not have access to the information provided previously in this section. Some apparent criticisms appear next. You may add others.

1. The phrase, "The client," is not necessary. It would have been fine to use an incomplete sentence.
2. The use of the word "often" is not precise. Does this mean every day, three times a week, or once every hour?
3. What is meant by the word "angry"? What behavior is the writer describing? Did the client hit, kick, get red in the face?
4. In what kind of basketball activity was the client engaged? Was this a scheduled game, a team practice, or an informal pickup game?
5. The word "always" is not precise. Does this mean the client never stops?
6. The terms "pacing" and "uncooperative" are not defined. What exactly was the client doing?
7. The expression "more psychotic than before" employs jargon (i.e., psychotic) and lacks precision (i.e., more than before).
8. Finally, the writer failed to record the date and time and to sign the entry.

How to Write a Progress Note

Below is another progress note. Look it over. Is it superior to the previous example? If so, in what ways?

Unable to sit for 5 minutes while teams were being organized for basketball game during informal recreation for the unit in the gym. Instead, rapidly walked back and forth in front of bleachers where others were sitting. Said he did not wish to play, but decided to participate when told he would have to sit and watch others, or return to the unit if he chose not to take part. Displayed anger 2 times during 15-minute game. Once kicked ball when teammate missed a pass and once shoved opposing player when client felt he was fouled. Appeared to experience verbal hallucinations throughout 10-minute group processing following the game. Kept mumbling about "Going to Heaven or Hell." 10-16-13, 1235, David Austin, CTRS.

Progress Note Content

The problem-oriented records format, of course, stipulates that each entry should be related to a problem and outlines the information that needs to appear. Some agencies, however, adapt or modify the POR system. Others use narrative notes. Even those using the POR system may find some guidelines helpful in preparing progress notes.

Problems. Just what sort of information should be contained in progress notes? A good beginning place is to consider the problems on which the client is working. How is the client responding to the treatment or rehabilitation program? Are interventions accomplishing the stated specific behavioral objectives in the plan? Is he or she changing? What does the client report in terms of his or her reaction to the program? Does he or she indicate feeling improvement?

Symptoms. What about symptoms? Have there been episodes you have observed? What was the severity? What was the frequency? Duration? When was the onset? What precipitating factors were involved? What aggravating factors were noted? Relieving factors? Associated symptoms?

Confusion or aggression. Were client behaviors such as confusion or aggression observed? When did this occur? Under what circumstances? What precipitating factors were involved? What specific behaviors were observed? What did you do? How did the client respond to your actions? (Potter & Perry, 1995)

General progress. Peterson and Stumbo (2000, p. 280) have offered the following list of guidelines for the relevance of content for progress notes:

- Progress toward attainment of client goal
- Regression from attainment of client goal
- New patterns of behavior
- Consistency of behavior
- Verbal information provided by the client
- Successful or unsuccessful attempts at a task
- Appropriate or inappropriate interactions with staff, peers, visitors
- Client responses to questions, instructions, requests
- Initiative with actions, ideas, problem solving, decision making
- Follow-through or lack of follow-through with commitment

Behaviors. Different categories of behavior are utilized in various types of settings for the reference of those writing progress notes. Through my personal observation of materials prepared by agencies, it seems that there are several broad categories of behavior that recreational therapists employ as guides to writing progress notes. Frequently used categories seem to be participation, performance, interpersonal relationships, personal habits, and state of consciousness and/or mental activity. These major categories follow along with items that relate to them.

Participation
- Interest in activities
- Extent and nature of involvement
- Attention shown (attention span)
- Appropriateness of energy output
- Initiative in choosing activities
- Attitude expressed toward own participation
- Attitude toward rules, winning, competition

Performance
- Level of performance
- Quality of performance
- Hindering factors
- Ability to make decisions
- Quality of judgment
- Ability to express self adequately
- Ability to express self appropriately
- Physical movement (e.g., slow, rigid)
- Use of any device or adaptive equipment
- Attitude expressed toward own performance
- Ability to follow rules and directions
- Special incidents
- Summary of change and performance

Interpersonal Relationships
- Relationships with recreational therapists and others (e.g., dependency, hostility)
- Acceptance of limits
- Manipulative
- Passive, aloof, or withdrawn
- Reserved, insecure, timid, or shy
- Outgoing, confident, or extroverted
- Ability to make friends
- Acceptance by others
- Agreeable, cooperative, or helpful
- Resistive or stubborn
- Verbalizes appropriately

Personal Habits and Appearances
- Appropriateness of dress
- Grooming
- Cleanliness and neatness
- Concern with appearance
- Walk or gait
- Tics, rituals, habitual movements

State of Consciousness and/or Mental Activity
- Orientation to time
- Orientation to place

- Orientation to persons or objects
- Preoccupied (responsiveness)
- Slow in answering or thinking
- Distracted by others or events
- Ability to remember (retention)
- Hallucinations or delusions
- Intellectual functioning
- Stability of mood

A Final Comment on Client Documentation

Documentation is regulated by both federal and state agencies and is influenced by accreditation bodies. For reimbursement, both **Medicare** and **Medicaid** require documentation to show that care was needed. In long-term care, both **Centers for Medicare and Medicaid Services (CMS)** regulations and the **Omnibus Budget Reconciliation Act (OBRA)** stipulate staff must complete the **Minimum Data Set for Resident Assessment and Care Screening (MDS)**, which includes a section on activity pursuit patterns. Information from the MDS is then the basis for another federally mandated form, the **Resident Assessment Protocol Summary (RAP)**. When examining agency practices, accreditation organizations review charts to confirm that documentation systems are functioning properly. Examples of accreditation organizations include, the **Joint Commission on Accreditation of Healthcare Organizations (JCAHOV)** and the **Commission on Accreditation of Rehabilitation Facilities (CARF)** (*Charting Made Incredibly Easy!* 2010).

Incident Report Documentation

As discussed in Chapter 5, one of the basic ethical principles for healthcare professionals is the principle of nonmaleficence, which means "do not harm." Yet to err is human. Healthcare professionals, including recreational therapists, do occasionally make human errors in their practice. Sometimes clients do something that leads to their injury or they may leave the facility against medical advice. Occasionally, equipment may malfunction, a vehicular accident may happen, or other events may occur that are inconsistent with what is normal or expected. *Incident reports* (sometimes termed unusual occurrence reports) allow for the reporting of such unusual or adverse events for the purpose of investigating these events and, through risk management programs, taking steps to avoid such occurrences in the future within the setting.

An examination of events leading up to the incident can be made by analyzing incident reports in order to determine what could have been done that might have altered the outcome from occurring. Of large concern in analysis of incident reports are factors that contribute to human errors. Latent factors that may exacerbate the potential for human error include heavy workloads, inadequate knowledge, lack of experience, inadequate supervision, a stressful environment, rapid organizational change, poor communication systems, inadequate maintenance of equipment or buildings, and incompatible goals (such as those that exist when there is a conflict between finance and client needs) (Vincent, Taylor-Adams, & Stanhope, 1998).

Healthcare facilities typically provide employees with a paper or online incident report form on which to report incidents that are inconsistent with normal or expected operations. Specific examples of incidents include injuries, bruises, falls, elopements or walk-aways, medication errors, treatment errors, equipment malfunction, vehicular accidents, death, attempted suicides, violent or aggressive acts, incidents involving the use of physical restraints, accusations of abuse, and incidents where criminal actions are alleged. Policies usually require the incident report to be made as soon as possible, or within 24 hours of the occurrence of the event. For an incident form to be filled out, an actual injury does not have to occur if the potential for injury is evident to the staff member completing the report (e.g., the occurrence of a "near miss"). (Administrative Policy, 2008; Graves, 2002).

As noted previously in this chapter's segment on guidelines for writing progress notes, the incident report is not a part of the client's health record. It is confidential and kept separate from the client's chart. Typically incident report forms include (a) the date and time the event happened; (b) facts involving findings at the scene (i.e., visual and material information); (c) care given before and following the incident; (d) comments by the client; (e) who was notified; and (f) preventive steps taken (Stumbo & Peterson, 2009, p. 348). Even though incident reports are internal reports which are separate from health or medical records, courts have ruled that they may be open to review by both sides in a law suit (Yoder-Wise, 2011).

When a recreational therapist or any healthcare professional becomes aware of an incident, he or she has the responsibility of documenting the circumstances surrounding the event on the incident form provided by the agency. The report should provide a brief account of the incident—recording only the facts, not opinions. Blame should not be apportioned for the incident (Guidelines for the Completion of the Incident Report Form, nd).

Principles in the Teaching/Learning Process

Many situations require the recreational therapists to help clients to learn. In fact, much of what is done in recreational therapy can be thought of as educational as clients learn to acquire and apply knowledge and analyze and evaluate information (cognitive skills), develop self-awareness in terms of values, attitudes, and opinions (affective skills), gain and refine abilities that require the integration of mental and muscular activities (psychomotor skills), and learn skills for human interaction (social skills).

Basic Teaching/Learning Principles

There is not a set formula for learning, but there are basic principles that can be used to guide the teaching/learning process. The principles that follow have been drawn from Alfaro-LeFevre (2010); Blattner (1981); Dainow and Bailey (1988); Kibler, Barker, and Miles (1970); Marriner (1983); McEwen & Willis (2007); Mosey (1973); Potter and Perry (1995); Ramont & Niedringhaus (2008); Stumbo (2005/2006), Stumbo (2011); and Taylor et al., (2008).

1. **Start at the level of the client and move at a rate that is comfortable**. It is important to assess the client's ability so the leader will not place too much or too little demand on the client. The rate of learning will vary, so the recreational therapist must be prepared to adjust instruction accordingly.
2. **Individual differences must be given consideration.** Each client is an individual and will learn in a unique way. Individuals differ in their abilities, backgrounds, interests, and ages. Intellectual capacities, physical health, and energy levels are ability factors demanding consideration. Educational and cultural background also influence learning, as does the level of client interest in the particular activity. Additionally, the individual must perceive the activity being learned to be age appropriate or it will likely be rejected. Finally, readiness plays a large part in learning. If the client does not have

the physical and cognitive development to cope with the learning situation, he or she will probably fail.

3. **Learning styles differ.** Some clients are visual learners (e.g., reading, viewing pictures or models). Other clients are oral learners (e.g., talking and discussing). Others are auditory learners (e.g., listening). Still others are kinesthetic learners (e.g., learn by active learning experiences). Wise recreational therapists will adapt to the client's preferred style Instead of using the one which appeals most to them.

4. **Active engagement and participation are essential for learning.** Active participation in planning for and engaging in learning means the client has a thorough involvement in the total learning process. It may be said that the best teaching is the least teaching. People do learn by doing, so it is generally better to engage them actively in learning to the fullest possible degree. This is true for the learning of psychomotor, affective, and social learning as well as cognitive learning. After all, it is what the learner does—not the instructor—that determines learning.

5. **Reinforcement strengthens learning.** People tend to repeat the things that they enjoy or find rewarding. Teaching new behaviors then depends on clients finding the behaviors rewarding. Therefore, the recreational therapist should strive to provide social reinforcement when clients perform appropriately. Usually social reinforcers take the form of attention, encouragement, and approval. Another reinforcer comes in the form of the client feeling mastery or a sense of accomplishment. Extrinsic rewards, such as money or food, may also be used to reinforce behaviors. The timing in delivering all types of reinforcers is critical to their success. Rewards have the most effect when administered immediately after the behavior. When new behaviors are initially being learned, a continuous schedule of reinforcement should be used. Once the behavior has been established, it does not need to be rewarded each time it is performed. It is possible to reward the client infrequently. (More detailed information on reinforcement as a technique is found in Chapter 2.)

6. **Opportunities for trial and error can enhance learning.** Trial-and-error learning allows the learner to use a variety of approaches until he or she finds one that works. Of course, trial-and-error learning works best in an atmosphere that allows the time and freedom for people to work things out for themselves. Errors are perceived as a natural part of the learning process, and clients are not told what they should do. The recreational therapist must remain flexible when using the trial-and-error approach in order to encourage inventive problem solving.

7. **Imitation and modeling can enhance learning.** When making projects, clients should be shown models or examples of what they are to produce at the end of the learning experience. For example, a completed arts-and-craft project might be displayed so that clients have an idea of what the finished product will be like. In teaching sports activities the leader can demonstrate proper form, or audiovisuals can be used to show clients correct methods. Social behaviors for adults and play behaviors for children can be gained more quickly if the learner can see a model demonstrate the desired behavior. As discussed in Chapter 2, modeling can also be combined with reinforcement to make it an even more potent means to learning.

8. **Practice facilitates learning.** Repetition helps to set in new skills or behaviors. The actual amount of practice needed to master a new skill or behavior will vary with the level of complexity of that skill or behavior. Recreational therapists must remember that clients are sometimes taught new skills but are not given enough time to practice them. Therefore, recreational therapy programs should offer many informal opportunities for clients to try new recreational and social skills. It may be that the recreational therapist

will help the client to arrange for post-discharge opportunities to practice while undergoing treatment.

9. **Feedback facilitates learning.** Leaders should provide learners with feedback as they learn and practice new skills. This feedback can take the form of positive reinforcement for doing well, encouragement for trying hard, or corrective instruction that will allow the client to improve. The general thought of many clients is that "no news is bad news." Therefore, it is critical to provide regular feedback to clients who are acquiring and practicing new skills.

10. **Clients should know what is to be learned and why they are learning it.** Our clients, as all learners, need to have prelearning preparation. They must be prepared for what is coming and the reasons for learning. Little learning will occur if clients do not understand what it is they are supposed to learn and why they are being taught something new. The learner has to see the importance or applicability of the skill or knowledge in order to be motivated to learn.

11. **Move from simple to the complex.** A general rule of learning is to move the learner from the simple toward the complex, from the familiar to the unfamiliar, and from concrete to abstract. However, Mosey (1973) stresses that those instructing should not fall into the trap of teaching meaningless parts that learners are somehow supposed to connect to a whole on their own. She gives the example of teaching clients how to use public transportation as a natural detail of a pleasurable outing instead of taking the client on a meaningless trip for the sake of learning how to ride the city bus.

12. **Perception affects learning.** A client's perceptions come about as a result of the brain's processing of stimuli received through the sense organs. Maturation and learning both impact on the client's perceptions of the environment. A child may miss subtle cues, or an older adult may perceive things much differently than a relatively young helping professional. Also, a person with sensory problems may experience difficulty in receiving stimuli. Therefore, the recreational therapist must become aware of possible client problems in receiving sensory impulses (e.g., sight, hearing) as well as differing perceptions on the part of individual clients.

13. **Anxiety and arousal affect learning.** Some anxiety, in the form of general arousal and interest, positively affects learning, but too much anxiety or arousal can interfere with the learning process. The recreational therapist must attempt to identify the optimal level of arousal for each client and gear the learning situation accordingly. Many clients require an accepting, nonjudgmental atmosphere in which to learn and try out new skills and behaviors. They learn best with individual instruction or in a small group where support and cooperation are emphasized. Once the skill is acquired, they may be ready to practice or perform gradually the skill in larger and larger groups. It is the role of the recreational therapist to judge, with the client, what pace is appropriate for each individual.

14. **Relate new learning to existing knowledge.** There needs to be a link between what the client is learning and his or her present knowledge so new skills may be logically connected with what is already known. The recreational therapist needs to build on the client's existing knowledge. This calls for the recreational therapist to conduct an assessment in order to determine existing knowledge.

15. **Sensory stimulation can aid learning.** The use of a combination of sensory experiences (sight, sound, touch, smell, taste) together with varied teaching strategies (e.g., role playing, audiovisual aids) may promote learning. We learn better when more than one of our senses is activated.

16. **Timing affects learning.** Teaching needs to be timed to coincide with the client's readiness to learn. The best learning will occur when the client is attentive, receptive, and alert. At times, side effects of drugs can interfere with the client's readiness to learn, so it becomes important for the recreational therapist to be aware of possible side effects of medication. Also, clients will retain skills or information best when there is a relatively short period of time between the initial learning and the actual use of the skill or information.

17. **Enthusiasm is contagious.** Clients will be more apt to remain interested in learning if the recreational therapist is enthusiastic about the area of learning. The recreational therapist should not remain stationary behind a lectern or desk, but should be an active teacher/therapist who makes eye contact with clients, uses gestures, and varies his or her voice tone and intensity. Teaching and learning are fun and should be approached with enthusiasm.

18. **Match teaching strategies to clients' needs.** Psychomotor skills are perhaps best taught through demonstration and practiced under supervision. Group discussion may prove effective when adult clients are exploring leisure values. Information on leisure resources might be provided to adolescents by means of an interactive computer program or a question-and-answer session. Play skills may be better taught to children with mental retardation through imitation and modeling rather than explanation. Regardless of the group you are working with, choose a teaching strategy that fits them and the skill or knowledge being taught.

19. **The relevance of the learning to the learner's needs and problems is key.** The learner has to determine what is relevant to him or her. Meaningful information is much better learned than that learned through rote memorization.

20. **Learning can be painful.** Learning is growth producing and growth involves change, which can provoke anxiety. It is therefore more comfortable and easier for learners to continue their behaviors rather than to learn new ways of behaving.

21. **Learning involves emotions as well as intellect.** There are emotional aspects involved in learning due to change and outcomes being involved. It can be a painful process when change is hard and a joyful one when positive outcomes result. Therapists should plan learning experiences that build on the client's successes.

22. **The environment affects learning.** The environment should be conducive to learning. To maximize learning, for example, the area should not be too hot or too cold and it should be free from noise and other distractions (e.g., interruptions).

Summary of Teaching/Learning Principles

The basic principles of teaching/learning have been presented to help recreational therapists facilitate client learning. Remember, however, that every principle presented will take on a different level of emphasis or importance with each individual client and each new learning situation. Learning is obviously far more complex than is reflected by the traditional teacher-learner paradigm, where the teacher's role is that of dispenser of information for eagerly awaiting learners. Certainly the role of the recreational therapist as a leader is far greater than this as he or she helps clients to find ways to learn.

It has been reported by Dainow and Bailey (1988) "that people generally remember 10% of what they read, 20% of what they hear, 30% of what they see, 50% of what they hear and see, 70% of what they say and write, and 80% of what they say as they do something" (p. 4). If this is true, people need a variety of means to learn. There are any number of strategies available to help clients to learn. These include modeling behaviors for clients, demonstrating techniques, lectures, group discussions, panel discussions, role-playing, programmed instructional materials, computer-instructional programs, printed material, games, group processing, and other experiential education approaches. When carrying out these strategies, "active participation" and "learning by doing" are key phrases for the recreational therapist who strives to actively engage the client in educational experiences that have recreation properties. Learning and enjoyment should go hand in hand.

Motivating Client Change: Transtheoretical Model and Motivational Interviewing

Because motivation is a fluctuating state of readiness to change, it can be influenced. We occasionally hear from therapists (including recreational therapists) that clients must motivate themselves and, therefore, they have no responsibility to motivate their clients. Such thinking is not only negative, it dodges the responsibility of therapists to employ motivational strategies when challenged by "unmotivated" or "resistant" clients. As Miller and Rollnick (1991) have written, "motivation for change does not simply reside within the skin of the client, but involves an interpersonal context" (p. 35). They go on to state:

As a therapist, you are not a passive observer of your clients' motivational states. You are an important determinant of your clients' motivation. "Lack of motivation" is a challenge for your therapeutic skills, not a fault for which to blame your clients. (p. 35)

What is occurring when a client is unmotivated is that the therapist is using strategies that are inappropriate for the client at the time. Once the therapist understands where the client is in the process of change, he or she can begin to facilitate change.

No matter the problem (e.g., problems in drinking or self-esteem), people pass through a similar series of gradual steps or stages in the process of change. Researchers Prochaska and DiClemente (1982) integrated concepts from other models of behavior change into their transtheoretical model (TTM). TTM is a helpful model for understanding the stages clients pass through. Stages included in their model are (1) precontemplation; (2) contemplation; (3) preparation; (4) action; and (5) maintenance (See Table 8.2).

DiClemente and Velasquez (2002) have summarized the stage process:

In this model change is viewed as a progression from an initial precontemplation stage, where the person is not currently considering change; to contemplation, where the individual undertakes a serious evaluation of considerations for or against change; and then to preparation, where planning and commitment are secured. Successful accomplishment of these initial stage tasks lead to taking action to make the specific behavioral change; if successful, action leads to the final and fifth stage of change, maintenance, in which the person works to maintain and sustain long-term change. (p. 201)

DiClemente and Velasquez (2002) have gone on to explain:

Individuals move from being unaware or unwilling to do anything about the problem to considering the possibility of change, then to becoming determined and prepared to make the change, and finally to taking actions and sustaining or maintaining the change over time. (p. 202)

Because the TTM is a stage-based model, it is sometimes referred to as the "stages of change model" (Albery, 2008). Prochaska and DiClemente's stages can be conceptualized as circular process, or following one another as parts of a wheel. As seasoned therapists know, it is not unusual for clients to go through the stages several times before maintaining stable change. In order to keep a realistic perspective and keep their clients from becoming disheartened when relapse occurs, Miller and Rollnick (1991) tell their clients dealing with addiction: "Each slip or relapse brings you one step closer to recovery" (p. 15).

Motivation then is an important part of therapists' responsibilities and a central task in working with clients. In order to motivate clients, therapists need to take different approaches, depending on which stage the client is in within the change process outlined by Prochaska and DiClemente. In sum, the recreational therapist needs (1) to understand the stages that people go through during change; (2) to assess "where the client is" in going through the stages; and (3) to employ timely strategies that are appropriate for each stage in order to help the client to change.

Precontemplation

During the precontemplation stage, clients are not yet thinking about changing their behavior. At this stage, they do not understand that their behavior is destructive and they may not even acknowledge having a problem or concern. DiClemente and Velasquez (2002) have discussed the "4 Rs" that mark precontemplation: reluctance, rebellion, resignation, and rationalization. *Reluctant precontemplators* lack the knowledge that would motivate change. Therefore, empathic feedback, delivered with sensitivity, can be a good approach with them. *Rebellious precontemplators* do not want others to make decisions for them. Therefore, offering choices for these clients is a good strategy. *Resigned precontemplators* are overwhelmed by their situations and have given up hope of change. A strategy with these clients is to provide them with a sense of hope and to explore barriers to change. While resigned precontemplators have no answers, *rationalizing precontemplators* have all the answers. They have reason after reason why their problem or concern is not really a problem or concern for them. Expressing empathy and engaging in reflective listening are strategies for those who rationalize.

In general, it is good to keep in mind that while precontemplators can be motivated to move to the contemplation stage, it is best to not be too aggressive in approaches in working with them because confrontation with them is likely to be met with few results. They certainly do not want to be "lectured" or told what to do. What is needed is to raise doubts about problems or concerns and risks involved with maintaining their current behavior. As DiClemente and Velasquez (2002) have indicated: "They can be coaxed, encouraged, informed, and advised. We cannot make precontemplators change, but we can help motivate them to move to comtemplation" (p. 208).

Contemplation

Once clients become aware of their problem or concern, they enter the contemplation stage. Ambivalence typifies this stage as contemplators go back and forth between reasons to change or stay the same. Clients see that a problem or concern exists and think they might consider changing their behavior at some time in the future but are not ready to commit. DiClemente and Velasquez (2002) have suggested it is critical "for contemplators to receive accurate information about their behavior and potential benefits of change and personal feedback about the effect the behavior is having on their lives" (p. 209). They go on to state that it is important to "accentuate the positive" and to instill hope in clients that change is possible. The strategy for therapists is to tip the balance toward change by providing reasons for change, pointing out risks of not changing, and strengthening the clients' feelings of self-efficacy or their beliefs in their abilities to carry out change-related tasks. To increase self-efficacy, it may be helpful to explore any past barriers clients have faced during any prior attempts at change and help them to see themselves as having had "some success" rather than as having been "a failure" (Miller & Rollnick, 1991, p. 196).

Preparation

During this stage, clients are committed to take steps to end a problem behavior or begin to engage in positive behavior. They are on the verge of change but change is not necessarily automatic. Ambivalence may yet be present. They may need guidance to develop an effective plan of action. Guiding clients may involve offering options to clients by "gently suggesting strategies that have worked for other people" (DiClemente & Velasquez, 2002, p. 211).

The therapist should assess each client's level of commitment to determine if the client needs to increase his or her commitment to a plan of action. Discussing potential barriers may strengthen the client's resolve, as well as help develop client strategies to cope with anticipated barriers. Even with a strong commitment, success is not guaranteed. It may be important for the client to build coping skills during this stage. Therefore, a good strategy for the therapist is to help the client to explore his or her course of action in order to focus on details that could derail the plan.

Action

During the action phase, the client has formulated a plan and has begun to implement it. He or she is meeting his or her concern or problem head on. Therapists at this stage may take the role of offering confirmation of the client's plan, monitoring client activities, supporting the client's efforts, and helping increase the client's sense of self-efficacy. Increases in feelings of self-efficacy can be developed by providing messages that the client can change if he or she truly wishes to do so, by reaffirming the client's decisions, and by offering information about successful models (perhaps through contacts with former clients). In general, during the action stage, the therapist needs to engender an "I can" attitude on the part of the client and help the client to take steps toward change. Once the client is confident, it may be that the therapist will no longer be needed.

Maintenance

The final stage of successful change is that of maintenance. During this stage, the client's new behaviors are becoming established. It may be that, during this time, a client will require not only encouragement or support, but he or she may need further skills training as old behaviors are given up and new ones are established. In general, it is the therapist's role to help the client to identify and use strategies that will prevent relapse.

Relapse and Recycling

Relapse is possible during both the action and maintenance stages. Usually relapses do not occur overnight but are gradual slips toward old behaviors. Relapse can have a number of causes. These may include a strong temptation, relaxing of the client's guard, or the client testing himself or herself. Such slides backward often erode feelings of self-efficacy. It is the therapist's role to help the client not to become demoralized because of the relapse and to help the client to "recycle" or to renew the processes of contemplation, determination, and action. Strategies include providing empathetic understanding about the relapse, giving feedback about the length of time needed for stable change, and exploring reasons for the relapse (Miller & Rollnick, 1991).

A Final Thought on the TTM

Prochaska and DiClemente's (1982) Transtheoretical Model has been deemed "an exciting model for those interested in enhancing behavior change" and one that "deserves attention from researchers and practitioners alike" (Glanz, Lewis, & Rimer, 1990, pp. 152, 153). It is a practical model that offers a theoretical basis for practice in recreational therapy in that once a client's stage has been determined, the recreational therapist can select appropriate strategies to help the client progress in changing.

Table 8.2

Stages of Transtheoretical Model (TTM)

Precontemplation:	Not planning any changes in foreseeable future.
Contemplation:	Having acknowledged problem. Is considering change.
Preparation:	Planning steps in the near future. May be starting to make small changes.
Action:	Plans are put into action. Actively involved in changing. Engaging in new behaviors.
Maintenance:	Working to maintain change over time. Preventing relapse, consolidating gains, integrating new behaviors into lifestyle.

Adapted from Berman, A., Snyder, S. J., Kozier, B., & Erb, G. (2008). *Fundamental of nursing* (8th ed.). Upper Saddle River, NJ: Pearson Prentice Hall, p. 281; Niven, N. (2006). *The psychology of nursing care* (2nd ed.). New York: Palgrave MacMillan, p. 368.

Motivational Interviewing

Motivational interviewing (MI) was developed as an empirically based method of interacting with clients with substance abuse. The MI method is based on the notion that clients are often ambivalent about change and this ambivalence affects their readiness to change their behavior (Miller & Rollnick, 2002). Closely connected to motivational interviewing (MI) is the transtheoretical model (TTM) that provides part of the framework on which motivational interviewing rests. This connection is evident in comments made by DiClemente and Velasquez (2002) in the second edition of Miller and Rollnick's book titled *Motivational Interviewing: Preparing People for Change*. These authors wrote:

TTM, in particular the stages of change aspect of the model, has played an integral role in the development of motivational interviewing and brief interventions using a motivational approach....The TTM view of behavior change as a series of gradual steps that involve multiple tasks and require different coping activities rather than a single dimension—or an "all or none" process—has led to a significant change in the way behavioral health professionals conceptualize health behavior change.... Thus, motivational interviewing can be used to assist individuals to accomplish the various tasks required to transition from the precontemplation stage through the maintenance stage. (p. 202).

According to DiClemente and Valasquez, perhaps the most apparent connection between MI and the TTM stages of change is the application of motivational interviewing with clients who are in the precontemplation and contemplation stages. Regardless of when motivational interviewing techniques are applied, they are based on four guiding principles known by the acronym RULE (Rollnick, Miller, & Butler, 2008):

Resist the righting reflex. What has been termed the "righting reflex" is a natural tendency of the helping professional to fix the client's problems by imposing solutions. Instead, the client should not be pushed into doing "the right thing." Instead, the client must be allowed to choose what to do.

Understand and explore the client's motivation. The second guiding principle is that of the importance of involving clients in exploring their concerns, perceptions, and motivations. Clients are not only encouraged to discuss what they see as their reasons to change but also how they might envision themselves making the changes. Making the reasons for change their own and picturing themselves making changes provides an internal motivation for change.

Listen with empathy. To draw out clients so they may determine their courses of action requires empathetic listening skills. Of course, showing empathy requires the helper to have the ability to identify with the client's concerns and emotions and to display these understandings to the client.

Empowering the client and encouraging hope and optimism. The helper encourages clients to explore how to make differences in their health. Clients are then helped to understand that their plans are achievable and that they have the ability to act on their plans to bring about changes.

Recreational therapists who employ the RULE guiding principles do not tell their clients what they should be doing. Instead, they guide clients toward self-discovery. They strive to become engaged with their clients in order to help them to independently set goals and determine how to achieve them. Through this process, clients come to sense the strengths and resources they possess that will help them to achieve their goals and they become activated to use these strengths and resources to bring about changes.

Teamwork

Teams vs. Groups

Teams are more than a group of people working together. Members of committees and task forces work together, but these groups may not truly constitute teams because they may lack teamwork. For teamwork to occur there must be a high level of interdependence and shared responsibility among members who feel accountable to one another and who are committed to work together in order to achieve a defined purpose.

Porter-O'Grady and Malloch (2013) have written:

Teamwork operates very much like a well-designed and structured symphony. The discipline of effective teams very much represents a dance. It is the obligation of the team leader within a collaborative work model to carefully and judiciously plan the character and content of the team's work and anticipate how the team will accomplish that work. (p. 252)

Concepts Involved in Teamwork

Teamwork includes concepts such as (a) interaction and communication, (b) interdependence and collaboration, (c) shared problem solving and decision making, (d) efficient and effective use of members' talents, (e) integration and accountability, and (f) goal specification and commitment. Such concepts bring the end result of (1) benefiting the workplace because goals are accomplished and (2) benefiting members of the team through positive feelings about being a part of a successful team.

Team members interact and communicate regularly with one another. Members hold meetings to exchange ideas in order to reach their goals. Those in well-functioning groups have learned to create a group atmosphere of trust and support. There is a regular flow of information among the group members.

Interdependence and collaboration are evident in well-working teams. Members are not competitive but, instead, are willing to give of themselves in order to produce a team effort. People rely on one another and work together in order to produce an outcome that is more than they could achieve independently. Interdependence and collaboration lead to members making the most of each individual's talents as they mutually work for the good of the team.

Interactions based on free communications and a spirit of working together produce a climate where ideas can be generated, problems can be solved, and decisions can be made. Because group members make decisions together, they feel ownership of them and are more likely to be committed to collectively carrying them out. Feelings of having a mutual purpose and of being accountable to the team naturally surface under these circumstances. Team members do not want to let one another down.

Teams in Health Care Settings

There are various types of teams found in health care settings. The "interdisciplinary team" or "treatment team" is one that may come to mind first. This team is made up of those who work with clients. In today's health care world interdisciplinary teams have been termed by Porter-O'Grady and Malloch (2013) to be the "cornerstone" of client care. These authors have explained that there has been a shift toward interdisciplinary teams because of the realization of the complexities of care under the broad based biopsychosocial approach that has been widely adopted by health care agencies. No one discipline is seen to have all the answers to meet client needs. An interdisciplinary team represents a variety of means to address client needs through a team-based collaborative approach.

Such an interdisciplinary approach is in sharp contrast to the early days of health care's hierarchical system where physicians dominated. Bishop (2009) emphasized this point when she wrote: "Medical dominance no longer remains socially appropriate (If it ever was) but is in fact unworkable in today's society where professionals have their own codes of practice and must fit their contributions to care within the jigsaw of a complete care programme that seeks to meet the demands of a rising consumer movement" (p. 9).

Additional teams may be established for any number of functions ranging from quality improvement to handling management and administration responsibilities. No matter the type of team, working effectively within teams is an important role for the recreational therapist. At times, the recreational therapist will assume the role of team facilitator. At other times, the recreational therapist will be in the role of team member.

Tips for Team Facilitators

While we usually think of team leaders as the primary facilitators, other members of the team from time to time can take on the role of facilitator. Therefore, the tips that follow may sometimes be used by members of the team other than the designated leader. Team facilitators can do a number of things to help the team to become successful. Drawn primarily from Porter-O'Grady and Malloch (2013), along with Harper and Harper (1992) and Johnson and Johnson (1997), these include the following:

Helping the team to understand its mission and to formulate goals. Teams that become successful are clear about their purpose. Knowing and understanding why their team exists allows members to take the next step of defining the goals and tasks of the team. Through the process of developing an understanding of their purpose and goals, members become personally committed to the team's purpose and goals and begin to have ownership of them.

Review the team's goals and progress toward them with team members regularly. A good practice is the frequent celebration of even small successes by the team. Such celebrations bring the team closer together and remind members of the team's long-term goals.

Arranging for regular interactions among members of the team. Of course, team meetings need to be regularly scheduled so the team comes together. Relatively frequent meetings are particularly important early in the team's development so that members have a chance to get to know each other and to begin to bond. The first meeting is especially important, because it will likely set a tone for what follows. Therefore, leaders need to think about how they present themselves and be sure not to take an authoritarian approach. The meeting room should be a place conducive to creating a comfortable atmosphere in which members can get to know each other as equals. Additionally, means of communication, such as telephones, fax machines, and electronic mail, need to be provided so members can interact outside of meeting times.

Providing structure for the group by helping to establish clear rules of conduct. Group leaders cannot provide too much structure or members will feel they are being controlled. At the same time, effective teams need rules of conduct to direct actions during their meetings. Areas for ground rules include attendance, confidentiality, open and honest discussion, constructive confrontation, opportunity for participation by everyone, contributions by all members to the work of the group, and maintaining focus on the team's mission and goals. Two very practical means to providing structure are for the leader to prepare and distribute an agenda before team meetings and to begin and end meetings on time.

Manage team conflicts early and well. The leader should not become overwhelmed by conflicts. In fact, the leader must expect conflicts will arise. Early action will help prevent generalization of the problem. Address conflicts and issues in a calm fashion, as they are a normal part of team processes. As much as possible, the leader should anticipate possible conflicts and plan for them with an appropriate response prior to their occurrence. This should include watching for behaviors of individuals that stand in opposition to the effectiveness of the team.

Providing feedback on performance. Means to evaluate the progress of the team in terms of reaching its goals need to be provided. The team has to be accountable for its performance. Feedback should offer recognition for achievement and means to identify problems for correction. A means for this is to schedule frequent sessions for team processing. In these sessions, the team can explore its pluses and minuses and discuss steps to improve its performance. Individuals need to be accountable for their individual performances as well. Provisions should be made to offer honest and timely feedback to individuals so they can be reinforced for their positive behaviors and assisted to correct behaviors that prevent them from achieving their optimal levels of performance. Finally, it is important to have frequent team celebrations, as well as occasions to recognize individuals for their contributions to the success of the team. Celebrations add to the level of team pride, as well as providing individuals with personal satisfaction for a job well done.

Helping members to develop their team skills. Members need training on both task skills and teamwork skills. Formal training sessions should be scheduled to keep task skills sharp or to enhance them. Likewise, training on being a good team member can improve team functioning. Communications training for members is especially important. During team meetings, the facilitator needs to recognize and reinforce the team efforts displayed by the team.

Caring for the people you lead and being sensitive to their needs. The team leader should not act to gain personal recognition or to meet his or her ego needs. Instead, a good leader strives to demonstrate to team members that he or she cares about them. One of the most important ways to show caring is to listen carefully to team members by paying attention to what is verbally and nonverbally communicated. Demonstrating active listening skills also serves as a model for other team members. Additionally, caring leaders are considerate of the opinions of others. Being sensitive to the needs of others on the team involves continually monitoring the group to determine what the team needs. Where is the group in terms of its development? What feelings are members expressing? What specific needs are being revealed (for more agreement, more fun, more success)? Finally, a caring and sensitive leader expresses thanks to members of the team when appreciation is due. The leader must remember that team members' successes need to be frequently rewarded and encouraged.

Table 8.3

Don'ts in Team Leadership

1. Oversupervise the team or over control the team processes.
2. Criticize or punish team members in front of others.
3. Take the work of team members as if it belongs to you.
4. Ignore either internal or external dynamics that can Impact on the team.
5. Allow the team to get tied up in peripheral issues that impede their work.
6. Let the team members forget their work serves a purpose and has value.
7. Take all the credit for the team's accomplishments.
8. Identify members of the team as "my" people.
9. Overwork the team.
10. Neglect to provide time for relationship building among team members, including social interactions and celebrations of success.
11. Limit information or access to resources that might be helpful to the team in achieving its goals.

Source: Porter-O'Grady, T., & Malloch, K. (2013). *Leadership in nursing practice.* Burlington, MA: Jones & Bartlett Learning.

Tips for Team Members

Drawn primarily from the work of Harper and Harper (1992) are the following tips for team members:

Members are good communicators. Good communicators listen to everyone on the team, attempting to understand others' points of view. They communicate openly and honestly while avoiding the stereotyping of others and, thus, respecting individual differences and cultural diversity.

Members are active listeners. Good communicators recognize that listening to their fellow team members is important and it is worth taking the time to do so. They display active listening skills such as making good eye contact, leaning forward toward the member speaking, using paraphrasing and other listening responses so the speaker knows he or she is being heard, and listening for feelings as well as for facts. Of course, being active listeners implies that members will not hold side conversations while others are talking.

Members respect others and have trust in them. Team members know and respect the strengths (i.e., skills and knowledge) of others on the team and attempt to draw out those strengths. Members have trust in one another and build this trust by being honest in expressing thoughts and feelings.

Members realize that conflict is a part of team life but work toward consensus. It is important to the success of the group that a variety of views are put forth because it is healthy to explore divergent ideas. At the same time, the team needs to work toward consensus, and once a decision is made, the team needs to stand united behind the decision.

Members are team players. Members strive toward the team's goals and try not to hurt the team but to enhance it. They truly believe in (i.e.,"own") the goals of the team and are willing to place the team's goals ahead of their individual gains. Members also have to maintain the "togetherness" of the team by not putting down others (e.g., "That's dumb," "You don't understand," or "You can't be serious!") but, instead, by encouraging other team members (e.g., "Good for you," "That's a good point," and "Right on!"). Positive comments from others enhance self-esteem and encourage members to have even more pride in the team and their place on it.

If both team facilitators and team members skillfully fulfill their roles, it is likely that work teams will be highly successful. Such teamwork should result in a coordinated effort in which the team attains its goals.

Advocacy

It has been stated that for any profession that advocacy "is less an option than a mandate" (Locke, Myers, & Herr, 2001, p.93). Because of the necessity for helping professionals to stand up for their professions and their clients, the term advocacy has today become a buzzword. Yet, few helping professionals, including recreational therapists, have received training for advocacy.

Because the term is still relatively new to many, confusion may exist as to just what is meant by advocacy. Some see advocacy as just lobbying for self-interests or interests that are political in nature (Shore, 1998). This is not a valid understanding of advocacy as it is conceived by helping professionals. Locke and his colleagues (2001) have explained that the term advocacy is derived from the Latin, *ad vocare*, which carries the connotation of being "inspired, dedicated, and noble" (p.92). They go on to state that: "Related French and Latin origins of the term incorporate more contemporary notions of speaking or acting for or on behalf of a person, an idea, a principle, a cause or a policy..." (p.92). In short, advocacy is making a reasoned argument to obtain something from those in power (Bateman, 2000).

There are a number of types of advocacy in which recreational therapists may engage. Perhaps the one that first comes to mind when thinking of helping professionals is advocating for a client or small group of clients in order to assure that they receive rights or benefits to which they are entitled. This is termed *case advocacy*. Recreational therapists may become involved in case advocacy in representing their clients' interests or in guiding their clients in helping them to protect their rights. A second type of advocacy for which we may prepare our clients is known as *self-advocacy*. The nature of this advocacy is that a person, or group of persons, act in their own behalf to gain rights or meet needs. Self-advocacy has become a particularly important area for persons with disabilities in the fight for their rights. *Internal advocacy* is advocacy done by those employed by an agency in order to alter policies and practices within that agency. At one time, recreational therapists had to advocate in order to be included as equal members of interdisciplinary teams. This would be a form of internal advocacy. *Community advocacy* is advocacy directed toward organizing the community to meet the needs of those in the community who are experiencing similar problems. For example, community advocacy may involve organizing the community to address accessibility concerns of persons with disabilities. *Legislative advocacy* attempts to influence legislation in order to bring about services or provide resources for those who have been deprived of them. Because of the impact that legislation may have on the ability of professions to deliver services to clients, legislative advocacy has become a priority area today for most professional associations. *Professional advocacy* is advocating for a profession. This type of advocacy is typically accomplished through a professional association, such as the American Therapeutic Recreation Association (ATRA) or the Canadian Therapeutic Recreation Association (CTRA). Such organizations may advocate for any number of causes to improve service delivery to clients. For instance, advocacy efforts produced today's credentialing program administered by the National Council for Therapeutic Recreation Certification (NCTRC). For the interested reader, Bateman (2000) and Ezell (2001) offer additional information on types of advocacy. These resources were the primary ones used for this discussion.

The critical importance of advocacy is being recognized by a number of helping professions. For example, Silver (2001), a psychologist, has exclaimed that "...psychologists have an obligation to pursue activities that protect professional practice, specifically, advocacy for professional psychology" (p.1009). He has gone on to state that, "I am committed to the belief that a certain portion of the professional psychologist's time should be devoted to professional association activities" (p.1013).

Should such a commitment be expected of all helping professionals? Locke and his colleagues (2001) have argued that those in the counseling profession must become active advocates or face being left out of the public policy process. They have written:

> Without appropriate advocacy for the counseling profession, mental health legislation, managed care, and other public and private policies can severely restrict and jeopardize counselors' sanctions and responsibilities to serve...even to the point of professional extinction. (p. 93)

It appears that recreational therapists should have similar concerns to those expressed by Locke and his colleagues. It would seem that only if recreational therapy professionals are included in policies can they help their clients. Professional organizations in recreational therapy have begun to provide their members with training in the area of legislative advocacy. For many years, the American Therapeutic Recreation Association (ATRA), for example, used its Mid-Year Forum in Washington, D.C., to prepare its members to conduct legislative and professional advocacy.

No matter the type, it is likely that recreational therapists in the future will be engaged in advocacy. It will become more and more critical to prepare both students and professionals in recreational therapy to work in the area of advocacy. It will be necessary to (a) understand just what constitutes advocacy, (b) realize the types or areas of advocacy, (c) know problems and needs that can be met by advocacy, (d) build understandings of issues of importance, (e) learn who the target groups are who hold the power and will need to be influenced, and (f) develop and employ strategies to influence those in power.

Ezell (2001) has proposed an action model for advocacy efforts. His model begins with *identification of the problem or needs*. At this point, the advocate realizes that a problem or need must be addressed. The second stage is to *conduct advocacy homework*. This involves gaining a deep understanding of the situation. The next stage in the model is to *select advocacy target(s)*. In this stage the advocate determines which identity holds the power to correct the problem or meet the needs. For instance, this might be an agency, a community, or a legislative body. The final stage is *choosing tactics to employ*. This is the plan of action that may involve "specific change activities such as lobbying legislators, testifying at a community hearing, persuading an agency executive, holding a news conference, or filing a friend-of-the-court brief in a lawsuit," as Ezell (2001, p. xx) has explained. Throughout the entire course of events, the advocate must monitor and evaluate to determine how the process is working.

Only in recent years has the recreational therapy profession begun to focus on advocacy. Thus some recreational therapists are just beginning to come to understand the importance of advocacy. It is my hope that this introduction to advocacy may serve as a catalyst for those in the profession of recreational therapy who are not now involved in advocacy to become engaged in this area of leadership. Elsewhere (Austin, 2011a) I have stated my position on advocacy:

> I have come to believe that advocating for our profession is a responsibility that all recreational therapists should assume. If we don't speak out for our profession, who will? In the end, by advocating for our profession, we are advocating for our clients as we push for public policies and legislation that will lead to more and better recreational therapy services being available for our clients. (p. 78)

One way in which professionals can begin to advocate is to become active members of their professional organizations (e.g., ATRA and ATRA Chapters) and, eventually, become a board member or officer. As Porter-O'Grady and Malloch (2013) have indicated: "Because much of public advocacy is undertaken by professional organizations, participation in the organization strengthens its capacity to speak for the best interests of the population for which it advocates" (p. 27).

International Classification of Functioning Disability and Health (ICF)

Following nine years of revision by the World Health Organization (WHO), the International Classification of Functioning, Disability and Health (ICF) was approved on May 22, 2001, by 191 WHO Member States composing the World Health Assembly (World Health Organization, 2008). The approval of the ICF has been termed "a landmark event for medicine and society" (Stucki & Grimby, 2004, p. 5). Peterson (2010) has remarked that "the ICF holds great promise for affecting how all of health care thinks about functioning, disability, and health" (p. 188).

Because readers will likely encounter both the expressions ICD and ICF, a brief review of these separate but complementary WHO classification systems seems to be in order. The WHO Family of International Classifications (WHO—FIC) is composed of both: (a) the WHO International Classification of Diseases–10th Revision (ICD-10); and (b) the ICF.

The ICD "is the global standard to report and categorize diseases, health-related conditions and external causes of disease and injury in order to compile useful health information related to deaths, illness and injury (mortality and morbidity)," according to the World Health Organization (2008). The ICD can therefore be used to compile basic health statistics and to compare occurrences between countries.

The ICF is broader in nature than the ICD and has direct applications in rehabilitation. It was constructed as a complement to the ICD classification, focusing on the *functioning associated with health conditions*. The ICF is a scientifically based approach that establishes common language to describe a large number of health conditions while placing an emphasis on functional health and disability (Peterson, 2010).

Nathan (2010) has explained:

ICF was developed by WHO to accompany the WHO's International Statistical Classification of Diseases and Related Health Problems (ICD-10: WHO, 1992). It is designed to provide information on the broad array of disease and health conditions categorized in the ICD-10. Emphasizing the importance of functional health as well as disability, the ICF describes health and health related states from the perspective of the body (by classifying body functions and body structures associated with health and disease states as specified in ICD-10) as well as from the perspective of the individual and society (by classifying activities and participation associated with health and disease states as specified in ICD-10). (p. xxvi)

Similarly, the Centers for Disease Control and Prevention (2006) has interpreted the ICF by stating that "people with a 'disabling' condition can be healthy regardless of the disease or disorder involved. To address this issue...the World Health Organization General Assembly developed a new health classification system, similar to the ICD....The new classification system, *2001 International Classification of Functioning, Disability, and Health* (ICF; http://www.who.int) helps understand why two people with the same diagnostic condition have different health outcomes or experiences." Because of its application to rehabilitation in recreational therapy, the focus of this section is on the ICF.

Wide Acceptance of the ICF

The ICF has become "the generally accepted framework to describe functioning in rehabilitation" which Stucki and his colleagues (2002, p. 281) predicted it would be in an article shortly after its approval. Because the ICF has become accepted worldwide as a classification system, those in recreational therapy need to grasp a basic understanding the ICF.

What has made the ICF so proclaimed and so widely embraced? The answer to this question is that the ICF provides a new approach to understanding clients. This new approach is reflected by two statements from the WHO. The first is from the 2002 WHO publication titled *Toward a Common Language for Functioning, Disability and Health: ICF*. It reads:

ICF (International Classification of Functioning, Disability and Health) is named as it is because of its stress is on health and functioning, rather than on disability. Previously, disability began where health ended; once you were disabled, you were in a separate category. We want to get away from this kind of thinking. We want to make ICF a tool for measuring functioning in society, no matter what the reason for one's impairments. So it becomes a much more versatile tool with a much broader area of use than a traditional classification of health and disability. This is a radical shift. From emphasizing people's disabilities, we now focus on their level of health.

The second WHO statement on the nature of the ICF reads:

The ICF puts the notions of "health" and "disability" in a new light. It acknowledges that every human being can experience a decrement in health and thereby experience some degree of disability. Disability is not something that only happens to a minority of humanity. The ICF thus "mainstreams" the experience of disability and recognizes it as a universal human experience. By shifting the focus from cause to impact it places all health conditions on an equal footing allowing them to be compared using a common metric—the ruler of health and disability. Furthermore ICF takes into account the social aspects of disability and does not see disability only as "medical" or "biological" dysfunction. By including Contextual Factors, in which environmental factors are listed, ICF allows to record the impact of the environment on the person's functioning. (World Health Organization, 2008)

Schneidert, Hurst, Miller, and Ustun's (2003) statement regarding the ICF likewise is reflective of the innovative approach brought by the ICF. They wrote:

The ICF is a classification that allows a comprehensive and detailed description of a person's experience of disability, including the environmental barriers and facilitators that have an impact on the person's functioning. The recognition of the central role played by environmental factors has changed the locus of the problem and, hence, focus of intervention, from the individual to the environment in which the individual lives. Disability is no longer understood as a feature of the individual, but rather as the outcome of an interaction of the person with a health condition and the environmental factors. (p. 11)

The National Center for Health Statistics explained the new approach of the ICF this way:

Functioning and disability are viewed as a complex interaction between the health condition of the individual and the contextual factors of the environment as well as personal factors. The picture produced by this combination of factors and dimensions is of "the person in his or her world." The classification treats these dimensions as interactive and dynamic rather than linear or static. It allows for an assessment of the degree of disability, although it is not a measurement instrument. It is applicable to all people, whatever their health condition. The language of the ICF is neutral as to etiology, placing the emphasis on function rather than condition or disease. (National Center for Health Statistics, 2008)

Finally, Stucki and Grimby (2004) wrote this about the ICF:

The ICF is not only a language for health professions, but for patients too. The ICF provides a language of potential interest to us all, since, during a lifetime, virtually everybody will develop a health condition, including not only diseases, but also congenital anomalies, trauma and aging. In line with this view, the ICF overcomes the distinction between healthy and disabled. Instead, functioning is seen along a (illness–wellness) continuum that is potentially relevant to all. (p. 5)

ICF Allows a Reconceptualization of Health and Disability

Thus, the ICF allows health professionals to reconceptualize notions of health and disability. From the quotes presented, it is apparent that the ICF is much more positive than prior classification systems, including WHO's own International Classification of Impairments, Disabilities and Handicaps (ICIDH) (World Health Organization, 1980a). The previous ICIDH classification system followed a traditional medical model that placed the emphasis of any intervention solely on the individual to the neglect of the environment. The wider aspects of society and social organization were ignored under the old system. Schneidert, Hurst, Miller, and Ustun (2003) explained: "This medicalization and individualization of the problems of disability leads to interventions medical in nature and policies targeting individuals rather than social organization and environment" (p. 590).

The older ICIDH "considered the negative consequences of diseases but the ICF considers the people's abilities—the ICIDH was cast in terms of impairments, disabilities and handicaps (all negative states), but the ICF is cast in terms of functioning, activities and participation," according to Darzins, Fone, and Darzins (2006, p. 128). These authors have gone on to explain that "the ICF enables coding of normal, as well as abnormal body structure and function, activities and participation. *This change* (from the ICIDH) reflects the important concept that health is more than just an absence of illness. The ICF also introduces a system for considering the environmental factors that influence how people live. What people can do in 'optimal' environments is labeled their 'capacity,' and what they actually do in their usual environments is labeled their 'performance'" (pp. 128–129).

Schneidert, Hurst, Miller, and Ustun (2003) have drawn clear distinctions between the ICIDH and ICF. They wrote:

The conceptualization of the role of environment in disability has undergone a significant change from ICIDH to ICF. In ICIDH, environment was a submerged and secondary aspect of the classification. In ICF, environment is an independent and integral component of the classification. The conceptualization provided in the ICF makes it impossible to understand disability without consideration and description of the environmental factors.

The focus, similarly, has shifted in the conceptualization of intervention. The ICIDH focused intervention on changing the individual to fit societal expectations. The ICF focuses intervention where it is most appropriate. This includes interventions aimed at the individual, as well as and, most importantly, at society to eliminate barriers and develop facilitators. (p. 594)

ICF Components

The ICF has two parts. Each part has two components. Part 1 is Functioning and Disability, with the components of (a) Body Functions and Structures and (b) Activities and Participation. Part 2 is Contextual Factors, with the components of (c) Environmental Factors and (d) Personal Factors.

In Part 1, both the terms functioning and disability are used as umbrella terms. In ICF, the term *functioning* "refers to all body functions, body structures, activities, and participation, while disability is similarly an umbrella term for impairments, activity limitations and participation restrictions," according to the World Health Organization (2002).

Body functions include physiological functions and psychological functions of body systems. Body structures include anatomical parts of the body, including organs, limbs, and their components. If an individual has a significant deviation or loss in body function or body structure it is termed an *impairment*. Activity is conceived to be the execution of a task or action by an individual, while participation is seen as involvement in a life situation. *Activity limitations* include difficulties an individual may have in executing activities. Participation restrictions are problems an individual may experience in involvement in life situations. (Peterson, 2010; World Health Organization, 2002). Stokes (2011) identified four key components in Part 1 as (1) Body functions: physiological functions of the body systems; (2) Body structures: anatomical parts of the body such as organs, limbs, and their components; (3) Activity execution of a task or action by an individual; and (4) Participation: involvement in a life situation (p. 13).

In Part 2, *Contextual Factors* are made up of *environmental factors* and *personal factors*. *Environmental factors* are external factors in the environmental such as social attitudes, architectural accessibility, terrain, climate, and legal and social structures. Personal factors are internal and include gender, age, coping styles, profession, education, social background, experiences, behavioral pattern, and character, as well as other factors that may influence how disability is experienced by a person (World Health Organization, 2002).

Employing the identified components of Part 1 and Part 2, the ICF classification system follows a coding scheme to classify individuals' health characteristics. This system allows the person's functioning and disability to be assessed, along with the contextual factors represented within the environment and personal factors inherent within the individual. Thus, as indicated by Kearney and Pryor (2004), "The ICF provides a structure for examining the connections among body systems, functional outcomes and social participation" (p. 166). In doing so, the ICF offers a framework for health professionals to address activity limitations and participation restrictions that are associated with impairments (Kearney & Pryor, 2004).

The ICF and Mental Health

Many recreational therapists work in mental health. These RTs should be aware that the ICF has application not only in physical rehabilitation but in psychiatric rehabilitation as well. Peterson (2010) has detailed applications of the ICF conceptual framework in conducting assessments and interventions with clients in mental health. In his book he outlines how the diagnoses of the *Diagnostic and Statistical Manual of Mental Disorders* (DSM) do not capture the entire picture in mental health and functioning. He highlights the importance of contextual factors in disability, health, and functioning and how the ICF's biopsychosocial approach is sensitive to contextual factors and can complement the DSM by providing "considerable additional information" (p. 164) to the DSM.

Peterson (2010) has explained:

When mental disorders are addressed not only by diagnosis but also with clear descriptions of related Impairments, Activity Limitations, Participant Restrictions, and Contextual Factors (Environmental and Personal), the overall picture of health becomes more complete. Mental Disorders can be described more clearly using impairments in Body Functions, and the manifestation of disability in context can be illustrated using the concepts of Activity Limitations and Participant Restrictions. (p.164)

He goes on to state:

With a more complete conceptualization of health and functioning, more precise intervention targeting can occur through accurate identification of activity limitations and participant restrictions. Appropriate treatments can be selected with the understanding of the treatment context (Environmental and Personal Factors). In addition, given that the ICF was created to describe functioning and health as well as disability, strengths in functioning and health will also inform the selection of treatments that build on strengths as well as address difficulties. (p. 164)

ICF and Recreational Therapy

The potential impact of the ICF on rehabilitation for their practice has not been lost on those in the recreational therapy profession. An article by Porter and VanPuymbroeck (2007) has provided an introduction to the ICF and how it can be incorporated into clinical practice in recreational therapy. In an extensive article, Howard, Browning, and Lee (2007) have described components of the ICF that are particularly pertinent to recreational therapy, as well as identifying literature that connects the ICF to various diagnoses and treatment settings. These authors conclude their article with the statement that: "The ICF presents an excellent framework to describe and conceptualize TR (or RT) practice" (p. 77).

Heyne and Anderson (2012) have written about the ICF and RT:

At the level of social and environmental contexts, the ICF acknowledges the vital role of activities and participation in health and well-being. This area addresses a person's capacity and performance in a number of life areas (e.g., learning, communication, self-care), including recreation and leisure. Activities identified under recreation and leisure consist of informal or organized play and sports, physical fitness, relaxation, crafts and hobbies, reading for enjoyment, playing musical instruments, and tourism, among several others. (p. 118)

A major contribution to the literature on the ICF and recreational therapy is Porter and burlingame's (2006) 770 page book titled, *Recreational Therapy Handbook of Practice: ICF-Based Diagnosis and Treatment*. This work begins by providing an introduction to and overview of the ICF. It then covers the ICF coding scheme, explaining the ICF is a classification system, not a tool for assessment. A section on diagnosis follows in which 30 diagnoses common in recreational therapy practice are discussed. The coverage of the diagnoses includes recreational therapy interventions indexed to appropriate ICF codes. A third section of the book is titled "Treatment and the ICF Model." An impressive amount of information is presented on each ICF code. This is information that may be used by any healthcare professional. A fourth section, "Recreational Therapy Treatment Issues," covers RT equipment, concepts, techniques, and assessments while relating them to the ICF. The book concludes with appendices that include the ICF Model and a glossary of terms. Porter and burlingame are to be congratulated for providing the recreational therapy profession with such extensive coverage of the topic of the ICF. The handbook is an excellent resource for recreational therapists wishing to employ the ICF.

The ICF has been formally endorsed by at least one professional organization in recreational therapy. At their 2005 Annual Conference in Salt Lake City, the Board of Directors of the American Therapeutic Recreation Association (ATRA) gave its support to the ICF. In a news release, then ATRA President Bryan McCormick was quoted as saying: "Our association is pleased to endorse the International Classification of Function and see it as a valuable tool in our treatment services" (ATRA News Release, 2005).

Final Thoughts on ICF

The World Health Organization's International Classification of Functioning, Disability and Health (ICF) offers a positive approach to rehabilitation. It does not adhere to the traditional medical model. Instead, it is holistic in nature, following a biopsychosocial approach. Most of all, its focus is on health characteristics and client strengths instead of the individual's impairment.

The ICF appears to share many similarities with the Health Protection/Health Promotion Conceptual Model of Recreational Therapy (e.g., holistic approach, biopsychosocial model, illness/wellness continuum, effect of the environment, strengths-based approach, health protection and promotion) which was presented in Chapter 4. It would be instructive to examine the Health Protection/Health Promotion Model and other conceptual models in recreational therapy to determine similarities and differences between them and the ICF. Such analysis would help to determine conceptual connections between the ICF and recreational therapy as described in the models. Stamm, Cieza, Machold, Smolen and Stucki (2006) have already completed such a study in which they found links between the ICF and conceptual occupational therapy models.

Leadership and Understanding Transactions: The Social Psychology of Recreational Therapy

There are a number of applications of knowledge from social psychology that can be made within recreational therapy leadership. With familiarity with the literature of social psychology, recreational therapists may better understand both dynamics that related to the development of client concerns and leadership processes involved in the provision of interventions applied with clients.

Self-views, learned helplessness, the self-fulfilling prophecy, labeling, loneliness, self-efficacy, and attributional processes are topics of concern in understanding leader transactions with clients.

Self-Views

Following an extensive review of the literature, Swann, Chang-Schneider, and McCarty (2007) concluded "people's self-views do matter" (p. 92). One's views of self do seem to play a large role in influencing behavior. For instance, one's self-views (i.e., self-concept and self-esteem) affect whether a particular situation is viewed as routine, challenging, or threatening. If we perceive ourselves positively, we are apt to enter into new experiences and challenges. Conversely, perceiving oneself as inadequate can be debilitating (Borden & Stone, 1976; Iso-Ahola, 1980). Psychologists (Bjorkvik et. al, 2008) have suggested that regardless of the psychological diagnosis that therapists should consider the client's self-esteem because "self-esteem plays a core role in psychopathology by perpetuating dysfunctional perceptions and maladaptive behaviours" (p. 55).

Self-Concept and Self-Esteem

A question that often arises when discussing self-views is how self-concept differs from self-esteem. Most authorities concur that self-esteem represents how people regard themselves or value themselves. Self-esteem "refers to an individual's sense of his or her value or worth, or the extent to which a person values, approves of, appreciates, prizes, or likes himself or herself," Adler and Stewart (2004) have written. Baccus, Baldwin, and Packer (2004) have stated, "A person's self-esteem is typically viewed as the sum of his or her conscious self-evaluative thoughts and feelings" (p. 498). In short, self-esteem describes how favorable persons feel about themselves. Positive feelings result when our self-esteem is bolstered by what we perceive to be good evaluations from others (i.e., being valued or accepted). Negative feelings occur when our self-esteem is deflated. When we feel good about ourselves, we perceive ourselves as having the ability to take on and meet the challenges we encounter in life. Negative evaluations of ourselves, however, can lead to a sense of devaluation or rejection with accompanying feelings such as loneliness, guilt, anxiety, or depression (Leary, 1999; Mann et al., 2004).

Mann and his colleagues (2004) wrote, "Self-concept is defined as the sum of an individual's beliefs and knowledge about his/her personal attributes and qualities" (p. 357). Thus self-concept is generally viewed as a more global concept than self-esteem. It is the overall mental image or self-description people have of themselves. Willoughby and Polatajko (1996) stated, "Self-esteem is considered to be the overall value that one places on oneself as a person...where self-concept is viewed as the body of self-knowledge that individuals possess about themselves." Yet, Swann, Chang-Schneider and McClarty (2007) have rightly emphasized that both self-esteem and self-concept share emotional and cognitive elements. They have written that "self-esteem is a cognition about the self (e.g., a belief about how worthwhile one is) as well as a feeling, so too are self-concepts emotional (e.g., people care enormously about personal attributes they deem important) as well as cognitive" (p. 86).

While self-esteem may be seen as a "state" (i.e., a temporary feeling) most theories of self-esteem portray it as a stable trait. Heatherton and Wyland (2003) explained why self-esteem is largely viewed as a trait. They wrote that "if you have high self-esteem today, you will probably have high self-esteem tomorrow. From this perspective, self-esteem is stable because it slowly builds over time through personal experiences, such as repeatedly succeeding at various tasks or continually being valued by significant others" (p. 224).

Sources of self-esteem: What influences self-esteem? As may be surmised from Heatherton and Wyland's (2003) explanation, there are generally thought to be two sources of self-esteem. One is personal experiences (i.e., successes or failures) that lead us to beliefs about our competency or ability. Perhaps the notion of self-esteem arising from personal experiences is a primary way by which many understand the development of self-esteem. The second source of self-esteem that may be less known but seemingly has great potential for application in recreational therapy. The other source of the development of self-esteem is others' reactions to us. People internalize others' views of them or they perceive themselves as significant others view them. As Heatherton and Wyland indicated this influence on self-esteem is one "in which self-appraisals are viewed as inseparable from social milieu" (p. 221).

An extensive review of the empirical research literature by Leary (1999) has confirmed the social nature of self-esteem. He found a large amount of evidence to indicate the critical part that our perceptions of others' reactions to us have in affecting self-esteem.

Our levels of self-esteem are highly sensitive to the way that others accept us. Self-esteem development may certainly be affected by successful performances that are reacted to positively by significant others. In this instance, we feel accepted by others who are important to us. Of course, poor performances met with negative evaluations by significant others can adversely affect self-esteem as well. Such negative evaluations can lead us to feelings of rejection. This "looking glass self," as George Herbert Mead (1934) originally termed it, is the central process that affects self-esteem, according to Leary (1999). He has emphasized that the *primary determinate of self-esteem* is how others evaluate us or how we are perceived by other people. Leary (1999) has declared, "Human beings are motivated to preserve, protect, and occasionally enhance the degree to which they are accepted, included, and valued by other people. The self-esteem system is involved in the process of monitoring and regulating people's self-acceptance" (p. 216).

Thus, social inclusion, or being accepted by others, appears to be the key factor in self-esteem. Leary (1999) amplified on this notion when he wrote: "Contrary to theories that conceptualize self-esteem as purely personal evaluation of one's own characteristics, research suggests that people's self-esteem is far more sensitive to others' reactions to them than to how they see themselves" (p. 213).

Leary (1999) has explained that people are primarily motivated to gain acceptance and be included by others. But being accepted and included has the "side effect" of enhancing self-esteem. He has explained that "events that raise self-esteem are those that increase a person's perceptions of being accepted and included—achievement, recognition, compliments, admiration, and the like" (p. 210).

High and low self-esteem. Individuals' levels of self-esteem can have a tremendous impact on them. As Mann and his colleagues (2004) have written: "These powerful, inner influences provide an internal guiding mechanism, steering and nurturing individuals through life, and governing their behavior" (p. 357).

Leary (1999) has explained, "People with relatively high self-esteem tend to believe that they are generally acceptable individuals and that other people value their relationships with them" (p. 210). Heatherton and Wyland (2003) indicated those with high self-esteem are "psychologically happy and healthy." These authors went on to write about those with high self-esteem: "They feel good about themselves, they are able to cope effectively with challenges and negative feedback, and they live in a social world in which they believe that people value and respect them" (p. 219).

Those with low self-esteem hold entirely different self-views. Leary has described them in this way: "People with relatively low self-esteem walk through life assuming that they are less acceptable and that other people value their relationships less if not expressly devalue them" (p. 210). Heatherton and Wyland (2003) portrayed those with low self-esteem to "see the world through a more negative filter (than those with high self-esteem), and their general dislike for themselves colors their perceptions of everything around them. Substantial evidence shows a link between self-esteem and depression, shyness, loneliness, and alienation—low self-esteem is aversive for those who have it" (p. 219).

Leary is, of course, describing trait self-esteem. All of us, no matter our normal levels of self-esteem, have experienced times when we have felt "on top the world" following the recognition of an achievement of some kind. At other times, we have felt "lower than a snake" (an expression my daughter used to use) when we have been rejected. Having experienced the highs and lows of acute self-esteem, most of us can relate to the feelings of people whose normal levels of self-esteem are relatively high, or in the case of many of our clients, are relatively low.

People who have high self-esteem feel secure in their interpersonal relationships. Because of their feelings of security, they feel comfortable seeking out social memberships, even in prestigious groups or clubs. Memberships in prestigious groups reinforces their feelings of being accepted by others who are important to them. Unfortunately, many of our clients have relatively low self-esteem. These persons have had events in their lives that have lead them to believe that they are not accepted by others, and in fact, are devalued. Their feelings of insecurity may lead them to become socially isolated in order to protect their fragile self-esteem (Leary, 1999). For example, they may avoid participation in recreation activities for fear of being rejected by others.

Due to the chronic nature of low self-esteem it is not easily for those experiencing it to change. Thus, recreational therapists should not expect "quick fixes" when working with clients who have low self-esteem due to feelings of being devalued, rejected and excluded.

Ramifications for therapy. The notion presented by Leary (1999) on the dynamics of self-esteem has direct clinical implications. He proposes that low self-esteem should only rarely be regarded as the central presenting problem. Instead, client problems relate to feeling devalued or rejected by others. Self-esteem represents only a sort of barometer that reflects people's feelings of self-worth that result from the perceived evaluations of significant others. Or low self-esteem may be seen as a symptom of the problem of not being accepted and valued by those whose evaluations people count most.

Because clients' self-esteem is largely based on how they believe significant others evaluate them, an intervention recreational therapists may employ is that of helping clients with low self-esteem to feel valued and accepted, which will produce resulting improvement in self-esteem. One important means of developing feelings of being valued and accepted (and therefore to enhance self-esteem) is giving positive evaluations following a client's successful performance of an activity that is important to him or her. The recreational therapist must keep in mind that he or she can have a great impact on a client's perceptions of being valued (and therefore experiencing enhanced self-esteem) and regularly strive to provide feedback that is both positive and realistic.

One of the best interventions that recreational therapists can introduce for clients with low self-esteem is helping them to develop skills and behaviors that will produce positive responses from others in order to allow them to be accepted and included by others. If destructive or inappropriate behaviors have caused others to avoid or reject them, clients need to learn acceptable behaviors. Self-esteem will be enhanced when individuals are perceived by others to be socially acceptable and they respond accordingly. As Leary (1999) has indicated, "Everyone needs relationships, and everyone needs to feel that they are accepted by the important people in their lives. To help clients pursue ways of promoting social acceptance seems a valid clinical goal" (p. 216).

Gergen and Gergen (1986) have suggested three strategies to maintain or strengthen self-esteem. These strategies involve (a) protecting self-esteem by avoiding negative social comparisons, (b) building self-esteem by helping clients to assume new roles, and (c) improving self-esteem by helping clients to realize their social distinctiveness.

As the Gergens' strategies are presented, the reader is invited to see how these strategies fit with the notion presented by Leary (1999) that self-esteem is based on perceptions of how accepting others are of the person. He, of course, sees the achievement of social acceptance as the key clinical outcome with self-esteem being an accompanying result.

The first strategy presented by the Gergens involves avoiding negative social comparisons. They suggest that therapists need to bear in mind that clients will be making social comparisons that feed into their self-views. Placing a client in situations where everyone else is clearly superior in some way (e.g., possessing a highly developed recreational skill) can negatively impact self-esteem as clients will not feel they are seen in a positive light (i.e., are not positively evaluated by others) or belong with those who are superior in some way (i.e., are not accepted by others). Therefore, the therapist must analyze situations carefully to avoid assigning a client into a group where he or she will likely pale in comparison to others.

A second strategy proposed by the Gergens is that of having clients assume social roles that may be used as a means to positively affect self-views. It may be very therapeutic for the therapist to help a client to enter into a social role with which he or she does not feel comfortable, if in the judgment of the therapist the client will achieve success. For example, if a client is reluctant to join in a recreational group because he or she is shy, encouraging participation by the client may lead to feelings of newfound confidence when the client is able to achieve success within the group and, thus, feel he or she belongs (i.e., achieves social acceptance).

Because people identify themselves with those things that they perceive as being special or distinctive about themselves, the Gergens suggest the therapist can use this human trait to positively influence self-views. For example, the therapist can help clients to realize positive characteristics about themselves that others commonly value but that have not been a part of the clients' consciousness. If a client is a particularly good athlete or a sharp dresser, the therapist can emphasize these positive characteristics that set the client apart. Clients who have collections as hobbies may be encouraged to make others aware of their interests because their collections represent symbols of their distinctive selves in which they can take pride. By emphatically focusing upon those things that are distinctive about clients, the therapist is providing the implication to clients that these things are evaluated positively by others and valued by others. Of course, the therapist must be honest in pointing out distinctions that others would truly appreciate because momentarily falsely inflating a client's self-esteem will not provide a meaningful clinical outcome. Long-term meaningful clinical outcomes will only result from clients truly experiencing feelings of being valued and accepted by others.

Finally, Leary (1999) has warned that simply providing means to increase social acceptance may not be the solution to all clients' problems. He has suggested therapists may sometimes need to intervene by helping "unfairly rejected clients understand that the self-esteem system is, by design, an indicator of others' reactions to them and, thus, their low self-esteem is nothing more than an accurate reflection of how others have treated them. At the same time, they must see that their self-esteem is not, as they likely assume, an index of their true worth as an individual" (Leary, p. 215).

Therefore, if low self-esteem is a symptom of unfair devaluation or rejection by others, clients need to come to understand that significant others are not providing the kind of feedback that they deserve. Leary has written, "Critical or uncaring parents, abusive spouses, and egocentric friends may induce low self-esteem in people who do not deserve it." He has gone on to state: "If they can view their low self-esteem as a product of other people's weaknesses and shortcomings rather than their own deficiencies, they may feel badly about how they have been devalued by significant others yet learn not to make the unwarranted leap to self-deprecation" (p. 215). Leary has suggested that those who have been mistreated should be encouraged to seek new relationships with persons who will value them.

This discussion of the social nature of influences on self-esteem is not to dismiss concerns for our clients' beliefs about their personal assessments of their abilities and competencies resulting from direct experiences in succeeding or not succeeding in a task, such as an activity or project in recreational therapy. Of course, recreational therapists will want to provide clients with opportunities to can gain personal success and thus feel better about themselves as a result of self-assessment. This approach to self-esteem enhancement has long been followed in recreational therapy and should certainly be maintained. The concept of the importance of the social influence on clients feeling valued and accepted is a perspective however that has not been a regular part of the approaches to self-esteem by recreational therapists. Yet this social view holds obvious promise as a basis for recreational therapists to help clients to enhance their self-esteem.

Self-Handicapping

We human beings are unique in our ability to think consciously about ourselves. Further, we not only have the ability to reflect about ourselves, we possess a tendency to evaluate ourselves and, in doing so, we attempt to protect and enhance our self-esteem. Healthy striving can lead to maintained or improved self-esteem as persons take on tasks, experience success, and perceive others value them. Unfortunately, unhealthy behaviors can also arise as individuals attempt to protect self-esteem through the mechanism of self-handicapping. The information in the following section on self-handicapping is taken from an outstanding presentation of the subject by Leary and Miller (1986).

Self-handicapping is the term that has been used to describe the action in which people actually arrange impediments that they can later blame for their poor performance. Strangely, people do not always want to admit the truth about themselves so they self-handicap by providing plausible excuses for their behavior. Self-handicapping allows them to avoid receiving negative information about themselves. The phenomenon may occur when the threat of failure is such that it would greatly shake confidence. For example, an individual may "pull an all-nighter" before an important examination to set up the opportunity to blame failure on lack of sleep. Another student may not study for an examination to ensure that any possible failure will be attributed to a lack of study, rather than a lack of personal competence.

Clients may self-handicap themselves by not putting effort into socializing with others so they can maintain that they would be successful in their social lives if they devoted enough effort to it. Self-handicapping can become a serious matter of maladaptive behavior. For instance, individuals may regularly take drugs, including alcohol, before any important event in order to blame any negative outcomes on a performance-debilitating drug. Others may become chronic underachievers by always expending less than maximum effort because of personal doubts about their abilities.

Maddison and Prapavessis (2007) have made an interesting point. They state that it is "possible that in avoiding evaluation of ability through self-handicapping, individuals may never actually know how much they can accomplish" (p. 212).

Self-Reported Handicap

Another related type of behavior is that of the *self-reported handicap*. This occurs when no actual inhibiting factor exists but, instead, the individual makes up an excuse to explain poor performance. For example, people sometimes use excuses that they "haven't played lately" or that "my muscles are really sore" when they do not do well in sports. A more serious occurrence of self-report handicapping is the person who chronically uses ill health as an excuse for not performing well. Hypochondriacs continually blame their failures on their lack of good health. Others may regularly report psychological symptoms, such as anxiety or job stress, which cause them not to perform adequately.

Realizing that clients may engage in self-handicapping and self-reported handicapping can be useful information for the recreational therapist. When clients, for instance, do not give a task their best effort, the recreational therapist may recognize that the individual is threatened by the situation and is, therefore, entering into self-handicapping behavior in order to save face. The client may need additional support in order to try out the new behavior. Clients who use self-report handicapping also feel a threat to their self-esteem. Knowing the dynamics of self-report handicaps will help the recreational therapist to understand clients' behaviors so he or she may assist clients to deal in a more adaptive way with the situation.

Learned Helplessness

The notion that we, as human beings, strive for control over ourselves and our environment is deeply rooted in our western culture (Austin, 2002d). As a matter of fact, the extent of discrepancy that exists between our perceived and desired levels of control may be seen as an indication of our degree of social adjustment (Grzdlak, 1985).

Both anecdotal material (Gatchel, 1980) and research reviews (e.g., Kleiber, Walker, & Mannell, 2011; Leary & Miller, 1986) have shown that experiencing a lack of control over adverse life situations produces a sense of uncontrollability. Repeated failure to affect outcomes that will allow one to escape adverse conditions can produce feelings of inadequacy, leading to the conclusion that no matter how much energy is expended, the situation is futile and the person is helpless to alter things (Stroebe, 2011).

The debilitating effect of such a perceived lack of control over events has been termed *learned helplessness.* Cemalcilar, Canbeyli, and Sunar (2003) defined learned helplessness: "When experience with uncontrollable events leads to the expectation that future events will also be uncontrollable, disruption in motivation, emotion, and learning may occur" (p. 65). These authors went on to explain learned helplessness can appear in the behavioral, motivational, cognitive, and emotional domains. They wrote: "Broadly speaking, the behavioral and motivational effects include passivity, giving up, and procrastination; the cognitive effects include decreased problem-solving, frustration, and lowered self-esteem; and the emotional deficits usually involve dysphasia or depressed mood following negative outcomes" (p. 66).

Stroebe (2011) has explained the theory behind the learned helplessness model:

The basic assumption is that when people or animals experience an event that they cannot control, they develop an expectation of lack of control in similar future situations. This learning results in the helplessness syndrome consisting of motivational, cognitive and emotional deficits; if the persons or animals have learned that the escape from aversive stimulation occurs independent of responses, they will not try very hard to initiate a response that can produce relief; they will react to the traumatic experience first with fear and then depression. On the basis of the similarity of the symptoms of learned helplessness and depression, Seligman proposed that learned helplessness was a major cause of reactive depression. (pp. 251, 252)

Helplessness and control. Much of the initial research work on helplessness was accomplished by Martin Seligman and his colleagues (Seligman, 1980), who first studied dogs and their reaction to painful, uncontrollable shocks and later conducted studies with human subjects. With humans, Seligman's efforts centered on the effect helplessness may have in bringing about depression.

One of the most frequently cited works on helplessness was the classic study done by Langer and Rodin (1976). The study was completed in a nursing home, a setting in which many patients feel a lack of control over their environment. In the study, residents were given opportunities for personal responsibility (e.g., taking care of a plant) and for decision making (e.g., to decide which night of the week to view a movie). The sense of control gained from these relatively small opportunities to exercise control apparently had a markedly positive effect. In contrast to a comparison group, the residents who were given control over their environment were more alert, had higher levels of participation in activities, and exhibited a greater sense of general well-being.

The study demonstrated that residents of institutions do not have to be doomed to a life of helplessness but may benefit from opportunities to gain a sense of perceived control. In light of such findings, it is unfortunate that much of what occurs in institutions, hospitals, and other health care settings can lead to feelings of helplessness. Too often, interactions with health professionals foster feelings of helplessness in clients due to condescending behaviors, paternalistic approaches, and the mystification that surrounds many health care processes.

While we may suppose that today's health care facilities may no longer foster helplessness, research by Ice (2002) suggests that, at least in nursing homes, there is room for improvement. A prior study (Gottesman & Bourestom, 1974) had found that nursing home residents spent 56% of their day confined to their rooms doing virtually nothing. Because institutional environments can lead to learned helplessness (see Voelkl, 1986), Ice wished to determine whether the situation had changed from the time of the original study. Unfortunately, this researcher's findings were not much different than what had been reported 25 years previously. Despite organized recreation programs being available, it was common for residents to spend the majority of their day alone in their room in inactivity. One conclusion the researcher reached was that studies need to be completed to determine what type of activities are needed to provide nursing home residents with a sense of control and a meaningful life.

From Ice's study it seems apparent that just having activities available is not enough. This could lead one to the conclusion that it is the approach to the provision of activities that is key in avoiding helplessness. The next section discusses helplessness and possible approaches in the provision of recreational therapy services that may permit clients a sense of control and prevent helplessness from occurring.

Helplessness and recreational therapy. Recreational therapy can represent the antithesis of the controlling environment often imposed on health care clients. Within recreational therapy individuals are given opportunities to escape the normal routines of the health care facility and to feel in control of their environments. Clients in recreational therapy programs become involved in experiences in both mastering challenges and learning to endure frustration. In doing so, individuals learn that they are able to affect the world and deal with its consequences. They learn to accept personal responsibility for their actions through these experiences, from which they develop healthy self-regard. (Iso-Ahola, 1980; Kleiber, Walker, & Mannell, 2011).

Austin (2002, pp. 106-110) has listed general principles that leaders of recreational therapy programs may use to assist clients to retain or regain a sense of control. The first principle is for *leaders to portray an optimistic attitude that clients' sense of control is changeable.* Even with clients who feel helpless, it is important that recreational therapists exude optimistic perspectives. A second principle is for leaders to *offer the antithesis of a controlling environment.* Rather than remove control from clients, recreational therapists strive to leave as much control as possible with their clients. A third principle is for *leaders to help clients increase feelings of self-efficacy.* When clients experience mastery they gain feelings of self-accomplishment that lead them toward greater self-efficacy with ensuing feelings of control. A fourth principle is closely related to the third principle. It is for *leaders to build on client strengths.* Recreational therapy should amplify client strengths during activities. Mastery and success experiences resulting from client strengths produce feelings of self-efficacy and feelings of control. A fifth principle is for *leaders to offer opportunities for clients to obtain and build social support.* Receiving social support from others can offer clients feelings of comfort and relief from stress, which may assist them to retain or regain personal control. The sixth principle is for *leaders to provide opportunities for mood enhancement.* Positive mood states can be gained from participation in recreation and leisure experiences. Mood enhancement tends to positively affect feelings of control. The final of Austin's principles is for *leaders to build optimism in clients.* Opportunities for self-determination tend to create optimism in clients. Optimistic perspectives lead clients toward experiencing a sense of control.

Psychological reactance. While helplessness may be a common reaction to feeling that a situation is beyond control, sometimes individuals do not become helpless in the face of perceived loss of control but, instead, experience **reactance**. In Walker's (2001) book on control and the psychology of health, she has suggested that years ago Taylor (1979) made a valid point when it was stated that "good" patients (who are compliant and passive) may be feeling helpless whereas "bad" patients (who are angry, demanding, and complaining) are in a state of reactance.

Psychological reactance is the opposite of learned helplessness. Instead of giving up, as people do when they become learned helpless, those exhibiting reactance resist when their freedom of choice is threatened. Kleiber, Walker, and Mannell (2011) have explained: "When a specific freedom is eliminated or threatened, the individual will evaluate that freedom more favorably and be motivated to re-establish it" (p. 147). Wortman and Brehm (1975) have hypothesized that individuals initially respond with reactance in order to overcome threats to freedom and control. If, however, they continually encounter failure in their efforts, they respond with weaker reactions until they eventually become completely frustrated, depressed, and experience helplessness. Research findings by Mikulincer (1988) and Roth and Kubal (1975) supported Wortman and Brehm's hypothesis.

It appears that when people first encounter difficulty, they may exhibit reactance. If, however, repeated attempts to gain control over the situation fail, motivation is reduced and they begin to believe the situation is truly beyond their abilities to live with or change. At that point, they experience helplessness and accompanying feelings of depression (Leary & Miller, 1986; Mikulincer, 1988).

The Self-Fulfilling Prophecy

Our prejudices can provide us with expectations that can set into motion self-fulfilling prophecies. For example, if Dave, the group leader, believes his group members "are unable to take care of themselves," he may treat them in a condescending way. Such an approach only leads the group members to be dependent. Thus Dave's original prejudice is confirmed (Gergen & Gergen, 1986). By acting in accord with his expectations, Dave "got what he expected." Perhaps he was able to inform his colleagues that "I told you so!"

Sometimes the self-fulfilling prophecy is referred to as the *self-fulfilling expectation*. Others term it the *Pygmalion effect,* after the Greek sculptor whose statue of a great beauty came alive due to his expectations (Gergen & Gergen, 1986). The classic study on the self-fulfilling prophecy was done by Rosenthal and Jacobson (1992) and was first published in 1968. These researchers randomly identified elementary schoolchildren as "spurters" and informed their teachers that "reliable tests" had indicated these students (actually chosen at random) would show rapid intellectual gains during the school year.

The researchers thus established positive expectations for these children in the minds of the teachers. Did teacher expectations cause teachers to treat these students differently in a way that would lead to a self-fulfilling prophecy? Yes, it appeared so. Intelligence tests at the end of the school year indicated the "spurters" showed significant gains, not because they were actually more gifted but because their teachers expected them to do better. Observations of the teachers revealed that they were unwittingly responsible for the outcome by paying more attention to the "high achievers" and rewarding them for behaviors that were not rewarded in other children.

While there was a happy ending to the Rosenthal and Jacobson experiment, negative expectations can also come true, as illustrated by Dave's leadership with the clients he encouraged to be dependent. Leaders of recreational therapy groups must be aware of possible prejudice, or preformed expectations, so they do not fall into the trap of the self-fulfilling prophecy. They also need to be aware that clients' self-expectations can play a role in the outcome of treatment or rehabilitation. If clients expect to improve, they will be more likely to do so. If they do not expect positive outcomes, improvement is far less likely (Sheras & Worchel, 1979).

Labeling

Leaders' transactions with clients can be influenced by the application of labels to clients. We usually associate labeling with the act of assigning a negative categorical term to an individual, often causing stigmatization. For instance, to label a client "mentally ill" could result in having him or her perceived as an inadequate person possessing negative traits.

Rosenhan's investigation. In what has perhaps become the best known study of labeling, Rosenhan (1973) investigated the effects of having people labeled as schizophrenic. He and his colleagues gained admission to psychiatric hospitals by exhibiting symptoms of schizophrenia, including complaints of vague auditory hallucinations. Once admitted, they dropped all pretenses of being schizophrenic. Staff, however, were not able to perceive the researchers' behavior as normal. The diagnostic label so strongly influenced staff members that whatever the researchers did was seen to reflect pathology. Eventually, the researchers were released, but even so, they were still officially labeled as having schizophrenia that was "in remission."

Negative labeling and staff reaction. Labeling a person, whether or not the label is reliable, can obviously affect others' responses to the labeled individual. Damaging effects can result if staff devalue the person due to a diagnostic label to which they have attached negative connotations. Staff, for instance, should never perceive the client as being "a deviant" or someone who is not equal to them. Such perceptions cause staff to be uncaring and act unprofessionally. This type of reaction by staff can lead the client to feel diminished and inadequate. This is, of course, very wrong. All clients are persons of worth and must be treated with dignity and respect.

Labeling and therapy. Recreational therapists also must never allow themselves to fall into the trap of perceiving individuals to represent the stereotype reflected by a diagnostic category. Stereotyping a client on the basis of the classification of a disorder or disability does not, of course, take the individual's uniqueness into account. It puts the focus on categorical differences instead of on the person. Thus, recreational therapists must be on guard against the dangers of labeling clients.

Each client needs to be treated as a unique and worthwhile human being with individual limitations and abilities. This does not mean that diagnoses (a type of labeling) should be avoided. Well-grounded diagnoses may serve valid legal and administrative purposes, enabling clients to receive care and agencies to organize services. Nevertheless, factual information regarding each client's abilities, needs, and desires—instead of a general label or diagnostic category—should form the basis for planning interventions for individuals.

In fact, labeling can even produce positive effects, according to psychologist Jeana Magyar-Moe (2009) who wrote:

> Although there are many potential problems associated with labeling people, positive outcomes can be achieved through the labeling process as well. Labels can have positive effects and be very enabling when they are used to identify more than just problems or deficits in human functioning. Indeed, when strengths and resources are labeled in addition to weakness and deficits, even the labeling of psychological disorders can have positive effects.

Loneliness

Who suffers from loneliness? The truth is that all of us have been lonely at one time or another. Studies have found that more than 25% of respondents admitted feeling very lonely within the past few weeks or month (Duck, 1998; Shultz, 1988). It has been reported that of those under 18 years of age, 80% had experienced loneliness and 40% of those over age 65 had been lonely. Loneliness is a chronic state for an estimated 15-30% of the population (Hawkley & Cacioppo, 2010). Of individuals with severe mental illnesses, more than one-half have problems with loneliness (Perese & Wolf, 2005).

Catttan and her colleagues (2005) have noted an increasing recognition of the importance of programs to reduce loneliness and increase the well-being of lonely clients. Unfortunately, loneliness seems to have been largely neglected in the literature of recreational therapy.

At-risk groups. If you are a university student away from home, you can no doubt relate to the topic of loneliness because students typically feel lonely when they begin their studies at a new school (Duck, 1998). At-risk groups for loneliness include adolescents, individuals who are dying, persons with chronic or socially unacceptable illnesses or body image problems, those who have undergone the loss of significant relationships, and people who have relocated geographically (Shultz, 1988, p. 397). Hospitalization can bring on or intensify feelings of loneliness because people are removed from their normal environments and support systems (Shives, 1998). Older people are particularly at risk for loneliness according to any number of authorities (Cattan et al., 2005; Cornwell & Waite, 2009; Golden et al., 2009; Martina & Stevens, 2006; O'Luanaigh & Lawlor, 2008; Pettigrew & Roberts, 2008; Shankar & McMunn, 2011; Theeke, 2009).

Health problems and loneliness. It is important for recreational therapists to understand that loneliness and health problems are often closely associated. Authorities have reported negative physical, psychological, and social correlates of loneliness. These include cardiovascular effects, malnutrition, sleep disturbance, diminished immunity, elevated blood pressure, dementia, depression, hopelessness, suicide, personality disorders, psychoses, low self-esteem, substance abuse, obesity, Alzheimer's disease, impaired cognitive functioning, decreased physical activity, fewer social contacts, and increased mortality in older adults (Cacioppo, Fowler, & Christakis, 2009; Golden et al., 2009; Hawkley & Cacioppo, 2010; O'Luanigh & Lawlor, 2008; Pettigrew & Roberts, 2008; Shankar, McMunn, Banks, & Steptoe, 2011; Theeke, 2009; Wilson et al., 2007).

Expectations define loneliness. Most of us can define loneliness on some level because we have experienced it firsthand. It is more than being alone, although isolation can be involved. Loneliness and social isolation are related concepts. They are however distinct. Hawkley and Cacioppo (2010) explained this distinction:

> Loneliness is synonymous with perceived social isolation, not with objective social isolation. People can live relatively solitary lives and not feel lonely, and conversely, they can live an ostensibly rich social life and feel lonely nevertheless. Loneliness is defined as a distressing feeling that accompanies the perception that one's social needs are not being met by the quantity or especially the quality of one's social environment. (p. 218)

Likewise, Shankar, McMunn, Banks, and Steptoe (2011) wrote:

> Individuals who live alone, have few friends or family, and have limited contact with people are viewed as being socially isolated. Loneliness or perceived social isolation is believed to be its psychological counterpart. While social isolation is an objective, quantitative measure of network size and diversity, and frequency of contact, loneliness is a qualitative, subjective evaluation related to individuals' expectations of and satisfaction with the frequency and closeness of contacts. (p. 377)

Similarly, Masi and his colleagues (2011) have stated that social isolation "reflects an objective measure of social interactions and relationships, whereas loneliness reflects perceived social isolation or outcast. Accordingly, loneliness is more closely associated with the quality than the number of relationships" (p. 219). Golden and her colleagues (2009) perhaps most succinctly described the difference between loneliness and social isolation when they stated, "Loneliness is the subjective experience of social isolation. It has been defined as an unpleasant subjective state of sensing a discrepancy between the desired amount of companionship or emotional support and that which is available in the person's environment" (p. 694).

"The critical feature of loneliness," according to Duck (1998), "is a discrepancy between what we're doing and what we expect or hope to do" (p. 24). Most of us would concur with Shultz (1988) that "loneliness results from deficiencies in a person's social relationships; it is subjective and often not directly related to social isolation; and it causes unpleasant feelings" (p. 382) such as despair, dejection, and depression.

Mood and social behavior. Transactions may be marked by a lack of caring for oneself or others. The lonely person may be moody, engage in self-deprecating acts, hold a morbid preoccupation with death, express suicidal ruminations or gestures, or experience social isolation and, perhaps, withdrawal from reality (Perko & Kreigh, 1988, p. 360).The social behaviors of people who are lonely tend to differ from others in three ways. The first difference is that lonely persons often hold a negative outlook toward themselves and others. The second difference is that lonely individuals exhibit social-skills deficits. Finally, their social behavior is superficial. They act more inhibited and less intimate than others (Leary & Miller, 1986).

Loneliness and therapy. As previously indicated, little attention has been given to loneliness in the recreational therapy literature. Evidence-based strategies are generally lacking in the professional literature of other disciplines as well (Cattan, White, Bond, & Learmouth, 2005; Martina & Stevens, 2006; Pettigrew & Roberts, 2008).

Hawkley and Cacioppo's (2010) review of the literature did reveal four main types of interventions have been employed to combat loneliness. The four are (a) enhancement of social skills, (b) the provision of social support, (c) increasing opportunities for social interaction, and (d) addressing maladaptive social cognitions. Martina and Stevens (2006) and Cattan, White, Bond, and Learmouth (2005) have reported that group interventions (rather than individual interventions) have been most effective. These findings provide direction for recreational therapists in working with clients who are lonely.

Lonely clients often have problems relating to others due to social-skills deficiencies. Recreational therapists can serve as role models by modeling effective social skills when interacting with clients who are lonely. Further, recreational therapists can conduct social-skills training or refer clients to social-skills training groups.

Recreational therapists can also offer social support to clients (The following section of this chapter covers social support in detail.). It would seem that trust building would be an important first step for recreational therapists to take with clients who are lonely. Creating a warm, caring atmosphere will allow these clients to become comfortable with you and themselves. To indicate a sense of caring, touch can be used in the form of patting the client on the shoulder or laying a hand on the client's wrist or arm (Perko & Kreigh, 1988). Because clients are likely to suffer pain and hurt as they try out new social skills and gain confidence in their abilities, recreational therapists will need to remain supportive. At the same time, recreational therapists will need to slowly decrease clients' dependence (Shultz, 1988). Social support can take several forms. For example, clients living at home may be encouraged to have an animal to provide companionship.

People who are lonely report that they feel shy and awkward in social situations. They also take fewer social risks than others. Some are so self-focused that it keeps them from responding to others' needs and feelings. Recreational therapists can help these individuals by providing opportunities for social interaction during recreational activities. Such occasions allow clients to develop friendship skills and to practice social skills. Another strategy is to help the client to make new relationships through participation in community organizations and activities.

Following participation in activities, recreational therapists can process what happened in the activity (See Chapter 7 for specific group processing techniques). Within group processing, clients can address maladaptive social cognitions (e.g., "People do not like me," or "I cannot function in a group of people."). Leisure counseling is another approach recreational therapists may employ to help clients to address maladaptive social cognitions (See Chapter 3 for information on leisure counseling).

While limited in number, some specific interventions for loneliness have been reported in the literature. Banks and Banks (2002) reported on a study of the effects of animal-assisted therapy (AAT) on loneliness in elderly clients in long-term care facilities. A weekly session of AAT for 6 weeks was found to reduce loneliness as measured by a standardized instrument.

Two studies using reminiscence therapy have been conducted by researchers in Taiwan. Following 6 to 10 reminiscence therapy sessions it was reported elderly participants who lived alone in the community experienced lessened loneliness, significantly raised self-esteem, and improved general life satisfaction. The researchers explained that participants who retold and shared life experiences began to see others shared similar life events and psychological problems as they did. Additionally, the researchers believed those in the group felt emotional support from other group members (Liu, Lin, Chen, & Huang, 2007). Chiang and her colleagues (2010) reported on the effects of eight reminiscence therapy sessions conducted over a period of two months with elderly people who were institutionalized. Reminiscence therapy improved participants' feelings of loneliness, helped to ameliorate depression, promoted socialization, and brought about feelings of accomplishment.

Australian researchers Pettigrew and Roberts (2008) conducted a study with elderly persons living in the community to determine those social and solitary pastimes that would ameliorate feelings of loneliness. Through an interview process there emerged four major activities that participants reported reduced their experiences of loneliness. Identified were two social activities. These were interacting with friends and family for emotional support and taking part in eating and drinking rituals as a means to maintaining social contacts. Two solitary activities that had loneliness reducing properties were reported to be reading books and newspapers and gardening. The authors claimed the activities in which interviewees participated permitted "them to engage in pastimes that have the potential to be challenging, stimulating, and rewarding, and therefore were effective in the management of age-related loneliness" (p. 308). While no more specific explanations of the therapeutic effects were given by the researchers, recreational therapists may wish to employ similar activities as those described to determine their value in reducing clients' loneliness.

Whatever approaches are employed by recreational therapists to assist clients to reduce loneliness, a key finding from an extensive review of the literature suggests that group programs need to heavily involve participants in planning, developing, and delivering the programs if the interventions are to be effective (Cattan, White, Bond, & Learmouth, 2005). While the literature review was done for interventions for older persons, the principle of client involvement would seem to have application for loneliness interventions for any group of participants. Certainly the approach to engage clients is in keeping with the traditions of recreational therapy. As I have written elsewhere, "I believe that perhaps better than any other therapy, recreational therapy has the ability to engage clients." I went on to state: "Recreational therapists involve clients in their own planning so that they have a say in determining in which programs they will take part. Thus, clients' preferences are honored within recreational therapy" (Austin, 2011, p. 85).

In summary, the literature of recreational therapy to a large degree neglects interventions to combat loneliness. To compound the situation, evidence-based strategies are lacking in the literature of kindred professions as well. Nevertheless, there are approaches to loneliness reduction that have been suggested within the literature of professions related in recreational therapy. Also, there are a limited number of studies on facilitation techniques often used by recreational therapists (i.e., animal-assisted therapy and reminiscence therapy) that recreational therapists may use as a basis for practice.

We do know from the available literature on loneliness that group interventions have been effective and for groups to be productive, leaders need to actively involve participants. Further, it has been suggested that recreational therapists can assist clients in the development of social skills and can offer clients social support. Trust building in a warm, caring atmosphere offers a basis for the provision of programs that allow positive social interaction. In such programs, clients may build friendship skills and practice social skills while feeling supported by the recreational therapist and other members of the group. Creating such a therapeutic environment provides a foundation for clients to address maladaptive social cognitions. While clients are building their skills and confidence in their abilities, the recreational therapist needs to remain supportive and slowly decrease client dependency.

Social Support

Social networks are made up of those with whom an individual interacts. Social support is the perception that at least some persons in the social network are supportive of the individual in meeting the individual's needs. Recreational therapy professor Bryan McCormick (2002) has completed research on social support and has defined social support as *"the provision of material, emotional, or informational resources through social relationships that aid an individual in functioning"* (p. 50, italics his).

Thus while social support depends on individuals having social networks, it involves more than simply having social ties. Social support involves the perception that others care about them, have esteem for them, and are willing to provide material, emotional, or informational aid to them (McCormick, 2002). Material aid, for instance, might be loaning a car or money. Emotional aid might take the form of being assured that a problem was not the individual's fault. Informational aid might include making suggestions on how to proceed when problem solving. A specific type of informational support is appraisal support where the information relates to the person's self-evaluation. For instance, a person may use another individual to compare himself or herself to as a source of information in completing self-evaluation (Stroebe, 2011).

Social relationships can affect both mental and physical health. As Stroebe (2011) has stated, "There is now a great deal of evidence that the availability of social support is associated with a reduced risk of mental illness and physical illness, and even mortality" (p. 280).

Walker (2001) has emphasized the need for possessing adequate social skills to permit the building of social relationships, which help to maintain good mental health. He wrote: "Characteristics of those who lack social skills include lack of self-esteem and assertiveness. These happen to be characteristics of many people with mental health problems, including anxiety and depression. It would thus appear that those most in need of social support are among those least likely to receive it" (p. 130).

Uchino (2004) has written that "…the strength of social bonds manifests in the joy, sense of acceptance, and resources we experience as a part of our relationships. This not only promotes positive mental health, but can also influence how long one lives" (p. 182). While it might be assumed that social support would impact on psychological well-being, it may be a surprise to many that "social support predicts lower mortality rates" (Uchino, 2004, p. 170).

Unfortunately, recreational therapy clients often lack social networks from which they may obtain social support. McCormick (2002) has explained that work by Lyons has suggested "the effect of illness on social relationships is such that it tends to reduce network size, to constrict the range of functions of relationships, and to decrease the availability of valued relationships" (p. 62).

Social support and therapy. Recreational therapists relate to the provision of social support for clients in at least two ways. Those who work in activity leadership roles with clients may be perceived to provide direct social support to clients in nurturing roles as "professional friends" or "surrogate friends." Particularly those clients who lack a social network of friends and family may rely on recreational therapists to provide social support. Initial provision of social support by recreational therapists may be appropriate, but it is important for clients to expand their social network through natural social relationships and not to become dependent on recreational therapists as their primary means for social support.

The other way that recreational therapists relate to social support is assisting clients to build social networks from which they may obtain social support. At first, this may include getting clients started in participating in activity groups within the agency or facility. In many cases recreational therapists will also assist clients to develop the leisure and social skills needed to as a foundation to become participants in groups. Later, recreational therapists may be involved in helping clients to become a part of community recreational groups in which they can meet others, develop friendships, and begin to build their social networks. Such community integration is particularly important for persons with psychiatric disabilities because their perceptions of whether they possess social support have been found to be a key to their feelings of subjective well-being (Prince & Gerber, 2005).

Social Facilitation

Social facilitation is the notion that the presence of others can have a facilitating or constraining effect on someone. Kleiber, Walker, and Mannell (2011) have explained that *social facilitation theory* "is based on the premise of 'the more the merrier' when the task/activity to be performed or engaged in is familiar and well-learned; on the other hand, the more of a crowd there is to witness the learning or performance of an unfamiliar task or skill, the more disruptive and self-consciousness-inducing it is" (p. 306).

Psychologist Robert Zajonc (1965) indicated why in some instances the presence of others enhances performance and in other instances there is a deteriorating effect on performance. Zajonc explained emotional arousal has an enhancing effect on people when they perform well-learned tasks. However, emotional arousal has a diminishing effect on performance when tasks are poorly-learned. It is simply that the dominant response comes out when emotional arousal is experienced. Some term the enhancing effect as social facilitation and the diminishing effect to be social inhibition (Austin, 2011).

Ramifications of social facilitation for recreational therapy. The implications for practice in recreational therapy are that therapists should provide opportunities for clients to perform well-learned tasks with others or in front of an audience. Conversely, if a client is just beginning to learn a new skill it would be best for that individual to learn the skill in a one-on-one learning environment, or at least in a very small group. In short, recreational therapists should put clients in situations where well-learned tasks can be enhanced by the presence of others and keep clients protected from an audience effect when they are first developing the skill.

Self-Efficacy

Self-referent thoughts play a central role in mediating behavioral change, according to Bandura's (1986) self-efficacy theory. Clients' personal evaluations of their abilities (i.e., their efficacy judgments) directly affect how they cope with their problems. "A person's efficacy expectancies describe that person's beliefs about his or her particular skills and capabilities, and they determine how the person reacts behaviorally, cognitively, and emotionally to problematic events," according to Leary and Miller (1986, p. 188).

Self-efficacy beliefs can have "a profound motivational effect on the adoption of behaviour," according to Albery (2008). Clients' expectations of themselves largely determine how willing they will be to deal with their problems, how much effort they will be willing to expend, and whether they will make a perseverant effort. Those who are self-doubters are likely to express little effort and will give up quickly if their initial efforts are not productive. Those with high efficacy expectations are apt to face their difficulties with determination, to exert maximum effort, and to persevere even when frustration is encountered.

Perceived capabilities. The critical influence that personal efficacy has in people's lives was expressed by Bandura (1986), when he stated: "Among the different aspects of self-knowledge, perhaps none is more influential in people's everyday lives than conceptions of their personal efficacy" (p. 390). Bandura defined personal efficacy, or self-efficacy, as follows:

> Perceived self-efficacy is defined as people's judgments of their capabilities to organize and execute courses of action required to attain designated types of performances. It is concerned not with the skills one has but with judgments of what one can do with whatever skills one possesses. (p. 391)

Response-outcome expectancy. Bandura went on to draw a distinction between personal efficacy judgments and response-outcome expectancy. Personal efficacy is the person's expectation that he or she can be successful in accomplishing a certain behavior or level of performance. It is the individual's subjective judgment that he or she can accomplish the sought end. Bandura gives the example of someone believing that he or she can high-jump six feet.

The **response-outcome expectancy** deals with the consequence of the act, not the actual performance of the behavior. In Bandura's illustration, the outcome expectancy for the high jumper might include anticipated applause, social recognition, trophies, and self-satisfaction.

Either one's expectations of personal competence or one's expectation of the consequences of performing an act can lead to dysfunctional behavior. For example, a young woman who is shy may avoid a social contact either because of feeling a lack of social competence or because of a belief that no matter how she performs in the interaction, the outcome will be rejection (Leary & Miller, 1986).

Too often, it seems that our clients believe performing a specific behavior will result in certain positive consequences; however, they will not attempt the behavior because they have self-doubts about their abilities to actually accomplish the act. Too often, they avoid difficult tasks, put forth little effort, give up quickly when faced with frustration, dwell on what they perceive to be their personal deficiencies (which detracts attention from the demands of the task), decrease their expectations, and undergo feelings of stress and anxiety (Bandura, 1986, p. 395). This behavior is dysfunctional because it prevents them from facing and taking on their problems and entering into challenging and enriching leisure activities that would allow them to develop their potentialities.

How do people gain the self-knowledge on which self-efficacy rests? Whether valid or invalid, efficacy judgments are based on four sources of information: performance, vicarious experiences, verbal persuasion, and physiological arousal (Bandura, 1986).

Performance. The most potent source on which efficacy expectations are built is the client's own performance accomplishments. In general, repeated successes increase perceived self-efficacy, while continual failures decrease perceived self-efficacy. It should be added, however, that the individual's interpretation of his or her performance is a key. If successful performance is not viewed as a success by the individual, it will not have a positive impact on perceived self-efficacy. Making attributions to internal, stable, global, and, particularly, controllable factors will most likely lead the client to positive beliefs about his or her abilities (Leary & Miller, 1986).

Vicarious experience. Although not as influential as mastery experiences, modeling can affect self-efficacy. We partly judge our capabilities by comparing ourselves to others. Observing others who are similar model successes provides information that raises judgments regarding our capacities. Seeing similar others fail lowers our self-expectations.

Verbal persuasion. Efforts at verbal persuasion do not always work because sometimes we do not believe what others tell us about our capabilities. The impact of persuasive efforts will likely be influenced by how credible the persuaders are seen as being. The more confident we are in those offering verbal persuasion, the more impact they will have.

Physiological arousal. Situations that increase feelings of anxiety and arousal to a high level are apt to be read as being problematic and create fear about our abilities. Moderate levels of arousal tend to facilitate performance and, thus, carry more positive expectations (Bandura, 1986).

Once persons have gained information that leads them to believe that they have the capabilities for success, this can produce positive outcomes. As Bandura (1997) has stated, "People's beliefs that they can motivate themselves and regulate their own behavior plays a crucial role in whether they even consider changing detrimental health habits or pursuing rehabilitation activities" (p. 279). Individuals' levels of self-efficacy have been found to predict health behaviors such as losing weight, quitting smoking, exercising regularly, and benefiting from treatment and rehabilitation programs (Bandura, 1997).

Self-efficacy and therapy. What can the recreational therapist do with this background on self-efficacy during transactions with clients? Most evident is that knowledge of self-efficacy might be used to facilitate behavioral change by influencing clients' perceptions of personal efficacy. As previously noted, clients too often do not have confidence in their abilities to perform the behaviors of which we as therapists know they are capable. The recreational therapist can help the client to enhance his or her perception of personal efficacy through means of the four factors that influence self-efficacy.

Iso-Ahola (1984), in a discussion of leisure counseling and self-efficacy, and Savell (1986), in an article on recreational therapy programming and self-efficacy, have offered suggestions for helping clients to enhance personal efficacy expectations. At the top of their lists is to encourage clients to participate in activities that allow mastery experiences and build a sense of personal accomplishment. In doing so, the initial exposure should result in a positive experience. Success in beginning endeavors will provide clients with the courage to attempt something more challenging. Skill levels can be increased as client abilities and confidence grow.

When using vicarious experiences, the models should be similar to the clients and be observed to gain success through their persistence after encountering and overcoming difficulty. When the clients see others enjoy success despite difficulties, they will be encouraged to stick with difficult tasks. Verbal persuasion needs to come from a respected source. In a case cited by Iso-Ahola, wives of men who were postcoronary patients provided strong verbal persuasion. Savell has mentioned the use of discussions or exercises to allow clients to clarify their own thoughts so they may persuade themselves of their potentials.

Physiological arousal may be managed through any of a number of stress-reduction techniques discussed in Chapter 3, including relaxation techniques and biofeedback. Reducing clients' feelings of arousal can enhance self-efficacy.

As Leary and Miller (1986) have indicated, many therapeutic approaches utilize more than one of the four self-efficacy information sources. For example, the learning of relaxation techniques not only reduces arousal but provides for the mastery of a new skill. Savell (1986) has suggested that recreational therapy approaches should employ all four of the factors identified by Bandura.

Finally, recreational therapists need to understand four components that are inherent in the process of personal change. The first component involves clients having information about the risk of not changing their behavior. This, in itself, however, is not enough. Many health education programs fail because they do not go beyond the information stage. The second component involves efficacy expectations. As has been previously discussed, personal efficacy must be built to a level great enough that individuals are confident of their abilities so they do not give up when immediate results are not produced. A strong sense of personal efficacy can be built through experiences. Therefore, it is important for recreational therapists to provide clients with the third component. That component is the provision of opportunities to practice their new behaviors in situations that are similar to those they will likely encounter in their everyday lives. The fourth component involves the social influences that can aid or retard personal change. Recreational therapists need to be sure that social supports are in place for their clients because the positive (or negative) reactions of others can affect client behaviors. Clients are not apt to succeed if left on their own without a positive social support system (Bandura, 1995).

Bandura's (1986; 1997) self-efficacy theory offers recreational therapists insights into their clients' behaviors, as well as practical means to help clients to overcome difficulties. Even though a check of PsychInfo in 2012 found more than 22,000 articles have been written on self-efficacy, few recreational therapy researchers have applied the construct in their work in studying interventions (Richeson, 2006; Wise, 2002).

Researchers outside of recreational therapy have however conducted studies that have direct ramifications for recreational therapy. British researchers (Ashford, Edmunds, & French, 2010) conducted a meta-analysis to identify the best ways to change self-efficacy in order to promote physical activity. They discovered vicarious experiences and the provision of feedback were effective techniques to increase physical activity self-efficacy. Interestingly, they reported that even though vicarious experiences had a large effect on self-efficacy, it was rarely used by those attempting to increase physical activity self-efficacy. The provision of participants with feedback, either on their past performances or comparing their performances with others, was highly effective.

Li and his colleagues (2001) studied the effect of tai chi with a population of physically inactive older adults. They found tai chi practice resulted in increased levels of physical function and perceived physical capability.

Attributional Processes

Although attribution theory began to enjoy popularity during the 1970s, it was first introduced by Fritz Heider (1944) in the mid-1940s (Shaw & Costanzo, 1982). Heider believed that people's perceptions of the causation of events had a great impact on their social behaviors (Gergen & Gergen, 1986).

Causes for events. Shaw and Costanzo (1982) defined the processes of making attributions:

Put most broadly, attributional processes are those processes governing a perceiver's attention to thought about and apprehension of perceived events. The events that serve as objects of perception might consist of the actions of social others, one's own actions, and/or environmentally produced effects. Attribution theory is typically concerned with the processes and schema invoked by the perceiver in assigning causes to these events. (p. 232)

Attribution theory, therefore, involves the processes through which we try to infer causes for events from our observations. We engage in attributional processes to explain the events that occur in our lives. These explanations (or attributions) have significant psychological consequences. Our reactions to emotional events, our self-regard, our judgments of ourselves and others, and our expectations about the future are all subject to the influences of our causal attributions (Leary & Miller, 1986). We decide what other people are like based on our inferences from behaviors we observe and, most important for recreational therapy, we seek explanations for events that occur in our own lives. These self-attributions have important consequences on our subsequent behaviors and feelings.

Internal and external attributions. Our attributions may be either internal or external. Making **internal attributions** places the cause of the events with us. Cause is perceived to be due to our personality dispositions, abilities, or the amount of effort expended. **External attributions** place the cause with the situation in which the event occurred. For instance, if we do well on an examination, we might likely attribute our success to internal causes, such as our intelligence or our preparation for the exam. If, however, we do poorly, we might make an external attribution by saying that the exam items were "ambiguous" (Leary & Miller, 1986).

The tendency to attribute successes to internal causes and attribute failures to external causes is termed the *self-serving bias* (Niven, 2006). Certainly each of us has engaged in self-serving bias when we have "made ourselves look good" by attributing a positive outcome to us or attributing a bad outcome to external factors.

The tendency to overestimate the role of personal dispositions and overlook situational causes is termed the *fundamental attributional error* (Brehm, Kassin, & Fein, 2005; Kleiber, Walker, & Mannell, 2011). For example, therapists may blame clients for unfortunate things that happen to them, while ignoring situational causes.

In addition to internality (i.e., internal versus external causes), causes may be organized around three dimensions. These are stability, globalization, and control. Causes may be perceived to be stable (long-term) or unstable, global (affecting many parts of our lives) or specific, and under our control or uncontrollable (Leary & Miller, 1986).

You may already be thinking that some of the phenomena previously discussed in this section of the chapter on transactions may be related to attributional processes. For instance, our self-esteem will likely be enhanced when we have success and we make internal, stable, global attributions and perceive the outcome to be under our control. Labeling ourselves or other persons (e.g., as "deviants" or "losers") may cause us to attribute all negative behaviors to personality dispositions, rather than to situations. The self-fulfilling prophecy can be explained by the labels we place on people that raise or lower our expectations of them, causing us to make original false perceptions true. Helplessness occurs when we perceive a sense of uncontrollability. Our feelings of self-efficacy may be directly affected by self-attributions (e.g., internal or external, stable or unstable, under our control or not within our control) when we interpret our performance.

Self-attributions and therapy. Because of the importance of attributional processes, most approaches to psychotherapy use attributional analysis and seek to allow the client to reinterpret his or her problems. Making *reattributions* allows the client to generate explanations (attributions) for experiences that are not as threatening as those initially identified. For instance, the client comes to see something as being caused by a situation and not by his or her personality. Another reattribution would be having the client view a negative event as an isolated incident rather than something consistent in his or her behaviors.

Some clients are plagued by chronic attributional patterns that cause problems for them. For example, persons who are chronically depressed magnify negative happenings and minimize successes. Those with low self-esteem often externalize successes and internalize failures. Such chronic patterns are not easily overcome, but with treatment, clients can change their attributional styles. Changing self-blaming habits is apt to involve more than being supportive and allowing clients to gain successes. Learning to persist and try harder can be an important lesson in the face of adversity. If clients only are given opportunities for successes, they may give up quickly when faced with adversity. Above all, if clients can be led to see themselves as being capable of overcoming their problems, they may establish a sense of control and self-efficacy that will allow them to conquer their problems. In all approaches to therapy, it is critical that clients begin to perceive their problems to be changeable and controllable (Leary & Miller, 1986).

Recreational therapy can, of course, help clients gain confidence in their skills and abilities through providing opportunities for success. However, when rewarding successes, the activity leader must employ minimal external rewards so an *overjustification effect* (Lepper & Greene, 1975) does not occur. Overjustification is rewarding the person with an external incentive (e.g., trophy) for doing something he or she finds intrinsically rewarding and, in doing so, produces a change so the person is participating for the external reward, rather than being intrinsically motivated (e.g., taking part for the pure joy found in participating; Kleiber, Walker, & Mannell, 2011). The recreational therapist needs to be on guard to let the individual retain as much internal control as possible.

Recreational therapists can likewise help clients to learn to cope with outcomes that do not result in success and encourage clients not to give up, but to put forth additional effort or try new strategies. Finally, recreational therapists can help clients to make reattributions, as is often done in psychotherapy. For example, clients can come to believe that a skill they have had difficulty mastering is not really so important after all, or that winning is not critical (since one-half of the teams lose every event!). Research by Dieser and Ruddell (2002) has demonstrated that recreational therapists can have an impact on client attributions.

Reading Comprehension Questions

1. What are the purposes for having client records?
2. How do source-oriented and problem-oriented records differ?
3. What does SOAP stand for?
4. Do you understand the guidelines for progress note writing? Can you apply them?
5. What categories of behavior might you use in making observations for progress notes?
6. Do you understand the principles for the teaching/learning process?
7. Can you give examples of how you might apply one or more of these principles?
8. How can recreational therapists employ Prochaska and DiClemente's Model to motivate client change?

9. Explain the relationship between motivational interviewing and the Transtheoretical Model.

9. Explain how teams are more than groups of people working together. What are tips to help team members work better together?

10. Do you agree that advocacy is a necessary professional activity? Explain.

11. What is the ICF and which organization developed it?

12. Explain how the approach of the ICF differs from the traditional medical model.

13. Explain why the recreational therapist should consider self-concept in client transactions.

14. By what means do people form self-concepts?

15. What is self-handicapping?

16. What is learned helplessness?

17. What are ways recreational therapists can decrease helplessness?

18. What is reactance?

19. What are concerns related to labeling?

20. What is the Pygmalion effect?

21. How can recreational therapists help lonely clients?

22. How can leaders help clients to develop social networks? Social support?

23. Can you explain social facilitation theory?

24. What is self-efficacy? How can leaders in recreational therapy promote it?

25. How can leaders use information about attributional processes in transactions with clients?

Chapter 9

Clinical Supervision

■ Chapter Purpose

The term *clinical supervision* has appeared in the literature of recreational therapy only within the past 25 years or so. The first publication on clinical supervision appeared in the literature of our profession in 1986 when *The Journal of Expanding Horizons in Therapeutic Recreation* published the article titled, "Clinical Supervision in Therapeutic Recreation," which I authored (Austin, 1986). Today the importance of clinical supervision is beginning to become recognized within the world of recreational therapy. Nevertheless, it is alarming that many recreational therapists have not received specific training in giving or receiving clinical supervision. It is safe to say that the training of recreational therapists to do clinical supervision lags far behind many other professions. Compounding the situation, surprisingly little attention has been given to clinical supervision in the literature of recreational therapy. In an effort to help remedy the neglect of clinical supervision in recreational therapy, this chapter presents an introduction to clinical supervision and information about the actual roles and functions of the supervisor and supervisee.

■ Key Terms

- Clinical supervision
- Skill development model of supervision
- Personal growth model of supervision
- Integrative model of supervision
- Dual relationship
- Informed consent

- Multiculturalism
- Diversity
- Triadic Supervision
- Formative Evaluation
- Summative Evaluation

■ Objectives

- Comprehend the nature of clinical supervision.
- Understand the goals and rationale for clinical supervision.
- Know elements that define the clinical supervision process.
- Distinguish between clinical supervision and administrative supervision.
- Distinguish between clinical supervision and therapy.
- Recognize ethical considerations in clinical supervision.
- Recognize the roles and functions of supervisors and supervisees.
- Know the stages experienced in clinical supervision.

- Know the methods and procedures for conducting clinical supervision.
- Know steps in setting up and monitoring a clinical supervision program.

The Purposes of Clinical Supervision

Clinical supervision has two broad purposes. One is to facilitate the personal and professional development of the supervisee receiving supervision. The second is improved client care and treatment through proper implementation of the agency's clinical program. As indicated by Aasheim (2011), "effective supervision serves the dual purpose of protecting client welfare and helping the supervisee develop and maintain clinical skills" (p. 30).

The supervisor helps the supervisee to acquire and refine clinical practice skills and to grow as a professional. This supervision is an ongoing process that begins during initial field placements and never ends, because even the master clinician always has more to learn. As Morton-Cooper and Palmer (2000) have indicated, "clinical supervision should continue throughout professional life" (p. 149).

Accountability is the aim of the second purpose. It is the function of the clinical supervisor to assure that the therapeutic intents of the clinical program are accomplished. Supervisors make certain that the purposes and goals of the intervention plan (e.g., treatment, rehabilitation, or care program) are achieved. Aasheim (2011) has suggested that clinical supervision "is intended to protect the welfare of the supervisee's clients above all else" (p. 6).

A Dynamic Process

Clinical supervision then may be defined as a joint relationship in which the supervisor assists the supervisee to develop himself or herself in order to deliver the highest possible level of clinical service while promoting accountability in the agency's clinical program. Williamson (1961), an early advocate for clinical supervision, has offered perhaps the most complete definition of clinical supervision found in the literature:

> Supervision is a dynamic enabling process by which individual workers who have direct responsibility for carrying out some part of the agency's program plans are helped to make the best use of knowledge and skills, and to improve their abilities so that they do their jobs more effectively and with increasing satisfaction to themselves and the agency. (p. 19)

Four elements define the clinical supervision process, according to Hart (1982):

1. Clinical supervision implies an ongoing relationship between the supervisor and supervisee. Such a continuing relationship is necessary because the supervisee is engaged in a develop mental process in order to function at a higher level of clinical practice.
2. The clinical supervisor need not be the managerial or administrative supervisor. In fact, it may be argued that general managerial or administrative supervision and clinical supervision should remain separate functions.
3. Strategies and skills needed in the delivery of treatment, rehabilitation, or care programs are the central concern during clinical supervision sessions. While the content of clinical

supervision sessions may be wide ranging, it pertains to effective clinical practice behaviors.

4. The primary thrust of clinical supervision always is on the behavior of the supervisee as he or she interacts with clients and staff.

Added to this list might be the gatekeeping role played by clinical supervisors. As indicated by any number of authors (e.g., Aasheim, 2011; Corey, Haynes, Moulton, & Muratori, 2010; Malone, 2009), supervisors are responsible for keeping unprepared and unethical practitioners from practicing and therefore from doing possible harm to clients.

Cutcliffe, Butterworth, and Proctor (2001) have posited a number of what they perceive to be necessary elements in clinical supervision. These parameters are found in Table 9.1. The reader is encouraged to read over these now (as an introduction to clinical supervision) and then review them again following having read the remainder of the chapter (to determine if the characteristics have taken on additional meaning).

Table 9.1

Characteristics of Clinical Supervision

Clinical supervision is:

- supportive;
- safe, because of clear, negotiated agreements by all parties with regard to the extent of limits of confidentiality;
- centered on developing best practice for service users;
- brave, because practitioners are encouraged to talk about the realities of their practice;
- a chance to talk about difficult areas of work in an environment where the person attempts to understand;
- an opportunity to ventilate emotion without comeback;
- the opportunity to deal with material and issues that practitioners may have been carrying for many years (the chance to talk about issues which cannot easily be talked about elsewhere and that may have been previously unexplored);
- not to be confused with or amalgamated with managerial supervision;
- not to be confused with or amalgamated with personal therapy/counseling;
- regular;
- protected time;
- offered equally to all practitioners;
- a committed relationship from those involved;
- separate and distinct from mentorship;
- a facilitative relationship;
- challenging;
- an invitation to be self-monitoring and self-accountable;
- at times hard work and at others enjoyable;
- the supervisee learning to become a reflective practitioner;
- an activity that continues throughout one's professional life.

Adapted from Cutcliffe, J. R., Butterworth, T., & Proctor, B. (2001). *Fundamental themes in clinical supervision.* New York: Routledge, pp. 3, 4.

Skills related to the achievement of client objectives remain at the heart of clinical supervision. On occasion, however, clinical supervision involves issues related to teamwork or to maintaining positive relationships in working with other staff in order to conduct a successful clinical program.

Any clinician who works with clients can profit from receiving clinical supervision because all have the potential for continual development. Even master clinicians (i.e., those with advanced preparation and extensive supervised experience) can improve their clinical functioning. Therefore, supervisees can range from beginning students to practitioners with years of experience. Of course, the frequency and emphasis of supervision will vary according to the background of those being supervised. Supervising emerging therapists is likely to require supervisors to take on larger roles than they would with more experienced supervisees (Kaslow, 1986).

The Status of Clinical Supervision

Clinical supervision is an emerging area in recreational therapy that is just beginning to be recognized as a key element in successful clinical practice. One study (Witman & Ligon, 2011a) revealed that only 37% of the recreational therapists surveyed received clinical supervision. Visits to clinical sites in recent years however substantiate that the importance of clinical supervision has become acknowledged by a number of health care disciplines. It has been particularly accepted during the past 35 to 40 years as a critical aspect of clinical practice by counselors, clinical psychologists, psychiatrists, and psychiatric social workers. No doubt these clinicians have recognized the benefits of clinical supervision that have widely appeared in the literature (e.g., Bishop, 2007; Begat & Severinsson, 2006; Edwards et al., 2006; Jones, 2008) and are summarized in Table 9.2.

Table 9.2

Benefits of Clinical Supervision

- Reduced emotional exhaustion
- Reduced occupational stress
- Reduced sick leave
- Reduced burnout
- Reduced feelings of professional isolation
- Increased job satisfaction and staff morale
- Increased feelings of support
- Increased confidence
- Increased awareness of solutions to clinical problems
- Increased self-awareness
- Increased reflective practice
- Enhanced feelings of accomplishment
- Improved recruitment
- Improved retention

Sources: Bishop, V. (2007). Literature review: Clinical supervision evaluation studies. In V. Bishop (Ed.), *Clinical supervision in practice* (2nd ed.). New York: Palgrave MacMillan (pp. 151–152); Driscoll, J., & O'Sullivan, J. (2007). The place of clinical supervision in modern healthcare. In J. Driscoll (Ed.), *Practicing clinical supervision* (2nd ed.). New York: Bailliere Tindall Elsevier, p. 20; Jones, J. M. (2008). Clinical supervision in nursing. *The Clinical Supervisor*, 24(1-2), 149-162.

The importance of clinical supervision has been widely recognized by college and university faculty who prepare students for careers in recreational therapy, according to the results of a national survey by Gruver and Austin (1990). The overwhelming majority of faculty responding to the survey indicated it is essential to provide classroom instruction in clinical supervision to both undergraduate and graduate students. Almost 80% (79.1%) felt it is essential for undergraduates, while 92.7% felt it is essential for graduate students. Unfortunately, the same study revealed that only about 50% of the colleges and universities were actually preparing students to give and receive clinical supervision.

A study by Jones and Anderson (2004), of Certified Therapeutic Recreation Specialists, found that only a small percentage had been provided training in clinical supervision. Further, these researchers revealed that most practitioners were not giving or receiving clinical supervision. Jones and Anderson's findings lead them to conclude for those in the profession to provide effective and ethical services "clinical supervision needs to be recognized by the therapeutic recreation field as a necessary competency to ensure that the best possible services are offered to clients. In order for this to occur, the knowledge of and the ability to perform clinical supervision needs to be included in ...university curricula" (p. 345).

Why has clinical supervision remained a largely neglected area in recreational therapy? There are a number of speculations that may be offered in response to this question.

One possible reason for the lack of earlier interest by recreational therapists in clinical supervision may be that practitioners did not take themselves seriously as clinicians. Simply providing recreation opportunities for clients does not require clinical supervision since clinical intents are not sought. Today, however, the clinical nature of recreational therapy is apparent within the field. The formation of the American Therapeutic Recreation Association, university accreditation standards established under the Commission on Accreditation of Allied Health Education Programs, and rapid growth in the literature of the profession related to clinical practice are reflective of a high level of clinical activity.

Another possible reason for the absence of interest in clinical supervision may simply have been a lack of information on the topic within the literature of recreational therapy. Hopefully, coverage in textbooks such as this one, articles in professional journals, and workshops and conference sessions on clinical supervision will supply practitioners and educators with information on the topic.

Bond and Holland (1998) have explained that the term, clinical supervision, itself may get in the way of understanding what it is. First, the prefix, clinical, may sometimes be confused with the term medical when clinical is used only to pertain to aspects of giving care or intervening with clients and not with applications of the medical model. Second, the term, supervision, may have negative connotations associated with it such as "keeping an eye on someone." Similarly, Bishop (2007b) has suggested that the word supervision "smacks of 'overseeing'" (p. 11) and hierarchical managerial control. Further, Bishop has observed: "It is undoubtedly this lack of differentiation between managerial and clinical supervision that has hindered many in taking clinical supervision forward" (p. 15). Finally, she has emphatically stated: "Clinical supervision is not a camouflage to hide hierarchical domination. It is a mechanism to empower practitioners and requires time and investment" (p. 21).

Clinical Supervision versus Administrative Supervision

A distinction can be drawn between clinical supervision and management or administrative supervision. Clinical supervision focuses on skills and strategies needed to reach objectives with clients. In contrast, management or administrative supervision deals with overseeing, directing, and evaluating all staff work, as well as ensuring that the staff follows agency policies and procedures. The administrative supervisor stresses organizational effectiveness and efficiency in seeing that staff arrive at work on time, structure and meet their schedules, correctly order and check out supplies and equipment, and so forth (Austin, 1986; Bradley, 1989). Corey, Haynes, Moulton, and Muratori (2010) clearly stated the distinction between the two types of supervision when they wrote, *"Clinical supervision* focuses on the work of the supervisee in providing services to clients."* And *"Administrative supervision* focuses on the issues surrounding the supervisee's role and responsibilities in the organization as an employee: personnel matters, timekeeping, documentation, and so forth" (p. 3).

It is my belief that administrative supervision and clinical supervision should be kept distinct and separate. The authoritative nature of administrative supervision (with administrative power) simply gets in the way of establishing the cooperative, helping relationship that must exist as a part of clinical supervision. In many respects, the process of clinical supervision parallels the therapist-to-client relationship. The supervisor must remain attentive to helping the supervisee meet his or her needs while maintaining a supportive atmosphere. The supervisee must feel free to be open and honest in his or her communications with the supervisor. While many agencies have supervisees receiving both their administrative and clinical supervision from the same individual, I would urge managers to give every consideration to keeping the two types of supervision separate. My position is shared by Bond and Holland (1998) who have authored a book on clinical supervision. They wrote, "Management supervision and clinical supervision are different functions and should not be undertaken by the same person." They go on to state that "any embodiment of clinical supervision within management will be liable to cause confusion and mistrust and lead to mixed messages about its aims and potential" (p. 18).

Similarly, Aasheim (2011) has written this about the dilemma when the clinical supervisor is also the managerial supervisor:

> These supervisors who are both managerial and clinical supervisors are in a dual relationship with their supervisee/employee. In these cases, agency or administrative needs may take precedence above clinical focus and supervisee development, and the supervisor's two roles may be in direct opposition. For instance, clinical supervisors often make great efforts to ensure the supervisee feels safe and comfortable to discuss times of professional incompetence and needed development. However, many supervisees may find it difficult to divulge professional weaknesses to their direct manager who has great control and influence over their ability to be promoted, given a raise or bonus, approved for vacation time, and the like. (p. 100)

Clinical Supervision and Therapy

While several of the elements of psychotherapy are found in clinical supervision, clinical supervision should not be confused with therapy. Both therapy and clinical supervision involve a helper and someone receiving help. Both are characterized by fear, anxiety, and resistance to change. Both take place in a nonjudgmental environment (Kahn, 1979; O'Toole, 1996).

Both, in short, are helping processes. But they differ in purpose and approach. The purpose of therapy is to resolve personal problems or inner conflicts. The purpose of clinical supervision is the improvement of clinical performance. The focus of therapy is on personal experiences and problems, while the focus of clinical supervision is work with clients. Change in therapy deals with the exploration and resolution of personal difficulties, while change in clinical supervision concerns behaviors, thoughts, or feelings that affect clients (Kahn, 1979; Malone, 2009; O'Toole, 1996; U.S. Department of Health and Human Services, 2009).

Table 9.3

Clinical Supervision is NOT . . .

- a management activity allowing for the overseeing of subordinates
- linked to the disciplinary process
- exclusively concerned with time-keeping, ranges of pay, and hours of duty
- about having the supervisee's work controlled, directed, or managerially evaluated
- a punitive or gratuitously negative experience for the supervisor
- a continuous discussion of mistakes, failing, or errors on the part of supervisee, without being balanced by a discussion or the supervisee's professional strengths and the positive aspects of his (or her) work

---

Adapted from Bishop, V. (2007). Clinical supervision: What is it? Why do we need it? In V. Bishop (Ed.), *Clinical supervision in practice* (2nd ed.) (pp. 14, 15). New York: Palgrave MacMillan.

Howard (2008) has written that effective clinical supervisors do not enter into therapy with supervisees:

> They wisely observe the boundary between therapy and supervision, maintaining that personal growth should not be the primary goal of supervision; rather it is an instrumental one that it can work in the service of making the supervisee a better practitioner. The focus should thus be upon the effects of these aspects upon the work rather than the events themselves. (p. 107)

As noted by Platt-Koch (1986), "The supervisor should not probe any more deeply into personal conflicts than is necessary to support the therapist's (i.e., supervisee's) professional role" (p.10). If a supervisee's personal difficulties interfere to a large extent with working with clients, the supervisor should discuss the possibility of the supervisee seeking help from a trained counselor or psychotherapist.

Models for Clinical Supervision

Corey, Haynes, Moulton, and Muratori (2010) have presented the Integrated Developmental Model (IDM) of clinical supervision originally created by Stoltenberg, McNeill, and Delworth (1998). The IDM presents three levels of supervisee development with a corresponding role of the supervisor for each level. Level 1 is the level for entry-level supervisees who need much structure and direction from the supervisor. Level 2 supervisees have developed to the point that they are more self-reliant but still need help from the supervisor in dealing with their own personal issues that affect their clinical functioning. Level 3 supervisees have obtained some amount of confidence in their abilities and therefore their relationship with their supervisor is a more collegial one in which they seek consultation in problem solving.

The IDM model is similar to Hart's (1982) proposed three models of clinical supervision which is used as the primary source for the discussion of models for clinical supervision that follows. These are the skill development model, the personal growth model, and the integrative model. Pearson (2004) framed these as teaching, counseling, and consulting.

The **skill development model** utilizes a teacher-student relationship between the supervisor and supervisee while emphasizing knowledge of professional roles and methods. Here the supervisor functions as an expert clinician who draws on his or her knowledge to teach the supervisee. The supervisee establishes his or her professional identity while learning leadership roles such as leading groups or administering client assessments. Supervisees acquire clinical skills that enable them to conduct therapy or rehabilitation programs. Examples of clinical skills include establishing client relationships, making diagnostic judgments, delivering interventions, and making referrals. Supervisees also learn to conceptualize aspects of client cases.

The **personal growth model** employs a relationship between the supervisor and supervisee that closely resembles a counselor-client relationship. The supervisor does not engage in deep psychotherapy, but does counsel the supervisee to help develop insights into self and affective sensitivity. One area under insight into self is that of understanding one's own needs so that personal needs remain in their proper place and do not take precedent over the needs of clients. A second area is learning to deal with "shocking" subjects such as child abuse, drug use, violence, and incest. A final area under insight into self is learning to deal with strong emotional reactions to situations (e.g., encountering hostility) or clients (e.g., countertransference) through discussions with the supervisor. Under affective sensitivity fall examination of the supervisee's interpersonal relationship patterns and how he or she affects others.

The third and final model is the **integrative model**, which builds on the first two models. Here the supervisor consults and collaborates with the supervisee. The integrative model employs a collaborative relationship between the supervisor and supervisee in order to integrate skill development and personal awareness into effective relationships with clients. This model is used with advanced students and experienced therapists. It utilizes a mutual effort between the supervisor and supervisee in which they share information regarding clinical practice and make and test hypotheses about client cases.

Hart's models would seem to have application to clinical supervision within recreational therapy. Certainly, the skill development model is commonly employed in the training of student interns in recreational therapy. The personal growth model is perhaps less established in recreational therapy but has apparent implications for use with both interns and emerging professionals. The integrative model is undoubtedly least employed in recreational therapy. As the use of clinical supervision spreads in recreational therapy, however, greater utilization of the integrative model might be anticipated.

Roles of Clinical Supervisors

Bradley (1989, pp. 302-307) identified three roles for clinical supervisors. These roles closely parallel Hart's (1982) three models of supervision and the Integrated Developmental Model (IDM) of Stoltenberg, McNeill, and Delworth (1998). Similar to Pearson (2004), the three roles for clinical supervisors proposed by Bradley are teacher, counselor, and consultant. Within the teacher role, the supervisor intends to instruct the supervisee in clinical practice skills.

The Teaching Role
Teaching activities include
- observing the supervisee in clinical practice;
- identifying interventions to enhance the supervisee's performance;

- applying interventions through demonstrations, modeling, and other teaching techniques;
- explaining rationales that underlie interventions and clinical strategies; and
- interpreting important events that occur during clinical sessions.

The Counselor Role

Within the counselor role, the supervisor intends to facilitate the supervisee's self-growth as a clinician. Specific activities include

- exploring the supervisee's feelings about clinical and supervisory sessions,
- exploring the supervisee's feelings regarding specific techniques or interventions,
- facilitating self-exploration by the supervisee of worries or concerns regarding clinical sessions,
- helping the supervisee evaluate personal competencies and areas for growth, and
- providing opportunities for the supervisee to discuss his or her effect on others and his or her use of defenses.

The Consulting Role

Within the consultant role, the supervisor intends to allow the supervisee to exert control over the interaction and to encourage choice and responsibility on the part of the supervisee. Specific activities include

- offering alternative interventions or conceptualizations for the supervisee to consider;
- encouraging brainstorming of strategies and interventions;
- discussing client problems, motivations, etc.;
- attempting to satisfy supervisee needs during clinical supervision sessions; and
- allowing the supervisee to control and structure the supervision session.

Different roles are, of course, called for with various supervisees. For example, emerging supervisees (e.g., students and young staff) are likely to require the supervisor to take the teacher and counselor roles. More experienced supervisees (e.g., staff experienced in clinical practice) are apt to need the supervisor to fulfill the consultant role.

Clinical Supervisor Traits

Of course, there is no one set of characteristics that constitute the makeup of an "ideal" clinical supervisor. Supervisees come with a variety of needs and different levels of development, and each has his or her individual personality. Therefore, the ideal supervisor will be the one who has the best match with the supervisee's needs, developmental level, and personality. There are nevertheless some core characteristics of clinical supervisors. A minimum qualification for the clinical supervisor is possessing the skills of a master clinician.

Becoming a master clinician involves gaining the professional competencies to perform at a high level and then polishing these skills during several years of experience. Generally, master clinicians hold a master's degree and have had a number of years of experience under a well-prepared clinical supervisor. Possessing such a background should bring with it the confidence and professional assurance needed in a supervisory position. In addition to feeling comfortable with his or her abilities, the clinical supervisor should have the respect of the colleagues and administrators with whom he or she works (Bradley, 1989).

Beyond being well prepared, self-assured, and respected, what specific characteristics should the clinical supervisor possess? A number of authors, including Aasheim (2011),

Bond and Holland (1998), Corey, Haynes, Moulton, & Muratori, 2010; Falender (2004), Johns (2004), Kaslow (1986), Malone (2009), and Platt-Koch (1986), have addressed this question. The discussion that follows is based on the comments of these authors.

Commitment. A successful clinical supervisor will have a firm sense that the purpose of the clinical supervision relationship is facilitating the personal and professional development of the supervisee and improving the agency's clinical program by promoting its proper implementation. The clinical supervisor has a keen interest in training and supervision. He or she is committed to the supervisory relationship to make sure its purpose is realized and that It is characterized by trust and respect. In short, the ideal supervisor is invested in the clinical supervision program and the supervisee.

An authority. The clinical supervisor holds power by virtue of his or her clinical expertise but does not exercise control over the supervisee. Instead, mutual support between the supervisor and supervisee is apparent and an atmosphere is promoted that is comfortable for the supervisee.

Empathy and caring. The clinical supervisor must have a genuine concern for the growth and development of the students and fellow professionals whom he or she supervises. Closely related is having the quality of being a caring and supportive person. Creating a supportive atmosphere is a hallmark of good supervision. The effective supervisor is empathetic, warm, and genuine. He or she gives honest feedback and helps supervisees work toward resolution of problems. He or she encourages exploration of new behaviors, involves supervisees in the supervisory process, and helps supervisees to move toward greater independence. In so doing, the supervisor builds rapport and trust with his or her supervisees. The supportive function is one of the most important aspects of supervision (Holloway, 1995). As Bond and Holland (1998) have suggested, "clinical supervision should be about empowerment and not control, hence emphasizing that the route to professional accountability is through building confidence and self-esteem, which in turn requires careful, supportive feedback" (p. 14).

Communication skills. Closely related to empathy and caring is being an active listener. The clinical supervisor must have well-developed attending skills and responding skills. It is critical that the supervisor be able to give constructive feedback. In short, he or she must possess the communication skills covered in Chapter 6.

Openness. The successful supervisor is available and approachable. He or she is characterized as being nonthreatening, nonauthoritarian, nonjudgmental, tactful, understanding, accepting, and possessing a good sense of humor. He or she expresses confidence in the abilities of the supervisees and is not afraid to engage in self-disclosure with their supervisees if he or she feels it will be helpful. In general, the good clinical supervisor is not defensive but, instead, expresses a sense of openness. He or she is open to new ideas and is willing to examine his or her own feelings, thoughts, and attitudes.

Areas of knowledgeable. The effective clinical supervisor must have a wealth of clinical experiences on which to draw. He or she must be aware of clinical, legal, ethical, and diversity issues. Further, the supervisor needs to be able to integrate theory and practice. He or she also needs to know how to use intervention or teaching techniques with supervisees, such as knowing when to encourage risk-taking on the part of the supervisee. The individual is able not only to supply the right facts or information at the correct times, but to also motivate and inspire supervisees to try new behaviors and to challenge themselves. Finally, the successful supervisor needs to have the abilities of a good consultant to help supervisees to assess situations themselves and to arrive at reasoned actions.

Education and training. Additionally, the effective clinical supervisor needs to be professionally prepared to do clinical supervision. To do clinical supervision in recreational therapy with university students, minimum credentials should include a bachelor's degree in recreational therapy or therapeutic recreation, certification (i.e., Certified Therapeutic Recreation Specialist), and a minimum of two-years of experience. Graduate preparation in recreational therapy is preferred. Specific instruction in doing clinical supervision needs to be a part of the clinical supervisor's university preparation. It should also be expected that those doing clinical supervision regularly complete continuing education experiences (e.g., workshops, conferences) in supervisory theory and practice. Hoffman (1994) termed the lack of formal training for clinical supervisors the "dirty little secret" of mental health professions, and she has suggested that those who practice clinical supervision without formal training are doing so unethically. It seems that recreational therapy needs to examine the ethical issue of clinical supervision being done by those who may lack education and training in the area.

One forward step for recreational therapy was taken when Hutchins (2005/2006) completed a study to identify the competencies required of clinical supervisors who provide supervision for recreational therapy internship experiences. This researcher identified 54 competencies needed by the clinical supervisors to successfully supervise university interns. Based on her findings, Hutchins has recommended the establishment of internship supervisor standards for the profession.

Table 9.4

Desirable and Undesirable Traits of Clinical Supervisors

Desirable Traits
- Has strong clinical skills and knowledge
- Establishes an accepting climate for supervision
- Shows interest in training supervisees
- Invests himself or herself in the supervision process
- Is empathic
- Is flexible
- Is available
- Possesses good relationship skills
- Is experienced as a clinician

Undesirable Traits
- Lacks interest in developing and training supervisees
- Is not available
- Is not flexible
- Lacks openness to new ideas and approaches to cases
- Has limited clinical knowledge and skills
- Is unreliable
- Gives unhelpful, inconsistent feedback

Table 9.4 (cont.)

- Is not empathic
- Lacks structure
- Lacks a sense of ethics

Source: Barnett, J. E., Erickson Cornish, J. A., Goodyear, R. K., & Lichtenberg, J. W. (2007). Commentaries on the ethical and effective practice of clinical supervision. *Professional Psychology Research and Practice, 38*(3), 268-275.

Self-Assessment for Clinical Supervisors

Aasheim (2011, p. 54) suggests potential clinical supervisors ask themselves major two questions. The first is "What is my motivation for providing supervision?" Aasheim has warned that because clinical supervision can be high risk and low reward that supervisors need to be internally motivated to develop emerging professionals or consult with colleagues and see the position as one that holds potential for professional fulfillment. The second question is "Do I truly have the time and availability to engage in supervision?" Clinical supervision takes a great deal of time and to be an effective supervisor involves being available to the supervisee at almost any time of the working day. Also there will be demands for training, continuing education, and required documentation.

Van Ooijen (2000, pp. 127, 128) has provided an extensive self-assessment questionnaire for those contemplating becoming clinical supervisors. The following questions are drawn from those posed by van Ooijen. It is recommended that those considering providing clinical supervision address each of these questions.

Self-assessment questions concerning *knowledge* include "How much supervision training have you had?"; "How much do you know about the purpose, function, goals, and process of clinical supervision?"; "How much do you know about theories and models?"; "How much do you know about different supervisory roles?"; and "Do you know enough to teach others?"

Under the topic of *skills* questions include "How easy is it for you to develop a supportive working alliance?"; "Can you help the supervisee to buy into a framework for supervision?"; "How good are your active listening skills?"; "Can you maintain boundaries of time and topic?"; "Can you use questions appropriately to help the reflection process?"; "How confident are you regarding challenge and confrontation while remaining supportive?"; and "How good are you at getting the supervisee to focus?"

Under *attitudes* self-assessment questions include "Do you feel pressured to appear competent?"; "Do you have a tendency to be authoritarian or to dominate?"; "Are you warm and open with those you supervise?"; "Are you generally caring and empathetic?"; "Do you tend to feel a need to rescue the supervisee?"; "To what extent have you developed an identity as a supervisor?"; "Do you feel the need to be 'all-knowing; and all-seeing'?"; and "Do you find it difficult to be honest?"

Under *self-awareness* questions include "How aware are you of your relevant knowledge and skills?"; "How aware are you of your own strengths and weaknesses?"; "How aware are you of projective identification?"; and "How aware are you of your impact on supervisees?"

Under *experience self-assessment* questions include "Do you have experience as a supervisor?"; "Do you have experience supervising people from different cultures?"; and "Do you have the academic and clinical experience necessary to help others to develop their clinical skills?"

Developmental Stages of Supervisors

Should individuals choose to do clinical supervision, what will they likely experience in their own growth and development? There was little literature to address this question until C. Edward Watkins, of the University of North Texas, first focused on the developmental stages clinical supervisors go through. In his 1990 article, Watkins presented a four-stage model commencing with the beginning supervisor and ending with becoming an assured, competent supervisor. The first stage is *role shock*. A crisis in confidence will often bring about the "imposter phenomenon" where novice supervisors do not feel they are capable and that they are pretending to be something they are not. Here new supervisors' confidence suffers as they becomes aware of weaknesses and feel unprepared. At this stage, they are just beginning to gain awareness of their impact on supervisees, their supervisory style, and their sense of identification with the supervisory role. Table 9.5 lists a number of struggles faced by beginning supervisors. Due to all this, they are apt to have little tolerance for ambiguity and to cling to "rules" and "procedures" in order to do things "right." Happily, with time, experience, and support from other new supervisors, as well as seasoned supervisors, novice supervisors typically recover from their role shock and move out of the first stage into Stage 2 or the recovery and transition stage.

Table 9.5

Struggles of Beginning Supervisors

- Developing one's identity as a supervisor
- Setting priorities for what is important in supervision
- Conquering self-doubt
- Setting appropriate boundaries and maintaining some distance
- Learning what supervisors do instead of just giving answers
- Juggling the various goals and roles of supervision
- Providing feedback to supervisees in a constructive manner
- Discovering how to let supervisees come up with their own answers
- Finding one's own style and realizing there is no one right way to supervise
- Helping supervisees accept responsibility for and have trust in the supervision process
- Creating a safe and accepting atmosphere
- Avoiding becoming the supervisee's therapist
- Making the transition from supervisee to supervisor and not over identifying with the supervisee
- Lacking self-confidence to know what to do as a supervisor
- Knowing how to handle supervisees' serious clinical mistakes
- Hesitating to play the role of expert
- Having expectations and goals for supervision that are too high and unrealistic when supervising veteran clinicians

---

Source: Corey, G., Haynes, R., Moulton, P., & Muratori, M. (2010). *Clinical supervision in the helping professions* (2nd ed.). Alexandria, VA: American Counseling Association, pp. 255-256.

In the *recovery and transition stage* supervisors begin to realize they possess positive qualities and start to settle into the supervisory role. Their confident begins to build as they can legitimately see themselves in the role of supervisor. While still not fully confident in their abilities, they begin to relax and put less distance between them and their supervisees.

Stage 3 is that of *role consolidation* in which supervisors further develop, gaining greater understandings of, and confidence, in their roles as supervisors. At this point, supervisors have developed more realistic views of their abilities and styles, as well as their impacts on supervisees. They begin to assume that they are qualified to be supervisors. They become comfortable in their roles and feel free to venture into the use of new techniques. Stage 4 is *role mastery*. At this stage supervisors experience a level of skill from which they gain a sense of mastery. They are no longer threatened by mistakes they make and know how to approach problems encountered in supervision. They are comfortable with themselves in their supervisory roles and know they are subject to human frailties so they are not expected to be perfect. In short, they have gained a perspective on their work as supervisors so they can have a sense of humor about themselves and enjoy meeting the challenges inherent in working with supervisees.

Thus, while novice clinical supervisors are apt to suffer from an initial crisis of confidence, it is heartening to realize that progression through the various stages is likely to help them to develop into creditable supervisors who can exert their influences to assist supervisees in gaining and improving skills and in providing quality care. Recreational therapists who ask themselves the tough questions about their desire to do supervision and then decide to become clinical supervisors should be encouraged that while they will encounter developmental tasks along the way, they can become autonomous supervisors who have much to offer to the growth and development of emerging professionals and to clinical problem solving with colleagues.

Benefits of Providing Clinical Supervision

Page and Wosket (1994) and Williams (1995) have noted that clinical supervisors benefit from their responsibilities by developing personal awareness and new insights that can enhance their own clinical work. For instance, the supervisor can come to understand how the supervisee might have acted more therapeutically and then apply this discovery in his or her own clinical practice. Thus, by supervising the supervisee, the clinical supervisor can reexamine his or her own performance at a distance, allowing an opportunity for self-reflection and personal growth. Page and Wosket have also mentioned that doing clinical supervision provides a change of pace for the supervisor by taking him or her away from often emotionally draining clinical work to the more intellectually stimulating area of clinical supervision.

Ethical Concerns in Clinical Supervision

Corey, Haynes, Moulton, and Muratori (2010) have warned that "It is essential that supervisors teach and model ethical and professional behavior for their supervisees" (p. 145). These authors stipulate that professional ethics must take a central place from the very beginning of every supervisor/supervisee relationship. Aasheim (2011) has indicted that a "key function of clinical supervision is to ensure that the supervisees are engaging in sound ethical practices" (p 7). What follows are specific ethical concerns in clinical supervision.

Nonmaleficence

The principle of **nonmaleficence** deals with ensuring that no harm is done. For clinical supervisors, this involves being competent to assume a supervisory role (Corey, Haynes, Moulton, & Muratori, 2010; Page & Wosket, 1994). A fundamental question that each clinical supervisor must address is "Am I qualified to do clinical supervision?" Should an individual not yet possess the skills, knowledge, and clinical background to conduct clinical supervision, he or she would not be on sound ethical ground in accepting a supervisory assignment. The individual would be exceeding his or her abilities and, thus, be placing the supervisee in jeopardy.

New recreational therapists are understandably often anxious to do clinical supervision, particularly with student interns. It is commendable that new recreational therapists wish to engage in helping relationships with students. However, before entering into supervisory responsibilities, a professional needs to complete a thorough self-assessment to determine if he or she possesses the necessary characteristics to do clinical supervision. Once a complete assessment has been conducted and it has been determined that an individual has the qualities needed to become an effective clinical supervisor, the person must gain the preparation required to conduct clinical supervision. This preparation may be gained through supervisory training provided by his or her agency, through workshops offered by professional societies, or through courses and other educational experiences conducted by colleges and universities (Corey, Haynes, Moulton, & Muratori, 2010).

Dual Relationships

A second area of ethical concern in clinical supervision is that of **dual relationships** between supervisor and supervisee. In the *Handbook of Counseling Supervision,* Borders and Leddick (1987) discussed three types of dual relationships: (1) the supervisor and supervisee are sexually involved; (2) the supervisor takes on the role of being the supervisee's therapist; and (3) there is a degree of closeness beyond the normal supervisory relationship (separate from sexual contact) that creates a danger of the development of a dual relationship.

Sexual contact. The sexual contact issue is clear in terms of ethical considerations. As Bernard (1987) has stated: "There seems to be no defensible argument for the ethics of sexual involvement between supervisor and supervisee" (p. 53). Should the two persons who are in clinical supervision become sexually attracted to one another, a new supervisory arrangement should be established to ensure that the supervisee is supervised objectively. Of course, clinical supervisors should also take responsibility for seeing that their supervisees are not sexually involved with clients.

Other intimacy concerns. The other two areas of dual relationship are less clear-cut in terms of ethics. There are sometimes instances in which focusing on personal issues is appropriate during supervision when issues interfere with the supervisee's ability to serve clients. In these instances, it may be necessary for the supervisor to discuss the supervisee's personal issues. However, the supervisor should not engage in extended counseling. To determine exactly when further discussion is not appropriate involves judgment on the part of the supervisor.

The third area of dual relationships also involves judgment on the part of the supervisor. There is nothing wrong with becoming close friends with those with whom you share a great deal in common. However, the supervisor must constantly monitor his or her actions to be certain that a dual relationship has not evolved. There is an obvious problem with remaining objective should a relationship develop beyond the supervisor-supervisee relationship. Should this occur, the supervisor needs to closely examine the situation to determine if an alternative supervisory arrangement should be made for the supervisee (Bernard, 1987; Bradley, 1989).

A final dual relationship. Another ethical dilemma is the clinical supervisor's dual relationship when he or she is both a mentor to, and evaluator of, the supervisee. For instance, the clinical supervisor may encourage the supervisee to be open and self-disclose. The supervisee may well divulge information that could later be used in a critical manner when the clinical supervisor assumes the role of evaluator. In cases such as this, it may not be possible to completely avoid conflict (Bernard, 1987).

Issues of Informed Consent

By virtue of the clinical supervision, the supervisor is involved in an indirect relationship with the supervisee's clients. It is, therefore, incumbent on the supervisor or supervisee to inform clients of the supervisory arrangement and gain the clients' consent for this to take place if a student intern is to be engaged in clinical practice with them. This is called *informed consent.* Clients need to be led to understand that students are in time-limited assignments and be told the extent of their assignments. If any special arrangements are made to observe or evaluate the performance of the supervisee, clients participating in the session need to be informed. For example, if the supervisor is to attend an activity that he or she does not normally attend, or if a special arrangement is made to video a session, these arrangements need to be discussed with clients. In general, clients need to be informed about any aspect of the supervisory relationship that could affect the clients' willingness to participate (Bernard, 1987; Bradley, 1989).

As with clients, supervisors need to be concerned with informed consent with student interns. Interns need to be informed of all conditions they must meet in order to successfully complete their training. Supervisors themselves should also operate with informed consent regarding the great responsibility, accountability, and even culpability they assume when they agree to do clinical supervision (Bernard, 1987).

Confidentiality Concerns

The clinical supervisor has the ethical responsibility to see that communications between him or her and the supervisee are kept confidential. Therefore, particularly in the case of students, there needs to be an agreed-upon procedure in place so the supervisee will know if information is to be shared with a third party (such as a university faculty member). Similarly, clients need to know if confidential information about them will be shared with the clinical supervisor. The topic of confidentiality needs to be covered at the beginning of the supervisor-supervisee relationship and the supervisee-client relationship.

Safeguarding the Rights of Future Clients

A final ethical concern is that clinical supervisors of university interns have the responsibility to safeguard future clients (Spielman, 1998). If the clinical supervisor does not believe the intern is ready to assume the role of working with clients as a professional, he or she has the ethical responsibility to inform the intern and the intern's university faculty supervisor.

Concluding Statement on Ethics and Clinical Supervision

The U.S. Department of Health and Human Services (2009) has emphasized ethical standards for clinical supervisors are not a cookbook. Ethical principles tell us what to do but not always how to do it. As may be ascertained from the discussion in this section on ethical concerns in clinical supervision, ethical issues are normally not simple matters. Ethical dilemmas are apt to occasionally arise even with the best planning. Knowing some of the key areas of ethical concern can, however, allow clinical supervisors and supervisees to anticipate ethical matters and deal with them before they become problematic.

Supervisees' Development and Supervisory Relationships

Three levels of clinical supervision have been proposed by Stoltenberg, McNeill, and Delworth (1998). In *Level 1*, supervisees are conceptualized as being relatively inexperienced and dependent on the supervisor but full of hope and motivation to become competent clinicians. They are also imitative and anxious, lack self-awareness, engage in categorical thinking, and over-accommodate to the supervisor, who is perceived to be an "all-knowing" expert. Supervisees, at this level, tend to focus on their own needs related to their personal feelings and thoughts about their own behaviors, and therefore, lack awareness of their clients' needs and interpersonal dynamics. A principal function of the supervisor is to provide the structure needed to keep the normal anxiety of the supervisee at a manageable level.

In *Level 2*, supervisees are seen to be less imitative and more assertive while striving for greater independence, but suffer from a dependency-autonomy conflict. Supervisees' motivational levels fluctuate as they become more confused and less confident about the effectiveness of their interventions. The supervisor functions to help the supervisee deal with the dependency-autonomy conflict and become more independent in his or her clinical functioning.

In *Level 3*, supervisees have an increased sense of personal identity and self-confidence. They have accepted themselves and are no longer defensive as they function relatively independently from the clinical supervisor. Their motivational levels are much more consistent, as they are not as susceptible to pessimism or undue optimism. The function of the supervisor is largely consultation with the supervisor following the lead of the supervisee in determining the content of supervision.

Loganbill, Hardy, and Delworth (1982) have indicated that the best-suited supervisor is someone who has a higher level of competence and maturity and greater clinical experience than the supervisee. It is suggested that supervision from an individual with these characteristics will be more readily accepted than it would be from someone lacking the status afforded by possessing a higher level of competence, maturity, and experience. It is, therefore, important to complete an initial assessment of the supervisee to determine at which of the three levels (Level 1, Level 2, or Level 3) he or she is functioning. This assessment will help ensure that a match can be made so that the supervisee receives supervision from someone who is functioning at a higher level.

Other variables that may influence the supervisory relationship are demographic factors, theoretical orientations, and personality dimensions. The impact of gender, sex-role attitudes, race, ethnic background, and social class are demographic variables that should be considered when matching supervisees with supervisors. Differences in theoretical orientations have been found to create conflict between supervisees and supervisors; therefore, consideration needs to be given to this aspect when assigning supervisees. Finally, personality clashes can interfere with the supervisor-supervisee relationship, so the personalities of individuals who might be placed together need to be taken into account.

Multiculturalism and Diversity

As indicated by Corey, Haynes, Moulton, and Muratori (2010): "A multicultural perspective provides a conceptual framework that recognizes the complex diversity of a pluralistic society while at the same time suggesting bridges of shared concern that bind culturally different individuals to one another" (p. 122). Today, within recreational therapy, a multicultural perspective is seen to be vital.

There are good reasons for adopting a multicultural perspective. A major one is that all clients and staff should be treated with respect and dignity no matter their cultural identities. This is just social justice. Another reason is that both the United States and Canada have become culturally diverse countries which are expected to become even more diverse in the future. So recreational therapists are likely to serve and work with persons from a number of different diversity groups.

The director of the U.S. Census Bureau has indicated that for the United States groups comprising ethnicity and race identities are increasing rapidly (U.S. Census Bureau, 2011). By 2030, ethnic and racial minorities will constitute 42% of the U.S. population (Rand, 2010). By 2050, it is anticipated that there will be a "majority minority" where ethnic and racial minorities will be in the majority (Malveaux, 2012).

Canada is also experiencing growing racial diversity. It has been reported by Statistics Canada (2005) that "Under the low- and high-growth scenarios for the projections, Canada could have between 11.4 million and 14.4 million persons belonging to a visible minority group by 2031, more than double the 5.3 million reported In 2006. The rest of the population, in contrast, is projected to increase by less than 12%."

As an essential part of recreational therapy, clinical supervision needs to reflect a multicultural focus. According to Falender and her colleagues (2004), a key component in clinical supervision is:

> Recognition that attention to diversity in all of its forms (e.g., age, disability, ethnicity, gender, gender identity, race, religion, sexual orientation, religion, socioeconomic status, etc.) relates to every aspect of the supervision process and requires specific competence. (p. 775)

A responsibility of the recreational therapy clinical supervisor is to see his or her supervisees recognize and respect the role diversity takes within clinical supervision. Supervisors need to help supervisees to gain basic understandings of diversity, to maintain positive approaches in their interactions with a diversity of clients, and to acknowledge the role of diversity will likely play in the supervisor/supervisee relationship (Barnett, Erickson Cornish, Goodyear, & Lichtenberg, 2007).

Of course, before attempting to prepare culturally competent supervisees, supervisors must develop their own personal cultural competence. This involves accepting the fundamental principle that others' views (e.g., beliefs, values, attitudes) are likely to often vary from those the supervisor holds. In addition, the supervisor needs to engage in self-examination to become aware of the personal views he or she holds toward individuals from various diverse groups. This examination should not be limited to thinking in terms of unitary groups, such as African Americans and Whites. Instead, it should consider the full range of diversity characteristics including age, disability, race, ethnicity, gender, gender identity, sexual orientation, language, national origin, religion, and socioeconomic status (Falender, et al., 2004).

To assure supervisees become culturally competent practitioners, the supervisor should discuss diversity with supervisees within supervisory sessions. These sessions should be structured in ways that will help them to examine their culturally influenced beliefs, values, and behaviors and to consider how these may affect their interactions with their clients and the supervisor.

Because the discussion of cultural diversity may be awkward for both the supervisor and supervisee, Corey and his colleagues (2010) have suggested that before discussing cultural identities that supervisors may wish to "talk about talking" about culture to set ground rules and clarify expectations. Discussion of the supervisory contact can be an ideal time to introduce the topic as an area of development for the supervisee and to introduce expectations of the supervisee related to multiculturalism. Initial sessions of supervision can then be used for supervisors and supervisees to explore concepts of multiculturalism and their cultural similarities and differences. A number of questions to facilitate multicultural conversations have been proposed in the clinical supervision literature.

Questions posed in a 2009 U.S. Department of Health and Human Services publication for clinical supervisors to ask to supervisees include "What did you think when you saw my last name?"; "What did you think when you found my culture was X, when yours is Y?"; "How did you feel about this difference?"; and "What did you do in response to this difference?"

Questions suggested by Constantine (2003) for supervisors to use with supervisees include "What demographic variables do you use to identify yourself?"; "What worldviews (e.g., values, assumptions, and biases) do you bring to supervision based on your cultural identities?"; and "What struggles and challenges have you faced working with clients who were from different cultures than your own?"

An extensive list of questions have been proposed by Corey and his colleagues (2010). These include the following:

- How do you describe your ethnic identity? What does it mean to you to identify with this group?
- What are the various cultural groups to which you belong? What ones seem to take on the most importance in your life?
- How do you think your culture affects the way you see your role as a therapist, your choice of theoretical orientation, diagnosis, and treatment? What parts of your clinical approach do you most strongly identify with and why?
- Can you identify at this time, ways in which our cultural differences or similarities may affect our supervisory relationship?
- How would you rate your knowledge of and comfort with discussing cultural issues?
- If you find discussions about culture uncomfortable, can you identify what it is that you find awkward or threatening? Where might you have learned this fear?
- What types of academic training, professional conferences, workshops, or seminars have you completed in the area of multicultural practice? (p. 128)

Of course, each individual supervisor will have to determine whether these or other questions are most appropriate for them to ask as a part of his or her overall personal approach to multiculturalism. It is however important that the topic is not neglected because of anxiousness on the part of the supervisor. It is critical that supervisors themselves develop cultural competency, that they model cultural sensitivity in all discussions of diversity, and, finally, that they display sincere concern for the development of culturally competency in supervisees.

The Supervisory Alliance With Emerging Professionals

Through the supervisory relationship, the student intern or emerging recreational therapist supervisee will grow from dependency to a relatively autonomous practitioner. By means of the helping relationship with his or her clinical supervisor, the supervisee will master and refine specific clinical skills, increase abilities to conceptualize client cases and concerns, become aware of the therapeutic use of self in the therapeutic process, and learn to translate theory into practice (Bradley, 1989; Corey, Haynes, Moulton, & Muratori, 2010).

When viewed in these terms, the critical nature of the relationship between the supervisor and supervisee looms large indeed. In fact, Malone (2009) has exclaimed the relationship is far more important to effective supervision than are the methods and techniques used by the clinical supervisor.

Pre-assessment

Because of the critical nature of the clinical supervision process, a great deal of planning is required on the part of the supervisor to assure that the relationship begins with as good a start as possible. Before meeting with the supervisee, the supervisor will want to begin to assess the supervisee's clinical skills.

The supervisee may be asked to complete a self-assessment on a form provided by the agency, or the supervisee may be requested to draft a statement to indicate strengths he or she may possess, areas of skill deficiency, and areas of concern on which he or she wishes to focus (Borders & Leddick, 1987). Many additional means of assessment might be used as well. Among these are transcripts from which to assess the course preparation of the supervisee, the supervisee's résumé, and communications from those familiar with the supervisee's developmental level. For example, a university faculty member could supply information as to the level on which the student supervisee would be functioning. Such information could be extremely useful when supervising graduate student interns, whose backgrounds may vary widely.

Initial Supervisory Sessions

Another step toward orchestrating a solid supervisory relationship is a well-conducted first session between the supervisor and supervisee. This meeting is an excellent opportunity for the two parties to discuss their expectations about the supervisory relationship. The initial session also sets the tone for the working relationship that will follow, so it is important for the supervisor to begin to establish rapport and display an organized, reassuring approach with the supervisee.

Table 9.6

Tips for Supervisors in Establishing a Productive Relationship with Supervisees

---

- Treat supervisees with respect, be open and honest about what you do and do not know.
- Work at developing a spirit of mutual trust and collaboration.
- Listen diligently to what the supervisees are both saying and not saying, and try to tune into their fears, struggles, and hopes.
- Have a clear understanding of the purpose and the limits of the supervisory relationship.
- Be available especially by being fully present during the supervisory session and by making sure that this is "protected time" that is free from interruptions.
- Be willing to seek consultation when you are unfamiliar with the topic under discussion.
- Be clear on the boundaries of the relationship.
- Have a clear understanding of your values, beliefs, and attitudes regarding the range of typical issues that come up in supervision, including multicultural issues.
- Discuss with your supervisees their values and beliefs and how values and beliefs may affect the supervisory relationship.

Adapted from Corey, G., Haynes, R., Moulton, P., & Muratori, M. (2010). *Clinical supervision in the helping professions* (2nd ed.). Alexandria, VA: American Counseling Association, p. 59.

As Bradley (1989) has stipulated, the goals of the initial supervisory conference should be to establish clear understandings about the structure of clinical supervision and the nature of the supervisory relationship, and to create a supportive supervisor-supervisee relationship. Realistically, it may take several supervisory sessions to accomplish these goals. Therefore, it is better to discuss what will occur in initial supervisory sessions or the initial phase of supervision, rather than in a single supervisory meeting.

What types of expectations need to be made clear regarding the structure of supervision and the nature of the supervisory relationship? Bradley (1989), Borders and Leddick (1987), and Corey, Haynes, Moulton, and Muratori (2010) have provided a number of specific suggestions of items that should be covered during initial supervisory sessions. These include the following:

- Time required at the agency (if supervisee is completing practicum or internship).
- Supervisee's schedule, including the frequency, length, and location of supervisory meetings.
- The structure and nature of supervisory sessions.
- The number and type of clients and programs with which the supervisee will be involved.
- How audio recordings, videos, case notes, and observations will be used in supervision.
- How the supervisee will be evaluated and the criteria employed in evaluation.
- Field site visit requirements and the organization and structure for the visits.
- Legal and ethical issues related to clinical practice.
- Procedures to be followed in case of an emergency situation (e.g., suicide attempt).
- Plans for any group supervision.
- Determination of supervisee's areas for professional growth and development.
- Establishment of the supervisee's learning goals, together with a plan to achieve the goals and measure outcomes.
- Review of expectations of the agency in terms of presentations, papers, or assignments.
- Review of expectations of college or university requirements, if the supervision is provided as part of a practicum or internship.
- Expectations of the supervisee's need to complete formal and informal self-evaluations.
- Expectations of the supervisor in regard to formal and informal evaluations.
- If the supervisor is providing administrative supervision as well as clinical supervision, or if the supervisor must submit an evaluation of the student supervisee to a university, he or she needs to discuss problems inherent in the contradictory roles of clinical supervisor and evaluator.

Fox (1983, p. 39) developed a set of questions to guide initial supervisory sessions between the supervisor and supervisee. While not as detailed as those items provided in the previous section, supervisors and supervisees may find Fox's questions useful to the process of clarifying expectations, particularly in regard to establishing learning goals for the supervisee and planning to achieve them. Fox's questions are listed below:

1. What do we expect from each other?
2. What can we give to each other?
3. Are our goals the same?
4. Can we achieve them?
5. How can we achieve them?
6. What constraints exist?
7. How will we know when we have achieved the goals?

In addition to establishing clear expectations about the supervision structure and the supervisory relationship, the supervisor wishes to establish a reassuring, supportive relationship with the supervisee during initial conferences. In this regard, Malone (2009) has proposed "the three A's of supervision" which are (1) acceptance, (2) approval, and (3) affirmation. Time should be devoted in the first meeting for allowing the supervisee to describe his or her background. Areas that may be covered are types of previous experiences, familiarity with recreational therapy settings, influences on present philosophy of practice, reasons for becoming a recreational therapist, and motivation for seeking the present growth experience. This process not only shows interest in the individual but provides information that will prove useful in the assessment of the supervisee. The supervisor should reciprocate by providing background information on himself or herself as it relates to the experiences of the supervisee. The supervisor should also demonstrate his or her qualifications for performing the role of clinical supervisor.

Issues of concern for the supervisee should also be dealt with during the initial phase of supervision. Time needs to be given to an exploration of the supervisee's expectations of supervision. Time also needs to be devoted to acknowledging and discussing the supervisee's fears regarding evaluation. Finally, the supervisee should have time to ask the supervisor about his or her background and approach to assure the supervisee is comfortable with the person who will be providing supervision.

A supportive relationship will probably only begin to be formed during the initial supervisory session, or even during the initial phase of supervision. This point has been discussed by Bradley (1989), who has written:

> ... a supportive supervisor-supervisee relationship unfolds throughout the length of supervision and is reinforced by positively perceived supervisor behavior. Supervisees reportedly value supervisors who call them by name, use humor in the supervisory sessions, allow observations, share...experiences, help the supervisee develop strengths and a personal...style, and lead the supervisee to realize that developing new skills is an awkward process. (p. 330)

In summary, as a result of initial supervisory sessions, the supervisor and supervisee will have formed the foundations for their working relationship and established clear expectations for the supervisory process. In doing so, they will have completed an assessment of the supervisee's clinical skills and knowledge as a basis for establishing learning goals for the supervisee. An important aspect to be considered when establishing clear expectations during the initial phase of supervision is the development of learning goals for the supervisee. Within the following section, the process of establishing learning goals and using them to guide the supervisory process is discussed.

Supervision Goals

Establishing learning goals for the supervisee can be helpful in both clarifying expectations and building the supervisor-supervisee relationship. First, working together on establishing the goals fosters a spirit of cooperation between the supervisor and supervisee. Second, the involvement of the supervisee increases the likelihood that he or she will be committed to accomplishing the goals. Third, goal achievement can be a positive motivational factor to inspire the supervisee. Fourth, the goal-setting process in clinical supervision serves as a model for the supervisee to follow in setting goals with clients.

Finally, the formulation of a goals set provides structure to guide the clinical supervision process (Borders & Leddick, 1987).

When beginning the goal formulation process, it may be necessary to discuss the purposes of establishing goals so that the supervisee comprehends the importance of goals to planning and evaluation. Sometimes the supervisee recognizes it is necessary to set goals, but does not understand the connection between each goal and actions required to reach a goal and ways to stipulate goal attainment (Bradley, 1989).

Because a great deal of information may be available as a result of the assessment, the supervisor needs to guard against being overwhelmed by the amount that the supervisee must learn. As with clients, goals need to be chosen that are realistic and achievable. The supervisor will probably have to guide the supervisee in selecting goals that coincide with the supervisee's needs and degree of readiness to master a specific skill or knowledge. Goals can be prioritized and sequenced so that they are manageable. It is also important to keep in mind that goals can be rewritten to reflect the supervisee's growth and additional information gained about the supervisee by the supervisor (Borders & Leddick, 1987).

Learning goals should each reflect an end result in a fashion similar to stipulating goals for clients. Therefore, each goal will be written as a behavior that the supervisee will display. As with the achievement of client goals, several enabling objectives may be used to break down goals into their component parts. According to Fox (1983, p. 40), learning goals should be

- specific;
- explicit;
- feasible in regard to capacity, opportunity, and resources;
- realistic and attainable;
- seen in light of constraints;
- related to the task formulated;
- modifiable over time;
- measurable; and
- ordered into priority.

Fox (1983, pp. 46-48) outlined eight steps to be followed in developing a goal-oriented contract to direct the supervisory process. Rather than contract, sometimes the expression "individual development plan" (IDP) or "professional development plan" (PDP) is employed to describe the goals, policies, timeline, and system of evaluation (U.S. Department of Health and Human Services, 2009). Whether or not a formal contractual agreement is drawn up or an IDP or PDP is developed, the steps offer a helpful procedure to be used in the formulation of goals and the planning of learning activities to achieve goals and planning evaluation activities to assess outcomes. The supervisor and supervisee

1. generate baseline information,
2. specify their focus and expectations,
3. set priorities for goals,
4. identify observable behavioral characteristics and describe how increased knowledge and skill will be exhibited by the supervisee,
5. delineate their respective roles and explain their responsibilities,
6. discuss the content of the supervisory program,

7. agree on a time frame, and
8. specify criteria for a step-by-step evaluation of the achievement of goals and their transferability into practice.

Baseline Information

In Fox's first step, the supervisor and supervisee generate baseline information that indicates the initial performance or knowledge level of the supervisee. Various approaches can be used in this assessment in addition to discussions between the supervisor and supervisee. These include the use of self-reports from the supervisee, role-plays, observations, audio recordings, videos, and reports from other staff or faculty. Through such means of assessment, the supervisor and supervisee arrive at agreement on needs areas and baseline functioning in the areas.

Focus and Expectations

The supervisor and supervisee then specify their focus and expectations. Here they record what they ultimately hope to achieve. This step answers the question: What is to be accomplished and in what time frame? The supervisor and supervisee then proceed to set priorities for the goals.

Priorities

Goals are ordered in importance. Next, the supervisor and supervisee identify observable behavioral characteristics and describe how increased knowledge and skill will be exhibited by the supervisee. This critical step puts into concrete terms the evidence of achievement of each goal. This step answers the question: How will the worker show improved skills or knowledge?

Delineation

During the fifth step, the supervisor and supervisee delineate their respective roles and explain their responsibilities. They decide who will do what. The question here is: What am I willing to offer or do?

Discussion

The supervisor and supervisee discuss the content of the supervising program. Specific learning strategies or interventions are identified.

Time Frame

In the next to last step, the supervisor and supervisee agree on a time frame. Questions to be answered include "How much time will it take to achieve the goals?"; "How much time will be devoted in each meeting to accomplish the task?"; and "In what sequence will the goals be achieved?"

Evaluation

The final step is that of specifying criteria for a step-by-step evaluation of the achievement of goals and transferability into practice. Methods for measuring change are agreed upon. This step answers the question, "How will progress be measured?"

Application of Fox's Procedure

While there are places of overlap within the steps proposed by Fox (1983), the procedure offers guidelines that may be adopted in order to facilitate the work of supervisors and supervisees. It may be, however, that supervisors may wish to modify Fox's procedure in order to fit their personal style.

It would seem that Fox's steps to establishing learning goals, learning activities, and evaluation procedures best apply to the supervision of supervisees who are at Stoltenberg, McNeill, and Delworth's (1998) Level 1 (i.e., still new and emerging supervisees) or Level 2 (i.e., supervisees who are still becoming independent). To use Hart's (1982) models of supervision and Bradley's (1989) supervisor roles, these Level 1 and Level 2 supervisees would profit from a skill development model (with the supervisor in a teaching role) or personal growth model (with the supervisor in a counselor role).

Those supervisees at Stoltenberg, McNeill, and Delworth's Level 3 (i.e., confident with developed skill levels) would be advanced students or experienced therapists who would fit into the integrative model of supervision proposed by Hart (1982). They would use the supervisor more as a consultant who might assist them in case conceptualization and in determining therapeutic approaches, particularly with difficult cases.

Having said that supervisees work at three levels, and, therefore, the type of supervision should match their developmental needs, it must be remembered that supervisees are not static. They do change over time.

Facilitation of the Learning Environment

The supervisor has the task of arranging learning conditions that contain adequate structure and support to optimize the supervisee's learning. The amount of structure and support provided will vary according to the developmental level of the supervisee (Bradley, 1989). Topics covered in this section are how the developmental level of the supervisee affects the structure for learning, methods for supervisory interventions, modalities for clinical supervision, and contracts in clinical supervision.

Developmental Level of Supervisee

As discussed earlier in the chapter, the supervisor may assume the role of teacher, counselor, or consultant. The assumption of a particular role is largely dictated by the developmental level of the supervisee. Emerging professionals (i.e., students, new practitioners) generally need to focus their attention on achieving clinical practice skills, so they are very task oriented and dependent on the supervisor, who assumes the role of their teacher.

These supervisees, therefore, respond positively to structured teaching methods such as completing assigned readings, attending didactic presentations, observing senior therapists conduct sessions, doing role playing, listening to suggestions for appropriate client interventions, and discussing the connection between theory and practice. Due to their typically high levels of anxiety, they also appreciate receiving support and reassurance from their supervisors (Borders & Leddick, 1987).

It does need to be noted that not all persons who are in this early stage of development are young adults. Supervisees who are middle aged or older will likely experience the same anxiety that the young person experiences. Unlike their younger counterparts, however, they may have deeply ingrained habits and behavioral patterns that the supervisor must recognize. The supervisor must also recognize that adult learners may have been functioning with a relatively high degree of independence and autonomy. It may be difficult and threatening for them to relinquish their independent functioning and become dependent on the supervisor in order to learn new skills and knowledge.

Adult learners thus present a somewhat different challenge for the supervisor, who may need to adjust his or her teaching approach to meet their unique characteristics (Bradley, 1989). For example, some of the teaching interventions normally employed with more advanced supervisees may be used occasionally with adult learners. Less directive approaches to teaching are typically preferred by supervisees who are experienced and have gained competence and confidence. They are apt to view the supervisor more as a resource person than an instructor and desire to enter into conversations with the supervisor regarding theoretical issues and case conceptualizations. Further, they are likely to take more responsibility for their learning than those who are less advanced and desire to enter into more of a peer-like relationship with the supervisor.

The more advanced supervisee is also likely to want the supervisor to be more frank about personal issues that may impact on his or her clinical work (Borders & Leddick, 1987). The supervisor's assessment of the developmental level of the supervisee will obviously be very helpful in determining the type of learning environment that will be optimal for his or her supervisee.

Methods for Supervisory Interventions

There are a number of interventions that supervisors may employ. Some of these already mentioned include reading assignments, didactic presentations, observations of senior staff, receiving suggestions for appropriate client interventions, and discussions of theory and practice. Other possible interventions are discussions of cases and activities, observations of sessions, critiques of audio and video recordings of sessions, role playing, conjoint interviewing, and co-leadership of individual or group sessions. In addition, supervisors may give specific instruction on cognitive skills, such as writing case recordings or preparing individual intervention plans. Normally, following readings and didactic instruction, supervisors review the work of supervisees and then offer feedback (Borders & Leddick, 1987; Corey, Haynes, Moulton, & Muratori, 2010; Platt-Koch, 1986).

Modalities for Clinical Supervision

There are two primary modalities or formats for conducting clinical supervision. They are the individual and group meetings. The *individual conference* is the most widely used modality and the format that perhaps most of us have as an image when thinking about clinical supervision. Here the supervisor and supervisee meet face-to-face. The individual conference has been termed by Druss (2007, p. 215) as "the backbone" of clinical supervision programs. Individual supervisory sessions are typically scheduled on a weekly or biweekly basis, although sometimes sessions are monthly. They typically last about an hour.

The second modality is *group meetings*. They too are regularly scheduled, often on a biweekly basis in order to supplement individual conferences. Within the group structure, several supervisees often work together on a particular skill. The group method lends itself to teaching skills and may, therefore, be chosen as a means to instruct new supervisees who are learning clinical practice skills and techniques. The group meeting also is commonly used with more advanced supervisees who may do group processing. The main drawback with the group meeting is that it may be difficult to meet the diverse needs of supervisees within a group situation.

A relatively new form of group supervision is *triadic supervision*. In triadic supervision two supervisees meet with one supervisor. If the supervisor is trained in triadic supervision, this format can lighten the load of the supervisor provided there is a good match between the supervisor and supervisees. Still, working with two supervisees at a time can be challenging. While triadic supervision holds promise, additional testing is required before it can be fully accepted as a method of supervision. A final type of group meeting is *peer supervision*. Within peer supervision groups, therapists with advanced clinical practice skills meet with one another to provide clinical supervision. Such supervision may be completed in dyads or in small groups. (Aasheim, 2011; Corey, Haynes, Moulton, & Muratori, 2010).

In instances where an appropriate clinical supervisor is not available at the supervisee's agency, technology-assisted techniques may be employed as an alternative method to face-to-face supervision. Options include doing clinical supervision using a variety of technologies such as the telephone, video conferencing, and online supervision using computer mediated communication tools such as electronic mail and Internet chat (Driscoll & Townsend, 2007).

Contracts and Individual Development Plans in Clinical Supervision

It has been found that it is helpful to have guidelines and responsibilities of the supervisor and supervisee clearly established so that both know what is expected. Agreement on guidelines and responsibilities is known as the *clinical supervision contract*. These are commonly written and signed by both parties.

Van Ooijen (2000) has suggested major areas within a contract. These areas are (a) *logistics or ground rules* to include meeting times, lengths, and locations and arrangements for cancellations or postponements; (b) *limits and boundaries* dealing with topics such as confidentiality, storing of notes or other documents, and the notion that the focus will be on the work of the supervisee and not the person as it would be in therapy; (c) *accountability* where the question of who is accountable for what is addressed (e.g., Does the supervisor report an intern's progress to the university?); (d) *aims and goals* include agreement on the purpose of the supervision and goals that have been developed; (e) *responsibilities* has to do with whether the supervisor or supervisee sets the agenda for sessions; and (f) *preferred process* addresses the questions: What should be the balance between support and challenge? How and when will evaluation of the supervision take place? (pp. 42–48)

Similar to the contract is the *individual development plan* (sometimes referred to as a professional development plan). An IDP follows a similar format to the contract. They are often developed using a form provided by the agency that has space for describing the goals for the plan; a section to list the knowledge, skills, and attitudes needed to reach the goals; another section to list the activities the supervisee will complete to achieve each goal; and a final section to stipulate evaluation procedures for demonstrating proficiency. Forms typically contain signature lines for both the supervisor and supervisee. As in the case of the contract, both the supervisor and supervisee should maintain copies of the IDP (U.S. Department of Health and Human Services, 2009).

Clinical Supervision Evaluation

Two major categories of evaluation are *formative evaluation* and *summative evaluation*. Formative evaluation is the continuous process of giving direct feedback to the supervisee in order to facilitate skill development and professional growth. It should occur throughout supervision on a regular basis. It is the constant, ongoing evaluation provided by the supervisor. Summative evaluation is the formal part of evaluation that provides an overall perspective of strengths, limitations, and areas for possible improvement (U.S. Department of Health and Human Sevices, 2009).

Both the supervisor and supervisee can benefit from formal evaluation sessions. For student interns, formal evaluations are typically held halfway through the experience (i.e., midterm) and at the conclusion of the experience (i.e., final evaluation). Any number of approaches can be used to structure the evaluation session. Evaluation instruments are commonly supplied by universities. Often the supervisor completes an instrument on the supervisee, and the supervisee is called upon to complete an evaluation of the supervisor. Generally, the supervisor first reviews his or her evaluation of the supervisee and then the student goes over his or her evaluation of the supervisor.

Another approach to evaluation is to review the supervisee's learning goals in an effort to determine progress in their attainment. This procedure helps the supervisee to see the gains he or she has made during the period of clinical supervision and to set goals for the future. The supervisor can serve as a model for the supervisee by engaging in self-evaluation, inviting feedback, and being open to criticism. The supervisee can be helpful to the supervisor by providing honest feedback that will assist the supervisor to adjust or modify his or her approach in the future.

Whatever approach is taken to evaluation in clinical supervision, it should be clearly delineated from the beginning of supervision in the supervision contract or individual development plan. As Corey and his colleagues (2010) indicated, "Supervisees have a right to be informed in writing of the procedures for evaluation, which include how and when it will occur, what the consequences of a serious negative evaluation might be, what recourse supervisees will have to correct any deficiencies identified, what they can do if they would like to challenge the evaluation results, and what the course of appeal is in the case of an extremely negative evaluation with which they do not agree" (pp. 222-223).

Borders and Leddick (1987) remind us that the helping relationships between supervisors and supervisees closely parallel the relationships between helping professionals and clients in discussing the final evaluation session as a termination session and a new beginning. They write,

> The final supervision session is similar to the termination session with a client, in that it can be an important catalyst for change, not just the end. Therapeutic termination sessions with clients have three functions: (a) summarizing progress toward goals, (b) discussing how changes will be maintained and identifying "next steps" for continued growth, and (c) achieving a sense of closure in the relationship. (p. 60)

Setting Up a Clinical Supervision Program

Before launching a new clinical supervision program, it is important that the senior administration indicate support for the program both verbally and in writing. Their communications should indicate their rationale for instigating the clinical supervision program (U.S. Department of Health and Human Services, 2009).

Bond and Holland (1998) have offered a six-stage model for setting up and maintaining a clinical supervision program. The first stage is that of *information sharing*. In this beginning stage there needs to be an assessment to determine the amount of interest and expertise in clinical supervision among the staff. A general meeting may be held if the number of staff is relatively small or a working group from a larger staff can meet to get started. Discussion and literature should be used to create understandings of clinical supervision.

The second stage is that of *skills training*. Staff are provided training in giving and receiving clinical supervision. A consultant may be employed to conduct tailor-made training for staff. Alternatives are for staff to take university courses on clinical supervision or to develop self-training in small groups.

Stage three involves *deciding on the modalities* for clinical supervision. Staff must determine how they wish to structure the program. Will a weekly 60-minute, individual, one-on-one meeting be used? Or will group or peer supervision be a better choice for the organization? The pros and cons of each approach will need to be discussed and a modality selected.

Stage four involves a *pilot program being implemented*. The modality selected is tested during this phase. Criteria for success have to be identified so staff can evaluate at the end of this stage. It is suggested that three to six clinical supervision meetings be conducted before the final evaluation of the pilot test is conducted.

The fifth stage is that of *evaluation and redesign*. Here the evaluation is actually conducted following the evaluation criteria previously identified. Changes are then made based on findings from this evaluation.

The sixth and final stage is *establishing and monitoring the program*. Once the program has been redesigned, a monitoring system needs to be developed. Perhaps some of the previously used evaluation methods can be adapted to use in the monitoring process. Of course, staff will want to continually refine and further develop their clinical supervision program to best meet their needs.

Chapter Summary

Clinical supervision is an evolving area in recreational therapy. Happily, its importance has begun to become more recognized. All who work directly with clients, from the newest student to the most seasoned senior staff member, can profit from clinical supervision because all enjoy the potential to grow, and no helping professionals ever reach the stage where they have all the answers. Within this chapter, an attempt has been made to explain clinical supervision and its potentially powerful impact on clinical practice. Hopefully, both future supervisors and supervisees will profit from the information offered in the chapter so that, ultimately, clients may benefit by receiving the highest level of clinical services that can be provided.

Reading Comprehension Questions

1. Have those entering careers in recreational therapy received preparation for giving and receiving clinical supervision?
2. Do university faculty value clinical supervision?
3. Why has recreational therapy only recently embraced clinical supervision, even though a number of helping professions have been using clinical supervision for several years?
4. Can you define clinical supervision in your own words? Tell what elements define the clinical supervision process?
5. What purposes does clinical supervision serve?
6. How does clinical supervision differ from managerial or administrative supervision?
7. What are similarities and differences between clinical supervision and therapy?
8. Describe the three models of supervision proposed by Hart.
9. Describe three roles for clinical supervisors.
10. What is a fundamental ethical question for any individual considering being a clinical supervisor?
11. What are dual relationships? Do you agree with the comments made about dual relationships in the chapter?
12. What is informed consent?
13. Why does confidentiality need to be discussed at the beginning of any helping relationship?

14. What are three levels of clinical supervision?
15. What are the characteristics of the individual who is best suited to do clinical supervision?
16. How do you define multiculturalism? Do you agree the concept of multiculturalism is accepted in RT?
17. When considering cultural competence within supervision, why is it important for the supervisor and supervisee to educate each other regarding their orientations, beliefs, and values?
18. Explain the nature and importance of the supervisor-supervisee relationship.
19. Why is the first supervisory session important?
20. What should be covered during initial supervisory sessions?
21. Why are learning goals important in clinical supervision?
22. What stages do supervisees pass through?
23. How does the supervisee's developmental level relate to the type of structure and support provided by the supervisor?
24. Identify methods for supervisory interventions.
25. What are the major modalities or formats for doing clinical supervision?
26. What is triadic supervision?
27. What is peer supervision?
28. What technologies offer alternatives to face-to-face supervision?
29. What is commonly included in clinical supervision contracts (or individual development plans)?
30. Describe the model proposed by Bond and Holland for setting up a clinical supervision program.

Chapter 10

Health and Safety Considerations

Joan K. Austin, PhD, RN, FAAN
David W. Dunn, MD.
Heather Lien, MSN, FNP-BC, CDE

█ Chapter Purpose

There are common physical occurrences or conditions that may threaten clients' health or physical safety. Diabetes mellitus, epilepsy, and long-term psychotropic drug use are examples of conditions that may affect a client's ability to participate safely in an activity. This chapter presents health and safety information to be considered when providing services for clients who have a seizure disorder, who are receiving medication for diabetes mellitus, or who are being treated with psychotropic drugs for the treatment of mental illness. Information is also provided regarding special mechanical aids upon which some clients must rely and which must be considered when providing recreational therapy services. Finally, information is presented on safety precautions when working with persons with HIV/AIDS.

Because diabetes mellitus is a chronic disease affecting approximately 26 million people, more than 8% of the population (American Diabetes Association,72012) in the United States, and because the treatment for diabetes mellitus can produce life-threatening side effects in the patient, basic information on diabetes mellitus and its management is necessary for the recreational therapist. In addition, complications from the disease can cause conditions such as blindness/visual impairment, loss of sensation, pain, and temperature changes, which will affect a client's ability to participate in specific activities. The first section of this chapter presents information on diabetes mellitus.

Another possible threat to clients' safety can occur during a seizure. Approximately 1 in 26 people will develop epilepsy during their lifetime (Hesdorffer et al., 2010). Epilepsy sometimes occurs simultaneously with other conditions affecting the brain, such as intellectual impairment and cerebral palsy. Thus the recreational therapist needs basic information regarding seizures, their usual treatment, and first-aid measures. Information regarding seizures is presented in the second section of the chapter.

Another section in the chapter is devoted to the client who takes psychotropic drugs for the treatment of mental health problems. Many recreational therapists come into contact with these clients at mental health facilities. However, clients from any of the clinical populations may receive psychotropic drugs. Consequently, recreational therapists who work with a variety of populations will come into contact with clients receiving psychotropic drugs. Clients who receive these drugs may experience side effects that should be taken into consideration when recreational activities are planned and provided. Information on commonly prescribed psychotropic drugs includes desired effects, side effects, and possible implications for the practice of recreational therapy.

General guidelines for recreational therapists to follow when working with clients who use mechanical aids such as braces, crutches, and wheelchairs also are presented. Clients who are elderly or who have common physical conditions such as arthritis, broken bones, spinal cord injuries, cerebral palsy, cancer, and muscular dystrophy often have physical limitations requiring mechanical aids, either temporarily or permanently. Recreational therapists who work in hospital settings, nursing homes, assisted living facilities, rehabilitation centers, camps for children with physical disabilities, and institutions for persons who are severely intellectually impaired serve clients with physical limitations. Information regarding possible safety hazards and implications for providing services are given. In addition, step-by-step guides for transferring clients from a wheelchair to a bed and from a bed to a wheelchair are provided. The final section provides safety guidelines for the recreational therapist when working with clients with HIV/AIDS.

■ Key Terms

- T1 diabetes mellitus
- Hyperglycemia
- Partial seizures
- Desired effect
- Psychotropic drugs
- Tardive dyskinesia

- T2 diabetes mellitus
- Hypoglycemia
- Generalized seizures
- Side effect
- Antipsychotics
- Safety precaution

■ Objectives

- Appreciate the importance of client safety needs resulting from physical disorders, physical limitations, or effects of drugs.
- Know causes and first-aid treatment of side effects of glucose lowering agents used to treat diabetes mellitus.
- Know first-aid treatment for different types of seizures.
- Describe desired effects and side effects of selected drugs (antiepileptics, antipsychotics, antidepressants, antimania agents, antianxiety agents, and stimulants).
- Recognize safety considerations for clients who use mechanical aids during recreational activities.
- Recognize safety considerations for the recreational therapist when transferring clients and when serving clients with HIV/AIDS.

Throughout the chapter, the emphasis is on providing information for the recreational therapist that will facilitate client and therapist safety. Common physical disorders and limitations that could result in client injury have been selected for presentation. The information is practical in nature and builds on information presented in introductory courses in recreational therapy and first-aid courses.

Diabetes Mellitus

Diabetes mellitus is a group of metabolic diseases characterized by hyperglycemia resulting from defects in insulin secretion, insulin action, or both. The chronic hyperglycemia of diabetes is associated with long-term damage, dysfunction, and failure of various organs, especially the eyes, kidneys, nerves, heart, and blood vessels (American Diabetes Association, 2012).

Diabetes mellitus occurs when there is an absolute or relative lack of body insulin. Body (endogenous) insulin normally controls glucose levels in the body within a specific range. Normal fasting blood glucose (BG) is under 100 mg/dl and under 140mg/dl two hours after a meal. Insulin facilitates glucose transport from the blood stream into cells, and insufficient insulin will cause the body to experience an elevated level of glucose in the blood stream. This physiological phenomenon is called *hyperglycemia*. Symptoms may include increased urination (as the body attempts to excrete the extra glucose), increased thirst (because of fluid loss through urination), weight loss, and fatigue. There are two major classifications of diabetes mellitus, Type 1 (T1) and Type 2 (T2). Although both types are due to insufficient insulin and will produce hyperglycemia, the disease mechanisms are a bit different, as are treatment modes and potential complications.

Type 1 Diabetes Mellitus

T1 diabetes develops when the body's immune system destroys pancreatic beta cells, the only cells in the body that make the hormone insulin that regulates blood glucose. To survive, people with T1 diabetes must have insulin delivered by injection or a pump. T1 diabetes has been referred to in the past as "juvenile diabetes" or "insulin-dependent diabetes." Those names are misleading because T1 can occur at any age and insulin may also be used in T2 treatment as well. At the time of T1 diagnosis, most people present with a rapid onset of symptoms over a period of days or weeks. These symptoms include those mentioned above and are often quite dramatic. If left untreated, the symptoms usually worsen to also include stomach pains, nausea, and vomiting, and may progress to a physiological state of metabolic acidosis, coma, and death. These symptoms may also occur during the course of the disease if insulin replacement is insufficient. Approximately 5% of all diabetes in the United States is T1. Treatment requires insulin injections and food intake sufficient to match the needs of activity level and growth.

Type 2 Diabetes Mellitus

T2 diabetes mellitus accounts for approximately 90 to 95% of all cases of diabetes. Typically, T2 is most often diagnosed in adults over 40, although a growing percentage of adolescents or young adults are being diagnosed with T2. In T2 diabetes, there are at least three significant areas of pathophysiology and therefore treatment often involves an approach of not only attention to healthy eating and exercise, but also combination medications. The three primary problems in T2:

1. Reduced insulin production: Beta cells located in the pancreas initially increase insulin production, but over time production decreases to point that insulin must be replaced. Even with insulin as part of treatment, the diagnosis does not change from T2 to T1.
2. Increased insulin resistance: Liver, muscle, and fat cells require insulin to transport glucose into the cell where it is used for energy production. In T2 these cells are not able to link up to insulin properly, and therefore glucose cannot get in the cells.

3. Dysfunctional liver release of stored glucose as a result of diminishing insulin production and insulin resistance.

In T2 about 80% of people are overweight. Symptoms of T2 are almost always gradual in onset. Some of these changes, if occurring in mid-life, can be mistaken for aging: fatigue, vision changes, increased urination, and thirst. A person with this type of diabetes is at very high risk for heart attacks and strokes, so treatment is aimed at reducing cardiovascular risks, which includes lipid management, smoking cessation, blood pressure control, exercise, obtaining and maintaining a healthy weight, and a healthy diet in terms of both quality and quantity.

Medication Management for Diabetes

The treatment for T1 diabetes has always been insulin replacement. The only newer therapy is using insulin in combination with another pancreatic hormone (Amylin) known to augment insulin effects. This combination therapy is not in widespread use. For about 20% of people with T2, diet, losing excess weight, and exercise may initially be sufficient to improve blood glucose control, but for others, oral medications may also be necessary. Additional agents for T2 are becoming available to more specifically target any one or more of the three major problem areas as previously noted. Ultimately, approximately 50% of people with T2 will require insulin.

Side Effects of Glucose-Lowering Agents

If persons with diabetes are participating in supervised recreation opportunities, the personnel need to be aware of the medications that the diabetic participant may be using. The glucose lowering agents (GLAs) can best be categorized by whether or not they lower blood glucose (BG) levels *directly* or *indirectly.* These work in several different ways to help T2 diabetes be better controlled and to lower BG levels (see Table 10.1). When agents are combined, there will most always be a direct glucose lowering effect, and treatment for hypoglycemia (low BG) is always consumption of glucose containing foods and products (See Table 10.1).

This concept is significant to whether or not a person's glucose lowering treatment regimen is likely to predispose him/her to low BG or **hypoglycemia** (a BG level of less than 70 mg/dl).

The common early warning signs and symptoms of low blood glucose include light sweating, shakiness, change in mood, or thought patterns. When BG levels are very low, the person will exhibit irrational thoughts and behaviors. Severe hypoglycemia may lead to erratic behavior, loss of consciousness, and seizures. The person with diabetes who participates in a planned recreational activity will likely already be aware of and have experienced low BG at some earlier point. The diabetic participant should be aware of the hypoglycemic possibility and know how to prevent or treat these situations. This means that the recreational therapist should make sure that diabetic clients have easy access to rapidly absorbed glucose at all times, especially during exercise or increased activity.

The three main causes of hypoglycemia are as follows:

1. Too much of a glucose-lowering agent
2. Not enough food (e.g., not eating enough, skipping meals, delaying meals), particularly at the time of maximum activity of a glucose-lowering agent.
3. Physical activity without eating enough food before, during, and after exercise.

Hypoglycemia is also more likely to occur in those who keep their BG in near-normal range, but it is not necessarily a problem, as long as symptoms are detected early and treated appropriately. Those with longstanding diabetes may experience a diminished awareness of hypoglycemia symptoms, and therefore frequent BG monitoring (self-administered finger stick for a drop of blood that is placed into a strip that is read by a glucose meter) is an important part of daily management. BG monitoring is encouraged before meals, before and after activity, and whenever the person feels hypoglycemic or that BG levels are out of range (high or low). Diminished awareness of hypoglycemia may also occur in those who aim to keep their BG levels within a normal range ("tight control") at all times.

Those with T2 diabetes who take direct GLAs or agents in combination may also experience hypoglycemia from the above noted causes. Older adults may be particularly vulnerable to long acting GLAs, and if hypoglycemia occurs, they will not only need initial or even emergency hypoglycemia treatment, but also continued 24-hour observation for recurrence of the problem.

Table 10.1

Available Glucose-Lowering Agents (GLAs)

Direct GLAs

Injected Agents

Insulins are used for insulin replacement or to supplement endogenous insulin. They are injected into fatty (subcutaneous) tissue for daily insulin replacement.

Note: action times noted are approximate and vary depending on insulin species source—animal or human—and individual absorption and metabolism

- *Rapid-acting insulins.* There are three rapid-acting insulins available: Novolog/Aspart, Humalog/Lispro, Gluilisine/Apidra.
  These insulins are quickly absorbed (10–20 minutes) and have an action profile of about 3–5 hours with maximum effect 1–3 hours after injecting. These insulins are analogues of regular insulin meaning that regular insulin has been modified to be absorbed quickly and to be given with meals to cover the rise of glucose that occurs with eating.
- *Short-acting,* called regular insulin (starts to work in about 30–60 minutes, has its maximum effect in approximately 2–4 hours, and has a duration of about 6–8 hours.
- *Intermediate-acting insulin.* NPH (neutral protamine Hagedorn) is regular insulin with substance added to prolong the duration of action. Starts to act in approximately 1–2 hours after injecting it; has a maximum effect in about 4–6 hours (varies by product: Eli Lilly NPH notes 2–8 hours, Novo Nordisk NPH notes 4–12 hours; duration of action varies per product: Eli Lilly NPH, 14–24 hours, Novo Nordisk NPH, 24 hours. NOTE: author's clinical experience with this insulin is onset of about 2 hours, maximum effect in 4–6 hours, during which meals should not be missed or delayed, duration of about 10 hours.
- **Long-acting insulins.** There are two available: Glargine/Lantus (manufactured by Sanofi-Aventis) and Detemir/Levemir (manufactured by Novo Nordisk). These long-acting analogs (modified regular insulin) are intended to provide all-day background insulin, and action onset is slow and may last up to 24 hours; however, many people take two injections per day (about every 12 hours) to provide stable basal insulin.

Table 10.1 (cont.)

- **Amylin mimetic.** Amylin is used with insulin in selected people because it augments and thereby lowers the needed daily dose of insulin. It can cause mild to serious nausea, as well as hypoglycemia. Brand name: Pramlintide acetate/Symlin.
- **Incretin mimetic.** This injected agent stimulates insulin production and is thought to perhaps preserve beta cell (in pancreas) function. When combined with another oral agent such as a sulfonylurea, hypoglycemia may be significant. Nausea is the most common side effect. Brand name: Exenatide/Byetta.

Oral Agents

Sulfonylureas. Used primarily to stimulate the production of body's own insulin.
Brand names:
Amaryl (glimepiride)
Diabinese (Cholopropamide)
DiaBeta (glyburide)
Micronase (glyburide)
Glynase (glyburide)
Glucotrol (glipizide)
Glucotrol XL (extended release glipizide)

All vary in onset and duration, but may be long lasting, particularly in elderly or people with kidney dysfunction. If hypoglycemia occurs, it may be long lasting and require repeated treatment with quick-acting carbohydrates, or if severe can require emergency medical treatment.

Meglitinides. Also stimulate insulin secretion; they act quickly and are preferred if person is allergic to sulfa. Brand name: Repaglinide/Prandin.

Phenylalanine derivatives. Similar to sulfonylureas and meglitinides to increase insulin secretion. Brand name: Nateglinide/Starlix.

DPP-4 Inhibitors. Enhances the incretin system–interaction between the stomach and the pancreas, and therefore regulates beta and alpha cells of the pancreas. Brand name: Sitagliptin phosphate/Januvia.

Indirect GLAs

Note: if taken as monotherapy, these agents are not likely to cause hypoglycemia, but when combined with direct GLAs, the glucose-lowering effect may be greatly enhanced.

Biguanides. Used to reduce liver release of stored glucose.
Brand names:
Metformin (generic)
Metformin/Glucophage
Riomet (Metformin solution)
Glucophage XR (extended release tablets)

Table 10.1 (cont.)

Alpha-glucosidase inhibitors. Slow digestion of carbohydrates and therefore the rise in BG after a meal.
> Brand names:
>> Acarose/Precose
>> Miglitol/Glyset

Thiazolidinediones (also called glitazones or TZDs). Improve insulin resistance, so that insulin and glucose are better utilized.
> Brand names:
>> Rosiglitazone/Avandia
>> Pioglitazone/Actos

Managing Hypoglycemia Reactions

Hypoglycemia may be mild, moderate, or severe. Mild instances are easily treated with fast-acting carbohydrate (see Table 10.2) and recovery is rapid—within 30 to 60 minutes. Moderate hypoglycemia may require repeated administration of rapidly absorbed carbohydrates. Severe episodes are those during which the person cannot safely swallow or may even lose consciousness.

All hypoglycemia requires immediate treatment; however, most individuals who manage diabetes with medications will have experienced hypoglycemia, will recognize the symptoms, and will seek treatment by eating foods that are quick-acting carbohydrates. Most should carry glucose tablets, sugar packets, or hard candies with them just in case hypoglycemia occurs. (See Table 10.2 for amounts.) For the newly diagnosed or those new to the experience of hypoglycemia, there may be a tendency to over treat with large candy bars, cake, or juice.

How Activity or Exercise May Affect Glucose Levels

Exercise and activity improves overall glucose metabolism in non-diabetic and diabetic alike. Exercise of moderate intensity and duration will improve how the body uses insulin, and if sufficient insulin is available, the result will most likely be lower glucose levels. The routine cautions, of course, apply to having medical evaluation prior to exercise, as well as judiciously choosing the type, level, and length of time of an activity as would apply to any participant (appropriate to age, comorbidities, and fitness level). Exercise and activity need to be considered in terms of the type of activity, the intensity, and duration. The acronym FITT may be helpful to remember the key things to consider: Frequency, Intensity, Type, and Timing. For people taking GLAs, "timing" has two meanings: the length of time that an activity is done and the timing of the activity in relation to when GLAs would be having an effect.

If treatment for a participant with T2 diabetes is diet and exercise only, there is no concern about blood levels of glucose dropping too low during recreational activity, and if glucose levels are not well controlled, the BG may even rise during exercise. However, for the person with diabetes who is taking GLAs, there is a challenge to maintain a balance

Table 10.2

Quick-Acting Carbohydrates Used in Hypoglycemia Treatment

Approximate amounts noted below are equal to 10 or 15 grams of carbohydrate and is considered to be a single treatment dose.

- 4–6 oz. of carbohydrate-containing liquids (e.g., unsweetened fruit juices, carbonated drinks)
- 5–6 LifeSavers candies
- 1 tablespoon of honey or Karo syrup
- 4 teaspoons or packets of granulated sugar or 6 half-inch sugar cubes (this might be more palatable in water, but can be eaten as is)
- 3 commercial glucose tablets

Commercially Prepared Fast-Acting Glucose Products:

- BD glucose tablets—3 tablets equals one dose and 15 grams of carbohydrate.
- Dex 4:
  - Tablets—4 tablets equals one dose and 16 grams of carbohydrate.
  - Gel—1 tube is equal to one dose and is 15 grams of carbohydrate.
- Glucose shot—1 bottle is equal to one dose and is 15 grams of carbohydrate.
- GlucoBurst glucose gel—1 bottle is one dose and is 15 grams of carbohydrate.
- Glutose 15 (one dose tube) or Glutose 45 (a three-dose tube), has 24 grams of carbohydrate per dose.
- InstaGlucose—one tube is one dose and has 24 grams of carbohydrates.
- ReliOn—glucose tablets

After a dose of quick-acting carbohydrate is administered, symptoms should begin to improve. If no significant improvement (BG > 70 mg/do), repeat the dose every 10 to 15 minutes until symptoms subside. Moderate hypoglycemia will also respond to the above choices, but the treatment may need to be repeated after 10 to 15 minutes. Overtreatment with glucose will most likely result in spike BG that is equally undesirable.

If the person is confused, combative, and unwilling to swallow, it may be necessary to give glucagon (a substance that must be given by injection and that stimulates the liver to release glucose). Glucagon is injected into the fatty (subcutaneous) tissue and should be administered by someone who has been coached through the process beforehand. Glucagon may cause nausea and vomiting, so turn the person on his/her side after administering so as to avoid aspiration.

Severe hypoglycemia occurs when the person has impaired consciousness or is unconscious and cannot swallow. The treatment needed is to call 911 and, if available, administer glucagon (injected intramuscularly or subcutaneously). Trained medical emergency personnel may need to administer intravenous glucose.

Glucagon. Used to treat moderate or severe hypoglycemia, it is available in kits at local pharmacies. People who may be called upon to use this drug should be instructed beforehand in its preparation and administration.

between having enough insulin to supply energy to muscles, as well as the right balance of glucose and insulin to avoid either hypoglycemia or hyperglycemia.

Exercise or activity of a short duration and at low intensity is unlikely to have significant effect on raising or lowering glucose levels. However, if the activity is sustained, and there are sufficient GLAs on board, the effect will be most likely to lower BG.

If glucose control is consistently poor (elevated over 180 mg/dl most of the time and elevated going into the activity), the result is more likely to be continued or worsened hyperglycemia at the end of the activity. This is because sustained exercise will stimulate a complex process of release of counter-regulatory hormones (glucagon, cortisol, growth hormone, norepinephrine, and epinephrine) that trigger the body to secrete its own stores of glucose from the liver and energy from fat. The body does this to assure that the muscles have a steady supply of glucose for energy needs. If blood glucose is high prior to exercise and there is insufficient insulin to transport glucose into the cell, then exercise will create an additional rise in BG. It is preferred that the BG be 250 mg/dl or less before moderate or vigorous exercise is undertaken. This target number may need to be modified for those persons with T1 diabetes who are undertaking exercise as part of weight-loss and glucose-reduction treatment, and physician guidelines would be helpful.

If a person with diabetes that is managed on GLAs engages in physical exercise, then he or she should make certain that sufficient food has been eaten to match the action profile of the medications. For example, if a glucose lowering agent is known to have a strong effect (peak) in about six hours after taking, then a dose taken at 8:00 a.m. would exert that effect sometime during or after the lunch time. Lunch would be an important meal that should not be skipped or delayed. This matching of meals to the medication action profile will help avoid hypoglycemic episodes.

Caveat: Those in relatively good glycemic control who also take GLAs may find that activity/exercise that is sustained or moderately intense over a period of 30 minutes may experience improvement in insulin sensitivity that begins during the exercise and lasts for many hours after the activity is stopped. Those with T1 (and well controlled T2 who are taking GLAs) who are participating in moderate to vigorous exercise should consume approximately 15 grams of carbohydrate for every 30 minutes of the activity. This means the participant needs to come prepared with quick acting carbohydrates and be willing to stop the activity briefly and eat/drink.

Stepped approach to glycemic management during activity:

1. Test BG before, 30 minutes into, and immediately after exercise.
2. A BG test of >250 before exercise (in T1) should be delayed until levels are under 200.
3. 15 to 30 grams of carbohydrate for every 30 minutes of sustained exercise.
4. Monitor BG every two to three hours after activity to assess for hypoglycemia.

An exercise medical management plan: Managing BG levels with GLAs before, during and after exercise can be offered in a specific management plan by the participant's health care provider. This is a strategy that considers the major effects of exercise and tailors the plan to the specific person.

Other Exercise or Activity Safety Considerations

Because diabetes can cause chronic complications involving eyes, nerves, kidney, and blood vessels, it is important that individuals with diabetes be medically evaluated before undertaking an exercise or activity program. Those with kidney or eye damage may need to participate in only low-impact activities that do not involve straining, lifting, or jarring behaviors. About 60% to 70% of people with diabetes have mild to severe forms of nervous system damage. The results of such damage include impaired sensation or pain in the feet or hands, slowed digestion of food in the stomach, carpal tunnel syndrome, or other nerve problems. Those who have nerve and muscle changes in their feet may need special foot protection or limited lower extremity impact activity, such as swimming. They should also be encouraged to examine their feet daily for sores, cuts, or blisters or any signs of infection.

Dietary Needs

The main problem in diabetes is that glucose (sugars) is not metabolized normally because there is either no insulin or the body does not use its own insulin well. Therefore, dietary needs are primarily focused on making certain that the person has a healthy (quality) food intake each day in the amounts (quantity) needed for activity and growth, with limited amounts of foods that are simple sugars. For those who manage their diabetes with medications, there will be an additional issue of timing food to match the glucose-lowering medications. Timing, for those on diabetes medications, also pertains to not skipping meals or delaying meals beyond the time when meals are expected.

Dietary needs during activity have been noted earlier. The major points are to be certain that there are adequate carbohydrates available during the activity/exercise period if the activity is going to be of moderate intensity for more than 30 minutes. 15–30 grams of carbohydrate may need to be eaten every 30 minutes of sustained activity, and carbohydrate requirements may be increased in the hours after moderate to vigorous activity, and/or a reduction of GLAs may need to be considered in the 6 to 12 hours after moderate or vigorous activity. There is a growing evidence base regarding diabetes and the athlete that examines the physiology and management strategies when applied to training and competition environments while using the newest GLAs. Journals such as *Diabetes Care* and *Diabetes* provide relevant articles on the topic, and a nationwide organization, called Insulin dependence (www.Insulindependence.org) can provide information and help for those wanting to participate in all types and levels of activities.

Seizures

Epilepsy is a disorder that is characterized by recurrent seizures. A seizure is believed to occur when a group of abnormal brain cells fire at the same time. Sometimes the abnormal firing or discharge spreads in the brain. Whatever the abnormal brain cells control in the body determines the nature of the seizure. For example, if the cells control movement of the right arm, the right arm could have repetitive movements.

Partial Seizures

There are many different types of seizures that can be classified into two large groups—partial and generalized. **Partial seizures** occur when the discharge from the abnormal brain cells remains in only one section of the brain. When the discharge involves most or all of the brain, a generalized seizure occurs.

Partial seizures can be broken down into two divisions—elementary and complex. Elementary partial seizures involve only one section of the brain and the person does not lose consciousness. An example would be the seizure described earlier where the client had repetitive jerking of one arm. Complex partial seizures involve parts of the brain that control thought processes. The person is not unconscious but experiences reduced consciousness. The person sometimes describes the seizure as being in a fog. In a complex partial seizure the person may make senseless movements such as walking around while pulling at his or her clothes, smacking his or her lips repeatedly, or speaking in an unintelligible manner. Complex partial seizures generally last a few minutes and are often followed by confusion and loss of memory during the seizure (Freeman, Vining, & Pillas, 1990; Nordli, 2008).

Generalized Seizures

In **generalized seizures,** there is a loss of consciousness. If the loss is brief, the seizure is called a petit mal or absence seizure. The *absence seizure* generally lasts a few seconds and usually consists of the staring or rolling back of the eyes. To an observer, the seizure may be seen as a brief lapse in activity. An absence seizure begins and ends abruptly.

Another type of generalized seizure is the *tonic-clonic,* or what used to be called the grand mal seizure. Typically the person loses consciousness, stiffens all over, has jerking movements of the arms and legs, and has loss of urine. At the onset, the person temporarily stops breathing and the skin may become pale or bluish. The breathing resumes during the jerking (tonic and clonic) phase. Following the seizure, the person is often sleepy and may have muscle soreness. The tonic-clonic seizure may be frightening to watch and generally seems to last longer than it does. The usual time is 2 to 3 minutes (Freeman, Vining, & Pillas, 1990; Nordli, 2008).

Epilepsy Syndromes

Patients with recurrent seizures are usually said to have an epilepsy syndrome. The epilepsy syndrome is defined by the type of seizures the person experiences, the changes seen on electroencephalogram, the effects on learning and behavior, and the etiology and prognosis of the disorder. A new classification scheme lists syndromes by age of onset, etiology, or distinct combination of symptoms and signs (Berg et al., 2010).

Seizure First-Aid Treatment

Because there are different types of seizures, first-aid procedures vary. In addition, some people have more than one type of seizure. Therefore, it is necessary for the recreational therapist to find out from the client or the client's family what typically happens during the seizure, how long seizures usually last, whether there is loss of consciousness, and whether there are any symptoms before the unconsciousness occurs.

The primary concern for the recreational therapist is the safety of the client. Generally, no first aid is necessary for any seizure except the tonic-clonic seizure. The lapses in the absence seizures are so short, they are generally not dangerous. Normal safety precautions for crossing streets and bicycling should be sufficient. During complex partial seizures, it may be necessary to guide the person if his or her reactions could result in danger. It also might be helpful to give an explanation to observers in order to help them understand that the person with epilepsy does not have control over his or her actions.

Tonic-clonic seizures may be unpleasant to watch and will often precipitate in the observer a feeling of needing to do something. The most important thing for the recreational therapist is to keep calm. This is especially important if the seizure occurs around a large group of people because anxiety and panic could spread among the group. If the client is sitting or standing, ease the person to the floor and loosen any constricting clothing. Do not try to stop the seizure or try to revive the client. Once the seizure has started, it cannot be stopped. Do *not* under any circumstances try to force anything between clenched teeth. People do not swallow their tongues during a seizure, and a great deal of damage can be done to the teeth and mouth.

It is also helpful to clear the area around the person of any hard objects so he or she will not inadvertently inflict self-harm with the seizure movements. Turning the head to the side may help the release of saliva. Call 911 if the seizure lasts for more than 5 minutes, or if the client passes from one seizure to another without gaining consciousness (a condition called status epilepticus). Status epilepticus is rare, but does require immediate medical treatment. Status epilepticus in generalized tonic-clonic seizures is life threatening.

Medical attention *is* also necessary for a seizure in any client who is *not* known to have seizures, even if the seizure does not last very long and the client appears unharmed. The cause of the seizure may be an underlying medical problem (e.g., hypoglycemia, brain infection) that may require further attention. Thus, the recreational therapist should be knowledgeable about the client's medical history. Other times that medical assistance would be needed are (a) seizure occurring in the water; (b) the person is pregnant, injured, or diabetic; and (c) the person does not regain consciousness after the shaking has stopped (Epilepsy Foundation, 2008). After the seizure, someone should stay with the client until he or she is fully awake and no longer is confused.

The recreational therapist should be matter-of-fact about the seizure with both the person who had the seizure and those who watched it. It is important to get back to business as usual to decrease the possibility of embarrassment for the client who has had the seizure.

Activity Restrictions

Because recreational therapy often involves physical activity, the question regarding activity restriction is regularly encountered. There are no firm rules for the recreational therapist to follow. The International League Against Epilepsy does recommend avoiding scuba diving and sky diving, but allows participation in most other sports and recreational activities as long as common-sense precautions are followed. Information from the client or the client's family regarding the nature and frequency of the seizures is an important consideration when decisions are made about the appropriateness of the activities. In addition, recommendations from the client's physician in regard to contact sports and swimming must be followed. It must be pointed out that there is risk in living, and the client should not be unduly restricted or overprotected. The recreational therapist should weigh three factors—seizure control, seizure type, and the nature of the activity—when determining risk versus benefit for the client with epilepsy. Each will be covered separately.

With medication, approximately 50% of people with epilepsy are seizure-free, and an additional 25 to 30% have fairly good seizure control. Only about 20 to 25% of people with epilepsy fail to achieve significant seizure control from medication. Some persons with poorly controlled epilepsy experience daily seizures. Generally, normal safety precautions suffice for clients who enjoy good seizure control. The recreational therapist should find out how often the client has been having seizures. Ask if the client is taking the medication regularly because failure to do so can result in seizures.

The nature of the seizures also determines the need for activity restrictions. Some clients have seizures only during sleep (nocturnal seizures) and, consequently, need no restrictions. Seizures such as absence, elementary-partial, and complex-partial impose very few, if any, restrictions on the client's activities. Instructions may have to be repeated for the client with absence or complex partial seizures because he or she may miss hearing or seeing something during the seizures. In addition, activities such as bicycling should be confined to bike paths and parks that are away from busy streets. During swimming, the recreational therapist should make sure that the client swims with someone who is aware of the nature of the seizures and can get help if needed. Basic safety rules for everyone apply.

Tonic-clonic seizures, however, can subject the client to harm if they occur while swimming. A generalized tonic-clonic seizure often begins with a quick inhalation. If the client is under water, he or she could breathe in water. Swimming can be hazardous for clients with poorly controlled tonic-clonic seizures; they should be closely monitored. All personnel who are swimming with the client with epilepsy should be aware of the seizure disorder and know first-aid procedures.

When a seizure does occur during swimming, the client should be supported so his or her head is out of the water to reduce the chance of getting water in the lungs. As soon as possible, the client should be taken out of the water and examined immediately to determine if artificial respiration is necessary. Even if the client seems fully recovered, medical attention should be obtained to protect the safety of the client. Seizures in the water can be very dangerous, and medical attention is essential to determine if there are any ill effects on the client.

If a client strikes his or her head forcefully against a hard object during any seizure, the client may develop a head injury. Because symptoms of a head injury such as headache, sleepiness, confusion, and weakness may be similar to symptoms occurring normally after a seizure, medical attention should be obtained for the client.

Any activities that require continued attention, such as climbing or horseback riding, may also need to be avoided by the client with poorly controlled tonic-clonic seizures. If the client has regular seizures, a hard hat may provide needed protection during bicycling or horseback riding.

The recreational therapist must assess each client with epilepsy and the activity individually. Guidance from medical personnel should be sought and followed. Regardless of the seizure type, people who have been seizure-free for six months to two years usually have no restrictions and are given permission to drive an automobile.

Antiepileptic Drug Therapy

The major treatment for seizures today is the long-term intake of antiepileptic drugs (AED). Other treatments have been tried with limited success. Since the 1920s, a ketogenic diet consisting of food high in fat and low in carbohydrates has been used. Acupuncture and biofeedback are being used experimentally today to determine their potential for use. Vagal nerve stimulation therapy has been approved as adjunctive therapy for partial seizures in adults and adolescents. Neurosurgery is an option for some partial seizures that are difficult to control. The majority of people with epilepsy regularly take AEDs to control seizures. Therefore, the recreational therapist should be knowledgeable about the effects of the most commonly used AEDs.

The **desired effect** of an AED is to make the brain less apt to seize. The goal of AED therapy is to get a sufficient amount of drug into the bloodstream to prevent or reduce seizures. Occasionally, clients take more than one drug daily to achieve optimal seizure control. In order to maintain the proper blood level, the AED must be taken at regular intervals. Provisions must be made by the recreational therapist for the client to receive drugs during prolonged activities such as field trips and overnight camping. AEDs are taken orally unless the client is unable to do so because of illness such as nausea and vomiting. If the AED cannot be taken orally, provisions must be made for medical personnel to give the drug in another manner. If too many doses are omitted, the client will be at risk for seizures.

All drugs may cause effects in addition to the desired effect for which they are being prescribed. Unfortunately, AEDs have some of these **side effects**. The most common side effects include somnolence, dizziness, unsteadiness, double vision, and behavioral changes. It is important that the recreational therapist be aware of possible side effects when assessing, planning, implementing, and evaluating activities for the client. Each client should be

Table 10.3

Anticonvulsant Drugs

Standard Agents

1. Carbamazepine (Tegretol). Possible side effects: sedation, unsteady gait, anemia, infections
2. Ethosuximide (Zarontin). Possible side effects: nausea, lethargy, dizziness, weight loss, headache, skin rashes
3. Phenobarbital (Luminal, Mysoline). Possible side effects: sedation, lethargy, mental dullness, hyperactivity, skin rash
4. Phenytoin (Dilantin). Possible side effects: unsteady gait, slurred speech, drowsiness, fatigue, gum swelling, skin rash, hair growth, anemia, infections
5. Valproic acid (Depakote). Possible side effects: nausea and vomiting, decreased liver function, decreased platelets, unsteady gait, weight gain.

New Agents

1. Gabapentin (Neurontin). Possible side effects: sedation, lethargy, hyperactivity, irritability, dizziness, headache
2. Lamotrigine (Lamictal). Possible side effects: skin rash, lethargy, stomach upset, unsteady gait, respiratory infections
3. Levetiracetam (Keppra). Possible side effects: drowsiness, behavioral changes
4. Oxcarbazepine (Trileptal). Possible side effects: headache, stomachache, dizziness, rash
5. Tiagabine (Gabitril). Possible side effects: dizziness, lethargy, nervousness, tremor, stomach upset
6. Topiramate (Topamax). Possible side effects: sedation, psychomotor slowing, slow speech, memory troubles, dizziness, unsteadiness, nausea, numbness
7. Zonisamide (Zonegran). Possible side effects: unsteadiness, depression, renal stones

Sources: Pellock (1998); Browne & Holmes (2004)

---

assessed individually because not everyone experiences side effects, and some may only experience them temporarily. The recreational therapist must assess which side effects the client is experiencing. For example, a client who suffers from dizziness and an unsteady gait would have difficulty with an activity that required physical agility. In addition, the recreational therapist may be the first to recognize a side effect, such as extreme drowsiness, that may need medical attention.

The most commonly prescribed AEDs, along with their possible side effects, are listed in Table 10.3. The table gives two names for each drug. The name that is listed first is the generic name. Each drug has only one generic name, which is never changed and is the same in all countries. The name that appears in parentheses is the trade name or the brand name. A drug can have many brand names. Except for phenobarbital, brand names are probably more familiar to you than the generic name, because brand names are promoted by drug companies and are generally easier to pronounce. Generic names usually reflect the chemical makeup of the drug and are harder to pronounce and remember.

It can be seen that the recreational therapist must be familiar with first aid and safety precautions for seizures and with possible side effects of AEDs in order to maintain client safety during recreation activities. The goal for therapy is seizure control with a minimum of side effects. With seizures that are very difficult to control, some clients are forced to tolerate side effects from more than one drug. The recreational therapist should report side effects to the client, the client's family, or medical personnel. Sometimes drugs can be changed if a side effect is potentially harmful. Assessment of side effects should be made and the information used when planning, implementing, and evaluating client care.

Psychotropic Drugs

Many recreational therapists provide services for clients who suffer from emotional disturbance or mental illness. In addition to other therapies such as psychotherapy and recreational therapy, most of these clients receive medication to reduce the symptoms of the mental illness. These drugs have an effect on the psychic function of the client and are known collectively as **psychotropic drugs**.

In this section, basic information is presented on the five major classes of psychotropic drugs: antipsychotic, antidepressant, antimania, antianxiety, and stimulants. It is important to realize that the information is about what usually happens when a client takes a drug regularly. The effects on any given individual may be different. Therefore, individual assessment for side effects must be completed before planning therapeutic recreation strategies.

Each class of drugs will be covered individually. Names of the common major drugs will be listed. Generic names will be presented first; brand names will appear in parentheses. The desired effects, possible side effects, and potential implication for the recreational therapist are also given.

Antipsychotic Drugs

The first **antipsychotic drug**, chlorpromazine (Thorazine), was introduced in 1952. Since that time, many antipsychotic drugs have been used in the treatment of psychotic patients. These drugs have revolutionized the treatment of schizophrenia and have been credited with dramatically reducing the number of patients in psychiatric institutions in the United States.

Uses

The major reason that antipsychotics are prescribed is to reduce the symptoms of schizophrenia, schizoaffective disorder, and bipolar disorder so that patients can better take care of themselves and function in society. Today there are a large number of antipsychotics for the physician to choose from when treating psychotic patients. Table 10.4 lists generic names, brand names, and the desired effects of commonly used antipsychotic medications.

Some of the antipsychotic drugs are also approved for the treatment of autistic disorder in school-age children and for bipolar disorder or schizophrenia in adolescents. The newer atypical antipsychotics are being used off label to reduce severe aggression and irritability in children. The main side effects in children and adolescents are weight gain and sedation.

Unfortunately, antipsychotic drugs have a wide range of side effects. One of the earliest side effects is drowsiness. It is usually temporary and lasts only one or two weeks. Low blood pressure also can occur as a side effect, particularly in low potency antipsychotics such as chlorpromazine and thioridazine. Symptoms of low blood pressure, which are dizziness and weakness, usually occur upon rising from a lying or sitting position. Movement disorders are often side effects of the high potency typical antipsychotic drugs such as haloperidol. These movement disorders are listed in Table 10.5. The newer atypical antipsychotic drugs cause fewer problems with movement, but have caused more weight gain. The recreational therapist should avoid activities that require alertness and muscular coordination from these clients and watch these clients carefully so they avoid falling. If the client is on an atypical antipsychotic, the therapist should monitor and limit dietary intake.

Table 10.4

Antipsychotic Drugs

Typical Antipsychotics

1. Chlorpromazine (Thorazine)
2. Thioridazine (Mellaril)
3. Fluphenazine (Prolixin)
4. Thiothixene (Navane)
5. Haloperidol (Haldol)
6. Primozide (Orap)

Atypical Antipsychotics

1. Clozapine (Clozaril)
2. Risperidone (Risperdal)
3. Olanzapine (Zyprexa)
4. Quetiapine (Seroquel)
5. Ziprasidone (Geodon)
6. Aripiprazole (Abilify)

Desired Effects

Major actions include the reduction of symptoms of psychosis (i.e., hallucinations, delusions, disordered thinking processes, and social withdrawal). The antipsychotic drugs have been used in the pervasive developmental disorders for reducing hyperactivity, emotional quieting, and decreased anxiety, and in Tourette's syndrome to decrease tics.

Source: Schatzberg & Nemeroff (1998); Findling (2008)

Extrapyramidal Side Effects (EPS)

A major side effect of the antipsychotic medications is extrapyramidal movements. Soon after starting the medications, patients may develop an acute dystonia (a stiff, fixed posturing) or akathisia (a restlessness and need to move constantly). Later, patients may develop Parkinson's-like symptoms such as tremor or a slow stiff gait or tardive dyskinesia (frequent irregular, choreiform movements). Acute dystonia often resolves after intravenous diphenhydramine [Benadryl]. Parkinson's-like movements may respond to drugs such as benztropine [Cogentin], trihexyphenidyl [Artane], or diphenhydramine. After stopping antipsychotics, patients may develop a withdrawal dyskinesia. Extrapyramidal side effects were more common with the older first generation antipsychotics such as haloperidol

Table 10.5

Antipsychotic Drugs Side Effects

Extrapyramidal Side Effects (EPS)

- Motor restlessness where the client cannot stop moving (akathisia).
- Involuntary jerking and bizarre movements of muscles in the face, neck, tongue, eyes, arms, and legs.
- Tremors, muscle weakness, and fatigue.
- Parkinson-like symptoms such as rigidity, drooling, difficulty in speaking, slow movement, and an unusual gait when walking, where the client has trouble slowing down.

Tardive Dyskinesia (TD)

- Abnormal mouth motion such as lip smacking, chewing, sucking, moving the tongue in and out of the mouth quickly, and pushing out the cheeks.
- Involuntary movements of the jaw, increased blinking, and spasms of muscles in the face, neck, back, eyes, arms, and legs.

Other Side Effects

- Drowsiness	- Edema
- Low blood pressure	- Weight gain
- Nausea	- Feminizing effects
- Vomiting	- Menstrual irregularities
- Rash	- Blurred vision
- Dry mouth	- Constipation
- Urinary retention	- Seizures
- Blood destruction	- Skin discoloration
- Photosensitivity (especially with Thorazine)	- Fever
	- Drop in blood cell count (especially with Clozapine)

Sources: Appleton (1988); Newton et al. (1978); Schatzberg & Nemeroff (1998)

---

than with the newer second generation antipsychotics such as olanzapine, risperidone, or ziprasidone. The annual incidence of tardive dyskinesias in patients on second generation antipsychotics is less than 2% in younger adults and 5-10% in older adults (Correll et al., 2004). Table 10.5 describes the most common extrapyramidal side effects. The recreational therapist must be familiar with side effects of antipsychotic medications and should regularly assess each client to determine which, if any, side effect will affect the planning of recreation activities.

Knowledge of the potential side effects of antipsychotic drugs can guide the assessment of the client by the recreational therapist. In addition, being aware that side effects may subside or be replaced by other side effects indicates the necessity of reassessment. When extrapyramidal symptoms (see Table 10.5) are present, activities that require physical agility, such as bike riding, climbing, and gymnastics, should be avoided. Even hiking down a steep hill can be potentially harmful for a client with a Parkinson's-like gait. Supervision by personnel should be increased for those clients. Clients with tremors, muscle weakness, and fatigue may need to participate at a slower pace and have frequent opportunities for rest.

Some activities may not be particularly dangerous, but they subject the client to increased frustration. For example, activities that require good hand-eye coordination or clear vision can be frustrating. If the activity includes using needles or sewing with a sewing machine, the activity becomes potentially harmful. Aiming at a target, reading, and writing are potentially frustrating for clients who suffer from blurred vision or motor restlessness.

One side effect that occurs, especially with Thorazine, is photosensitivity, which means the skin becomes increasingly sensitive to burning by the sun. The recreational therapist should check with medical personnel before the client is allowed to participate in an outside activity with maximum exposure to sunlight, such as swimming. A sunscreen should be applied. For activities in the sun, clients should wear sunglasses, protective clothing, and sunscreen lotion on exposed areas if they are receiving Thorazine (Schatzberg & Nemeroff, 2009).

Patients on the newer atypical antipsychotic medications may have an increase in appetite with resultant weight gain. They have also caused an increase in blood glucose and lipids putting patients at risk for the development of type 2 diabetes mellitus. The recreation therapists can help design activities to assist in weight reduction and can encourage patients to modify their diet to limit caloric intake.

Antidepressant Drugs

Several classes of drugs are available for the treatment of depressive disorders. These drugs can also be used for attention deficit hyperactivity disorder, enuresis (bedwetting), obsessive-compulsive disorder, and anxiety disorders. The different drugs are probably equally effective, but vary in their side effects. (See Table 10.6 for a list of common antidepressants.) The serotonin reuptake inhibitors most often are used initially because they lack serious side effects. Most of the agents take about three weeks to become effective. They should relieve feelings of sadness, irritability, hopelessness, trouble sleeping, changes in appetite, decreased concentration, and guilt associated with depression.

Side effects. The side effects of the tricyclic and heterocyclic agents are lethargy, dry mouth, blurred vision, constipation, weight gain, decreased blood pressure, and changes in heart rate and rhythm. The serotonin reuptake inhibitors cause upset stomach, diarrhea, headache, nervousness, sleepiness, and impaired sexual functioning. Bupropion can cause restlessness, insomnia, and, rarely, seizures. All of these drugs can lead to mania in clients with bipolar (manic-depressive) disorder.

Antimania Drugs

Lithium is the oldest drug used for the treatment of mania and the manic phase of manic-depression psychoses. Lithium is an element that is administered as a salt. Common brand names include Eskalith and Lithobid (McVoy & Findling, 2012). The antiepileptic drugs, called mood stabilizers by psychiatrists, are used to treat mania and depression in bipolar disorder. Currently, valproate, carbamazepine, oxcarbazepine, and lamotrigine are the AEDs most often employed.

Mania is a mood disorder characterized by a subjective feeling of elation. The person usually engages in endless activity and experiences a decreased need for sleep. Usually, the person speaks quickly, as if under pressure to do so, and has flights of ideas, where many unrelated topics are mentioned, one after another. Mania can progress to involve grandiose delusions, hallucinations, and paranoia.

Table 10.6

Antidepressants

Drugs

Tricyclic antidepressants
1. Imipramine (Tofranil)
2. Amitriptyline (Elavil)
3. Desipramine (Norpramin)
4. Nortriptyline (Pamelor)

Heterocyclic antidepressants
1. Trazadone (Desyrel)
2. Nefazadone (Serzone)

Serotonin reuptake inhibitors
1. Fluoxetine (Prozac)
2. Sertraline (Zoloft)
3. Paroxetine (Paxil)
4. Fluvoxamine (Luvox)
5. Citalopram (Celexa)
6. Escitalopram (Lexapro)

Others
1. Buproprion (Wellbutrin)
2. Venlafaxine (Effexor)
3. Mirtazapine (Remeron)
4. Duloxetine (Cymbalta)

Desired Effect
Relief of feelings such as hopelessness, sadness, helplessness, anxiety, worthlessness, and fatigue that are associated with depression.

Sources: Appleton (1988); Schatzberg & Nemeroff (1998); Findling (2008)

Currently acute mania is treated with a mood stabilizer [lithium, divalproex, carbamazepine, oxcarbamazepine, lamotrigine], an antipsychotic [olanzapine, risperidone, quetiapine, ziprazsidone, aripiprazole], or a combination of the two. Mood stabilizers decrease the severity and frequency of manic episodes. To avoid the side effects of weight gain and metabolic syndrome, an attempt is made to use mood stabilizers for maintenance treatment (American Psychiatric Association, 2002; Kowatch et al., 2005).

Side effects. Generally, the side effects of lithium are mild and are related to the level of lithium in the bloodstream. Early side effects include thirst, increased urine, decreased appetite, nausea, vomiting, diarrhea, and a fine tremor. These side effects usually do not persist with continued therapy. However, higher lithium levels in the blood can be very dangerous; symptoms include muscular weakness, blurred vision, drowsiness, and ringing in the ears. Excessively high levels can lead to convulsions, coma, and death. The recreational therapist's recognition of the side effects can help ensure the clients' safety by encouraging the client to seek medical attention if higher-level symptoms occur.

Antianxiety Drugs

Antianxiety drugs or minor tranquilizers are used to treat clients who suffer from excessive anxiety and tension. They also are used for short-term therapy for insomnia. The antianxiety drugs are listed in Table 10.7. Buspirone is used for anxiety and hyperactivity. The benzodiazepines are used for anxiety and insomnia. In addition, they have been used to lessen symptoms of drug withdrawal. Lorazepam and diazepam have anticonvulsant effects and are given intravenously to treat status epilepticus.

Patients with anxiety disorders usually receive a combination of psychotherapy, either behavioral therapy or cognitive-behavioral therapy, and medication. The antidepressant serotonin reuptake inhibitors are often the first choice agents because they have fewer side effects. The tricyclic antidepressant drugs also have been used for treatment of generalized anxiety disorder.

Side effects. The most common side effect of the benzodiazepines is drowsiness. Other side effects include dizziness, muscular incoordination, muscle weakness, skin rash, menstrual irregularities, and weight gain. Withdrawal reactions after prolonged use also have been found. Buspirone may cause dizziness, lethargy, upset stomach, and headache.

The recreational therapist would need to assess the individual client for side effects such as drowsiness or dizziness before planning activities that require alertness and muscular agility. Side effects of the antianxiety drugs are usually temporary and generally do not limit the recreational activities of the client.

Table 10.7

Antianxiety Drugs

Drug

Azapirone
Buspirone (BuSpar)

Benzodiazepines
Alprazolam (Xanax)
Clonazepam (Klonopin)
Lorazepam (Ativan)
Serotonin reuptake inhibitors (see Table 10-6)
Tricyclic antidepressants (see Table 10-6)

Desired Effect
Reduction of anxiety, relaxation of skeletal muscles, relief of symptoms of tension and insomnia, and anticonvulsant properties.

Sources: Newton et al. (1978); Appleton (1988); Schatzberg & Nemeroff (1998); Findling (2008)

Drugs for ADHD

The stimulants are used to treat attention-deficit/hyperactivity disorder (ADHD) and occasionally for oppositional defiant disorder and conduct disorder. They should help clients concentrate, attend, and stay organized and should reduce distractibility, hyperactivity, and impulsivity. The two groups are amphetamines and methylphenidate. There are short (about

4 hours) acting, intermediate acting (7–8 hours), and long (10–12 hours) acting agents. The agents are listed in Table 10.8. They are effective in approximately 80-90% of children with ADHD.

The most common side effects of the stimulants are decreased appetite, insomnia, headache and stomachache. Irritability and depression may occur, particularly in the children under 6 years of age. Occasional side effects are tics, nervous picking at the skin, and increased pulse or blood pressure. Hallucinations can occur rarely in children taking appropriate doses. Hallucinations also can occur with very excessive doses or in clients with early schizophrenia or bipolar disorder.

If the stimulants are not effective or if they cause unacceptable side effects, nonstimulant medications may be used. Atomoxetine (Strattera) is approved for children and adolescents with ADHD. It can be taken once or twice a day. The main side effects are stomachache and decreased appetite, lethargy, and occasionally irritability. Some of the older antidepressants such as bupropion (Wellbutrin) and the tricyclic antidepressants may improve attention and reduce hyperactivity. Clonidine and guanfacine help reduce hyperactivity but are not as good for inatttention. The main side effect of both clonidine and guanfacine is lethargy. New, long acting forms of clonidine and guanfacine have been approved as once-a-day adjunct treatments for symptoms of ADHD.

Table 10.8

Drugs for ADHD

Drug

Stimulants

Methylphenidate
Short acting (Ritalin, Methylin, Focalin)
Intermediate acting (Ritalin SR, Ritalin LA, Metadate CD, Methylin ER)
Long acting (Concerta, Focalin XR, Daytrana)
Amphetamines
Short acting (Dexedrine, Dextrostat)
Intermediate acting (Dexedrine spansule, Adderall)
Long acting (Adderall XR and Vyvanse)

Nonstimulants

Atomoxetine (Strattera)
Bupropion (Wellbutrin)
Tricyclic antidepressants (imipramine, nortriptyline)
Alpha adrenergics (clonidine, guanfacine)
Desired effect
Improved attention and concentration, reduced distractibility, impulsivity, and hyperactivity

---

Source: Findling (2008)

Mechanical Aids

Many individuals have either permanent or temporary conditions that limit their physical mobility and require the use of mechanical aids. Mechanical aids include equipment such as braces, crutches, walkers, and wheelchairs that are used to assist clients in carrying out their activities of daily living. The use of mechanical aids allows the client to be as independent as possible. This section will present general guidelines for the recreational therapist to follow when working with the client.

Safety for both the recreational therapist and the client is the prime consideration. Helping clients who have limited mobility is a major source of back injury for health care professionals. To avoid injury recreational therapists should not lift more than 35 pounds unless they have proper equipment or assistance from another person. To prevent back injuries it is also important to avoid twisting of the spine or stooping with the hips and knees straight. Twisting can be prevented by facing the direction of the movement squarely and moving the client directly toward or away from the center of gravity (Berman & Snyder, 2012). In general, recreational therapists should use their legs rather than their backs when lifting or helping clients move.

Every client differs in weight, disability, and size. Therefore, each client should be individually assessed to determine his or her abilities and specific needs for assistance. The first general rule to follow, if possible, is *always consult with the client or the client's family regarding how much and what kind of assistance is needed.* Clients live with their mechanical aids and have safe and efficient routines that they follow. Even when clients have only recently developed the physical limitation, safe techniques have usually been taught to them by health care personnel prior to their participation in recreational therapy activities. Extra caution will be needed for clients who have impaired cognition or confusion because they might not be able to provide accurate information about what kind of assistance they need or be able to follow instructions. For these clients, it is best to obtain information about them from medical personnel or the family.

Braces, Crutches, and Walkers

Clients who use *braces, crutches,* or *walkers* have limited physical mobility and reduced weight-bearing ability in their legs. The recreational therapist must assess each client's abilities prior to planning activities. Information should be sought from the chart, other medical and professional personnel, and the client. Assessment should include observation of the client to determine how well the client handles the mechanical aid in his or her activities of daily living. The recreational therapist should assess how much balance the client has in various positions, whether one side of the body is weaker than the other, and how much physical endurance is present. The amount of physical endurance will affect how long the client can participate in more strenuous activities. If fatigue occurs, the client may be more apt to have an accident. In addition, clients who lack physical strength or mobility in both upper and lower extremities are less able to regain their balance or catch themselves if they begin to fall.

The recreational therapist should conduct a physical inspection of the environment to insure client safety. Loose rugs, debris, and uneven or steep paths can make mobility more difficult for clients using mechanical aids. Paths that have sharp drops should be avoided.

The condition of the mechanical aid should also be observed. Equipment should be inspected to make sure that it is in safe condition and has no missing or loose pieces. Crutches and walkers should have secured rubber tips covering the base. Crutches should also have rubber covers over the shoulder piece and hand piece. Wheelchairs should have wheels that lock.

Clients may develop reddened or pressure areas from lack of circulation or irritation from the mechanical aid. The recreational therapist, especially in long-term activities such as camping, is often responsible for assessment of the client's skin. The client cannot always be relied on to know if pressure exists because of loss of feeling in the area. If any reddened or broken areas are observed, the recreational therapist should call it to the attention of the client and medical personnel as soon as possible so proper measures can be taken to prevent further problems such as skin infection.

Clients who use braces, crutches, or walkers generally need minimal to moderate assistance. Ask the client or the client's family about the amount and type of assistance needed. Adequate assessment by the recreational therapist should result in recreational activities in which the client can participate safely. Clients may need assistance with stairs, especially if they use a walker. The nature of the assistance depends on the type of physical disability, the length of time the client has had limited mobility, and other conditions. For example, an elderly client suffering from a recent stroke may need maximum assistance with stairs, and a child who has had leg braces for several years may need no assistance.

Before the recreational therapist helps any client with a mechanical aid, the client should be told exactly what the recreational therapist is trying to do. The use of a safety belt is especially helpful when clients are having problems maintaining balance.

When the client using crutches ascends stairs, the client should place the crutches under the unaffected side and grasp the banister with the free hand. The unaffected foot is lifted to the step above. Then, supporting the weight on the unaffected foot, the client pulls the crutches onto the step. The process is repeated until the client reaches the top of the stairs. To go down the stairs, the client again positions himself or herself so that the banister is on the affected side and both crutches are on the other side. The client places the crutches on the step below and at the same time swings his or her affected foot out over the step. The client would support his or her body weight with a hand on the banister and the crutches and step down with the unaffected foot. The process is repeated until the bottom of the stairs is reached. When helping clients with stairs, a general safety rule is to keep below them on the steps. When they are going up the stairs, you would follow them; when going down the stairs, you would be in front of them.

Catheters and Collection Bags

Clients who have loss of bladder function may have an indwelling urinary catheter and a collection bag. Urinary appliances are most common in the hospital or rehabilitation settings. When working with the client, care should be taken to avoid pulling on the catheter because the pressure may irritate the bladder opening and predispose the client to an infection. It is imperative that the tubing and collection bag always remain *below* the level of the bladder. Lifting the appliance above the bladder will cause the urine to flow back into the bladder and possibly cause an infection.

Wheelchairs

When working with clients who are *wheelchair users*, ask them how the wheelchair works and what kind of assistance is needed, if any. Wheelchairs come in various styles. Armrests and footrests may be removable; some wheelchairs are self-propelled, depending on the needs of the clients. All wheelchairs should have brakes or locks on the wheels. Become familiar with the wheelchair before working with the client.

It is important to observe safety rules when transporting a client in a wheelchair. Safety precautions include locking the wheels of the wheelchair when it is not in motion. In addition, the wheels should be locked when the client is getting in and out of the chair or when the client is being transported in the wheelchair inside a van. Always make sure that you have a good grasp on the handles of the wheelchair. Seat belts should be used to secure the client in the chair and avoid the possibility that the client can tumble forward at a sudden stop. When maneuvering over bumps and curbs, tilt the wheelchair back slightly by applying pressure on one of the tilting rods on the back of the chair. If you are pushing a wheelchair down a steep ramp, turn yourself and the chair around and proceed down the ramp backward. Your body will help control the speed of the wheelchair.

Wheelchair users who have full use of their arms may only need assistance when faced with an architectural barrier such as a flight of stairs. Except in the case of children, two people are usually needed to transport the client in the wheelchair up and down stairs. If the client is heavy, three people may be needed. The wheelchair is taken up the stairs backward and down the stairs frontward. The people assisting should be positioned in front and in back of the wheelchair. The chair should be balanced on the large wheels and lifted by the handgrips in back and the rods holding the footrests in front. The large wheels of the wheelchair are eased on the stairs one step at a time. If able, the person in the wheelchair can help by holding on to the large side of the wheels to help keep the wheelchair from going down the stairs too quickly (eHow, 2012).

Some clients who are wheelchair users prefer to go it alone on the stairs. Generally, they fold up their chairs and move one step at a time by using their arms to lift their buttocks up and down the stairs, taking their chair with them.

Transferring clients

In some settings, the recreational therapist may be asked to assist in transferring a client from a bed to a wheelchair or chair or from a chair into the bed. There are many methods to use for transferring clients. One common method that might be used by the recreational therapist to transfer a client safely from a wheelchair to a bed is presented in Figure 10.1.

Transferring the client from the bed to the wheelchair is usually easier because less lifting is required. Again, there are many methods. One common method to use is presented in Figure 10.2.

The same basic steps presented in Figures 10.1 and 10.2 can be used to transfer a client between chairs and between a wheelchair and a toilet. The distances between equipment should always be minimized. When transferring a client between chairs or between a wheelchair and a toilet, there should be about a 40-degree angle between the objects. If one side of the client's body is weaker than the other, the client should be moved toward the stronger side. The client will be able to assist more with the motion if he or she is moving toward the stronger side. The recreational therapist should remember to keep his or her feet spread about shoulders' width apart and to flex the knees. Proper body positioning allows the muscle groups to work together and prevents injury to the recreational therapist. Arm, shoulder, back, and stomach muscles should be used to pull. To avoid back strain when lifting, recreational therapists should use the major muscle groups of the thighs, knees, arms, abdomen, and pelvis (Berman & Snyder, 2012).

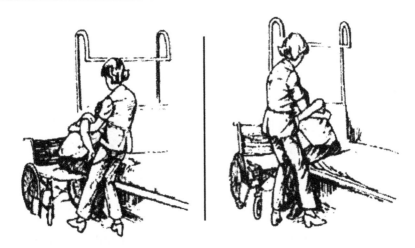

Figure 10.1. Transferring a Client from a Wheelchair to a Bed

1. Minimize the distance between the wheelchair and the bed by placing the chair adjacent and parallel to the bed.
2. Lock the wheels on the wheelchair and the bed if the bed has wheels.
3. Raise the footrests and remove the armrest near the bed.
4. Stand in front of the client with your feet shoulders' width apart. Your outside foot should be between the footrests.
5. Flex your knees.
6. Place your palms on either side of the client's rib cage.
7. Have the client put his or her arms on your elbows and hug your arms to assist.
8. Use your shoulder, arm, stomach, and back muscles to pull and your leg muscles to lift the client from the chair. Your knees should stabilize the client's knees.
9. Pivot your whole body to swing the client onto the bed.
10. Position the client in bed.

HIV/AIDS

Acquired immunodeficiency syndrome (AIDS) is caused by a virus, referred to as the human immunodeficiency virus (HIV). When an antibody against the virus is found in the blood, it indicates the person has been infected by the virus. The immune system, which defends the body's health, is progressively weakened by the HIV. One main effect of the HIV infection is a reduction in the immune system's key infection fighters in the blood (CD4 positive T cells). After exposure, some people experience flu-like symptoms for a few weeks. In many others the disorder begins with no symptoms, progresses to an early symptomatic stage in which the person experiences flu-like symptoms such as fever, headache, tiredness, and enlarged lymph nodes. These early symptoms generally last from

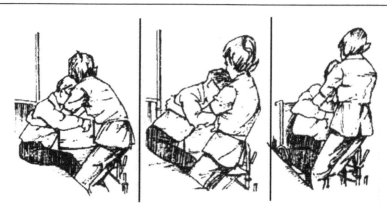

Figure 10.2. Transferring a Client from a Bed to a Wheelchair

1. Minimize the distance between the wheelchair and the bed by placing the wheelchair adjacent and parallel to the bed.
2. Lock the wheels on the wheelchair and the bed (if the bed has wheels).
3. Raise the footrests and remove the armrest near the bed.
4. Face the head of the bed. Spread your feet about shoulders' width apart. Place one forearm under the knees of the client and place your other forearm under the client's shoulder.
5. Assist the client to the sitting position by pivoting the client on his or her buttocks and swinging his or her legs over the edge of the bed. The client should be sitting on the edge of the bed.
6. Stand in front of the client and block his or her knees with your own. Your feet should be spread shoulders' width apart. The outside foot should be midway between and in front of the footrest.
7. Place your palms on either side of the client's rib cage.
8. Have the client put his or her arms on your elbows and hug your arms to assist.
9. Use your shoulder, arm, stomach, and back muscles to pull the client off the bed.
10. At the same time, pivot the client and lower the client into the chair, flexing your knees.
11. Position the client securely onto the wheelchair.

one week to a month. The length of time for the onset of more severe symptoms varies widely with some people having symptoms within a few months and others not having them for 10 or more years. Nevertheless, during this time the virus is actively multiplying and attacking the immune system. Symptoms during this period include lack of energy, weight loss, fever, opportunistic infections (e.g., candidiasis, cervical dysplasia, herpes zoster, pelvic inflammatory disease), short-term memory loss, and peripheral neuropathy. AIDS is the most advanced stage; in the late symptomatic stage, every organ system can be involved and there are symptoms of severe opportunistic infections and life-threatening cancers (Flaskerud & Ungvarski, 1999; WebMD 2012).

Because people can be infected with HIV many years before they have symptoms, it is important that the recreational therapist be aware of how HIV is transmitted. HIV is not transmitted through casual contact, such as touching, hugging, using swimming pools or toilet seats, or sharing sports equipment (Centers for Disease Control and Prevention, 2008). HIV is transmitted through contact with contaminated body fluids and safety precautions should be taken (see next section).

Safety Precautions

The Occupational Safety and Health Administration (OSHA) is concerned with keeping working environments safe. OSHA has standards to deal with infection control in healthcare settings. Standard Precautions have replaced the earlier "Universal Precautions." All health care settings are required to have safety procedures in place and to train all employees in their use. It is important for recreational therapy students to be familiar with the procedures at each health care setting before they begin working with clients.

Because it is not always possible to know when a client has an infection, the Centers for Disease Control and Prevention (CDC) has identified Standard Precautions (CDC 2012a,b) to be used for all patients (Ramont & Niedringhaus, 2008). Standard Precautions include procedures such as hand hygiene; employing protective equipment (e.g., gloves, facemasks); respiratory hygiene; practices for injections; and handling contaminated equipment. Recreational therapists need to employ hand hygiene procedures such as washing hands with alcohol-based rubs or soap and water when working with clients. Hand hygiene procedures should be used before and after touching all clients and when recreational therapists come into contact with any bodily fluids or dressings even when the recreational therapist uses gloves. If a recreational therapist is engaged in an activity in which a client's skin is broken, the client should be immediately separated from others to reduce the chance of contamination. The recreational therapist should use latex, vinyl, or rubber gloves to avoid direct contact with blood while attending to the wound and wash his/her hands after removing gloves. It is important to remember to have gloves and antiseptic towelettes available for activities in which hand-washing facilities are not available.

Chapter Summary

Providing recreational therapy services for clients requires knowing about each client's health and safety needs. Clients who have diabetic reactions or seizures may experience episodes that threaten their health and physical safety. Other clients who receive long-term drug therapy with psychotropic drugs may experience side effects that affect their ability to participate in recreational therapy activities. Finally, clients who use mechanical aids may need assistance from the recreational therapist. To assist the client safely and efficiently, the recreational therapist must know proper transferring techniques and how to handle blood. This chapter has provided general information and basic guidelines for the recreational therapist to use when working with clients.

Reading Comprehension Questions

1. What are the main causes of hypoglycemia and hyperglycemia?
2. What precautions should the recreational therapist take when planning extended activities for clients with diabetes mellitus?
3. What is the first-aid treatment for each type of seizure?
4. What are the main factors to consider when planning activities for the client who is subject to tonic/clonic seizures?

5. Which side effects of antiepileptic drugs and psychotropic drugs necessitate changes in activities due to safety considerations?
6. What are the main safety considerations for clients who use mechanical aids?
7. What are some basic principles to follow when lifting or transferring clients who have physical limitations?
8. What precautions should be followed when coming into contact with blood?

References

Aasheim. L.(2011). *Practical clinical supervision for counselors: An experiential guide*, New York: Springer.

Abell, J. E., Hootman, J. M., Zack, M. M., Moriarty, D., & Helmick, C. G. (2005). Physical activity and health-related quality of life among people with arthritis. *Journal of Epidemiology and Community Health, 59*, 380-385.

Acterberg, J. (1985). *Imagery in healing: Shamanism and modern medicine*. Boston, MA: Shambhala.

Adams, E. R., & McGuire, F. (1986). Is laughter the best medicine? A study of the effects of humor on perceived pain and affect. *Activities, Adaption, & Aging, 8*(3/4), 157-175.

Adams, M., Caldwell, K., Atkins, L., & Quin, R. (2012). Pilates and mindfulness: A qualitative study. *Journal of Dance Education, 12*(4), 123-130.

Addis, M. E., & Martell, C. R. (2004). *Overcoming depression one step at a time: The new behavioral approach to getting your life back*. Oakland, CA: New Harbinger Publications.

Adinolfi, A. A., McCourt, W. F., & Geoghegan, S. (1976). Group assertiveness training for alcoholics. *Journal of Studies on Alcohol, 37*(3), 311-320.

Adler, N., & Stewart, J. (2004). Self-Esteem. Retrieved from http://www.macses.ucsf.edu/Research/Psychosocial/notebook/selfesteem.html

Adler, T. (1989). Funnybone connected to cognition, physiology. The *APA Monitor, 20*(5), 16.

Administrative Policy. (2008). Incident reports policy no. 200.5, Page 1. Retrieved from http://optionsfs.org/admin/pdfs/200-5-1.pdf

Aguilera, D. (1967). Relationships between physical contact and verbal interaction between nurses and patients. *Journal of Psychiatric Nursing, 5*, 5-21.

Albery, I. (2008). *Key concepts in health psychology*. Boston, MA: Sage. Retrieved from http://www.credoreference.com/book/sageukhp

Alderman, R. B. (1974). *Psychological behavior in sport*. Philadelphia, PA: W. B. Saunders.

Alfaro-LeFevre, R. (2010). *Applying nursing process: A tool for critical thinking*. Philadelphia, PA: Wolters Kluwer/ Lippincott Williams & Wilkins.

Allgood, M. R., & Marriner-Tomey, A. (1997). *Nursing theory: Utilization and application*. St. Louis, MO: Mosby.

Allsop, J. A., & Dattilo, J. (2000). Therapeutic use of t'ai chi ch'uan. In J. Dattilo (Ed.), *Facilitation techniques in therapeutic recreation* (pp. 245-271). State College, PA: Venture.

Altan, L., Korkmaz, N., Dizdar, M., & Yurtkuran, M. (2011). Effect of Pilates training on people with ankylosing spondylitis. *Rheumatology International, 32*(7), 2093-2099.

Alvarez, A. G.,& Stauffer, G. A. (2001). Musings on adventure therapy. *Journal of Experiential Education, 24*(2), 85-91.

Alzahrani, M. A., Dean, C. M., Ada, L., Dorsch, S., & Canning, C. G. (2012). Mood and balance are associated with free-living physical activity of people after stroke residing in the community. *Stroke Research and Treatment, 2012*, Article ID 470648, 8 pages.

Alzheimer's Association. (2012). 2012 Alzheimer's disease facts and figures. Retrived from http://www.alz.org/documents_custom/2012_facts_figures_fact_sheet.pdf

Amarsi, Y. (2002). Evidence-based nursing: Perspective from Pakistan. *Reflections on Nursing Leadership, 28*(2), 28, 29, & 46.

American College of Sports Medicine. (2001). Appropriate intervention strategies for weight loss and prevention of weight regain for adults. *Medicine and Science in Sports and Exercise, 33*(12), 2145-2156.

American Diabetes Association. (2003). Physical activity/exercise and diabetes mellitus. *Diabetes Care, 26*, 573-577.

American Diabetes Association, Inc. (2004). *Therapy for diabetes mellitus and related disorders* (4th ed.). Clinical Education Series, Alexandria, VA: Author.

American Diabetes Association. (2007) Retrieved from http://www.diabetes.org/diabetes-statistics.jsp

American Diabetes Association, Inc. (2008). *Medical management of type 1 diabetes* (5th ed.). Clinical Education Series. Alexandria, VA: Author.

American Diabetes Association, Inc. (2009). *Intensive diabetes management* (4th ed.) Clinical Education Series. Alexandria, VA: Author.

American Diabetes Association, Inc. (2013). Diabetes Statistics. Retrieved from http://www.diabetes.org/diabetes-basics/diabetes-statistics/

American Heart Association. (2011). What is cardiovascular disease (heart disease)? Retrieved from http://www.heart.org/HEARTORG/Caregiver/Resources/WhatisCardiovascularDisease/What-is-Cardiovascular-Disease_UCM_301852_Article.jsp

American Psychiatric Associaiton. (2002). Practice guidelines for the treatment of patients with bipolar disorder (revision). *American Journal of Psychiatry, 159*(suppl), 1-50.

American Therapeutic Recreation Association. (2000). *Standards for the practice of therapeutic recreation.* Alexandra, VA: American Therapeutic Recreation Association.

American Therapeutic Recreation Association. (2001). Code of ethics. [Online]. Available at www.atra-tr.org/ethics.html

Anderson, J. W., Liu, C., & Kryscio, R. J. (2008). Blood pressure response to Transcendental Meditation: A meta-analysis. *American Journal of Hpertension, 21*(3), 310-316.

Anderson, L., & Heyne, L. (2013). *Therapeutic recreation practice: A strengths approach.* State College, PA: Venture.

Anderson, R. A. (1978). *Stress power!* New York: Human Sciences Press.

Andrews, L. W. (2005). *Stress control for peace of mind.* New York: Main Street.

Andrews, M., Angone, K. M., Cray, J. V., Lewis, J. A., & Johnson, P. H. (1999). *Nurses handbook of alternative & complementary therapies.* Springhouse, PA: Springhouse Corporation.

Annema, J-H., Verstraete, M., Abee;e. V. V., Desmet, S., & Geerts, D. (2010). Videogames in therapy: A therapist's perspecive. *Proceedings of the 3rd International Conference on Fun and Games. AMC,* pp. 94-98.

Anselmo, J. (2013). Relaxation. In B. M. Dossey & L. Keegan (Eds.), *Holistic nursing: A handbook for practice* (pp. 327-361). Burlington, MA: Jones & Bartlett Learning.

Antai-Otong, D. (2007). *Nurse-client communication: A life span approach.* Boston, MA: Jones and Bartlett.

Apostolo, J., & Kolcaba, K. (2009). The effects of guided imagery on comfort, depression anxiety, and stress of psychiatric inpatients with depressive disorders. *Archives of Psychiatric Nursing, 23*(6), 403-411.

App, B., Bulleit, B. A., & Jaskolka, A. R. (2006). Touch communicates distinct emotions. *Emotion, 6*(3), 528-533.

Appleton, W. S. (1988). *Practical clinical psychopharmacology* (3rd ed.). Baltimore, MD: Williams & Wilkins.

Appleton, V. (2012). Laughter yoga specialist serves people with disabilities. Retrieved from http://www.disabled-world.com/fitness/exercise/yoga/laughter-yoga.php

Aproberts, A. (2000). Calling Dr. Video. *The Herald-Times,* Bloomington, IN, April 1, 2000, p. D1.

Arbuthnott, K. D., Arbuthnon, D. W., & Rossiter, L. (2001). Guided imagery and memory: Implications for psychotherapists. *Journal of Counseling Psychologty, 49*(3), 123-132.

Ardell, B. (1977). *High-level wellness: An alternative to doctors, drugs, and disease.* Berkeley, CA: Ten Speed Press.

Argyle, M. (2001). *The psychology of happiness* (2nd ed.). New York, NY: Taylor & Francis Inc.

Arnold, E. (2007). Communicating in groups. In E. C. Arnold, & K. U. Boggs (Eds.), *Interpersonal relationships: Professional communication skills for nurses* (5th ed.) (pp. 260–287). St. Louis, MO: Saunders Elsevier.

Arnold, E., & Boggs, K. (2007). *Interpersonal relationships: Professional communication skills for nurses.* (5th ed.). St. Louis, MO: Saunders Elsevier.

Ashe, M. C., Miller, W. C., Eng, J. J., & Noreau, L. (2009). Older adults, chronic disease and leisure-time physical activity. *Gerontology, 55,* 64-72.

Asher, B. (1998). Getting back to basics: Health-care experts giving horticulture therapy a fresh look. *The Herald-Times,* Boomington, IN, April 2, 1998 (pp. D1, D4).

Ashford, S., Edmunds, J., & French, D. P. (2010). What is the best way to change self-efficacy to promote lifestyle and recreational physical activity? A systematic review with meta-analysis. *British Journal of Health Psychology, 15,* 265-288.

Askins, J. (1997). Gone fishin'. *Team Rehab Report, 8*(3), 35-37.

Aspinwall, L. G., & Staudinger, U. M. (Eds.). (2003). *A psychology of human strengths.* Washington, D.C.: American Psychological Association.

Associated Press. (2002). Canada's population grows 4% in 5 years. Sarasota *Herald-Tribune,* p.10A, March 13, 2002.

Atalay, A. S., & Meloy, M. G. (2011). Retail therapy: A strategic effort to improve mood. *Psychology & Marketing, 28*(6), 638-660.

Atkinson, M. (2005). *A practical guide to self-massage.* London: Cico Books.

ATRA News Release. (2005). *ATRA affirms support of ICF.* Alexandria, VA: American Therapeutic Recreation Association.

ATRA. (2009). *ATRA code of ethics.* Retrieved from http://atra-online.com/displaycommon. cfm?an=1&subarticlenbr=91

Austin, D. R. (1971). Catharsis theory: How valid is therapeutic recreation? *Therapeutic Recreation Journal, 5*(1), 30, 31, 44, 45.

Austin, D. R. (1986). Clinical supervision in therapeutic recreation. *Journal of Expanding Horizons in Therapeutic Recreation, 1,* 7-13.

Austin, D. R. (1987). Therapeutic recreation. In A. Graefe, & S. Parker (Eds.), Recreation and leisure: An introductory handbook (pp. 155-158). State College, PA: Venture.

Austin, D. R. (1991). *Therapeutic recreation: Processes and techniques* (2nd ed.). Urbana, IL: Sagamore.

Austin, D. R. (1997). Recreation therapy education: A call for reform. In D. M. Compton (Ed.), *Issues in therapeutic recreation: Toward the new millennium* (2nd ed.) (pp. 193-209). Urbana, IL: Sagamore.

Austin, D. R. (1998). The Health Protection/Health Promotion Model. *Therapeutic Recreation Journal, 32*(2), 109-117.

Austin, D. R. (2001a). *Glossary of recreation therapy and occupational therapy.* State College, PA: Venture.

Austin, D. R. (2001b). Introduction and overview. In D. R. Austin, & M. E. Crawford (Eds.), *Therapeutic recreation: An introduction* (3rd ed.) (pp.1-21). Boston, MA: Allyn and Bacon.

Austin, D. R. (2002a). This I believe…In D. R. Austin, J. Dattilo, & B. P. McCormick (Eds.), *Conceptual foundations for therapeutic recreation* (pp. 313-314). State College, PA: Venture.

Austin, D. R. (2002b). A call for training in physical activity. In D. R. Austin, J. Dattilo, & McCormick, B. P. (Eds.), *Conceptual foundations for therapeutic recreation* (pp. 225-234). State College, PA: Venture.

Austin, D. R. (2002c). Conceptual models in therapeutic recreation. In D. R. Austin, J. Dattilo, & B. P. McCormick (Eds.), *Conceptual foundations for therapeutic recreation* (pp. 1-30). State College, PA: Venture.

Austin, D. R. (2002d). Control: A major element in therapeutic recreation. In D. R. Austin, J. Dattilo, & B. P. McCormick (Eds.), *Conceptual foundations for therapeutic recreation* (pp. 93-114). State College, PA: Venture.

Austin, D. R. (2002e). The therapeutic relationship. In D. R. Austin, J. Dattilo, & B. P. McCormick (Eds.), *Conceptual foundations for therapeutic recreation* (pp. 115-132). State College, PA: Venture.

Austin, D. R. (2005-2006). The changing contextualization of therapeutic recreation: A 40-year perspective. *Annual in Therapeutic Recreation, 14*, 1–11.

Austin, D. R. (2009). *Therapeutic recreation: Processes and techniques* (2nd ed.). Urbana, IL: Sagamore.

Austin, D. R. (2011a). *Lessons learned: An open letter to recreational therapy students and practitioners.* Urbana, IL: Sagamore.

Austin, D. R. (2011b). Reformulation of the Health Protection/Health Promotion Model. *American Journal of Recreation Therapy, 10*(3), 19-26.

Austin, D. R., & Binkley, A. L. (1977). A summary of the curriculum plan for the master of science in recreation: Options in therapeutic recreation. Unpublished report. Department of Recreation and Park Administration. Bloomington, IN: Indiana University.

Austin, D. R., & Crawford, M. E. (2001). *Therapeutic recreation: An introduction* (3rd ed.). Needham Heights, MA: Allyn & Bacon.

Austin, D. R., & Szymanski, D. J. (1985). Burnout or burnbright. *Camping Magazine, 57*(7), 26-28.

Austin, D. R., & Voelkl, J. E. (1986). Effects of social support and locus of control on camp staff burnout. *Camping Magazine, 58* (7), 18-21.

Austin, E. N., Johnston, Y., & Morgan, L. L. (2006). Community gardening in a senior center: A therapeutic intervention to improve the health of older adults. *Therapeutic Recreation Journal, 40*(1), 48-57.

Autry, C. E. (2001). Adventure therapy with girls at-risk: Responses to outdoor experiential activities. *Therapeutic Recreation Journal, 35*(4), 289-306.

Avedon, E. M. (1974). *Therapeutic recreation service: An applied behavioral science approach.* Englewood Cliffs, NJ: Prentice-Hall.

Ayers, S., Colman, J., & DeSalvatore, G. (n.d.). *The parent-child activity group manual.* Storehan, MA: New England Memorial Hospital.

Azar, B. (1997). Quelling today's conflict between home and work. *Monitor on Psychology, 28*(7), 1 & 16.

Azar, B. (2010). Another reason to break a sweat: In addition to boosting your brainpower, exercise may fend off and even alleviate cognitive ills, including Alzheimer's disease, research suggests. *Monitor on Psychology, 41*(6), 36-38.

Azar, B. (2011). Positive psychology advances with growing pains. *Monitor on Psychology, 42*(4), 32-36.

Baccus, J. R., Baldwin, M. W., & Packer, D. J. (2004). Increasing implicit self-esteem through classical conditioning. *Psychological Science, 15*(7), 498–502.

Bacon, S. (1983). *The conscious use of metaphor in Outward Bound.* Denver: Colorado Outward Bound School.

Bae, B. G., Oh, S. H., Park, C. O., Noh, S., Noh, J. Y., Kim, K. R., & Lee, K. H. (2012). Progressive muscle relaxation therapy for atophic dermatitis: Objective assessment of efficacy. *Acta Derm Venereol, 92*, 57-61.

Baikie, K. A., & Wilhelm, K. (2005). Emotional and physical health benefits of expressive writing. *Advances in Psychiatric Treatment, 11*, 338-346.

Baker, R., Holloway, J., Larsson, A., Hartman, L. C., Pearce, R., Scherman, B., Johnsson, S., … & Owens, M. (2003). Effects of multi-sensory stimulation for people with dementia. *Journal of Advanced Nursing, 43*(5), 465-477.

Bal, B. S. Singh, K., & Vaz, W. (2011). Effects of 4-week yogasanas training on balance and agility in adolescent girls. *International Journal of Sports Science and Engineering, 5*(2), 85-92.

Ball, E. L. (1970). The meaning of therapeutic recreation. *Therapeutic Recreation Journal, 4*(1), 17,18.

Bandura, A. (1986). *Social foundations of thought and action: A social cognitive theory.* Englewood Cliff, NJ: Prentice-Hall.

Bandura, A. (Ed.). (1995). *Self-efficacy in changing societies.* New York, NY: Cambridge University Press.

Bandura, A. (1997). *Self-efficacy: The exercise of control.* New York, NY: W. H. Freeman and Company.

Banks, G., Bernhardt, J., Churilov, L., & Cumming, T. B. (2012). Exercise preferences are different after stroke. *Stroke Research and Treatment, 2012*, Article ID 890946, 9 pages.

Banks, M. R., & Banks, W. A. (2002). The effects of animal-assisted therapy on loneliness in an elderly population in long-term care facilities. *The Journal of Gerontology, 57A*, M428-M432.

Banks, M. R., Willoughby, L. M., & Banks, W. A. (2008). Animal-assisted therapy and loneliness in nursing homes: Use of robotic versus living dogs. *Journal of the American Medical Directors Association, 9*, 173-177.

Baranow, J., Dolan, B., & Watts, D. (2011). *The healing art of writing.* San Francisco, CA: University of California Medical Humanities Consortium.

Baranowski, T., Baranowski, J., Thompson, D., & Buday, R. (2011). Behavior science in video games for children's diet and physical activity change: Key research needs. *Journal of Diabetes Science and Technology, 5*(2), 229-233.

Baranowski, T., Buday, R., Thompson, D. I., & Baranowski, J. (2008). Playing for real: Video games and stories for health-related behavior change. *American Journal of Preventative Medicine, 34*(1), 74-82.

Barbour, K. A., Edenfield, T. M., & Blumenthal, J. A. (2007). Exercise as a treatment for depression and other psychiatric disorders. *Journal of Cardiopulmonary Rehabilitation and Prevention, 27,* 359-367.

Barker, S. B., & Dawson, K. S. (1998). The effects of animal-assisted therapy on anxiety ratings of hospitalized psychiatric patients. *Psychiatric Services, 49,* 797-801.

Barlett, C. P. (2009). Video game effects--confirmed, suspected, and speculative: A review of the evidence. *Simulation & Gaming, 40*(2), 377-403.

Barnes & Noble. (2007). *Quamut how-to-guide to stretching.* New York: Author.

Barnes & Noble. (2007). *Quamut how-to-guide on tai chi.* New York: Author.

Barnes & Noble. (2007). *Quamut how-to-guide on yoga.* New York: Author.

Barnes, E. K., Sack, A., & Shore, H. (1973). Guidelines to treatment approaches: Modalities and methods for use with the aged. *The Gerontologist, 13,* 515-522.

Barnes, V. A., Treiber, F. A., & Johnson, M. H. (2004). Impact of Transcendental Meditation on ambulatory blood pressure in Afriacn-American adolescents. *American Journal of Hypertension, 17*(4), 366-369.

Barnes, V. A., Treiber, F. A., Turner, J. R., Davis, H., & Strong, W. B. (1999). Acute effects of Transcendental Meditation1 on hemodynamic functioning in middle-aged adults. *Psychosomatic Medicine, 61*(4), 525-531.

Barnett, J. E., Erickson Cornish, J. A., Goodyear, R. K., & Lichtenberg, J. W. (2007). Commentaries on the ethical and effective practice of clinical supervision. *Professional Psychology Research and Practice, 38*(3), 268-275.

Barnum, B. S. (1998). *Nursing theory: Analysis, application, evaluation* (5th ed.). Philadelphia, PA: Lippincott.

Baron, R. A., & Byrne, D. (1994). *Social psychology: Understanding human interaction* (7th ed.). Boston, MA: Allyn and Bacon.

Barrett, B., Hayney, M. S., Muller, D., Rakel, D., Ward, A., Obast, C.N., ...& Coe, C. L. (2012). Meditation or exercise for preventing acute respiratory infection: A randomized controlled trail. *Annals of Family Medicine, 10*(4), 337-346.

Barton, J., & Pretty, J. (2010). What is the best dose of nature and green exercise for improving mental health? A multi-study analysis. *Environmental science & technology, 44*(10), 3947-3955.

Basak, C., Boot, W. R., Voss, M. W., & Kramer, A. F. (2008). Can training in a real-time strategy video game attenuate cognitive decline in older adults? *Psychology and Aging, 21*(4),

Bateman, N. (2000). *Advocacy skills for health and social care professionals.* Philadelphia, PA: Jessica Kingsley Publishers.

Beal, B. M., Bohlen, J. M., & Raudabaugh, J. N. (1976). *Leadership and dynamic group action.* Ames, IA: The Iowa State University Press.

Beale, J. (2003). *Aromatherapy.* Permacharts from Mindsource Technologies Inc.

Bean, J. F., Vora, A., & Frontera, W. R. (2004). Benefits of exercise for community-dwelling older adults. *Archives of Physical Medicine and Rehabilitation, 86*(Suppl. 3), S31-S42.

Beard, M. T., & Bidus, D. R. (1968), A study of the effects of remotivation on social competence, social interests and personal neatness. *Journal of Psychiatric Nursing and Mental Health Services, 6*(4), 197-201.

Beaudouin, N. M., & Keller, M. J. (1994). Aquatic-Solutions: A continuum of services for individuals with physical disabilities in the community. *Therapeutic Recreation Journal, 28*(4), 193-202.

Beck, A. M. (2000). The use of animals to benefit humans: Animal-assisted therapy. In A. H. Fine (Ed.), *Handbook on animal-assisted therapy: Theoretical foundations and guidelines for practice* (pp. 21-40). San Diego, CA: Academic Press.

Becker, B. E. (2009). Aquatic therapy: Scientific foundations and clinical rehabilitation applications. *PM&R, 1,* 859-872.

Becker, B. E., & Cole, A. J. (1997). *Comprehensive aquatic therapy.* Boston, MA: Butterworth-Heinemann.

Becker, I. (2000). Uses of yoga in psychiatry and medicine. In P. R. Muskin (Ed.), *Complementary and alternative medicine and psychiatry* (pp. 107-146). Washington, D.C.: American Psychiatric Press.

Beckman, H., Regier, N., & Young, J. (2007). Effect of workplace laughter groups on personal efficacy beliefs. *The Journal of Primary Prevention, 28*(2), 167-183.

Bedini, L. A., & Phoenix, T. I. (1999). Addressing leisure barriers for caregivers of older adults: A model leisure wellness program. *Therapeutic Recreation Journal, 33*(3), 222-240.

Bedini, L. A., Williams, L., & Thompson, D. (1995). The relationship between burnout and role stress in therapeutic recreation specialists. *Therapeutic Recreation Journal, 29*(3), 163-174.

Begat, I., & Severinsson, E. (2006). Reflection on how clinical nursing supervision enhances nurses' experiences of well-being related to their psychosocial work environment. *Journal of Nursing Management, 14*(8), 610-616.

Begley, S. (2008). This is your brain on a videogame. *Newsweek.* Retrieved from http://www.newsweek.com/id/134298

Beland, B. (2001). Bibliotherapy and pediatrics. Educational session. New Orleans: American Therapeutic Recreation Association Annual Conference, August 31, 2001.

Belkin, G. S. (1988). *Introduction to counseling* (3rd ed.). Dubuque, IA: Wm. C. Brown.

Bemelmans, R., Gelderblom, G. J., Junker, P. & de White, L. (2012). Socially assistive robots in elder care: A systematic review into effects and effectiveness. *Journal of the American Medical Directors Association, 13*(2), 114-120.

Benfer, B. A., & Schroder, P. J. (1985). Nursing in the therapeutic milieu. *Bulletin of the Menninger Clinic, 49*(5), 451-465.

Bennett, H. J. (2003). Humor in medicine. *Southern Medical Journal, 96*(12), 1257-1261.

Bennett, M. J. (2001). *The empathic healer: An endangered species?* San Diego, CA: Academic Press.

Bennett, M. P. (2008). Humor and laughter may influence health: III. Laughter and health outcomes. *eCAM, 5*(1), 37-40.

Bennett, M. P., & Lengacher, C. (2008). Humor and laughter may influence health: III. Laughter and health outcomes. *Evidence-Based Complementary and Alternative Medicine, 5*(1), 37-40.

Bennett, M. P., Zeller, J. M., Rosenberg, L., & McCann, J. (2003). The effect of mirthful laughter on stress and natural killer cell activity. *Alternative Therapies, 9*(2), 38-44.

Benson, H. (1975). *The relaxation response.* New York: Avon Books.

Berg, A., Berkovic, S. E., Brodie, M., Cross, J. H., Van Emde Boas, W.,...& Scheffer, I. E. (2010). Revised terminology and concepts for organization of seizures and epilepsies: Report of the ILAE Commission on Classification and Terminology, 2005-2009. *Epilepsia, 51,* 676-685.

Berger, B. G. (1987). Stress levels of swimmers. In W. P. Morgan, & S. E. Goldston (Eds.), *Exercise and mental health.* New York: Hemisphere.

Berger, B. G. (1994). Coping with stress: The effectiveness of exercise and other techniques. *Quest, 46,* 100-119.

Beringer, A., & Martin, P. (2003). On adventure therapy and the natural worlds: Respecting nature's healing. *Journal of Adventure Education and Outdoor Learning, 3*(1), 29-40.

Berk, R. A. (2001). The active ingredients in humor: Psychophysiological benefits and risks for older adults. *Educational Gerontology, 27,* 323-339.

Berkowitz, L. (1972). *Social psychology.* Glenview, IL: Scott, Foresman and Company.

Berkowitz, L. (1978). Sports competition and aggression. In W. F. Staub (Ed.), *An analysis of athlete behavior.* Ithaca, NY: Movement Publications.

Berman, A., & Snyder, S. (2012). *Kozier & Erb's fundamentals of nursing* (9th ed.). Upper Saddle River, NJ: Prentice Hall.

Berman, A., Snyder, S. J., Kozier, B., & Erb, G. (Eds.). (2008). *Kozier & Erb's fundamental of nursing: Concepts, process and practice* (8th ed.). Upper Saddle River, NJ: Pearson Prentice Hall.

Berman, D. S., & Davis-Berman, J. (2005). Positive psychology and outdoor education. *Journal of Experiential Education, 28*(1), 17-24.

Bernard, J. M. (1987). Ethical and legal considerations for supervisors. In L. D. Borders, & G. R. Leddick (Eds.), *Handbook of counseling supervision.*

Bernardo, L. M., (2007). The effectiveness of Pilates training in healthy adults: An appraisal of the research literature. *Journal of Bodywork and Movement Therapies, 11,* 106-110.

Berne, E. (1964). *Games people play: The psychology of human relationships.* New York: Grove Press, Inc.

Bernstein, D. A., & Borkovec, T. D. (1973). *Progressive relaxation training: A manual for the helping professions.* Champaign, IL: Research Press.

Bernstein, L., & Bernstein, R. S. (1985). *Interviewing: A guide for health professionals* (4th ed.). Norwalk, CT: Appleton-Century-Crofts.

Bias, K. K., & Hayes, J. S. (2011). *Professional nursing practice* (6th ed.). Boston, MA: Pearson.

Biddiss, E., & Irwin, J. (2010). Active video games to promote physical activity in children and youth. *Archives of Pediatrics & Adolescent Medicine, 164*(7), 664-672.

Biech, E. (Ed.). (2008). *Trainer's warehouse book of games.* San Francisco, CA: Pfeiffer.

Bierma, J. (1998). *Remotivation group therapy: Handbook for the basic course.* York Harbor, ME: NRTO, Inc.

Biley, F. C. (2000). The effects on patient well-being of music listening as a nursing intervention: A review of the literature. *Journal of Clinical Nursing, 9,* 668-677.

Birdee, G. S., Wayne, P. M., Davis, R. B., Phillips, R. S., & Yeh, G. Y. (2009). T'ai Chi and Qigong for health: Patterns of use in the United States. *The Journal of Alternative and Complementary Medicine, 15*(9), 969-973.

Birrell, J., & Henderson, M. (1986). The psychological approach. In C. Hume, & I. Pullen (Eds.), *Rehabilitation in psychiatry.* New York: Churchill Livingstone.

Bishop, V. (2007). Literature review: Clinical supervision evaluation studies. In V. Bishop (Ed.), *Clinical supervision in practice* (2nd ed.) (pp. 141-158). New York: Palgrave Macmillan.

Bishop, V. (2007b). Clinical supervision: What is it? Why do we need it? In V. Bishop (Ed.), *Clinical supervision in practice* (2nd ed.) (pp. 1-26). New York: Palgrave Macmillan.

Bishop, V. (2009). *Leadership for nursing and allied health care professionals.* New York: Open University Press.

Biswas-Diener, R. (2010). *Practicing positive psychology coaching.* Hoboken, NJ: John Wiley & Sons.

Biswas-Diener, R., & Dean, B. (2007). *Positive psychology coaching: Putting the science of happiness to work for you clients.* Hoboken, NJ: John Wiley & Sons.

Bjorkvik, J., Biringer, E., Eikeland, O., & Nielsen, G. H. (2008). Predicting self-esteem in psychiatric outpatients, *Nordic Psychology, 60*(1), 43-57.

Black, K., & Lobo, M. (2008). A conceptual review of family resilience factors. *Journal of Family Nursing, 14*(1), 33-55.

Blackham, G. J. (1977). *Counseling: Theory, process, and practice.* Belmont, CA: Wadsworth.

Blair, D. K., & Coyle, C. (2005). An examination of multicultural competencies of entry-level Certified Therapeutic Recreation Specialists. *Therapeutic Recreation Journal, 39*(2), 139-157.

Blais, K., & Hayes, J. S. (2011). *Professional nursing practice: Concepts and perspectives*   (6th ed.).   Upper Saddle River, NJ: Pearson.

Blatner, A. (1999). Psychodramatic methods in psychotherapy. In D. J. Wiener (Ed.), *Beyond talk therapy: Using movement and expressive techniques in clinical practice* (pp. 125-143). Washington, D.C.: American Psychological Association.

Blatner, A. (2000). *Foundations of psychodrama.* New York: Springer.

Blatner, A., & Blatner, A. (1988). *The art of play: An adult's guide to reclaiming imagination and spontaneity.* New York: Human Sciences.

Blattner, B. (1981). *Holistic nursing.* Englewood Cliffs, NJ: Prentice-Hall.

Boggs, K. U. (2007). Documentation in the age of the electronic health record. In E. C. Arnold & K. U. Boggs (Eds.), *Interpersonal relationships: Professional communication skills for nurses* (5th ed.) (pp. 498-518). St. Louis, MO: Saunders.

Bolander, V. B., & Manville, J. A. (2008). Communication. In J. A. Manville, & C. G. Huerta (Eds.), *Health promotion in nursing* (2nd ed.) (pp. 78-95). Clifton Park, NY: Thomson Delmar Learning.

Bonadies, V. (2004). A yoga therapy program for AIDS-related pain and anxiety: Implications for therapeutic recreation. *Therapeutic Recreation Journal, 38*(2), 148-166.

Bonadies, V. (2009). Guided imagery as a therapeutic recreation modality to reduce pain and anxiety. *Therapeutic Recreation Journal, 43*(2), 43-55.

Bond, M., & Holland, S. (1998). *Skills of clinical supervision for nurses: A practical guide for supervisees, clinical supervisors, and managers.* Philadelphia, PA: Open University Press.

Bonitz, V. (2008). Use of physical touch in the "talking cure": A journey to the outskirts of psychotherapy. *Psychotherapy Theory, Research, Practice, Training, 45*(3), 391-404.

Borden, G. A., & Stone, J. D. (1976). *Human communication: The process of relating.* Menlo Park, CA: Cummings.

Borders, L. D., & Leddick, G. R. (1987). *Handbook of counseling supervision.* Alexandria, VA: Association for Counselor Education and Supervision.

Bouchard, C., Blair, S. N., & Haskell, W. L. (2012). Why study physical activity and health? In C. Bouchard, S. N. Blair, & W. L. Haskell (Eds.), *Physical activity and health* (2nd ed.) (pp. 3-20). Champaign, IL: Human Kinetics.

Bourne, E. J., Brownstein, A., & Garano, L. (2004). *Natural relief for anxiety.* Oakland, CA: New Harbinger.

Bowler, D. E., Buyung-Ali, L. M., Knight, T. M., & Pullin, A. S. (2010). A systematic review of evidence for the added benefit to health of exposure to natural environments. *BMC, Public Health, 10* Retrieved from http//www.biomedcentral.com/1471-2458/10/456

Boyd, M. A. (2008). *Psychiatric nursing: Contemporary practices* (4th ed.). Philadelphia, PA: Wolters Kluwer/Lippincott Williams & Wilkins.

Bradley, L. J. (1989). *Counselor supervision: Principles, process, and practice* (2nd ed.). Muncie, IN: Accelerated Development.

Brammer, L. M., & MacDonald, G. (2002). *The helping relationship: Process and skills* (8th ed.). Boston, MA: Allyn and Bacon.

Branden, N. (1985). *To see what I see and know what I know: A guide to self-discovery.* New York, NY: Bantam Books.

Brandon, L. J. (1999). Promoting physically active lifestyles in older adults. *Journal of Physical Education, Recreation & Dance, 70*(6), 34-37.

Brazzelli, M., Saunders, D. H., Greig, C. A., & Mead, G. E. (2012). Physical fitness training for patients with stroke: Updated review. *Stroke, 43*, e39-e40.

Brehm, S. S., Kassin, S., & Fein, S. (2005). *Social psychology* (6th ed.). Boston: Houghton-Mifflin.

Brenneke, H. F. (2001). Autogenic training. In R. Corsini (Ed.), *Handbook of innovative therapy* (2nd ed.) (pp. 38-45). New York: John Wiley & Sons.

Brightbill, C. K. (1966). *Educating for leisure-centered living.* Harrisburg, PA: Stackpole.

Brill, N. I., & Levine, J. (2002). *Working with people: The helping process* (7th ed.). Boston, MA: Allyn and Bacon.

Broach, E., & Dattilo, J. (2001). Effects of aquatic therapy on adults with multiple sclerosis. *Therapeutic Recreation Journal, 35*(2), 141-154.

Broach, E., & Dattilo, J. (2003). The effects of aquatic therapy on strength of adults with multiple sclerosis. *Therapeutic Recreation Journal, 37*(3), 224-239.

Broach, E., & Dattilo, J. (2011a). Aquatic therapy. In J. Dattilo & A. McKenney (Eds.), *Facilitation techniques in therapeutic recreation* (2nd edition) (pp. 69-110). State College, PA: Venture.

Broach, E., & Dattilo, J. (2011b). Assistive technology. In J. Dattilo & A. McKenney (Eds.), *Facilitation techniques in therapeutic recreation* (2nd ed.) (pp. 111-152). State College, PA: Venture.

Broach, E., Dattilo, J., & Loy, D. (2000). Therapeutic use of exercise. In J. Dattilo (Ed.), *Facilitation techniques in therapeutic recreation* (pp. 355-383). State College, PA: Venture.

Broach, E., Dattilo, J., & McKenney, A. (2007). Effects of aquatic therapy on perceived fun and enjoyment experiences of participants with multiple sclerosis. *Therapeutic Recreation Journal, 41*(3), 179-200.

Brodie, S. J., & Riley, F. C. (1999). An exploration of the potential benefits of pet-facilitated therapy. *Journal of Clinical Nursing, 8*, 329-337.

Bronikowska, M., Bronikowski, M., & Schott, N. (2011). "You think you are too old to play?" Playing games and aging. *Human Movement, 12*(1), 24-30.

Brown, D. W. (1999). *Therapeutic massage: A practical introduction.* San Diego, CA: Thunder Bay Press.

Brown, K. (2005). Using motion pictures to enhance counselor effectiveness in conducting grief training. Unpublished doctoral dissertation. Texas Tech University.

Brown, S. J. (1999). *Knowledge for health care practice: A guide to using research evidence.* Philadelphia, PA: W. B. Saunders.

Browne, T. R., & Holmes, G. L. (2008). *Handbook of epilepsy* (4th ed.). Philadelphia, PA: Lippincott Williams & Wilkins.

Brownlee, S., & Dattilo, J. (2002). Therapeutic massage as a therapeutic recreation facilitation technique. *Therapeutic Recreation Journal, 36*(4), 369-381.

Brownlee, S., & Dattilo, J. (2011). Therapeutic massage. In J. Dattilo & A. McKeney (Eds.). *Facilitation techniques in therapeutic recreation* (2nd ed.) (pp. 349-373). State College, PA: Venture.

Brutsche, M. H., Grossman, P., Muller, R. E., Wiegand, J., Pello, Baty, F., & Ruch, W. (2008). Impact of laughter on air trapping In severe chronic obstructive lung disease. *International Journal of COPO, 3*(1), 185-192.

Buckle, J. (1997). *Clinical aromatherapy in nursing.* San Diego, CA: Singular.

Buckle, J. (2007). Literature review: Should nursing take aromatherapy more seriously? *British Journal of Nursing, 16*(2), 116-120.

Buckle, J. (2013). Aromatherapy. In B. M. Dossey & L. Keegan (Eds.). *Holistic nursing: A handbook for practice* (6th ed.) (pp. 563-581). Burlington, MA: Jones & Bartlett Learning.

Buettner, L. L., Fitzsimmons, S., & Barba, B. (2011). Animal-assisted therapy for clients with dementia. *Journal of Gerontological Nursing, 37*(5), 10-15.

Buettner, L. L., Wang, Y. C, Stevens, K., Jessup, H., & Magrinat, G. C.(2011). Perceived benefits of animal-assisted therapy in the oncology waiting room. *American Journal of Recreation Therapy, 10*(4), 25-34.

Buffart, L. M., van Uffelen, J. G. Z., Riphagen, I. I., Brug, J., van Mechelen, W., Brown, W.J., & Chinapaw, M. J. M. (2012). Physical and psychological benefits of yoga in cancer patients and survivors, a systematic review and meta-analysis of randomized control trails. *BMC Cancer, 12*(1), 559-586.

Buffone, G. W. (1997). Future directions: The potential for exercise as therapy. In M. L. Sachs, & G. W. Buffone (Eds.), *Running as therapy.* Northvale, NJ: Jason Aronson Inc.

Bulechek, G. M. (1999). *Nursing interventions: Effective nursing treatments* (3rd ed.). Philadelphia, PA: W. B. Saunders Company.

Bullock, C. C. (1987). Recreation and special populations. In A. Graefe, & S. Parker (Eds.), *Recreation: An introductory handbook* (pp. 203-207). State College, PA: Venture.

Bullock, C. C. (1998). The Leisurability model: Implications for the researcher. *Therapeutic Recreation Journal, 32*(2), 97-102.

Bullock, C. C., Austin, D. R., & Lewko, J. H. (1980). Leadership behavior in therapeutic recreation settings. In G. Hitzhusen, J. Elliott, D. J. Szymanski, & M. G. Thompson (Eds.), Expanding horizons in therapeutic recreation (Vol. 7) (pp. 135-139). Columbia, MO: University of Missouri.

Bullock, C. C., & Mahon, M. J. (1997). *Introduction of recreation services for people with disabilities.* Urbana, IL: Sagamore.

Bullock, C. C., Mahon, M. J., & Killingsworth. (2010). *Introduction to recreation services for people with disabilities* (3rd ed.). Urbana, IL: Sagamore.

Burbach, F. R. (1997). The efficacy of physical activity interventions within mental health services: Anxiety and depressive disorders. *Journal of Mental Health, 6*(6), 543-567.

Burkhardt, M. A., & Nathaniel, A. K. (2008). *Ethics and issues in contemporary nursing* (3rd ed.). Clifton Park, NJ: Thomson Delmar Learning.

burlingame, j. (1998). Clinical practice models. In F. Brasile, T. K. Skalko, & j. burlingame (Eds.), *Perspectives in recreational therapy: Issues of a dynamic profession* (pp. 83-106). Ravensdale, WA: Idyll Arbor, Inc.

burlingame, j., & Blaschko, T. M. (2002). *Assessment tools for recreation therapy: Red book #1* (3rd ed.). Ravensdale, WA: Idyll Arbor.

burlingame, j., & Skalko, T. K. (1997). *Idyll Arbor's glossary for therapists.* Ravensdale, WA: Idyll Arbor.

Burnside, I., & Haight, B. (1994). Reminiscence and life review: Therapeutic interventions for older people. *Nurse Practitioner, 19*(4), 55-61.

Burton, G., & Dimbleby, R. (1990). *Teaching communication* (2nd ed.). New York: Routledge.

Bury, T. (1999). Evidence-based healthcare explained. In T. Bury, & J. Mead (Eds.), *Evidence-based healthcare: A practical guide for therapists* (pp. 3-25). Oxford: Butterworth-Heinemann.

Bussing, A., Michalsen, A., Khalsa, S. B. S., Telles, S., & Sherman, K. J. (2012). Effects of yoga on mental and physical health: A short summary of reviews. *Evidence-Based Complementary and Alternative Medicine, 2012,* Article ID 165410, 7 pages.

Cable, T. T., & Udd, E. (1988). Therapeutic benefits of a wildlife observation program. *Therapeutic Recreation Journal, 22*(4), 65-70.

Cabral, P., Meyer, H. B., & Ames, D. (2011). Effectiveness of yoga therapy as a complementary treatment for major psychiatric disorders: A meta-analysis. *The Primary Care Companion for CNS Disorders, 13*(4). 16 pages. Retrieved from http://www.ncbi.nih.gov/pmc/articles/PMC3219516/?report

Cacioppo, J. T., Fowler, J. H., & Christakis, N. A. (2009). Alone in the crowd: The structure and spread of loneliness in a large social network. *Journal of Personality and Social Psychology, 97*(6), 977-991.

Cain, D. J. (2002). Defining characteristics, history, and evolution of humanistic psychotherapies. In D. J. Cain, & J. Seeman (Eds.), *Humanistic psychotherapies: Handbook of research and practice* (pp. 3-54). Washington, D.C.: American Psychological Association.

Caldwell, K., Harrison, M., Adams, M., & Triplett, N. T. (2009). Effect of Pilates and taiji quan training on self-efficacy, sleep quality, mood, and physical performance of college students. *Journal of Bodywork and Movement Therapies, 13,* 155-163.

Caldwell, L. L. (2001). Reflections on therapeutic recreation and youth: Possibilities for broadening horizons. *Therapeutic Recreation Journal, 35*(4), 279-288.

Caldwell, L. L., Adolph, S., & Gilbert, A. (1989). Caution! Leisure counselors at work: Long-term effects of leisure counseling. *Therapeutic Recreation Journal, 23*(3), 41-49.

Callaghan, P. (2004). Exercise: A neglected intervention in mental health care? *Journal of Psychiatric and Mental Health Nursing, 11,* 476-483.

Caminiti, G., Volterrani, M., Marazzi, G., Cerrito, A., Massaro, R., Arisi, A. Franchinl, A., Sposato, B., & Rosano, G. (2011). Tai Chi enhances the effects of endurance training in the rehabilitation of elderly patients with chronic heart failure. *Rehabilitation Research and Practice,* Article ID 761958, 6 pages.

Campbell, T., & Jones, E. (2000). Aromatherapy. In R. A. Charman (Ed.), *Complementary therapies for physical therapists* (pp. 231-246). Boston, MA: Butterworth-Heinemann.

Camping, P. (2001). Therapeutic communities. *Advances in Psychiatric Treatment, 7,* 365-372.

Campos, L., & McCormick, P. (1980). *Introduce yourself to transactional analysis: A TA primer* (5th ed.). Stockton, CA: San Joaquin TA Institute.

Capuzzi, D., Gross, D., & Friel, S. E. (1990). Recent trends; group work with elders. *Generations,* January 1, 1990.

Carlson, C. R., & Hoyle, R. H. (1993). Efficacy of abbreviated progressive muscle relaxation training: A quantitative review of behavioral medicine research. *Journal of Consulting and Clinical Psychology, 61*(6), 1059-1067.

Carpenter, S. (2001). A new reason for keeping a diary. *Monitor on Psychology, 32*(8), 68-70.

Carr, A. (2000). *Family therapy: Concepts, process and practice.* New York: John Wiley & Sons.

Carrington, P. (1993). Modern forms of meditation. In P. M. Lehrer, & R. L. Woolfolk (Eds.), *Principles and practices of stress management* (2nd ed.). New York: The Guilford Press.

Carruthers, C., & Hood, C. D. (2007). Building a life of meaning through therapeutic recreation: The Leisure and Well-Being Model, Part 1. *Therapeutic Recreation Journal, 41*(4), 276-297.

Carson, R. C., Butcher, J. N., & Mineka, S. (2000). *Abnormal psychology and modern life* (11th ed.). Boston, MA: Allyn and Bacon.

Carson, V. B., & Trubowitz, J. (2006). Relevant theories and therapies for nursing practice. In E. M. Varcarolis, V. B. Carson, & N. C. Shoemaker (Eds.), *Foundations of psychiatric mental health nursing: A clinical approach* (5th ed.). St. Louis, MO: Saunders Elsevier.

Carter, M., & Stephenson, J. (2012). The use of multi-sensory environments in schools servicing children with severe disabilities. *Journal of Developmental and Physical Disabilities, 24,* 95-109.

Carter, M. J., & Messerly, D. (2001). Therapy in a bag: Arts and crafts interventions. In G. Hitzhusen, & L. Thomas (Eds.), *Expanding horizons in therapeutic recreation XIX.* Columbia: University of Missouri, pp. 112-122.

Carter, M. J., Van Andel, G. E., & Robb, G. M. (1995). *Therapeutic recreation: A practical approach* (3rd ed.). Prospect Heights, IL: Waveland.

Carter, M. J., Van Andel, G. E., & Robb, G. M. (2003). *Therapeutic recreation: A practical approach* (3rd ed.). Prospect Heights, IL: Waveland.

Carter, M. J., Van Andel, G. E., & Robb, G. M. (2011). *Therapeutic recreation: A practical approach* (4th ed.). Prospect Heights, IL: Waveland.

Cass, M. A. (1993). *Adventure therapy: Therapeutic applications of adventure programming.* Dubuque, IA: Kendall/Hunt.

Cassetta, R. A. (1993). Healing through caring touch. *The American Nurse,* July/August, p.18.

Castleman, M. (2000). *Blended medicine: The best choices in healing.* New York: Rodale.

Cattan, M., White, M., Bond, J., & Learmouth, A. (2005). Preventing social isolation and loneliness among older people: A systematic review of health promotion interventions. *Aging & Society, 25,* 41-67.

Cautela, J. R. (1990). *Behavior analysis forms for clinical intervention, volume 1.* Cambridge, MA: Cambridge Center for Behavioral Studies.

Cautela, J. R., & Groden, J. (1978). *Relaxation.* Champaign, IL: Research Press.

Cemalcilar, Z., Canbeyli, R., & Sunar, D. (2003). Learned helplessness. therapy, and personality traits: An experimental study. *The Journal of Social Psychology, 143*(1), 65-81.

Center for Disease Control. (1987). Recommendations for prevention of HIV transmission in health-care centers. MMWR, 36, suppl. 25.

Center for Pet Therapy. (n.d.). Center for pet therapy highlights third annual therapeutic recreation forum of New York State Recreation and Park Society. New York: Author.

Centers for Disease Control and Prevention (2006). New standard for assessing health status of people with disabilities: International Classification of Functioning, Disability and Health. Retrieved from http://www.cdc.gov/hcbddd/dh/assessingheatlh.htm

Centers for Disease Control and Prevention. (2008). How HIV is and is not transmitted. Retrieved from http://www.cdc.gov/hiv/resources/qa/hoax1.htm

Centers for Disease Control and Prevention. (2010). Physical activity is essential to healthy aging. Retrieved from http://www.edc.gov/physicalactivity/everyone/guidelines/olderadults.html

Centers for Disease Control and Prevention. (2011a). Adult obesity facts. Retrieved from http://www.cdc.gov/obesity/data/adult.html

Centers for Disease Control and Prevention. (2011b). How much physical activity do children need? Retrieved from http://www.cdc.gov/physicalactivity/everyone/guidelines/children.html

Centers for Disease Control and Prevention. (2011c). How much physical activity do adults need? Retrieved from http://www.cdc.gov/physicalactivity/everyone/guidelines/adults.html

Centers for Disease Control and Prevention. (2011d). How much physical activity do older adults need? Retrieved from http://www.cdc.gov/physicalactivity/everyone/guidelines/olderadults.html

Centers for Disease Control and Prevention. (2011e). Physical activity for arthritis. Retrieved from http://www.cdc.gov/arthritis/pa_factsheet.htm

Centers for Disease Control and Prevention. (2011f). Obesity: Halting the epidemic by making health easier. Retrieved from http://www.cdc.gov/chronicdisease/resources/publications/AAG/obesity.htm

Centers for Disease Control and Prevention. (2012a). Basic infection control and prevention plan for outpatient oncology settings. IV. Standard precautions. Retrieved from http://www.cdc.gov/HAI/settings/outpatient/basic-infection-control-prevention-plan-2011/standard-precautions.html

Centers for Disease Control and Prevention. (2012b). Basic infection control and prevention plan for outpatient oncology settings. I. Fundamental principles of infection prevention. Retrieved from http://www.cdc.gov/HAI/settings/outpatient/basic-infection-control-prevention-plan-2011/fundamental-of-infection-prevention.html

Centers for Disease Control and Prevention. (2012c). Basics about childhood obesity. Retrieved from http:www.cdc.gov/obesity/childhood/basics.html

Centers for Disease Control and Prevention. (2012d). Causes and consequences. Retrieved from http://www.cdc.gov/obesity/adult/causes/index.html

Centers for Disease Control and Prevention. (2012e). Stroke fact sheet. Retrieved from http://www.cdc.gov/dhdsp/data_statistics/fact_sheets/fs_stroke.htm Centers for Disease Control and Prevention. (2012e). Defining overweight and obesity. Retrieved from http://www/cdc.gov/obesity/adult/defining.html

Chakravorty, D., Trunnell, E. P., & Ellis, G. D. (1995). Ropes course participation and postactivity processing in transient depressed mood on hospitalized adult psychiatric patients. *Therapeutic Recreation Journal, 29*(2), 104-113.

Chan, S. W., Thompson, D. R., Chau, J. P .C., Tam, W. W. S., Chiu, I. W. S., & Lo, S. H. S. (2010). The effects of multisensory therapy on behaviour of adult clients with developmental disabilities—a systematic review. *International Journal of Nursing Studies, 47*(1), 108-122.

Chartier, M. R. (1981). Clarity of expression in interpersonal communication. *Journal of Nursing Administration, 11*(7), 42-48.

Charting made incredibly easy! (4th ed.). (2010). Philadelphia, PA: Lippincott Williams & Wilkins.

Chen, H., & Guo, X. (2008). Obesity and functional disability among elder Americans. *Journal of the American Geriatric Society, 56*(4), 689-694.

Chen, K-M., Chen, M-H., Lin, M-H., Fan, J-T., Lin, H-S.,& Li, C-H. (2010a). Effect of yoga on sleep quality and depression in elders in assisted living facilities. *Journal of Nursing Research, 18*(1), 53-61.

Chen, K-M., Fan, J-T., Wang, H-H., Wu, S-J., Li, C-H., & Lin, H-S. (2010b). Silver yoga exercises improved physical fitness of transitional frail elders. *Nursing Research, 50*(5), 364-370.

Chen, K-M., Hsu, Y-C., Chen, W-T., & Tseng, H-F. (2007). Well-being of institutionalized elders after Yang-style Tai Chi practice. *Journal of Clinical Nursing, 16*, 845-852.

Chen, K-M., & Tseng, W-S. (2008). Pilot-testing the effects of a newly-developed silver yoga exercise program for female seniors. *Journal of Nursing Research, 16*(1), 37-45.

Chen, W-C., Chu, H., Lu, R-B., Chou, Y-H., Chen, C-H., Chang, Y-C., O'Brien, A.P., & Chou, K-R. (2009). Efficacy of progressive muscle relaxation training in reducing anxiety in patients with acute schizophrenia. *Journal of Clinical Nursing, 18*, 2187-2196.

Cherniss, C. (1980). *Professional burnout in human service organizations.* New York: Praeger.

Cherry, B., & Bridges, R. A. (2005). Staffing and nursing care delivery models. In B. Cherry & S. R. Jocob (Eds.), *Contemporary nursing: Issues, trends, and management* (3rd ed.) (pp. 443-466). St. Louis, MO: Elsevier Mosby.

Chiang, K-J., Chu, H., Chang, H., Chung, M., Chen, C., Chiou, H., & Chou, K. (2010). The effects of reminiscence therapy on psychological well-being, depression, and loneliness among the institutionalized aged. *International Journal of Geriatric Psychiatry, 25*, 380-388.

Child Life Program. (2007). Mount Sinai Department of Pediatrics. Retrieved from http://www.mssm.edu/peds/spec_clife.shtml

Childs, A. (2000). Therapeutic touch. In R. A. Charman (Ed.), *Complementary therapies for physical therapists* (pp. 100-107). Boston: Butterworth-Heinemann.

Chinn, P. L., & Kramer, M. K. (1999). *Theory and nursing: Integrated knowledge development* (5th ed.). St. Louis: Mosby.

Christopher, C.J., & Cochrane, L.M. (1999). Physical activity and asthma. *Current Opinion In Pulmonary Medicine, 5*(1), 68-76.

Churchill, J.D., Galvez, R., Colcombe, S., Swain, R.A., Kramer, A.F., & Greenough, W.T. (2002). Exercise, experience and the aging brain. *Neurobiology of Aging, 23*, 941-955.

Clark, C.C. (2009). *Group leadership skills* (5th ed.). New York: Springer.

Coats, B. (1989). *Runner's World training log.* Emmaus, PA: Rodale.

Cohen, R. G., & Lipkin, G. B. (1979). *Therapeutic group work for health professionals.* New York: Springer.

Cohen, S. S. (1987). *The magic of touch.* New York: Harper & Row.

Colberg, S. R. (2012). Physical activity: The forgotten tool for type 2 diabetes management. *Frontiers in Endocrinology, 31*(3), Article 70, 1-6.

Cole, M. B. (1993). *Group dynamics in occupational therapy.* Thorofare, NJ: SLACK Incorporated.

Cole, M. B. (2005). *Group dynamics in occupational therapy* (3rd ed.). Thorofare, NJ: SLACK Incorporated.

Colgrove, Y. S., Sharma, N., Kluding, P., Potter, D., Imming, K., VandeHoef, J., Stanhope, J., Hoffman, K., & White, K. (2012). Effect of yoga on motor function in people with Parkinson's Disease: A randomized, controlled pilot study. *Journal of Yoga & Physical Therapy, 2*(2). Retrieved from http://www.omicsonline.org/2159-7595/2157-7595-2-112.php?aid=6073

College of Respiratory Therapists of Ontario. (2005). Professional practice guidelines: Documentation. Retrieved from http://www.crto.on.ca/pdf/documentation-ppg.pdf

Collins, C. C., & O'Callaghan. (2008). The impact of horticultural responsibility on health indicators and quality of life in assisted living. *Hort-Technology, 18*(4), 611-618.

Colton, H. (1983). *Touch therapy.* New York: Zebra Books, Kensington.

Combs, A. W. (1989). *A theory of therapy.* Newbury Park, CA: Sage.

Combs, M. L., & Slaby, D. A. (1977). Social skills training with children. In B. B. Lahey, & A. E. Kazdin (Eds.), *Advances in clinical child psychology*, 1. New York: Plenum Press.

Complete guide to documentation (2nd ed.). (2008). Philadelphia, PA: Lippincott Williams & Wilkins.

Complete guide to Pilates, yoga, meditation, stress relief. (2006). New York: Barnes & Noble.

Compton, D., Witt, P. A., & Sanchez, B. (1980). Leisure counseling. *Parks and Recreation, 15*(8), 23-27.

Cone, J. D. (2001). *Evaluating outcomes: Empirical tools for effective practice.* Washington, D.C.: American Psychological Association.

Conn, V. S., Minor, M. A., Burks, K. J., Rantz, M. J., & Pomeroy, S. H. (2003). Integrative review of physical activity intervention research with aging adults. *Journal of the American Geriatrics Society, 51*(8), 1159-1168.

Connolly, M. L. (1977). Leisure counseling: A values clarification and assertive training approach. In A. Epperson, P. A. Witt, & G. Hitzhusen (Eds.), *Leisure counseling: An aspect of leisure education.* Springfield, IL: Charles C. Thomas.

Conrad, A., & Roth, W.T. (2007). Muscle relaxation therapy for anxiety disorders: It works but how? *Journal of Anxiety Disorders, 21*, 243-264.

Constable, J. F., & Russell, D. W. (1986). The effect of social support and the work environment upon burnout among nurses. *Journal of Human Stress, 12*(2), 20-26.

Constantine, M. G. (2003). Multicultural competencies in supervision: Issues, processes, and outcomes. In D. B. Pope-Davis, H. L. K. Coleman, W. M. Liu, & R. L. Toporek (Eds.). *Handbook of multicultural competencies: In counseling and psychology* (pp. 383-391). Thousand Oaks, CA: Sage.

Conyers, J. K., Malkin, M. J., & Yang, H. (2011). An exploratory study on the effects of Nintendo Wii™ balance board on balance retraining and body mass index of adolescents with a traumatic brain injury. *American Journal of Recreation Therapy, 10*(2), 38-48.

Cook, A. M., & Hussey, S. M. (2002). *Assistive technologies: Principles and practices* (2nd ed.). St. Louis, MO: Mosby.

Cooke, B., & Ernst, E. (2009). Aromatherapy: A systematic review. *British Journal of General Practice, 50*, 493-496.

Coopersmith, S. (1967). *The antecedents of self-esteem.* San Francisco, CA: W. H. Freeman and Company.

Corbin, C. B, Lindsey, R., Welk, G. J., & Corbin, W. R. (2001). *Fundamental concepts of fitness and wellness.* Boston, MA: McGraw Hill.

Corbin, D. E., & Mental-Corbin, J. (1983). *Reach for it: A handbook of exercise and dance activities for older adults.* Dubuque, IA: Eddie Bowers.

Corey, G. (2012). *Theory and practice of group counseling* (8th ed.). Belmont, CA: Brooks/Cole.

Corey, G., Haynes, R., Moulton, P., & Muratori, M. (2010). *Clinical supervision in the helping professions* (2nd ed.). Alexandria, VA: American Counseling Association.

Corey, M. S., & Corey, G. (2006). *Groups: Process and practice* (7th ed.). Pacific Grove, CA: Thomson Brooks/Cole.

Coriolano Appell, I. P., Perez, V. R., de Maio Nascimento, M., & Appell Coriolano, H. J. (2012). The Pilates method to improve body balance in the elderly. *Archives of Exercise in Health and Disease, 3*(3), 188-193.

Cory, L., McKenney, A., & Marsden, S. (2011). Therapeutic use of animals. In J. Dattilo & A. McKenney (Eds.), *Facilitation techniques in therapeutic recreation* (2nd ed.)(pp. 403-440.). State College, PA: Venture.

Cormier, S., & Hackney, H. (2005). *Counseling strategies and interventions* (6th ed.). Boston, MA: Pearson.

Cormier, W. H., & Cormier, S. (1998). *Interviewing strategies for helpers: Fundamental skills and cognitive behavioral interventions* (4th ed.). Pacific Grove, CA: Brooks/Cole.

Cornwell, E. Y., & Waite, L. J. (2009). Social disconnectedness, perceived isolation, and health among older adults. *Journal of Health and Social Behavior, 50*(1), 31-58.

Correll, C. U., Leucht, S., & Kane, J. M. (2004). Lower risk for tardive dyskinesia associated with second-generation antipsychotics: A systematic review of 1-year studies. *American Journal of Psychiatry, 161*, 414-425.

Cotman, C. W., & Berchtold, N. C. (2002). Exercise: A behavioral intervention to enhance brain health and plasticity. *Trends In Neurosciences, 25*(6), 295-301.

Cotman, C. W., & Engesser-Cesar, C. (2002). Exercise enhances and protects brain function. *Sport Sciences Reviews, 30*(2), 75-79.

Cousins, N. (1979). *Anatomy of an illness.* New York: Bantam Books.

Cousins, N. (1983). *The healing heart.* New York: Avon Books.

Cowen, E. L., & Kilmer, R. P. (2002). Positive psychology: Some pluses and some open issues. *Journal of Community Psychology, 30*(4), 449-460.

Cox, R. H. (2002). *Sport psychology: Concepts and applications* (5th ed.). Boston, MA: McGraw-Hill Higher Education.

Craig, J. V., & Smyth, R. L. (2007). *The evidence-based practice manual for nurses* (2nd ed.). Philadelphia: Churchill Livingstone Elsevier.

Craighead, L. W., Craighead, W. E., Kazdin, A. E., & Mahoney, M. J. (1994). *Cognitive and behavioral interventions.* Boston, MA: Allyn and Bacon.

Crain, D. J. (2002). Defining characteristics, history, and evolution of humanistic psychotherapies. In D. J. Crain, & J. Seeman (Eds.), *Humanistic psychotherapies: Handbook of research and practice* (pp. 3-54). Washington, D.C.: American Psychological Association.

Cramer, H., Lauche, R., Haller, H., Langhorst, J., Dobos, G., & Berger, B. (2011). "I'm more in balance": A qualitative study of yoga for patients with chronic neck pain. *The Journal of Alternative and Complementary Medicine, 18*, 1-7.

Creasia, J. L., & Friberg, E. E. (2010). *Conceptual foundations: The bridge to professional nursing practice* (5th ed.). Philadelphia, PA: Elsevier.

Creek, J. (2010). *The core concepts of occupational therapy.* Philadelphia, PA: Jessica Kingsley Publishers.

Crider, D. A., & Klinger, W. R. (2001). *Stretch your mind and body: Tai chi as an adaptive activity.* State College, PA: Venture.

Critchley, D. L. (1995). Play therapy. In B. S. Johnson (Ed.), *Child, adolescent and family psychiatric nursing.* Philadelphia, PA: J. B. Lippincott Company.

Crizzle, A. M., & Newhouse, I.J . (2006). Is physical exercise beneficial for persons with Parkinson's Disease? *Clinical Journal of Sport Medicine, 16*(5), 422-425.

Cronan, M. K., Shinew, K. J., & Stodolska, M. (2008). Trail use among Latinos: Recognizing diverse uses among a specific population. *Journal of Park and Recreation Administration, 26*(1), 62-86.

Cruz-Ferreira, A., Fernandes, J., Gomes, D., Bernardo, L. M., Kirkcaldy, B. D., Barbosa, T. M., & Silva, A. (2011). Effects of Pilates-based exercises on life satisfaction, physical self-concept and health status in adult women. *Women & Health, 51*, 240-255.

Cruz-Ferreira, A., Fernandes, J., Laranjo, L., & Bernardo, L.M. (2011). A systematic review of the effects of Pilates method of exercise in health people. *Archives in Physical Medicine and Rehabiitation, 92*, 2071-2081.

Csikszentmihalyi, M. (1996). *Creativity.* New York: Harper Collins.

Cutcliffe, J. R., Butterworth, T., & Proctor, B. (2001). *Fundamental themes in clinical supervision.* New York: Routledge.

Dahnke, M., & Dreher, H. M. (2006) Defining ethics and applying the therories. In V. D. Lachman (Ed.), *Applied ethics in nursing* (pp. 3-13). New York: Springer.

Dainow, S., & Bailey, C. (1988). *Developing skill with people: Training for person-to-person client contact.* New York: Wiley.

Dalgas, U., Stenager, E., & Ingermann-Hansen, T. (2008). Multiple sclerosis and physical exercise; Recommendations for the application of resistance-, endurance- and combined training. *Multiple Sclerosis, 14*, 35-53.

Danesh, H., Serban, S., Herrera, J. (2011). Yoga as an intervention for low back pain. *Current Concepts and Treatment Strategies, 27*(4), 1-11.

d'Angelo, R. (2002). Aromatherapy. In S. Shannon (Ed.), *Handbook of complementary and alternative therapies in mental health* (pp. 71 - 92). San Diego, CA: Academic Press.

Danhauer, S. C., Mihalko, S. L., Russell, G. B., Campbell, C. R., Felder, L., Daley, K., & Levine, E. A. (2009). Restorative yoga for women with breast cancer: Findings from a randomized pilot study. *Psycho-Oncology, 18*(4), 360-368.

Darzins, P., Fone, S., & Darzins, S. (2006). The International Classification of Functioning, Disability and Health can help to structure and evaluate therapy. *Australian Occupational Therapy Journal, 53*, 127-131.

Dattilo, J. (2008). *Leisure education program planning: A systematic approach* (3rd ed.). State College, PA: Venture.

Dattilo, J., Kleiber, D. A., & Williams, R. (1998). Self-determination and enjoyment enhancement: A psychologically based service delivery model for therapeutic recreation. *Therapeutic Recreation Journal, 32*, 258-271.

Dattilo, J., & McKenney, A. (2011). *Facilitation techniques in therapeutic recreation* (2nd ed.). State College, PA: Venture.

Dattilo, J., & Murphy, W. D. (1987). Facilitating the challenge in adventure recreation for persons with disabilities. *Therapeutic Recreation Journal, 21*(3), 14-21.

Dattilo, J., & Williams, R. (2011). Leisure education. In J. Dattilo & A. McKenney (Eds.), *Facilitation techniques in therapeutic recreation* (2nd ed.) (pp. 187-220). State College, PA: Venture.

Dattilo, J., Williams, R., & Cory, L. (2003). Effects of computerized leisure education on knowledge of social skills of youth with intellectual disabilities. *Therapeutic Recreation Journal, 37*(2), 142-155.

Dattilo, J., & Wingate, I. (2011). Therapeutic use of T'ai Chi. In J. Dattilo & A. McKenney (Eds.), *Facilitation Techniques in Therapeutic Recreation* (2nd ed.) (pp. 283-318). State College, PA: Venture.

Dattilo, J., & Wolfe, B. (2002). Behavior modification in therapeutic recreation: Observing behaviors and applying consequences. In D. R. Austin, J. Dattilo, J., & B. P. McCormick (Eds.), *Conceptual foundations for therapeutic recreation* (pp. 31-48). State College, PA: Venture.

David, D. (1990). Reminiscence, adaptation, and social context in old age. *International Journal of Aging and Human Development, 30*(3), 175-188.

Davidhizar, R., & Giger, J. N. (1997). When touch is *not* the best approach. *Journal of Clinical Nursing, 6*, 203-206.

Davis, J. B. (1997). Garden stroll offers therapeutic benefits. The *Denver Post*, Nov. 27, 1997, p. 4E.

Davis, M., Eshelman, E. R., & McKay, M. (2008). *The relaxation and stress reduction workbook* (6th ed.). Oakland, CA: New Harbinger.

Davis, P. (1995). Aromatherapy: An a-z. New York: Barnes & Noble Books.

DeAngelis, T. (2012). A second life for practice? *Monitor on Psychology, 43*(3), 48-51.

Dearholt, S. L., & Dang, D. (2012). *Johns Hopkins nursing evidence-based practice: Model and guidelines* (2nd ed.). Indianapolis: Sigma Theta Tau International.

Debriefing cooperative games. (nd). Retrieved from http://peacegamesnetwork.googlepages.com/DebriefingCooperativeGames.pdf

Deci, E. L., & Ryan, R. M. (1985). *Intrinsic motivation and self-determination in human behavior.* New York: Plenum Press.

DeCourcey, M., Russell, A. C., & Keister, K. J. (2010). Animal-Assisted Therapy. *Dimensions of Critical Care Nursing, 29*(5), 211-214.

Deig, L. (1989). Reminiscence. Unpublished paper. Bloomington, IN: Indiana University.

DeNoon, D. J. (2010). Study: People who spend most leisure time sitting die soonest. Retrieved from http://women.webmd.com/news/20100722/sit-more-die-sooner

Deplanque, D., Masse, I., Libersa, C., Leys, D., & Bordet, R. (2012). Previous leisure-time physical activity dose dependently decreases ischemic stroke severity. *Stroke Research and Treatment, 2012*, Article ID 614925, 6 pages.

DeSalvatore, H. G. (1989). Therapeutic recreators as family therapists: Working with families on a children's psychiatric unit. *Therapeutic Recreation Journal, 23*(2), 23-29.

DeSalvatore, H. G., & Rosenman, D. (1986). The parent-child activity group: Therapeutic activities to use in parent-child interactions. *Child Care Quarterly, 15*, 211-222.

Deschenes, N., Clark, H. B., Herrygers, J., Blase, K., & Wagner, R. (2010). *Transition to independence process (TIP) system: Module 1: Strengths discovery and needs assessment.* Retrieved from http://www.tipstars.org/Portals/0/pdf/Mod1-StrengthsDiscovery.pdf

Deslandes, A., Moraes, H., Ferreira, C., Veiga, H., Silveira, H., Mouta, R., …& Laks, J. (2009). Exercise and mental health: Many reasons to move. *Neuropsychobiology, 59*, 191-198.

Devine, M. A.(2011). Expressive arts as therapeutic media. In J. Dattilo & A. McKenney (Eds.), *Facilitation techniques in therapeutic recreation* (2nd ed.) (pp. 153-186). State College, PA: Venture.

Dhikav, V., Karmarkar, G., Gupta, M., & Anand, K. S. (2007). Yoga in premature ejaculation: A comparative trail with fluoxetine. *The Journal of Sexual Medicine, 4*, 1726-1732.

Dhikav, V., Karmarkar, G., Verma, M., Gupta, M., Mittal, D., & Anard, K. (2010). Yoga in male sexual functioning: A noncomparative pilot study. *The Journal of Sexual Medicine, 7*, 3460-3466.

DiClemente, C. C., & Velasquez, M. M. (2002). Motivational interviewing and stages of change. In W. R. Miller, & S. Rollnick (Eds.), *Motivational interviewing: Preparing for change* (2nd ed.) (pp. 201-216). New York: The Guilford Press.

Diebert, A. N., & Harmon, A. J. (1977). *New tools for changing behavior.* Champaign, IL: Research Press.

Dieleman, H., & Huisingh, D. (2006). Games by which to learn and teach about sustainable development: Exploring the relevance of games and experimental learning for sustainability. *Journal of Cleaner Production, 14*(9), 837-847.

Dieser, R. B., & Ruddell, E. (2002). Effects of attribution retraining during therapeutic recreation on attributions and explanatory styles of adolescents with depression. *Therapeutic Recreation Journal, 36*(1), 35-47.

DiPietro, L. (2012). Physical activity, fitness, and aging. In C. Bouchard, S. N. Blair, & W. L. Haskell (Eds.), *Physical activity and health* (2nd ed.) (pp. 303-316). Champaign, IL: Human Kinetics.

Ditor, D. S., Latimer, A. E., Martin Ginis, K. A., Arbour, K. P., McCartney, N., & Hicks, A. L. (2003). Maintenance of exercise participation in individuals with spinal cord injury: Effects on quality of life, stress and pain. *Spinal Cord, 41*, 446-450.

Dolbier, C. L., & Rush, T. E. (2012). Efficacy of abbreviated progressive muscle relaxation in a high-stress college sample. *International Journal of Stress Management, 19*(1), 48-68.

Doman, G., Wilkinson, R., Dimancescu, M. D., & Pelligra, R. (1993). The effect of intense multi-sensory stimulation on coma arousal and recovery. *Neuropsychological Rehabilitation, 3*(2), 203-212.

Donaghy, M. E. (2007). Exercise can seriously improve mental health: Fact or fiction? *Advances in Physiotherapy, 9*, 76-88.

Donaldson, S. I., Csikszentmihalyi, M., & Nakamura, J. (2011). *Applied positive psychology.* New York: Psychology Press.

Dossey, B. M., Keegan, L., & Guzzetta, C. E. (2000). *Holistic nursing: A handbook for practice* (3rd ed.). Gaithersburg, MD: Aspen Publishers, Inc.

Dowing, G. (1972). *The message book.* New York: Bookworks/Random House.

Dreifuss, F. E. (1988). What is epilepsy? In H. Reisner (Ed.), *Children with epilepsy.* Kensington, MD: Woodbine House.

Driscoll, J., & O'Sullivan, J. (2007). The place of clinical supervision in modern healthcare. In J. Driscoll (Ed.), *Practising clinical supervision* (2nd ed.) (pp. 3-26). New York: Bailliere Tindall Elsevier.

Driscoll, J., & Townsend, A. (2007). Alternative methods in clinical supervision: Beyond the face-to-face encounter. In J. Driscoll (Ed.), *Practising clinical supervision* (2nd ed.) (pp. 141-162). New York: Bailliere Tindall Elsevier.

Driver, S., O'Connor, J., Lox, C. & Rees, K. (2004). Evaluation of an aquatic programme on fitness parameters of individuals with a brain injury. *Brain Injury, 18*, 847-859.

Druss, R. G. (2007). Intensive supervision. *American Journal of Psychiatry, 164*(2), 215-216.

Du, B., & King, J. (1998). Tai chi: A conditioning exercise. *Recreation and Parks in South Carolina, 13*(1), 6, 7.

Duchene, P. M. (2008). Lifestyle and recreation. In S. P. Hoeman (Ed.), *Rehabilitation nursing: Prevention, intervention, and outcomes* (4th ed.) (pp. 586-593). St. Louis, MO: Mosby Elsevier.

Duck, S. (1998). *Human relationships* (3rd ed.). London: SAGE Publications.

Duckworth, A. L., Steen, T. A., & Seligman, M. E. P. (2004). Positive psychology in clinical practice. *Annual Review of Clinical Psychology, 1*, 629-651.

Dunham, G. (2011). The future at hand: Mobile devices and apps in clinical practice. *The ASHA Leader*, April 5, 2011, 2 pages.

Dunn, H. L. (1961). *High-level wellness.* Arlington, VA: R. W. Beatty.

Dunn, J. D. (1989). Guidelines for using published assessment procedures. *Therapeutic Recreation Journal, 23*(2), 59-69.

Dupuis, S. L., & Pedlar, A. (1995). Family leisure programs In institutional care settings: Buffering the stress of caregivers. *Therapeutic Recreation Journal, 29*(3), 184-205.

Durana, C. (1998). The use of touch In psychotherapy: Ethical and clinical guidelines. *Psychotherapy, 35*(2), 269-280.

Dusay, J. M., & Dusay, K. M. (1984). Transactional analysis. In R. J. Corsini (Ed.), *Current psychotherapies* (3rd ed.). Itasca, IL: F. E. Peacock.

Dusek-Girdano, D. (1979). Stress reduction through physical activity. In D. Girdano, & G. Everly (Eds.), *Controlling stress and tension: A holistic approach.* Englewood Cliffs, NJ: Prentice-Hall.

Duxbury, J. (2000). *Difficult patients.* Boston, MA: Butterworth-Heinemann.

Dvorak, D. (nd). Laughter yoga—newest exercise craze. Retrieved from http://www.nywellnessguide.com/yoga/070515-LaughingYoga.asp

Dyer, J. A., & Stotts, M. L. (2005). *Handbook of remotivation therapy.* Binghamton, NY: The Haworth Press, Inc.

Eaton, M., Michell-Bonair, I. L., & Friedman, E. (1989). The effect of touch on nutritional intake of chronic brain syndrome patients. *Journal of Gerontology, 41*, 611-616.

Edelman, C., & Mandle, C. (2006). *Health promotion throughout the lifespan* (6th ed.). Philadelphia, PA: Mosby/Elsevier.

Edelwich, J., & Brodsky, A. (1980). *Burn-out: Stages of disillusionment in the helping professions.* New York: Human Science Press.

Edwards, D., Burnard, P., Hannigan, B., Cooper, L., Adams, J., Juggessur, T., Fothergil, A., & Coyle, D. (2006). Clinical supervision and burnout: The influence of clinical supervison for community mental health nurses. *Journal of Clinical Nursing, 15*(8), 1007-1015.

Egan, G. (2009). *The skilled helper: A problem-management approach to helping* (9th ed.). Belmont, CA: Brooks/Cole.

eHow. (2012). How to get down the stairs in a wheelchair. Retrieved from http://www.ehow.com/how_5084755_down-stairs-wheelchair.html

Eisenberg, S., & Delaney, D. J. (1986). *The counseling process* (2nd ed.). Chicago: Rand McNally College Publishing Company.

Eisenberg, S., & Patterson, L. E. (1977). *Helping clients with special concerns.* Chicago: Rand McNally College Publishing Company.

Ekkekakis, P., Hall, E. E., VanLanduyt, L. M., & Petruzzello, S. J. (2000). Walking in (affective) circles: Can short walks enhance affect? *Journal of Behavioral Medicine, 23*(3), 245-275.

Elings, M. (2006). People-plant interaction. In J. Hassink & M. van Dijk (Eds.), *Farming for health* (pp. 43-55). New York: Springer.

Eliopoulos, C. (2005). Complementary and alternative healing. In B. Cherry, & S. R. Jocob (Eds.), *Contemporary nursing: Issues, trends, & management* (3rd ed.) (pp. 338 - 356). St. Louis, MO: Elsevier Mosby.

Ellis, A. (1976). Rational-emotive therapy. In V. Binder, A. Binder, & B. Rimland (Eds.), *Modern therapies.* Englewood Cliffs, NJ: Prentice-Hall.

Ellis, A. (2000). Rational emotive behavior therapy. In R. J. Corsini, & D. Wedding (Eds.), *Current psychotherapies* (6th ed.) (pp. 168-204). Itasca, IL: F. E. Peacock Publishers, Inc.

Ellis, G. D. (1987). A comparison of major assessment paradigms. Unpublished table. Salt Lake City: University of Utah.

Ellis, M. J. (1973). *Why people play.* Englewood Cliffs, NJ: Prentice-Hall.

Ellmo, W., & Graser, J. (1995). *Adapted adventure activities.* Dubuque, IA: Kendall/Hunt.

Emerson, D., Sharma, R., Chaudhry, S., & Turner, J. (2009). Truma-sensitive yoga: Principles, practice, and research. *International Journal of Yoga Therapy, 19,* 123-128.

Emery, K., De Serres, S. M., McMillan, A., & Cote, J. N. (2010). The effects of a Pilates training program on arm-trunk posture and movement. *Clinical Biomechanics, 25,* 124-130.

Emtner, M., Herala, M., & Stalenheim, G. (1996). High-intensity physical training in adults with asthma: A 10-week rehabilitation program. *CREST Journal, 109*(2), 323-330.

Epilepsy Foundation of America. (1975). *Basic statistics on the epilepsies.* Philadelphia, PA: F. A. Davis Company.

Epilepsy Foundation of America. (2008). First aid. Retrieved from http://www.epilepsyfoundation.org/about/firstaid/index.cfm

Epilepsy school alert. (1974). Landover, MD: Epilepsy Foundation of America.

Erdman, L. (1991). Laughter therapy for patients with cancer. *Oncology Nursing Forum, 18,* 1359-1363.

Erikson, K. I., Voss, M. S., Prakash, S., Basak, C. Szabo, A. Chaddock, L., Kim, J. S., ... & Kramer, A. F. (2010). Exercise training increases size of hippocampus and improves memory. *Proceedings of the National Academy of Sciences, 108*(7), 3017-3022.

Eshref, H. (1999). *Easy exercises to relieve stress.* London: Frances Lincoln Limited.

Esterling, B. A., L'Abate, L., Murry, E. J., & Pennebaker, J. W. (1999). Empirical foundations for writing In prevention and psychotherapy: Mental and physical outcomes. *Clinical Psychology Review, 19*(1), 79-96.

Eveik, D., Yigit, I., Pusak, H., & Kavuncn, V. (2008). Effectiveness of aquatic therapy in the treatment of fibromyalgia syndrome: A randomized controlled open study. *Rheumatology International, 28,* 885-890.

Ewert, A. (1987). Research in outdoor adventure: Overview and analysis. *The Bradford Papers Annual, 2,* 15-28.

Ewert, A. W., McCormick, B. P., & Voight, A. E. (2001). Outdoor experiential therapies: Implications for TR practice. *Therapeutic Recreation Journal, 35*(2), 107-122.

Ewert, A., Voight, A., & Harnishfeger, B. (2002). An overview of therapeutic outdoor programming. In D. R. Austin, J. Dattilo, & B. P. McCormick (Eds.) (pp. 133-150). *Conceptual foundations in therapeutic recreation.* State College, PA: Venture.

Ezell, M. (2001). *Advocating in the human services.* Stamford, CT: Brooks/Cole.

Falender, C. A., Erickson Cornish, J. A., Goodyear, R., Hatcher, R., Kaslow, N.J., Leventhal, G., Shafranske, E., ...& Grus, C. (2004).Defining competencies in psychology supervision: A consensus statement. *Journal of Clinical Psychology, 60*(7), 771-785.

Farnsworth, B. J., & Biglow, A. S. (1997). Psychiatric care management. In J. Haber, B. Krainovich-Miller, A. L. McMahon, & P. Price-Hoskins (Eds.), *Comprehensive psychiatric nursing* (5th ed.). St. Louis, MO: Mosby.

Fave, A., & Massimini, F. (2004). Bringing subjectivity into focus: Optimal experiences, life themes, and person-centered rehabilitation. In P. A. Linley & S. Joseph (Eds.), *Positive psychology in practice* (pp. 581-597). Hoboken, NJ: John Wiley & Sons.

Fawcett, J. (1995). *Analysis of conceptual models of nursing.* Philadelphia, PA: F. A. Davis Co.

Feeley, N., & Gottlieb, L. N. (2000). Nursing approaches for working with family strengths and resources. *Journal of Family Nursing, 6*(1), 9-24.

Feil, N. (2002). *The validation breakthrough: Simple techniques for communicating with people with "Alzheimer's-type dementia"* (2nd ed.). Baltimore, MD: Health Professions Press.

Feinglass, J., Thompson, J. A., He, X. Z., Witt, W., Chang, R. W., & Baker, D. W. (2005). Effect of physical activity on functional status among older middle-age adults with arthritis. *Arthritis & Rheumatism, 53*(6), 879-885.

Feldman, R. S. (1995). *Social psychology.* Englewood Cliffs, NJ: Prentice Hall.

Femal, H. (2012). Healing gardens: Beneficial for patients and staff. *American Therapeutic Recreation Association Newsletter, 28*(1), 3-4.

Ferrini, A. F., & Ferrini, R. L. (2000). *Health in the later years* (3rd ed.). Boston, MA: McGraw Hill.

Fick, K. M. (1993). The influence of an animal on social interactions of nursing home residents in a group setting. *The American Journal of Occupational Therapy, 47*(6), 529-534.

Fidler, G. S., & Fidler, J. W. (1954). *Introduction to psychiatric occupational therapy.* New York: The MacMillan Company.

Field, C. (1989). Reminiscing. Unpublished paper. Bloomington, IN: Indiana University.

Field, T. (1998). Massage therapy effects. *American Psychologist, 53*(12), 1270 - 1281.

Field, T. (2010). Touch for socioemotional and physical well-being: A review. *Developmental Review, 30,* 367-383.

Field, T. (2011). Yoga clinical research review. *Complementary Therapies in Clinical Practice, 17,* 1-8.

Field, T., Diego, M., Cullen, C., Hartshorn, K., Gruskin, A., Hernandez-Reif, M., & Sunshine, W. (2004). Carpal tunnel syndrome symptoms are lessened following massage therapy. *Journal of Bodywork and Movement Therapies, 8,* 9-14.

Field, T., Diego, M., Hernandez-Reif, M., & Shea, J. (2007). Hand arthritis pain is reduced by massage therapy. *Journal of Bodywork and Movement Therapies, 11,* 21-24.

Field, T., Hernandez-Reif, M., Hart, S., Quintino, O., Drose, L., Field, T., Kuhn, C., & Schanberg, S. (1997). Sexual abuse effects are lessened by massage therapy, *Journal of Bodywork and Movement Therapies, 1,* 65-66.

Fikes, C. R. (1976). A description of leisure counseling services in Texas community mental health and mental retardation centers. Unpublished master's thesis. Denton, TX: North Texas State University.

Fillingim, R. B., & Blumenthal, J. S. (1993). The use of aerobic exercise as a method of stress management. In P. M. Lehrer, & R. L. Woolfolk (Eds.), *Principles and practice of stress management* (2nd ed.). NY: The Guilford Press.

Finsch, N. C., & Finsch, L. E. (1998*). Psychiatric mental health nursing: Understanding the client as well as the condition.* Albany, NY: Delmar.

Finsch, N. C., & Frisch, L. E. (2006). *Psychiatric mental heatlh nursing* (3rd ed.). Clifton Park, NY: Thomson Delmar Learning.

Fiore, K. (2012). Exercise benefits In diabetes upheld. *MedPageToday.* Retrieved from http://medpagetoday.com/ Endocrinology/Diabetes/34077

Fitzhugh, E. C., Klein, D., & Hayes, G. (2008). Leisure-time physical activity participation among older adults: Implications for therapeutic recreation specialists. *Annual in Therapeutic Recreation, 16,* 117-128.

Flaskerud, J., & Ungvarski, P. (1999). *Overview and update of HIV disease in HIV/AIDS: A guide to primary care management* (4th ed.). Philadelphia: W. B. Saunders.

Fleming, M., & Bohnel, E. (2009). Use of feature film as part of psychological assessement. *Professional Psychology: Research and Practice, 40*(6), 641-647.

Fletcher, T. B., & Scott, H. J. (2002). Adventure-based counseling: An innovation in counseling. *Journal of Counseling & Development, 80*(3), 277-286.

Flowers, B. J., & Davidov, B. J. (2006). The value of multiculturalism. *American Psychologist, 61*(6), 581-594.

Flowers, B. J., & Richardson, F. C. (1996). Why is multiculturalism good? *American Psychologist, 51,* 609-621.

Flynn, J. M., & Heffron, P. B. (1988). *Nursing: From concept to practice* (2nd ed.). Norwalk, CT: Appleton & Lange.

Flynn, P. A. R. (1980). *Holistic health.* Bowie, MD: Robert J. Brady Co.

Fontaine, K. L., & Kaszubski, W. (2004). *Absolute beginner's guide to alternative medicine.* Indianapolis, IN: Sams Publishing.

Ford, C. W. (1992). *Where healing waters meet touch: Mind and emotion through the body.* Barrytown, NY: Station Hill Press.

Ford, D. H., & Urban, H. B. (1963). *Systems of psychotherapy.* New York: John Wiley & Sons.

Ford, E. S. (2012). Does exercise reduce inflammation? Physical activity and c-reactive protein among U.S. adults. *Epidemiology, 13*(5), 561-568.

Ford, E. S., Heath, G. W., Mannino, D. M., & Redd, S. C. (2003). Leisure-time physical activity patterns among U.S. adults with asthma. *CHEST Journal, 124*(2), 432-437.

Forkner, D. J. (1996). Clinical pathways: Benefits and liabilities. Available at http://www.springnet.com/ce/m611a. htm

Forsblom, A., Laitinen, S., Sarkamo, T., & Tervaniemi, M. (2009). Therapeutic role of music listening in stroke rehabilitation. *Annals of the New York Academy of Sciences, 1169*(1), 426-440.

Fortney, L., & Taylor, M. (2010). Meditation in medical practice: A review of the evidence and practice. *Primary Care Clinical Office Practice, 37,* 81-90.

Foster, G. D., Wadden, T. A., Makris, A. P., Davidson, D., Sanderson, R. S., Allison, D. B., & Kessler, A. (2003). Primary care physician attitudes about obesity and treatment. *Obesity Research, 11*(10), 1168-1177.

Fox, R. (1983). Contracting in supervision: A goal-directed process. *The Clinical Supervisor, 1*(1), 37-49.

Frank, J. D., & Frank, J. B. (1991). *Persuasion and healing* (3rd ed.). Baltimore, MD: The Johns Hopkins University Press.

Franks, C. M. (2006). Behavior therapy. In J. L. Ronch, W. Van Ornum, & N. C. Stilwell (Eds.), *The counseling sourcebook* (pp. 28-43). New York: The Crossroad Publishing Company.

Fredrickson, B. L. (2001). The role of positive emotions in positive psychology: The broaden-and-build theory of positive emotion. *American Psychologist, 56,* 218-226.

Fredrickson, B. L. (2009). *Positivity.* New York: Three Rivers Press.

Fredrickson, B., & Joiner, T. (2002). Positive emotions trigger upward spirals toward emotional well-being. *Psychological Sciences, 13*, 172 – 175.

Freeman, J. M., Vining, E. P. G., & Pillas, D. J. (1990). *Seizures and epilepsy in childhood: A guide for parents.* Baltimore, MD: Johns Hopkins University Press.

Freeman, L. W. (2001a). Meditation. In L. W. Freeman, & G. F. Lawlis (Eds.), *Mosby's complementary and alternative medicine: A research-based approach* (pp. 166-179). St. Louis, MO: Mosby.

Freeman, L. W. (2001b). Therapeutic touch: Healing with energy. In L. W. Freeman, & G. F. Lawlis (Eds.) *Mosby's complementary and alternative medicine: A research-based approach* (pp. 493-506). St. Louis, MO: Mosby.

Freeman, P., & Zabriskie, R. B. (2003). Leisure and family functioning in adoptive families: Implications for therapeutic recreation. *Therapeutic Recreation Journal, 37*(1), 73-93.

French, J., & Raven, B. (1959). The basis for social power. In D. C. Artwright (Ed.), *Studies in social power.* Ann Arbor, MI: Institution for Social Research.

Freudenberger, H. (1975). The staff burnout syndrome in alternative institutions. *Psychotherapy: Theory, research, and practice, 12,* 73-83.

Friedman, H. J. (1985). Horticulture in the treatment of recovering alcoholics. *Leisure Information Quarterly, 11* (3), 5, 6.

Frisch, C. F., & Frisch, L. E. (2002). Individual psychotherapy. In N. C. Frisch, & L. E. Frisch (Eds.), *Psychiatric mental health nursing* (2nd ed.) (pp. 669-681). Albany, NY: Delmar.

Frisch, N. C., & Frisch, L. E. (2006). *Psychiatric mental health nursing* (3rd ed.). Clifton Park, NY: Thomson Delmar Learning.

Frisch, M. B. (2006). *Quality of life therapy: Applying a life satisfaction approach to positive psychology and cognitive therapy.* Hoboken, NJ: John Wiley & Sons.

Frisch, N. C. (2002). Complementary and somatic therapies. In N. C. Frisch, & L. E. Frisch (Eds.), *Psychiatric mental health nursing* (2nd ed.) (pp. 743-757). Albany, NY: Delmar.

Froeliger, B. E., Garland, E. L., Modlin, L. A., & McClernon, F. J. (2012). Neurocognitive correlates of the effects of yoga meditation practice on emotion and cognition: A pilot study. *Frontiers in Integrative Neuroscience, 6,* Article 48, 11 pages. Retrieved from http://www.ncbi.nlm.nih.gov/pmc/articles/PMC3405281/pdf/ fnint-06-00048.pdf

Fry, W. F. (1993). Introduction. In W. F. Fry & W. A. Salameh (Eds.), *Advances in humor and psychotherapy.* Sarasota, FL: Professional Resource Press.

Fry, W. F., & Salameh, W. A. (Eds.). (1993). *Advances in humor and psychotherapy.* Sarasota, FL: Professional Resource Press.

Frye, V., & Peters, M. (1972). *Therapeutic recreation: Its theory, philosophy and practice.* Harrisburg, PA: Stackpole Books.

Funderburk, J.A., & Callis, S. (2010). Aquatic intervention effect on quality of life prior to obesity surgery: A pilot study. *Annual in Therapeutic Recreation, 18,* 66-77.

Furstenburg, F. F., Rhodes, P. S., Powell, S. K., & Dunlop, T. (1984). The effectiveness of pet therapy on nursing home patients suffering with dementia. *Gerontologist, 24,* 245.

Gable, S. L., & Haidt, J. (2005). What (and why) is positive psychology? *Review of General Psychology, 9*(2), 103-110.

Gallace, A., & Spence, C. (2008). The science of interpersonal touch: An overview. *Neuroscience and Biobehavioral Reviews, 14,* 248-259.

Gamberini, L., Barrrfesi, G., Majer, A., & Scarpetta, F. (2008). A game a day keeps the doctor away: A short review of computer games in mental health care. *Journal of Cyber Therapy & Rehabilitation, 1*(2), 127-145.

Garcia-Aymerich, J., Lang, P., Benet, M., Schnohr, P., & Anto, J. M. (2006). Regular physical activity reduces hospital admission and mortality in chronic obstructive pulmonary disease: A population based cohort study. *Thorax, 61,* 772-778.

Garland, K., Beer, E., Eppingstall, B., & O'Connor, D. W. (2007). A comparison of two treatments of agitated behavior In nursing home residents with dementia: Simulated Family presence and preferred music. *American Journal of Geriatric Psychiatry, 15*(6), 514-521.

Gass, M. A. (1993). *Adventure therapy.* Dubuque, IA: Kendall-Hunt.

Gatchel, R. J. (1980). Perceived control: A review and evaluation of therapeutic implications. In A. Baum & J. E. Singer (Eds.), *Advances in environmental psychology: Volume 2. Applications of perceived control.* Hillsdale, NJ: Lawrence Erlbaum Associates, Publishers.

Gayle, J. (1989). Reminiscence as a therapeutic intervention. Unpublished paper. Bloomington, IN: Indiana University.

Geist, T. S. (2011). Conceptual framework for animal Assisted Therapy. *Child & Adolescent Social Work Journal, 28,* 243-256.

Gelkopf, M. (2011). The use of humor in serious mental illness: A review. *Evidence-Based Complementary and Alternative Medicine, Volume 2011*, Article ID 342837, 8 pages.

Gelkopf, M., Gonen, B., Kurs, R., Melamed, Y., & Bleich. (2006). The effect of humorous movies on Inpatients with chronic schizophrenia. *The Journal of Nervous and Mental Disease, 194*(11), 880-883.

Gelkopf, M., Kreitler, S., & Sigal, M. (1993). Laughter In a psychiatric ward: Somatic, emotional, social and clinical influences on schizophrenic patients. *Journal of Nervous and Mental Disorders, 181*(5), 283-289.

Gelkopf, M., Sigal, M., & Kremer, R. (1994). The use of humor for improving social support In a psychiatric ward. *Journal of Social Psychology, 134,* 175-182.

George, J. B. (2011). *Nursing theories* (6th ed.). Boston, MA: Pearson.

George, R. L., Cristiani, T. S. (1995). *Counseling theory and practice* (4th ed.). Boston, MA: Allyn and Bacon.

Gerdner, L. (1997). An individualized music intervention for agitation. *Journal of the American Psychiatric Nurses Association, 3,* 177-184.

Gergen, K. J. (1971). *The concept of self.* New York: Holt, Rinehart and Winston.

Gergen, K. J., & Gergen, M. M. (1986). *Social psychology* (2nd ed.). New York: Springer Verlag.

Gervais, M., & Wilson, D. S. (2005). The evolution and functions of laughter and humor: A synthetic approach. *The Quarterly Review of Biology, 80*(4), 395-430.

Getchell, B. (1994). *Shape up: The fitness handbook.* Lincolnwood, IL: NTC/Contemporary Publishing Company.

Getz, D. (2002). Increasing cultural competence in therapeutic recreation. In D. R. Austin, J. Dattilo, & B. P. McCormick, (Eds.), *Conceptual foundations for therapeutic recreation* (pp. 151-164). State College, PA: Venture.

Ghafari, S., Ahmadi, F., Nabavi, M., Anoshirvan, K., Memarian, R., & Rafatbakhsh, M. (2009). Effectiveness of applying progressive muscle relaxation technique on quality of life of patients with multiple sclerosis. *Journal of Clinical Nursing, 18,* 2171-2179.

Ghueckauf, R. L., & Quittner, A. L. (1992). Assertiveness training for disabled adults in wheelchairs: Self-report, role-play, and activity pattern outcomes. *Journal of Consulting and Counseling Psychology, 60*(3), 419-425.

Gibson, J. L., Ivancevich, J., & Donnelly, J. H. (2000). *Organizations: Behavior, structure, processes* (10th ed.). Boston, MA: Irwin McGraw-Hill.

Gilbert, A. A. (2010). Teaching students to become self-reflective practitioners. *Therapeutic Recreation Journal, 44*(4), 303-309.

Gilkey, W. A. (1986). *Biofeedback: Leaning to relax.* Bloomington, IN: South Central Community Mental Health Center, Inc.

Gillis, H. L., & Simpson, C. (1993). Project choices: Adventure-based residential drug treatment for court-referred youth. In M. A. Gass (Ed.), *Adventure therapy: Therapeutic applications of adventure programming.* Dubuque, IA: Kendall/Hunt.

Girdano, D. A., Everly G. S., & Dusek, D. E. (1997). *Controlling stress and tension: A holistic approach* (5th ed.). Boston: Allyn and Bacon.

Gladding, S. T. (2002). *Family therapy history, theory, and practice* (3rd ed.). Upper SaddRiver, NJ: Merrill Prentice Hall.

Glanz, K., Lewis, F. M., & Rimer, B. K. (1990). *Health behavior and health education.* San Francisco, CA: Jossey-Bass Publishers.

Glasser, W. (1965). *Reality therapy: A new approach to psychiatry.* New York: Harper and Row.

Glasser, W. (1976). Reality therapy. In V. Binder, A. Binder, & B. Rimland (Eds.), *Modern therapies.* Englewood Cliffs, NJ: Prentice-Hall.

Glasser, W., & Wubbolding, R. (1995). Reality therapy. In R. J. Corsini, & D. Wedding (Eds.), *Current psychotherapies* (5th ed.). Itasca, IL: F. E. Peacock.

Glicken, M. D. (2004). *Using the strengths perspective in social work practice: A positive approach for the helping professions.* Boston, MA: Pearson Education.

Glueckauf, R. L, & Quittner, A. L. (1992). Assertiveness training for disabled adults in wheelchairs: Self-report, role-play, and activity pattern outcomes. *Journal of Consulting and Clinical Psychology, 60*(3), 419-425.

Gonzalez, M. T., Hartig, T., patil, G. G., Martinsen, E. W., & Kirkevold, M. (2010). Therapeutic horticulture In clinical depression: A prospective study of active components. *Journal of Advanced Nursing, 66*(9), 2002-2013.

Gonzalez, M. T., Hartig, T., patil, G. G., Martinsen, E. W., & Kirkevold, M. (2011). A prospective study of existential issues in therapeutic horticulture depression. *Issues in Mental Health Nursing, 32,* 73-81.

Gonzalez, M. T., Hartig, T., patil, G. G., Martinsen, E. W., & Kirkevold, M. (2011a). A prospective study of group cohesiveness in therapeutic horticulture for clinical depression. *International Journal of Mental Health Nursing, 20,* 119-129.

Golden, J., Conroy, R. M., Bruce, I., Denihan, A., Greene, E., Kirby, M., & Lawlor, B. A. (2009). Loneliness, social support networks, mood and well-being in community-dwelling elderly. *International Journal of Geriatric Psychiatry, 24,* 694-700.

Gordon, C., & Gergen, K. J. (1968). *The self in social interaction.* New York: John Wiley & Sons.

Gordon, T. (2001). *Leader effectiveness training: L.E.T.* New York: Perigee Books.

Gottesman, L. E., & Bourestom, N. C. (1974). Why nursing homes do what they do. *Gerontologist, 14,* 501-506.

Graf, D. L., Pratt, L. V., Hester, N., & Short, K. R. (2009). Playing active video games increases energy expenditure in children. *Pediatrics, 124*(2), 534-540.

Graham-Pole, J. (2002). The creative arts: What role do they play? In S. Shannon (Ed.), *Handbook of complementary and alternative therapies in mental health* (pp. 475 - 495). San Diego: Academic Press.

Granath, J., Ingvarsson, S., von Thiele, U., & Lundberg, U. (2006). Stress management: A randomized study of cognitive behavioural therapy and yoga. *Cognitive Behaviour Therapy, 35*(3), 3-10.

Grandgeorge, M., & Hausberger, M. (2011). Human-animal relationships: From daily life to animal-assisted therapies. *Ann 1st Super Sanita, 47*(4), 397-408.

Graner, B. (2007). Aromatherapy for you and your patient. *American Nurse Today, 2*(9), 53 - 54.

Graves, A. M. (2002). Incident report forms and policies. NursingManagers.com. Retrieved from http://www. hospitalsoup.com/public/incidentsmh.pdf

Graves, L. E. F., Ridgers, N. D., Williams, K., Stratton, G., Atkinson, G., & Cable, N. T. (2010). The physiological cost and enjoyment of Wii Fit in adolescents, young adults, and older adults. *Journal of physical activity and health, 7*, 383-401.

Gray, D. E. (1975). The future of American society. In J. F. Murphy (Ed.), *The epilogue to recreation and leisure services.* Dubuque, IA: Wm. C. Brown.

Green, J. (2011). Fitness training for clients with muscular dystrophy. Retrieved from http://www.ncpad.org/yourwrites/fact_sheet.php?sheet=857&view=all&print=yes

Greenspan, A. I., Wolf, S. L., Kelley, M. E., & O'Grady, M. (2007). Tai chi and perceived health status in older adults who are transitionally frail: A randomized controlled trail. *Physical Therapy, B7*(5), 525-535.

Griffith, J. M., Hasley, J. P., Liu, H., Severn, D. G., Conner, L. H., & Adler, L. E. (2008). Qigong stress reduction in hospital staff. *The Journal of Alternative and Complementary Medicine, 14*(8), 939-945.

Groff, D., & Dattilo, J. (2011). Adventure therapy. In J. Dattilo & A. McKenney (Eds.), *Facilitation techniques in therapeutic recreation* (2nd ed.) (pp. 15-42). State College, PA: Venture.

Grohol, J. M. (2008). Doctors use Wii games for physical therapy. Retrieved from http://psychcentral.com/blog/archives/2008/02/10/doctors-use-wii-games-for-physical-therapy

Gronlund, N. E. (1985). *Stating behavioral objectives for classroom instruction* (3rd ed.). London: The MacMillan Company.

Gross, S., & Anthony, K. (2003). *Technology in counseling and psychotherapy: A practitioner's guide.* New York: Palgrave MacMillan.

Grossman, A. H., & Caroleo, O. (1996). Acquired immunodeficiency syndrome (AIDS). In D. R. Austin, & M. E. Crawford (Eds.), *Therapeutic recreation: An introduction* (2nd ed.). Boston: Allyn & Bacon.

Group processing. (nd). Retrieved from http://csl.iupui.edu/does/Group%20Processing.doc

Growing Confidence—Horticulture and Stroke Recovery. (1993). *Stroke connection.* Golden Valley, MI: Courage Center.

Gruver, B. M., & Austin, D. R. (1990). The instructional status of clinical supervision in therapeutic recreation curricula. *Therapeutic Recreation Journal, 24* (2), 18-24.

Grzdlak, J. L. (1985). Desire for control: Cognitive, emotional and behavioral consequences. In F. L. Denmark (Ed.), *Social/ecological psychology and the psychology of women.* New York: Elsevier Science.

Guidance for the Completion of the Incident Report (nd). Retrieved from http://www.suffolk.gov.uk/NR/rdonlyres/5AAA9F0B-A423-4D46-8D0f-329178452E27/0/GuidancefortheCompletionoftheIncidentForm. doc

Gunn, S. L., & Peterson, C. A. (1978). *Therapeutic recreation program design.* Englewood Cliffs, NJ: Prentice Hall.

Gussen, J. (1967). The psychodynamics of leisure. In P. A. Martin (Ed.), *Leisure and mental health: A psychiatric viewpoint.* Washington, D.C.: American Psychiatric Association.

Haans, A., & IJssenisteijn, W. (2006). Mediated social touch: A review of current research and future directions. *Virtual Reality, 9*, 149-159.

Haans, A., & IJssenlsteijn, W. A. (2009). The virtual Midas touch: Helping behavior after a mediated social touch. *IEEE Transactions on Haptics, 2*(3), 138-140.

Haaz, S., & Bartlett, S. J. (2011). Yoga for arthritis: A scoping review. *Rheumatic Diseases Clinics of North America, 37*(1), 33-46.

Haber, J. (1997a). Stress theory and intervention. In J. Haber, B. Krainovich-Miller, A. L. McMahon, & P. Price-Hoskins (Eds.), *Comprehensive psychiatric nursing* (5th ed.) (pp. 239-260). St. Louis, MO: Mosby.

Haber, J. (1997b). Therapeutic communication. In J. Haber, B. Krainovich-Miller, A. L. McMahon, & P. Price-Hoskins, *Comprehensive psychiatric nursing* (5th ed.) (pp. 121-142). St. Louis, MO: Mosby.

Haber, J., Leach-McMahon, A., Price-Hoskins, P., & Sideleau, B. F. (1992). *Comprehensive psychiatric nursing* (4th ed.). St. Louis, MO: Mosby.

Hadjistravropoulos, H. D., & Asmundson, G. J. G. (2009). Clinical health psychology. In D. C. S. Richard & S. K. Huprich (Eds.). *Clinical Psychology* (pp. 351-378). Boston, MA: Elsevier.

Hagedorn, R. (1997). *Foundations for practice in occupational therapy* (2nd ed.). New York: Churchill Livingstone.

Haglund, L., Ekbladh, E., Thorell, L-H., & Hallberg, I. (2000). Practice models of Swedish psychiatric occupational therapy. *Scandinavian Journal of Occupational Therapy, 7*, 107-113.

Haidt, J. (2006). *The happiness hypothesis.* New York: Basic Books.

Hales, D., & Hales, R. E. (1995). *Caring for the mind: The comprehensive guide to mental health.* New York: Bantam Books.

Hall, E. T. (1966). *The hidden dimension.* New York: Doubleday/Anchor.

Haller, R. L., & Kramer, C. L. (2006). *Horticultural therapy methods.* New York: The Haworth Press.

Hallstrand, T. S., Bates, P. W., & Schoene, R. B. (2000). Aerobic conditioning in mild asthma decreases the hyperpnea of exercise and improves exercise and ventilatory capacity. *CHEST Journal, 118*(5), 1460-1469.

Hamilton, E. J., & Austin, D. R. (1992). Future perspectives of therapeutic recreation. *Annual in Therapeutic Recreation, 3,* 72-79.

Hansen, E. (2010). Yoga for seniors with arthritis: A pilot study. *International Journal of Yoga Therapy, No. 20,* 55-60.

Hansen, J. C., Warner, R. W., & Smith, E. M. (1980). *Group counseling: Theory and process* (2nd ed.). Chicago: Rand McNally College Publishing Company.

Hansmann, R., Hug, S-M., & Seeland, K. (2007). Restoration and stress relief through physical activities in forests and parks. *Urban Forestry & Urban Greening, 16*(4), 213-225.

Harper, A., & Harper, B. (1992). *Skill-building for self-directed team members: A complete course.* Mohegan Lake, NY: MW Corporation.

Harper, F. D. (1984). Jogotherapy: Jogging as psychotherapy. In M. L. Sachs, & G. W. Buffone (Eds.), *Running as therapy: An integrated approach.* Lincoln, NE: University of Nebraska Press.

Harris, E. (1981). Antidepressants: Old drugs, new uses. *American Journal of Nursing, 81*(7), 1308-1309.

Harris, T. A. (1976). Transactional analysis: An introduction. In V. Binder, A. Binder, & B. Rimland (Eds.), *Modern therapies.* Englewood Cliffs, NJ: Prentice-Hall.

Hart, C. E. F., & Tracy, B. L. (2008). Yoga as steadiness training: Effects on motor variability In young adults. *Journal of Strength and Conditioning Research, 22*(5), 1659-1668.

Hart, G. M. (1982). *The process of clinical supervision.* Baltimore, MD: University Park Press.

Hartz, G. W., & Splain, D. M. (1997). *Psychosocial intervention in long-term care: An advanced guide.* New York: The Haworth Press.

Hauser, W. A., & Hesdorffer, D. C. (1990). *Epilepsy: Frequency, causes and consequences.* Landover, MD: Epilepsy Foundation of America.

Havens, M. D. (1992). *Bridges to accessibility: A primer for including persons with disabilities in adventure curricula.* Dubuque, IA: Kendall/Hunt.

Hawkin, M., & Ozuna, J. (1979). Practical aspects of anticonvulsant therapy. *American Journal of Nursing, 79*(6), 1062-1068.

Hawkley, L. C., & Cacioppo, J. T. (2010). Loneliness matters: A theoretical and empirical review of consequences and mechanisms. *Annals of Behavioral Medicine, 40,* 218-227.

Hayashi, T., & Murakami, K. (2009). The effects of laughter on post-prandial glucose levels and gene expression In type 2 diabetic patients. *Life Sciences, 85,* 185-187.

Hayashi, T., Tsum, S., Iburi, T., Tamanaha, T., Yamagami, K., Ishibashi, R., Hori, M., … & Murakami, K. (2007). Laughter up-regulates the genes related to NK cell activity In diabetes. *Biomedical Research, 28*(6), 281-285.

Hayes, N. (2001). *Teach yourself applied psychology.* London: Teach Yourself Books.

Hays, K. F. (1999). *Working it out: Using exercise in psychotherapy.* Washington, D.C.: American Psychological Association.

Hazzard, A., Celano, M., Collins, M., & Markov, Y. (2002). Effects of STARBRIGHT World on knowledge, social support, and coping in hospitalized children with sickle cell disease and asthma. *Children's Health Care, 31*(1), 69-86.

Heatherton, T. F., & Wyland, C. L. (2003). Assessing self-esteem. In S. J. Lopez & C. R. Snyder (Eds.), *Positive psychology assessment: A handbook of models and measures.* Washington, DC: American Psychological Association.

Heavey, B. (2002). A life in balance. *Modern Maturity, 45*(2), 61-68.

Heider, F. (1944). Social perception and phenomenal causality. *Psychological Review, 51,* 358-374.

Henderson, S. (1980). A development in social psychiatry: The systematic study of social bonds. *The Journal of Nervous and Mental Disease, 168*(2), 63-69.

Herbert, I. (2008). Exercising judgment: The psychology of fitness. *Observer, 21*(1), pp. 13-17.

Herlihy-Chevalier, B. (2005). What is remotivation therapy? In J. A. Dyer & M. L. Stotts, M. L. (Eds.). *Handbook of remotivation therapy* (pp. 13-170. Binghamton, NY: The Haworth Press.

Herrington, L., & Davies, R. (2005). The influence of Pilates training on the ability to contact the Transversus Abdominis muscle in asymptomatic Individuals. *Journal of Bodywork and Movement Therapies, 9,* 52-57.

Hershberger, P. J. (2005). Prescribing happiness: Positive psychology and family medicine. *Family Medicine, 37*(9), 630-634.

Herz, R. S. (2009). Aromatherapy facts and fictions: A scientific analysis of olfactory effects on mood, physiology and behavior. *International Journal of Neuroscience, 119,* 263-290.

Hesdorffer, D. C., Logroscino, G., Benn, E. K. T., Katri, N., Cascino, G., & Hauser, W. A. (2011). Estimating risk for developing epilepsy: A population-based study in Rochester, Minnesota. *Neurology 76*(1), 23-27.

Hesley, J. W. & Hesley, J. G. (2001). *Rent two films and let's talk in the morning: Using popular movies in psychotherapy* (2nd ed.). New York: John Wiley & Sons.

Hewitt, C. (1988). Training in social skills. In M. Willson (Ed.), *Occupational therapy in short-term psychiatry* (2nd ed.). New York: Churchill Livingstone.

Hewitt, J. (1985). *Teach yourself relaxation.* New York: Random House.

Heyne, L. A., & Anderson, L. S. (2012). Theories that support strengths-based practice in therapeutic recreation. *Therapeutic Recreation Journal, 36*, 106-128.

Heywood, L. A. (1978). Perceived recreative experience and relief of tension. *Journal of Leisure Research, 10*, 86-97.

Higginbotham, H. N., West, S. G., & Forsyth, D. R. (1988). *Psychotherapy and behavior change: Social, cultural, and methodological perspectives.* New York: Pergamon Press.

Hill, C., Vowles, D., Craig, D. & Fyson, N. (2001). *The Hamlyn encyclopedia of alternative health.* London: Octopus Publishing Group Limited.

Hill, C. E. & O'Brien, K. M. (1999). *Helping skills: Facilitating, exploration, insight, and action.* Washington, D.C.: American Psychological Association.

Hill, L., & Smith, N. (1990). *Self-care nursing: Promotion of health* (2nd ed.). Norwalk, CT: Appleton & Lange.

Hillman, C. H., Erickson, K. I., & Kramer, A. F. (2008). Be smart, exercise your heart: Exercise effects on brain and cognition. *Nature Review, 9*, 58-65.

Hirsch, S. M., von Rosenberg, R., Phelan, C., & Dudley, H. K. (1978). Effectiveness of assertiveness training with alcoholics. *Journal of Studies on Alcohol, 39*(1), 89-97.

Hoeger, W. W., & Hoeger, S. A. (2011). *Lifetime physical fitness & wellness: A personalized program.* Belmont, CA: Wadsworth.

Hoffman, L. W. (1994). The training of psychotherapy supervisors: A barren scape. *Psychotherapy in Private Practice, 13*, 23-42.

Hogg, J., & Raynes, N. V. (1987). Assessing people with mental handicap: An introduction. In J. Hoog & N. V. Raynes (Eds.), *Assessment in mental handicap.* Cambridge, MA: Brookline Books.

Hollin, C. R., & Trower, P. (Eds.). (1986). *Handbook of social skills training: Volume 2.* New York: Pergamon Press.

Holloway, E. L. (1995). *Clinical supervision: A systems approach.* Thousand Oaks, CA: SAGE.

Holmes, M. D., Chen, W. Y., Feskanich, D., Kroenke, C. H., & Colditz, G. A. (2005). Physical activity and survival after breast cancer diagnosis. *Journal of the American Medical Association, 293*(20), 2479-2486.

Hope, K. (1997). Using multi-sensory environments with older people with dementia. *Journal of Advanced Nursing, 25*, 780-785.

Hooker, S. D., Freeman, L. H., & Stewart, P. (2002). Pet therapy research: A historical review. *Holistic Nursing Practice, 17*(1), 17-23.

Hootman, J. M. (2012). Physical activity, fitness, and joint and bone health. In C. Buchard, S. N. Blair, & W. L. Haskell (Eds.). *Physical Activity and Health.* (2nd ed.) (pp. 245-255). Champaign, IL: Human Kinetics.

Hoozer, H. V., Ruther, L., & Craft, M. (1982). *Introduction to charting.* Philadelphia, PA: J. B. Lippincott.

Horner, A. J. (1993). Occupational hazards and characterological vulnerability: The problem of "burnout." *The American Journal of Psychoanalysis, 53* (2), 137-142.

Horton, J., Clance, P. R., Sterk-Elifson, C., & Emshoff, J. (1995). Touch in psychotherapy: A survey of patients' experiences. *Psychotherapy, 32*, 443-457.

Howard, D., Browning, C., & Lee, Y. (2007). The International Classification of Functioning, Disability and Health: Therapeutic recreation code sets and salient diagnostic core sets. *Therapeutic Recreation Journal, 41*(1), 61 - 81.

Howard, F. (2008). Managing stress or enhancing wellbeing? Positive psychology's contributions to clinical supervision. *Australian Psychologist, 43*(2), 105-113.

Howe, C. Z. (1984). Leisure assessment instrumentation in therapeutic recreation. *Therapeutic Recreation Journal, 18* (2), 14-24.

Howie, A. R. (2000). *Starting a visiting-animal group.* Olympia, WA: Providence Health System.

Hultsman, J. T., Black, D. R., Seehafer, R. W., & Hovell, M. F. (1987). The Purdue stepped approach model: Application to leisure counseling service delivery. *Therapeutic Recreation Journal, 21*(4), 9-22.

Human Kinetics. (2011). Physical inactivity: The biggest public health problem of the 21st century. Retrieved from http://www.humankinetics.com/sitename/DAM/069/Physical_Inactivity_Presenation1.pdf

Hurkmans, H. L., van den Berg-Emons, R. J., & Stam, H. J. (2010). Energy expenditure in adults with cerebral palsy playing Wii Sports. *Archives of Physical Medicine and Rehabilitation, 91*, 1577-1581.

Hurwitz, D. C, Morgenstern, H., & Chiao, C. (2005). Effects of recreational physical activity and back exercises on low back pain and psychological distress: Findings from the UCLA low back pain study. *American Journal of Public Health, 95*(10), 1817-1824.

Huss, A. J. (1977). Touch with care or a caring touch? *The American Journal of Occupational Therapy, 31*(1), 11-18.

Hutchins, D. (2011). Assertiveness training. In N. J. Stumbo & B. Wardlaw (Eds.), *Facilitation of therapeutic recreation services* (pp. 237-245). State College, PA: Venture.

Hutchins, D. A. (2005/2006). Competencies required for effective clinical supervision during the therapeutic recreation internship. *Annual in Therapeutic Recreation, 14*, 114-130.

Hutchinson, S. L., Bland, A. D., & Kleiber, D. A. (2008). Leisure and stress-coping: Implications for therapeutic recreation practice. *Therapeutic Recreation Journal, 42*(1), 9-23.

Hutchinson, S. L., & Dattilo, J. (2001). Processing: Possibilities for therapeutic recreation. *Therapeutic Recreation Journal, 35*(1), 43-56.

Hutchinson, S. L., Doble, S., Warner, G., & MacPhee, C. (2011). Lessons learned from Take Care: A brief leisure education intervention for caregivers. *Therapeutic Recreation Journal, 45*(3), 121-134.

Hutchinson, S. L, LeBlanc, A., & Booth, R. (2002). "Perpetual problem-solving: An ethnographic study of clinical reasoning in a therapeutic recreation setting." *Therapeutic Recreation Journal, 36*(1), 18-34.

Huth, M. M., Broome, M. E., & Good, M. (2004). Imagery reduces children's post-operative pain. *Pain, 110*(1-2), 439-448.

Ice, G. H. (2002). Daily life in a nursing home: Has it changed in 25 years? *Journal of Aging Studies, 16*, 345-359.

Ilhan, M. N., Durukan, E., Taner, E., Maral, I., & Bumin, M. A. (2007). Burnout and its correlates among nursing staff: Questionnaire survey. *Journal of Advanced Nursing, 61*(1), 100 - 106.

Innes, K. E., & Selfe, T. K. (2012). The effect of a gentle yoga program on sleep, mood, and blood pressure in older women with restless legs syndrome (RLS): A preliminary randomized controlled trail. *Evidence-Based Complementary and Alternative Medicine, 2012.*

Institute of Medicine. (2001). *Crossing the quality chasm: A new health system for the 21st Century.* Washington: Institute of Medicine.

Indian Epilepsy Association. (1996). *Yoga for epilepsy.* Indore, India: Indian Epilepsy Association.

Irez, G. B., Ozdemir, R. A., Evin, R., Irez, S. G., & Korkusuz, F. (2011). Integrating Pilates exercise Into an exercise program for 65+ year-old women to reduce falls. *Journal of Sports Science and Medicine, 10*, 105-111.

Irwin, M. L. (2008). Physical activity interventions for cancer survivors. *British Journal of Sports Medicine, 43*, 32-38.

Irwin, M. R., Olmstead, R., & Motivala, S. J. (2008). Improving sleep quality in older adults with moderate sleep complaints: A randomized controlled trail of Tai chi chih. *Sleep, 31*(7), 1001-1008.

Ismail, A. H., & Trachtman, L. E. (1973). Jogging the imagination. *Psychology Today, 6*(10), 78-82.

Iso-Ahola, S. E. (1980). Perceived control and responsibility as mediators of the effects of therapeutic recreation on the institutionalized aged. *Therapeutic Recreation Journal, 14*(1), 36-43.

Iso-Ahola, S. E. (1984). Social psychological foundations of leisure and resultant implications for leisure counseling. In E. T. Dowd (Ed.), *Leisure counseling: Concepts and applications.* Springfield, IL: Charles C. Thomas.

Iso-Ahola, S. E. (1989). Motivation for leisure. In E. L. Jackson, & T. L. Burton (Eds.), *Understanding leisure and recreation: Mapping the past, charting the future.* State College, PA: Venture.

Itin, C. M. (2001). Adventure therapy—critical questions. *Journal of Experiential Education, 24*(2), 80-84.

IU Health. (2013). Stroke. Retrieved from http://iuhealth.org/neuroscience-center/specialities/stroke/?gclid=CM33q_6d8LQCFcU-Mgodn24AGQ

Ivey, A. E., Ivey, M. B., & Simek-Morgan, L. (1993). *Counseling and psychotherapy: A multicultural perspective* (3rd ed.). Boston, MA: Allyn and Bacon.

Ivey, A. E., Ivey, M. B., & Simek-Morgan, L. (1997). *Counseling and psychotherapy: A multicultural perspective* (4th ed.). Boston: Allyn and Bacon.

Jack, S. J., & Ronan, K. R. (2008). Bibliotherapy practice and research. *School Psychology International, 29*(2), 161-182.

Jackson, C., & Latini, C. (2013). Touch and hand-mediated therapies. In B. M. Dossey & L. Keegan (Eds.), *Holistic nursing: A handbook for practice* (6th ed.) (pp. 417-437). Burlington, MA: Jones & Bartlett.

Jacobson, J. M., & James, A. (2001). Ethics: Doing right. In N. J. Stumbo (Ed.), *Professional issues in therapeutic recreation: On competence and outcomes* (pp. 237-248). Urbana, IL: Sagamore.

Jacobson, M., & Ruddy, M. (2004). *Open to outcome: A practical guide for facilitating & teaching experiential reflection.* Oklahoma City, OK: Wood 'N' Barnes Publishing & Distribution.

Jahnke, R., Larkey, L., Rogers, C., Etnier, J., & Lin, F. (2010). A comprehensive review of health benefits of qigong and tai chi. *American Journal of Health Promotion, 24*(6), e1-e25.

Jake, L. (2001). Bibliotherapy applications for recreation therapy. Interlink Feature Article, pp.1-3. Retrieved from http:// www.recreationtherapy.com/articles/bibliotherapy.htm

James, C. (2008). Casual video gaming reduces stress. Retrieved from http://www.vnunet.com/vnunet/news/2215423/casual-video-gaming-reduces

James, M., & Jongward, D. (1996). *Born to win: Transactional analysis with Gestalt experiments.* Reading, MA: Addison-Wesley.

Janssen, I. (2012). Physical activity, fitness, and cardiac, vascular, and pulmonary morbidities. In C. Bouchard, S. N. Blair, & W. L. Haskell (Eds.). *Physical Activity and Health* (2nd ed.) (pp. 185-195). Champaign, IL: Human Kinetics.

Jarrott, S. E., Kwack, H. R., & Relf, D. (2002). An observational assessment of a dementia-specific horticulture therapy program. *Hort-Technology, 12*(3), 403-410.

Jayson, S. (2012). Americans report a decrease in stress for the first time in five years, maybe because it's just the new normal. *USA Today,* January 11, 2012, Section D, pp. D1-D2.

Jenaro, C., Flores, N., & Arias. (2007). Burnout and coping in human service practitioners. *Professional Psychology: Research and Practice, 38*(1), 80-87.

Johns, C. (2004). *Becoming a reflective practitioner* (2nd ed.). Malden MA: Blackwell.

Johnson, B. S. (1995). *Child, adolescent & family psychiatric nursing.* Philadelphia, PA: J.B. Lippincott.

Johnson, D. W., & Johnson, F. P. (1997). *Joining together: Group therapy and group skills* (6th ed.). Boston, MA: Allyn and Bacon.

Johnson, E. G., Larsen, A., Ozawa, H., Wilson, C. A., & Kennedy, K. L. (2007). The effects of Pilates-based exercise on dynamic balance in healthy adults. *Journal of Bodywork and Movement Therapies, 11*, 238-342.

Johnson, K. A., Bland, M. K., & Rathsam, S. M. (2002). Taking root: The development of a hospital garden. *Parks & Recreation, 37*(1), 61-64.

Johnson, R. A. (1999). Reminiscence therapy. In G. M. Bulechek, & J. C. McCloskey (Eds.), *Nursing interventions: Effective nursing treatments* (3rd ed.) (pp. 371-384). Philadelphia, PA: W. B. Saunders.

Jones, D. B., & Anderson, L. S. (2004). The status of clinical supervison in therapeutic recreation: A national study. *Therapeutic Recreation Journal, 38*(4), 329 - 347.

Jones, J. J., & Pfeiffer, J. W. (Eds.). (1972). *What to look for in groups. The 1972 annual handbook for group facilitators.* Iowa City, IA: University Associates.

Jones, J. M. (2008). Clinical supervision in nursing. *The Clinical Supervisor, 24*(1-2), 149-162.

Jones, S. (2000). *Talking about health and wellness with patients.* New York: Springer.

Jorgensen, I. S., & Nafstad, H. F. (2004). Positive psychology: Historical, philosophical, and epistemological perspectives. In P. A. Linley & S. Joseph (Eds.), *Positive psychology in practice* (pp. 15 - 34). Hoboken, NJ: John Wiley & Sons.

Jung, Y., Li, K. J., Janissa, N. S., Gladys, W. L. C., & Lee, K. M. (2009). Games for a better life: Effects of playing Will games on the well-being of seniors in a long-term care facility. *Proceedings of the Sixth Australasian Conference on Interactive Entertainment. ACM.*

Juniper, D. (2003). Leisure counselling in stress management. *Work Study, 52*(1), 7-12.

Juniper, D. (2005). Leisure counselling, coping skills and therapeutic applications. *British Journal of Guidance & Counseling, 33*(1), 27-36.

Kahn, E. M. (1979). The parallel process in social work: Treatment and supervision. *Social Casework, 60*(9), 520-528.

Kam-Tim, S., & Orme-Johnson, D. W. (2001). Three randomized experiments on the longitudinal effects of the Transcendental Meditation technique on cognition. *Intelligence, 29*, 419-440.

Kamwendo, K., Askenbom, M., & Wahlgren, C. (1999). Physical activity in the life of the patient with rheumatoid arthritis. *Physiotherapy Research International, 4*(4), 278-292.

Kanfer, F. J., & Goldstein, A. P. (1991). *Helping people change: A textbook of methods* (4th ed.). New York: Pergamon Press.

Kang, M., & Johnson, K. K. P. (2011). Retail therapy: Scale development. *Clothing and Textiles Journal, 29*(1), 3-19.

Kanji, N., White, A., & Ernst, E. (2004). Autogenic training reduces anxiety after coronary angioplasty: A randomized clinical trail. *American Health Journal, 147*(3), K1-K4.

Kanji, N., White, A. R., & Ernst, E. (2005). Autogenic training for tension type headaches: a systematic review of controlled trials. *Complementary Therapies in Medicine, 14*(2), 144-150.

Kaplan, H. I., & Sadock, B. (1995). *Comprehensive textbook of psychology/VI* (6th ed.). Baltimore, MD: Williams & Weilkins.

Karras, B. (1987). Music and reminiscence: For groups and individuals. In B. Karras (Ed.), *You bring out the music in me: Music in nursing homes.* New York: The Haworth Press.

Kasl-Godley, J., & Gatz, M. (2000). Psychosocial interventions for individuals with dementia: an integration of theory, therapy, and a clinical understanding of dementia. *Clinical psychology review, 20*(6), 755-782.

Kaslow, F. W. (1986). Supervision, consultation and staff training—creative teaching/learning processes in the mental health profession. In F. W. Kaslow (Ed.), *Supervision and training: Models, dilemmas and challenges.* New York: The Haworth Press.

Kato, P. M. (2010). Video games in health care: Closing the gap. *Review of General Psychology, 14*(2), 113-121.

Kearney, P. M., & Pryor, J. (2004). The International Classification of Functioning, Disability and Health (ICF) and nursing. *Journal of Advanced Nursing, 46*(2), 162-170.

Keays, K. S., Harris, S. R., Lucyshyn, J. M., & MacIntyre, D. L. (2008). Effects of Pilates exercises on shoulder range of motion, pain, mood, and upper-extremity function In women living with breast cancer: A pilot study. *Physical Therapy, 88*(4), 494-508.

Kelland, J. (Ed.). (1995). *Protocols for recreation therapy programs.* State College, PA: Venture.

Kelley, H. H. (1950). The warm-cold variable in first impressions of persons. *Journal of Personality, 18*, 431-439.

Kelley, J. (Ed.). (1981). *Recreation programming for visually impaired children and youth.* New York: American Foundation for the Blind.

Kelly, J. R. (1982). *Leisure: An introduction.* Englewood Cliffs, NJ: Prentice Hall.

Kelly, L. M., & Mosher-Ashley, P. M. (2002). Combining reminiscence with journal writing to promote greater life satisfaction In an assisted-living community. *Activities, Adaptations & Aging, 26*(4), 35-46.

Kelly, M. (2005). Aquatic exercise for children with cerebral palsy. *Developmental Medicine & Child Neurology, 47*, 838-842.

Kelly, P. (2009). *Essentials of nursing leadership and management.* Boston, MA: Cengage Learning.

Kemper, K. J., & Danhauer, S. C. (2005). Music as therapy. *Southern Medical Journal, 98*(3), 282-288.

Kennard, D. (1998). *An introduction to therapeutic communities.* Philadelphia, PA: Jessica Kingsley.

Kennedy, D. D. (1995). Have a laugh! Have a healthy laugh! *Nursing Forum, 30*(1), 25-30.

Kermani, K. (1996). Autogenic training. In J. Jacobs (Ed.), *The encyclopedia of alternative medicine* (pp. 168-173). Boston: Journey Editions.

Kerse, N., Elley, C. R., Robinson, E., & Arroll, B. (2005). Is physical activity counseling effective for older people? A cluster randomized, controlled trail in primary care. *Journal of the American Geriatrics Society, 53*, 1951-1956.

Keville, K. (2009). Aromatherapy and essential oils. In A. Rost (Ed.) *Natural healing wisdom and know-how* (pp. 119-136). New York: Black Dog & Leventhal.

Keyes, C. L. M., & Haidt, J. (Eds.). (2003). *Flourishing: Positive psychology and the life well-lived.* Washington, D.C.: American Psychological Association.

Keysor, J. J. (2003). Does late-life physical activity or exercise present or minimize disablement? A critical review of the scientific evidence. *American Journal of Preventive Medicine, 25*, 129-136.

Khalsa, S. B. S. (2004). Yoga as a therapeutic intervention: A bibliometric analysis of published research studies. *Indian Journal of Physiology and Pharmacology, 48*(3), 269-285.

Kibler, R. J., Barker, L. L., & Miles, D. T. (1970). *Behavioral objectives and instruction.* Boston, MA: Allyn and Bacon.

Kidd, S. A., Miller, R., Boyd, G. M., & Cardena, I. (2009). Relationship between humor, subversion, and genuine connection among persons with severe mental illness. *Qualitative Health Research, 19*(10), 1421-1430.

Kielhofner, G. (1997). *Conceptual foundations of occupational therapy* (2nd ed.). Philadelphia, PA: F. A. Davis.

Kielhofner, G. (2005). A scholarship of practice: Creating discourse between theory, research and practice. *Occupational Therapy in Health Care, 19*(1/2), 7-16.

Kielhofner, G. (2007). Respecting both the "occupation" and the "therapy" in our field. *American Journal of Occupational Therapy, 61*(4), 479-482.

Kielhofner, G. (2009). *Conceptual foundations of occupational therapy* (4th ed.). Philadelphia, PA: F. A. Davis.

Kileff, J., & Ashburn, A. (2005). A pilot study of the effect of aerobic exercise on people with moderate disability multiple sclerosis. *Clinical Rehabilitation, 19*, 165-169.

Killen, K. H. (1977). *Management: A middle-management approach.* Boston, MA: Houghton-Mifflin.

Kim, J., & Van Puymbroeck, M. (2011). Providing cultural competent therapeutic recreation for East Asian immigrant clients. *Annual In Therapeutic Recreation, 19*, 114-124.

King, I. M. (1971). *Toward a theory of nursing.* New York: John Wiley and Sons.

Kinney, J. S., Kinney, T., & Witman, J. (2004). Therapeutic recreation modalities and facilitation techniques: A national study. *Annual in Therapeutic Recreation, 13*, 59-79.

Kinney, J. S., Warren, L., Kinney, T., & Witman, J. (1999). Use of therapeutic modalities and facilitation techniques by therapeutic recreation specialists in the northeastern United States. *Annual in Therapeutic Recreation, 8*, 1-11.

Kleiber, D. A., Walker, G. J., & Mannell, R .C. (2011). *A social psychology of leisure* (2nd ed.). State College, PA: Venture.

Klein, P. J., & Adams, W. D. (2004). Comprehensive therapeutic benefits of Taiji: A critical review. *American Journal of Physical Medicine and Rehabilitation, 83*, 735-745.

Kloubec, J. A. (2010). Pilates for improvement of muscle endurance, flexibility, balance, and posture. *Journal of Strength and Conditioning Research, 24*(3), 661-667.

Knafl, K., & Grey, M. (2008). Clinical translational science awards: Opportunities and challenges for nurse scientists. *Nursing Outlook, 56*(3), 132-137.

Knickerbocker, I. (1969). Leadership: A conception and some implications. In C.A. Gibb (Ed.), *Leadership* (pp?). Baltimore: Peguin Books.

Knobloch, S., & Zillman, D. (2002). Mood management via the digital jukebox. *Journal of Communication, 52*(2), 351-366.

Knowles, M., & Knowles, H. (1972). *Introduction to group dynamics* (rev. ed.). Chicago, IL: Follett.

Kolasinski, S. L., Garfinkel, M., Tsal, A. G., Matz, W., Van Dyke, A., Schumacher, H. R. (2005). Iyengar yoga for treating symptoms of osteoarthritis of the knees: A pilot study. *The Journal of Alternative and Complementary Medicine, 11*(4), 689-693.

Kollak, I. (2009). *Yoga for nurses.* New York: Springer.

Kongable, L. G., Buckwalter, K. C., & Stolley, J. M. (1989). The effects of pet therapy on the social behavior of institutionalized Alzheimer's clients. *Archives of Psychiatric Nursing, 3*(4), 191-198.

Kopelowicz, A. K., Liberman, R. P., & Zarate, R. (2006). Recent advances in social skills training for schizophrenia. *Schizophrenia Bulletin, 32*(S1), S12-S23.

Korkmaz, N. (2010). Effects of Pilates exercises on the social physical concern of patients with fibromyalgia syndrome: A pilot study. *Turkish Journal of Rheumatology, 25*, 201-207.

Kovel, J. (1976). *A complete guide to therapy: From psychoanalysis to behavior modification.* New York: Pantheon Books.

Kowatch, R. A., Fristad, M., Birmaher, B., Wagner, K. D., Findling, R. I. & Hellander, J. D. (2005). Bipolar disorder: Treatment guidelines for children and adolescents with bipolar disorders. *Journal of the Academy of Child and Adolescent Psychiatry, 44*, 213-235.

Kraus, R. G., Carpenter, G., & Bates, B. (1989*). Recreation leadership and supervision: Guidelines for professional development* (2nd ed.). Dubuque, IA: Wm. C. Brown.

Krefling, L. H. (1985). The use of conceptual models in clinical practice. *Canadian Journal of Occupational Therapy, 52*, 173-178.

Krieger, D. (1979). *The therapeutic touch: How to use your hands to help or to heal.* Englewood Cliffs, NJ: Prentice-Hall.

Kruger, K. A., & Serpell, J. A. (2010). Animal-assisted interventions mental health: Definitions and theoretical foundations. In A. H. Fine (Ed.), *Handbook on animal-assisted therapy: Theoretical foundations and guidelines for practice* (2nd ed.) (pp. 33-48). Philadelphia, PA: Elsevier.

Kuhlman, T. L. (1993). Humor in stressful milieus. In W. F. Fry, & W. A. Salameh (Eds.), *Advances in humor and psychotherapy.* Sarasota, FL: Professional Resource Press.

Kunstler, R., Greenblatt, F., & Moreno, N. (2004). Aromatherapy and hand massage: Therapeutic recreation interventions for pain management. *Therapeutic Recreation Journal, 38*(2), 133-147.

Kunstler, R., & Stavola Daly, F. (2010). *Therapeutic recreation leadership and programming.* Champaign, IL: Human Kinetics.

Kurtz, M. M., & Mueser, K. T. (2008). A meta-analysis of controlled research of social skills training for schizophrenia. *Journal of Counseling and Clinical Psychology, 76*(3), 491-504.

Kutner, B. (1971). The social psychology of disability. In W. S. Neff (Ed.), *Rehabilitation psychology.* Washington D.C.: American Psychological Association, Inc.

Laatsch, L., Harrington, D., Hotz, G., Marcantuono, J., Mozzoni, M. P., Walsh, V., & Hersey, K. P. (2007). An evidence-based review of cognitive and behavioral rehabilitation treatment studies in children with acquired brain injury. *Journal of Head Trauma Rehabilitation, 22*(4), 248-256.

Lai, C. Y. (2003). The use of multisensory environments on children with disabilities: A literature review. *International Journal of Therapy & Rehabilitation, 10*(8), 358-363.

Lake, J. (2002). Qigong. In S. Shannon (Ed.), *Handbook of complementary and alternative therapies for mental health* (pp. 183 - 207). San Diego, CA: Academic Press.

Lakowski, T., & Long, T. (2011). *Proceedings: Physical activity and sport for people with disabilities.* Washington, DC: Georgetown University Center for Child and Human Development.

Lammers, D. (2008). Video games: Gaming into shape with the new "Wii Fit." *The Bloomington Herald-Times,* Section D, May 22, 2008, D8.

LaMonte, M. J., & Blair, S. N. (2012). Physical activity, fitness, and mortality rates. In C. Bouchard, S. N. Blair, & W. L. Haskell (Eds.), *Physical activity and health* (2nd ed.) (pp. 167-184). Champaign, IL: Human Kinetics.

Lamport, N. K., Coffey, M. S., & Hersch, G. I. (1996). *Activity analysis and application* (3rd ed.). Thorofare, NJ: SLACK Incorporated.

Lampropoulos, G. K., Kazantzis, N., & Deane, F. P. (2004). Psychologists' use of motion pictures in clinical practice. *Professional Psychology: Research and Practice, 35*(5), 535- 541.

Lancioni, G. E., Cuvo, A. J., & O'Reilly, M. F. (2002). Snoezelen: An overview of research with people with developmental disabilities and dementia. *Disability and Rehabilitation, 24*(4), 175-184.

Lange, C., Unnithan, V., Larkam, E., & Latta, P. M. (2000). Maximizing the benefits of Pilates-inspired exercise for learning functional motor skills. *Journal of Bodywork and Movement Therapies, 4*(2), 99-108.

Langer, E. J., & Rodin, J. (1976). The effects of choice and enhanced personal responsibility for the aged: A field experiment in an institutional setting. *Journal of Personality and Social Psychology, 34*, 191-198.

Langhammer, B., & Lindmark, B. (2012). Functional exercise and physical fitness post stroke: The importance of exercise maintenance for motor control and physical fitness after stroke. *Stroke Research and Treatment, 2012,* Article ID 864835, 9 pages.

Lanningham-Foser, L., Foster, R. C., McCrady, S. K., Jensen, T. B., Mitre, N., & Levine, J. A. (2009). Activity promoting games and increased energy expenditure. *Journal of Pediatrics, 154*(6), 819-823.

Larrabee, J. H. (2009). *Nurse to nurse evidence-based practice.* New York: McGraw Hill Medical.

Larson, E. B., Wang, L., Bowen, J. D., McCormick, W. C., Teri, L., Crane, P., & Kukull, W. (2006). Exercise is associated with reduced risk for incident dementia among persons 65 years of age and older. *Annals of Internal Medicine, 144*(2), 73-81.

Lau, D. C. W. (2007). Synopsis of the 2006 Canadian clinical practice guidelines on the management and prevention of obesity in adults and children. *Canadian Medical Association Journal, 176*(8), 1103-1106.

Laughter Medicine (nd). Retrieved from http://www.laughteryoga.org/

Lavallee, A. (2006). Chat therapy: Patients seek help via instant messaging. *Wall Street Journal,* March 28, 2006. Retrieved from http://www.mytherapynet.com/public/PR/wsj.asp?referral=PEMAIN

Laver, K., Ratcliffe, J., George, S., Burgess, L., & Crotty, M. (2011). Is the Nintendo Wii Fit acceptable to older people? A discrete choice experiment. *BMC Geriatrics, 11*(1), 64-70.

Law, M., & MacDermid, J. (2008). *Evidence-based rehabilitation: A guide to practice* (2nd ed.). Thorofare, NJ: SLACK Incorporated.

Lazarus, A. A. (1989). *The practice of multimodal therapy.* Baltimore, MD: The Johns Hopkins University Press.

Lazarus, A. A. (1992). The multimodal approach to the treatment of minor depression. *American Journal of Psychotherapy, 46*(1), 50-57.

Lazarus, A. A. (2000). Multimodal therapy. In R. J. Corsini, & D. Wedding (Eds.), *Current psychotherapies* (6th ed.) (pp. 340-374). Itasca, IL: F. E. Peacock.

Leary, M. R. (1999). The social and psychological importance of self-esteem. In R. M. Kowalski, & M. R. Leary (Eds.), *The social psychology of emotional and behavioral problems: Interfaces of social and clinical psychology* (pp. 197-221). Washington, D.C.: American Psychological Association.

Leary, M. R., & Miller, R. S. (1986). *Social psychology and dysfunctional behavior: Origins, diagnosis, and treatment.* New York: Springer-Verlag.

Leatherdale, S. T., Woodruff, S. J., & Manske, S. R. (2010). *American Journal of Health Behavior, 34*(1), 31-35.

LeCroy, C. W., & Archer, J. (2001). Teaching social skills: A board game approach. In C. Schaefer & S. E. Reid (Eds.), *Game play: Therapeutic use of childhood games* (2nd ed.) (pp. 331-334). New York: John Wiley.

Lee, B. (1993). Tai chi chuan exercise for reducing stress: A study at a clinical setting. Unpublished dissertation, Clemson University, South Carolina.

Lee, J., Lim, N., Yang, E., & Lee, S. M. (2011). Antecedents and consequences of three dimensions of burnout in psychotherapists: A Meta-Analysis. *Professional Psychology: Research and Practice, 42*(3), 252-258.

Lee, Y. (1998). Critique of Austin's Health Protection and Health Promotion Model. *Therapeutic Recreation Journal, 32*(2), 118-123.

Lee, Y., Henningfeld, A. G., & Tabourne, C. E. (2012). Life review program as a therapeutic recreation modality. *Annual in Therapeutic Recreation, 20,* 59-67.

Lee, Y., & McCormick, B. P. (2002). Toward evidence-based therapeutic recreation practice. In D. R. Austin, J. Dattilo, & B. P. McCormick (Eds.), *Conceptual foundations for therapeutic recreation* (pp. 165-181). State College, PA: Venture.

Lee, Y., Tabourne, C., & Yoon, J. (2008). Life review program as a therapeutic recreation intervention for Korean elderly with Alzheimer's disease: Qualitative analysis. *Annual in Therapeutic Recreation, 16,* 171-180.

Lehrer, P. M., & Woolfolk, R. L. (Eds.). (1993). *Principles and practice of stress management* (2nd ed.). New York: Guilford Press.

Leitner, M. J., & Leitner, S. F. (1985). Recreation leadership principles. Activities, *Adaptation, & Aging, 7*(3/4), 25-41.

Leitner, M. J., & Leitner, S. F. (2005). The use of leisure counselling as a therapeutic technique. *British Journal of Guidance & Counseling, 33*(1), 37-49.

Leitner, M. J., & Leitner, S. F. (2012). *Leisure in later life* (4th ed.). Urbana, IL: Sagamore.

Lemmens, P. M. C., Brokken, D., Crompvoets, F. M. H., van den Eerenbeemd, & de Vries, G-J. (2010). Tactile experiences. In A. Nijholt, E. O. Dijk, P. M. C. Lemmens, & S. Luitjens (Eds.). *EuroHaptics 2010: Proceedings of the EuroHaptics 2010 Special Symposium* (pp. 11-17). Amsterdam.

Leopold, A. A. O., Avelar, N. C. P., Passos, G. B., Santana, N. A. P., Teixera, V. P., de Lima, V. P., & de Melo Vitorno, D. F. (2013). Effect of Pilates on sleep quality and quality of life of sedentary population. *Journal of Bodywork and Movement Therapies, 17*(1), 5-10.

Leopoldino, A. A., Avelar, N. C., Passos, G. B., Santano, N. A., Teixeria, V. P., de Lima, V. P., & de Melo Vitorino, B. F. (2013). Effects of Pilates on sleep quality and quality of life of sedentary population. *Journal of Bodywork and Movement Therapies, 17*(1), 5-10.

Lepper, M. R., & Greene, D. (1975). Turning play into work: Effects of adult surveillance and extrinsic rewards on children's intrinsic motivation. *Journal of Personality and Social Psychology, 33,* 25-35.

Le Roux, M. C., & Kemp, R. (2009). Effect of a companion dog on depression and anxiety levels of elderly residents in a long-term care facility. *Psychogeriatrics, 9,* 23-26.

Leshan, L. (1999). *How to meditate.* New York: Little, Brown & Company.

Letts, L., Minezes, J., Edwards, M., Berenyl, J., Moros, K., O'Neill, & O'Toole, C. (2011). Effectiveness of interventions designed to modify and maintain abilities of people with Alzheimer's disease and related dementias. *The American Journal of Occupational Therapy, 65*(5), 505-513.

LeUnes, A. D., & Nation, J. (1996). *Sport psychology: An introduction* (2nd ed.). Chicago: Nelson-Hall.

Leung, C. M., Lee, G., Cheung, B., Kwong, E., Wing, Y. K., Kas, C. S., & Lau, J. (1998). Karaoke therapy in the rehabilitatin of mental patients. *Singapore Medical Journal, 39*(4), 166-168.

Leung, R. W. M., Alison, J. A., McKeough, Z. J., & Peters, M. J. (2011). A study design to investigate the effect of short-term Sun-style Tai Chi in improving functional exercise capacity, physical performance, balance, and health related quality of life in people with Chronic Obstructive Pulmonary Disease (COPD). *European Respiratory Journal, 32*(2), 267-272.

Levy, K. N. (2009). Psychodynamic and psychoanalytic psychotherapy. In D. C. S. Richard & S. K. Huprich (Eds.), *Clinical Psychology* (pp. 181-214). Boston, MA: Elsevier.

Li, F., Harmer, P., McAuley, E., Fisher, K. J., Duncan, T. E., & Duncan, S. C. (2001). Tai chi, self-efficacy, and physical function in the elderly. *Prevention Science, 2*(4), 229-239.

Li, M., Chen, K., & Mo, Z. (2002). Use of qigong therapy in the detoxification of heroin addicts. *Alternative Therapies, 8*(1), 1-9.

Li, R. K. K. (1981). Activity therapy and leisure counseling for the schizophrenic population. *Therapeutic Recreation Journal, 15*(4), 44-49.

Liberman, R. P. & Martin, T. (1988). Social skills training. *Psychiatric Rehabilitation of Chronic Mental Patients.* pp. 147-198.

Lidell, L. (2002). *The book of massage.* New York: A Fireside Book.

Lim, N., Kim, E. K., Kim, H., Yang, E. & Lee, S. M. (2010). Individual and work-related factors influencing burnout of mental health professionals: A meta-analysis. *Journal of Employment Counseling, 47*, 86-96.

Limond, J., & Leeke, R. (2005). Practitioner review: Cognitive rehabilitation for children with acquired brain injury. *Journal of Child Psychology and Psychiatry, 46*(4), 339-352.

Linden, W. (1993). The autogenic training method of J. H. Schultz. In P. M. Lehrer, & R. L. Woolfolk (Eds.), *Principles and practices of stress management* (2nd ed.). New York: The Guilford Press.

Linley, P. A., & Joseph, S. (Eds.). (2004). *Positive psychology in practice.* Hoboken, NJ: John Wiley & Sons.

Linley, P. A., & Joseph, S. (2004a). Applied positive psychology: A new perspective for professional practice. In P. A. Linley & S. Joseph (Eds.), *Positive psychology in practice* (pp. 3-12). Hoboken, NJ: John Wiley & Sons.

Linley, P. A., & Joseph, S. (2004b). Toward a theoretical foundation for positive psychology in practice. In P. A. Linley, & S. Joseph (Eds.), *Positive psychology in practice* (pp. 713 – 731). Hoboken, NJ: John Wiley & Sons.

Liu, S., Lin, C., Chen, Y., & Huang, X. (2007). The effects of reminiscence group therapy on self-esteem, depression, loneliness and life satisfaction of elderly people living alone. *Taiwan Journal of Medicine, 12*, 133-142.

Livingston, G., Johnston, K., Katona, C., Paton, J., & Lyketsos, C. G. (2005). Systematic review of psychological approaches to the management of neuropsychiatric symptoms of dementia. *American Journal of Psychiatry, 162*(11), 1996-2021.

Lloyd, J. (2012). Alzheimer's risk falls with activity. *USA Today,* April 19, 2012, p. 3A.

LoBello, J. (nd). Gardening from a wheelchair. Retrieved from http://www.christopherreeve.org/site/c.mtKZKgMWKwG/b.5300837/k.7D2E/Gardening_from_a_Wheelchair.htm

Locke, D. C., Myers, J. E., & Herr, E. L. (2001). *The handbook of counseling.* Thousand Oaks: Sage.

Lolak, S., Connors, G. L., Sheridan, M. J., & Wise, T. N. (2008). Effects of progressive muscle relaxation training on anxiwty and depression in patients enrolled in an outpatient pulmonary rehabilitation program. *Psychotherapy and Psychosomatics, 77,* 119-125.

Lotan, M., & Gold, C. (2009). Meta-analysis of the effectiveness of individual intervention in the controlled multisensory environment (Snoezelen) for individuals with Intellectual disabilities. *Journal of Intellectual & Developmental Disability, 34*(3), 207-215.

Li, F., Harmer, P., McAuley, E., Fisher, K. J., Duncan, T. E., & Duncan, S. C. (2002). Tai chi, self-efficacy, and physical function in the elderly. *Prevention Science, 2*(4), 229-239.

Lin, Y., Wu, M., Yang, C., Chen, T., Hsu, C., Chang, Y., Tzeng, W. C., Chou, Y. H., & Chou, K. R. (2008). Evaluation of assertiveness training for psychiatric patients. *Journal of Clinical Nursing, 17*(21), 2875-2883.

Lippincott Manual of Nursing Practice. (2007). *Documentation.* Philadelphia: Wolters Kluwer/Lippincott Williams & Wilkins.

Loganbill, C., Hardy, E., & Delworth, U. (1982). Supervision: A conceptual model. *The Counseling Psychologist, 10,* 3-42.

Lolak, S., Connors, G. L., Sheridan, M. J., & Wise, T. N. (2008). Effects of progressive muscle relaxation training on anxiety and depression in patients enrolled in an outpatient pulmonary rehabilitation program. *Psychotherapy and Psychosomatics, 77*(2), 119-125

Lombardi, F., Taricco, M., De Tanti, A., Telaro, E., & Liberati, A. (2002). Sensory stimulation of brain-injured individuals in coma or vegetative state: Results of a Cochrane systematic review. *Clinical Rehabilitation, 16,* 464-472.

Long, G. L., Higgins, P. G., & Brady, D. (1988). *Psychosocial assessment: A pocket guide for data collection.* Norwalk, CT: Appleton & Lange.

Longo, D. C., & Williams, R. A. (1986). *Clinical practice in psychosocial nursing: Assessment and intervention* (2nd ed.). New York: Appleton-Century-Crofts.

Lou, M. F. (2001). The use of music to decrease agitated behaviour of the demented elderly: The state of the science. *Scandinavian Journal of Caring Science, 15*(2), 165-173.

Luckmann, J., & Sorensen, K. C. (1980). *Medical-surgical nursing: A psychophysiologic approach* (2nd ed.). Philadelphia, PA: W. B. Saunders.

Luckner, J. L., & Nadler, R. S. (1995). Processing adventure experiences: It's the story that counts. *Therapeutic Recreation Journal, 29*(3), 175-183.

Luckner, J. L., & Nadler, R. S. (1997). *Processing the experience: Strategies to enhance and generalize learning* (2nd ed.). Dubuque, IA: Kendall/Hunt.

Luft, J. (1984). *Group processes: An introduction.* Mountain View, CA: Mayfield.

Lumsden, L. (1986). *The healing power of humor.* Bloomington, IN: South Central Community Mental Health Centers, Inc.

Lynch, J. (1989). Relax to the max. *Runner's World, 24*(3), 39, 40.

Lyons, R. F., Sullivan, M. J. L., Ritvo, P. G., & Coyne, J. C. (1995). *Relationships in chronic Illness and disability.* Newbury Park, CA: Sage.

Lysycia, J. (2008). *Superstretch.* New York: Sterling.

Maas, J., & Verheij, R. A. (2007). Are health benefits of physical activity in natural environments used In primary care by general practitioners in the Netherlands? *Urban Forestry & Urban Greening, 6*(4), 227-233.

Macrae, J. (1993). *Therapeutic touch: A practical guide.* New York: Alfred A. Knopf.

Maddi, S. R. (1996). *Personality theories: A comparative analysis* (6th ed.). Pacific Grove, CA: Brooks/Cole.

Maddison, R., & Prapavessis, H. (2007). Self-handicapping in sport: A self-presentation strategy. In S. Jowett & D. Lavallee (Eds.), *Social psychology in sport* (pp. 208 - 231). Champaign, IL: Human Kinetics.

Madori, L. L. (2007). *Therapeutic thematic arts programming for older adults.* Baltimore, MD: Health Professions Press.

Mager, R. F. (1997). *Preparing instructional objectives: A critical tool in the development of effective instruction* (3rd ed.). Atlanta: The Center for Effective Performance, Inc.

Magyar-Moe, J. L. (2009). Labeling (positive effects). In S. J. Lopez (ed.). *Encyclopedia of Positive Psychology.* Hoboken, NJ: Wiley-Blackwell. Retrieved from http://site.ebrary.com/lib/lub/Doc?id=10301299&ppg=587.

Makwana, J. J., & Patil, P. J. (2012). Premature ejaculation: A comparative analysis between joga and stop-start. *Indian Journal of Research and Reports in Medical Sciences, 2*(3), 17-20.

Malkin, M. J., & Cook, A. B. (1997). Cognitive therapy techniques in recreation therapy and leisure education for individuals with depression. In G. L. Hitzhusen, & L. Thomas (Eds.), *Expanding horizons in therapeutic recreation XVII: Selected papers from the 1995-96 midwest symposium on therapeutic recreation* (pp. 54-68). Columbia: University of Missouri.

Malkin, M. J., & Kastrinos, G. (1997). Integration of cognitive therapy techniques with recreational therapy. In D. M. Compton (Ed.), *Issues in therapeutic recreation: Toward the new millennium* (2nd ed.) (pp. 445-460). Urbana, IL: Sagamore.

Malkin, M. J., Lloyd, L. F., & Gerstenberger, D. (2011). Benefits of therapeutic horseback riding for an adolescent female with traumatic brain injury. *American Journal of Recreation Therapy, 10*(2), 17-28.

Malkin, M. J., Phillips, R. W., & Chumbler, J. A. (1991). The family lab: An interdisciplinary family leisure education program. *Annual in Therapeutic Recreation, 2,* 25-36.

Maloff, C., & Wood, S. M. (1988). *Business and social etiquette with disabled people.* Springfield, IL: Charles C. Thomas.

Malone, W. J. (2009). Clinical supervision: We are more than bosses...we are leaders. Retrieved from http://www.canville.net/malone/home-study-course-200903.pdf

Malveaux, J. (2012). Blacks must adjust to changing times. *USA Today,* February 17, 2012, 9A.

Manini, T. M., Everhart, J. E., Patel, K. V., Schoeller, D. A., Colbert, L. H., Visser, M., Tylavsky, F.,... & Harris, T.B. (2006). Daily activity energy expenditure and mortality among older adults. *JAMA, 296*(2), pp. 171-179.

Mann, M., Hosman, C., Schaalma, H., & de Fries, N. (2004). Self-esteem in a broad-spectrum approach for mental health promotion. *Health Education Research, 19*(4), 357-372.

Manocha, R. (2000). Why meditation? *Australian Family Physician, 29*(12), 1135-1138.

Marcer, D. (1986). *Biofeedback and related therapies in clinical practice.* Rockville, MD: Aspen.

Mark, G. F. (2001). *Six healing movements: Qigong for health, strength, longevity.* Boston, MA: YMCA Publication Center.

Marriner, A. (1983). *The nursing process: A scientific approach to nursing care* (3rd ed.). St. Louis, MO: Mosby.

Martens, R. (1975). *Social psychology and physical activity.* New York: Harper & Row.

Martin, D., & Wilhite, B. (2003). Understanding meaning: A writing intervention to explore the personal relevance of recreation and leisure participation. *American Journal of Recreation Therapy, 2*(1), 49 - 55.

Martin, R. A. (2001). Humor, laughter, and physical health: Methodological issues and research findings. *Psychological Bulletin, 127*(4), 504-519.

Martina, C. M. S., & Stevens, N. L. (2006). Breaking the cycle of loneliness? Psychological effects of a friendship enhancement program for older adults. *Aging & Mental Health, 10*(5), 467-475.

Mascott, C. (2004). *The therapeutic recreation stress management primer.* State College, PA: Venture.

Masi, C. M., Chen, H., Hawkley, L. C., & Cacippo, J.T . (2011). A meta-analysis of interventions to reduce loneliness. *Personality and Social Psychology Review, 15*(3), 219-266.

Maslach, C. (1982). *Burnout: The cost of caring.* Englewood Cliffs, NJ: Prentice-Hall.

Maslach, C., & Leiter, M. P. (1997). *The truth about burnout: How organizations cause personal stress and what to do about it.* San Francisco, CA: Jossey-Bass.

Maslach, C., & Leiter, M. P. (2005). Reversing burnout: How to rekindle your passion for your work. Stanford University, Center for Social Innovation. Retrieved from http://findarticles.com/p/articles/mi_qa5307/is_200501/ai_n21384852/print

Maslach, C., & Leiter, M. P. (2008). Early predictors of job burnout and engagement. *Journal of Applied Psychology, 93*(3), 498 - 512.

Maslow, A. H. (1970). *Motivation and personality* (2nd ed.). New York: Harper & Row.

Mason, L. J. (2001). *Guide to stress reduction.* Berkeley, CA: Celestial Arts.

Mattson, R. H. (1998). Medical management of epilepsy in adults. *Neurology, 51*(Suppl 4), S15-S20.

Maville, J. A., & Huerta, C. G. (2008). *Health promotion in nursing* (2nd ed.). Clifton Park, NY: Thomson Delmar Learning.

Maxwell-Hudson, C. (1988). *The complete book of massage.* New York: Random House.

Maxwell-Hudson, C. (1996). *Pocket massage for stress relief.* New York: DK Publishing.

Mayeroff, M. (1971). *On caring.* New York: Harper & Row.

Mayo Clinic. (2006). Job burnout: Know the signs and symptoms. Retrieved from http://www.mayoclinic.com/print/burnout/WL00062/METHOD=print

Mayo Clinic. (2012). Stroke complications. Retrieved from http://www.mayoclinic.com/health/stroke/D500150/DSECTION=complications

McBride, G. (1983). Teachers, stress, and burnout. In R. E. Schmid, & L. M. Nagata (Eds.), *Contemporary issues in special education.* New York: McGraw-Hill.

McCabe, P., Lippert, C., Weiser, M., Hilditch, M., Hartridge, C., & Villamere, J. (2007). Community reintegration following acquired brain Injury. *Brain Injury, 21*(2), 231-257.

McCaffrey, R. M., Hanson, C., & McCaffrey, W. (2010). Garden walking for depression: A research report. *Holistic Nursing Practice, 24*(5), 252-259.

McCaffrey, R. & Locsin, R. C. (2002). Music listening as a nursing intervention: A symphony of practice. *Holistic Nursing Practice, 16*(3), 70-77.

McCallie, M. S., Blum, C. M., & Hood, C. J. (2006). Progressive muscle relaxation. *Journal of Human Behavior in the Social Environment, 13*(3), 51-66.

McCormick, B. P. (2002). Social support in therapeutic recreation. In D.R. Austin, J. Dattilo, & B.vP. McCormick (Eds.), *Conceptual foundations for therapeutic recreation* (pp. 49-72.). State College, PA: Venture.

McCrone, S. H. (1991). Resocialization group treatment with the confused institutionalized elderly. *Western Journal of Nursing Research, 13*(1), 30-45.

McDavid, J. W., & Harari, H. (1968). *Social psychology, individuals, groups, societies.* New York: Harper & Row.

McDowell, C. F. (1980). Leisure counseling issues: Reviews, overviews, & previews. In F. Humphrey, J. D. Kelley, & E. J. Hamilton (Eds.), *Facilitating leisure development for the disabled: A status report on leisure counseling.* College Park, MD: University of Maryland.

McDowell, C. F. (1984). Leisure: consciousness, well-being, and counseling. In E. T. Dowd (Ed.), *Leisure counseling: Concepts and applications.* Springfield, IL: Charles C. Thomas.

McEwen, M., & Wills, E. M. (2007). *Theoretical basis for nursing* (2nd ed.). Philadelphia, PA: Lippincott Williams & Wilkins.

McEwen, M., & Willis, E. M. (2011). *Theoretical basis for nursing* (3rd ed.). Philadelphia, PA: Wolters Kluwer Health/Lippincott Williams & Wilkins.

McFarland, K. M., & Wasli, E. L. (1986). *Nursing diagnosis and process in psychiatric nursing.* Philadelphia, PA: J. B. Lippincott.

McGarry, T. J., & Prince, M. (1998). Implementation of groups for creative expression on a psychiatric unit. *Journal of Psychosocial Nursing, 36*(3), 19-24.

McGuire, F., Boyd, R., & Tedrick, R. T. (1995). Preventing caregiver burnout. *Recreation Focus, 3*(1), 4.

McHugh, R. K., & Barlow, D. H. (2010). The dissemination and implementation of evidence-based psychological treatments. *American Psychologist, 65*(2), 73-84.

McKay, M., & Fanning, P. (2008). *Progressive relaxation and breathing.* (Audio CD). Oakland, CA: New Harbinger.

McKechnie, A. A., Wilson, F., Watson, N., & Scott, D. (1983). Anxiety states: A preliminary report on the value of connective tissue massage. *Journal of Psychosomatic Research, 27,* 125-129.

McKechnie, G. E. (1974). Psychological foundations of leisure counseling: An empirical strategy. *Therapeutic Recreation Journal, 8* (1), 4-16.

McKenney, A., & Dattilo, J. (2011). Values clarification. In J. Dattilo & A. McKenney (Eds.), *Facilitation techniques in therapeutic recreation* (2nd ed.) (pp. 593-614). State College, PA: Venture.

McKenney, A., Dattilo, J., Cory, L., & Williams, R. (2004). Effects of a computerized therapeutic recreation program on knowledge of social skills of male youth with emotional and behavioral disorders. *Annual in Therapeutic Recreation, 8,* 12-23.

McKenzie, M. D. (2000). How are adventure education programs achieved? A review of the literature. *Australian Journal of Outdoor Education, 5*(1), 19-28.

McKinney, A., Dustin, D., & Wolff, R. (2001). The promise of dolphin-assisted therapy. *Parks & Recreation, 36*(5), 46-50.

McNeil-Haber, F. M. (2004). Ethical considerations of nonerotic touch in psychotherapy with children. *Ethics & Behavior, 14*(2), 123-140.

McVoy, M., & Findling, R.L. (2012). *Clinical manual of child and adolescent psychopharmacology.* Washington, DC: American Psychiatric Publishing.

Mead, G., Bernhardt, J., & Kwakkel, G. (2012). Stroke: Physical fitness, exercise, and fatigue. *Stroke Research and Treatment, 2012,* Article ID 632531, 2 pages.

Mead, G. H. (1934). *Mind, self, and society.* Chicago: University of Chicago Press.

Meehan, T. C. (1999). Therapeutic touch. In G. M. Bulechek, & J. C. McCloskey (Eds.), *Nursing interventions: Effective nursing treatments* (3rd ed.) (pp. 173-188). Philadelphia, PA: W. B. Saunders.

Meixsell, J. J. (2005). Remotivation programing: The first fifty years. In J. A. Dyer & M. L. Stotts (Eds.), *Handbook of remotivation therapy* (pp. 7-12). Binghamton, NY: Haworth.

Melnyk, B. M., Fineout-Overholt, E., Giggleman, M., & Cruz, R. (2010). Correlates among congitive beliefs, EMP implementation, organizational culture, cohesion and job satisfaction in evidence-based practice mentors from a community hospital system. *Nursing Outlook, 58,* 301-308.

Melson, G. F., Kahn, P. H., Beck, A., & Friedman, B. (2009). Robotic pets In human lives: Implications for human-animal bond and for human relationships with personified technologies. *Journal of Social Issues, 65*(3), 545-567.

Menard, L. A. (2011). A review of innovative apps for students with communication needs. *American Journal of Recreation Therapy, 10*(2), 29-37.

Menninger, W. C. (1960). *Recreation and mental health*. Recreation and psychiatry. New York: National Recreation Association.

Meyer, M. W. (1962). The rationale of recreation as therapy. *Recreation in treatment centers* (Vol. 1). Washington, D.C.: National Therapeutic Recreation Society, National Recreation and Park Association.

Meyerhardr, J. A., Giovannucci, E. L., Holmes, M. D., Chan, A. T., Chan, J. A., Colditz, G. A., & Fuchs, C. S. (2006). Physical activity and survival after colorectal cancer diagnosis. *Journal of Clinical Oncology, 24*(22), 3527-3534.

Meyers, L. (2008). Recommended readings: Psychologists share the contents of their self-help shelves. *Monitor on Psychology, 39*(1), 26-27.

Mikulincer, M. (1988). Reactance and helplessness following exposure to unsolvable problems: The effects of attributional style. *Journal of Personality and Social Psychology, 54*, 679-686.

Miller, E. E. (1986). *Self-imagery: Creating your own good health*. Berkeley, CA: Celestial Arts.

Miller, K., Dierks, T., Van Puymbroeck, M., Schalk, N., Williams, L., Damush, t., & Schmid, A. (2011). Poster 73: Therapeutic yoga: Impact on pain and physical impairments after stroke. *Archives of Physical Medicine and Rehabilitation, 92*, 1713.

Miller, M. (1989). *Documentation in long-term care*. Alexandria, VA: National Therapeutic Recreation Society, National Recreation and Park Association.

Miller, W. R., & Rollnick, S. (1991). *Motivational interviewing: Preparing people to change addictive behavior*. New York: The Guilford Press.

Miller, W. R., & Rollnick, S. (2002). *Motivational interviewing: Preparing people to change* (2nd ed.). New York: The Guilford Press.

Milne, A. (1999). *Counseling*. Lincolnwood, IL: NTC/Contemporary.

Minor, M. A., Webel, R. R., Kay, D. R., Hewett, J. E., & Anderson, S. K. (1989). Efficacy of physical conditioning exercise in patients with rheumatoid arthritis and osteoarthritis. *Arthritis & Rheumatism, 32*, 1396-1405.

Mitchell, L. A., MacDonald, R. A. R., Knussen, C., Serpell, M. G. (2007). A survey investigation of the effects of music listening on chronic pain. *Psychology of Music, 35*(1), 37-57.

Mizuno-Matsumoto, Y., Kobashi, S., Hata, Y., Ishikawa, O., & Asano, F. (2008). Horticulture therapy has beneficial effects on brain functions in cerebrovascular disease. *International Journal of Intelligent Computing In Medical Sciences and Imaging Processing, 2*, 169-182.

Moadel, A. B., Shah, C., Wylie-Rosett, J., Harris, M.S., Petel, S. R., Hall, C. B., & Sparano, J. A. (2007). Randomized control trail of yoga among a multiethnic sample of breast cancer patients: Effects on quality of life. *Journal of Clinical Oncology, 25*(28), 4387-4395.

Mobily, K. E. (2009). Role of exercise and physical activity In therapeutic recreation service. *Therapeutic Recreation Journal, 43*(2), 9-26.

Mobily, K. E. (2011). Physical activity. In N.J. Stumbo & B. Wardlaw (Eds.), *Facilitation of therapeutic recreation services* (pp. 247-255). State College, PA: Venture.

Mokone, S. (2000). Qi gong and tai chi in physical therapy. In R. A. Charman (Ed.), *Complementary therapies for physical therapists*. Boston: Butterworth-Heinemann.

Monroe, J. E. (1987). Family leisure programming. *Therapeutic Recreation Journal, 21*(3), 44-51.

Monsen, R. B. (2002). Children playing. *Journal of Pediatric Nursing, 17*(2), 137,138.

Moon, L. M. (2010). Benefits of aquatic exercise for persons living with a mental illness at Eastern State Hospital. *ATRA Newsletter, 26*(3), 2-3.

Moore, A., & Malinowski, P. (2008). Meditation, mindfulness and cognitive flexibility. *Consciousness and Cognition, 18*, 176-186.

MoraMarco, J. (2000). *The way of walking*. Lincolnwood, IL: Contemporary Books.

Moraska, A., & Chandler, C. (2008), Changes in clinical parameters in patients with tension-type headache following massage therapy: A pilot study. *The Journal of Manual & Manipulative Therapy, 16*(2), 106-112.

Morgan, S. (1996). *Helping relationships in mental health*. New York: Chapman & Hall.

Morrison, I., Bjornsdotter, M., & Olausson, H. (2011). Vicarious responses to social touch in posterior insular cortex are tuned to pleasant caressing speeds. *The Journal of Neuroscience, 31*(26), 9554-9562.

Morse, G., Salyers, M. P., Rollins, A. L., Monroe-DeVita, M., & Pfahler, C. (2012). Burnout in mental health services: A review of the problem and its remediation. *Administrative and Policy in Mental Health, 39*, 341-352.

Morton-Cooper, A., & Palmer, A. (2000). *Mentoring, preceptorship and clinical supervision* (2nd ed.). London: Blackwell Science.

Mosak, H., & Maniacci, M. (1993). An "Adlerian" approach to humor and psychotherapy. In W. F. Fry, & W. A. Salameh (Eds.), *Advances in humor and psychotherapy*. Sarasota, FL: Professional Resource Press.

Mosey, A. C. (1973). *Activities therapy*. New York: Raven Press.

Mostert, S., & Kesselring, J. (2002). Effects of a short-term exercise training program on aerobic fitness, fatigue, health perception and activity level of subjects with multiple sclerosis. *Multiple Sclerosis, 8*, 161-168.

Motl, R. W., & Gosney, J. L. (2008). Effect of exercise training on quality of life in multiple sclerosis: A meta-analysis. *Multiple Sclerosis, 14*, 129-135.

Motl, R. W., McAuley, E., & Snook, E. M. (2005). Physical activity and multiple sclerosis: A meta-analysis. *Multiple Sclerosis, 11*, 459-463.

Moyer, C. A., Rounds, J., & Hannum, J. W. (2004). A meta-analysis of massage therapy research. *Psychological Bulletin, 130*(1), 3-18.

Mrkic, L. (2011). *The prevalence of evidence-based practice by the Certified Therapeutic Recreation Specialist in the interrvention planning process for client treatment.* Unpublished master's thesis. Richmond, KY: Eastern Kentucky University.

MTD Training. (2010a). *Advanced communication skills.* Training & Ventus Publishing ApS.

MTD Training. (2010b). *Effective communication skills.* Training & Ventus Publishing ApS.

Moss, D. (2002). Biofeedback. In S. Shannon (Ed.), *Handbook of complementary and alternative therapies in mental health* (pp. 135 - 158). San Diego, CA: Academic Press.

Mueser, K. T., & Glynn, S. M. (1999). *Behavioral family therapy for psychiatric disorders* (2nd ed.). Oakland, CA: New Harbinger.

Muller, B., & Armstrong, H. (1975). A further note on the "running treatment" for anxiety. *Psychotherapy: Theory, research, and practice, 12*(4), 385-367.

Mulveaux, J. (2012). Blacks must adjust to changing times. *USA Today*, February 17, 2012, 9A.

Mundy, J., & Odum, L. (1979). *Leisure education: Theory and practice.* New York: John Wiley and Sons.

Munson, C. E. (2002). *Handbook of clinical social work supervision* (3rd ed.). New York: The Haworth Social Work Practice Press.

Munson, W. W., & Munson, D. G. (1986). Multimodal leisure counseling with older people. *Activities, Adaption & Aging, 9*(1), 1-15.

Murphy, J. F. (1975). *Recreation and leisure services.* Dubuque, IA: Wm. C. Brown.

Murphy, J. F., Williams, J. G., Niepoth, E. W., & Brown, P. D. (1973). *Leisure service delivery system: A modern perspective.* Philadelphia, PA: Lea & Febiger.

Murray, R. B., & Baier, M. (1993). Use of the therapeutic milieu in a community setting. *Journal of Psychosocial Nursing, 31*(10), 11-16.

Murray, R. B., & Huelskoetter, M. M. W. (1987). *Psychiatric/mental health nursing* (2nd ed.). Norwalk, CT: Appleton & Lange.

Murray, R. B., & Huelskotter, M. M. W. (1991). *Psychiatric/mental health nursing* (3rd ed.). Norwalk, CT: Appleton & Lange.

Murray, S. B. (1997). The benefits of journaling. *Parks & Recreation, 32*(5), 68-75.

Myers, D. G. (1996). *Social psychology* (5th ed.). New York: McGraw-Hill.

Nadler, R. S., & Luckner, J. L. (1997). *Processing the adventure experience: Theory and practice.* Dubuque, IA: Kendall/Hunt.

Nakamura, J., & Csikszentmihalyi, M. (2004). The construction of meaning through vital engagement. In C. L. M. Keyes and J. Haidt (Eds.), *Flourishing: Positive psychology and the life well-lived* (pp. 83-104). Washington, D.C.: American Psychological Association.

Narrow, B. W., & Buschle, K. B. (1987). *Fundamentals of nursing practice* (2nd ed.). New York: John Wiley & Sons.

Nathan, A. A., & Mirviss, S. (1998). *Therapy techniques using the creative arts.* Ravensdale, WA: Idyll Arbor.

Nathan, P. E. (2010). Forward. In D. B. Peterson (Eds.), *Psychological aspects of functioning, disability, and health* (pp. xxv-xxvii). New York: Springer.

National Center for Complementary and Alternative Medicine. (2010a). *Massage therapy: An introduction.* Retrieved from http://nccam.nih.gov/health/massageintroduction.htm

National Center for Complementary and Alternative Medicine (2010b). *Tai chi: An introduction.* Retrieved from http://nccam.nih.gov/health/taichi/Introduction.htm National Center for Complementary and Alternative Medicine. (2012a). *Meditation: An introduction.* Retrieved from http://nccam.nih.gov/health/meditation.overview.htm

National Center for Complementary and Alternative Medicine. (2012b). *Relaxation techniques for health: An introduction.* Retrieved from http://nccam.nih.gov/health/stess/relaxation,htm

National Center for Complementary and Alternative Medicine. (2012c). *Yoga for health.* Retrieved from http://nccam.nih.gov/health/yoga/introduction.htm

National Center for Health Statistics. (2008). Classifications of diseases and functioning & disability. Retrieved from http://www.cdc.gov/nchs/about/otheract/icd9/icfhome.htm

National Center on Physical Activity and Disability. (2005). Gardening. Retrieved from http://www.ncpad.org/gardening/

National Council for Therapeutic Recreation Certification. (2007). *2007 NCTRC job analysis report.* New City, NY: National Council for Therapeutic Recreation Certification.

National Diabetes Information Clearing House. (2007). National diabetes statistics. Retrieved from http://diabetes.niddk.nih.gov/dm/pubs/statics/index.htm#allages

National Institute on Aging. (2008). Exercise: A guide from the National Institute on Aging. Retrieved from http://www.nia.nih.gov/HealthInformation/Publications/ExerciseGuide/default.htm

National Institute on Aging. (2010). *Exercise & physical activity*. Gaithersburg, MD: National Institute of Health, Publication No. 09-4258.

Neal, M., & Barton Wright, P. (2003). Validation therapy for dementia. *Cochrane Database of Systematic Reviews*, Issue 3. Art. No. CD001394.DOI: 10.1002/14651858.CD001394.

Neale, T. (2011). Aerobic exercises good for asthma patients. *MedPageToday*. Retrieved from http:www.medpagetoday.com/tbprint.cfm?tbid=29257

Netz, Y., Wu, M. J., Becker, B. J., & Tenenbaum, G. (2005). Physical activity and psychological well-being in advanced age: A meta-analysis of intervention studies. *Psychology and Aging, 20*(2), 272-284.

Neven, N. (2006). *The psychology of nursing care* (2nd ed.). New York: Palgrave Macmillan.

New York University Langone Medical Center. (2012). Relaxation therapies. Retrieved from http://surgery.med.nyu.edu/contents?ChuckIID=37435

Newes, S., & Bandoroff, S. (2004). What is adventure therapy. *Coming of age: The evolving field of adventure therapy*, pp. 1-30.

Ng, B. F. L., Lo, P. M. T., & Chan, A. S. B. (2009). Field trail of using remotivation therapy in adult psychiatry. *HKJOT Abstracts. Hong Kong Journal of Occupational Therapy, 19*(2), A11.

Ng, B. H. P. & Tsang, H. W. H. (2009). Psychphysiological outcomes of health qigong for chronic conditions: A systematic review. *Psychophysiology, 46*, 257-269.

Nidich, S. I., Rainforth, M. V., Haaga, D. A. F., Hagelin, J., Salerno, J. W., Travis, F., Tanner, M., ... & Schneider, R.H. (2009). A randomized controlled trail on effects of the transcendental meditation program on blood pressure, psychological distress, and coping in young adults. *American Journal of Hypertension, 22*(12), 1326-1331.

Nicholi Jr, A. M. (1988). *The new Harvard guide to psychiatry*. Cambridge, MA: Belknap Press.

Niles, S., Ellis, G., & Witt, P. A. (1981). Attribution scales: Control, competence, intrinsic motivation. In G. Ellis, & P. A. Witt (Eds.), *The leisure diagnostic battery: Background conceptualization and structure*. Denton, TX: North Texas State University, Division of Recreation and Leisure Studies.

Nimer, J., & Lundahl, B. (2007). Animal-assisted therapy: A meta-analysis. *Anthrozoos, 20*(3), 225-238.

Nintendo (2008). Wii Fit. Kyoto, Japan: Nintendo.

Niven, N. (2006). *The psychology of nursing care* (2nd ed.). New York: Palgrave MacMillan.

Nordli, D. R. (2008). Classification of epilepsies in childhood. In J. M. Pellock, B. F. D. Bourgeois, & W. E. Dodson (Eds.), *Pediatric epilepsy: Diagnosis and treatment* (3rd ed.) (pp. 137-146). New York, NY: Demos Medical Publishing.

Novotney, A. (2009). Yoga as a practice tool. *Monitor on Psychology, 40*(10), 38-42.

Novotney, A. (2010). Lights, camera, action! *Monitor on Psychology, 41*(7), 58-60.

Nugent, E. (1995). Try to remember . . . Reminiscence as a nursing intervention. *Journal of Psychosocial Nursing, 33*(11), 7-11.

Oakley, W. C., & Freeman, A. (2009). Cognitive-behavioral therapy: Breadth, range and diversity. In D. C. S. Richard & S. K. Huprich (Eds.), *Clinical psychology* (pp. 281-308). Boston: Elsevier.

O'Connell, B., Gardner, A., Takase, M., Hawkins, M.T., Ostaszkiewicz, J., Ski, C., & Josipovic, P. (2007). Clinical usefulness and feasibility of using Reality Orientation with patients who have dementia in acute care settings. *International Journal of Nursing Practice, 13*, 182-192.

Okun, B. F. (2002). *Effective helping: Interviewing and counseling techniques* (6th ed.). Pacific Grove, CA: Brooks/Cole.

Okun, B. F., & Kantrowitz, R. E. (2008). *Effective helping: Interviewing and counseling techniques* (7th ed.). Belmont, CA: Thomson, Brooks/Cole.

Olson, O. C. (1988). *Diagnosis and management of diabetes mellitus* (2nd ed.). New York: Raven Press.

O'Luanaigh, C. O., & Lawlor, B. A. (2008). Loneliness and the health of older people. *International Journal of Geriatric Psychiatry, 23*, 1213-1221.

O'Morrow, G. S. (1971). The whys of recreation activities for psychiatric patients. *Therapeutic Recreation Journal, 5* (3), 97-103+.

O'Morrow, G. S. (1976). *Therapeutic recreation: A helping profession*. Reston, VA: Reston.

O'Morrow, G. S. (1980). *Therapeutic recreation: A helping profession* (2nd ed.). Reston, VA: Reston.

O'Morrow, G. S., & Carter, M. J. (1997). *Effective management in therapeutic recreation service*. State College, PA: Venture.

O'Morrow, G. S., & Reynolds, R. P. (1989). *Therapeutic recreation: A helping profession* (3rd ed.). Englewood Cliffs, NJ: Prentice-Hall.

Ornstein, R., & Sobel, D. (1989). *Healthy pleasures.* New York: Addison-Wesley.

O'Toole, A. W. (1996). Designing a graduate program in psychiatric-mental health nursing. In S. Lego (Ed.), *Psychiatric nursing: A comprehensive reference* (2nd ed.). Philadelphia: J. B. Lippincott.

Owen, B. D. (1980). How to avoid that aching back. *American Journal of Nursing, 80*(5), 894-897.

Pace, T. W. W., Negi, L. T., Adame, D. D., Cole, S. P., Sivilli, T. I., Brown, T. D., Issa, M. J., & Raison, C. L. (2008). Effect of compassion meditation on neuroendocrine, Innate Immune and behavioral responses to psychosocial stress. *Psychoneuroendocinology, 34*(1), 87-98.

Pachana, N. A., & Arathoon, M. (2003). Passive therapeutic gardens: A study on an inpatient geriatric ward. *Journal of Gerontological Nursing, 29*, 4-10.

Page, S., & Wosket, V. (1994). *Supervising the counselor: A cyclical model.* New York: Routledge.

Palley, L. S., O'Rouke, P. P., & Niemi, S. M. (2010), Mainstreaming animal-assisted therapy. *ILAR Journal, 51*(3), 199-207.

Palmer, L. L., & Sadler, R. R. (1979). The effects of a running program on depression in rehabilitation clients. Unpublished research report. Fisherville, VA: Research Utilization Laboratory, Woodrow Wilson Rehabilitation Center.

Paluska, S. A., & Schwenk, T. L. (2000). Physical activity and mental health. *Sports Medicine, 29*(3), 167-180.

Panesar, N., & Valachova, I. (2011). Yoga and mental health. *Australasian Psychiatry, 19*(6), 538-539

Panksepp, J. (2000). The riddle of laughter: Neural and psychoevolutionary underpinnings of joy. *Current Directions in Psychological Science, 9*(6), 183-186.

Panman, R., & Panman, S. (2006). Group counseling and therapy. In J. L. Ronch, W. Van Ornum & N. C. Stilwell (Eds.), *The counseling sourcebook* (pp. 44 - 59). New York: The Crossroad Publishing Company.

Parham, D. (1987). Toward professionalism: The reflective therapist. *American Journal of Occupational Therapy, 41*, 555-561.

Paris, M., & Hoge, M. A. (2010). Burnout in the mental health workforce: a review. *Journal of Behavioral Health Services Research, 37*, 519-528.

Parke, R. D., & Sawin, D. B. (1975). *Aggression: Causes and controls.* Homewood, IL: Learning Systems Company.

Parker, R., Ellison, C., Kirby, T., & Short, M. J. (1975). The comprehensive evaluation in recreation therapy scale: A tool for patient evaluation. *Therapeutic Recreation Journal, 9*(4), 143-152.

Patrick, P. K. S. (1981). *Health care worker burnout: What it is, what to do about it.* Chicago: An Inquiry Book.

Paulose, M. J. (2011). The healing power of well-being. *Acta Neuropsychiatrica, 23*, 145-155.

Patterson, I. (2004). Snoezelen as a casual leisure activity for people with a developmental disability. *Therapeutic Recreation Journal, 38*(3), 289-300.

Patterson, M. M. (2012). Touch: Vital to patient-physician relationships. *Journal of the American Osteopathic Association, 112*(8), 485.

Patton, D. (2006). Reality orientation: Its use and effectiveness within older person mental health care. *Journal of Clinical Nursing, 15*(11), 1440-1449.

Paris, M., & Hoge, A. A. (2009). Burnout in the mental health workforce: A review. *Journal of Behavioral Health Services & Research, 37*(4), 519-528.

Payne, R. A. (2005). *Relaxation techniques: A practical handbook for the health care professional* (3rd ed.). New York: Elsevier Limited.

Pearson, Q. M. (2004). Getting the most of clinical supervision: Strategies for mental health. *Journal of Mental Health Counseling, 26*(4), 361-373.

Pedlar, A., Hornibrook, T., & Haasen, B. (2001). Patient focused care: Theory and practice. *Therapeutic Recreation Journal, 35*(1), 15-30.

Penedo, G. J., & Dahn, J. R. (2005). Exercise and well-being: A review of mental and physical health benefits associated with physical activity. *Current Opinion in Psychiatry, 18*, 189-193.

Pender, N. J. (1982). *Health promotion in nursing practice.* Norwalk, CT: Appleton-Century-Crofts.

Pender, N. J., Murdaugh, C. L., & Parsons, M. A. (2002). *Health promotion in nursing practice* (4th ed.). Upper Saddle River, NJ: Prentice Hall.

Peng, W., Crouse, J. C., & Lin, J. H. (2013). Using active video games for physical activity promotion: A systematic review of the current state of research. *Health Education & Behavior, 40*(3), 1-22.

Pennebaker, J. W. (1997). Writing about emotional experiences as a therapeutic process. *Psychological Science, 8*(3), 162-166.

Pennebaker, J. W. (2004). Theories, therapies, and taxpayers: On the complexities of the expressive writing paradigm. *Clinical Psychology: Science and Practice, 11*(2), 138-142.

Pennebaker, J. W., & Beall, S. K. (1986). Confronting a traumatic event: Toward an understanding of inhibition and disease. *Journal of Abnormal Psychology, 95*, 274-281.

Penner, D. (1989). *Eldercise.* Reston, VA: The American Alliance for Health, Physical Education, Recreation & Dance.

Pep up your life: A fitness book for seniors. (n.d.). Washington D.C.: American Association of Retired Persons.

Peregoy, J., & Dieser, R. (1997). Multiculturalism awareness in therapeutic recreation: Hamlet living. *Therapeutic Recreation Journal, 31*(3), 173-187.

Peregoy, J. J., Schliebner, C. T., & Dieser, R. B. (1997). Diversity issues in therapeutic recreation. In D. Compton (Ed.), *Issues in therapeutic recreation: Toward the new millennium* (2nd ed.) (pp. 275-298). Urbana, IL: Sagamore.

Perese, E. F., & Wolf, M. (2005). Combating loneliness among persons with severe mental illness: Social network interventions' characteristics, effectiveness, and applicability. *Issues in Mental Health Nursing, 26*, 591-609.

Perkins School for the Blind. (n.d.). *Horticulture program.* Watertown, MA.

Perko, J. E., & Kreigh, H. Z. (1988). *Psychiatric and mental health nursing* (3rd ed.). Norwalk, CT: Appleton & Lange.

Peterson, C. A., & Gunn, S. L. (1984). *Therapeutic recreation program design* (2nd ed.). Englewood Cliffs, NJ: Prentice-Hall.

Peterson, C., Park, N., & Seligman, M. E. P. (2006). Greater strengths of character and recovery from illness. *The Journal of Positive Psychology, 1*(1), 17-26.

Peterson, C. A., & Stumbo, N. J. (2000). *Therapeutic recreation program design* (3rd ed.). Boston, MA: Allyn and Bacon.

Peterson, C., & Seligman, M.E.P. (2004). *Character strengths and virtues. A handbook and classification.* New York: Oxford University Press/Washington, D.C.: American Psychological Association.

Peterson, D. B. (2010). *Psychological aspects of functioning, disability, and health.* New York: Springer.

Peterson, M., & Loy, D. P. (2008). Comparing the effectiveness of animal intervention, digital music relaxation, and humor on the galvanic skin response of individuals with Alzheimer's disease: Implications for recreational therapy. *Annual in Therapeutic Recreation, 16*, 129-142.

Pettigrew, S., & Roberts, M. (2008). Addressing loneliness in later life. *Aging in Mental Health, 12*(3), 302-309.

Pettit, J. W., Kline, J. P., Gencoz, T., Gencoz, F., & Joiner, T. E. (2001). Are happy people healthier? The specific role of positive affect in predicting self-reported health symptoms. *Journal of Research in Personality, 35*(4), 521-536.

Pfeiffer, E. F., & Galloway, J. A. (1988). Type II diabetes mellitus and oral hypoglycemic agents. In J. A. Galloway, J. H. Potvin, & C. R. Shuman (Eds.), *Diabetes mellitus* (9th ed.). Indianapolis: Lilly Research Laboratories.

Phelan, J. E. (2008). Exploring the use of touch In the psychotherapeutic setting: A phenomenological review. *Psychotherapy Theory, Research, Practice Training, 46*(1), 97-111.

Phend, C. (2011). Add a mile to walk off diabetes risk. *MedPageToday*. Retrieved from http://www.medpagetoday.com/tbprint.cfm?tbid=24336

Phillips, W. T., Kiernan, M., & King, A. C. (2001). The effects of physical activity on physical and psychological health. *Handbook of health psychology.* Baum, A, Revenson, TA, and Singer, JE, eds. Mahwah, NJ: Erlbaum, 627-657

Phillips, E. M., Schneider, J. C., & Mercer, G. R. (2004). Motivating elders to initiate and maintain exercise. *Archives of Physical Medicine and Rehabilitation, 85*(Suppl. 3), S52-S57.

Phrompaet, S., Paungmali, A., Pirunsan, U., & Sifilertpisan, P. (2011). Effects of Pilates training on lumbo-pelvic stability and flexibility. *Asian Journal of Sports Medicine, 2*(1), 7 pages.

Pichot, T. (2012). *Animal-assisted brief therapy: A solution-focused approach* (2nd ed.). New York: Routledge.

Pilon, B. A. (1998). Clinical pathways. In J. J. Fitzpatrick (Ed.), *Encyclopedia of nursing research* (pp. 92-93). New York: Springer.

Pilu, A., Sorba, M., Havdoy, M.C., Floris, A. L., Mannu, F., Seruis, M. L., Velluti, C., Carpiniello, B., Salvi, M., & Carta, M. G. (2007). Efficacy of physical activity in the adjunctive treatment of major depressive disorders: Preliminary results. *Clinical Practice and Epidemiology in Mental Health, 3*(8). Retrieved from http://www.cpementalhealth.com/content/3/1/8.

Pinson, B. (2002). Touch in therapy: An effort to make the unknown known. *Journal of Contemporary Psychotherapy, 32*(2/3), 179-196.

Plasqui, G. (2008). The role of physical activity In rheumatoid arthritis. *Psychology & Behavior, 94*, 270-275.

Platt-Koch, L. M. (1986). Clinical supervision for psychiatric nurses. *Journal of Psychosocial Nursing, 26*(1), 7-15.

Ploughman, M. (2008). Exercise is brain food: The effects of physical activity on cognitive function. *Developmental Neurorehabilitation, 11*(3), 236-240.

Polkki, T., Pietila, A-M., Vehvilainen,-Julkunen, K., Laukkala, H., & Kiviluoma, K. (2008). Imagery-Induced relaxation in children's postoperative pain relief: A randomized pilot study. *Journal of Pediatric Nursing, 23*(3), 217-224.

Porter, H. R., & burlingame, j. (2006). *Recreational therapy handbook of practice: ICF-based diagnosis and treatment.* Enumclaw, WA: Idyll Arbor.

Porter, H. R., Shank, J., & Iwasaki, Y. (2012). Promoting a collaborative approach with recreational therapy to Improve physical activity engagement in type 2 diabetes. *Therapeutic Recreation Journal, 46*(3), 202-217.

Porter, H. R., & Van Puymbroeck, M. (2007). Utilization of the International Classification of Functioning, Disability, and Health within therapeutic recreation practice. *Therapeutic Recreation Journal, 41*(1), 47-60.

Porter, P. A., & Perry, A. G. (2009). *Fundamentals of nursing* (7th ed.). St. Louis, MO: Mosby Elsevier.

Porter-O'Grady, T., & Malloch, K. (2013). *Leadership in nursing practice.* Burlington, MA: Jones & Bartlett Learning.

Posthuma, B. W. (2002). *Small groups in counseling and therapy: Process and leadership* (4th ed.). Boston, MA: Allyn and Bacon.

Potter, P. A., & Perry, A. G. (1995). *Basic nursing: Theory and practice* (3rd ed.). St. Louis, MO: Mosby.

Pratt, A. C. (2004). Retail therapy. *GeoForum, 35*(5), 519-521.

Preidt, R. (2013). Health. HealthDay Story. Retrieved from www.nim.nih.gov/medlineplus/news/fullstory_133058.html

Prerost, F. (1987). Health locus of control, humor, and reduction in aggression. *Psychological Reports, 61*, 887-896.

Pressman, S. D., & Cohen, S. (2005). Does positive affect influence health? *Psychological Bulletin, 131*(6), 925-971.

Price, M. J. (1983). Insulin and oral hypoglycemic agents. *Nursing Clinics of North America, 18*(4), 687-705.

Priest, S., & Gass, M. A. (1997). *Effective leadership in adventure programming.* Champaign, IL: Human Kinetics.

Primack, B. A., Carroll, M. V., McNamara, M., Klem, M. L., King, B., Rich, M., Chan, C. W., & Nayak, S. (2012). Role of video games in improving health-related outcomes. *American Journal of Preventive Medicine, 42*(6), 630-638.

Prince, P. N., & Gerber, G. J. (2005). Subjective well-being and community integration among clients of assertive community treatment. *Quality of Life Research, 14*, 161-169.

Prochaska, J. O., & DiClemente, C. C. (1982). Transtheoretical therapy: Toward a more integrative model of change. *Psychotherapy: Theory, Research and Practice, 19*, 276-288.

Provine, R. R. (2000). *Laughter: A scientific investigation.* New York: Penguin Books.

Purtilo, R. B., & Haddad, A. M. (2002). *Health professional and patient interactions.* Philadelphia, PA: W. B. Saunders.

Purtilo, R. B., Haddad, A. M., & Doherty, R. (2013). *Health professional and patient interaction* (8th ed.). St. Louis: Elsevier Saunders.

Quanty, M. B. (1976). Aggression catharsis: Experimental investigations and implications. In R. G. Green, & E. C. O'Neal (Eds.), *Perspectives on aggression.* New York: Academic Press.

Raglin, J. S. & Wilson, G. S. (2012). Exercise and its effects on mental health. In C. Bouchard, S. N. Blair & W. L. Haskell (Eds.), *Physical activity and* health (2nd ed.) (pp. 331-342). Champaign, IL: Human Kinetics.

Ram, F. S. F., Robinson, S. M., & Black, P. N. (2000). Effects of physical training in asthma: A systematic review. *British Journal of Sports Medicine, 34*, 162-167.

Ram, F. S. F., Robinson, S. M., Black, P. N., & Picot, J. (2005). Physical training for asthma. *Cochrane Database of Systematic Reviews* 2005, Issue 4. Art. No.: CD001116. DOI: 10.1002/14651858.CD001116.pub2.

Ramont, R. P., & Maldonado Niedringhaus, D. (2008). *Fundamental nursing care* (2nd ed.) Upper Saddle River, NJ: Pearson.

Rand, A. B. (2010). New realities of aging. *AARP Bulletin*, December 2010, p. 34.

Rappe, E., & Kivela, S. (2005). Effects of garden visits on long-term care residents as related to depression. *Research Reports: Horticulture Technology, 15*, 298-303.

Rappe, E., Kivela, S-L., & Rita, H. (2006). Visiting outdoor green environments positively impacts self- rated health among older people in long-term care. *Hort-Technology, 16*(1), 55-59.

Rashid, T., & Ostermann, R. F. (2009). Strength-based assessment in clinical practice. *Journal of Clinical Psychology, 65*(5), 488-498

Raskin, N. J., & Rogers, C. R. (2000). Person-centered therapy. In R. J. Corsini, & D. Wedding (Eds.), *Current psychotherapies* (6th ed.) (pp. 133-167). Itasca, IL: F. E. Peacock.

Rawlins, R. P., Williams, S. R., & Beck, C. K. (1993). *Mental health-psychiatric nursing: A holistic life-cycle approach* (3rd ed.). St. Louis, MO: Mosby Year Book.

Rawson, H. E. (1978). Short-term residential therapeutic camping for behaviorally disordered children ages 6-12: An academic remediation and behavioral modification approach. *Therapeutic Recreation Journal, 12*(4), 17-23.

Reader, M., Young, R., & Connor, J. P. (2005). Massage therapy improves the management of alcohol withdrawal syndrome. *The Journal of Alternative and Complementary Medicine, 11*(2), 311-313.

Reddy, N. (2006). Top six benefits of Pilates exercises. Retrieved from http://www.articlealley.com/article_87831_23.html

Reed, K. L., & Sanderson, S. N. (1992). *Concepts of occupational therapy* (3rd ed.). Baltimore: Williams & Wilkins.

Reference guide to handbooks and annuals. (1999). San Francisco, CA: Pfeiffer.

Rees, L., Marshall, S., Hartridge, C., Mackie, D., & Weiser, M. (2007). *Brain Injury, 21*(2), 161-200.

Reilly, D. E. (1978). *Teaching and evaluating the affective domain in nursing programs.* Thorofare, NJ: Charles B. Slack.

Remington, R. (2002). Calming music and hand massage with agitated elderly. *Nursing Research, 51*(5), 317-323.

Reynolds, R. P., & Arthur, M. H. (1982). Effects of peer modeling and cognitive self-guidance on the social play of emotionally disturbed children. *Therapeutic Recreation Journal, 16*(1), 33-40.

Rezaeei, V., & Ghofrani, M. (2012). Effect of two-month Pilates exercises on lumbar hyperlordosis of 15-18 year old girl students. *Annals of Biological Research, 3*(6), 2667-2672.

Richardson, E.D.(1998). Adventure-based therapy and self-efficacy theory: Test of treatment model of late adolescents and depressive symptomatology. (Doctorial dissertation) Virginia Polytechnic Institute and State University. Blacksburg, VA. Retrieved from: http://scholar.lib.vt.edu/theses/available/etd-041299.

Richardson, C. R., Faulkner, G., McDevitt, J., Skrinar, G. S., Hutchinson, D. S., & Piette, J. D. (2005). Integrating physical activity into mental health services for persons with serious mental illness. *Psychiatric Services, 56*(4), 324-331.

Richeson, N. E. (2003). Effects of animal-assisted therapy on agitated behaviors and social interactions of older adults with dementia. *American Journal of Alzheimer's Disease and Other Dementias, 18*(6), 353-358.

Richeson, N. E. (2006). Effects of a pedometer-based intervention on the physical performance and mobility-related self-efficacy of community-dwelling older adults: An interdisciplinary preventive health care intervention. *Therapeutic Recreation Journal, 40*(1), 18-32.

Richeson, N. E., & McCullough, W. T. (2003). A therapeutic recreation intervention using animal-assisted therapy: Effects on the subjective well-being of older adults. *Annual in Therapeutic Recreation, 12*, 1-6.

Rick, S. I., Pereira, B., & Burson, K. A. (2012). The benefits of retail therapy: Choosing to buy reduces residual sadness. Available at SSRN2119576.

Ridenour, D. (1983). *Wellness: Building toward maximal health*. Bloomington, IN: South Central Community Mental Health Center.

Ridley, C. R., Mendoza, D. W., Kanitz, B. E., Angermeier, L., & Zenk, R. (1994). Cultural sensitivity in multicultural counseling: A perceptual schema model. *Journal of Counseling Psychology, 41*, 125-135.

Riehl, J. P., & Roy, C. (1980). *Conceptual models for nursing practice* (2nd ed.). New York: Appleton-Century-Crofts.

Rimmer, J. H., & Yamaki, K. (2006). Obesity and intellectual disability. *Mental Retardation and Developmental Disabilities, 12*, 22-27.

Ringness, T. A. (1975). *The affective domain in education*. Boston, MA: Little, Brown and Company.

Robb, G. M. (Ed.). (1980). Outdoor and adventure programs: Complementing individual education programs and treatment plan objectives. *Practical Pointers, 4*(1), 1-23.

Robb, G. M., Leslie, J., & McGowan, M. L. (n.d.). *Sequential outdoor challenge activities*. Bloomington, IN: Indiana University.

Robb, S., Boyd, M., & Pristash, C. L. (1980). A wine bottle, plant, and puppy: Catalysis for social behavior. *Journal of Gerontological Nursing, 6*(12), 721-728.

Robb, S. S., Stegman, C. E., & Wolanin, M. O. (1986). No research versus research with compromised results: A study of validation therapy. *Nursing Research, 35*(2), 113-118.

Robitaille, S. (2010). *The illustrated guide to assistive technology and devices; Tools and gadgets for living independently*. New York: Domos Medical Pub.

Rogers, C. R. (1961). *On becoming a person: A therapist's view of psychotherapy*. Boston, MA: Houghton-Mifflin.

Rogers, K., & Gibson, A.L. (2009). Eight-week traditional mat Pilates training-program effects on adult fitness characteristics. *Research Quarterly for Exercise and Sport, 80*(3), 569-574.

Rohnke, K. (1989). *Cowstails and cobras II*. Dubuque, IA: Kendall/Hunt.

Roland, C. C., Keene, T., Dubois, M., & Lentini, J. (1988). Experiential challenge program development in the mental health setting. *The Bradford Papers Annual, 3*, 66-77.

Roland, C. C., Summers, S., Friedman, M. J., Barton, G. M., & McCarthy, K. (1987). Creation of an experiential challenge program. *Therapeutic Recreation Journal, 21*(2), 54-63.

Rollnick, S., Miller, W. R., & Butler, C. C. (2008). *Motivational interviewing in healthcare: Helping patients change behavior*. New York: Guilford Press.

Rosenberg, W., & Donald, A. (1995). Evidence-based medicine: An approach to clinical problem solving. *British Medical Journal, 310*, 1122-1226.

Rosenhan, D. L. (1973). On being sane in insane places. *Science, 179*, 250-258.

Rosenthal, D., Teague, M., Retish, P., West, J., & Vessell, R. (1983). The relationship between work environment attributes and burnout. *Journal of Leisure Research, 15*, 125-135

Rosenthal, R., & Jacobson, L. (1992). *Pygmalion in the classroom: Teacher expectation and pupils' intellectual development*. New York: Irvington.

Ross, R., & Janssen, I, (2012). Physical activity, fitness, and obesity. In C. Bouchard, S. N. Blair, & W. L. Haskell (Eds.), *Physical activity and health* (2nd ed.) (pp. 197-214). Champaign, IL: Human Kinetics.

Rote, S. (1990). Alterations in immunity and inflammation. In K. L. McCance & S. Huether (Eds.), *Pathophysiology: The biologic basis for disease in adults and children (Rothert & Daubert)*. St. Louis, MO: C. V. Mosby.

Roth, S., & Kubal, L. (1975). The effects of noncontingent reinforcement on tasks of differing importance: Facilitation and learned helplessness effects. *Journal of Personality and Social Psychology, 32*, 680-691.

Rothert, E. A., & Daubert, J. R. (1981). *Horticulture therapy at a physical rehabilitation facility*. Glencoe, IL: Chicago Horticulture Society.

Rowe, C. J., & Mink, W. D. (1993). *An outline of psychiatry* (10th ed.). Madison, WI: Brown and Benchmark.

Rupert, P. A., & Morgan, D. J. (2005). Work setting and burnout among professional psychologists. *Professional Psychology: Research and Practice, 36*(5), 544-550.

Rupert, P. A., Stevanovic, P., & Hunley, H. A. (2009). Work-family conflict and burnout among practicing psychologists. *Professional Psychology: Research and Practice, 40*(1), 54-61.

Russell, J. (2005). *Introduction to psychology for health careers*. Cheltenham, UK: Nelson Thomas Ltd.

Russell, K. C. (2000). Exploring how the wilderness therapy process relates to outcomes. *Journal of Experiential Education, 23*(3), 170-176.

Russell, K. C. (2006). Brat camp, boot camp, or...? Exploring wilderness therapy program theory. *Journal of Adventure Education and Outdoor Learning, 6*(1), 51-68.

Russoniello, C. V. (2001). Biofeedback: Helping people gain control of their health. *Parks & Recreation, 36*(12), 24-30.

Russoniello, C. V., O'Brien, K. O., Parks, J. M. (2009). EEG, HRV and psychological correlates while playing Bejeweled II: A randomized controlled study. *Cyber Therapy and Telemedicine, 7*, 189-192.

Sachs, J. (1997). *Nature's Prozac: Natural therapies and techniques to rid yourself of anxiety, depression, panic attacks and stress*. Englewood Cliffs, NJ: Prentice-Hall.

Saebu, M. (2010). Physical disability and physical activity: A review of the literature on correlates and associations. *European Journal of Adapted Physical Education, 3*(2), 37-55.

Sallis, J. F. (2011). Potential vs actual benefits of exergames. *Archives of Pediatrics & Adolescent Medicine, 165*(7), 667-678.

Salmon, P. (2001). Effects of physical exercise on anxiety, depression, and sensitivity to stress: A unifying theory. *Clinical Psychology Review, 21*(1), 33-61.

Sames, K. M. (2005). *Documenting occupational therapy practice*. Upper Saddle River, NJ: Pearson.

Sanchez, V. C. Lewinsohn, P. M., & Larson, D. W. (2012). Assertion training: Effectiveness in the treatment of depression. *Journal of Clinical Psychology, 36*(2), 526-529.

Sancier, K. M. (1996). Medical applications of Qigong. *Alternative Therapies, 2*(1), 40-46.

Sancier, K. M. (1999). Therapeutic benefits of qigong exercises in combination with drugs. *The Journal of Alternative and Complementary Medicine, 5*(4), 383-389.

Sancier, K. M., & Holman, D. (2004). Commentary: Multifaceted health benefits of medical qigong. *The Journal of Alternative and Complementary Medicine, 10*(1), 163-165.

Sands, H., & Minters, F. C. (1977). *The epilepsy fact book*. Philadelphia, PA: F. A. Davis.

Sarkamo, T., Tervaniemi, M., Laitinen, S., Forsblom, A., Soninila, S., Mikkonen, M., Autti, T., ... & Hietanen, M. (2008). Music listening enhances cognitive recovery and mood after middle cerebral artery stroke. *Brain, 131*, 866-876.

Satir, V. (1972). *Peoplemaking*. Palo Alto, CA: Science and Behavioral Books.

Savell, K. (1986). Implications for therapeutic recreation leisure-efficacy: Theory and therapy programming. *Therapeutic Recreation Journal, 20*(1), 41-52.

Sayre-Adams, J. & Wright, S. G. (2001). *The theory and practice of therapeutic touch*. St. Louis: Churchill Livingstone.

Scanland, S. G., & Emershaw, L. E. (1993). Reality orientation and validation therapy: Dementia, depression, and functional status. *Journal of Gerontological Nursing, 19*(6), 7-11.

Scarf, M. (1980). The promiscuous woman. *Psychology Today, 14*(2), 78-87.

Schatzberg, A. F., & Nemeroff, C. B. (2009). *The American psychiatric press textbook of psychopharmacology* (4th ed.). Washington, D.C.: American Psychiatric Press.

Schaub, B. G., & Burt, M. M. (2013). Imagery. In B. M. Dossey & L. Keegan (Eds.). *Holistic nursing: A handbook for practice* (6th ed.) (pp. 363-395). Burlington, MA: Jones & Bartlett Learning.

Schimel, J. L. (1993). Reflections on the function of humor in psychotherapy, especially with adolescents. In W. F. Fry & W. A. Salameh (Eds.), *Advances in humor and psychotherapy*. Sarasota, FL: Professional Resource Press.

Schleien, S. J., & Wehman, P. (1986). Severely handicapped children: Social skills development through leisure skills programming. In G. Cartledge, & J. F. Miburn (Eds.), *Teaching social skills to children* (2nd ed.). New York: Pergamon Press.

Schmid, A. A., Van Puymbroeck, M. W., Altenburger, P. A., Schalk, N. L., Dierks, T. A., Miller, K. K., Damush, T. M., Dravata, D. M., & Willieams, L. S. (2012). Poststroke balance improves with yoga: A pilot study. *Stroke, 43*(9), 2402-2407.

Schmid, A. A., Van Puymbroeck, M. W., & Koceja, D. M. (2010). Effect of a 12-week yoga intervention on fear of falling and balance In older adults: A pilot study. *Archives of Physical Medicine and Rehabilitation, 9*(4), 576-583.

Schmidt, N. A., & Brown, J. M. (2009). *Evidence-based practice for nurses*. Boston, MA: Jones and Bartlett.

Schmokel, C. (1980). An alternative to the Premack principle. Unpublished paper. Bloomington, IN: Indiana University.

Schmuck, R. A., & Schmuck, P. A. (1997). *Group processes in the classroom* (7th ed.). Madison, WI: Brown & Benchmark.

Schneider, R. H., Staggers, F., Alexander, C. N., Sheppard, W., Rainforth, M., Kondwant, K., Smith, S., & King, C. G. (1995). A randomized controlled trail of stress reduction for hypertension in older African Americans. *Hypertension, 26*, 820-827.

Schneidert, M., Hurst, R., Miller, U., Ustun, B. (2003). The role of environment in the International Classification of Functioning, Disability and Health (ICF). *Disability and Rehabilitation, 25*(11-12), 588-595.

Schoel, J., Prouty, D., & Radcliffe, P. (1988). *Islands of healing: A guide to adventure-based counseling*. Hamilton, MA: Project Adventure.

Schofield, W. (1964). *Psychotherapy: The purchase of friendship*. Englewood Cliffs, NJ: Prentice-Hall.

Schofield, W. (1986). *Psychotherapy: The purchase of friendship* (2nd ed.). New Brunswick: Transaction Books.

Scholl, J. C., & Ragan, S. L. (2003). The use of humor in promoting positive provider-patient interactions in a hospital rehabilitation unit. *Health Communication, 15*(3), 319-330.

Schor, J. (2010). Emotions and health: Laughter really is good medicine. *Natural Medical Journal, 2*(1), 1-4.

Schulman, E. D. (1991). *Intervention in human services: A guide to skills and knowledge* (4th ed.). New York: Macmillan.

Schultz, D. (1977). *Growth psychology: Models of the healthy personality*. New York: D. Van Nostrand.

Schwartzberg, S. L., Howe, M. C., & Barnes, M. A. (2008). *Groups: Applying the functional group model*. Philadelphia, PA: F. A. Davis.

Scogin, F. (1998). Bibliotherapy: A nontraditional intervention for depression. In *Innovative behavioral healthcare for older adults: A guidebook for changing times* (pp. 129-144). San Francisco, CA: Jossey-Bass.

Scott, E. (2011a). Gratitude journal: How to maintain a gratitude journal for stress relief. Retrieved from http://stress.about.com/od/positiveattitude/ht/gratitude_journ.htm

Scott, E. (2011b). The benefits of journaling for stress management. Retrieved from http://stress.about.com/od/generaltechniques/p/profilejournal.htm

Scott, J., & Clare, L. (2003). Do people with dementia benefit from psychological interventions offered on a group basis? *Clinical Psychology and Psychotherapy, 10*, 186-196.

Seaward, B. L. (2002). *Managing stress: Principles and strategies for health and well-being* (3rd ed.). Boston, MA: Jones and Bartlett.

Segal, D. (2005). Relationships of assertiveness, depression, and social support among older nursing home residents. *Behavior Modification, 29*(4), 689-695.

Sekendiz, B., Altun, O., Korkusuz, F., & Akin, S. (2007). Effects of Pilates exercise on trunk strength, endurance and flexibility in sedentary adult females. *Journal of Bodywork and Movement Therapies, 11*, 318-326.

Seligman, M. E. P. (1980). Fall into helplessness. In J. D. Samtic (Ed.), *Abnormal psychology: A perspective approach.* Wayne, NJ: Avery Publishing Group Inc.

Seligman, M. E. P. (2002). *Authentic happiness: Using the new positive psychology to realize your potential for lasting fulfillment.* New York: Free Press.

Seligman, M. E. P. (2011). *Flourish: A visionary new understanding of happiness and well-being.* New York: Free Press.

Seligman, M. E. P. (1998). *Learned optimism: How to change your mind and your life* (2nd ed.). New York: Pocket Books.

Seligman, M. E. P., Steen, T. A., Park, N., & Peterson, C. (2005). Positive psychology progress: Empirical validation of interventions. *American Psychologist, 60*, 410-421.

Seligman, M. E .P., & Csikszenmihalyi, M. (2000). Positive psychology: An introduction. *American Psychologist, 55*, 5-15.

Seligman, M. E. P., & Csikszenmihalyi, M. (2001). Reply to comments. *American Psychologist, 56*, 89-90.

Shahidi, M., Moutahed, A., Modabbernia, A., Mojtahed, M., Shafiabady, A., Delavar, A., & Honari, H. (2011). Laughter yoga versus group exercise program in elderly depressed women: A randomized controlled trail. *International Journal of Geriatric Psychiatry, 26*, 322-327.

Shanafelt, T. D., Boone, S., Tan, L., Dyrbye, L. N., Solie, W., Satele, D., West, C. P., Sloan, J., & Oreskovich, M. R. (2012). Burnout and satisfaction with work-life balance among U.S. physicians relative to the general U.S. population. *Archives of Internal Medicine.*

Shanahan, L., McAllister, L., & Curtin, M. (2009). Wilderness adventure therapy and cognitive rehabilitation: Joining forces for youth with TBI. *Brain Injury, 23*(13-14), 1054-1064.

Shankar, A., McMunn, A., Banks, J., & Steptoe, A. (2011). Loneliness, social isolation, and behavioral and biological health indicators in older adults. *Health Psychology, 30*(4), 377-385.

Shank, J. W. (1985). Bioethical principles and the practice of therapeutic recreation in clinical settings. *Therapeutic Recreation Journal, 19*(4), 31-40.

Shank, J. W., & Coyle, C. (2002). *Therapeutic recreation in health promotion and rehabilitation.* State College, PA: Venture.

Shank, J. W., & Kennedy, D. W. (1976). Recreation and leisure counseling: A review. *Rehabilitation Literature, 37* (9), 258-262.

Shank, J. W., & Kinney, T. (1987). On the neglect of clinical practice. In C. Sylvester, J. L. Hemingway, R. Howe-Murphy, K. Mobily, & P. A. Shank (Eds.). *Philosophy of therapeutic recreation: Ideas and issues* (pp. 65-75). Alexandria, VA: National Recreation and Park Association.

Shankar, A., & McMunn, A. (2011). Loneliness, social isoloation, and behavioral and biological health indicators in older adults. *Health Psychology, 30*(4), 377-385.

Shannon, C., Wahl, P., Rhea, M., & Dyehouse, J. (1988). The nursing process. In C. K. Beck, R. P. Rawlins & S. R. Williams (Eds.), *Mental health-psychiatric nursing: A holistic life-cycle approach* (2nd ed.). St. Louis, MO: C.V. Mosby.

Shapiro, D., Cook, I. A., Davydov, D. M., Ottaviani, C., Leuchter, A. F., & Abrams, M. (2007). Yoga as a complementary treatment of depression: Effects of traits and moods on treatment outcomes. *eCAM, 4*(4), 493-502.

Shapiro, D. H., & Astin, J. (1998). *Control therapy: An integrated approach to psychotherapy, health and healing.* New York: John Wiley & Sons.

Sharp, C., Smith, J. V., & Cole, A. (2002). Cinematherapy: Metaphorically promoting therapeutic change. *Counseling Psychology Quarterly, 15*(3), 269-276.

Shaw, M. E., & Costanzo, P. R. (1982). *Theories of social psychology* (2nd ed.). New York: McGraw-Hill.

Shealy, C. N. (1999). *The complete illustrated encyclopedia of alternative healing therapies.* Boston, MA: Element Books.

Shedden, M., & Kravitz, L. (2006). Pilates exercise: A research-based review. *Journal of Dance Medicine & Science, 10*(3&4), 111-116.

Sheldon, K., & Dattilo, J. (1997). Multiculturalism in therapeutic recreation: Terminology clarification and practical suggestions. *Therapeutic Recreation Journal, 31*(3), 148-158.

Sheldon, K. M., & Lyubomirsky, S. (2004). Achieving sustainable new happiness: Prospects, practices, and prescriptions. In P. A. Linley & S. Joseph (Eds.), *Positive psychology in practice (127-145)*. Hoboken, NJ: John Wiley & Sons.

Sheras, P. L., & Worchel, S. (1979). *Clinical psychology: A social psychological approach.* New York: Van Nostrand Reinhold.

Shibata, T., & Wada, K. (2011). Robot therapy: A new approach for mental healthcare of the elderly: A mini-review. *Gerontology, 57,* 378-386.

Shiina, A., Nakazato, M., Mitsumori, M., Koizumi, H., Shimizu, E., Fujisaki, M., & Iyo, M. (2005). An open trail of outpatient group therapy for bulimic disorders: Combination program of cognitive-behavioral therapy with assertiveness training and self-esteem enhancement. *Psychiatry and Clinical Neurosciences, 59*(6), 690-696.

Shinn, M., Rosario, M., Morch, H., & Chestnut, D. E. (1984). Coping with job stress and burnout in human services. *Journal of Personality and Social Psychology, 46,* 864-876.

Shives, L. R. (1998). *Basic concepts of psychiatric-mental health nursing* (4th ed.). Philadelphia, PA: Lippincott.

Shoemaker, N. C., & Lala, C. (2006). In E. M. Varcarolis, V. B. Carson, & N. C. Shoemaker (Eds.), *Foundations of psychiatric mental health nursing: A clinical approach* (5th ed.). St. Louis, MO: Saunders Elsevier.

Shore, M. F. (1998). Beyond self-interest: Professional advocacy and the integration of theory, research, and practice. *American Psychologist, 55*(4), 474-479.

Shorvon, S. S. (2010). *Handbook of epilepsy treatment* (3rd ed.). Oxford, UK: Wiley-Blackwell.

Shultz, C. (1988). Loneliness. In C. K. Beck, R. P. Rawlins, & S. R. Williams (Eds.), *Mental health-psychiatric nursing*. St. Louis, MO: C. V. Mosby.

Sigal, R. L., Kenny, G. P., Wasserman, D. H., Castaneda-Sceppa, C., & White, R. D. (2006). Physical activity/exercise and type 2 diabetes: A consensus statement from the American Diabetes Association. *Diabetes Care, 29*(6), 1433-1438.

Silver, J. K., & Morin, C. (2008). *Understanding fitness: How exercise fuels health and fights disease.* Westport, CT: Praeger.

Silver, R. J. (2001). Practicing professional psychology. *American Psychologist, 56*(11), 1008-1013

Silverman, L. H. (1998). *The therapeutic potential of museums: A guide to social service/museum collaboration.* Bloomington, IN: Institute of Museum and Library Services.

Silverman, S. (1998). The effects of tai chi and traditional locomotor exercises on senior citizens' motor control. *The Journal of Physical Education, Recreation & Dance, 69*(9), 9.

Silverthorne, C., Khalsa, S. B. S., Gueth, R., DeAvilla, N., & Pansini, J. (2012). Respiratory, physical, and psychological benefits of breath-focused yoga for adults with severe traumatic brain injury (TBI): A brief pilot study report. *International Journal of Yoga Therapy, No. 22,* 47-51.

Simon, J. M. (1988). Therapeutic humor: Who's fooling who? *Journal of Psychosocial Nursing and Mental Health Services, 26*(4), 8-12.

Simon, S. B., Howe, L. W., & Kirschenbaum, H. (1995). *Values clarification.* New York: Warner.

Simon, S. B., & Olds, S. W. (1977). *Helping your children learn right from wrong: A guide to values clarification.* New York: McGraw-Hill.

Sjosten, N. & Kivela, S. L. (2006). The effect of physical exercise on depressive symptoms among the aged: A systematic review. *International Journal of Geriatric Psychiatry, 21,* 410-418.

Skerrett, K. (2010). Extending family nursing: Concepts from positive psychology. *Journal of Family Nursing, 16*(4), 487-502.

Skokols, D. (2003). The ecology of human strengths. In L. Aspinwall & U. M. Staudinger (Eds.), *The psychology of human strengths: Fundamental questions and future directions for a positive psychology* (pp. 331-343). Washington, D.C.: American Psychological Association.

Smalheiser, M. (1996). T'ai chi ch'uan. In J. Jacobs (Ed.), *The encyclopedia of alternative medicine.* Boston, MA: Journey Editions.

Smith, C. E., Holcroft, C., Rebeck, S. L., Thompson, N. C., & Werkowitch, M. (2000). Journal writing as a complementary therapy for reactive depression: A rehabilitation teaching program. *Rehabilitation Nursing, 25*(5), 170-176.

Smith, D. J. (1998). Horticultural therapy: The garden benefits everyone. *Journal of Psychosocial Nursing, 36*(10), 14-21.

Smith, J. C. (1993). *Understanding stress and coping.* New York: MacMillan.

Smith, J. C. (2005). *Relaxation, meditation, and mindfulness: A mental health practitioner's guide to new and traditional approaches.* New York: Springer.

Smith, K. (1999). *Massage.* London, UK: Duncan Baird.

Smith, K., & Smith, E. (2005). Intergrating Pilates-based core strengthening into older adult fitness programs: Implications for practice. *Topics in Geriatric Rehabilitation, 21*(1), 57-67.

Smith, M., Jaffe-Gill, E., Segal, J., & Segal, R. (2007). Preventing burnout: Signs, symptoms, and strategies to avoid it. Retrieved 6/10/2008 from http://www.helpguide.org/mental/burnout_signs_symptoms.htm

Smith, M. J., & Liehr, P. R. (Eds.). (2008). *Middle range theory for nursing* (2nd ed.). New York: Springer.

Smith, N., & Oliver, N. (1998). Is laughter the best medicine? *American Journal of Nursing, 98*(12), 12, 13.

Smith, R. E., & Smoll, F. L. (1997). Coaching the coaches: Youth sports as a scientific and applied behavioral setting. *Current Directions in Psychological Science*, 6(1), 16-21.

Smith, R. W. (2002). Leaders in therapeutic recreation: David R. Austin. In D. R. Austin, J. Dattilo, & B. P. McCormick (Eds.), *Conceptual foundations for therapeutic recreation* (pp. 320-321). State College, PA: Venture.

Smith, R. W., Austin, D. R., Kennedy, D. W., Lee, Y., & Hutchison, P. (2005). *Inclusive and special recreation: Opportunities for persons with disabilities* (5th ed.). Boston, MA: McGraw-Hill.

Smith, S. (1992). *Communications in nursing*. St. Louis, MO: Mosby Year Book.

Smith, T. (1987). Foster families and adventure/challenge therapy. *The Bradford Papers Annual, 2*, 65-72.

Smith, T. E., Roland, C. C., Havens, M. D., & Hoyt, J. A. (1992). *The theory and practice of challenge education.* Dubuque, IA: Kendall/Hunt.

Smither, R. (2009). Existential and humanistic psychotherapies. In D. C. S. Richard, & S. K. Huprich (Eds.), *Clinical Psychology* (pp. 309-329). Boston, MA: Elsevier.

Smyth, J. M., Nazarian, D., & Arigo, D. (2008). Expressive writing in the clinical context. In *Emotion Regulation* (pp. 215-233).

Sneegas, J. J. (1989). Social skills: An integral component of leisure participation and therapeutic recreation services. *Therapeutic Recreation Journal*, 23(2), 30-40.

Snider, M. (2008). Miracle-Gro for brains. emporiagazette.com. Retrieved from http://johnratey.typepad.com/blog/2008/03/miracle-gro-for.html

Snyder, M., & Lindquist, R. (2006). *Complementary/alternative therapies in nursing* (5th ed.). New York: Springer.

Sohlberg, M. M., & Mateer, C. A. (2001). *Cognitive rehabilitation: An integrative neuropsychological approach.* New York: The Guilford Press.

Soloman, G. (1995). *The motion picture prescription: Watch this movie and call me in the morning: 200 movies to help you heal life's problems.* Santa Rosa, CA: Aslan.

Solomon, G. (2000). *Reel therapy: How movies can help you overcome life's problems.* New York: Lebhar-Friedman.

Solomon, G. E., & Plum, F. (1976). *Clinical management of seizures: A guide for the physician.* Philadelphia, PA: W. B. Saunders.

Soltys, F. G., & Coats, L. (1995). The SolCos model: Facilitating reminiscence therapy. *Journal of Psychosocial Nursing*, 33(11), 21-26.

Song, R., Lee, E-O., Lam, P., & Bae, S-C. (2003). Effects of Tai Chi exercise on pain, balance, muscle strength, an perceived difficulties in physical functioning in older women with osteoarthritis: A randomized clinical trial. *The Journal of Rheumatology*, 30(9), 2039-2044.

Sova, R. (2000). Bringing new clients to your facility with aquatic therapy and rehab. *Parks & Recreation*, 35(11), 74-78.

Spacapan, S., & Oskamp, S. (1988). *The social psychology of health.* Newbury Park, CA: SAGE.

Spector, A., Orrell, M., Davies, S., & Woods, B. (2001). Can Reality Orientation be rehabilitated? Development and piloting of an evidence-based programme of cognition-based therapies for people with dementia. *Neuropsychological Rehabilitation*, 11(3/4), 377-397.

Spector, A., Thorgrimsen, L., Woods, B., Royan, L., Davies, S., Butterworth, M., & Orrell, M. (2003). Efficacy of evidence-based cognitive stimulation therapy programme for people with dementia. *British Journal of Psychiatry*, 183, 244-254.

Spielman, M. B. (1998). Ethics: To do the right thing. In F. Brasile, T. K. Slalko, & j. burligame (Eds.), *Perspectives in recreational therapy: Issues of a dynamic profession* (pp. 63-80). Ravensdale, WA: Idyll Arbor.

Spilner, M. (2002). Walking is powerful medicine. *Runner's World.* Retrieved from http://www.runnersworld.com/article/0,7120,s6-238-261--1684-1-3-2,00.html

Stamm, T. A., Cieza, A., Machold, K., Smolen, J. S., & Stucki, G. (2006). Exploration of the link between concepatul occupational therapy models and the International Classification of Functioning, Disability and Health. *Australian Occupational Therapy Journal*, 53, 9-17.

Stanley, J., & Kasson, I. (n.d.). *Guidelines for interviewing applicants and parents.* Trenton, NJ: Office on Community Recreation for Handicapped Persons, State of New Jersey Department of Community Affairs.

Stanley-Hermanns, M., & Miller, J. (2002). Animal-assisted therapy. *AJN*, 102(10), 69-76.

Stanton, C. M., Kahn, P. H., Severson, R. L., Ruckert, J. H., & Gill, B. T. (2008). Robotic animals might aid in the social development of children with autism. *2008 3rd ACM/IEEE International Conference*, pp. 271-278.

Statistics Canada. (2005). Study: Projections of the diversity of the Canadian population 2006 to 2031. Retrieved from http://www.statcan.gc.ca/daily-quotidien/100309/dq100309a-eng.htm

Stein, F., & Cutler, S. K. (1998). *Psychosocial occupational therapy: A holistic approach.* San Diego: Singular.

Steiner, C. M. (1974). *Scripts people live: Transactional analysis of life scripts.* New York: Grove Press.

Stephens, T. (1978). *Social skills in the classroom.* Columbus, OH: Cedars.

Stetter, F., & Kupper, S. (2002). Autogenic training: A meta-analysis of clinical outcome studies. *Applied Psychophysiology and Biofeedback*, 27(1), 45-98.

Stevens, J. O. (1988). *Awareness: Exploring, experimenting, and experiencing.* London, UK: Eden Grove Editions.

Stokes, E. K. (2011). *Rehabilitation outcome measures.* New York: Churchill Livingstone.

Stokols, D. (2003). The ecology of human strengths. In L. G. Aspinwall & U. M. Staudinger (Eds.), *A psychology of human strengths: Fundamental questions and future directions for a positive psychology* (pp. 331-343). Washington, DC: American Psychological Association.

Stigsdotter, U. A., & Grahn, P. (2003). Experiencing a garden: A healing garden for people suffering from burnout diseases. *Journal of Therapeutic Horticulture, 14*, 60-69.

Stoltenberg, C. (1981). Approaching supervision from a developmental perspective: The counselor-complexity model. *Journal of Counseling Psychology, 28*, 59-65.

Stoltenberg, C., McNeill, B., & Delworth, U. (1998). *IDM supervision: An integrated developmental model of supervising counselors and supervisors.* San Francisco, CA: Jossey-Bass.

Stone, C. F. (2003). Exploring cultural competencies of Certified Therapeutic Recreation Specialists: Implications for education and training. *Therapeutic Recreation Journal, 37*(2), 156-174.

Stone, W. L., & Stone, C. G. (1952). *Recreation leadership.* New York: The Williams Frederick Press.

Stoyva, J. M., & Budzynski, T. H. (1993). Biofeedback methods in the treatment of anxiety and stress disorders. In P. M. Lehrer & R. L. Woolfolk (Eds.), *Principles and practice of stress management* (2nd ed.). New York: The Guilford Press.

Strean, W. B. (2009). Laughter prescription. *Canadian Family Physician, 55*, 965-967.

Street, R. L., Gold, W. R., & Manning, T. (1997). *Health promotion and interactive technology: Theoretical applications and future directions.* Mahwah, NJ: Lawrence Erlbaum Associates.

Streeter, C. C., Gerberg, P. L., Saper, R. B., Ciraulo, D. A., & Brown, R. P. (2012). Effects of yoga on the autonomic nervous system, gamma-aminobutyric-acid, and allostasis in epilepsy, depression, and post-traumatic stress disorder. *Medical Hypotheses, 2012*, 9 pages, dol: 10.1016/j.mehy.2012.01.021. Retrieved from http://scholar.google.com/scholar?start=208q=miller+PTSD+yoga&hl=en&as_sdt=0,34

Streeter, C. C., Whitfield, T. H., Owen, L., Rein, T., Karrri, S. K., Yakhkind, A., Perilmutter, R., ... & Jensen, J. E. (2010). Effects of yoga versus walking on mood, anxiety, and brain GABA levels: A randomized controlled MRS study. *The Journal of Alternative and Complementary Medicine, 16*(11), 1145-1152.

Stroebe, W. (2011). *Social psychology and health.* Berkshire, GBR: Open University Press. Retrieved from http://site.ebrary.com/lib/lub/Doc?id=10604358&ppg=267

Stuart, C. (2006). *The illustrated guide to massage and aromatherapy.* London, UK: Hermes House.

Stuart, G. W. (2001a). Cognitive behavioral therapy. In G. W. Stuart & M. T. Laraia (Eds.), *Principles and practices of psychiatric nursing* (7th ed.) (pp. 658-672). St. Louis, MO: Mosby.

Stuart, G. W. (2001b). Evidence-based psychiatric nursing practice. In G. W. Stuart & M. T. Laraia (Eds.), *Principles of psychiatric nursing* (7th ed.) (pp. 76-87). St. Louis, MO: Mosby.

Stuber, M., Hilber, S. D., Mintzer, L. L., Castaneda, M., Glover, D., & Zeltzer, L. (2007). Laughter, humor, and pain perception in children: A pilot study. *eCAM, 6*(2), 271-276.

Stucki, G., & Grimby, G. (2004). Foreword: Applying the ICF in medicine. *Journal of Rehabilitation Medicine, Supplement. 44*, 5-6.

Stucki, G., Cieza, A., Ewert, T., Kostanjsek, N., Chatterji, S., & Ustun, T. B. (2002). Application of the International Classification of Functioning, Disability and Health in clinical practice. *Disability and Rehabilitation, 24*(5), 281-282.

Stuifbergen, A. K., Blozis, S. A., Harrison, T. C., & Becker, H. A. (2006). Exercise, functional limitations, and quality of life: A longitudinal study of persons with multiple sclerosis. *Archives of Physical Medicine and Rehabilitation, 87*, 935-943.

Stumbo, N. J. (1991). Selected assessment resources: A review of instruments and references. *Annual in Therapeutic Recreation, 2*, 8-24.

Stumbo, N. J. (2002). *Client assessment in therapeutic recreation services.* State College, PA: Venture.

Stumbo, N. J. (2005/2006). Application of learning theory to leisure education. *Annual in Therapeutic Recreation, 14*, 25-41.

Stumbo, N. J. (2011). Instructional techniques. In N. J. Stumbo & B. Wardlaw (Eds.), *Facilitation of therapeutic recreation services* (pp. 87-113). State College, PA: Venture.

Stumbo, N. J., Carter, M. J., & Kim, J. (2004). National therapeutic recreation curriculum study part A: Accreditation, curriculum, and internship characteristics. *Therapeutic Recreation Journal, 38*(1), 32-52.

Stumbo, N. J., & Peterson, C. A. (1998). The Leisurability Model. *Therapeutic Recreation Journal, 32*(2), 82-96.

Stumbo, N. J., & Peterson, C. A. (2004). *Therapeutic recreation program design* (4th ed.). San Francisco, CA: Pearson.

Stumbo, N. J., & Peterson, C. A. (2009). *Therapeutic recreation program design* (5th ed.). San Francisco, CA: Pearson.

Stumbo, N. J., & Wardlaw, B. (2011). Social skills training. In N. J. Stumbo & B. Wardlaw (Eds.), *Facilitation of therapeutic recreation services* (pp. 189-217). College Park, PA: Venture.

Sue, D. W. & Sue, D. (2003). *Counseling the culturally diverse.* New York: Wiley. Sugarman, D. (1988). Adventure education for people who have disabilities: A critical review. *The Bradford Papers Annual, 3*, 27-37.

Sugumaran, A., & Prakash, A. (2011). Wii can rehabilitate? *Geriatric Medicine,* April, 2011, 228-229.

Suhr, J., Anderson, S., & Tranel, D. (1999). Progressive muscle relaxation in the management of behavioral disturbance in Alzheimer's Disease. *Neuropsychological Rehabilitation, 9*(1), 31-44.

Sullivan, F. R., Bird, E. D., Alpay, M., & Cha, J-H J. (2001). Remotivation therapy and Huntington's disease. *Journal of Neuroscience Nursing, 33*(3), 136-142.

Sundeen, S. J., Stuart, G. W., Rankin, E. A. D., & Cohen, S. A. (1998). *Nurse-client interaction: Implementing the nursing process* (6th ed.). St. Louis: Mosby.

Sung, H., Chang, S., Lee, W., & Lee, M. (2006). The effects of group music with movement intervention on agitated behaviours of institutionalized elders with dementia in Taiwan. *Complementary Therapies in Medicine, 14,* 113-119.

Swackhamer, A. H. (1995). Alternatives: Complementary therapies: It's time to broaden our practice. *RN, 58*(1), 49-51.

Swann, W. B., Chang-Schneider, C., & McClarty, K. L. (2007). Do people's self-views matter? *American Psychologist, 62*(2), 84-94.

Swanwick, T., & McKimm, J. (2011). *ABC of clinical leadership.* Hoboken, NJ: BMJ Books.

Sylvester, C. D. (1982). Exploring confidentiality in therapeutic recreation practice: An ethical responsibility in need of a response. *Therapeutic Recreation Journal, 16*(3), 25-34.

Sylvester, C. D. (1985). An analysis of selected ethical issues in therapeutic recreation. *Therapeutic Recreation Journal, 19*(4), 8-21.

Sylvester, C., Voelkl, J. E., & Ellis, G. D. (2001). *Therapeutic recreation programming: Theory and practice.* State College, PA: Venture.

Szymanski, D. J. (1989). Hardiness and burnout in the staff of summer residence camps. Unpublished dissertation. Bloomington, IN: Indiana University.

Taber, K. H., Redden, M., & Hurley, R. A. (2007). Functional anatomy of humor: Positive affect and chronic mental illness. *The Journal of Neuropsychiatry and Clinical Neuroscience, 19,* 358-362.

Tabourne, C. E. S. (1995). The life review program as an intervention for an older adult newly admitted to a nursing home facility: A case study. *Therapeutic Recreation Journal, 29*(3), 228-236.

Takata, N. (1974). Play as a prescription. In M. Reilly (Ed.), *Play as exploratory learning: Studies of curiosity behavior.* Beverly Hills, CA: Sage.

Tamparo, C. T. & Lindh, W. Q. (2000). *Therapeutic communications for health professionals* (2nd ed.). Albany, NY: Delmar.

Tanner, L. (2008a). Doctors use Wii games for rehab therapy. *USA Today 2,* February 9, 2008.

Tanner, L. (2008b). New form of physical therapy: Wii games. Retrieved from http:www.livescience.com/health/080209-ap-wii-therapy.html.

Tatum, N. G., Igel, C. C., & Bradley, R. C. (2009). Effect of therapeutic yoga on balance and the ability to transfer from the floor in an older adult population. *International Journal of Yoga Therapy, No. 19,* 69-75.

Taylor, S. E. (1979). Hospital patient behavior: Reactance, helplessness, or control. *Journal of Social Issues, 35,* 156 - 184.

Taylor, S. E., Kimeny, M. E., Reed, G. M., Bower, J. E., & Gruenewald, T. L. (2000). Psychological resources, positive illusions, and health. *American Psychologist, 55*(1), 99-109.

Taylor, C. R., Lillis, C., & LeMone, P. (2001). *Fundamentals of nursing: The art and science of nursing care.* Philadelphia, PA: Lippincott Williams & Wilkins.

Taylor, C., Lillis, C., LeMone, P., & Lynn, P. (2008). *Fundamentals of nursing* (6th ed.). Philadelphia, PA: Lippincott Williams & Wilkins.

Taylor-Piliae, R. E., Haskell, W. L., Waters, C. M., & Froelicher, E. S. (2006). Change in perceived psychosocial status following a 12-week Tai Chi exercise programme. *Journal of Advanced Nursing, 54*(3), 313-329.

Teen Health. (2007). Nemours Foundation. Retrieved from http://www.kidshealth.org/PageManager.jsp?dn=Kid sHealth&lic=1&ps=207&cat_id=20.

Terjestam, Y., Jouper, J., & Johansson, C. (2010). Effects of scheduled qigong exercise on pupil's well-being, self-image, distress, and stress. *The Journal of Alternative and Complementary Medicine, 16*(9), 939-944.

Thayer, S. (1988). Close encounters. *Psychology Today, 22*(3), 30-36.

Theeke, L. A. (2009). Predictors of loneliness in U.S. adults over age sixty-five. *Archives of Psychiatric Nursing, 23*(5), 387-396.

Thompson, D., Baranowski, T., Buday, R., Buday, R., Baranowski, J., Thompson, V., Jago, R., & Griffith, M. J. (2010). Serious video games for health: How behavioral science guided the development of a serous video game. *Simulated Gaming, 41*(4), 587-606.

Thompson, G. T. (1996). Structuring your department to manage coverage and reimbursement. In D. Wagner, B. Kennedy & A. Pritchard (Eds.), *Recreational therapy: The next generation of reimbursement* (pp. 1-18). Hattiesburg, MS: American Therapeutic Recreation Association.

Thompson, P. S., Buchner, D., Pina, I. L., Balady, G. J., Williams, M. A., Marcus, B. H., Berra, K., ... & Wegner, N. D. (2003). Exercise and physical activity In the prevention and treatment of atherosclerotic cardiovascular disease. *Arterioscler, Thrombosis, and Vascular Biology, 23,* e42-e49.

Thornton, S., & Brotchie, J. (1987). Reminiscence: A critical review of the empirical literature. *British Journal of Clinical Psychology, 26,* 93-111.

Tierney, M. B. (2013). Older adults can use Pilates for healing and wellness benefits. *ADVANCE for Physical Therapy & Rehab Medicine.* Retrieved from http://physical-therapy.advanceweb.com/Editorial/Content/PrintFriendly.aspx?CC=238802

Tilbrook, H. E., Cox, H., Hewitt, C. E., Kang'ombe, A. R., Chuang, L-H., Jayakody, S., Aplin, J. D.,... & Torgerson, D. J. (2011). Yoga for chronic low back pain: A randomized trial. *Annals of Internal Medicine, 155*(9), 1-9.

Tillett, J., & Ames, D. (2010). The uses of aromatherapy in women's health. *Journal of Perinatal & Neonatal Nursing, 24*(3), 238-245.

Timberlake, W., & Allison, J. (1974). Response deprivation: An empirical approach to instrumental performance. *Psychological Review, 81*, 146-164.

Tinsley, H. E., & Tinsley, D. J. (1981). An analysis of leisure counseling models. *The Counseling Psychologist, 9*, 45-53.

Titlebaum, H. (1988). Relaxation. In Zahourek, R. P. (Ed.), *Relaxation and imagery: Tools for therapeutic communication and intervention.* Philadelphia: W. B. Saunders.

Toglia, J. P., & Golisz, K. M. (1990). *Cognitive rehabilitation: Group games and activities.* Tucson, AZ: Therapy Skill Builders.

Torres, A. (2008). Cognitive effects of videogames on older people. *ZON Digital Games 2008,* 19-27.

Toseland, R. W., & Rivas, R. F. (2005). *An introduction to group work practice* (5th ed.). Boston, MA: Pearson.

Townsend, J. A., & Zabriskie, R. B. (2010). Family leisure among families with a child in mental health treatment: Therapeutic Recreation Implications. *Therapeutic Recreation Journal, 44*(1), 11-34.

Townsend, M. C. (2000). *Psychiatric mental health nursing: Concepts of care* (3rd ed.). Philadelphia, PA: F. A. Davis.

Townsend, M. C. (2009). *Psychiatric mental health nursing: Concepts of care in evidence-based practice* (6th ed.). Philadelphia, PA: F. A. Davis.

Trenholm, S., & Jensen, A., (2000). *Interpersonal communication* (4th ed.). Belmont, CA: Wadsworth.

Tsao, J. C. I. (2007). Effectiveness of massage therapy for chronic, non-malignant pain: A review. *Advance Access Publications, 4*(2), 165-179.

Tubbs, S. L., & Moss, S. (2010). *Human communication: Principles and context* (12th ed.). New York: McGraw-Hill.

Tuckman, B. W., & Jensen, M. A. C. (1977). Stages of small group development revisited. *Group and Organizational Studies, 2,* 419-427.

Turner-Stokes, L. (2008). Evidence for the effectiveness of multidisciplinary rehabilitation following acquired brain injury: A synthesis of two systematic approaches. *Journal of Rehabilitation Medicine, 40*, 691-701.

Tusek, D., Church, J. M., & Fazio, V. W. (1997). Guided imagery as a coping strategy for perioperative patients. *AORN, 66*(4), 644-649.

Uchino, B. N. (2004). *Social support and physical health: Understanding the health consequences of relationships.* New Haven: Yale University Press.

Ullman, K. (2011). Fitness key to longevity. *MedPageToday.* Retrieved from http://medpagetoday.com/tbprint. efm?tbid=30027

Ulrich, P. M., & Lutgendorf, S. L. (2002). Journaling about stressful events: Effects of cognitive processing and emotional expression. *Annals of Behavioral Medicine, 24*(3), 244-250.

Umpierre, D., Ribeiro, P. A. B., Kramer, C. K., Leitao, C. B., Zucatti, A. T. N., Azevedo, M. J., Gross, J. I., Ribeiro, J. P., & Schaan, B. D. (2011). Physical activity advice only or structured exercise training and association with HbA1c levels in type 2 diabetes: A systematic review and meta-analysis. *Journal of the American Medical Association, 305*(17), 1790-1799.

Unstress your life. (1987). Stanford, CT: Longmeadow Press.

U.S. Census Bureau. (2011). The director's blog. Retrieved from http://blogs.census.gov/directorsblog/2011/03/index.html

U.S. Department of Health and Human Services. (2008). *At-a-glance: A fact sheet for professionals.* ODPHP Publication No. U0043. Retrieved from www.health.gov/paguidelines

U.S. Department of Health and Human Services. (2008). *2008 physical activity guidelines for Americans.* Washington, DC: U.S. Department of Health and Human Services.

U.S. Department of Health and Human Services. (2009). *Clinical supervision and professional development of the substance abuse counselor.* Rockville, MD.

U.S. Department of Health and Human Services. (2000). *Healthy people 2010* (Conference Edition, in Two Volumes). Washington, DC: U.S. Department of Health and Human Services.

Vagnoli, L., Caprilli, S., Robiglio, A., & Messeri, A. (2005). Clown doctors as a treatment for preoperative anxiety in children: A randomized, prospective study. *Pediatrics, 116*(4), e563-e567.

Van Andel, G. E. (1998). TR Service Delivery and TR Outcome Models. *Therapeutic Recreation Journal, 32*(3), 180-193.

Vancampfort, D., De Hert, M., Knapen, J., Maurissen, K., Raepsaet, J., Declox, S., Remans, S., & Probst, M. (2011). Effects of progressive muscle relaxation on state anxiety and subjective well-being in people with schizophrenia: A randomized controlled trail. *Clinical Rehabilitation, 25*(6), 567-575.

Vancampfort, D., Probst, M., Skjaerven, L.H., Catalan-Matamoros, D., Lundvik-Gyllensten, A., Gomez-Conesa, A., Ijnterma, R., & De Hert, M. (2012). Systematic review of the benefits of physical therapy within a multidisciplinary care approach for people with schizophrenia. *Physical Therapy, 92*(1), 11-23.

van der Watt, G., & Janca, A. (2008). Aromatherapy in nursing and mental health. *Contemporary Nurse, 30*(1), 69-75.

van Duijnhoven, H. J. R., De Kam, D. Hellebrand, W., Smulders, E., Geurts, A. C. H., & Weerdesteyn, V. (2012). Development and process evaluation of a 5-week exercise program to prevent falls in people after stroke: The FALLS program. *Stroke Research and Treatment, 2012,* Article ID 407693, 7 pages.

van Ooijen, E. (2000). *Clinical supervision: A practical approach*. New York: Churchill Livingstone.

Van Puymbroeck, M., Payne, L. L., & Hiseh, P-C. (2007). A phase 1 feasibility study of yoga on the physical health and coping of informal caregivers. *Advance Access Publication, 4*(4), 519-529.

Van Puymbroeck, M., Schmid, A., Miller, K., & Schalk, N. (2012). Improved activity, participation, and quality of life for individuals with chronic stroke following an 8-week yoga intervention. *BMC Complementary and Alternative Medicine* 2012 12(Suppi 1):039. Retrieved from http://www.biomedcentral.com/1472-6882/12/S1/039

Van Puymbroeck, M., Smith, R., & Schmid, A. (2011). Yoga as a means to negotiate physical activity constraints in middle-aged and older adults. *International Journal on Disability and Human Development, 10*(2), 117-121.

Varcarolis, E. M. (2006). Assessment strategies and the nursing process. In E. M. Varcarolis, V. B. Carson, & N. C. Shoemaker (Eds.), *Foundations of psychiatric mental health nursing: A clinical approach* (5th ed.). St. Louis: Saunders Elsevier.

Veenstra, J., Brasile, F., & Stewart, M. (2003). Perceived benefits of aquatic therapy for multiple sclerosis participants. *American Journal of Recreation Therapy, 2*, 33-48

Velde, B. P., Cipriani, J., & Fisher, G. (2005). *Australian Occupational Therapy Journal, 52*, 43-50.

Vera, F. M., Manzaneque, J. M., Maldonado, E. F., Carranque, G. A., Rodriguez, F. M., Blanca, M. J., & Morell, M. (2009). Subjective sleep quality and hormonal modulation in long-term yoga practitioners. *Biological Psychology, 81*, 164-168.

Vernon, W. M. (1972). *Motivating children: Behavior modification in the classroom*. New York: Holt, Rinehart and Winston, Inc.

Vikesland, G. (2006). Employee burnout. Retrieved from http://www.employer-employee.com/Burnout.html

Vincent, C., Taylor-Adams, S., & Stanhope, N. (1998). Framework for analyzing risk and safety in clinical medicine. *British Medical Journal, 316*(7138), 1154 - 1157.

Visceglia, E., & Lewis, S. (2011). Yoga therapy as an adjunctive treatment for schizophrenia: a randomized, controlled pilot study. *The Journal of Alternative and Complementary Medicine, 17*(7), 601-607.

Voelkl, J. E. (1986). Effects of institutionalization upon residents of extended care facilities. *Activities, Adaptation and Aging, 8*, 37-46.

Voner, L. (2005). *Massage: Everything you need to relax, rejuvenate, and relieve stress*. Avon, MA: Adams Media.

Vortherms, R. (1991). Clinically improving communication through touch. *Journal of Gerontological Nursing, 17*(5), 6-10.

Voss, M. W., Nagamatsu, L. S., Lin-Ambrose, T., & Kramer, A. F. (2011). Exercise, brain, and cognition across the life span. *Journal of Applied Physiology, 111*, 1505-1513.

Wada, K., & Shibata, T. (2008). Social and physiological influences of robot therapy in a care house. *Interaction Studies, 9*(2), 258-276.

Wanda, K., Shibata, T., Musha, T., & Kimura, S. (2008). Robot therapy for elders affected by dementia: Using personal robots for pleasure and relaxation. *IEEE Engineering In Medicine and Biology Magazine, IEEE, 27*(3), 53-60.

Wanda, K., Shibata, T., Saito, T., & Tanie, K. (2004). Effects of robot-assisted activity for elderly people and nurses at a day service center. *Proceedings of the IEEE, 92*(11), 1780-1787.

Walker, J. (2001). *Control and the psychology of health*. Philadelphia, PA: Open University Press.

Walters, C. (1998). *Aromatherapy: An illustrated guide*. Boston, MA: Element Books.

Walton, K. G., Fields, J. Z., Levitsky, D. K., Harris, D. A., Pugh, N. D., & Schneider, R. H. (2004). Lowering cortisol and CVD risk In postmenopausal women. *Annual of the New York Academy of Sciences, 1032*, 211-215.

Walton, K. G., Schneider, R. H., & Nidich, S. (2004). Review of controlled research on Transcendental Meditation program and cardiovascular disease. *Cardiology in Review, 12*(5), 262-266.

Waltzlawick, P., Beavin, J. H., & Jackson, D. D. (1967). *Pragmatics of human communication: A study of interactional patterns and paradoxes*. New York: W. W. Norton & Company.

Wang, C., Schmid, C. H., Kalish, R., Yinh, J., Goldenberg, D. L., & McAlindon, T. (2010). A randomized trial of tai chi for fibromyalgia. *New England Journal of Medicine, 363*(8), 743-754.

Wang, J-J. (2007). Group; reminiscence therapy for cognitive and affective function of demented elderly in Taiwan. *International Journal of Geriatric Psychiatry, 22*, 1235-1240.

Wang, M-Y., Greendale, G. A., Kazadi, & Salem, G. J. (2012). Yoga improves upper-extremity function and scapular posturing in persons with hyperkyphosis. *Journal of Yoga & Physical Therapy, 2*(3).

Wang, Y. (2008), Physical activities and health-related quality of life in older adults: Findings from the BRFSS 2000. *Annual In Therapeutic Recreation, 16*, 105-116.

Warburton, D. E. R., Nicol, C. W., & Bredin, S. S. D. (2006). Health benefits of physical activity: The evidence. *Canadian Medical Association Journal, 174*(6), 801-809.

Watkins, C. E. (1990). Development of the psychotherapy supervisor. *Psychotherapy, 27*(4), 553-560.

Watson, J. B. (1913). Psychology as the behaviorist views it. *Psychological Review, 20*, 158-177.

Watt, L. M., & Cappeliez, P. (2000). Integrative and instrumental reminiscence therapies for depression in older adults: Intervention strategies and treatment effectiveness. *Aging & Mental Health, 4*(2), 166 - 177.

Waughfield, C. G., & Burckhalter, T. S. (2002). *Mental health concepts*. New York: Delmar.

WebMD. (2012). *HIV/AJDS symptoms*. Retrieved from http://www.webmd.com/hivaids/guide/hiv-symptoms

Wehman, P. (1977). Application of behavior modification techniques to play problems of the severely and profoundly retarded. *Therapeutic Recreation Journal, 11*(1), 16-21.

Wehman, P., & Rettie, C. (1975). Increasing actions on play materials by severely retarded women through social reinforcement. *Therapeutic Recreation Journal, 9*(4), 173-178.

Wehmeyer, M. L. (1996). Self-determination as an educational-outcome: Why it is important to children, youth and adults with disabilities? In D. J. Sands & M. L. Wehmeyer (Eds.), *Self-Determination across the life span: Independence and choice for people with disabilities* (pp.15-34). Baltimore, MD: Paul H. Brookes.

Weiner, B. (Ed.). (1974). *Achievement and motivation and attribution theory.* Morristown, NJ: General Press.

Weisenberg, M., Raz, T., & Hener, T. (1998). The influence of film-induced mood on pain perception. *Pain, 73*(3), 365-375.

Weiss, C. R. (1989). TR and reminiscing: The pursuit of elusive memory and the art of remembering. *Therapeutic Recreation Journal, 23*(3), 7-18.

Weiss, C. R., & Kronberg, J. (1986). Upgrading TR service to severely disoriented elderly. *Therapeutic Recreation Journal, 20*(1), 32-42.

Weiss, C. R., & Thurn, J. M. (1987). A mapping project to facilitate reminiscence in a long-term care facility. *Therapeutic Recreation Journal, 21*(2), 46-53.

Weiss, T. C. (2012). Laughter yoga: Good medicine for seniors. Retrieved from http://ww.disabled-world.com/fitness/exercise/yoga/laughter.php

Welsh, L., Kemp, J. G., & Roberts, R. G. D. (2005). Effects of physical conditioning on children and adolescents with asthma. *Sports Medicine, 35*(2), 127-141.

West, O. (1990). *The magic of massage: A new and holistic approach.* Mamaroneck, NY: Hastings House Book Publishers.

Weuve, J., Kang, J. H., Manson, J. E., Breteler, M. M. B., Ware, J. H., & Grodstein, F. (2004). Physical activity, including walking, and cognitive function in older women. *Journal of the American Medical Association, 292*(12), 1454-1461.

What on Earth is a Snoezelen room? (2002). *Active Living, 10*(6), 38.

Weybright, E. H., Dattilo, J., & Rusch, F. R. (2010). Effects of an Interactive video game (Nintendo Wii) on older women with mild cognitive Impairment. *Therapeutic Recreation Journal, 44*(4), 271-287.

Whitaker, D. S. (1985). *Using groups to help people.* New York: Routledge & Kegan Paul.

Whitaker, D. S. (2001). *Using groups to help people* (2nd ed.). Philadelphia, PA: Taylor & Francis.

Whitcher, S. J., & Fisher, J. D. (1979). Multidimensional reaction to therapeutic touch in a hospital setting. *Journal of Personality and Social Psychology, 37,* 87-96.

White, L. J., & Dressendorfer, R. H. (2004). Exercise and multiple sclerosis. *Sports Medicine, 34*(15), 1077-1100.

Whitman, J. P., & Munson, W. W. (1992). Outcomes of adventure programs for adolescents in psychiatric treatment. *Annual in Therapeutic Recreation, 3,* 44-57.

Wichrowski, M., Whiteson, J., Haas, F., Mola, A., & Rey, M. J. (2005). Effects of horticulture therapy on mood and heart rate in patients participating in an inpatient cardiopulmonary rehabilitation program. *Journal of Cardiopulmonary Rehabilitation, 25,* 270-274.

Widmer, M. A. & Ellis, G. D. (1998). The Aristotelian Good Life Model: Integration of values into therapeutic recreation service delivery. Therapeutic *Recreation Journal, 32,* 290-302.

Widmeyer, W. N., Bray, S. R., Dorsch, K. D., & McGuire, E. J. (2002). Explanations for the occurrence of aggression: Theories and research. In J. M. Silva & D. E. Stevens (Eds.), *Psychological foundations of sport* (pp. 352-379). Boston, MA: Allyn and Bacon.

Wilhite, B., Keller, M. J., & Caldwell, L. (1999). Optimizing lifelong health and well-being: A health enhancing model of therapeutic recreation. *Therapeutic Recreation Journal, 33,* 98-108.

Wilkinson, J. M. (2007). *Nursing process and critical thinking* (4th ed.). Upper Saddle River, NJ: Pearson/Prentice Hall.

Wilkinson, J., & Canter, S. (1982). *Social skills training manual.* New York: John Wiley & Sons.

Wilkinson, N., Ang, R. P., & Goh, D. H. (2008). Online video game therapy for mental health concerns: A review. *International Journal of Social Psychiatry, 54*(4), 370-382.

Williams, A. (1995). *Visual & active supervision: Roles, focus, technique.* New York: W. W. Norton & Company.

Williams, A. K. (2005). Motivation and dementia. *Topics in Geriatric Rehabilitation, 21*(2), 123-126.

Williams, C. L., & Davis, C. M. (2005). *Therapeutic interaction in nursing.* Boston, MA: Jones and Bartlett.

Williams, E. M. (2005). Reality orientation, remotivation, and validation therapy: Comparison of use in older people with dementia. In B. Haight & F. Gibson (Eds.), *Working with older adults: Group processes and techniques* (4th ed.) (pp. 161-174). Sudbury, MA: Bartlett.

Williams, K. A., Petronis, J., Smith, J., Goodrich, D., Wu, J., Ravi, N., Doyle, E. J., ... & Steinbert, L. (2005). Effects of Iyengar yoga therapy for chronic low back pain. *Pain, 115,* 107-117.

Williamson, M. (1961). *Supervision: New patterns and processes.* New York: Associated Press.

Willison, B. G., & Masson, R. L. (1986). The role of touch in therapy: An adjunct to communication. *Journal of Counseling and Development, 64,* 497-500.

Willoughby, C., & Polatajko, H. (1996). The importance of self-esteem: Implications for Practice. Retrieved from http://www.canchild.ca/Default.aspx?tabod=132

Willson, M. (1987). *Occupational therapy in long-term psychiatry* (2nd ed.). Edinburgh: Churchill Livingstone.

Wilson, J. F. (2010). The relationship of outdoor recreation and gardening with depression among individuals with disabilities. Master's thesis, Utah State University, *All Graduate Theses and Dissertations*. Paper 1311. Retrieved from http://digitalcommoms.usu.edu/etd/1311

Wilson, R. S., Krueger, K. R., Arnold, S. E., Schneider, J. A., Kelly, J. F., Barnes, L. L., Tang, Y., & Bennet, D. A. (2007). Loneliness and risk of Alheimer's disease. *Archives of General Psychiatry, 64*(2), 234-240.

Wilson, S. L., & McMillan, T. M. (1993). A review of the evidence for the effectiveness of sensory stimulation treatment for coma and vegetative states. *Neuropsychological Rehabilitation, 3*(2), 149-160.

Wilson, S. L., Powell, G. E., Elliot, K., & Thwaites, H. (1993). Evaluation of sensory stimulation as a treatment for prolonged coma—seven single experimental case studies. *Neuropsychological Rehabilitation, 3*(2), 191-201.

Winn, W. A. (1982). Physical challenge approaches to psychotherapy. In E. T. Nickerson, & K. S. O'Laughlin (Eds.), *Helping through action-oriented therapies*. Amherst, MA: Human Resource Development Press.

Wise, J.B. (2002). Social cognitive theory: A framework for therapeutic recreation practice. *Therapeutic Recreation Journal, 36*(4), 335 - 351.

Witman, J. P. (1987). The efficacy of adventure programming in the development of cooperation and trust with adolescence in treatment. *Therapeutic Recreation Journal, 21*(3), 22-29.

Witman, J. P., & Lee, L. L. (1988). Social skills training for adults in psychiatric treatment: A program model. *Journal of Expanding Horizons in Therapeutic Recreation, 3*, 18-28.

Witman, J., & Ligon, M. (2011a). Evaluation benchmarks in recreational therapy practice. *American Therapeutic Recreation Association Newsletter, 27*(3), 1-3.

Witman, J., & Ligon, M. (2011b). *Reflection, recognition, reaffirmation: An engaging frame of reference for leisure education* (2nd ed.). Enumclaw, WA: Idyll Arbor.

Witman, J., & Ligon, M. (2011c). The status of assessment in recreational therapy: A data-based quiz. *American Therapeutic Recreation Association Newsletter, 27*(1), 1-4.

Witman, J. P., & Munson, W. W. (1992). Outcomes of adventure programs for adolescents in psychiatric treatment. *Annual in Therapeutic Recreation, 3*, 44-57.

Witt, P. A., & Ellis, G. D. (1987). *The leisure diagnostic battery users manual*. State College, PA: Venture Publishing, Inc.

Wolfe, B.D., Dattilo, J., & Gast, D.L. (2003). Effects of a token economy system within the context of cooperative games on social behavior of adolescents with emotional and behavioral disorders. *Therapeutic Recreation Journal, 37*(2), 124-141.

Wolfe, R. A., & Riddick, C. C. (1984). Effects of leisure counseling on adult psychiatric outpatients. *Therapeutic Recreation Journal, 18*(3), 30-37.

Wolz, B. (2005). Cinema therapy: Using the power of Imagery in films for the therapeutic process. Retrieved from http://www.shamonjgifts.com/wp-content/uploads/2011/11/cinematherqpy.pdf

Wong, F. W. H. (2009). Chart audit: Strategies to improve quality of nursing documentation. *Journal for Nurses in Staff Development, 25*(2), E1-F6.

Woods, B. (2002). Reality Orientation: A welcome return? *Age and Ageing, 31*, 155-156.

Woods, B., Aguirre, E., Spector, A. E., & Orrell, M. (2012). Cognitive stimulation to improve cognitive functioning in people with dementia (Cochrane Review). *The Cochrane Library, Issue 2.*

Woods, B., Spector, A., Jones, C., Orrell, M., & Davies, S. (2005), Reminiscence therapy in dementia. *Cochrane Database of Systematic Reviews, 4*, 1-31.

Woods, J. (2012). Exercise boosts school performance with kids with ADHD. *Psych Control*. Retrieved from http://psychcentral.com/news/2012/10/17/exercise-boosts-school-performance-for-kids-with-adhd/46162.html

Woods, M. L. (1971). Development of a pay for recreation procedure in a token economy. *Mental Retardation, 2* (1), 54-57.

Woods, W. (nd) What is "Laughter Yoga"? Retrieved from http://209.85.165.104/search?q=cacje:eT3H1pqyuSgJ:laughter-yoga.ca/laughter_yoga.pdf

Woollams, S., Brown, M., & Huige, K. (1976). *Transactional analysis in brief*. Ann Arbor, MI: Huron Valley Institute.

Wooten, P. (2013). Humor, laughter, and play. In B. M. Dossey & L. Keegan (Eds.), *Holistic nursing: A handbook for practice* (6th ed.) (pp. 307-326). Burlington, MA: Jones & Bartlett.

World Health Organization. (2002). Toward a common language for functioning, disability and health: ICF. Geneva, Switzerland: World Health Organization. Retrieved from http://www.who.int/classifications/icf/beginners/bg.pdf

World Health Organization. (2008). International Classification of Functioning, Disability and Health (ICF). Retrieved from http://www.who.int/classifications.icf.en

Wortman, C. B., & Brehm, J. W. (1975). Responses to uncontrollable outcomes: An integration of reactance theory and the learned helplessness model. In L. Berkowitz (Ed.), *Advances in experimental social psychology* (Vol. 8). New York: Academic Press.

Wright, J., & Chung, M. C. (2001). Mastery or mystery? Therapeutic writing: A review of the literature. *British Journal of Guidance & Counseling, 29*(3), 278-289.

Wuang, Y-P, Chiang, C-S, Su, C-Y., & Wang, C-C. (2011). Effectiveness of virtual reality using Wii gaming technology in children with Down syndrome. *Research in Developmental Disabilities, 32*, 312-321.

Wubbolding, R. E. (1988a). Reality therapy: A method made for the recreation therapist. *ATRA Newsletter, 4*(6), 6,7.

Wubbolding, R. E. (1988b). *Using reality therapy*. New York: Harper & Row.

Wyatt, S. B., Winters, K. P., & Dubbert, P. M. (2006). Overweight and obesity: Prevalence, consequences, and causes of a growing public health problem. *American Journal of the Medical Sciences, 331*(4), 166-174.

Yaffe, R. M. (1998). The leisurability model: A response from a service perspective. *Therapeutic Recreation Journal, 32*(2), 103-108.

Yalom, I. D. (1995). *The theory and practice of group psychotherapy* (3rd ed.). New York: Basic Books.

Yamagami, T., Oosawa, M., Ito, S., & Yamaguchi, H. (2007). Effect of activity reminiscence therapy as brain-activating rehabilitation for elderly people with and without dementia. *Psychogeriatrics, 7*(2), 69-75.

Yan, J. H. (1995). The health and fitness benefits of tai chi. *The Journal of Physical Education, Recreation & Dance, 66*(9), 61-63.

Yang, K. (2007). A review of yoga programs for four leading risk factors of chronic diseases. *eCAM, 4*(4), 487-491.

Yang, H., & Poff, R. (2001). Virtual reality therapy: Expanding the boundaries of therapeutic recreation. *Parks & Recreation, 36*(5), 52-57.

Yeap, B. I., Leow, S. A., & Ng, J. (2008). Snoezelen room: The use of technology to reduce agitated behaviours among geriatric patients with schizophrenia, a literature review. *2008 Sigma Theta Tau International Conference.*

Yim, V. W. C., Ng, A. K. Y., Tsang, H. W. H., & Leung, A. Y. (2009). A review on the effects of aromatherapy for patients with depressive symptoms. *The Journal of Alternative and Complementary Medicine, 15*(2), 187-195.

Yoder-Wise, P. S. (2011). *Leading and managing in nursing* (5th ed.). St. Louis, MO: Elsevier Mosby.

Yorukoglu, A. (1993). Favorite jokes and their use in psychotherapy with children and parents. In W. F. Fry & W. A. Salameh (Eds.), *Advances in humor and psychotherapy*. Sarasota, FL: Professional Resource Press.

Young, C. (2005). "To touch or not to touch: That is the question": Doing effective body psychotherapy without touch. *Energy & Character, 34*, 1-23.

Young, C. (2007). The power of touch in psychotherapy. *International Journal of Psychotherapy.* pp. 1-8. Retrieved from http://www.courtenay-young.co.uk/courtenay/articles/The_Power_of_Touch.pdf

Young, J. (2001). When breathing becomes a bad habit: How to recognize it, how to change it. In G. Hitzhusen & L. Thomas (Eds.), *Expanding horizons in therapeutic recreation XIX* (pp. 141-149). Columbia, MO: University of Missouri.

Yura, H., & Walsh, M. B. (1988). *The nursing process* (5th ed.). Norwalk, CT: Appleton & Lange.

Yurcicin, S. (1995). Aquatics and the ATC. *Rehab Management, 8*(3), 50.

Yusuf, R. B., & Taharem, S. B. (2006). Bibliotherapy: A tool for primary prevention program with children and adolescents. Paper presented at the International Counseling Symposium on Drug Prevention and Rehabilitation, Kuala Lumpur, September 4-9, 2006, pp. 75-90.

Zabriskie, R. B. (2003). Measurement basics: A must for TR professionals today. *Therapeutic Recreation Journal, 37*(4), 330-338.

Zahourek, R. P. (1988). Imagery. In R. P. Zahourek (Ed.), *Relaxation & imagery: Tools for therapeutic communication and intervention*. Philadelphia, PA: W. B. Saunders.

Zajonc, R. B. (1965). Social facilitation. *Science, 149*, 269-274.

Zisser, H., Sueyoshi, M., Kingstein, K., Szigiato, A., & Riddell, M. C. (2012). Advances in exercise, physical activity, and diabetes mellitus. *The International Journal of Clinical Practice, 66*(Suppl. 175), 62-71.

Zixin, L., Li, Y., Zhengyi, G., Zhenyu, S., Honglin, Z., & Tongling, Z. (2000). *Qigong: Chinese medicine or pseudoscience?* Amherst, NY: Prometheus Books.

Zur, O. (2007). Touch in therapy and the standard of care in psychotherapy and counseling: Bringing clarity to illusive relationships. *The USA Body Psychotherapy Journal, 6*(2), 60-93.

Zur, O., & Nordmarken, N. (2004). To touch or not to touch: Rethinking the prohibition on touch in psychotherapy and counseling. Retrieved from http://www.drzur.com/touchintherapy.html

Zych, A., Yang, H., & Malkin, M. J. (2011). Perceived leisure satisfaction of participants In the Arthritis Foundation aquatic program. *American Journal of Recreation Therapy, 10*(2), 9-16.

Index

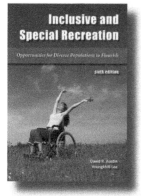
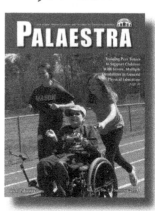